The Cambridge Companion to Video Game Music

Video game music has been permeating popular culture for over forty years. Now, reaching billions of listeners, game music encompasses a diverse spectrum of musical materials and practices. This book provides a comprehensive, up-to-date survey of video game music by a diverse group of scholars and industry professionals. The chapters and summaries consolidate existing knowledge and present tools for readers to engage with the music in new ways. Many popular games are analyzed, including *Super Mario Galaxy, Bastion, The Last of Us, Kentucky Route Zero* and the Katamari, Gran Turismo and Tales series. Topics include chiptunes, compositional processes, localization, history and game music concerts. The book also engages with other disciplines such as psychology, music analysis, business strategy and critical theory, and will prove an equally valuable resource for readers active in the industry, composers or designers, and music students and scholars.

MELANIE FRITSCH is Junior Professor in Media and Cultural Studies with a focus on Game Studies and related fields at Heinrich Heine University Düsseldorf. She is the author of *Performing Bytes: Musikperformances der Computerspielkultur* (2018).

TIM SUMMERS is Lecturer in Music at Royal Holloway, University of London. He is the author of *Understanding Video Game Music* (Cambridge, 2016) and *The Legend of Zelda: Ocarina of Time – A Game Music Companion* (2021).

Cambridge Companions to Music

Topics

Composers

The Cambridge Companion to Video Game Music

Edited by

MELANIE FRITSCH

Heinrich Heine University Düsseldorf

TIM SUMMERS

Royal Holloway, University of London

CAMBRIDGE
UNIVERSITY PRESS

CAMBRIDGE
UNIVERSITY PRESS

University Printing House, Cambridge CB2 8BS, United Kingdom

One Liberty Plaza, 20th Floor, New York, NY 10006, USA

477 Williamstown Road, Port Melbourne, VIC 3207, Australia

314–321, 3rd Floor, Plot 3, Splendor Forum, Jasola District Centre, New Delhi – 110025, India

79 Anson Road, #06–04/06, Singapore 079906

Cambridge University Press is part of the University of Cambridge.

It furthers the University's mission by disseminating knowledge in the pursuit of education, learning, and research at the highest international levels of excellence.

www.cambridge.org
Information on this title: www.cambridge.org/9781108473026
DOI: 10.1017/9781108670289

First published 2021

A catalogue record for this publication is available from the British Library.

ISBN 978-1-108-47302-6 Hardback
ISBN 978-1-108-46089-7 Paperback

Contents

Figures

Tables

Musical Examples

Contributors

LYDIA ANDREW is currently the Audio Director at Ubisoft Quebec, having previously worked as an Audio Director for Electronic Arts. Most recently, she has served as Audio Director for the *Assassin's Creed* games.

MICHAEL L. AUSTIN is Founding Director of the School of Music and Associate Professor of Music at Louisiana Tech University. His research encompasses a wide variety of topics concerning music, technology and the moving image. He is the editor of *Music Games: Performance, Politics, and Play* (2016).

BEN BABBITT is a composer and one-third of the game developer Cardboard Computer. Beyond his work for albums and film, he composed the music for *Kentucky Route Zero* (2013–2020).

THOMAS BÖCKER is the founder of Merregnon Studios. He has been conceiving, producing and promoting video game music concerts since 2003. He organized the first game music concert outside Japan and continues to produce orchestral game music albums featuring high-profile orchestras and ensembles.

ROB BRIDGETT is an author and audio director. His books, including *Game Audio Culture* (2013) and *From the Shadows of Film Sound* (2010), are informed by his professional work as audio director on titles including *Shadow of the Tomb Raider* (2018).

JAMES COOK is Lecturer in Music at Edinburgh University. As well as researching Early Music (especially music of the fourteenth to sixteenth centuries), he investigates the representation and use of Early Music in popular culture. He is a co-founder of the REMOSS (Representations of Early Music on Stage and Screen) study group.

K. J. DONNELLY is Professor of Film and Film Music at the University of Southampton. His books include *The Spectre of Sound: Music in Film and Television* (2005) and *Occult Aesthetics: Sound and Image Synchronization* (2013). He is the co-editor of *Music in Video Games: Studying Play* (2013).

MELANIE FRITSCH is Junior Professor in Media and Cultural Studies with a focus on Game Studies and related fields at Heinrich Heine University Düsseldorf. She is a member of the Ludomusicology Research Group, co-founder of the Society for the Study of Sound and Music in Games and the author of *Performing Bytes: Musikperformances der Computerspielkultur* (2018).

WILLIAM GIBBONS is Associate Professor of Musicology and Associate Dean of the College of Fine Arts at Texas Christian University. He is the author of *Unlimited Replays: Classical Music and Video Games* (2018) and co-editor of *Music in Video Games* (2013) and *Music in the Role-Playing Game* (2019).

MARK GRIMSHAW-AAGAARD is Obel Professor of Music at Aalborg University. He has published extensively on sound both in and beyond video games. He has edited books including *Game Sound Technology and Player Interaction* (2011), and the *Oxford Handbook of Virtuality* (2014) and *Oxford Handbook of Sound and Imagination* (2019).

IAIN HART completed his PhD on the semiotics of video game music at the University of Sydney. His research encompasses a variety of topics and approaches, though it is fundamentally concerned with the communicative functions of music. He has also researched music and genre in video games.

ANDRA IVĂNESCU is a Lecturer in Game Studies and Ludomusicology at Brunel University London. Beyond music her work also engages with key concepts in nostalgia, genre, gender studies and film studies. She is the author of *Popular Music in the Nostalgia Video Game: The Way It Never Sounded* (2019).

MICHIEL KAMP is Assistant Professor of Musicology at Utrecht University. His research takes hermeneutic and semiotic approaches to music in video games and related audiovisual media such as films and virtual reality. His recent publications include research on *Diablo III* and *Skyrim*.

ANDREW LEMON is a senior lecturer in Music and Sound Design at London South Bank University whose career has spanned multiple platforms including video games, film and art installations. He produces audio for mobile games and is active in the demoscene, as well as building custom music technology including one-off hardware synthesizers.

KENNETH B. MCALPINE is Melbourne Enterprise Fellow in Interactive Composition at Melbourne Conservatorium of Music. His research focuses on how technology changes the creation and consumption of music. He is the author of *Bits and Pieces: A History of Chiptunes* (2018) and has composed music for film, television and video games.

ELIZABETH MEDINA-GRAY is Assistant Professor of Music Theory at Ithaca College. Her research focuses on developing novel analytical approaches to music and sound in video games. She has illustrated her approaches through analysing games including *Flower*, *Portal 2* and *Legend of Zelda* games. She also edits the *Journal of Sound and Music in Games*.

GUY MICHELMORE is a composer for film, television and games. He is also the CEO of ThinkSpace Education, an online postgraduate degree provider in music and sound design, for film, games and television.

JAMES NEWMAN is Professor of Digital Media at Bath Spa University. He has published numerous books on games including *Videogames* (2004/ 2013), *Playing with Videogames* (2008) and *Best Before: Videogames, Supersession and Obsolescence* (2012). James is Senior Curator at the UK's National Videogame Museum and a co-founder of the 'Videogame Heritage Society' Subject Specialist Network.

JUNKO OZAWA is a video game composer and sound designer. She was a member of the influential Namco Sound Team and created sound for games including *Gaplus* (1984) and *The Tower of Druaga* (1984). Her innovative approaches to audio helped shape video game music in its formative years.

DANA PLANK is Lecturer in Music at Ohio State University. Her research interests include disability studies, music and identity, and the sacred music of Carlo Gesualdo. Apart from her PhD research on representations of disability in 8- and 16-bit video game soundscapes, she has also published research on the online culture of *Mario Paint Composer* and the musical national politics of *Tetris*.

STEVEN REALE is Professor of Music Theory at the Dana School of Music at Youngstown State University. His research interests include music in video games and music analysis, often in combination. He is the co-editor of *Music in the Role-Playing Game* (2019) and has published on games including *L. A. Noire* as well as theoretical topics such as metric dissonance in music.

HILLEGONDA C. RIETVELD is Professor of Sonic Culture at London South Bank University. Her research focuses on electronic dance music culture, in addition to electronic music and game music. She is the editor of *IASPM@Journal*, for the Association for the Study of Popular Music and the author of *This Is Our House: House Music, Cultural Spaces, and Technologies* (1998).

RICHARD STEVENS is Course Director for the postgraduate programmes in music and sound at Leeds Beckett University. His research interests include the impact of interactive music systems on the video game player experience. He is the co-author of *Game Audio Implementation* (2015) and *The Game Audio Tutorial* (2011) amongst other book chapters and articles on game sound and music.

TIM SUMMERS is Lecturer in Music at Royal Holloway, University of London. He is the author of *Understanding Video Game Music* (2016) and co-editor of *Ludomusicology: Approaches to Video Game Music* (2016), as well as other book chapters and articles on video game music.

RYAN THOMPSON is Professor of Practice at Michigan State University. His research focuses on intersections between gameplay and audio and he creates remixes of game music as part of OverClocked ReMix. His research has included work on *Final Fantasy*, *League of Legends* and music in e-sports events.

CHRIS TONELLI is Assistant Professor in History and Theory of Popular Music at the University of Groningen. His research interests include music and culture in Japan, unconventional vocal sound and popular music as mimesis. He is the author of *Voices Found: Free Jazz and Singing* (2020).

DUNCAN WILLIAMS is Lecturer in Acoustics and Audio Engineering at the University of Salford. He combines his research interests in psychoacoustics and the human responses to sound with a career as a composer. He is the co-editor of *Emotion in Video Game Soundtracking* (2018).

Preface

The editors are very grateful to Kate Brett, Commissioning Editor for Music at Cambridge University Press for her enthusiasm and support for the volume, along with her Assistant Editor Eilidh Burrett. Kate and Eilidh both provided encouragement and wisdom throughout the process of creating this volume.

We would like to thank our colleagues of the Ludomusicology Research Group, Mark Sweeney and Michiel Kamp, as well as the members of the Society for the Study of Sound and Music in Games. Their efforts have helped to create the academic community surrounding music in games, whose collaborative spirit has given rise to many of the ideas and findings shared in this book. We would similarly like to thank all of our authors for their generosity in writing contributions for this book.

Unlike most Cambridge Companions, this book deals primarily with music by living composers and artists. During the book's creation, some of the musicians whose music is discussed by the authors in this volume have been reported as making offensive statements and engaging in personal misconduct. The chosen case studies and examples are in no way an endorsement of the non-musical views of any of the creators mentioned here, nor should they be understood as commenting on the personal behaviour of individuals. We also respect the difficulty of separating art from the artist.

Game music research is a young field, and we hope that the knowledge gathered here from practitioners and researchers representing a diverse set of backgrounds will inspire readers' own explorations. As the field continues to grow, we hope to continue to welcome even more views and perspectives on this exciting music that reaches so many ears.

A Landmark Timeline of Video Game Music

This timeline presents a number of landmarks in the history of video game music. To avoid presenting a history that is inappropriately linear or giving a false impression of completeness, we have selected landmark moments that reveal the changing forms and technologies of game music, as well as game music's relationship with wider culture.

Year	Landmark		Contemporary technology and world events
1972	*Pong* (Atari)	Pitched sound is introduced into video games, with different notes linked to gameplay events.	The last mission of the Apollo space programme lands on the moon.
1975	*Western Gun/Gun Fight* (Taito/ Midway/Nutting)	Games begin to use distinctive melodies in the mid-1970s. This early example includes an excerpt of Chopin's 'Funeral March', when a character is killed.	The Altair 8800 is released in January, sparking the microcomputer revolution as the first commercially successful home computer.
1978	*Space Invaders* (Taito)	In likely the first example of continuous music reacting to the gameplay, the four-note ostinato in *Space Invaders* increases in tempo as the aliens advance.	The Camp David Accords are signed between Israel and Egypt.
1978	Yellow Magic Orchestra release an album of the same name	Yellow Magic Orchestra's first LP includes chip music, illustrating an early convergence between pop music and games. The single release 'Computer Game' subsequently influences early hip-hop and techno musicians in the USA.	
1979	'Space Invaders' song by Player (1) released	Using audio from *Space Invaders* and a bassline influenced by the game, this song becomes	Islamic revolution in Iran.

(*cont.*)

Year	Landmark		Contemporary technology and world events
		the inspiration for one of the first house records, 'On and On' by Jesse Saunders (1984).	
1981	*Frogger* (Konami/Sega)	*Frogger* is one of the earliest examples of a game where different pieces of music are cued depending on the game action.	First launch of NASA's space shuttle.
1981	'Pac-Man Fever' single by Buckner & Garcia	This novelty hit about *Pac-Man* finds chart success and is followed by a game-themed concept album of the same name in 1982.	
1982	Adoption of the MIDI 1.0 standard	MIDI establishes a standard way of communicating musical performance data. MIDI captures the instructions for performance, rather than the sonic output.	The Falklands Conflict erupts between the UK and Argentina.
1982	MOS 6581 SID chip is used as the sound chip for the Commodore 64	Designed by Robert Yannes, the SID chip offers composers great flexibility. Though it only features three main voices, composers can select waveforms for the channels and each has a wide pitch range. Beyond the Commodore, the SID chip in its several iterations and variations inspires musicians and becomes an important feature of the chiptune scene.	
1983	*Journey* (Bally/ Midway)	This arcade game, starring the band of the same name, features synthesized versions of Journey's music during the game. In the final level, an audio cassette built into the cabinet plays a looped, edited recording of Journey's 'Separate Ways'. This is not the first video game appearance of Journey: it is a successor to an earlier home console Journey game.	The first commercial mobile telephone call is made.
1983	*Moondust* (Creative/ Lanier)	One of the first so-called 'art games', created by Jaron Lanier for the Commodore 64,	

(*cont.*)

Year	Landmark		Contemporary technology and world events
		features generative music in an ambient style as a core part of the game's aesthetic.	
1984	*Ballblazer* (LucasArts)	In contrast to *Moondust*, *Ballblazer* features an algorithmically created theme song, 'Song of the Grid' by Peter Langston, in a rock style.	Bob Geldof and Midge Ure assemble a supergroup of musicians to perform a charity single under the name Band Aid.
1984	*Video Game Music* (LP)	Haruomi Hosono assembles the first commercial album of video game music, featuring captures and remixes of sound from Namco games.	
1986	*Dragon Quest Symphonic Suite* album	An album of *Dragon Quest*'s music is released, with the music arranged for orchestral performers. It marks the beginning of orchestral game music albums.	The Chernobyl nuclear power plant undergoes a catastrophic disaster.
1986	Special game music issue of the Japanese gaming magazine *Beep*	The Japanese gaming magazine *Beep* was first published in 1984. This special issue augments their audience significantly. After this issue the magazine features a regular section dedicated to game music.	
1986	*Soundmonitor*	Chris Hülsbeck releases his *Soundmonitor*, the first tracker program for users to create their own music, as a listing in the German computer magazine *64er*.	
1986	*OutRun* (Sega)	This arcade racing game by Sega is notable for several aspects, including its outstanding hardware and non-linear gameplay. It also allows players to choose the music to accompany their play. The music, composed by Hiroshi Kawaguchi, later inspires the synthwave genre called OutRun in the early 2000s,	

(*cont.*)

Year	Landmark		Contemporary technology and world events
		named in reference to 1980 aesthetics. *OutRun*'s music is played live by the Sega Sound Team (SST) during their concerts in the late 1980s.	
1987	Dragon Quest Concert in Tokyo	Koichi Sugiyama stages a 'Family Classic Concert' at Suntory Hall, Tokyo. The concert programmes his music from *Dragon Quest I* and *II* alongside Saint-Saëns's *Carnival of the Animals*. It is likely the first orchestral concert of video game music.	A West German teenager lands a light aircraft in Moscow's Red Square.
1987	*Dance Aerobics* (Bandai/Human, Nintendo)	This release for the Famicom/ NES is the first game to feature a floor mat controller, the Power Pad. It anticipates later dance games.	
1987	*Otocky* (Sedic/ASCII)	*Otocky* is a musical sidescroller shoot-'em-up game by Toshio Iwai for Nintendo's Famicom. It is notable for its generative soundtrack, co-created by the player while playing. It was never released outside Japan.	
1987	Commodore Amiga makes extensive use of the MOD music format	The Amiga uses a format for storing music which is similar to MIDI, but also includes the instrument samples in the files, as well as the note data, which creates significant possibilities for unique musical timbres.	
1988	*Soundtracker 2*	'Exterminator' of the Dutch hacker group Jungle Command hacks Karsten Obarski's *Soundtracker*, and rereleases it as freeware under his own name, making the playback routine public. It starts the soundtracker revolution, and other trackers are later built from it (like *NoiseTracker* and *ProTracker*).	The Morris Internet Worm, the first internet-spread malware, wreaks havoc.
1991	*Monkey Island 2: LeChuck's Revenge* (LucasArts)	LucasArts debut iMUSE, an interactive music system, demonstrating complex	The Cold War ends with the dissolution of the USSR.

(cont.)

Year	Landmark		Contemporary technology and world events
		adaptive music programming including branching, layering and alternative variations. It even allows music to dictate game timing.	
1991	General MIDI standard established	To combat the high degree of variation between sound cards and hardware, General MIDI presents a template of 128 instruments, so composers are able to address specific instruments in their sound files. This ensures that, for example, a part written for a violin always sounds as a violin.	
1992	*Streets of Rage II* (Sega)	*Streets of Rage II* is the second entry in Sega's side-scrolling beat-'em-up series and features a soundtrack inspired by 1990s club music, created by Yuzo Koshiro and Motohiro Kawashima.	Atari, Nintendo and Sega are all involved in lawsuits concerning reverse engineering and modification of games.
1994	Michael Jackson is engaged to write music for *Sonic the Hedgehog 3*	Video games begin to attract major pop stars to write music specifically for games. One of the world's most famous musicians is involved in *Sonic 3*. Ultimately he is uncredited in the released game. His contribution to the finished game would long be the subject of avid speculation. British band Right Said Fred promote *Sonic 3* with their song 'Wonderman'. Jackson appears in several games, including *Moonwalker* (1989) and *Space Channel 5* (1999).	Nelson Mandela becomes the first president of South Africa.
1995	*Wipeout* (Psygnosis)	*Wipeout* is released as a PlayStation launch title in Europe and features music from electronic music acts such as Orbital, The Chemical Brothers, Underworld and Leftfield. It is part of a wider	eBay and Windows 95 are launched.

(cont.)

Year	Landmark		Contemporary technology and world events
		approach of Sony to market the PlayStation to a more mature demographic than earlier games consoles.	
1996	*PaRappa the Rapper* (NanaOn-Sha)	This rhythm-based music game is created by music producer Masaya Matsuura and Rodney Greenblat. A comic-styled dog PaRappa learns to rap from several teachers. It is a commercial success on the PlayStation in Japan and is one of the starting points of the Japanese music game boom of the late 1990s.	Dolly the sheep is born, the first mammal cloned from a somatic cell.
1997	*The Lost World: Jurassic Park* (Dreamworks) (PlayStation and Saturn)	This game, with music by Michael Giacchino, is one of the first to use a recorded orchestra for the soundtrack, made feasible by the space and facilities of CD-based consoles.	Deep Blue beats Garry Kasparov in a chess match, the first computer to beat a current world champion.
1997	*Beatmania* (Konami)	The DJ-style rhythm game *Beatmania*, along with *PaRappa*, launches the Japanese game music boom. *Beatmania* lends its name to Konami's eponymous Bemani line of music games.	
1998	*Dance Dance Revolution* (Konami)	*Dance Dance Revolution* (released in Europe as *Dancing Stage*), part of Konami's Bemani series, becomes internationally successful and starts a long-running series of games. In 2012, Konami creates a special edition of the game with the American Diabetes Association, The National Foundation on Fitness, Sports, and Nutrition and the Let's Move! project for US schools' physical education classes. *Dance Dance Revolution* develops a very active fan community that engages in competitions all over the world.	Tencent and Google are founded.

(cont.)

Year	Landmark		Contemporary technology and world events
2000	*LSDJ* (*Little Sound DJ*)	Johan Kotlinski creates tracker software to turn a Game Boy into a synthesizer, allowing direct control of the Game Boy's five hardware sound channels with a straightforward interface. It becomes a staple of the chip-tune scene.	Apocalyptic predictions of the consequences of the Millennium Bug computer date error fail to materialize.
2001	*Grand Theft Auto III* (Rockstar)	With DVD storage as a dominant format, games could now include significantly more recorded and licensed music. *Grand Theft Auto III* features pre-existing music as part of in-game radio stations, complete with announcers and fictional adverts.	The United States suffers a terrorist attack on 11 September, prompting a controversial 'War on Terror'.
2001	Release of the album *Music inspired by Final Fantasy: The Hollywood Symphony Orchestra and Chorus Perform The Music of Nobuo Uematsu*	In the 1980s and 1990s, most game music albums are only available outside Japan as expensive imports or as bootleg MP3s. In 1997, Stephen Kennedy starts the 'Project Majestic Mix', a group of game music fans who want to produce an album. Via the project's website, the group select the music and fund the project with donations from other fans. Kennedy contacts Uematsu and Square to clarify issues of copyright and licensing. He is successful and the first album is released. It is followed by three more albums of music from Square games.	
2001	*Rez* (United Game Artists)	The game *Rez* is released (in Japan in a bundle with a peripheral called the Trance Vibrator) aiming at recreating the experience of a rave.	
2001	Virtual music by In Extremo in *Gothic* (Piranha Bytes)	The German medieval rock band In Extremo appears in the fantasy game *Gothic*, performing their live rendition of 'Herr	

(cont.)

Year	Landmark		Contemporary technology and world events
		Mannelig'. For non-German language releases the performance was deleted, because of copyright issues.	
2003	Symphonic Game Music Concert in Leipzig	Opening the Leipzig Games Convention, Thomas Böcker produces the first commercial game music concert outside Japan, starting an ongoing tradition of Western concerts of game music.	The Human Genome Project is completed.
2005	*Guitar Hero* (RedOctane)	Starting a craze for rhythm music games in the West, *Guitar Hero* captures the interest of a wide audience attracted by the performative possibilities of the game.	YouTube is launched.
2008	*Spore* (Maxis)	Procedural generation is central to the 'God game' *Spore*. It features an elaborate music system that procedurally generates music on the fly, rather than playing pre-composed music. Similar examples include *No Man's Sky* (2016).	A major financial crisis affects banks and economies around the globe.
2008	Karen Collins publishes *Game Sound*	The first academic volume dedicated to video game music and sound gives the area of study new legitimacy.	
2008	'Auto-Mario Wipeout' or 'X Day' on Nico Nico Douga	On May 13th, 2008, Japanese video platform Nico Nico Douga bulk-deletes fan-made Automatic Mario videos because of copyright infringement. Automatic Mario is a specific subgenre of remix videos using customized Super Mario World levels to recreate popular songs and other music.	
2008	'Symphonic Shades' concert is broadcast live	The WDR Rundfunkorchester, conducted by Arnie Roth, perform a concert dedicated to the game music of Chris Hülsbeck: "'Symphonic	

(cont.)

Year	Landmark		Contemporary technology and world events
		Shades" – Hülsbeck in Concert'. This is the first game music concert to be broadcast live on radio and streamed on the internet.	
2009	*DJ Hero* (FreeStyleGames)	DJ game featuring the music of artists such as Daft Punk, DJ AM, Grandmaster Flash, DJ Jazzy Jeff, and many more, some included as avatars in the game.	The cryptocurrency Bitcoin is launched.
2011	Christopher Tin's 'Baba Yetu' wins a Grammy Award	Written for *Civilization IV* (2005), and later rereleased on Tin's 2009 studio album, 'Baba Yetu' becomes the first music composed for a video game to win a Grammy Award. It was nominated in the category 'Best Instrumental Arrangement Accompanying Vocalist(s)'.	Anti-government protests spread across the Arab world, a phenomenon named the 'Arab Spring'.
2011	*Rocksmith* (Ubisoft)	*Rocksmith* is released, featuring the option to plug in a real guitar and advertising that players can learn to play the guitar through the game.	
2011	*Top Score*, a radio show/podcast dedicated to game music begins	Emily Reese begins a long-running programme celebrating game music and interviewing composers on Classical Minnesota Public Radio.	
2012	*Journey*'s soundtrack nominated for a Grammy award	Austin Wintory's music for *Journey* is nominated for 'Best Score Soundtrack for Visual Media', the first time a game score is nominated in this category.	The Higgs boson elementary particle is discovered.
2015	*Undertale* (Toby Fox)	The rise of digital distribution and open or free development tools prompts a blossoming of independent game development. In seeking a different approach to high-budget releases from major studios,	The Paris Agreement on climate change is negotiated at a United Nations climate conference.

(cont.)

Year	Landmark		Contemporary technology and world events
		many such games embrace retro or nostalgic aesthetics (both generally and musically). *Undertale* is one such example, modelled visually, sonically and ludically on RPGs of the 1980s.	
2018	AR K-pop live concert opens the *League of Legends* World Championships	As e-sports tournaments come to more closely emulate traditional sporting events, Riot Games opens its annual *League of Legends* World Championships with a spectacular show including an augmented reality performance by K-pop group K/DA.	According to the UN, more than half of the world's population is now using the internet.
2020	*Journal of Sound and Music in Games* published	An academic journal dedicated to the study of music and games is launched by the Society for the Study of Sound and Music in Games.	The world experiences a global pandemic of the Covid-19 virus.
2020	Travis Scott stages a concert in *Fortnite*	12.3 million players attend a virtual concert in a game. Though online games have been hosting performances since the mid-2000s, this event brought new attention to the format.	

Foreword: The Collaborative Art of Game Music

LYDIA ANDREW

I greatly welcome the opportunity to write this foreword to *The Cambridge Companion to Video Game Music*. The essays in this collection share ideas about this dynamic, shape-shifting, all-embracing discipline from multiple perspectives. That sharing is a communal, creative effort. In many ways, it is what video games themselves are all about.

Music is a key moment where the creative vision of player experience crystallizes. Whatever the genre of game, music can characterize avatars, it can enhance settings, it can deepen emotions and shape the pace of games.

Game music is an experience. It is not linear. Every change comes from a hook in gameplay, a decision of programming, a variation in the system based on the player's input. To create a consistent player experience, both diegetic and non-diegetic music, and the role of music within the larger soundscape, demand a through line deeply grounded in our response and engagement with the game. Research, creative expression and the ongoing search for ways to connect with our players: all are synergistic and raise issues of identity and psychology. One of the great, continuing pleasures of developing and playing video games is that this work is never done. This is what has most inspired me in my work on the *Assassin's Creed* brand, specifically *Syndicate* (2015) and *Odyssey* (2018).

Game music is a truly collaborative creative endeavour, which draws deeply on a range of people's skills. The music team works with world designers, animators, game designers, gameplay programmers and audio programmers, without speaking of the composers, musicians, arrangers, lyricists, researchers and the rest of the audio team (dialogue and sound effects) with whom they must liaise. The larger the scale of the game, the greater the challenges to consistency in the game architecture into which we all feed. But on smaller games too, the ultimate design of music is determined by the particular player experience a team collectively foresees. It is an emotional and creative vision that must first be defined.

For my part, that collaborative process begins with our early concept art, narrative outlines and gameplay ideas. These provide touchstones to discuss with the rest of the development team – the evocations, moods and themes that are the building-blocks of our living and breathing world. These in turn suggest paths of ever-deepening research.

For both *Syndicate* and *Odyssey*, we wanted a holistic design of music. We wanted diegetic and non-diegetic music to be symbiotic. Music speaks constantly of shared community – it is born of art and architecture, of commerce, beliefs, logistics, wider cultural life, even the weather of its locale. For *Syndicate*, that locale was mid-Victorian London, engine of innovation and modernity, and of the great social and psychological disruptions that go with them. A Londoner myself, I needed to hear experimentation, immediacy, aggression and something of that psychic dislocation in the style. Austin Wintory tuned into this. Aided by critical musicologist Prof. Derek Scott and traditional music producer Dave Gossage, we curated a selection of songs which captured the atmosphere of each district of London. For instance, light opera, military music and hymns for Westminster; pub singalongs and folk music for Whitechapel. From each selection, we further chose one song as the key motif for that district. Westminster became 'Abide with Me', and Whitechapel became 'My Name It Is Sam Hall'. Austin wove these motifs into the underbelly of the score, such that each melody echoes subtly throughout its district. Score and source fully intertwined.

Against this use of popular music for atmosphere, we used commissioned ballads to deepen the drama of the game story itself. The game's progression demands critical assassinations, so the band Tripod in Australia and Austin wrote original murder ballads, attuned to the personality of each victim, modelling them on popular Victorian storytelling songs. The intimate dance of death further informed the score – we hear small chamber ensembles, solo string instruments attached to characters, the light 'springiness' of waltzes and mazurkas, the immediacy of scherzo sketches.

For *Odyssey*, the world was larger and more complex.

The commissioned score took over two years to develop. The musical duo The Flight are multi-instrumentalists and producers as well as composers. We had to discover Ancient Greece together. Consequently, the research effort demanded was great. Little music survives from the Golden Age of Ancient Greece. We looked at ancient vases and sculptures for visual clues, and to ancient texts for lyrics and poetry. We wanted an intimate, handmade, acoustic feel. We found one sonic signature in the Aulos, a key instrument in ceremonies and festivals, reconstructed from archaeological findings. In exploring how this instrument was played, we came to appreciate its relevance to a modern audience. To do this, we combined voices and other instruments in such a way as to appeal to modern musical aesthetics and used this instrument at significant moments in our non-diegetic underscore.

The diegetic music also took two years to develop and followed multiple parallel tracks. For historical materials, I drew on the work of individual experts – musical anthropologists, archaeologists, highly skilled craftspeople who reconstruct ancient instruments, local Greek practitioners. On the one hand, we created facsimiles of ancient Greek songs based on texts of the period, such as the sea shanties for which melodies were devised by Dimitris Ilias of Chroma Musica and Giannis Georgantelis. On the other, we themed our choice of story songs, which reflect the specific narrative and character arc of the game, around the notion of *odyssey*. The lyrics for these were written by Emma Rohan, with music composed by Giannis Georgantelis. All this also fed back into the commissioned non-diegetic material.

Finally, there is the life of our game music outside the game. This is a new collaboration in itself. The music experience we deliver lives on through players' imaginations, in the many cover versions and reinventions players spawn. They reinterpret and share their work in the even wider context of social media. Many reworkings exist of the murder ballads and underscore from *Syndicate*. The first cover of the main theme track from *Odyssey* was uploaded before the game itself was released. This is a greater celebration of game music, seen also in the recent *Assassin's Creed Symphony* series and many other live music events. This community that has developed around game music is huge, ever-evolving and constantly energizing. It is perhaps appropriate that my brief remarks end with them.

Lydia Andrew
Quebec, March 2020

Introduction

MELANIE FRITSCH AND TIM SUMMERS

Video game music has been permeating popular culture for over forty years, at least since the titular aliens of *Space Invaders* arrived in 1978, accompanied by an ever-accelerating musical ostinato. Now, reaching hundreds of millions of listeners, game music has grown to encompass a diverse spectrum of musical materials and practices. Its instrumentation ranges from orchestras to rock bands, its contexts from bedroom televisions to concert halls, its materials from 'art music' to Top-40 pop, and its systems from generative music technologies to carefully handcrafted idiosyncratic musical structures.

No longer a novelty within electronic music technology, nor a poor relation of film music, game music engages huge audiences and large budgets, and is the site of innovative scholarship. As well as being a crucial component of the audiovisual interactive experience of video gaming, game music has also had a marked impact on broader popular culture. Simply put, video game music is an important aspect of the musical life of the late-twentieth and twenty-first centuries in the Western world, and has cross-fertilized with many musical genres. At the same time, game music highlights a long tradition of music and play that can be traced back to antiquity.

This volume is specifically concerned with game music. Nevertheless, in video games, it is often unhelpful to imply a hard-and-fast separation between music and other aspects of the audio output of games. Especially in earlier games, the same technology would be responsible for musical content as for other sonic elements. Even in modern examples, audio icons and musicalized sound effects are interstitially both sound effect and yet distinctly musical. Rather than using a restrictive definition of what qualifies as 'music', the book instead explores the diverse and multifaceted musicality of games. The discussions engage the whole range of musical materials, from long cues and fully fledged music games to sonic fragments that constitute only one or two pitches. In this way, we might better appreciate the full significance of music to the experience of playing video games.

Video Game Music Studies

Though video game music has long been the subject of (sometimes heated) discussion in college dorms, playgrounds, internet forums, conventions and anywhere gamers gather, academic studies of video game music primarily date from the mid-2000s. Despite some notable predecessors,[1] 2004–2008 saw a flurry of publications that would be foundational to the study of game music. Understandably, many initial studies engaged with games that trumpeted their engagement with music, like Dance Dance Revolution (1998–2019),[2] Grand Theft Auto's extensive use of licensed music from 2001 onwards[3] and music games including Guitar Hero (2005–2015).[4] Another early area of interest included the compositional challenges presented by early video game hardware.[5] Broader conceptual issues in game music were initially couched in terms of the relationship with film,[6] functionality[7] and ideas of immersion.[8] In 2008, Karen Collins published her landmark book *Game Sound: An Introduction to the History, Theory, and Practice of Video Game Music and Sound Design*, which continues to serve as

[1] See, for example, Matthew Belinkie, 'Video Game Music: Not Just Kid Stuff', *VGMusic.com*, 1999, accessed 8 April 2020, www.vgmusic.com/information/vgpaper.html.

[2] Joanna Demers, 'Dancing Machines: "Dance Dance Revolution", Cybernetic Dance, and Musical Taste', *Popular Music* 25, no. 3 (2006): 401–14; Jacob Smith, 'I Can See Tomorrow in Your Dance: A Study of Dance Dance Revolution and Music Video Games', *Journal of Popular Music Studies* 16, no. 1 (2004): 58–84.

[3] Kiri Miller, 'Jacking the Dial: Radio, Race, and Place in "Grand Theft Auto"', *Ethnomusicology* 51, no. 3 (2007): 402–38; Kiri Miller, 'Grove Street Grimm: Grand Theft Auto and Digital Folklore', *Journal of American Folklore* 121, no. 481 (2008): 255–85; and Kiri Miller, 'The Accidental Carjack: Ethnography, Gameworld Tourism, and Grand Theft Auto', *Game Studies* 8, no. 1 (2008).

[4] Dominic Arsenault, 'Guitar Hero: "Not Like Playing Guitar at All"?', *Loading . . .* 2, no. 2 (2008); Fares Kayali, 'Playing Music: Design, Theory, and Practice of Music-based Games' (PhD dissertation, Vienna University of Technology, 2008); Henry Adam Svec, 'Becoming Machinic Virtuosos: Guitar Hero, Rez, and Multitudinous Aesthetics', *Loading . . .* 2, no. 2 (2008).

[5] Karen Collins, 'Loops and Bloops: Music on the Commodore 64', *Soundscape: Journal of Media Culture* 8, no. 1 (2006); Karen Collins, 'Flat Twos and the Musical Aesthetic of the Atari VCS', *Popular Musicology Online*, 1 (2006); and Karen Collins, 'In the Loop: Confinements and Creativity in 8-bit Games', *Twentieth-Century Music* 4, no. 2 (2007), 209–27.

[6] Zach Whalen, 'Play Along – An Approach to Videogame Music', *Game Studies* 4, no. 1 (2004) and Zach Whalen, 'Case Study: Film Music vs. Video-Game Music: The Case of Silent Hill', in *Music, Sound and Multimedia: From the Live to the Virtual*, ed. Jamie Sexton (Edinburgh: Edinburgh University Press, 2007), 68–81.

[7] Kristine Jørgensen, '"What Are These Grunts and Growls Over There?" Computer Game Audio and Player Action' (PhD dissertation, Copenhagen University, 2007) and Kristine Jørgensen, 'Left in the Dark: Playing Computer Games with the Sound Turned Off', in *From Pac-Man to Pop Music: Interactive Audio in Games and New Media*, ed. Karen Collins (Aldershot: Ashgate, 2008), 163–76.

[8] Rod Munday, 'Music in Video Games', in *Music, Sound and Multimedia: From the Live to the Virtual*, ed. Jamie Sexton (Edinburgh: Edinburgh University Press, 2007), 51–67.

a cornerstone of game music studies.[9] This volume introduces key terminology and touches upon a huge variety of foundational ideas in game music studies. There is no better starting point for the reader new to this topic than *Game Sound*.

Since *Game Sound*, the field has continued to develop rapidly in a multitude of different directions. It is not uncommon to find university classes on video game music, while conferences, PhD dissertations and books on the topic are not unusual. The field has even grown to include an academic journal dedicated to the subject, the *Journal of Sound and Music in Games*. This companion aims to guide the reader through some of the main topics and ways of approaching game music, both in games, and the engagement with it beyond the games themselves.

Some discussions of game music have opted to use the term 'ludomusicology', a word originating in the work of Guillaume Laroche, Nicholas Tam and Roger Moseley.[10] The word is used to describe studies that engage with music and play, especially, though certainly not exclusively, through the lens of video games. While some game music scholars find the word problematic, with exclusionary and elitist overtones, it has served as a handy identifier to help with the visibility of research.

Beyond academics, game music practitioners have also revealingly written about their own experiences creating music for games. Prolific game composer George 'The Fat Man' Sanger wrote a book that defies easy categorization.[11] Encompassing autobiography, history, business advice, composition treatise and personal philosophy, the book is a revealing holistic insight into the life of a game composer. Other practitioners have written volumes that aim to pass

---

[9] Karen Collins, *Game Sound: An Introduction to the History, Theory and Practice of Video Game Music and Sound Design* (Cambridge, MA: MIT Press, 2008).

[10] On Guillaume Laroche and Nicholas Tam's use of the term see Tasneem Karbani, 'Music to a Gamer's Ears', *University of Alberta Faculty of Arts News* (22 August 2007), accessed 10 April 2020, https://web.archive.org/web/20070915071528/http://www.uofaweb.ualberta.ca/arts/news.cfm?story=63769 and Nicholas Tam, 'Ludomorphballogy', *Ntuple Indemnity* (7 September 2007), accessed 10 April 2020, www.nicholastam.ca/2007/09/07/ludomorphballogy/; Roger Moseley, 'Playing Games with Music, and Vice Versa: Performance and Recreation in Guitar Hero and Rock Band', in *Taking It to the Bridge: Music as Performance*, ed. Nicholas Cook and Richard Pettengill (Ann Arbor: University of Michigan Press, 2013), 279–318. Moseley used the term in 2008 for a paper, 'Rock Band and the Birth of Ludomusicology' delivered at the Annual Meeting of the SEM at Wesleyan University (28 October 2008) and at Music and the Moving Image, New York University (1 June 2008).

[11] George Sanger, *The Fat Man on Game Audio* (Indianapolis, IN: New Riders, 2003).

on their knowledge to aspiring composers,[12] or as part of the activity of reflecting on their own processes.[13]

Of course, published discourse about game music works alongside, and in tandem with the conversations about game music that occur in all kinds of other media. YouTube is a goldmine of excellent discussions and video essays about game music, forums like Discord and Twitch provide the opportunity for interactive conversations about game music, and journalists continually interview composers and report on popular opinion about the genre. We can also consider documentaries such as the Karen-Collins-directed *Beep* (2016), and *Diggin' in the Carts* (2014) by Nick Dwyer and Tu Neill. Academic game music studies exist as part of a broader ecosystem of discussions about video game music, each of which draws on, and contributes to, the others.

Video game music studies is a diverse area, and this book does not claim to represent all of the voices in the field. We have sought to balance summarizing existing knowledge with presenting some new perspectives, and to showcase conceptual thinking alongside more practical discussion. More than anything, we hope that this book will provide readers with a broad overview of the subject, and useful knowledge and tools for better understanding video game music, no matter how they engage with music – whether that be as listeners, composers, analysts or perhaps most importantly, as players.

Introductory Reading

Collins, Karen. *Game Sound: An Introduction to the History, Theory and Practice of Video Game Music and Sound Design*. Cambridge, MA: MIT Press, 2008.

Fritsch, Melanie. 'History of Video Game Music', in *Music and Game: Perspectives on a Popular Alliance*, ed. Peter Moormann. Wiesbaden: Springer, 2013, 11–40.

Grimshaw, Mark. 'Sound', in *The Routledge Companion to Video Game Studies*, ed. Bernard Perron and Mark J. P. Wolf (London: Routledge, 2016), 117–24.

Jørgensen, Kristine. 'Left in the Dark: Playing Computer Games with the Sound Turned Off', in *From Pac-Man to Pop Music: Interactive Audio in Games and New Media*, ed. Karen Collins. Aldershot: Ashgate, 2008, 163–76.

Whalen, Zach. 'Play Along – An Approach to Videogame Music.' *Game Studies* 4, no. 1 (2004).

---

[12] Winifred Phillips, *A Composer's Guide to Game Music* (Cambridge, MA: The MIT Press, 2014); Michael Sweet, *Writing Interactive Music for Video Games* (Upper Saddle River, NJ: Addison-Wesley, 2015); Chance Thomas, *Composing Music for Games* (Boca Raton, FL: CRC Press, 2016).

[13] Rob Bridgett, *From the Shadows of Film Sound. Cinematic Production & Creative Process in Video Game Audio.* (N.p.: Rob Bridgett, 2010).

PART I

Chiptunes

Introduction

MELANIE FRITSCH AND TIM SUMMERS

And three 'bips' disrupted the silence – this is how a written history of game sound might start. These famous 'bips' in three different pitches occurred when players hit the white pixel representing the ball with the controllable white bar representing the bat, when the ball bumped from the upper or lower border or when the ball went off screen in the first widely commercially successful arcade game, *Pong* (1972). These sounds were not produced with a sound chip, but by the voltage peaks of the circuits in the gaming machine: in other words, their origin was analogue. Three years later, the arcade game *Gun Fight* (in Japan and Europe released under the name *Western Gun*), created by Tomohiro Nishikado, included a monophonic version of the famous opening bars of Chopin's funeral march from his Second Piano Sonata, and was the first game to include a melodic line. Again three years later, Taito's arcade title *Space Invaders* (1978), also created by Nishikado, used a changing soundtrack for the first time. It drew attention to the possibilities that a dynamic approach towards sound and music provided in terms of enhancing the player's experience during play. The arcade cabinet produced its sounds using the Texas Instruments SN76477 sound chip that had come to market the same year. Such programmable sound generators (PSGs) were used to produce the sound and music for arcade titles, home consoles and home computers. Some of these chips came to fame, either as they were used widely and in many gaming devices, or because of their distinct sound, or both. Famous examples are General Instrument's AY-3–8910 (1978), the MOS Technology 6581/8580 SID (Sound Interface Device, 1981) Atari's POKEY (Pot Keyboard Integrated Circuit, 1982) and the Amiga Paula (1985). While these chips are usually each referred to under one name as one item, it is worthwhile noting that many of them were produced in several iterations and versions. Another early approach towards game music beside the use of PSGs was wavetable synthesis, most famously adopted by Namco with their Namco WSG (Waveform Sound Generator) for their 8-bit arcade-game system boards such as the Namco Pac-Man board (1980) or the Namco Galaga board (1981). From the mid-1980s FM synthesis (Frequency Modulation synthesis) was popular, particularly after the release of Yamaha's DX7 synthesizer, and became the standard for game sound until the mid-1990s, with Yamaha being one of the main hardware producers. Unlike the PSGs, which used set soundwaves to give particular timbres, FM synthesis allowed waveforms to be blended and altered, giving rise to a far greater variety of timbres.

Early programmable sound generators usually provided three to five voices in the form of square, triangle or sawtooth waves plus a noise channel. The music had to be written in machine code, namely in programming languages such as BASIC or Assembler, which meant that either a composer needed programming skills, a programmer needed musical skills or the two professions had to work together. As Andrew Schartmann describes it for Koji Kondo's *Super Mario Bros.* soundtrack on the NES:

The NES master's idea had to be translated into the language of computer code. And given that Kondo's music would be *perform*ed by a programmable sound generator, he couldn't rely on a human element to bring expression to his work. . . . For a video-game composer . . . a crescendo requires precise calculation: it is expressed in numbers ranging from 0 to 15, each of which represents a specific volume level. There is no continuum to work with, thus forcing composers to create the illusion thereof.[1]

That early game music composers only had a limited number of channels at hand oftentimes leads to the conclusion that early game music was limited in its expression by technology. And while this is certainly true for the sound aesthetics (as, for example, the use of real instrument samples wasn't possible until MIDI) and number of available channels, it is not for compositional quality. As early game composers such as Rob Hubbard, Junko Ozawa, Yuriko Keino, Martin Galway, Koji Kondo, Nobuo Uematsu, Yoko Shimomura, Jeroen Tel, Chris Hülsbeck and so many others have demonstrated, PSGs and WSGs can be used to create complex and exciting compositions, if the composer knows their instrument. Furthermore, by inventing their own programming routines and tricks,

---

[1] Andrew Schartmann, *Koji Kondo's Super Mario Bros. Soundtrack* (New York: Bloomsbury, 2015), 36.

these composers created sounds and music that were continuously pushing the boundaries. In addition, the players themselves entered this new playground early on.

Chiptune Culture from Old School to New School

Thanks to the coming of affordable and programmable home computers from the late 1970s like the Apple II, Sinclair ZX Spectrum or the Commodore 64, computer hardware and games found their way into private households. While some players used the possibilities of these open and programmable systems to create their own homebrew games, others aimed at cracking the standard copy protection of commercially distributed titles and competing with each other as to who could do it first. These cracked games were circulated within the community of enthusiasts, and were marked with so-called intros (also sometimes known as cracktros). These small programs started before the actual game, and usually showed the (oftentimes animated) name of the cracker group as well as scrolling text containing messages like greetings to other groups, all underscored by computer music. Driven by the idea of creating increasingly sophisticated intros and going beyond the apparent limits of the respective technologies' capacities, the creation of such little programs became a distinct practice in its own right, resulting in the emergence of the demoscene and the chip music scene. While the demosceners were interested in creating audiovisual real-time animations (demos), the chip musicians were only interested in the sonic aspects.

In this way a participatory music culture emerged, driven by an active and creative fan community, who did not just play the games, but also played *with* them and their material basis: the respective systems' technology. By hacking commercial products such as games, home computers and consoles, and inventing their own program routines and software tools, they continuously pushed the boundaries of the materials to create their own artefacts and performances. It was in 1986 that seventeen-year old Chris Hülsbeck published his 'Soundmonitor' in the German computer magazine *64er*. The 'Soundmonitor' was a program for the Commodore 64 based on his own MusicMaster-Routine, and allowed users to create music and exciting new sound effects with the Commodore's SID chip. It was easier to handle than commercial products such as the Commodore Music Maker, and is said to have been an inspiration for Karsten Obarski's 1987 'Ultimate Soundtracker', a music sequencer program for Amiga's Paula. The program was released as a commercial product, but, according to Johan Kotlinski, it was rather buggy and therefore did not achieve big sales. In 1988, the Dutch demo programmer Exterminator of the group Jungle Command hacked the program, improved it and rereleased it for free as Soundtracker 2 under his own name.

The most important change was that he made the playback routine public, so that anyone could incorporate Soundtracker songs into their own productions. It was a very shameless and illegal thing to do, but the fact is that it was the starting point for the Soundtracker revolution. Slowly, Soundtracker became the de facto standard within game programming and the demo scene.[2]

The demo- and chip music scene not only became a first touchpoint for later professional game music composers such as Chris Hülsbeck or Jesper Kyd, but also allowed musicians from other fields to take their first musical steps. For example, the producer and DJ Brian Johnson, known under his alias Bizzy B., also reported in interviews that home PCs such as Commodore's Amiga made his entry into the music business possible in the first place by being an affordable experimental platform and allowing him to create music even though he could not afford a studio. With Amigacore, for example, a separate subgenre was established. Known representatives included the Australian techno formation Nasenbluten from Newcastle, who also pioneered hardcore techno, gabber and cheapcore in Australia. Such interrelationships between chip music and other musical genres are still to be investigated.

Studying Chip Music

The study of sound chip-based game music from the 1970s and 1980s has been the subject of interest in game music research since the very beginning. Pioneers in the field such as Karen Collins,[3] Nils Dittbrenner,[4] Kevin Driscoll and Joshua Diaz[5] and many others have written about the history of chip music in games and investigated the ways in which aesthetics and

---

[2] Johan Kotlinski, *Amiga Music Programs 1986–1995*, 20 August 2009, 8. Last accessed 2 May 2020, http://goto80.com/chipflip/dox/kotlinski_(2009)_amiga_music_programs_89-95.pdf.

[3] Karen Collins, 'From Bits to Hits: Video Games Music Changes Its Tune', *Film International* 12 (2005), 4–19; Collins, 'Flat Twos and the Musical Aesthetic of the Atari VCS', *Popular Musicology Online* 1 (2006); Collins, *Game Sound: An Introduction to the History, Theory, and Practice of Video Game Music and Sound Design* (Cambridge, MA: The MIT Press, 2008).

[4] Nils Dittbrenner, *Soundchip-Musik: Computer- und Videospielmusik von 1977–1994*, Magister thesis, University of Lüneburg, 2005.

[5] Kevin Driscoll and Joshua Diaz, 'Endless Loop: A Brief History of Chiptunes', *Transformative Works and Cultures* 2 (2009).

compositional approaches have evolved. Documentaries such as *Beep*, by Collins herself, or Nick Dwyer's *Diggin' in the Carts*, focusing on Japanese game music, offer an abundance of valuable material and first-hand insights from practitioners such as Junko Ozawa, Chris Hülsbeck, Rob Hubbard and many others. Additionally, practitioners are regularly invited to share their knowledge at conferences and conventions, and at time of writing, James Newman is working on establishing a Game Sound Archive he founded in 2017 in collaboration with the British Library. The chip music scene has also been investigated by researchers,[6] was the topic of documentaries such as *Blip Festival: Reformat the Planet* (2008) and practitioners such as Anders Carlsson,[7] Leonard J. Paul,[8] Haruhisa 'hally' Tanaka[9] and Blake Troise[10] have recently shared their knowledge in publications.

Media archaeologist Stefan Höltgen points out the following issue with the research as conducted so far:

> Most research into computer sound hardware favors historiographical 're-narrations' . . . : the development of (sound) technology moves from the simple to the complex, from poor to better sound chips. Such evolution is often measured in terms of quantifiable attributes like year dates, sales figures, or technical elements (such as bandwidth, numbers of different wave forms, sound channels, filters etc.). Sometimes this perspective leads to the marginalization of (economically) unsuccessful systems[.][11]

Furthermore, as time goes by, the original hardware or entire systems become harder to find or unavailable, and researchers must depend on

---

[6] See, for example, Melanie Fritsch, *Performing Bytes: Musikperformances der Computerspielkultur* (Würzburg: Königshausen & Neumann, 2018), 252–67; Matthias Pasdzierny, 'Geeks on Stage? Investigations in the World of (Live) Chipmusic', in *Music and Game. Perspectives on a Popular Alliance*, ed. Peter Moormann (Wiesbaden: Springer, 2013), 171–90; Chris Tonelli, 'The Chiptuning of the World: Game Boys, Imagined Travel, and Musical Meaning', in *The Oxford Handbook of Mobile Music Studies*, Vol. 2, ed. Sumanth Gopinath and Jason Stanyek (New York: Oxford University Press, 2014), 402–26.

[7] Anders Carlsson, 'Chip Music: Low-Tech Data Music Sharing', in *From Pac-Man to Pop Music: Interactive Audio in Games and New Media*, ed. Karen Collins (Aldershot: Ashgate, 2008), 153–62.

[8] Leonard J. Paul, 'For the Love of Chiptune', in *The Oxford Handbook of Interactive Audio*, ed. Karen Collins, Bill Kapralos and Holly Tessler (New York: Oxford University Press, 2014), 507–30.

[9] Haruhisa 'hally' Tanaka, *All About Chiptune* (Tokyo: Seibundo-shinkosha, 2017).

[10] Blake Troise, 'The 1-Bit Instrument: The Fundamentals of 1-Bit Synthesis, Their Implementational Implications, and Instrumental Possibilities', *Journal of Sound and Music in Games* 1, no. 1 (2020): 44–74.

[11] Stefan Höltgen, 'Play that Pokey Music: Computer Archeological Gaming with Vintage Sound Chips', *The Computer Games Journal* 7 (2018): 213–30 at 214.

emulations for their investigations. Scholars have started to research these issues more broadly. Especially for older systems such as 1970s and 1980s arcade machines, home consoles, handhelds or home computers, a close investigation both of the respective sound chips and their features is necessary, as well as version histories and the features of the entire systems in which these chips were built. Looking at the technology, the 'instrument as such', firstly reveals the respective technological preconditions, and secondly furthers a more in-depth understanding of the compositional approaches and decisions both of contemporary game composers and chip music practitioners in the chip music scene.[12] Subsequently, another discussion is arousing more and more attention: the question of game and game sound preservation and accessibility.[13] In order to conduct such investigations, the hardware, software and the games must be available and functional. Emulations, recordings or watching gameplay videos can help when focusing on the mere compositions or describing how the music is played back during gameplay. But when it comes to understanding the original game feel, delivering the full original sonic experience including unintended sounds, some caused by the hardware used to create sounds and music – they fall short.

Furthermore, music making has not only made use of the dedicated means of production such as sound chips, but also the deliberate (mis-)use of other hardware components. As Höltgen puts it:

[C]omputers have never calculated in silence. Computer technology of the pre-electronic era emitted sound itself, . . . because where there is friction, there will be sound. This did not even change when the calculating machines became inaudible. Their peripherals have always made sounds with their motors (tape and floppy drives, printers, scanners), rotors (fans), movable heads (hard disk and floppy drives), or relays (in built-in cassette recorders and power supply choppers).[14]

Furthermore, these sounds were not just audible during gameplay; they were also used in themselves to create sounds and music, be it for games or in the form of playful practices that used the given material basis to create music such as chip music, floppy music, circuit bending and the like.

Subsequently, Höltgen suggests an alternative approach from the perspective of 'computer archaeology with its methods of measuring, demonstrating,

---

[12] See, for example, Nikita Braguinski, *RANDOM: Die Archäologie der Elektronischen Spielzeugklänge* (Bochum: Projekt Verlag, 2018).

[13] See, for example, James Newman, 'The Music of Microswitches: Preserving Videogame Sound – A Proposal', *The Computer Games Journal* 7 (2018): 261–78.

[14] Höltgen, 'Play that Pokey Music', 216.

and re-enacting technical processes'[15] – in other words, the scientific study of musical instruments and questions of historical performance practice needs to be pursued in ludomusicological discourse and teaching.

Further Reading

Braguinski, Nikita. *RANDOM: Die Archäologie der Elektronischen Spielzeugklänge.* Bochum: Projekt Verlag, 2018.

Collins, Karen. 'From Bits to Hits: Video Games Music Changes Its Tune.' *Film International* 12 (2005): 4–19.

Collins, Karen. 'Flat Twos and the Musical Aesthetic of the Atari VCS.' *Popular Musicology Online* 1 (2006).

Collins, Karen. *Game Sound: An Introduction to the History, Theory, and Practice of Video Game Music and Sound Design.* Cambridge, MA: The MIT Press, 2008.

Fritsch, Melanie. *Performing Bytes: Musikperformances der Computerspielkultur.* Würzburg: Königshausen & Neumann, 2018.

McAlpine, Kenneth B. *Bits and Pieces. A History of Chiptunes.* New York: Oxford University Press, 2018.

Newman, James. 'The Music of Microswitches: Preserving Videogame Sound – A Proposal.' *The Computer Games Journal* 7 (2018): 261–78.

Tanaka, Haruhisa 'hally'. *All About Chiptune.* Tokyo: Seibundo-shinkosha, 2017.

Troise, Blake. 'The 1-Bit Instrument. The Fundamentals of 1-Bit Synthesis, Their Implementational Implications, and Instrumental Possibilities.' *Journal of Sound and Music in Games* 1, no. 1 (2020): 44–74.

---

[15] Höltgen, 'Play that Pokey Music', 213.

1

Before Red Book: Early Video Game Music
and Technology

JAMES NEWMAN

The Rise and Rise of Video Game Music

There can be no doubt that interest in video game music has grown
considerably in recent years. It is notable that this passion is not reserved
only for the latest releases, but extends back to the earliest days of the form,
with as much praise heaped upon 1980s Commodore 64 or 1990s Amiga
500 music as on the high-profile symphonic soundtrack *du jour*.
Contemporary game developers, such as Terry Cavanagh, underscore
games like *vvvvvv* (2010) and *Super Hexagon* (2012) with soundtracks
that draw directly on the early home computing and console instrumentation and form. In doing so, they demonstrate their own fandom, as well as
a desire to draw on the distinctive aesthetics of early gaming and their
association with an era of putatively simple yet unabashedly complex
gameplay. We further note exhaustive online archival collections such as
the HVSC (High Voltage SID Collection) or VGMrips that gather together
music files extracted from original game code. For their part, enthusiastic
programmers expend extraordinary effort on the production of software
applications such as VGMPlay and Audio Overload, which are solely
dedicated to the task of playing back these music files with no care or
support for reproduction of graphics or gameplay.

The influence and impact of video game music is felt beyond the
community of game fans: contemporary artists such as Tokyo Machine
are fully fluent in the language of early video game music, while
Grandaddy's 'A.M. 180' (1998) and Beck's 'Girl' (2005) demonstrate
a bilingual mix of indie rock guitar instrumentation and 1980s video
game consoles. In addition, a litany of tracks directly sample from titles
as diverse as David Wise's 1995 Super Nintendo *Donkey Kong Country 2*
(on Drake's 2015 '6 God') and David Whittaker's 1984 Commodore 64
Lazy Jones (Zombie Nation's 1999 'Kernkraft 400').

To ease the process of accessing this sonic territory, contemporary
synthesizer and sampler manufacturers draw on the distinctive sounds of

early video game music in their banks of presets, programs and raw waveform data. Plogue's Chipsounds software instrument offers painstakingly detailed emulations and recreations of a host of home and arcade-game sound systems, while Korg's Kamata instrument explicitly references Namco's 1980s game music, even going as far as integrating presets designed by legendary composer and sound designer Junko Ozawa, as it 'reconstructs the C30 custom sound engine that swept the world in the 1980s . . . [and] lets you play the classic video game sounds of the past'.[1]

To palpably extend the impact of early video game sound into the present, some manufacturers build new machines explicitly influenced by the architectures and sonic fingerprints of specific systems, such as Mutable Instruments' Edges module that mimics the Nintendo NES, or Noise Engineering's Ataraxic Translatron that nods to the Atari VCS console. Some go further still in creating instruments that eschew emulation or simulation and instead are built around the physically extracted innards of old home computers and gaming consoles. For instance, Elektron's SIDStation and ALM Busy Circuits' SID GUTS repurpose the Commodore 64's Sound Interface Device (or SID chip) sound chip, while Twisted Electrons' AY3 module has at its heart two of General Instrument's AY-3–8912 chips, variants of which provided the sonic foundation of countless computers, consoles and arcade systems, including the Spectrum 128, Mattel Intellivision and Capcom's *1942* arcade game (1984).

But notwithstanding the enormity and creativity of the labour that continues to see these sounds celebrated and embedded into contemporary electronic music and gaming cultures, there remains little detailed historical work on early video game music. The few popular and scholarly histories of early game music that do exist are frequently based around discursive formulations and conceptualizations of technology that reinforce totalizing teleological narratives rather than add nuance to the picture.

This chapter suggests how we might arrive at a nuanced discussion of the role and function of technology in relation to video game sound and music. In doing this, the chapter will address some of the limitations of extant approaches, and outline some alternative ways of thinking that reconfigure the relationships between hardware, software and, crucially, the creative endeavour of composers, coders and sound designers.

---

[1] Korg, 'Kamata Wavetable Synthesizer', *korg.com*, 2016, accessed 8 April 2020, http://gadget.korg.com/kamata/index_en.php.

Early Video Game Sound: When or What?

Before we proceed with this analysis, it is essential to address what we mean by 'early' game sound and music. Surprisingly, this is a difficult task, with no universally agreed definition. While there are distinctive practices, tools, technologies and techniques that are characteristic of game music making and reproduction throughout the 1970s, 1980s and 1990s, these ultimately continue to be evident, and are in use to this day, albeit in different contexts. For instance, central to the definition of early video game music is the sound chip. Whether they took the form of a TV-connected console or handheld device, a general-purpose home computer or a dedicated arcade cabinet, gaming systems created in the first three decades of the medium's existence all generated their sound in real time via a sound chip. These specially designed pieces of silicon were effectively synthesizers capable of generating waveforms played back at specific pitches, with timing and durations specified by code created in advance by a composer and programmer. Just as a graphics chip takes data about colour, x-y coordinates and scrolling and processes them in real time to create images on screen, so too the sound chip responds to data in order to generate the game's aural components.

The references to data are important here, and the methods and working practices for dealing with sound chips are particularly noteworthy. Contemporary video game composers likely expect to work with a Digital Audio Workstation for composition and sound design, might have vast libraries of hardware or virtual instruments and effects and use a plethora of software tools like Wwise to facilitate the integration of sound, music and interactivity. Each of these tools typically offers a graphical user interface, or a physical set of controls in the case of hardware, which are typically assessed in terms of their 'user friendliness', as Pinch and Trocco note.[2] Composers working with 1980s sound chips found themselves in an altogether different situation. Crudely speaking, there were no tools save for those that they created themselves.

Commenting on the situation in the early 1980s when he began composing for the Commodore 64, Rob Hubbard observes,

There were no MIDI sequencers, no Trackers. We coded everything just in an Assembler. I used to load up a machine code monitor and literally display the bytes in real time. The music was all triggered on the raster interrupt and I would start

[2] Trevor Pinch and Frank Trocco, *Analog Days* (Cambridge, MA and London: Harvard University Press, 2002), 309–13.

changing the numbers in real time to alter the synth settings and musical notes. So, I would tend to work on four bar chunks that I would tend to repeat and I would sit on that Hex editor, changing things. I would sit and tweak all those numbers until I had the four bars pretty much the way that I wanted them to sound and that would let me continue on for another 16 bars ... [.][3]

Consumer-facing music-making hardware and software did exist, such as the *Commodore Music Maker* (1982), but these were too inefficient for use in game development, meaning that working with code remained the only viable solution. The experience of writing for the NES was very similar, as Manami Matsumae, who composed the soundtrack for the first *Mega Man* game, explains.

[N]owadays it's a lot simpler to get the data that you want to create, and if you need to make any changes, it's not that difficult. Back then, in order to put the musical data into the ROMs, and you had to convert the musical notes into numbers ... there were times when you'd have to put the entire game into ROM and test it, but there are also times when only the music had to go in.[4]

As Collins notes, the lack of any readily available or suitable tools, and the necessity to work either directly with machine code or via a code-oriented interface,

meant that most early games composers were in fact programmers working on other aspects of a game, or at best in rare cases, in-house programmer-musicians who had to work closely with programmers.[5]

Even when such tools were later developed, they still demanded a combination of computing and musical literacy. The 'Tracker' to which Hubbard refers, for instance, is a sequencing application that takes its name from Karsten Obarski's *The Ultimate Soundtracker*, developed in 1987 at German developer Rainbow Arts. The Tracker arose from the frustrations Obarski felt writing music for the Commodore Amiga, and derived its visual interface from the vertical piano roll.[6] Yet music and sound information was still entered as a series of hexadecimal values rather than as traditional musical notation and the Tracker's resemblance to a code listing

[3] Rob Hubbard, 'The Golden Days of Computer Game Music', *Assembly 2002 Helsinki*, 2002, accessed 8 April 2020, www.youtube.com/watch?v=DiPdjbsiQqM.

[4] Jeremy Parish, 'Manami Matsumae, the Maestro of Mega Man', *USGamer*, 20 January 2016, accessed 8 April 2020, www.usgamer.net/articles/manami-matsumae/page-2.

[5] Karen Collins, 'Flat Twos and the Musical Aesthetic of the Atari VCS', *Popular Musicology Online* 1 (2006a).

[6] Kevin Driscoll and Joshua Diaz, 'Endless Loop: A Brief History of Chiptunes', *Transformative Works and Cultures* 2 (2009).

was unavoidable. Of perhaps even greater significance than the interface was Obarski's implementation of the 'Module' or 'MOD' file format, which defined a collection of 'instruments' in the form of constituent samples, patterns that specified when and how the samples were played, and a list that set out the order in which those patterns would be played.

We will return to the importance of the interface between composer and sound chip later, but here we should note that the programming of sound chips to replay music in real time sits in stark contrast to systems such as the PlayStation 4 and Xbox One, for instance, which stream music from a hard disk, CD or from an online source. In these systems, music is not performed in real time by a sound chip responding to coded instructions but rather is prerecorded and played back in much the same manner as it might be played back on a CD player or portable music player. Accordingly, the scope of the musical creation is not defined by the capabilities of the sound chip, and might make use of any form of instrumentation available to the modern musician, composer, producer or recording engineer.

The utilization of prerecorded music in video games had been greatly precipitated by Sony's 1995 PlayStation console, which brought the first commercially successful mainstream implementation of audio streaming from a built-in CD drive. In addition to creating and commissioning original music, CD playback brought the possibility of licensing pre-existing tracks. Psygnosis's *Wipeout* (1995) led the charge, and serenaded players with the sounds of the Chemical Brothers and Orbital. Beyond this, some games even allowed players to swap out the game CD and its supplied soundtrack and replace it with a disc of their own, as with NanaOnSha's *Vib-Ribbon* (1999), in which the game's landscape was derived from an audio analysis of the CD audio content. The disc swapping possible with games like Namco's *Ridge Racer* (1993), and central to *Vib-Ribbon*, arose because the entirety of the game's program data could be loaded into the PlayStation's memory (rendering the disc is no longer necessary), and because the PlayStation console was able to decode standard audio CDs. Indeed, the PlayStation game discs were often supplied as 'Mixed Mode' discs, meaning there was one partition with game data and one with CD audio, making it also possible to playback game music in a consumer CD player. It was this adoption of the CD audio format, or what is technically termed the 'Red Book' audio standard, that represents perhaps the greatest shift in game music technology. It also serves as a clear pivot point for 'early' game music, as prior to this moment, music was generated and created in a markedly different manner, with different working practices and tools and audibly different results.

However, while this might seem like a neat delineation point, the launch of the PlayStation, Sega Saturn and subsequent home, portable and arcade systems employing prerecorded audio streaming did not mark the end of sound-chip-based music making or reproduction. Countless handheld systems such as Nintendo's Game Boy Advance and DS series as well as their Nintendo 64 home console continued to offer no optical disc streaming and, therefore, relied still on the use of sound chips not merely as an aesthetic choice but as a technical necessity.

If we use the widespread adoption of prerecorded music as a historical watershed, the definition might seem to be based as much around what it isn't as what it is; how it isn't produced, and which technologies and creative practices aren't deployed in its production, distribution and reception. Perhaps more accurately and more positively, however, we can define the era of 'early' game music as the period during which the use of real-time sound chips was the only way to create and hear game music, rather than the Mixed Mode discs and mixed economy of forms of streaming and sound chips that we identify from the mid-1990s onwards.

'Chiptunes' and the Flattening of Early Video Game Sound

One of the consequences of the increased popularity of early video game music has been its contemporary designation as 'chiptunes'. As McAlpine notes, the term appeared in the early 1990s, has grown in popularity since, and is now often used for any music created with sound chips (or the sounds of sound chips), whether produced today or thirty years ago.[7] Given the slippery nature of definitions based around temporality, perhaps this chronological ambiguity might be useful. However, even though 'chiptunes' has the distinct advantage of being in popular parlance, it brings with it some significant issues. From the perspective of the historian, the term 'chiptunes' has an unhelpful flattening effect. Quite simply, there is such a wide variety of 'chips' with which video game music is, has been, and can be made, that such a designation is helpful only in distinguishing it from music from disk or online streaming. 'Chiptunes' tells us nothing of the differences between the affordances of the Commodore 64, NES or *Space Invaders* arcade cabinet, or how composers and sound designers might investigate, harness and extend their potentialities.

---

[7] Kenneth B. McAlpine, *Bit and Pieces: A History of Chiptunes* (New York: Oxford University Press, 2018), 6.

This flattening effect is particularly troublesome given the tendency of current accounts of early video game music to deploy the language of 'bleeps' and 'blips' in their often pun-heavy titles (e.g., BBC Radio 4's *While My Guitar Gently Bleeps*, 2017).[8] The origin of this construction of early video game music is understandable as many of the very earliest home and arcade sound chips utilized in 1970s systems offered few of the sound-shaping tools such as filters, or fine-grained control over pitch and amplitude, that would become commonplace from the early 1980s. As such, raw waveforms were typical, and particularly square waves which, requiring only binary on–off instructions to generate, are the simplest to create. Certainly, such sounds are inescapably electronic, frequently associated with the sounds of sci-fi control panels burbling, and are unlikely to be heard outside the most experimental and avant-garde academic music-research labs. Indeed, if we take the Atari 2600 (1977) as an example, we find that the sound capabilities of the market-leading home video game console were decidedly challenging.[9] The system's TIA (Television Interface Adapter) made use of a 5-bit frequency divider, which generated a limited number of mathematically related, but often musically unrelated, pitches. As the opening lines of the *Atari 2600 Music And Sound Programming Guide* have it, 'It is difficult to do music on the Atari 2600 due to the limited pitch and two voices . . . many of the pitch values are not in-tune with others.'[10] Were we only to consider examples such as the 1984 Atari 2600 *Gyruss* soundtrack, we might well be forgiven for building a view of game music as bleeps and bloops (and fairly discordant ones at that). To compensate for the TIA's esoteric tuning, Garry Kitchen, the developer of Activision's 1983 *Pressure Cooker*, 'determined a set of pitches that the Atari TIA could reliably reproduce. He then hired a professional jingle writer to compose theme music using only those available pitches'.[11] Similarly, PC-compatibles and home computers like the ZX Spectrum were equipped with just a 'beeper' circuit primarily intended for system-alert sound effects. Yet, music and sound design of some sophistication and complexity was coaxed from the Spectrum, which speaks to the ingenuity of composers and programmers, and further complicates the idea of bleeping and blooping.[12]

---

[8] See www.bbc.co.uk/programmes/b07dlx8y (last accessed 15 October 2020).

[9] Nick Montfort and Ian Bogost, *Racing the Beam: The Atari Video Computer System* (Cambridge, MA: The MIT Press, 2009), 131.

[10] Paul Slocum, *Atari 2600 Music and Sound Programming Guide*, 2003, accessed 8 April 2020, http://qotile.net/files/2600_music_guide.txt.

[11] Driscoll and Diaz, 'Endless Loop'.

[12] See Kenneth B. McAlpine, 'The Sound of 1-bit: Technical Constraint and Musical Creativity on the 48k Sinclair ZX Spectrum', *GAME: The Italian Journal of Game Studies* 6 (2017).

Yet, so pervasive is the idea that early video game music is no more than a series of bleeps, it has become necessary to tackle it head on. Question 3 on the HVSC's FAQ list is telling: 'Isn't Commodore C64 music just silly beep-blop music?' The answer, unsurprisingly, is an emphatic 'no!' Surely the palpable sonic differences between the TIA, ZX Spectrum, NES and Commodore 64 demand a distinction between their 'bleeps'? In discussing the absence of fine-grained analysis, Altice notes that,

The output of the GameBoy, NES and Commodore 64 are now subsumed under the chiptune moniker, but the sonic character of those machines are far more unique than the Xbox 360, PlayStation 3, or Nintendo Wii. Games ported across those platforms will exhibit visual differences, but their soundtracks will remain the same. There is no 'sound' of the Xbox 360 any more than there is a 'sound' of an Onkyo CD player.[13]

One possible solution entails adopting an approach that focuses on the specificities of the particular sound chips in the Commodore 64, NES and Atari 2600 and conceiving of them not merely as musical instruments or constituents of gaming systems but as distinctive platforms for music and sound design in and of themselves. A 'platform studies' approach recognizes the significance and character of the base technological systems and the contribution their underlying design and capabilities make in defining the sound of the platform. As Arcangel et al. put it, 'Computers have personalities, shapes and architectures like a canvas that influence what we make.'[14]

Conceptualizing early video game music as 'chiptunes' conflates and smooths out differences between platforms, but a game converted from NES to Commodore 64 will sound as immediately and profoundly different as it will look and feel different. The NES's sound chip is recognizable, characterful and, most importantly, unlike that of the Commodore 64. The platforms contrast sonically in precisely the same way that Nintendo's joypad is unlike Commodore's keyboard and the NES's colour palette and display resolution are unlike the C64's. Indeed, if we look at the specification of the NES and Commodore 64 sound chips (see Table 1.1), we immediately begin to appreciate how these differences come to be so pronounced and why an approach that recognizes and foregrounds the specificity of design is so essential.

---

[13] Nathan Altice, *I Am Error: The Nintendo Family Computer/Entertainment System Platform* (Cambridge, MA: The MIT Press, 2015), 277.

[14] Cory Arcangel, Paul B. Davis and Joseph P. Beuckman, 'BEIGE as an Expert', (interview with Dragan Espenschied), *Post-Data*, 2001, accessed 8 April 2020, www.post-data.org/beige/beige_make.html.

Table 1.1 A comparison of five early video game sound chips

System	Chip	Channels	Waveforms	Notes
Nintendo NES/Famicom (1983)	**RP2A0X**	4	2 x pulse voices; 1 x triangle; 1 x noise	Additional 'DMC' channel can be used for sample playback. For pulse channels, pulse width can be set to 25, 50 and 75 per cent duty cycle. Amplitude variable between 15 fixed values (no amplitude over triangle channel).
Commodore 64 (1982)	**Sound Interface Device (SID Chip)**	3	All voices offer saw, triangle, pulse and noise waveforms (that can be combined). Waveforms can be varied per clock cycle. Pulse width is continuously variable.	Multimode Resonant Filter; per-voice amplitude ADSR envelopes; ring modulation, oscillator sync.
Sega Mega Drive/Genesis (1988)	**YM2612 Texas Instruments SN76489**	6 FM voices / 4	Four Operator Frequency Modulation (FM) / 3 square-wave generators and 1 noise generator	The Mega Drive uses two sound chips. The Texas Instruments SN76489 was also used in Sega's earlier Master System console.
PC-Compatibles (ALMSC released 1987)	**YM3812 AdLib Music Synthesizer Card (ALMSC)**	9 (or 6 plus 5 percussion instruments)	FM with sine waves; three other waveforms inc. pseudo sawtooth via waveshaping	PC-compatible sound card with dual mode operation offering either 9-voice melodic playback or 6 melodic voices plus 5 percussion instruments.
Commodore Amiga (1985)	**Paula**	4	8-bit PCM samples (techniques were developed to replay 14-bit samples by combining 2 channels)	Separate to the Paula chip, the Amiga contains an analogue low-pass filter. The filter can only be applied globally to all four channels. The Amiga has stereo audio output – the four channels are mixed in pairs and hard-panned to the left and right audio outputs.

Examining the specification in this way, as in Table 1.1, we begin to reveal not only that there are differences between the capabilities of sound chips but also that the differences can be of great significance. For example, the SID chip offered variable waveform oscillators, Multimode Filter (buggy and unpredictable as it was), Ring Modulation and per-voice ADSR amplitude envelopes unavailable on the NES's RP2A0X chip. On the other hand, the NES had more voices and a particularly characteristic and 'lo-fi' triangle waveform, so it would be unproductive to designate one platform better than another. It makes no sense to discuss these sound chips or sound-generation techniques as being better than one another, any more than it would make sense to have that debate about a guitar, flute or acoustic drum kit. That these instruments are markedly and audibly different is the key to understanding the call to disentangle the chips from the tunes. Examining them in this way, we begin to reveal not only some of the significant ways in which the gaming sound chips differ from one another but also how these differences materially affect the sonic fingerprint of the games created for the host system.

'Chiptunes' and the Oversimplification of the Sound of Sound Chips

While it is essential to recognize the distinctive nature of different sound chips and move away from the monolithic nature of *chip*tunes, it is important that we do not overstate the role of the chip in affecting the sound of a given gaming system. Of course, the SID chip's oscillators sound different to those of the NES. For that matter, different revisions of the SID chip sound different to one another, with the filters varying depending on the month of manufacture, just as the different iterations of the Game Boy and Mega Drive vary, with one version of the latter being labelled 'The Stinker'![15] However, although the SID Chip, RP2A0X, YM2612 and Paula all shape the sonic landscape of C64, NES, Mega Drive and Amiga respectively, the chips do not write the tunes. And many of the compositional, stylistic and sound-design techniques most commonly associated with chip music, or even with specific sound chips, are really better understood as interactions and improvisations between person and technology.

---

[15] Ace, 'GUIDE: A Complete Overview of the Many Sega Genesis/MegaDrive Models, Sega-16', *SEGA-16 Forum*, 2 July 2009, accessed 8 April 2020, www.sega-16.com/forum/showthread .php?7796-GUIDE-Telling-apart-good-Genesis-1s-and-Genesis-2s-from-bad-ones.

By way of example, the ability of the Amiga's sound chip, Paula, to play back samples, is certainly a distinctive, if not wholly unique feature of the platform. Paula's ability to replay samples certainly affords a different kind of compositional and sound-design style, but it is only one aspect of the characteristic sound of the Amiga. Those snippets of audio are replayed at a specific sample rate and bit depth, which gives them a characteristic, grainy, subjectively 'lo-fi' quality, especially when they are pitched away from the root note. This is also affected by the quality of the computer's DAC (Digital Audio Converter), which is responsible for outputting the sound in a form capable of being replayed to a TV set, speakers or headphones (indeed, it is here that the audiophile might take exception with Altice's point about CD players not having a distinct sound). Each step of the audio pathway imparts its own distortions and colouration, some pleasing, some intended, but all present.

But even this extension of the 'platform' to encompass the audio format conversions fails to recognize the brute fact that Paula doesn't create music. Paula's ability to replay samples might strongly imply a compositional workflow based around small snippets of sound acquired from original recordings, sound libraries or from other pieces of music, and this workflow might have much in common with the cut-up techniques of Steve Reich or the burgeoning hip-hop scene. However, whether Paula plays back the sound of a barking dog or a series of samples derived from Roland's (1987) D-50 synthesizer (as in the case of Andrew Barnabas's *SWIV* soundtrack, 1991) is the result of a complex series of aesthetic and technical decisions arrived at through the dialogue between composer, programmer and chip. The compositional decisions, solutions and compromises are negotiated with the affordances of the sound chip, the architecture of the system as a whole, and the amount of memory and processing resources afforded to the sound program by the development team. Interestingly, the availability of samples gives the video game composer access not only to a broader sonic palette but, as we hear with *SWIV*'s 'Decimation' theme, access to a sound palette immediately familiar from popular music. Laced with the sounds of the Roland D-50, *SWIV* is audibly connected to the industrial soundscapes of Jean-Michel Jarre's influential 1988 *Revolutions* album, for instance.

Yet, there is considerably more to explore than spec sheets and more to chiptunes than chips. Not only does each chip have an identifiable musical/ technical 'character', but also each composer/programmer bestows upon it a unique and equally identifiable personality born of specific compositional, sound design and technological interactions and intentions. In discussing her work on early Namco arcade games, Junko Ozawa notes how foundational this personalization can be, by pointing to her own library of hand-drawn waveforms meticulously laid out on squared paper.[16] Like the Amiga composer's *bricolage* of samples drawn from countless sources, these waveforms operate in dialogue with the sound chip's playback capabilities to define the sonic territory available to the composer. Ozawa's stamp of individuality is evident in her personalized waveforms.

Other composers forged their own distinct paths by rejecting the typical approaches to writing music for a particular chip. The NES's triangle waveform is often used to take on bassline duties, as we hear in the case of the overworld theme in *Super Mario Bros.* (1985). The triangle wave is suited to this function because of a lack of control over its amplitude (thereby offering fewer opportunities for dynamics) and its pitch range extends down to 27.3 Hz, unlike the two pulse voices that bottom out at 54.6 Hz. Yet, some composers challenge convention by utilising the triangle wave in a wholly different way. By rapidly modulating the pitch of the triangle, the single voice can do double duty: it can alternate between a pitched bassline note and a kick drum. When the drum note is reinforced with a burst from the chip's noise channel, the result is heard as combination of bass, kick and percussion. The effect was used extensively by Neil Baldwin (*Hero Quest*, 1991) and Tim Follin (*Silver Surfer*, 1990). Composers devised their own innovative ways of writing for the technology, resulting in a diversity of approaches to composing for even one type of chip.

Some composers took this approach even further. Some SID chip composers, such as Rob Hubbard, would use one chip channel to play multiple voices, and/or blend chip channels to create new hybrid sounds. For example, in *Commando* (1985), to create his percussion sounds, Hubbard changes the waveform of a channel every fiftieth of a second to create a single sound that combines a burst of noise followed by a swooping pitched 'tom' effect. Even though the SID chip only has three channels, Hubbard's *Commando* score does not limit itself to three discrete musical parts. Where the listener may hear the rhythm track as a single 'part', it is actually written and performed across multiple voices. Sometimes voice two performs a 'drum' hit and elsewhere the same sound is played on voice three, for example. This happens because, depending on the nature of the composition, voice two is

---

[16] RBMA (Red Bull Music Academy), 'Diggin' in the Carts: Episode 1: The Rise of VGM', *Red Bull Music Academy*, 2014, accessed 8 April 2020, http://daily.redbullmusicacademy.com/2014/10/diggin-in-the-carts-series.

not always available and may be 'busy' playing the bassline or counter-melody. It is clear from analysing the *Commando* theme that it is not a piece of music simply transcribed for the SID chip but, rather, is written with the specific capabilities and affordances of the chip in mind.[17] The piece's thick sonic texture is further enhanced by the frequent use of ornamentation characteristic of Hubbard's work. *Commando* only uses three channels, but by continually shifting the musical material across the three voices, making space to pack in other musical elements, it gives the listener the impression of more than three voices being present.

Martin Galway's soundtrack to *Wizball* (1987), by contrast, uses similar processes for different ends. Here, Galway doubles and offsets melodies across voices to simulate a delay or echo effect (common in recording-studio outboard racks but absent from the SID's specification).[18] What we hear in Galway and Hubbard's work, then, is as much a function of the SID chip as it is a reflection of their individual compositional characters. And so, when Guay and Arsenault note a tendency in 'chiptunes' towards busy 'baroque' ornamentation, this holds true only for some composers of early video game music.[19]

If we look to the NES, we see similar variations in musical style and form that are best read as reflections of differing artistic and aesthetic intentions and sensibilities. Koji Kondo's work on the *Super Mario Bros.* and The Legend of Zelda series takes a very particular approach to the RP2A0X sound chip. Unlike the work of Hubbard, whose extreme multiplexing sought to create the impression of a greater number of voices than were actually sounding, Kondo's NES themes are stripped back. Not bare or minimalistic, by any means, but neither disguising nor shying away from the presentation of a four-part composition of bassline (triangle), melody and countermelody (pulses) and percussion (noise). For McAlpine, Kondo's technique in *Super Mario Bros.* has its antecedents in the 'shell voicing' technique used by Art Tatum and Bill Evans that implies complex harmonies with just a few notes, and the syncopations and polyrhythms that are not entirely dissimilar to the rhythmic devices employed in Debussy's first *Arabesque*.[20]

---

[17] James Newman, 'Driving the SID Chip: Assembly Language, Composition, and Sound Design for the C64', *GAME: The Italian Journal of Game Studies* 6 (2017).

[18] Neil Baldwin, 'James Bond Jr (Eurocom/THQ 1991)', *DutyCycleGenerator*, 29 March 2009, accessed 8 April 2020, https://web.archive.org/web/20200325074309/http://dutycyclegenerator.com:80/.

[19] Louis-Martin Guay and Dominic Arsenault, 'Thumb-Bangers: Exploring the Cultural Bond Between Video Games and Heavy Metal', in *Heavy Metal Generations*, ed. Andy Brown and Kevin Fellezs (Oxford: Interdisciplinary Press, 2012), 105–15.

[20] McAlpine, *Bits and Pieces*, 120–1.

Of course, music is typically not the only sonic output of a game, but has to co-exist with sound effects in the game's soundscape. One question we might raise in relation to Kondo's *Super Mario Bros.* theme is why the jumping sound effect, triggered as Mario takes flight and heard with some frequency, should cut out the main melody line. The technical answer is simple. With only four channels available for music and sound effects, something has to give. Kondo's was but one of a number of strategies deployed throughout the 1980s and 1990s to combine music and 'interactive non-diegetic sound' as Collins puts it.[21] Some games reserved voices on the chip exclusively for sound effects (*The Human Race*, Mastertronic, Commodore 64, 1985), while others asked players to choose between music and sound effects (*Delta*, Thalamus, Commodore 64, 1987). But why replace the lead line rather than the counter-melody? One answer, favoured by McAlpine, connects the pitch of the jump sound effect with the key of the game's soundtrack.[22] As such, the harmonic integrity of the soundscape (if not the melody) is preserved and the sound effect is integrated into the music, joining the visual, sonic, haptic and ludic aspects of the game into one experiential whole.

What we see in these examples is not simply the result of different musicians imprinting themselves on an instrument through their differing sensibilities. Rather, the different approaches become encoded in the distinct software routines that are used to create and craft music.

Although it is tempting to view the 1980s or 1990s console, home computer or arcade-board sound chip as a synthesizer, if we consider the interfaces by which these sonic potentialities were accessed, they have little in common with the commercially available instruments used by musicians on stage and in studios at the time. The SID chip, for instance, presents itself as a series of data registers that can be read and written to. There are no inviting faders, sliders, potentiometers, or pitch and modulation wheels to be seen. All sound design is undertaken by accessing these data registers in hexadecimal. Similarly, in the 1980s, no visual compositional tools existed to help write, arrange or edit sequences of game music. Any tools had to be created for the task. Some musicians created their own bespoke sound design, composition and playback software routines – or 'drivers' as they are typically called – while others relied on the services of coders. Either way, these sound drivers play an immense role in defining the sound of the sound chip. These routines reveal, or make available, facets of the

---

[21] Karen Collins, 'In the Loop: Creativity and Constraint in 8-bit Video Game Audio', *Twentieth Century Music* 4, no. 2 (2007): 209–27, at 212.

[22] McAlpine, *Bits and Pieces*, 123.

sound chip's capability.[23] As Hubbard notes of his *Monty on the Run* (1985) composition, 'The middle section was an excuse to use the new pitch bend code that I wrote for this project.'[24] Similarly, Martin Galway, in-house composer at Ocean Software, describes how he was 'mastering the C64' as he was developing his drivers.[25]

Technical capabilities are transformed into musical utilities by the software driver. For instance, the SID chip's technical capability to stably control the pitch of its oscillators over a wide frequency range or to continuously vary the duty cycle of its pulse waves become the musical operation of *portamento*. A driver includes and omits musical and sound design features in accordance with the aesthetic judgement and predilections of the composer and sound designer. As new affordances are revealed, these features can be added to the driver to present them in a musically useful manner. Sometimes these are features unintended and unanticipated even by the creators of the sound chips themselves, as in the case of the SID chip's sample playback capability.

To speak of the sonic characteristic of a given sound chip is to tell only part of the story. Without sound driver routines written in software and acting as a mediating interface between the composer and silicon, the sound chip's features remain musically inaccessible data points on a specification sheet. As Chris Abbott observes, 'Rob Hubbard sounded very different from Martin Galway because they had to write their own synthesizer engine, as well as the music.'[26]

Perhaps the most persuasive example of the significance and personality of the sound driver in mediating and shaping the interface between musician and chip is found in the rapidly arpeggiating pseudochord. This musical device must surely rank as one of the most instantly recognizable features of 'chiptunes'. It consists of an arpeggio of two or more notes played at a speed so high that the individual tones almost appear to meld into a single chord. Almost, but not quite, which is what gives the figure a warbling or chirping effect a little like a mobile telephone ring, as the individual tones and their transients are still identifiable.

---

[23] For an analysis of Hubbard's early driver routine see Anthony McSweeney, 'Rob Hubbard's Music: Disassembled, Commented and Explained', *C=Hacking* 5 (1993), accessed 8 April 2020, www.ffd2.com/fridge/chacking/c=hacking5.txt.

[24] Andreas Wallström, 'Rob Hubbard Interview', *C64.com* (n.d.), accessed 8 April 2020, www.c64.com/interviews/hubbard.html.

[25] Andreas Wallström, 'Martin Galway Interview', *C64.com* (n.d.), accessed 8 April 2020, www.c64.com/interviews/galway_part_2.html.

[26] Flat Four, *Programme 3: Commodore Music*, Flat Four Radio, 2005, accessed 8 April 2020, www.mcld.co.uk/flatfour/chiptunes/commodore/.

The key here is that the design and operation of the sound driver for a video game are intimately related to those of the system processor, game program and TV standards. The sound driver is just one of the processes requiring access to the finite computing resources of the system. If we take the case of the typical 1980s console or home computer game, as graphics need to be drawn on screen fifty or sixty times a second (depending on the exact system and international TV specification) to create the impression of continuous, smooth motion, other elements of the program, including the sound driver, can run only when the processor is not busy undertaking these tasks. With the driver written to issue new instructions to the sound chip fifty times a second, this sets the maximum rate of change for the opening or closing of a filter, the adjustment of a waveform duty cycle or the pitch of a note. The effect of this is that the rapidity of the rapid arpeggiations that comprise the pseudochord is dictated not by any musically significant or even musically derived division, but rather by the driver's maximum speed of operation. Importantly, the maximum speed of arpeggiation does not necessarily reflect the extent of a sound chip's capability, and serves to underscore the significance of the driver in shaping the available features.

Yet, while arpeggiation has become almost emblematic of an entire genre of music, it is not endemic to any particular chip nor, indeed, is its use a product of or limited to sound chips. Rapid arpeggiation has been evident in monophonic music for many centuries, but here it is accelerated beyond the ability of even the most dexterous human player. More importantly, because this rapid changing of pitch is not a feature of the sound chip that is simply enabled or disabled, but rather is a function of the sound driver routine, its design and implementation is as personal and distinctive as any other sound-design or compositional device we might identify. So, where some composers use three- or even four-note arpeggios, some, such as Hubbard, often use just two. Indeed, where a composer writes just music with no need for graphics, game logic or user input, a sound driver may be written to run at a higher rate thereby offering increased resolution of sound manipulation and note retriggering. As such, though the pseudochord is characteristic of early game music, its implementation is always coloured by the driver and composer in question.

In addition to its flattening effect, then, the chiptune soubriquet is also problematic because it goes beyond setting focus on technology to giving it primacy. As such, the interactions and creative endeavours of the people who design the chips and the sound drivers and those who ultimately shape the technology are silenced. A focus on the machinery of music making is key to helping us avoid the tendency to generalization rightly identified by Altice. However, we must also exercise caution by ensuring that we do not separate the sound chip from the contexts of its design and use and inadvertently create a deterministic account that is deaf to the ways in which technologies are shaped. Similarly, by focusing on the ways in which the particular combinations of design decisions, technical and musical opportunities, quirks and affordances are revealed, harnessed and exploited in different ways by different composers and programmers, we offer ourselves an opportunity to account for the often chaotic and haphazard manner in which these investigations, innovations and musical inventions are arrived at.

Teleology, Linearity and the Tyranny of Limitations

Both popular and scholarly accounts of game music history display a tendency to centre on the inevitability of technological progress or evolution. These teleological approaches are based upon two interrelated principles. First, that there is an implied perfect or ideal state which this inexorable forward motion is heading towards. Second, that less advanced stages along this journey are characterized by limitations, which are progressively eradicated and rendered immaterial.[27]

Histories of early video game music typically present an evolutionary narrative that is both teleological and demonstrably written from a backward-facing perspective in which the limitations are evident given the bounty of what is now known to have followed. As such, rather than offer a study of early video game music and sound chips in terms of the ways in which foundational practices of design, composition and technique were established, they typically serve the purpose of a (brief) contextual 'prehistory' for contemporary practices. Popular accounts are more explicit in their conceptualization of progression in their titles. Both BBC Radio 3 (2018) and NPR (2008) have produced programmes entitled *The Evolution of Video Game Music*, for instance.

The orthodoxy of the technological timeline begins with the silence of early video games such as Steve Russell's *Spacewar!* (1962) before indefatigably

---

[27] Damian Kastbauer, 'Using Memorable, Iconic Sounds in Video Games', *Gamasutra*, 30 April 2013, accessed 8 April 2020, www.gamasutra.com/view/news/191426/Using_memorable_iconic_sounds_in_video_games.php.

moving along the pathway to the present, noting the series of significant milestones along the way. Early milestones typically include games such as Taito's coin-operated *Space Invaders* (1978), noted for including the first continuously playing soundtrack. This consisted of an ostinato pattern of four descending notes played in the bass register, and the tempo increased as the player cleared more invaders, making it the first example of interactive, or perhaps more accurately reactive, audio. For the first instance of a continuous melodic soundtrack, our attention is drawn to Namco's 1980 *Rally-X*, while Konami's 1981 *Frogger* added introductory and 'game over' themes linking music to the game state. The evolution of arcade sound is often articulated in terms of new chips (including the introduction of the numerous variants based around Yamaha FM or Frequency Modulation synthesis method), or the inclusion of greater numbers of sound chips working in parallel to provide increased polyphony (Konami's 1983 *Gyruss* included five of General Instrument's AY-3–8910 chips, for instance).

For home gaming, the evolutionary narrative is typically mapped to the successive 'generations' of consoles which move from the discordance of the Atari 2600's TIA, through the SID chip's synthesis, FM (e.g., Sega Mega Drive/Genesis which actually used a combination of Yamaha YM2612 along with the Texas Instruments SN76489 from the earlier Master System console), and sample playback (the Nintendo SNES/Super Famicom's Sony-designed S-SMP allowed 8 channels of 16-bit samples).

In the domain of general-purpose home computers, while it is ironic to note that the Atari ST was a fixture of commercial music recording studios,[28] it is the Commodore Amiga that is more commonly identified as key in the evolution of game music. This accolade arises from the development of the 'Tracker' software sequencers we noted above and the associated 'MOD' file format, which brought some degree of compatibility and portability.

In contrast, the PC-compatible games marketplace was characterized by a variety of competing sound cards such as the AdLib, Creative's Sound Blaster and peripherals such as the Roland MT32, offering differing playback quality, sound libraries and available effects (the MT32 included reverb, for instance). Where consoles provided a stable platform, the variety of potential PC-compatible sound cards created a situation whereby music might sound markedly different from one system to the next. In the

---

[28] Matt Anniss, 'Instrumental Instruments: Atari ST', *Red Bull Music Academy Daily*, 6 October 2017, accessed 8 April 2020, http://daily.redbullmusicacademy.com/2017/10/atari-st-instrumental-instruments/.

case of a game like LucasArts' *Monkey Island* (1990), although the PC speaker version is recognizably the same melody, when this is compared with its playback on a Roland SCC-1 card, it is rather easier to note the differences than the similarities.

Aside from the inevitable magnitude of the task, one issue we might immediately have with the timeline approach arises from the fact that, while games and systems unquestionably provide useful sites for investigation, their milestones entangle aesthetic, creative and technological endeavour and innovation. Nonetheless, such narratives remain powerfully seductive, not least because they chime neatly with the dominant discourses identifiable elsewhere in writing on video game history and, indeed, as deployed by the video games industry through its marketing and advertising messages.

As I have suggested elsewhere,[29] this narrative is not merely one that implies the existence of a continuum with its imaginary end point of gaming perfection, but is also one predicated on the supersession of successive generations of hardware. Simply put, each platform generation embarks on a journey beginning with its construction as mythical object of speculation, anticipation and desire through to an ultimate reconstruction as a series of weaknesses, limitations and failings that are rectified by its replacement. It becomes the baseline from which the next generation's performance is measured. Given the prevalence of this narrative and the ways in which new platforms and games are seen to improve upon their predecessors and render them obsolete, it is not surprising to find so much history of game music reproducing these formulations.

However, it is worth probing the efficacy of the conceit of limitations, particularly as its use in relation to early video game music is so prevalent that it seems almost to have become an uncontested truism. Much of what we have seen above, whether it be the use of the distinctive pseudochord or the waveform manipulation/multichannel drum design, can be explained as a response to the limitations of the SID chip and RP2A0X polyphony, just as Mario's occupation as a plumber can be explained as a response to the limitations of the NES colour palette and sprite resolution and the decision to clad him in overalls. On the other hand, these examples can equally be framed as manifest examples of the creativity and inventiveness of composers, programmers and character artists working within specific resource windows and working in dialogue with the technologies at their

---

[29] James Newman, *Best Before: Videogames, Supersession and Obsolescence* (London: Routledge, 2012).

disposal to shape their outcomes. That their creations, whether auditory or visual, appear to confound and exceed the boundaries of the 'limitations' is a testament to their ingenuity.

The incidence of looping is another area worthy of study in this regard. The construction of early video game music either as a single looping phrase, or as a series of nested loops, is for many commentators a defining feature of the form.[30] The reliance on looping is typically explained as a necessary compositional response to the limited availability of memory within which music data and driver code had to be stored. However, the tendency towards heavily looping sequences might also be read as a result of the iterative nature of compositional/coding practices.

This repetitious methodology is reflected in the unique needs of game scoring. Unlike a film score, background music for computer games in this era was designed to loop endlessly along with highly repetitious game play.[31]

In fact, in this final point there is a hint that, like Kondo's integration of the jump sound effect into the melodic top line, repetition in early video game music might be read as aesthetically and functionally matched to the often repetitive, iterative nature of the gameplay it supported. The four notes of *Space Invaders* are undoubtedly efficient, but they also suit the relentlessly cyclical nature of the gameplay just as *Super Mario Bros.*' repeating phrases suit gameplay and levels comprising repeating graphical and structural elements.

More than this, however, we might also re-evaluate whether some of what are presented as limitations truly were so, or have ever been truly remedied. Returning to drum design, achieving this through the rapid manipulation and alteration of an oscillators' waveform is a remarkable feat of ingenuity in sound design and creative thinking. It is also made possible because the SID chip's design allows the waveform of its oscillators to be altered at audio rate. It is possible to achieve this because the sound driver software provides an interface to that data register and enables the composer and sound designer to manipulate the SID's output accordingly. Is this example best understood as limited polyphony, with voices and waveforms accessed through an unforgiving interface? We might well argue that the SID chip was far from limited. Indeed, while modern replications and emulations of sound chips (such as the SID Guts, AY3

---

[30] See Karen Collins, 'Loops and Bloops: Music of the Commodore 64 Games', *Soundscapes* 8 (2006b) and Collins, 'In the Loop'.
[31] Driscoll and Diaz, 'Endless Loop'.

and Edges) provide altogether more user-friendly and tactile interfaces to the underlying hexadecimal data registers, the nature of these interfaces and protocols means that they actually offer considerably less precise control. The sound driver's interface may have lacked the tactility of the contemporary hardware synthesizer, but it did enable the composer, programmer and sound designer to effectively write directly to the silicon. If for no other reason than this, our discussion of the role of technology would greatly benefit from a radical rethinking of the centrality of limitations and the teleological, evolutionary process that implicitly frames early video game sound as a prototype or underdeveloped iteration of what would inevitably later come.

In this chapter, I hope to have demonstrated the importance of keeping an awareness of technology at the heart of our consideration of early video game music while simultaneously guarding against the rehearsal of the deterministic, teleological discourses so dominant within scholarly, popular and industry accounts. In particular, I hope to have foregrounded the ways in which contemporary analytical frames such as the centrality of overcoming or working with 'limitations' or the construction of 'chiptunes' actually serve to hinder our ability to create nuanced accounts of early video game sound and music.

| Chiptune, Ownership and the Digital Underground

KENNETH B. MCALPINE

Chiptune is an underground – and very distinctive – style of lo-fi electronic music that grew from the first generations of video game consoles and home computers in the late 1970s and early 1980s. Over the years, the style has grown in popularity to become the *chipscene*, a vibrant community of practitioners and fans who create, distribute and consume chip music.

However, while chiptune was defined by the sound chips and gameplay of that early 8-bit hardware, in the late 1980s the worlds of chiptune and gaming began to diverge as advances in technology and the changing practice of professional game development changed the way that video game music was produced and implemented, in turn shifting user expectations and killing the demand for chip music soundtracks.

This chapter explores how that transition occurred and helped to create a distinctive subculture, and it explores how attitudes to ownership and intellectual property in the scene were shaped, in part, by a reaction against the increasingly corporatized world of game development, and by the other countercultural movements that influenced it.

Introduction

Chiptune: for players of a certain age – and, as a child of the 1970s, I certainly count myself as one of them – it is the aural embodiment of video games. There is something about that raw, geometric sound that captures classic video gaming in its most immediate form, a distillation of pure gameplay. It represents a period of gaming in which technical and musical creativity combined in the most exquisite way, as video game programmer-composers ingeniously coaxed the primitive hardware – primitive, at least by today's standards – into feats of musicality that it had never been designed to achieve.[1]

---

[1] See, for example, James Newman, 'Driving the SID Chip: Assembly Language, Composition and Sound Design for the C64', *GAME: The Italian Journal of Game Studies* 1, no. 6 (2017), and my own

That period of game audio, however, was relatively short-lived. The programmable sound generators (PSGs) that served as the voice for the 8-bit machines – Atari's TIA and POKEY and Commodore's SID, for example – used simple digital sound synthesis.[2] While this gave those 8-bit soundtracks a unique and very characteristic sound, it was almost impossible to make those PSGs sound anything other than 'blippy'.

By the mid-1980s, in a drive towards greater sonic range and fidelity, the PSGs had largely been superseded and were beginning to be replaced by dedicated sample-based hardware, such as the Paula chip that provided the four-channel stereo soundtracks of Commodore's Amiga,[3] and FM and wavetable soundcards in IBM PCs and compatibles,[4] but it was the arrival of the CD-ROM drive, and particularly that of the Sony PlayStation, that created a fundamental shift in what players could expect from their video game soundtracks.

For some, it heralded the end of an era. Mark Knight, an industry veteran who got his break writing the *Wing Commander* (1990) soundtrack for the Commodore Amiga explains:

In my opinion . . . those new formats killed computer game music. It started with the PlayStation, when instead of being stuck by limitations which forced [composers] to create music in a certain style, in a certain way and using certain instrumentations, suddenly you could go into a recording studio, you could record an orchestra or a rock band or whatever you wanted, really, and then plonk it on a CD as Red Book audio. Suddenly game music didn't sound distinctive any more. It sounded like everything else.[5]

Just as an industry drive towards filmic realism and shifting audience expectations normalized colour cinema in the 1940s and '50s,[6] bringing an end to the era of black-and-white film and its brooding unreality, so

---

articles 'All Aboard the Impulse Train: A Retrospective Analysis of the Two-Channel Title Music Routine in *Manic Miner*', *The Computer Games Journal* 4, no. 3–4 (2015): 155–68 and 'The Sound of 1-bit: Technical Constraint and Musical Creativity on the 48k Sinclair ZX Spectrum', *GAME: The Italian Journal of Game Studies* 1, no. 6 (2017).

[2] In fact, although the PSGs generated their raw sounds digitally, many chips included analogue components in their signal paths. Commodore's SID, for example, employed digitally controlled analogue filters for post-trigger processing of sounds.

[3] Jimmy Maher, *The Future Was Here* (Cambridge, MA: The MIT Press, 2012), 192.

[4] Peter Ridge, *Sound Blaster: The Official Book* (New York: McGraw-Hill, 1994).

[5] Mark Knight, interview with author, 13 June 2017.

[6] Wheeler Winston Dixon, *Black and White Cinema: A Short History* (New Brunswick, NJ: Rutgers University Press, 2015).

too PSG music disappeared from video game soundtracks,[7] to be replaced by MIDI arrangements, sampled loops and licensed commercial tracks on CD-ROM.

It was a shift that saw video game music take on a more polished and commercial edge. The PlayStation racer *Wipeout* (1995), for example, featured a high-octane electronic soundtrack that was mostly written by composer Tim Wright with some tracks licensed from Leftfield, the Chemical Brothers and Orbital. Sony also licensed music from some non-mainstream acts to create an original soundtrack album that was released to promote the game at launch (Columbia Records, 1995).[8]

Colin Anderson, who, in the 1990s, was Head of Audio at DMA Designs, the company that created both *Lemmings* (1991) and *Grand Theft Auto* (*GTA*, 1997), described how that shift away from sound chips to full production music changed how he approached game audio.

Probably the most significant change was the fidelity of the audio that you could create. [Sampling and CD audio] gave you access to the same resources that the film and television industries would use ... and that meant for the first time you could use real recordings of real instruments, of real sound effects ... instead of having to synthesise them.[9]

One of the principal soundtrack innovations introduced by the GTA franchise was its in-game radio stations, a feature that created a sense of pervasiveness for its diegetic world, making it seem broader, richer and more multifaceted than the player's direct experience of it.

But, as Anderson continues,

On the downside, we lost interactivity for a while. The synth chips were particularly good because they were being coded at quite a low level. They were really good at responding to gameplay as it moved, and that went away when we started using CD and things like that ...

---

[7] At least for a time. Recently chiptune, along with 8-bit and pixel art, has seen something of a resurgence, as developers use these technologically obsolete approaches stylistically to impart a degree of retro-cool to contemporary games.

[8] In fact, *Wipeout* was part of a larger marketing strategy to build relationships with DJs, the music industry and fashion, and align Sony and its PlayStation console with 1990s club culture, which, at the time, was becoming more mainstream and represented a huge, untapped market. Arguably this soundtrack was a key component in positioning Sony, which at that time did not have a track record as an independent manufacturer in either console or video game development, as a major player alongside Sega and Nintendo.

[9] Colin Anderson, interview with author, 29 May 2017.

Expectations changed really quickly as well. Suddenly the novelty of, 'Hey! This has got a CD soundtrack', went away, and people were just like, 'OK, we expect that. Of course it's going to have a CD soundtrack. What else have you got?' It was a real game changer in that respect.[10]

That shift in end-user expectation proved to be a spur for further innovation, both in the way that music was utilized in games – the move back towards video games with real-time adaptive soundtracks, for example, was as much an industry response to that 'so what' factor as it was a desire to create tightly integrated interactive audiovisual experiences – and in how that music was acquired by developers.

For *GTA 1*, [all of the soundtrack material] was 100 per cent completely original material that we recorded in-house [largely] because we were this little software development house based in Dundee that nobody had ever heard of really, and at that time, if you approached the record companies and said, 'Would you like to license us some music for your games', they kind of laughed and said, 'Well, why would we ever want to do that? We're making ever so much money from selling CDs, thank you very much!' They just weren't interested.

In *GTA 2* that started to change. As soon as the game became successful, suddenly people turned up wanting their favourite tracks to be licensed, and [that commercial pressure] increased [with each subsequent release].[11]

If established artists were prepared to lend the weight of their brand and fan base to a game franchise, and perhaps even pay for the privilege, it is hardly surprising that developers and publishers would embrace that new commercial model, particularly in the high-budget blockbuster development space, where development times and budgets are often huge, raising significantly the overall cost and risk of production.[12]

  The age of PSG video game music, then, was brought to an end as much by the commercial realities of video game production as it was by the increasing technical capacity of home consoles. However, while chiptune might have disappeared from games, reports of its demise were greatly exaggerated. Chiptune was about to develop an edge, one that would set it in direct opposition to the corporate world of professional game development.

[10] Anderson, interview.
[11] Ibid.
[12] 'T. C.', 'Why Video Games Are So Expensive to Develop', *The Economist*, 25 September 2014, accessed 8 April 2020, www.economist.com/the-economist-explains/2014/09/24/why-video-games-are-so-expensive-to-develop.

Going Underground

Since the earliest days of gaming, software piracy had been a problem for publishers.[13] In the late 1970s and early 1980s, the issue was most pressing on tape- and disc-based machines like the Apple II, the Commodore C64 and later the Commodore Amiga and Atari ST, these media lending themselves more easily to analogue or direct digital duplication than did cartridges.

The industry responded directly and technologically to the threat, by combining a range of sophisticated copy protection routines with the threat of legal action against those who circumvented the copy protection to distribute the games.[14]

That stance created two parallel but overlapping worlds; on the one side the corporate world of the games industry, and on the other, the world of *crackers*, skilled coders whose self-appointed role it was to strip the copy protection from games and release neutered versions within days – and sometimes hours – of their official release.

Removing copy protection was a complex process, akin to surgically removing a non-vital organ that, nevertheless, forms part of a complex biosystem. The more complex the copy protection, the greater the surgical skill required to remove it. For the cracker this was the primary motivating force, not the resale value of the software or its functionality; they wanted to be able to demonstrate that they were nimbler and more skilled than those who designed the copy protection and all of the other crackers who were scrubbing up in countless other bedroom operating theatres.

Warez crackers, traders, and collectors don't pirate software to make a living: they pirate software because they can. The more the manufacturers harden a product, with tricky serial numbers and anticopy systems, the more fun it becomes to break. Theft? No: it's a game, a pissing contest; a bunch of dicks and a ruler. It's a hobby, an act of bloodless terrorism. It's 'Fuck you, Microsoft.'[15]

The first organized groups of crackers, or *cracking crews*, came out of Western Europe, specifically West Germany (JEDI) and the Netherlands (ABC Crackings) around 1983,[16] but by the mid-to-late 1980s crews were working across international borders to produce not only cracks, but

---

[13] Ron Honick, *Software Piracy Exposed* (Amsterdam: Elsevier, 2005), 215; Jacob A. Ratliff, *Integrating Video Game Research and Practice in Library and Information Science* (Hershey, PA: IGI Global, 2015), 121.

[14] Honick, *Software Piracy*, 151.

[15] David McCandless, 'Wares Wars', *Wired* 5, no. 4 (1997): 132–5 at 135.

[16] Markku Reunanen, Patryk Wasiak and Daniel Botz , 'Crack Intros: Piracy, Creativity, and Communication', *International Journal of Communication* 9 (2015): 798–817.

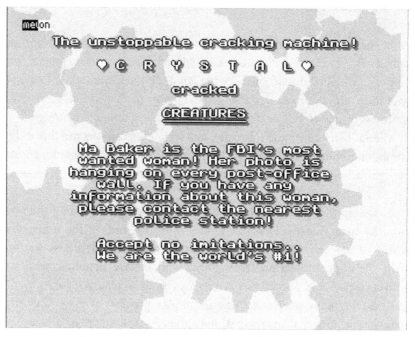

Figure 2.1 The Melon Dezign cracktro from their crack of Thalamus's *Creatures* (1993). The cracktro features the music of Mark Knight, credited as TDK. Note the use of the lyrics to Boney M's *Ma Baker*, an ironic nod towards the illicit practice of cracking. Cracking groups often riffed off pop culture references

sophisticated digital calling cards – crack intros, or *cracktros* – that were displayed onscreen as the games loaded. These combined scrolling text, algorithmically generated plasma and 3-D effects, and music to mark the technical achievements of the crack (see Figure 2.1).

The code to execute cracktros had to be compact and efficient to fit in the boot sectors of floppy disks, so that the cracked game could be uploaded and downloaded easily from bulletin board services via dial-up and rewritten to new floppies. The simple waveforms and sequences of PSG music, which could be stored as space-efficient single-cycle samples and tracker sequences for playback on sample-based systems, lent itself perfectly to this end. Chiptune became the sound of the digital underground.

Over time, the competition to demonstrate both coding virtuosity and graphical and musical creativity became more important than the cracks themselves. End users would actively seek out cracked software for the crack-tros, rendering the game an almost insignificant by-product of the cracking process.

The production and sharing of cracktros became an end in itself, and evolved into the *demoscene*, a distributed online community of digital arts practice dedicated to the production of complex real-time audiovisual displays.[17] That combination of anti-commercialism, a distinctive sense of community and a culture of sharing marks a definite point of departure of chiptune, as a constituent part of the crackscene and demoscene, from the increasingly professionalized and corporate approach to video game music production.

It also points to a difference in mindsets. On one side sits the corporate perspective, which recognizes that there is value – and cost – in the production of professional content, be that music or software, and that it is therefore justifiable for a company to protect its investment by using a combination of digital rights management (DRM) and litigation to ensure that only legitimate copies are in circulation.

Set against this, the Hacker Ethic, the core philosophy of hacking culture, which originated from Massachusetts Institute of Technology in the 1950s and 1960s,[18] sets out the intellectual counterpoint to this enterprise-driven process of making intellectual property out of everything, namely the 'belief that information sharing is a powerful good and that it is an ethical duty ... to share ... expertise by writing free software and facilitating access to information ... whenever possible'.[19]

But while that intellectual tension is most often framed and discussed in terms of the lone hacker against the multinational corporation, in practice, its impact can often be felt on a much smaller scale. As Mark Knight says:

A lot of chiptune artists today ... most of them [have] grown up with the idea that music is just something you share with people for free, so they're like, 'Yeah, but that's just how it is. Why do you have a problem with it?'... But CDs cost money to make. When I did my last album I spent nearly £1000 in software and hardware and that sort of thing. It'd be nice to be able to make that back.

It is frustrating that people complain that you're asking for money when you release an album for three quid. I'm kind of like, 'Yeah, do you drink coffee? So you will happily go and pay three quid for a cup of coffee but you're not happy to pay three quid for an album?' That really does frustrate me, because ... I've been learning my craft for years. That has value. I buy equipment, I buy strings and this, that and the other, but the concept ... people don't quite get it.[20]

[17] Markku Reunanen, 'How Those Crackers Became Us Demosceners', *WiderScreen* 17, nos. 1–2 (2014).

[18] Steven Levy, *Hackers, Heroes of the Computer Revolution, 25th Anniversary Edn* (Sebastopol, CA: O'Reilly Media, 2010), 23–31.

[19] Eric Raymond, *The New Hacker's Dictionary, Third Edition* (Cambridge, MA: The MIT Press, 1996), 234.

[20] Mark Knight, interview with author, 6 October 2015.

I would argue that it's not that people don't 'get it', it's that these perspectives lie at opposite ends of a continuum on which we all sit, and our position on it shifts, depending on context and whether we are predominantly creating or consuming.[21] It also points to a fundamental shift in how we collectively value intangible products, be they musical works or software.

An Open Letter to Hobbyists

Early in 1975, a young Bill Gates and his friend Paul Allen picked up the January copy of the news-stand magazine, *Popular Electronics*. On the cover was an Altair 8800. Manufactured by Micro Instrumentation and Telemetry Systems (MITS), the Altair, almost overnight, would become a commercial success: its designer, Ed Roberts, worked out that he needed to sell 200 machines to break even; within three months he had a backlog of 4,000 orders.[22]

Gates, then a Harvard undergraduate, had been following closely the growing phenomenon of personal computing, and had come to the conclusion that there was value in software as an indispensable counterpart to hardware. Sensing that the Altair represented a breakthrough moment, Gates and Allen called Roberts and offered to demonstrate a BASIC interpreter for the machine, hoping to contract with MITS as a key supplier. In fact, the pair didn't even have an Altair, let alone the BASIC interpreter that they were offering.[23]

Roberts agreed to meet them, and in the space of just a few weeks, Gates and Allen had developed an Altair emulator that ran on Harvard's PDP-10 mainframe, and then the BASIC interpreter. The first 'Micro-soft' agreement was sealed in April; Gates and Allen received US$3,000 immediately, with royalties of US$30 per copy of 4 K BASIC, and US$35 for 8 K BASIC for each subsequent sale.[24]

---

[21] There is, of course, another dimension to this debate, which has become particularly nuanced since digital content has become decoupled from physical media, and since recontextualized and reappropriated content has started to be freely shared on social media and media streaming platforms. This has fundamentally shifted notions of ownership, the emotional investment of consumers in content and the role that music and other electronic media have to play in our 'real' and 'virtual' identities.

[22] Thom Hogan, 'From Zero to a Billion in Five Years', *Infoworld* 3, no. 17 (1981): 6; Peggy Albrich Kidwell and Paul E. Ceruzzi, *Landmarks in Digital Computing: A Smithsonian Pictorial History* (Washington, DC: Smithsonian Institution Press, 1994).

[23] Jack Schofield, 'Paul Allen Obituary', *The Guardian*, 17 October 2018, accessed 8 April 2020, www.theguardian.com/technology/2018/oct/16/paul-allen-obituary.

[24] Centre for Computing History, 'Bill Gates and Paul Allen Sign a Licensing Agreement with MITS – Computing History', (n.d.), accessed 8 April 2020, www.computinghistory.org.uk/det/5946/Bill-Gates-and-Paul-Allen-sign-a-licensing-agreement-with-MITS/.

As they were about to discover, however, the early adopters of personal computing had a very different perspective from Micro-soft on the value of software. At one time, computer software was not something that was bought and sold. As computing hardware trickled out from research labs in the early 1950s, most end users wrote programs themselves, largely because none of the hardware manufacturers provided any for them to use. IBM's first production computer, for example, the 701, came with little more than a user manual.[25]

Developing applications was a major undertaking that required specialist support. Even relatively mundane programs required thousands of lines of code. They were difficult to debug and needed continual modification and improvement in response to the demands of a changing business environment.[26] Most companies maintained a team of programmers to service a single mainframe machine, a significant portion of the overall cost of maintaining and running a computer.

IBM, which, even in the 1950s was an old and well-established company, recognized that if that continued, 'the cost of programming would rise to the point where users would have difficulty in justifying the total cost of computing.'[27]

In response IBM created *SHARE*, a community of makers and consumers whose key mission was to share information and programs, thereby reducing the overall cost of computing, and in turn making IBM's machines a more attractive and cost-effective option.

From this group came many of the standardized notions of operational computing that continue through to the present day,[28] but so too did the idea that software could – and should – be something that was freely distributable. It was a commodity whose main value was in making the leasing of hardware more attractive, rather than as something that had value in its own right.

By the late 1960s, IBM had become the dominant player in mainframe systems. In much the same way as Microsoft achieved with its operating systems throughout the 1980s and 1990s,[29] IBM, by power of ubiquity, had

---

[25] Paul Armer, 'SHARE – a Eulogy to Cooperative Effort [1956]', *Annals of the History of Computing* 2 (1980): 122–9.

[26] Martin Campbell-Kelly, *From Airline Reservations to Sonic the Hedgehog* (Cambridge, MA: The MIT Press, 2003), 29.

[27] R. Blair Smith, 'The IBM 701 – Marketing and Customer Relations', *Annals of the History of Computing* 5 (1983): 170–2.

[28] Atsushi Akera, *Calculating a Natural World* (Cambridge, MA: MIT Press, 2006), 263.

[29] See, for example, for a comprehensive account of Microsoft's corporate dominance at this time, and the principles of anti-trust legislation, Jeffrey Eisenach and Thomas Lenard (eds), *Competition, Innovation and the Microsoft Monopoly: Antitrust in the Digital Marketplace* (Boston, MA: Kluwer, 1999).

created a de facto standard. By bundling software, IBM was able to provide users with a tight-knit group of products that would work seamlessly together, and that presented a problem: when the choice was to go with an IBM system, complete with training and support, or to try and bring together several applications from different suppliers that had not been proven to work together and which might receive uncoordinated updates and fixes from their individual manufacturers, most customers did not consider it a choice at all.

In 1967, the Antitrust Division of the US Department of Justice began an investigation of IBM, citing IBM's practice of bundling as evidence of the company's anti-competitive practice, and so, on 6 December 1968, IBM announced that it would unbundle the five major services – system engineering, education and training, field engineering, programming services and software packages – that it had previously included free with its hardware, and charge separately for them.[30]

And so it was, fresh in the wake of IBM's unbundling initiative, and with the concept of software as a saleable product still a relatively novel and untested idea, that Gates found himself colliding head-on with the established mindset that software should be free.

Gates had embarked on a national roadshow to demo the Altair and Microsoft's BASIC interpreter. At one event in Paolo Alto, Gates presented to a hotel packed with members of the Homebrew computing club, many of whom had already built an Altair and were waiting for MITS to release BASIC.[31] When they saw that the Altairs on display were all running BASIC off punched paper tape, one unnamed member 'borrowed' the tape and ran off a few copies. At the next Homebrew club meeting, there was a cardboard box filled with dozens of BASIC tapes for members to take, with just one condition: you had to make a couple of copies for each one you took.[32]

Gates was furious. He wrote an emotionally charged open letter, which set out both the tone and the agenda for the debate around intellectual property that has raged since (Figure 2.2).

History has demonstrated beyond doubt that Bill Gates and Paul Allen were right about the commercial potential of software as a commodity, but the continued growth of the underground *warez* scene, and the legitimate adoption of *freeware, Creative Commons* and *open source* as models for publishing and distribution suggest that attitudes around the sharing of digital content remain as strong as ever.

[30] Franklin Fisher, James McKie and Richard Mancke, *IBM and the US Data Processing Industry: An Economic History* (Westport, CT: Praeder, 1983), 175–7.

[31] Fred Moore, 'It's a Hobby', *Homebrew Computer Club Newsletter* 4, 7 June 1975, p. 1.

[32] Levy, *Hackers*, 192–3.

-2-

February 3, 1976

<u>An Open Letter to Hobbyists</u>

To me, the most critical thing in the hobby market right now is the lack of good software courses, books and software itself. Without good software and an owner who understands programming, a hobby computer is wasted. Will quality software be written for the hobby market?

Almost a year ago, Paul Allen and myself, expecting the hobby market to expand, hired Monte Davidoff and developed Altair BASIC. Though the initial work took only two months, the three of us have spent most of the last year documenting, improving and adding features to BASIC. Now we have 4K, 8K, EXTENDED, ROM and DISK BASIC. The value of the computer time we have used exceeds $40,000.

The feedback we have gotten from the hundreds of people who say they are using BASIC has all been positive. Two surprising things are apparent, however. 1) Most of these "users" never bought BASIC (less than 10% of all Altair owners have bought BASIC), and 2) The amount of royalties we have received from sales to hobbyists makes the time spent of Altair BASIC worth less than $2 an hour.

Why is this? As the majority of hobbyists must be aware, most of you steal your software. Hardware must be paid for, but software is something to share. Who cares if the people who worked on it get paid?

Is this fair? One thing you don't do by stealing software is get back at MITS for some problem you may have had. MITS doesn't make money selling software. The royalty paid to us, the manual, the tape and the overhead make it a break-even operation. One thing you do do is prevent good software from being written. Who can afford to do professional work for nothing? What hobbyist can put 3-man years into programming, finding all bugs, documenting his product and distribute for free? The fact is, no one besides us has invested a lot of money in hobby software. We have written 6800 BASIC, and are writing 8080 APL and 6800 APL, but there is very little incentive to make this software available to hobbyists. Most directly, the thing you do is theft.

What about the guys who re-sell Altair BASIC, aren't they making money on hobby software? Yes, but those who have been reported to us may lose in the end. They are the ones who give hobbyists a bad name, and should be kicked out of any club meeting they show up at.

I would appreciate letters from any one who wants to pay up, or has a suggestion or comment. Just write me at 1180 Alvarado SE, #114, Albuquerque, New Mexico, 87108. Nothing would please me more than being able to hire ten programmers and deluge the hobby market with good software.

Bill Gates

Bill Gates
General Partner, Micro-Soft

Figure 2.2 Bill Gates's *Open Letter to Hobbyists.* This letter sets out clearly the opposing perspectives of the hobbyist community, which had legitimately come to think of software as a freely shareable resource, and Gates's more corporate viewpoint, which sought to commoditize its value. This debate has, if anything, intensified, and has grown to incorporate all manner of intangible commodities, including music recordings

The Incentive to Share

While the technology of sharing is now different – chunks of data shared as torrent files as opposed to cardboard boxes of punched paper tapes – the nature and themes of the debate have remained remarkably consistent as they have played out across different domains and distribution media and at different points in time. Although there are some notable differences between software development and music publication and distribution, there are also some quite striking parallels. Both, for example, have forced legislators and the public to deal with new technologies that have challenged our fundamental assumptions of what constitutes publication and ownership.

At the turn of the century, piano rolls, for example, were considered to be part of the machinery of a player piano, like the mechanism of a music box, and so not subject to copyright law, despite the fact that the punched paper rolls, unlike a music box, were distinct from the playing mechanism and could easily be swapped for other rolls, which contained all of the detail of the original music manuscript, albeit in a mechanically encoded form.[33]

In 1978, novelist John Hershey, a member of the National Commission on the New Technological Uses of Copyrighted Works, argued, in a similar vein, that computer code is dramatically different from other copyright works because the ones and zeroes in a computer program are designed to have

no purpose beyond being engaged in a computer to perform mechanical work ... [A] program, once it enters a computer and is activated, does not communicate information of its own, intelligible to a human being ... The function of computer programs are [*sic*] fundamentally and absolutely different in nature from those of sound recordings, motion pictures, or videotapes. [These] produce for the human ear and/or eye the sounds and images that were fed into them and so are simply media for transmitting the means of expression of the writings of their authors.[34]

In some respects, chiptune represents both of these key characteristics: the machine code routines and data are no more than ones and zeroes designed to control electrical impulses in a machine, and, like the rolls of a player piano, they convey no meaning unless they are coupled with a PSG,[35] which provides the machinery necessary to turn that code into sound, and yet few creative coders would challenge the idea that in writing sound drivers and music data, they are encoding both the musical score and the performance characteristics that will realize a musical work; they are not simply performing routine mechanical tasks.

---

[33] Alex Cummings, *Democracy of Sound: Music Piracy and the Remaking of American Copyright in the Twentieth Century* (New York: Oxford University Press, 2013), 21.

[34] Michael Scott, *Scott on Information Technology Law, 2018 Supplement* (New York: Wolters Kluwer, 2018), 2–20.

[35] Or at least an emulation of a PSG.

However, such notions remain abstract until they are tested in law, and because of the anti-commercial sharing ethos that is prevalent in the chiptune community, chip musicians have generally been happy for others to appropriate, adapt and cover their work provided nobody makes any money from it.

In an interview, Ben Daglish,[36] the prolific C64 composer, described how he felt about new generations of chip musicians rediscovering and using his video game themes:

It's amazing that people are still listening to my stuff, still giving me recognition thirty years on . . . I'm most impressed by the guys who take my stuff and play it live. When I was writing for the SID chip, I could use notes that were never actually meant to be played by human beings [and] there are guys out there who have transcribed those pieces and turned them out as guitar solos . . . In the end, I think it's just nice to be appreciated without having to work for it myself![37]

There have, however, been instances where chiptunes have ended up in court: David Whittaker's soundtrack to the classic C64 game, *Lazy Jones* (1984), for example, was reused commercially without permission by the German techno outfit, Zombie Nation, who used it as the central hook in their track 'Kernkraft 400' (1999), while in 2007 Timbaland used elements of the demotune 'Acidjazzed Evening' (2002) in the Nelly Furtado track, '*Do It*' (2007).

In both instances the legal challenge failed, and in part, that failure stemmed from the fact that it was difficult to prove ownership and establish the mode of publication. In the early days of the games industry, in Europe and North America at any rate, nobody gave much thought to the value that was present in the intellectual property that comprised the game. Video game music was not something that was imagined to have distinct value, and in most cases, those soundtracks were commissioned verbally – often by telephone – and so today there is simply not the paperwork to go back and prove who owns what.

In some respects, that legal ambiguity presents a real challenge for video game historians who seek to document and archive the ephemeral elements of early gaming culture. Video Game History Foundation founder Frank Cifaldi notes that 'there is no alternative BUT piracy for, like, 99 per cent of

---

[36] Ben Daglish was one of the early pioneers of 8-bit video game music, and became particularly well known for his work on the Commodore C64, scoring works including *The Last Ninja* and *Auf Wiedersehen Monty*. Sadly, during the writing of this chapter, he died, on 1 October 2018. This chapter is dedicated to his memory.

[37] Interview with the author, 14 December 2015.

video game history' due to 'the completely abysmal job the video game industry has done keeping its games available'.[38]

That rarity argument – the idea that if the industry is either unwilling or unable to maintain legitimate access to a back catalogue, then end users are justified in using whatever means are available to source the material that they seek – is discussed more fully by Steven Downing,[39] and it represents another driver in the underground market for digital content, particularly when the boundaries between the legitimate and the illegitimate are fuzzy or uncontested.

The desire to accumulate and collect is a common feature in most fan communities,[40] and the chip music community is no exception. The High Voltage SID Collection (HVSC), for example, is an expansive and in-depth online repository of community-ripped C64 SID music files that combine both the copyrighted music data and the music driver code required to play it. It was created specifically to meet the growing demand for the specific sound of classic 1980s video game music in its original form as gamers migrated to new platforms that offered a different – more 'produced' – musical experience.

Collections like the HVSC represent the latest manifestation of a culture of illicit supply and demand that goes back to the very beginnings of the recording industry, when bootleggers, playing a role similar to the fans who rip SID music files for the HVSC, stepped in to provide consumer content that was not available through legitimate channels.

Bootleggers and Mixtapes

The term bootlegging rose to prominence in Prohibition-era America,[41] and it first started to be associated with the practice of music recording and distribution in the late 1920s, just as the culture of record collecting started to emerge. An article in *Variety* in April 1929, for example, notes that 'There is almost as big a market for bootleg disk records as there is for bootlegged books'.[42]

---

[38] Quoted in Kyle Orland, 'ROM Sites are Falling, But a Legal Loophole Could Save Game Emulation', *Ars Technica*, 21 August 2018, accessed 8 April 2020, https://arstechnica.com /gaming/2018/08/can-a-digital-lending-library-solve-classic-gamings-piracy-problem.

[39] Steven Downing, 'Retro Gaming Subculture and the Social Construction of a Piracy Ethic', *International Journal of Cyber Criminology* 5, no. 1 (2011): 750–72.

[40] Henry Jenkins, 'What Are You Collecting Now? Seth, Comics, and Meaning Management', in *Fandom*, ed. Jonathan Gray, C. Lee Harrington and Cornel Sandvoss (New York: New York University Press, 2017), 222–37.

[41] The term derives from the smugglers' practice of concealing illicit bottles of alcohol in the legs of their boots.

[42] *Variety*, 'Bootleg "Blue" Records Lure to College Boys', *Variety* XCIV, no. 13 (10 April 1929): 1.

Many of the recordings that fans were interested in collecting had been produced in low numbers by small or unstable companies, and major labels like RCA Victor and Columbia were not interested in keeping obscure records in production. Collectors' magazines sprouted up in the 1930s in response to the growing public interest, and this, in turn, boosted the collectors' market, with the value of individual recordings being determined largely by their rarity. Bootleggers began supplying the demand, sourcing and reproducing rare and deleted works without incurring any legal reaction.

Collecting and bootlegging, from the outset, existed in paradoxical symbiosis: fan culture depended on bootlegging, and yet bootlegging undermined the rarity value of the recordings it supplied. The relationship highlighted the long-term commercial value of a back catalogue at a time when the music industry still treated recordings as products of the moment, aimed at contemporary markets and abandoned as consumer tastes shifted.

By the late 1960s, the availability of quality portable recording equipment and cassette tapes meant that an increasing number of unauthorized recordings of live events began to surface. Bootlegs became a valuable commodity in the shadow cultural economy of fan culture that sat – from the perspective of the industry, at least – uncomfortably alongside the more mainstream commercial channels of popular music. It was an economy that relied on an honour system, where those who received tapes from fellow traders and collectors made multiple copies to pass on to others within the community, echoing the sharing culture of many other anti-commercial groups and in particular, the hacker code that had so incensed Bill Gates.

'Home Taping Is Killing Music', cried the British Phonographic Industry (BPI) as the 1980s dawned and twin cassette decks and blank tapes became more affordable, which in turn domesticated music duplication.[43] A few years earlier, in 1977, the BPI had estimated that the industry had suffered around £75 million in losses through lost revenue to home taping. A study released by CBS went further, blaming home taping for the loss of hundreds of millions of dollars of record sales, and industry commentators began to predict the death of music just as surely as Gates had predicted the death of professional software.[44]

---

[43] Kathleen McConnell, 'The Handmade Tale: Cassette-Tapes, Authorship, and the Privatization of the Pacific Northwest Independent Music Scene', in *The Resisting Muse: Popular Music and Social Protest*, ed. Ian Peddie (Aldershot: Ashgate, 2006), 163–76.

[44] Andrew Bottomley, '"Home Taping Is Killing Music": The Recording Industries' 1980s Anti-Home Taping Campaigns and Struggles over Production, Labor and Creativity', *Creative Industries Journal* 8, no. 2 (2015): 123–45.

It was a hard-hitting message that had little impact. It was at odds with consumer experience, who viewed home taping at worst as a victimless crime, but largely, thanks to the subversive DIY ethic of punk, primarily as an expressive and creative act. A whole culture and social infrastructure grew up around the mixtape,[45] allowing music lovers to spread the word about what they liked, to make statements about themselves or to reinvent themselves to others, or, in the days before the complex personality-matching algorithms of internet dating, to tentatively sound out the personal qualities of a potential life partner. The counter-slogan of mixtape culture? 'Home Taping is Skill in Music.'[46]

Home taping did not kill music, just as VHS did not kill the theatrical movie release. The emphasis of the rhetoric was wrong. It wasn't music itself that was under threat, but the commercial framework that surrounded it, and here, amateur taping and informal distribution did, slowly, begin to change the way that commercial music was produced and distributed: streaming content, peer-to-peer file sharing, aggregators, online music collections like the HVSC and netlabels have all changed the way we access and consume music, and all have their roots, at least in part, in the digital underground.

Rather than move with the times, however, and embrace and adapt to disruptive technologies and changing public attitudes towards content, particularly as music became decoupled from physical media and labels could no longer justify charging consumers for simply accessing content, the industry reacted slowly and heavy-handedly, targeting the technology and the cultures of practice that grew up around them. As early as 1974, the BPI had threatened legal action against 'hardware manufacturers whose advertising of tape equipment emphasises its potential for home-copying of copyrighted material such as recorded music'.[47] Ten years later, the BPI made formal complaints to both the Advertising Standards Authority (ASA) and the Independent Broadcasting Authority about Amstrad's advertising for their music centres, which highlighted the ease with which its two-in-one cassette deck could duplicate tapes. Their complaints were dismissed. The ASA pointed out that it was not unlawful 'to advertise [the] features and capabilities of lawfully constructed appliances'.[48]

---

[45] For a discussion of mixtape culture and video games, see Michael L. Austin, 'From Mixtapes to Multiplayers: Sharing Musical Taste Through Video Games', *The Soundtrack* 8, no. 1–2 (2015): 77–88.

[46] Bob Dormon, 'Happy 50th Birthday, Compact Cassette: How it Struck a Chord for Millions', *The Register*, 30 August 2013, accessed 8 April 2020, www.theregister.co.uk/2013/08/30/50_years_of_the_compact_cassette/.

[47] Bottomley, 'Home Taping', 234.

[48] Bottomley, 'Home Taping', 235.

What the BPI was trying to do, of course, was protect the interests of its members, but it was doing it by demonizing the fans who were their bread and butter, in the process stoking mistrust and disenchantment that would further erode the sell-through music market. It was a counterproductive attack aimed in the wrong direction. A survey by tape manufacturer Maxell, for example, showed that 'premium' cassette users, those who were apparently killing music, actually bought twice as many records as non-tape-users,[49] lending some credence to the notion that – amongst the fan community at any rate – collectors are likely to seek illicit copies for consumption to augment legitimate hardware and software that is bought for archival purposes.

Conclusion

Chiptune exhibits several significant links to and parallels with other, established areas of cultural practice. In particular, the increasing commercial pressures of video game development contributed – in part – to a schism between the production and consumption of video game music: this led, on the one hand, to an increasingly corporate and professionalized approach that has seen video game soundtracks evolve to become a tightly produced and interactive form of media music, and on the other, to chiptune becoming one element of a manifestation of a set of co-operative and anti-commercial community values that can trace its roots back through computer hacking to the bootleggers who supplied content for the early record-collecting community.

That anti-commercial ethos, however, and the pervasive culture of sharing, not just within the chipscene, but more broadly within the different subcultural groups that lurk beneath the increasingly corporate digital mainstream, certainly poses a challenge: as Bill Gates noted, who will create professional content – be that music or games or productivity software – if nobody is prepared to pay for it? History, however, suggests that content will still be produced both commercially and – to a very high standard – within deprofessionalized communities like the chip music scene.

That anti-commercial ethos, however, does impinge on the community itself, as musicians who invest heavily in the music they produce find themselves unable to recoup that investment by charging for product.

---

[49] Maxell, 'People Who Buy Maxell Tape Buy Twice As Many Records As People Who Don't', *Billboard*, 28 May 1983: 29. Similar arguments can be made about video games, where customers often purchased physical media copies for their software collection, and either made or sourced copies to play.

Perhaps more significantly still, the anti-commercial ethos provides the rationale for the continued adoption of stringent music DRM, which commercial publishers use to protect their intellectual property (IP). Again, however, history has demonstrated that while DRM may well reduce casual sharing, it seems to have little impact on piracy; instead, it primarily inconveniences legitimate customers by limiting what they can do with their legally purchased content.[50] As Dinah Cohen-Vernik et al. discuss, since DRM-restricted content is only ever purchased by legitimate users, only they 'pay the price and suffer from the restrictions ... Illegal users are not affected because the pirated product does not have DRM restrictions'.[51]

Contrary to conventional wisdom, then, it seems that because DRM restricts the legitimate buyer, thus making the product less valuable, and increases the cost of the product, the effect is that fewer people are willing to buy; instead they make an active decision to source their music illegally. That inconvenience may also play a role in driving new listeners to grass-roots subcultures like the chip music scene, where sharing is the default, and the boundaries between creation and consumption are less distinct.

But what of those scenes today? Interestingly, while both the chipscene and the demoscene evolved both conceptually and technically from video game hardware, it is the social and performative expressions of that hardware that have seen both scenes flourish into vibrant contemporary movements.

A hacked Nintendo Game Boy took the sound of chiptune from the desktop to the stage,[52] and created a new generation of chiptuners who brought with them new musical influences, particularly the sound of contemporary electronic dance music, giving the chip sound a harder, more aggressive edge.

In the intervening years, the scene has grown in scale – thanks largely to social media allowing geographically remote performers and audiences to form communities of practice – and in significance; the lo-fi sound of chip music has been adopted by a number of major commercial acts, including Beck, Kraftwerk and Jme.

---

[50] Cory Doctorow, 'What Happens with Digital Rights Management in the Real World?', *The Guardian Technology Blog*, 6 February 2014, accessed 8 April 2020, www.theguardian.com/technology/blog/2014/feb/05/digital-rights-management.

[51] Dinah Cohen-Vernik, Devavrat Purohit and Preyas Desaiecause, 'Music Downloads and the Flip Side of Digital Rights Management', *Marketing Science* 30, no. 6 (2011): 945–1126 at 1011–27.

[52] See Kenneth B. McAlpine, *Bit and Pieces: A History of Chiptunes* (New York: Oxford University Press, 2018).

In a similar way, interest in the demoscene has surged, reaching a peak of activity in the early 2010s, with the informal DIY parties of the late 1980s and early 1990s growing to become huge international stadium events attended by tens of thousands of people, all gripped by the spectacle of competitive creative coding.

Ultimately, however, while there are links in both chiptune and the demoscene with hacking, bootlegging, mixtapes and gaming, both groups exhibit a collective and very distinctive form of self-identity, and by staying true to their core ethos – of using technical constraint as a mechanism through which to explore creative expression – they demonstrate that there is value in creative ideas distilled down to their most fundamental form and expressed well.

Few members of the chipscene would disagree that a big part of chiptune's appeal comes from it being unconventional and musically heterodox, both in terms of its production and its sound, and these are characteristics that I think demonstrate that these scenes are distinctive and well-established subcultures. Chiptuners and demosceners are quite happy to occupy that space. After all, as one unnamed blogger is quoted as saying in an article in the *Pittsburgh Post-Gazette*: 'Hoping to god this genre never goes mainstream. It's too [expletive] brilliant to get run over by the masses.'[53]

---

[53] Dan Majors, 'Artist of the Chiptunes Genre Featured at Unblurred', *Pittsburgh Post-Gazette*, 2 June 2012, accessed 8 April 2020, www.post-gazette.com/ae/music/2012/06/01/Artist-of-the-chiptunes-genre-featured-at-Unblurred/stories/201206010264.

3

Waveform Wizard: An Interview with Composer Junko Ozawa

JUNKO OZAWA, TRANS. LYMAN GAMBERTON

Introduction

Junko Ozawa was born in 1960 in Saitama prefecture. After attending the Musashino College of Music as a student in the Musicology Department and graduating with a major in Instrumental Piano, she joined the Namco Corporation in 1983 (now Bandai Namco Entertainment). The first game she worked on was *Gaplus* (1984, the name was later changed to *Galaga 3* in the United States), and following this game, she was in charge of the music for *The Tower of Druaga* (1984, for which she also wrote the sound driver) and *Rolling Thunder* (1986), amongst several other games. She was also responsible for porting some of her game music from the arcade to the Famicom versions (e.g., *The Tower of Druaga*), and further created the music for games that Namco developed for other companies, including Nintendo's critically acclaimed rhythm game *Donkey Konga* (for the Nintendo GameCube, 2003). She is credited alongside Toshio Kai, Nobuyuki Ohnogi, Yuriko Keino and Yuu Miyake for the song 'Katamari On Namco' on the *Katamari Damacy – Touch My Katamari Original Sound Track 2* soundtrack release of the PlayStation Vita title *Touch My Katamari* (2011). Since leaving Namco in 2008, she has continued to compose music, alongside giving piano performances and doing a variety of musical activities.

The music she created for *Gaplus* and *The Tower of Druaga* was included in the second game music album ever made. Produced by Haruomi Hosono (famous member of the Japanese synthpop and computer music pioneers Yellow Magic Orchestra) and released in 1984, the album entitled *Super Xevious* contained music by Namco's female composers: Ozawa-sensei and the other major composer, Yuriko Keino. The success of this album and its predecessor *Video Game Music* released earlier the same year started the game music boom in Japan.[1] *Streets of Rage* composer Yuzo Koshiro, who is

---

[1] For further information, see Melanie Fritsch, 'Heroines Unsung: The (Mostly) Untold Story of Female Japanese Game Music Composers', in *Women's Music for the Screen: Diverse Narratives*

also often lauded for having an influence on 1990s electronic dance music, mentions Ozawa's *The Tower of Druaga* soundtrack in a video posting as one of the major inspirations for his own work. In 2016, the Danish indie rock duo The Raveonettes dedicated the song 'Junko Ozawa' to her and her work. Ozawa-sensei[2] herself appeared in Nick Dwyer's *Diggin' in the Carts* documentary series, in which she also talks about her work at Namco and presents her own wavetable library. While other major manufacturers worked with PSGs (programmable sound generators, as documented elsewhere in this book), Namco's customized arcade game boards created sound with built-in wavesound generators (WSGs), including the C15, and the later model C30, which featured a dedicated 8-channel wavesound generator. This allowed for the use of customized waveforms that Ozawa-sensei and her fellow Namco composers used to create a distinct and recognizable Namco sound. As is the case for many other female Japanese composers (see Chapter 21 by Lemon and Rietveld in this book),[3] her musical impact and legacy is still to be fully acclaimed in academic research.

Note from the editors: The following interview with Ozawa-sensei was conducted in the Japanese language, then translated back into English and brought into the form of an article. This would not have been possible without the dedicated and outstanding help and translations of Lyman Gamberton, to whom the editors owe their deep gratitude.

Becoming a Video Game Music Composer

The first time I touched a piano was when I was two years old. My sister, who is four years older than me, had begun to learn piano and so my parents brought one home. Although I begged my parents to let me take lessons, because I wanted to learn the same way my sister did, I was still too little and wasn't allowed to study properly. Imitating the pieces that my sister played, I played them in my 'own style'; and from around the time I was four years old, I was able to study under the guidance of a music teacher.

---

in *Sound*, ed. by Felicity Wilcox (New York: Routledge, in press); Chris Kohler, *Power-Up: How Japanese Video Games Gave the World an Extra Life* (Indianapolis: BradyGames, 2004); and Yōhei Yamakami and Mathieu Barbosa, 'Formation et développement des cultures autour de la "Geemu Ongaku"(1980–1990)', *Kinephanos* 5, no. 1 (2015): 142–60.

[2] 'Sensei' is used here as an honorific, indicating teacher or learned authority, in keeping with convention.

[3] See also Fritsch, 'Heroines Unsung.'

When I was in high school, a friend invited me to join a band they had started. I was the keyboardist. Although I only played one concert during my high school years, I resumed band-related activities from the time I started at university, and gradually I began to compose my own melodies. My harmony classes at university were also really interesting, and it was there that I developed a further interest in composition.

Because I majored in music at university, I wanted to have a job where I could use my musical skills and knowledge. I found Namco Ltd. through my search for companies that employed music majors. I was already familiar with them via their Micromouse events.[4] I thought I would be able to do interesting work there and so I sent in a job application. At that point in time, I was willing to do anything as long as it involved music – I didn't expect it to be video game music.

My first completed project was *Galaga 3*. While my senior (*senpai*)[5] was teaching me, I was able to compose slowly and by trial and error; there were barely any impediments. The method of entering musical data is different to the way a score is written, so I struggled a bit at the beginning – but every day was a fresh experience, and it was a lot of fun to, for example, create 60-second sound clips.

I think that recent video game music does not greatly differ from TV/ film music and so on, but when I was just starting out as a composer, game music was decisively different. For game music at that time, the whole point was that the 'performer' was a computer. Computers' strong point is that they can play music fast and accurately: the sound was completely different to what musical instruments had been able to do up until then. There is only a slight electronic tone to the sound. Because the number of output sounds is limited to three or eight, if a different sound occurs in the middle of the song, the vocal portion within the melody is completely cut out.[6] That is characteristic of this kind of game music.

---

[4] Notes are by the editors, unless otherwise indicated. For the rules of the Micromouse events see New Technology Foundation, 'Rules for Classic Micromouse' (*c*.2010), (last accessed 20 May 2020), www.ntf.or.jp/mouse/micromouse2010/ruleclassic-EN.html. On that page the following description of the events can be found: 'Micromouse Contest is a contest in which contestants enter their robots to compete for intelligence and speed while the robots negotiate a specified maze. A robot participating in this contest is termed a micromouse.'

[5] Translator's note: By 'senior', Ozawa-sensei is referring not to managerial or corporate-hierarchy-related 'senior composers', but to the senpai–kōhai dynamic, a specific form of hierarchical interpersonal relationship similar to that of a mentor and a mentoree – that is, they were **her** seniors, if not seniors in the company.

[6] Here Ozawa-sensei refers to the capacities of the Namco WSGs mentioned in the introduction of this chapter.

The most difficult thing is always being under pressure to meet a deadline. The music is created after the character development has finished: although the last part of the game's development period is busy no matter what, because the programmers and the art/design team's appointed deadlines get delayed, I have to make the music in what little time (barely any) I have before my deadline. The thing that brings me greatest joy is that many people all over the world are hearing the music I've composed as they play.

I can't really say if my musical style has been influenced by any particular musician, but an artist I do like is Stevie Wonder. If we're talking about composing video game music specifically, I think the greatest influences for me were songs from the various anime series I often watched on TV as a child.

Starting to Work at Namco

At that time, the places where you could play video games (they were called 'game centres') had a very bad image. They were the kind of places that elementary and middle schoolers would be told by their teachers and parents to avoid because they were dangerous – and since my parents were both teachers, I received fierce opposition, especially from my mother. While this was going on, Namco was working as a company to improve the image of the games industry. At that time, I thought the creative environment inside Namco was something really amazing. The latest computer equipment was set out for us, and there were very expensive musical instruments that you could not buy as an individual collector. Working every day with these great instruments, being told that I could use whichever ones I wanted, was my dream.

At first it was 'one composer per game' in terms of composition, but as the games got bigger, the number of melodies also increased, so we eventually composed as a group. The first thing I considered was songs that suited the game. The game's 'image' grew out of its time period, location, content etc. as I composed. When I first joined the company, I was hyper-aware of trying to make music that would not fall short of the expected standard, because the people who were already 'senior' composers were making really fantastic video game music.

Waveforms and Sound Driver

For the waveforms, I created software that added additional waveforms, or I analysed the waveform of the sound created by a synthesizer, using an oscilloscope or an FFT analyser.[7] Anyhow, amongst the many prototypes I'd created, I had about twenty that looked potentially useful. As for the sound driver, since my senior already had one, I kept reading and referencing it, and I added specifications that were easy for me to use. Since I understood how the programming language worked, it was not very difficult at all. Of course, that is because the driver my senior had made was already there; if I had had to make it from scratch, I think it would have been more of a struggle. When I created a sound driver by myself, it was satisfying to be able to put all of my own ideas into practice straight away, such as being able to change the tone in detail.

Because *The Tower of Druaga* is set in ancient Mesopotamia, neither techno nor contemporary music seemed appropriate. I thought that it should be classical music, something with a slightly 'Ancient Egyptian' atmosphere. When the knight character comes out, I thought it would be good to create a brave and solemn atmosphere. The melody is the image of the knight gallantly marching forwards.[8] At that time, the sound integrated circuit could not output more than eight sounds including the sound effects, so I did not plan to write an orchestral melody. But I can't help thinking that the sounds transformed into an orchestra inside the listener's head ...

The Status of Video Game Music in Japan in the Early 1980s

Regarding video game music at that time, I think that even the video game production companies themselves weren't very aware of it. Of the companies that made video games, Namco was very aware of the importance of video game music – they recruited composers as company employees and composed original melodies, but it was also a time when the machines made by other video game companies were playing 'ready-made' songs without any repercussions. (There should have been copyright issues.) Mr Haruomi Hosono, of the Japanese techno-unit Yellow Magic Orchestra,

---

[7] 'In the computer method, almost universally the mathematical tool to calculate the spectrum is a Fourier transform, usually a special form called the fast Fourier transform, FFT, which is particularly suited to computers. Thus, the digital method of spectrum analysis is often called an FFT analyzer.' Albert D. Helfrick, *Electrical Spectrum and Network Analyzers: A Practical Approach* (San Diego, CA: Academic Press Inc., 1991), 15.

[8] It is worth noting that *The Tower of Druaga* precedes *Dragon Warrior/Dragon Quest*, a game released for the Famicom with a soundtrack by Koichi Sugiyama that is oftentimes mentioned as the first classical-style game music.

produced Namco's *Xevious* as a musical album, but that was the very first album of video game music anywhere in the world.[9] In terms of how the record was marketed, it was put with the film soundtracks and in the techno music corner, since game music didn't yet exist as a genre. These days, first-class orchestras that usually play classical music often do eventually include video game music in their concert repertoires. It seems more people come to the video game music concerts than to the classical performances, and the orchestras say they want to continue doing these kinds of concerts in the future. The orchestras are happy because adults come along with kids for the video game music programmes.

About the Albums *Super Xevious* (1984) and *The Return of Video Game Music* (1985)

For both of those albums, the producer (Mr Haruomi Hosono) selected and arranged his favourite songs. Once everyone had decided the order of the songs, the engineer created the record by cutting and pasting songs from the game's circuit board. For *Super Xevious*, there is a special BGM (background music) for the player name and high score in *Gaplus* and *The Tower of Druaga*. As for *The Return of Video Game Music*, my essay is written inside the album notes.[10] At the time, we discussed it with the director: we decided that the game music we had composed would be the first A-side. For the B-side, we decided to put in the music that we had made but had not ended up using in a game and that we personally liked. Later, the B-side compositions by Ohnogi-san[11] were used in a game after all.

To record the music I brought the whole game machine to the recording studio, attached a clip cord to the foot of the IC[12] on the circuit board, and

---

[9] Here Ozawa-sensei refers to the album entitled *Video Game Music* (released in April 1984), which preceded *Super Xevious* by four months, and included music from Namco arcade games such as *Xevious, Pac-Man, Mappy, New Rally-X* and others. It did not include music by Ozawa-sensei.

[10] Translator's note: Ozawa-sensei does not elaborate further on the title of her essay or give any other details. The essay she is referring to is the one in the album liner notes called 'Making of Druaga Music'.

[11] Nobuyuki Ohnogi was also one of the Namco composers, who had started his career in the company in 1981, and is known for titles such as *Galaga, Mappy* and *New Rally-X*. He was also involved in the creation of the game music albums and after leaving Namco in 1985 continued working on similar album projects. See 'Nobuyuki Ohnogi', *Video Game Music Preservation Foundation* (c.2020), accessed 23 May 2020, www.vgmpf.com/Wiki/index.php/Nobuyuki%20Ohnogi.

[12] Integrated circuit.

recorded it with as little noise as possible before the sound was amplified. During the break, I watched the producer, sound engineer and other people fight over who got to play the game. I think these kinds of records were starting to be produced because video game music had become trendy worldwide, and because there was increasing focus on its originality.

The Current State of Video Game Music Education

I do not think there needs to be a specialist BA or other university degree, but I do think technology and research are necessary for attaching sound to image in the same way for films and television – so a class on coordinating image and music in video games could also be good.

If video games as a medium are an important part of popular culture, then I think video game music is certainly also important. In the future, I think games will not just be a part of 'culture', but will also play a role in physical convalescence and in medical treatment, and that they will become more interlinked with human life in general.

Further Reading

Fritsch, Melanie. 'Heroines Unsung: The (Mostly) Untold Story of Female Japanese Game Music Composers', in *Women's Music for the Screen: Diverse Narratives in Sound*, ed. Felicity Wilcox. New York: Routledge, in press.

Kohler, Chris. *Power-Up: How Japanese Video Games Gave the World an Extra Life*. Indianapolis: BradyGames, 2004.

Yamakami, Yôhei and Barbosa, Mathieu. 'Formation et développement des cultures autour de la "Geemu Ongaku" (1980–1990).' *Kinephanos* 5, no. 1 (2015): 142–60.

Video

Dwyer, Nick (dir.). *Diggin' in the Carts*. (2014). [Video documentary series] (accessed 23 May 2020). http://daily.redbullmusicacademy.com/2014/10/diggin-in-the-carts-series.

Koshiro, Yuzo. *What Led Me to Game Music? Talk About the Music of The Tower Of Druaga, Gradius, Space Harrier*. (2019). [Video] (accessed 23 May 2020) www.youtube.com/watch?v=tLqbixY5H0s.

PART II

Creating and Programming Game Music

Introduction

MELANIE FRITSCH AND TIM SUMMERS

Video game music is often sonically similar to film music, particularly when games use musical styles that draw on precedent in cinema. Yet there are distinct factors in play that are specific to creating and producing music for games. These factors include:

- technical considerations arising from the video game technology,
- interactive qualities of the medium, and
- aesthetic traditions of game music.

Apart from books and manuals that teach readers how to use particular game technologies (such as, for example, Ciarán Robinson's *Game Audio with FMOD and Unity*),[1] some composers and audio directors have written about their processes in more general terms. Rob Bridgett,[2] Winifred Phillips,[3] George Sanger,[4] Michael Sweet,[5] Chance Thomas,[6] and Gina Zdanowicz and Spencer Bambrick[7] amongst others have written instructive guides that help to convey their approaches and philosophies to music in games. Each of these volumes has a slightly different approach and focus. Yet all discussions of creating and producing game music deal with the three interlinked factors named above.

---

[1] Ciarán Robinson, *Game Audio with FMOD and Unity* (New York: Routledge, 2019).
[2] Rob Bridgett, *From the Shadows of Film Sound. Cinematic Production & Creative Process in Video Game Audio.* (N.p.: Rob Bridgett, 2010).
[3] Winifred Phillips, *A Composer's Guide to Game Music* (Cambridge, MA: The MIT Press, 2014).
[4] George Sanger, *The Fat Man on Game Audio* (Indianapolis, IN: New Riders, 2003).
[5] Michael Sweet, *Writing Interactive Music for Video Games* (Upper Saddle River, NJ: Addison-Wesley, 2015).
[6] Chance Thomas, *Composing Music for Games* (Boca Raton, FL: CRC Press, 2016).
[7] Gina Zdanowicz and Spencer Bambrick, *The Game Audio Strategy Guide: A Practical Course* (New York: Routledge, 2020).

Music is one element of the video game; as such it is affected by technical aspects of the game as a whole. The first part of this book considered how sound chip technology defined particular parameters for chiptune composers. Even if modern games do not use sound-producing chips like earlier consoles, technical properties of the hardware and software still have implications for the music. These might include memory and processing power, output hardware, or other factors determined by the programming. In most cases, musical options available to the composer/audio director are determined by the (negotiated) allocation of time, budget and computational resources to audio by the game directors. This complexity, as well as the variety of audio elements of a game, is part of the reason why large game productions typically have an 'audio director'. The role of the audio director is to supervise all sound in the game, managing the creation of sound materials (music, sound effects, dialogue), while co-ordinating with the teams programming other aspects of the game.

For smaller-sized productions such as mobile games, indie games or games that just do not use that much music, tasks conducted by an audio director are either outsourced and/or co-ordinated by a game producer. Additionally, in-house composers are rather uncommon; most composers do work-for-hire for a specific project, and are therefore oftentimes not permanent team members.[8]

Composers must consider how their music will interact with the other elements of the game. Perhaps chief amongst these concerns is the question of how the music will respond to the player and gameplay. There are a variety of ways that music might do so. A game might simply feature a repeating loop that begins when the game round starts, and repeats until the player wins or loses. Or a game might involve more complicated interactive systems. Sometimes the music programming is handled by specialist 'middleware' software, like FMOD and Wwise, which are specifically designed to allow advanced audio options. In any case, the composer and audio directors are tasked with ensuring that music fits with the way the material will be deployed in the context of the game.

Karen Collins has defined a set of terms for describing this music. She uses 'dynamic music', as a generic term for 'changeable' music; 'adaptive' for music that changes in reaction to the game state, not in direct response to the player's actions (such as music that increases in tempo once an in-game countdown timer reaches a certain value); and

---

[8] For challenges arising from this situation, see Phillips, *A Composer's Guide*.

'interactive' for music that does change directly as a result of the player's actions, such as when music begins when the player's avatar moves into a new location.[9]

Unlike the fixed timings of a film, games often have to deal with uncertainty about precisely when particular events will occur, as this depends on the player's actions. Composers frequently have to consider whether and how music should respond to events in the game. Musical reactions have to be both prompt and musically coherent. There are a great variety of approaches to the temporal indeterminacy of games, but three of the most common are loops, sections and layers.[10] Guy Michelmore, in Chapter 4 of this volume, outlines some of the challenges and considerations of writing using loops, sections and layers.

A less common technique is the use of generative music, where musical materials are generated on the fly. As Zdanowicz and Bambrick put it, 'Instead of using pre-composed modules of music', music is 'triggered at the level of individual notes'.[11] Games like *Spore*, *Proteus*, *No Man's Sky* and *Mini Metro* have used generative techniques. This approach seems best suited to games where procedural generation is also evident in other aspects of the game. Generative music would not be an obvious choice for game genres that expect highly thematic scores with traditional methods of musical development.

As the example of generative music implies, video games have strong traditions of musical aesthetics, which also play an important part in how game music is created and produced. Perhaps chief amongst such concerns is genre. In the context of video games, the word 'genre' is usually used to refer to the type of game (strategy game, stealth game, first-person shooter), rather than the setting of the game (Wild West, science fiction, etc.). Different game genres have particular conventions of how music is implemented. For instance, it is typical for a stealth game to use music that reacts when the player's avatar is discovered, while gamers can expect strategy games to change music based on the progress of the battles, and Japanese role-playing game (RPG) players are likely to expect a highly thematic score with character and location themes.

---

[9] Karen Collins, *Game Sound: An Introduction to the History, Theory and Practice of Video Game Music and Sound Design* (Cambridge, MA: The MIT Press, 2008), 183–5.

[10] Richard Stevens and Dave Raybould, *Game Audio Implementation: A Practical Guide Using the Unreal Engine* (Boca Raton, FL: CRC Press, 2016), 129–96.

[11] Zdanowicz and Bambrick, *Game Audio Strategy Guide*, 332.

K. J. Donnelly has emphasized that, while dynamic music systems are important, we should be mindful that in a great many games, music does not react to the ongoing gameplay.[12] Interactivity may be an essential quality of games, but this does not necessarily mean that music has to respond closely to the gameplay, nor that a more reactive score is intrinsically better than non-reactive music. Music that jumps rapidly between different sections, reacting to every single occurrence in a game can be annoying or even ridiculous. Abrupt and awkward musical transitions can draw unwanted attention to the implementation. While a well-made composition is, of course, fundamental, good implementation into the game is also mandatory for a successful score.

The genre of the game will also determine the cues required in the game. Most games will require some kind of menu music, but loading cues, win/lose cues, boss music, interface sounds and so on, will be highly dependent on the genre, as well as the particular game. When discussing game music, it is easy to focus exclusively on music heard during the main gameplay, though we should recognize the huge number of musical elements in a game. Even loading and menu music can be important parts of the experience of playing the game.[13]

The highly collaborative and interlinked nature of game production means that there are many agents and agendas that affect the music beyond the composer and audio director. These can include marketing requirements, broader corporate strategy of the game publisher and developer, and technical factors. Many people who are not musicians or directly involved with audio make decisions that affect the music of a game. The process of composing and producing music for games balances the technical and financial resources available to creators with the demands of the medium and the creative aspirations of the producers.

Further Reading

Collins, Karen. 'An Introduction to Procedural Audio in Video Games.' *Contemporary Music Review* 28, no. 1 (2009): 5–15.

---

[12] K. J. Donnelly, 'Lawn of the Dead: The Indifference of Musical Destiny in *Plants vs. Zombies*', in *Music in Video Games: Studying Play*, ed. K. J. Donnelly, William Gibbons and Neil Lerner (New York: Routledge, 2014), 151–65.

[13] On the process of creating menu music for *Shift 2*, see Stephen Baysted, 'Palimpsest, Pragmatism and the Aesthetics of Genre Transformation: Composing the Hybrid Score to Electronic Arts' Need for Speed Shift 2: Unleashed', in *Ludomusicology: Approaches to Video Game Music*, ed. Michiel Kamp, Tim Summers and Mark Sweeney (Sheffield: Equinox, 2016), 152–71.

Paul, Leonard J. 'Droppin' Science: Video Game Audio Breakdown', in *Music and Game: Perspectives on a Popular Alliance*, ed. Peter Moormann. Wiesbaden: Springer, 2013, 63–80.

Phillips, Winifred. *A Composer's Guide to Game Music*. Cambridge, MA: The MIT Press, 2014.

Zdanowicz, Gina and Bambrick, Spencer. *The Game Audio Strategy Guide: A Practical Course*. New York: Routledge, 2020.

4 | Building Relationships: The Process of Creating Game Music

GUY MICHELMORE

Even more than writing music for film, composing for video games is founded on the principle of interactive relationships. Of course, interactivity is particularly obvious when games use dynamic music systems to allow music to respond to the players. But it is also reflected more generally in the collaborative nature of game music production and the way that composers produce music to involve players as active participants, rather than simply as passive audience members. This chapter will outline the process of creating video game music from the perspective of the composer. The aim is not to provide a definitive model of game music production that applies for all possible situations. Instead, this chapter will characterize the processes and phases of production that a game composer will likely encounter while working on a project, and highlight some of the factors in play at each stage.

Beginning the Project

Though some games companies have permanent in-house audio staff, most game composers work as freelancers. As with most freelance artists, game composers typically find themselves involved with a project through some form of personal connection. This might occur through established connections or through newly forged links. For the latter, composers might pitch directly to developers for projects that are in development, or they might network at professional events like industry conferences (such as Develop in the UK). As well as cultivating connections with developers, networking with other audio professionals is important, since many composers are given opportunities for work by their peers.

Because of the technical complexity of game production, and the fact that games often require more music than a typical film or television episode, video games frequently demand more collaborative working patterns than non-interactive media. It is not uncommon for games to involve teams of composers. One of the main challenges of artistic collaborations is for each party to have a good understanding of the other's creative and technical processes, and to find an effective way to communicate. Unsurprisingly, one positive experience of a professional relationship often leads to another. As well as the multiple potential opportunities within one game, composers may find work as a result of previous fruitful collaborations with other designers, composers or audio directors. Since most composers find work through existing relationships, networking is crucial for any composer seeking a career in writing music for games.

Devising the Musical Strategy

The first task facing the composer is to understand, or help devise, the musical strategy for the game. This is a process that fuses practical issues with technical and artistic aspirations for the game. The game developers may already have a well-defined concept for the music of their game, or the composer might shape this strategy in collaboration with the developers.

Many factors influence a game's musical strategy. The scale and budget of the project are likely well outside the composer's control. The demands of a mobile game that only requires a few minutes of music will be very different from those of a high-budget title from a major studio that might represent years of work. Composers should understand how the game is assembled and whether they are expected to be involved in the implementation/integration of music into the game, or simply delivering the music (either as finished cues or as stems/elements of cues). It should also become clear early in the process whether there is sufficient budget to hire live performers. If the budget will not stretch to live performance, the composer must rely on synthesized instruments, and/or their own performing abilities.

Many technical decisions are intimately bound up with the game's interactive and creative ethos. Perhaps the single biggest influence on the musical strategy of a game is the interactive genre or type of game (whether it is a first-person shooter, strategy game, or racing game, and so on). The interactive mechanics of the game will heavily direct the musical approach to the game's music, partly as a result of precedent from earlier games, and partly because of the music's engagement with the player's interactivity.[1] These kinds of broad-level decisions will affect how much music is required for the game, and how any dynamic music should be deployed. For

---

[1] Paul Hoffert, *Music for New Media* (Boston, MA: Berklee Press, 2007), 16; Richard Stevens and Dave Raybould, *The Game Audio Tutorial* (Burlington, MA: Focal, 2011), 162–3.

instance, does the game have a main character? Should the game adopt a thematic approach? Should it aim to respond to the diversity of virtual environments in the game? Should it respond to player action? How is the game structured, and does musical development align with this structure?

Part of the creative process will involve the composer investigating these questions in tandem with the developers, though some of the answers may change as the project develops. Nevertheless, having a clear idea of the music's integration into the game and of the available computational/financial resources is essential for the composer to effectively begin creating the music for the game.

The film composer may typically be found writing music to a preliminary edit of the film. In comparison, the game composer is likely to be working with materials much further away from the final form of the product.[2] It is common for game composers to begin writing based on incomplete prototypes, design specifications and concept art/mood boards supplied by the developers. From these materials, composers will work in dialogue with the developers to refine a style and approach for the game. For games that are part of a series or franchise, the musical direction will often iterate on the approach from previous instalments, even if the compositional staff are not retained from one game to the sequel.

If a number of composers are working on a game, the issue of consistency must be considered carefully. It might be that the musical style should be homogenous, and so a strong precedent or model must be established for the other composers to follow (normally by the lead composer or audio director). In other cases, multiple composers might be utilized precisely because of the variety they can bring to a project. Perhaps musical material by one composer could be developed in different ways by other composers, which might be heard in contrasting areas of the game.

Unlike a film or television episode, where the composer works primarily with one individual (the director or producer), in a game, musical discussions are typically held between a number of partners. The composer may receive feedback from the audio director, the main creative director or even executives at the publishers.[3] This allows for a multiplicity of potential opinions or possibilities (which might be liberating or frustrating, depending on the collaboration). The nature of the collaboration may also be

---

[2] Michael Sweet, *Writing Interactive Music for Video Games* (Upper Saddle River, NJ: Addison-Wesley, 2015), 80.

[3] Winifred Phillips, *A Composer's Guide to Game Music* (Cambridge, MA: MIT Press, 2014), 136–7.

affected by the musical knowledge of the stakeholders who have input into the audio. Once the aesthetic direction has been established, and composition is underway, the composer co-ordinates with the audio director and/ or technical staff to ensure that the music fits with the implementation plans and technical resources of the game.[4] Of course, the collaboration will vary depending on the scale of the project and company – a composer writing for a small indie game produced by a handful of creators will use a different workflow compared to a high-budget game with a large audio staff.

Methods of Dynamic Composition

One of the fundamental decisions facing the composer and developers is how the music should react to the player and gameplay. This might simply consist of beginning a loop of music when the game round begins, and silencing the loop when it ends, or it might be that the game includes more substantial musical interactivity.

If producers decide to deploy more advanced musical systems, this has consequences for the finite technical resources available for the game as it runs. Complex interactive music systems will require greater system resources such as processing power and memory. The resources at the composer's disposal will have to be negotiated with the rest of the game's architecture. Complex dynamic music may also involve the use of middleware systems for handling the interactive music (such as FMOD, Wwise or a custom system), which would need to be integrated into the programming architecture of the game.[5] If the composer is not implementing the interactive music themselves, further energies must be dedicated to integrating the music into the game. In all of these cases, because of the implications for time, resources and budget, as well as the aesthetic result, the decisions concerning dynamic music must be made in dialogue with the game development team, and are not solely the concern of the composer.

The opportunity to compose for dynamic music systems is one of the reasons why composers are attracted to writing for games. Yet a composer's enthusiasm for a dynamic system may outstrip that of the producers or

---

[4] Phillips, *Composer's Guide*, 119; Sweet, *Interactive Music*, 55–6; Chance Thomas, *Composing Music for Games* (Boca Raton, FL: CRC Press, 2016), 52.

[5] Thomas, *Composing Music for Games*, 249–53.

even the players. And, as noted elsewhere in this book, we should be wary of equating more music, or more dynamic music, with a better musical experience.

Even the most extensive dynamic systems are normally created from relatively straightforward principles. Either the selection and order of musical passages is affected by the gameplay ('horizontal' changes), or the game affects the combinations of musical elements heard simultaneously ('vertical' changes). Of course, these two systems can be blended, and both can be used to manipulate small or large units of music. Most often, looped musical passages will play some part in the musical design, in order to account for the indeterminacy of timing in this interactive medium.

Music in games can be designed to loop until an event occurs, at which point the loop will end, or another piece will play. Writing in loops is tricky, not least when repetition might prompt annoyance. When writing looped cues, composers have to consider several musical aspects including:

- *Harmonic structure*, to avoid awkward harmonic shifts when the loop repeats. Many looped cues use a cadence to connect the end of the loop back to the beginning.
- *Timbres and textures*, so that musical statements and reverb are not noticeably cut off when the loop repeats.
- *Melodic material*, which must avoid listener fatigue. Winifred Phillips suggests using continual variation to mitigate this issue.[6]
- *Dynamic and rhythmic progression* during the cue, so that when the loop returns to the start, it does not sound like a lowering of musical tension, which may not match with in-game action.
- *Ending the loop* or transitioning to another musical section. How will the loop end in a way that is musically satisfying? Should the loop be interrupted, or will the reaction have to wait until the loop concludes? Will a transition passage or crossfade be required?

A game might involve just one loop for the whole game round (as in *Tetris*, 1989) or several: in the stealth game *Splinter Cell* (2002), loops are triggered depending on the attention attracted by the player's avatar.[7]

Sometimes, rather than writing a complete cue as a whole entity, composers may write cues in sections or fragments (stems). Stems can be written to sound one after each other, or simultaneously.

---

[6] Phillips, *Composer's Guide*, 166.

[7] Simon Wood, 'Video Game Music – High Scores: Making Sense of Music and Video Games', in *Sound and Music in Film and Visual Media: An Overview*, ed. Graeme Harper, Ruth Doughty and Jochen Eisentraut (New York: Continuum, 2009), 129–48.

In a technique sometimes called 'horizontal sequencing'[8] or 'branching',[9] sections of a composition are heard in turn as the game is played. This allows the music to respond to the game action, when musical sections and variations can be chosen to suit the action. For instance, the 'Hyrule Field' cue of *Legend of Zelda: Ocarina of Time* (1998) consists of twenty-three sections. The order of the sections is partly randomized to avoid direct repetition, but the set is subdivided into different categories, so the music can suit the action. When the hero is under attack, battle variations play; when he stands still, sections without percussion play. Even if the individual sections do not loop, writing music this way still has some of the same challenges as writing loops, particularly concerning transition between sections (see, for example, the complex transition matrix developed for *The Operative: No One Lives Forever* (2000)).[10]

Stems can also be programmed to sound simultaneously. Musical layers can be added, removed or substituted, in response to the action. Composers have to think carefully about how musical registers and timbres will interact when different combinations of layers are used, but this allows music to respond quickly, adjusting texture, instrumentation, dynamics and rhythm along with the game action. These layers may be synchronized to the same tempo and with beginnings and endings aligned, or they may be unsynchronized, which, provided the musical style allows this, is a neat way to provide further variation. Shorter musical fragments designed to be heard on top of other cues are often termed 'stingers'.

These three techniques are not mutually exclusive, and can often be found working together. This is partly due to the different advantages and disadvantages of each approach. An oft-cited example, *Monkey Island 2* (1991), uses the iMUSE music system, and deploys loops, layers, branching sections and stingers. *Halo: Combat Evolved* (2001), too, uses loops, branching sections, randomization and stingers.[11] Like the hexagons of a beehive, the musical elements of dynamic systems use fundamental organizational processes to assemble individual units into large complex structures.

Even more than the technical and musical questions, composers for games must ask themselves which elements of the game construct their

---

[8] Phillips, *Composer's Guide*, 188.
[9] Sweet, *Writing Interactive Music*, 149.
[10] Guy Whitmore, 'A DirectMusic Case Study for No One Lives Forever', in *DirectX 9 Audio Exposed: Interactive Audio Development*, ed. Todd M. Fay with Scott Selfon and Todor J. Fay (Plano, TX: Wordware Publishing, 2003), 387–415.
[11] Martin O'Donnell, 'Producing Audio for Halo' (presentation, Game Developers Conference, San Jose, 21–23 March 2002), accessed 8 April 2020, http://halo.bungie.org/misc/gdc.2002.music/.

music responds to, and reinforces. Musical responses inevitably highlight certain aspects of the gameplay, whether that be the avatar's health, success or failure, the narrative conceit, the plot, the environment, or any other aspect to which music is tied. Unlike in non-interactive media, composers for games must predict and imagine how the player will engage with the game, and create music to reinforce and amplify the emotional journeys they undertake. Amid exciting discussions of technical possibilities, composers must not lose sight of the player's emotional and cognitive engagement with the game, which should be uppermost in the composer's mind. Increased technical complexity, challenges for the composer and demands on resources all need to be balanced with the end result for the player. It is perhaps for this reason that generative and algorithmic music, as impressive as such systems are, has found limited use in games – the enhancement in the player's experience is not always matched by the investment required to make successful musical outcomes.

Game Music as Media Music

As much as we might highlight the peculiar challenges of writing for games, it is important not to ignore game music's continuity with previous media music. In many senses, game composers are continuing the tradition of media music that stretches back into the early days of film music in the late nineteenth century – that is, they are starting and developing a conversation between the screen and the viewer. For most players, the musical experience is more important than the technical complexities or systems that lie behind it. They hear the music as it sounds in relation to the screen and gameplay, not primarily the systematic and technical underpinnings. (Indeed, one of the points where players are most likely to become aware of the technology is when the system malfunctions or is somehow deficient, such as in glitches, disjunct transitions or incidences of too much repetition.) The fundamental question facing game composers is the same as for film composers: 'What can the music bring to this project that will enhance the player/viewer's experience?' The overall job of encapsulating and enhancing the game on an aesthetic level is more important than any single technical concern.

Of course, where games and films/television differ is in the relationship with the viewer/listener. We are not dealing with a passive viewer, or homogenous audience, but a singular participant, addressed, and responded to, by the music. This is not music contemplated as an 'other' entity, but a soundtrack to the player's actions. Over the course of the time taken to play through a game, players spend significantly longer with the music of any one game than with a single film or television episode. As players invest their time with the music of a game, they build a partnership with the score.

Players are well aware of the artifice of games and look for clues in the environment and game materials to indicate what might happen as the gameplay develops. Music is part of this architecture of communication, so players learn to attend to even tiny musical changes and development. For that reason, glitches or unintentional musical artefacts are particularly liable to cause a negative experience for players.

The connection of the music with the player's actions and experiences (whether through dynamic music or more generally), forges the relationship between gamer and score. Little wonder that players feel so passionately and emotionally tied to game music – it is the musical soundtrack to their personal victories and defeats.

Delivering the Music

During the process of writing the music for the game, the composer will remain in contact with the developers. The audio director may need to request changes or revisions to materials for technical or creative reasons, and the requirement for new music might appear, while the music that was initially ordered might become redundant. Indeed, on larger projects in particular, it is not uncommon for drafts to be ultimately unused in the final projects.

Composers may deliver their music as purely synthesized materials, or the score might involve some aspect of live performance. A relatively recent trend has seen composers remotely collaborating with networks of soloist musicians. Composers send cues and demos to specific instrumentalists or vocalists, who then record parts in live performance, which are then integrated into the composition. This blended approach partly reflects a wider move in game scoring towards smaller ensembles and unusual combinations of instruments (often requiring specialist performers). The approach is also well suited to scores that blend together sound-design and musical elements. Such hybrid approaches can continue throughout the compositional process, and the contributed materials can inform the ongoing development of the musical compositions.

Of course, some scores still demand a large-scale orchestral session. While the composer is ultimately responsible for such sessions, composers rely on a larger team of collaborators to help arrange and record orchestras. An orchestrator will adapt the composer's materials into written notation readable by human performers, while the composer will also require the assistance of engineers, mixers, editors and orchestra contractors to enable the session to run smoothly. Orchestral recording sessions typically have to be organized far in advance of the recording date, which necessitates that composers and producers establish the amount of music to be recorded and the system of implementation early on, in case this has implications for the way the music should be recorded. For example, if musical elements need to be manipulated independently of each other, the sessions need to be organized so they are recorded separately.

Promotion and Afterlife

Some game trailers may use music from the game they advertise, but in many cases, entirely separate music is used. There are several reasons for this phenomenon. On a practical level, if a game is advertised early in the development cycle, the music may not yet be ready, and/or the composer may be too busy writing the game's music to score a trailer. More conceptually, trailers are a different medium to the games they advertise, with different aesthetic considerations. The game music, though perfect for the game, may not fit with the trailer's structure or overall style. Unsurprisingly, then, game trailers often use pre-existing music.

Trailers also serve as one of the situations where game music may achieve an afterlife. Since trailers rely heavily on licensed pre-existing music, and trailers often draw on more than one source, game music may easily reappear in another trailer (irrespective of the similarity of the original game to the one being advertised).

Beyond a soundtrack album or other game-specific promotion, the music of a game may also find an afterlife in online music cultures (including YouTube uploads and fan remixes), or even in live performance. Game music concerts are telling microcosms of the significance of game music. On the one hand, they may seem paradoxical – if the appeal of games is founded on interactivity, then why should a format that removes such engagement be popular? Yet, considered more broadly, the significance of these concerts is obvious: they speak to the connection between players and music in games. This music is the soundtrack to what players feel is their own life. Why wouldn't players be enthralled at the idea of a monumental staging of music personally connected to them? Here, on a huge scale in a public event, they can relive the highlights of their marvellous virtual lives.

* * *

This brief overview of the production of music for games has aimed to provide a broad-strokes characterization of the process of creating such music. Part of the challenge and excitement of music for games comes from the negotiation of technical and aesthetic demands. Ultimately, however, composers aim to create deeply satisfying experiences for players. Game music does so by building personal relationships with gamers, enriching their lives and experiences, in-game and beyond.

5 | The Inherent Conflicts of Musical Interactivity in Video Games

RICHARD STEVENS

Within narrative-based video games the integration of storytelling, where experiences are necessarily directed, and of gameplay, where the player has a degree of autonomy, continues to be one of the most significant challenges that developers face. In order to mitigate this potential dichotomy, a common approach is to rely upon cutscenes to progress the narrative. Within these passive episodes where interaction is not possible, or within other episodes of constrained outcome where the temporality of the episode is fixed, it is possible to score a game in exactly the same way as one might score a film or television episode. It could therefore be argued that the music in these sections of a video game is the least idiomatic of the medium. This chapter will instead focus on active gameplay episodes, and interactive music, where the unique challenges lie. When music accompanies active gameplay a number of conflicts, tensions and paradoxes arise. In this chapter, these will be articulated and interrogated through three key questions:

- Do we score a player's experience, or do we direct it?
- How do we distil our aesthetic choices into a computer algorithm?
- How do we reconcile the players' freedom to instigate events at indeterminate times with musical forms that are time-based?

In the following discussion there are few certainties, and many more questions. The intention is to highlight the issues, to provoke discussion and to forewarn.

Scoring and Directing

Gordon Calleja argues that in addition to any scripted narrative in games, the player's interpretation of events during their interaction with a game generates stories, what he describes as an 'alterbiography'.[1] Similarly, Dominic Arsenault refers to the 'emergent narrative that arises out of the

---

[1] Gordon Calleja, *In-Game: From Immersion to Incorporation* (Cambridge, MA: The MIT Press, 2011), 124.

interactions of its rules, objects, and player decisions'[2] in a video game. Music in video games is viewed by many as being critical in engaging players with storytelling,[3] but in addition to underscoring any wider narrative arc music also accompanies this active gameplay, and therefore narrativizes a player's actions. In Claudia Gorbman's influential book *Unheard Melodies: Narrative Film Music* she identifies that when watching images and hearing music the viewer will form mental associations between the two, bringing the connotations of the music to bear on their understanding of a scene.[4] This idea is supported by empirical research undertaken by Annabel Cohen who notes that, when interpreting visuals, participants appeared 'unable to resist the systematic influence of music on their interpretation of the image'.[5] Her subsequent congruence-associationist model helps us to understand some of the mechanisms behind this, and the consequent impact of music on the player's alterbiography.[6]

Cohen's model suggests that our interpretation of music in film is a negotiation between two processes.[7] Stimuli from a film will trigger a 'bottom-up' structural and associative analysis which both primes 'top-down' expectations from long-term memory through rapid pre-processing, and informs the working narrative (the interpretation of the ongoing film) through a slower, more detailed analysis. At the same time, the congruence (or incongruence) between the music and visuals will affect visual attention and therefore also influence the meaning derived from the film. In other words, the structures of the music and how they interact with visual structures will affect our interpretation of events. For example, 'the film character whose actions were most congruent with the musical pattern would be most attended and, consequently, the primary recipient of associations of the music'.[8]

---

[2] Dominic Arsenault, 'Narratology', in *The Routledge Companion to Video Game Studies*, ed. Mark J. P. Wolf and Bernard Perron (New York: Routledge, 2014), 475–83, at 480.

[3] See, amongst others, Richard Jacques, 'Staying in Tune: Richard Jacques on Game Music's Past, Present, and Future', *Gamasutra*, 2008, accessed 8 April 2020, www.gamasutra.com/view/ feature/132092/staying_in_tune_richard_jacques_.php; Michael Sweet, *Writing Interactive Music for Video Games* (Upper Saddle River, NJ: Addison-Wesley, 2015); Simon Wood, 'Video Game Music – High Scores: Making Sense of Music and Video Games', in *Sound and Music in Film and Visual Media: An Overview*, ed. Graeme Harper, Ruth Doughty and Jochen Eisentraut (New York and London: Continuum, 2009), 129–48.

[4] Claudia Gorbman, *Unheard Melodies: Narrative Film Music* (London: BFI, 1987).

[5] Annabel J. Cohen, 'Film Music from the Perspective of Cognitive Science', in *The Oxford Handbook of Film Music Studies*, ed. David Neumeyer (New York: Oxford University Press, 2014), 96–130, at 103.

[6] Annabel J. Cohen, 'Congruence-Association Model and Experiments in Film Music: Toward Interdisciplinary Collaboration', *Music and the Moving Image* 8, no. 2 (2015): 5–24.

[7] Cohen, 'Congruence-Association Model'.

[8] Cohen, 'Congruence-Association Model', 10.

In video games the music is often responding to actions instigated by the player, therefore it is these actions that will appear most congruent with the resulting musical pattern. In applying Cohen's model to video games, the implication is that the player themselves will often be the primary recipient of the musical associations formed through experience of cultural, cinematic and video game codes. In responding to events instigated by the player, these musical associations will likely be ascribed to their actions. You (the player) act, superhero music plays, you are the superhero.

Of course, there are also events within games that are not instigated by the player, and so the music will attach its qualities to, and narrativize, these also. Several scholars have attempted to distinguish between two musical positions,[9] defining *interactive* music as that which responds directly to player input, and *adaptive* music that 'reacts appropriately to – and even anticipates – gameplay rather than responding directly to the user'.[10] Whether things happen because the 'game' instigates them or the 'player' instigates them is up for much debate, and it is likely that the perceived congruence of the music will oscillate between game events and players actions, but what is critical is the degree to which the player perceives a causal relationship between these events or actions and the music.[11] These relationships are important for the player to understand, since while music is narrativizing events it is often simultaneously playing a ludic role – supplying information to support the player's engagement with the mechanics of the game.

The piano glissandi in *Dishonored* (2012) draw the player's attention to the enemy NPC (Non-Player Character) who has spotted them, the four-note motif in *Left 4 Dead 2* (2009) played on the piano informs the player that a 'Spitter' enemy type has spawned nearby,[12] and if the music ramps up in *Skyrim* (2011), *Watch Dogs* (2014), *Far Cry 5* (2018) or countless other

---

[9] Scott Selfon, Karen Collins and Michael Sweet all distinguish between adaptive and interactive music. Karen Collins, 'An Introduction to Procedural Music in Video Games', *Contemporary Music Review* 28, no. 1 (2009): 5–15; Scott Selfon, 'Interactive and Adaptive Audio', in *DirectX 9 Audio Exposed: Interactive Audio Development*, ed. Todd M. Fay with Scott Selfon and Todor J. Fay (Plano, TX: Wordware Publishing, 2003), 55–74; Sweet, *Writing Interactive Music*.

[10] Guy Whitmore, 'Design with Music in Mind: A Guide to Adaptive Audio for Game Designers', *Gamasutra*, 2003, accessed 8 April 2020, www.gamasutra.com/view/feature/131261/design_with_music_in_mind_a_guide_.php; www.gamasutra.com/view/feature/131261/design_with_music_in_mind_a_guide_.php?page=2.

[11] The game may instigate an event, but it only does so because the player has entered the area or crossed a trigger point – so whether this is 'game'-instigated or 'player'-instigated is probably a matter of debate.

[12] If the motif is played on the strings then the player knows the 'Spitter' has spawned further away. Each special enemy in *Left 4 Dead 2* has a specific musical spawn sound: a two-note motif for the 'Smoker', a three-note motif for the 'Hunter', four for the 'Spitter', five for the 'Boomer', six for the 'Charger' and eight for the 'Jockey'.

games, the player knows that enemies are aware of their presence and are now in active pursuit. The music dramatizes the situation while also providing information that the player will interpret and use. In an extension to Chion's causal mode of listening,[13] where viewers listen to a sound in order to gather information about its cause or sources, we could say that in video games players engage in ludic listening, interpreting the audio's system-related meaning in order to inform their actions. Sometimes this ludic function of music is explicitly and deliberately part of the game design in order to avoid an overloading of the visual channel while compensating for a lack of peripheral vision and spatial information,[14] but whether deliberate or inadvertent, the player will always be trying to interpret music's meaning in order to gain advantage.

Awareness of the causal links between game events, game variables and music will likely differ from player to player. Some players may note the change in musical texture when crouching under a table in *Sly 3: Honor Among Thieves* (2005) as confirmation that they are hidden from view; some will actively listen out for the rising drums that indicate the proximity of an attacking wolf pack in *Rise of the Tomb Raider* (2015);[15] while others may remain blissfully unaware of the music's usefulness (or may even play with the music switched off).[16] Feedback is sometimes used as a generic term for all audio that takes on an informative role for the player,[17] but it is important to note that the identification of causality, with musical changes being perceived as either adaptive (game-instigated) or interactive (player-instigated), is likely to induce different emotional responses. Adaptive music that provides information to the player about game states and variables can be viewed as providing a *notification* or feed-forward function – enabling the player. Interactive music that corresponds more

---

[13] Michel Chion, trans. Claudia Gorbman, *Audio-Vision: Sound on Screen* (New York: Columbia University Press, 1994), 25–7.

[14] Richard Stevens, Dave Raybould and Danny McDermott, 'Extreme Ninjas Use Windows, Not Doors: Addressing Video Game Fidelity Through Ludo-Narrative Music in the Stealth Genre', in *Proceedings of the Audio Engineering Society Conference: 56th International Conference: Audio for Games*, 11–13 February 2015, London, AES (2015).

[15] The very attentive listener will note that the wolf drums also indicate the direction from which they are coming via the panning of the instruments.

[16] Music can also indicate ludic information through its absence. For example, in *L.A. Noire* (2011), when all clues have been collected in a particular location, the music stops.

[17] Axel Stockburger, 'The Game Environment from an Auditive Perspective', in *Proceedings: Level Up: Digital Games Research Conference (DiGRA)*, ed. Marinka Copier and Joost Raessens, Utrecht, 4–6 November 2003; Patrick Ng and Keith V. Nesbitt, 'Informative Sound Design in Video Games', *13 Proceedings of the 9th Australasian Conference on Interactive Entertainment*, 30 September–1 October 2013, Melbourne, Australia (New York: ACM, 2013) 9: 1–9: 9.

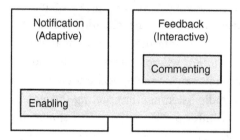

Figure 5.1 Notification and feedback: Enabling and commenting functions

directly to player input will likewise have an enabling function, but it carries a different emotional weight since this *feedback* also comments on the actions of the player, providing positive or negative reinforcement (see Figure 5.1).

The percussive stingers accompanying a successful punch in *The Adventures of Tintin: The Secret of the Unicorn* (2011), or the layers that begin to play upon the successful completion of a puzzle in *Vessel* (2012) provide positive feedback, while the duff-note sounds that respond to a mistimed input in *Guitar Hero* (2005) provide negative feedback. Whether enabling or commenting, music often performs these ludic functions. It is simultaneously narrating and informing; it is ludonarrative. The implications of this are twofold. Firstly, in order to remain congruent with the game events and player actions, music will be inclined towards a Mickey-Mousing type approach,[18] and secondly, in order to fulfil its ludic functions, it will tend towards a consistent response, and therefore will be inclined towards repetition.

When the player is web-slinging their way across the city in *Spider-Man* (2018) the music scores the experience of being a superhero, but when they stop atop a building to survey the landscape the music must logically also stop. When the music strikes up upon entering a fort in *Assassin's Creed: Origins* (2017), we are informed that danger may be present. We may turn around and leave, and the music fades out. Moving between these states in either game in quick succession highlights the causal link between action and music; it draws attention to the system, to the artifice. Herein lies a fundamental conflict of interactive music – in its attempt to be narratively congruent, and ludically effective, music can reveal the systems within the

---

[18] Mickey-Mousing 'consists of following the visual action in synchrony with musical trajectories (rising, falling, zigzagging) and instrumental punctuations of actions'. Chion, *Audio-Vision*, 121–2.

game, but in this revealing of the constructed nature of our experience it disrupts our immersion in the narrative world. While playing a game we do not want to be reminded of the architecture and artificial mechanics of that game. These already difficult issues around congruence and causality are further exacerbated when we consider that music is often not just scoring the game experience, it is directing it.

Film music has sometimes been criticized for a tendency to impose meaning, for telling a viewer how to feel,[19] but in games music frequently tells a player how to act. In the 'Medusa's Call' chapter of *Far Cry 3* (2012) the player must 'Avoid detection. Use stealth to kill the patrolling radio operators and get their intel', and the quiet tension of the synthesizer and percussion score supports this preferred stealth strategy. In contrast, the 'Kick the Hornet's Nest' episode ('Burn all the remaining drug crops') encourages the player to wield their flamethrower to spectacular destructive effect through the electro-dubstep-reggae mashup of 'Make it Bun Dem' by Skrillex and Damian 'Jr. Gong' Marley. Likewise, a stealth approach is encouraged by the James-Bond-like motif of *Rayman Legends* (2013) 'Mysterious Inflatable Island', in contrast to the hell-for-leather sprint inferred from the scurrying strings of 'The Great Lava Pursuit'. In these examples, and many others, we can see that rather than scoring a player's actual experience, the music is written in order to match an imagined ideal experience – where the intentions of the music are enacted by the player. To say that we are scoring a player experience implies that somehow music is inert, that it does not impact on the player's behaviour. But when the player is the protagonist it may be the case that, rather than identifying what is congruent with the music's meaning, the player *acts* in order for image and music to become congruent. When music plays, we are compelled to play along; the music directs us. Both Ernest Adams and Tulia-Maria Căşvean refer to the idea of the player's contract,[20] that in order for games to work there has to be a tacit agreement between the player and the game maker; that they both have a degree of responsibility for the experience. If designers promise to provide a credible, coherent world then the player agrees to behave according to a given set of predefined rules, usually determined by game genre, in order to maintain

---

[19] Royal S. Brown, *Overtones and Undertones: Reading Film Music* (Berkeley: University of California Press, 1994), 54.

[20] Ernest Adams, 'Resolutions to Some Problems in Interactive Storytelling Volume 1' (PhD Thesis, University of Teesside, 2013), 96–119; Tulia-Maria Căşvean, 'An Introduction to Videogame Genre Theory: Understanding Videogame Genre Framework', *Athens Journal of Mass Media and Communications* 2, no. 1 (2015): 57–68.

this coherence. Playing along with the meanings implicit in music forms part of this contract. But the player also has the agency to decide not to play along with the music, and so it will appear incongruent with their actions, and again the artifice of the game is revealed.[21]

When game composer Marty O'Donnell states 'When [the players] look back on their experience, they should feel like their experience was scored, but they should never be aware of what they did to cause it to be scored'[22] he is demonstrating an awareness of the paradoxes that arise when writing music for active game episodes. Music is often simultaneously performing ludic and narrative roles, and it is simultaneously following (scoring) and leading (directing). As a consequence, there is a constant tension between congruence, causality and abstraction. Interactive music represents a catch-22 situation. If music seeks to be narratively congruent and ludically effective, this compels it towards a Mickey-Mousing approach, because of the explicit, consistent and close matching of music to the action required. This leads to repetition and a highlighting of the artifice. If music is directing the player or abstracted from the action, then it runs the risk of incongruence. Within video games, we rely heavily upon the player's contract and the inclination to act in congruence with the behaviour implied by the music, but the player will almost always have the ability to make our music sound inappropriate should they choose to.

Many composers who are familiar with video games recognize that music should not necessarily always act in the same way throughout a game. Reflecting on his work in *Journey* (2012), composer Austin Wintory states, 'An important part of being adaptive game music/audio people is not [to ask] "Should we be interactive or should we not be?" It's "To what extent?" It's not a binary system, because storytelling entails a certain ebb and flow'.[23] Furthermore, he notes that if any relationship between the music and game, from Mickey-Mousing to counterpoint, becomes predictable then the impact can be lost, recommending that 'the extent to

---

[21] Gorbman identifies that film music is typically designed not to be consciously noticed or 'heard'. She identifies incongruence as one of the factors that violates this convention, along with technical mistakes, and the use of recognizable pre-existing music. Claudia Gorbman, 'Hearing Music', paper presented at the Music for Audio-Visual Media Conference, University of Leeds, 2014.

[22] Martin O'Donnell, 'Martin O'Donnell Interview – The Halo 3 Soundtrack', (c.2007), YouTube, accessed 13 October 2020, www.youtube.com/watch?v=aDUzyJadfpo.

[23] Austin Wintory, 'Journey vs Monaco: Music Is Storytelling', presented at the Game Developers Conference, 5–9 March 2012, San Francisco, accessed 20 October 2020, www.gdcvault.com/play/1015986/Journey-vs-Monaco-Music-is.

which you are interactive should have an arc'.[24] This bespoke approach to writing and implementing music for games, where the degree of interactivity might vary between different active gameplay episodes, is undoubtedly part of the solution to the issues outlined but faces two main challenges. Firstly, most games are very large, making a tailored approach to each episode or level unrealistic, and secondly, that unlike in other art forms or audiovisual media, the decisions about how music will act within a game are made *in absentia*; we must hand these to a system that serves as a proxy for our intent. These decisions in the moment are not made by a human being, but are the result of a system of events, conditions, states and variables.

Algorithms and Aesthetics

Given the size of most games, and an increasingly generative or systemic approach to their development, the complex choices that composers and game designers might want to make about the use of music during active gameplay episodes must be distilled into a programmatic system of events, states and conditions derived from discrete (True/False) or continuous (0.0–1.0) variables. This can easily lead to situations where what might seem programmatically correct does not translate appropriately to the player's experience. In video games there is frequently a conflict between our aesthetic aims and the need to codify the complexity of human judgement we might want to apply.

One common use of music in games is to indicate the state of the artificial intelligence (AI), with music either starting or increasing in intensity when the NPCs are in active pursuit of the player, and ending or decreasing in intensity when they end the pursuit or 'stand down'.[25] This provides the player with ludic information about the NPC state, while at the same time heightening tension to reflect the narrative situation of being pursued. This could be seen as a good example of ludonarrative consonance or congruence. However, when analysed more closely we can see that simply relying on the ludic logic of gameplay events to determine the music system, which has narrative implications, is not effective. In terms of the game's logic, when an NPC stands down or when they are killed the

---

[24] Ibid.
[25] Three examples demonstrate a typical way in which this is implemented within games. In *Deus Ex: Human Revolution* (2011), *Dishonored* and *Far Cry 3*, the music starts when the player has been spotted, and fades out when the NPC is no longer pursuing them.

outcome is the same; *they are no longer actively seeking the player* (Active pursuit = False). In many games, the musical result of these two different events is the same – the music fades out. But if as a player I have run away to hide and waited until the NPC stopped looking for me, or if I have confronted the NPC and killed them, these events should feel very different. The common practice of musically responding to both these events in the same way is an example of ludonarrative dissonance.[26] In terms of providing ludic information to the player it is perfectly effective, but in terms of narrativizing the player's actions, it is not.

The perils of directly translating game variables into musical states is comically apparent in the ramp into epic battle music when confronting a small rat in *The Elder Scrolls III: Morrowind* (2002) (Enemy within a given proximity = True). More recent games such as *Middle Earth: Shadow of Mordor* (2014) and *The Witcher 3: Wild Hunt* (2015) treat such encounters with more sophistication, reserving additional layers of music, or additional stingers, for confrontations with enemies of greater power or higher ranking than the player, but the translation of sophisticated human judgements into mechanistic responses to a given set of conditions is always challenging. In both *Thief* (2014) and *Sniper Elite V2* (2012) the music intensifies upon detection, but the lackadaisical attitudes of the NPCs in *Thief*, and the fact that you can swiftly dispatch enemies via a judicious headshot in *Sniper Elite V2*, means that the music is endlessly ramping up and down in a Mickey-Mousing fashion. In *I Am Alive* (2012), a percussive layer mirrors the player character's stamina when climbing. This is both ludically and narratively effective, since it directly signifies the depleting reserves while escalating the tension of the situation. Yet its literal representation of this variable means that the music immediately and unnaturally drops to silence should you 'hook-on' or step onto a horizontal ledge. In all these instances, the challenging catch-22 of scoring the player's actions discussed above is laid bare, but better consideration of the player's alterbiography might have led to a different approach. Variables are not

---

[26] The term ludonarrative dissonance was coined by game designer Clint Hocking to describe situations where the ludic aspects of the game conflict with the internal narrative. In his analysis of the game *BioShock*, he observes that the rules of the game imply 'it is best if I do what is best for me without consideration for others' by harvesting the 'Adam' from the Little Sisters characters in order to enhance the player's skill. However, in doing this the player is allowed to 'play' in a way that is explicitly opposed by the game's narrative, which indicates that the player should rescue the Little Sisters. As Hocking comments, '"helping someone else" is presented as the right thing to do by the story, yet the opposite proposition appears to be true under the mechanics'. Clint Hocking, 'Ludonarrative Dissonance in Bioshock', 2007, accessed 8 April 2020, http://clicknothing.typepad.com/click_nothing/2007/10/ludonarrative-d.html.

feelings, and music needs to interpolate between conditions. Just because the player is now 'safe' it does not mean that their emotions are reset to 0.0 like a variable: they need some time to recover or wind down. The literal translation of variables into musical responses means that very often there is no coda, no time for reflection.

There are of course many instances where the consideration of the experiential nature of play can lead to a more sophisticated consideration of how to translate variables into musical meaning. In his presentation on the music of *Final Fantasy XV* (2016), Sho Iwamoto discussed the music that accompanies the player while they are riding on a Chocobo, the large flightless bird used to more quickly traverse the world. Noting that the player is able to transition quickly between running and walking, he decided on a parallel approach to scoring whereby synchronized musical layers are brought in and out.[27] This approach is more suitable when quick bidirectional changes in game states are possible, as opposed to the more wholescale musical changes brought about by transitioning between musical segments.[28] A logical approach would be to simply align the 'walk' state with specific layers, and a 'run' state with others, and to crossfade between these two synchronized stems. The intention of the player to run is clear (they press the run button), but Iwamoto noted that players would often be forced unintentionally into a 'walk' state through collisions with trees or other objects. As a consequence, he implemented a system that responds quickly to the intentional choice, transitioning from the walk to run music over 1.5 beats, but chose to set the musical transition time from the 'run' to 'walk' state to 4 bars, thereby smoothing out the 'noise' of brief unintentional interruptions and avoiding an overly reactive response.[29]

These conflicts between the desire for nuanced aesthetic results and the need for a systematic approach can be addressed, at least in part, through a greater engagement by composers with the systems that govern their music and by a greater understanding of music by game developers. Although the

[27] Sho Iwamoto, '*Epic AND Interactive Music in "Final Fantasy XV"*', paper presented at the Game Developers Conference, 27 February–3 March 2017, San Francisco, accessed 15 October 2020, www.gdcvault.com/play/1023971/Epic-AND-Interactive-Music-in.

[28] The musical approaches referred to here as parallel and transitional are sometimes referred to respectively as Vertical Re-Orchestration and Horizontal Re-Sequencing (Kenneth B. McAlpine, Matthew Bett and James Scanlan, 'Approaches to Creating Real-Time Adaptive Music in Interactive Entertainment: A Musical Perspective', *The Proceedings of the AES 35th International Conference: Audio for Games*, 11–13 February 2009, London, UK), or simply as Vertical and Horizontal (Winifred Phillips, *A Composer's Guide to Game Music* (Cambridge, MA: The MIT Press, 2014), 185–202).

[29] 'Noise' in this instance refers to any rapid fluctuations in data that can obscure or disrupt the more significant underlying changes.

situation continues to improve it is still the case in many instances that composers are brought on board towards the end of development, and are sometimes not involved at all in the integration process. What may ultimately present a greater challenge is that players play games in different ways.

A fixed approach to the micro level of action within games does not always account for how they might be experienced on a more macro level. For many people their gaming is opportunity driven, snatching a valued 30–40 minutes here and there, while others may carve out an entire weekend to play the latest release non-stop. The sporadic nature of many people's engagement with games not only mitigates against the kind of large-scale musico-dramatic arc of films, but also likely makes music a problem for the more dedicated player. If music needs to be 'epic' for the sporadic player, then being 'epic' all the time for 10+ hours is going to get a little exhausting. This is starting to be recognized, with players given the option in the recent release of *Assassin's Creed: Odyssey* (2018) to choose the frequency at which the exploration music occurs.

Another way in which a fixed-system approach to active music falters is that, as a game character, I am not the same at the end of the game as I was at the start, and I may have significant choice over how my character develops. Many games retain the archetypal narrative of the Hero's Journey,[30] and characters go through personal development and change – yet interactive music very rarely reflects this: the active music heard in 20 hours is the same that was heard in the first 10 minutes. In a game such as *Silent Hill: Shattered Memories* (2009) the clothing and look of the character, the dialogue, the set dressing, voicemail messages and cutscenes all change depending on your actions in the game and the resulting personality profile, but the music in active scenes remains similar throughout. Many games, particularly RPGs (Role-Playing Games) enable significant choices in terms of character development, but it typically remains the case that interactive music responds more to geography than it does to character development. *Epic Mickey* (2010) is a notable exception; when the player acts 'good' by following missions and helping people, the music becomes more magical and heroic, but when acting more mischievous and destructive, 'You'll hear a lot of bass clarinets, bassoons, essentially like the wrong notes … '.[31] The 2016 game *Stories: The Path of Destinies* takes this idea further, offering moments of

[30] Barry Ip, 'Narrative Structures in Computer and Video Games: Part 2: Emotions, Structures, and Archetypes', *Games and Culture* 6, no. 3 (2011): 203–44.

[31] Jim Dooley, quoted in NPR Staff, 'Composers Find New Playgrounds in Video Games', *NPR. org*, 2010, accessed 8 April 2020, www.npr.org/blogs/therecord/2010/12/01/131702650/composers-find-new-playgrounds-in-video-games.

choice where six potential personalities or paths are reflected musically through changes in instrumentation and themes. Reflecting the development of the player character through music, given the potential number of variables involved, would, of course, present a huge challenge, but it is worthy of note that so few games have even made a modest attempt to do this.

Recognition that players have different preferences, and therefore have different experiences of the same game, began with Bartle's identification of common characteristics of groups of players within text-based MUD (Multi-User Dungeon) games.[32] More recently the capture and analysis of gameplay metrics has allowed game-user researchers to refine this understanding through the concept of player segmentation.[33] To some extent, gamers are self-selecting in terms of matching their preferred gaming style with the genre of games they play, but games want to appeal to as wide an audience as possible and so attempt to appeal to different types of player. Making explicit reference to Bartle's player types, game designer Chris McEntee discusses how *Rayman Origins* (2011) has a co-operative play mode for 'Socializers', while 'Explorers' are rewarded through costumes that can be unlocked, and 'Killers' are appealed to through the ability to strike your fellow player's character and push them into danger.[34] One of the conflicts between musical interactivity and the gaming experience is that the approach to music, the systems and thresholds chosen are developed for the experience of an average player, but we know that approaches may differ markedly.[35] A player who approaches *Dishonored 2* (2016) with an aggressive playstyle will hear an awful lot of the high-intensity 'fight' music; however a player who achieves a very stealthy or 'ghost' playthrough will never hear it.[36] A representation of the potential experiences of different player types with typical 'Ambient', 'Tension' and 'Action' music tracks is shown below (Figures 5.2–5.4).

---

[32] Richard Bartle, 'Hearts, Clubs, Diamonds, Spades: Players Who Suit MUDs', *Journal of MUD Research* 1, no. 1 (1996), accessed 13 October 2020, reproduced at http://mud.co.uk/richard/hcds.htm.

[33] Alessandro Canossa and Sasha Makarovych, 'Videogame Player Segmentation', presented at the Data Innovation Summit, 22 March 2018, Stockholm, accessed 13 October 2020, www.youtube.com/watch?v=vBfYGH4g2gw.

[34] Chris McEntee, 'Rational Design: The Core of Rayman Origins', *Gamasutra*, 2012, accessed 8 April 2020, www.gamasutra.com/view/feature/167214/rational_design_the_core_of_.php?page=1.

[35] Imagine two versions of a film: in one the main character is John McClane, while in another it is Sherlock Holmes. The antagonists are the same, the key plot features the same, but their approaches are probably very different, and necessitate a very different musical score.

[36] Playing a game with an extreme stealth approach is sometimes referred to as 'ghosting', and playing without killing any enemies a 'pacifist' run.

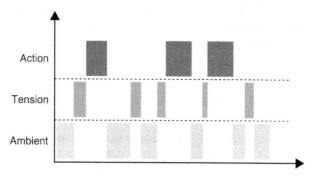

Figure 5.2 Musical experience of an average approach

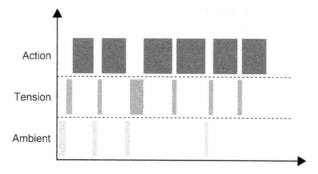

Figure 5.3 Musical experience of an aggressive approach

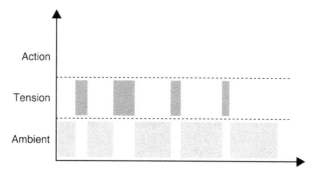

Figure 5.4 Musical experience of a stealthy approach

A single fixed-system approach to music that fails to adapt to playstyles will potentially result in a vastly different, and potentially unfulfilling, musical experience. A more sophisticated method, where the thresholds are scaled or recalibrated around the range of the player's 'mean' approach, could lead to a more personalized and more varied musical experience. This could be as simple as raising the threshold at which a reward stinger is played for the good player, or as complex as introducing new micro tension elements for a stealth player's close call.

Having to codify aesthetic decisions represents for many composers a challenge to their usual practice outside of games, and indeed perhaps a conflict with how we might feel these decisions should be made. Greater understanding by composers of the underlying systems that govern their music's use is undoubtedly part of the answer, as is a greater effort to track and understand an individual's behaviour within games, so that we can provide a good experience for the 'sporadic explorer', as well as the 'dedicated killer', but there is a final conflict between interactivity and music that is seemingly irreconcilable – that of player agency and the language of music itself.

Agency and Structure

As discussed above, one of the defining features of active gameplay episodes within video games, and indeed a defining feature of interactivity itself, is that the player is granted agency; the ability to instigate actions and events of their own choosing, and crucially for music – at a time of their own choosing. Parallel, vertical or layer-based approaches to musical form within games can respond to events rapidly and continuously without impacting negatively on musical structures, since the temporal progression of the music is not interrupted. However, other gaming events often necessitate a transitional approach to music, where the change from one musical cue to an alternate cue mirrors a more significant change in the dramatic action.[37] In regard to film music, K. J. Donnelly highlights the importance of synchronization, that films are structured through what he terms 'audiovisual cadences' – nodal points of narrative or emotional impact.[38] In games these nodal points, in particular at the end of action-based episodes, also have great significance, but the agency of the player to instigate these events at any time represents an inherent conflict with musical structures.

---

[37] Parallel forms or vertical remixing involve altering the volume of parallel musical layers in response to game events or variables. Horizontal forms or horizontal resequencing involve transitions from one musical cue to another. See references for further detailed discussion. See Richard Stevens and Dave Raybould, *Game Audio Implementation: A Practical Guide Using the Unreal Engine* (Burlington, MA: Focal Press, 2015) and Sweet, *Writing Interactive Music*.

[38] K. J. Donnelly, *Occult Aesthetics: Synchronization in Sound Film* (New York: Oxford University Press, 2014).

There is good evidence that an awareness of musical, especially rhythmic, structures is innate. Young babies will indicate negative brainwave patterns when there is a change to an otherwise consistent sequence of rhythmic cycles, and even when listening to a monotone metronomic pulse we will perceive some of these sounds as accented.[39] Even without melody, harmonic sequences or phrasing, most music sets up temporal expectations, and the confirmation of, or violation of expectation in music is what is most closely associated with strong or 'peak' emotions.[40] To borrow Chion's terminology we might say that peak emotions are a product of music's vectorization,[41] the way it orients towards the future, and that musical expectation has a magnitude and direction. The challenges of interaction, the conflict between the temporal determinacy of vectorization and the temporal indeterminacy of the player's actions, have stylistic consequences for music composed for active gaming episodes.

In order to avoid jarring transitions and to enable smoothness,[42] interactive music is inclined towards harmonic stasis and metrical ambiguity, and to avoiding melody and vectorization. The fact that such music should have little structure in and of itself is perhaps unsurprising – since the musical structure is a product of interaction. If musical gestures are too strong then this will not only make transitions difficult, but they will potentially be interpreted as having ludic meaning where none was intended. In order to enable smooth transitions, and to avoid the combinatorial explosion that results from potentially transitioning between different pieces with different harmonic sequences, all the interactive music in *Red Dead Redemption* (2010) was written in A minor at 160 bpm, and most music for *The Witcher 3: Wild Hunt* in D minor. Numerous other games echo this tendency towards repeated ostinatos around a static tonal centre. The music of *Doom* (2016) undermines rhythmic expectancy through the

---

[39] There is evidence that 'infants develop expectation for the onset of rhythmic cycles (the downbeat), even when it is not marked by stress of other distinguishing spectral features', since they exhibit a brainwave pattern known as mismatch negativity, which occurs when there is a change to an otherwise consistent sequence of events. István Winkler, Gábor P. Háden, Olivia Ladinig, István Sziller and Henkjan Honing, 'Newborn Infants Detect the Beat in Music', *Proceedings of the National Academy of Sciences* 106, no. 7 (2009): 2468–71 at 2468. The perception of a fictional accent when listening to a monotone metronome sequence is known as subjective rhythmization (Rasmus Bååth, 'Subjective Rhythmization', *Music Perception* 33, no. 2 (2015): 244–54).

[40] John Sloboda, 'Music Structure and Emotional Response: Some Empirical Findings', *Psychology of Music* 19, no. 2 (1991): 110–20.

[41] Chion, *Audio-Vision*, 13–18.

[42] Elizabeth Medina-Gray, 'Modularity in Video Game Music', in *Ludomusicology: Approaches to Video Game Music*, ed. Michiel Kamp, Tim Summers and Mark Sweeney (Sheffield: Equinox, 2016), 53–72.

use of unusual and constantly fluctuating time signatures, and the 6/8 poly-rhythms in the combat music of *Batman: Arkham Knight* (2015) also serve to unlock our perception from the usual 4/4 metrical divisions that might otherwise dominate our experience of the end-state transition. Another notable trend is the increasingly blurred border between music and sound effects in games. In *Limbo* (2010) and *Little Nightmares* (2017), there is often little delineation between game-world sounds and music, and the audio team of *Shadow of the Tomb Raider* (2018) talk about a deliberate attempt to make the player 'unsure that what they are hearing is score'.[43] All of these approaches can be seen as stylistic responses to the challenge of interactivity.[44]

The methods outlined above can be effective in mitigating the interruption of expectation-based structures during musical transitions, but the de facto approach to solving this has been for the music to not respond immediately, but instead to wait and transition at the next appropriate musical juncture. Current game audio middleware enables the system to be aware of musical divisions, and we can instruct transitions to happen at the next beat, next bar or at an arbitrary but musically appropriate point through the use of custom cues.[45] Although more musically pleasing,[46] such metrical transitions are problematic since the audiovisual cadence is lost – *music always responds after the event* – and they provide an opportunity for incongruence, for if the music has to wait too long after the event to transition then the player may be engaging in some other kind of trivial activity at odds with the dramatic intent of the music. Figure 5.5 illustrates the issue. The gameplay action begins at the moment of pursuit, but the music waits until the next juncture (bar) to transition to the 'Action' cue. The player is highly skilled and so quickly triumphs. Again, the music holds on the 'Action' cue until the next bar line in order to transition musically back to the 'Ambient' cue.

The resulting periods of incongruence are unfortunate, but the lack of audiovisual cadence is particularly problematic when one considers that these

---

[43] Rob Bridgett, 'Building an Immersive Soundscape in Shadow of the Tomb Raider – Full Q&A', *Gamasutra,* 2018, accessed 8 April 2020, www.gamasutra.com/blogs/ChrisKerr/20181108/329971/Building_an_immersive_soundscape_in_Shadow_of_the_Tomb_Raider__full_QA.php.

[44] These stylistic responses are also a product of the inflexibility of waveform-based recorded music. It is possible that we will look back on the era of waveform-based video game music and note that the affordances and constraints of the waveform have had the same degree of impact on musical style that the affordances and constraints of the 2A03 (NES) or SID chip (C64) had on their era.

[45] Game audio middleware consists of audio-specific tools that integrate into game engines. They give audio personnel a common and accessible interface that is abstracted from the implementations of each specific gaming platform. FMOD (Firelight Technologies) and Wwise (Audiokinetic) are two of the most commonly used middleware tools.

[46] Sweet, *Writing Interactive Music,* 167, 171.

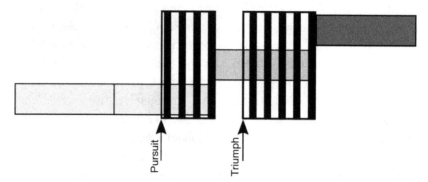

Figure 5.5 Potential periods of incongruence due to metrical transitions are indicated by the hatched lines

transitions are typically happening at the end of action-based episodes, where music is both narratively characterizing the player and fulfilling the ludic role of feeding-back on their competence.[47] Without synchronization, the player's sense of accomplishment and catharsis can be undermined. The concept of repetition, of repeating the same episode or repeatedly encountering similar scenarios, features in most games as a core mechanic, so these 'end-events' will be experienced multiple times.[48] Given that game developers want players to enjoy the gaming experience it would seem that there is a clear rationale for attempting to optimize these moments. This rationale is further supported by the suggestion that the end of an experience, particularly in a goal-oriented context, may play a disproportionate role in people's overall evaluation of the experience and their subsequent future behaviour.[49]

---

[47] Rigby and Ryan describe two distinct types of competence feedback; *sustained competence feedback* (during an episode) or *cumulative competence feedback* (at the conclusion of an episode). Richard M. Ryan and Scott Rigby, *Glued to Games: How Video Games Draw Us in and Hold Us Spellbound* (Santa Barbara: Praeger, 2010), 25.

[48] Hanson refers to this as 'mastery through compulsive repetition'. Christopher Hanson, *Game Time: Understanding Temporality in Video Games* (Bloomington, Indiana: Indiana University Press, 2018), 111.

[49] Daniel Kahneman has suggested that there are differences between the objective moment-to-moment evaluation of what he terms the 'experiencing self', and that of the more subjective 'remembering self' that retrospectively evaluates an experience. The remembering self neglects duration, and the experience is instead evaluated upon 'Peak' and 'End' experiences. Daniel Kahneman, *Thinking, Fast and Slow* (London: Penguin, 2012). There is further evidence that when activities are goal-oriented the 'End' is more dominant, that the achievement (or lack of achievement) of the goal will dominate evaluations of the experience more than any 'peak' experiences within it. Ziv Carmon and Daniel Kahneman, 'The Experienced Utility of Queuing: Real Time Affect and Retrospective Evaluations of Simulated Queues', Working paper, Duke University (1996). www.researchgate.net/publication/236864505_The_Experienced_Utility_of_Queuing_Experience_Profiles_and_Retrospective_Evaluations_of_Simulated_Queues.

The delay between the event and the musical response can be alleviated in some instances by moving to a 'pre-end' musical segment, one that has an increased density of possible exit points, but the ideal would be to have vectorized music that leads up to and enhances these moments of triumph, something which is conceptually impossible unless we suspend the agency of the player. Some games do this already. When an end-event is approached in *Spider-Man* the player's input and agency are often suspended, and the climactic conclusion is played out in a cutscene, or within the constrained outcome of a quick-time event that enables music to be more closely synchronized. However, it would also be possible to maintain a greater impression of agency and to achieve musical synchronization if musical structures were able to input into game's decision-making processes. That is, to allow musical processes to dictate the timing of game events. Thus far we have been using the term 'interactive' to describe music during active episodes, but most music in games is not truly interactive, in that it lacks a reciprocal relationship with the game's systems. In the vast majority of games, the music system is simply a receiver of instruction.[50] If the music were truly interactive then this would raise the possibility of thresholds and triggers being altered, or game events waiting, in order to enable the synchronization of game events *to* music.

Manipulating game events in order to synchronize to music might seem anathema to many game developers, but some are starting to experiment with this concept. In the *Blood and Wine* expansion pack for *The Witcher 3: Wild Hunt* the senior audio programmer, Colin Walder, describes how the main character Geralt was 'so accomplished at combat that he is balletic, that he is dancing almost'.[51] With this in mind they programmed the NPCs to attack according to musical timings, with big attacks syncing to a grid, and smaller attacks syncing to beats or bars. He notes 'I think the feeling that you get is almost like we've responded somehow with the music to what was happening in the game, when actually it's the other way round'.[52] He points out that 'Whenever you have a random element then you have an opportunity to try and sync it, because if there is going to be a sync point

---

[50] Richard Stevens and Dave Raybould, 'Designing a Game for Music: Integrated Design Approaches for Ludic Music and Interactivity', in *The Oxford Handbook of Interactive Audio*, ed. Karen Collins, Bill Kapralos and Holly Tessler (New York: Oxford University Press, 2014), 147–66.

[51] Colin Walder, 'Music: Action Synchronization', Wwise Tour, Warsaw 2016, accessed 13 October 2020, www.youtube.com/watch?v=aLq0NKs3H-k.

[52] Walder, 'Music: Action Synchronization'.

happen [*sic*] within the random amount of time that you were already prepared to wait, you have a chance to make a sync happen'.[53] The composer Olivier Derivière is also notable for his innovations in the area of music and synchronization. In *Get Even* (2017) events, animations and even environmental sounds are synced to the musical pulse. The danger in using music as an input to game state changes and timings is that players may sense this loss of agency, but it should be recognized that many games artificially manipulate the player all the time through what is termed dynamic difficulty adjustment or dynamic game balancing.[54] The 2001 game *Max Payne* dynamically adjusts the amount of aiming assistance given to the player based on their performance,[55] in *Half-Life 2* (2004) the content of crates adjusts to supply more health when the player's health is low,[56] and in *BioShock* (2007) they are rendered invulnerable for 1–2 seconds when at their last health point in order to generate more 'barely survived' moments.[57] In this context, the manipulation of game variables and timings in order for events to hit musically predetermined points or quantization divisions seems less radical than the idea might at first appear.

The reconciliation of player agency and musical structure remains a significant challenge for video game music within active gaming episodes, and it has been argued that the use of metrical or synchronized transitions is only a partial solution to the problem of temporal indeterminacy. The importance of the 'end-event' in the player's narrative, and the opportunity for musical synchronization to provide a greater sense of ludic reward implies that the greater co-influence of a more truly interactive approach is worthy of further investigation.

---

[53] Walder, 'Music: Action Synchronization'.

[54] Robin Hunicke and Vernell Chapman, 'AI for Dynamic Difficulty Adjustment in Games', in *Challenges in Game Artificial Intelligence: Papers from the AAAI Workshop*, ed. Dan Fu, Stottler Henke and Jeff Orkin (Menlo Park, California: AAAI Press, 2004), 91–6.

[55] Ernest Adams, *Fundamentals of Game Design*, 2nd ed. (Berkeley: New Riders, 2007), 347.

[56] Ben Serviss, 'Ben Serviss's Blog – The Discomfort Zone: The Hidden Potential of Valve's AI Director', *Gamasutra*, 2013, accessed 8 April 2020, www.gamasutra.com/blogs/BenServiss/20130207/186193/The_Discomfort_Zone_The_Hidden_Potential_of_Valves_AI_Director.php.

[57] Paul Hellquist, [tweet] (1 September 2017), accessed 13 October 2020, https://twitter.com/theelfquist/status/903694421434277888?lang=en. Game designer Jennifer Scheurle revealed many other game design 'secrets' or manipulations through responses to her Twitter thread (accessed 13 October 2020, https://twitter.com/gaohmee/status/903510060197744640), discussed further in her 2017 presentation to the New Zealand Game Developers Association. Jennifer Scheurle. 'Hide and Seek: Good Design is Invisible', presented at the New Zealand Game Developers Conference, Wellington, 6–8 September 2017, accessed 13 October 2020, www.youtube.com/watch?v=V0o2A_up1WA.

Conclusion

Video game music is amazing. Thrilling and informative, for many it is a key component of what makes games so compelling and enjoyable. This chapter is not intended to suggest any criticism of specific games, composers or approaches. Composers, audio personnel and game designers wrestle with the issues outlined above on a daily basis, producing great music and great games despite the conflicts and tensions within musical interactivity.

Perhaps one common thread in response to the questions posed and conflicts identified is the appreciation that different people play different games, in different ways, for different reasons. Some may play along with the action implied by the music, happy for their actions to be directed, while others may rail against this – taking an unexpected approach that needs to be more closely scored. Some players will 'run and gun' their way through a game, while for others the experience of the same gaming episode will be totally different. Some players may be happy to accept a temporary loss of autonomy in exchange for the ludonarrative reward of game/music synchronization, while for others this would be an intolerable breach of the gaming contract.

As composers are increasingly educated about the tools of game development and approaches to interactive music, they will no doubt continue to become a more integrated part of the game design process, engaged with not only writing the music, but with designing the algorithms that govern how that music works in game. In doing so there is an opportunity for composers to think not about designing an interactive music system for a game, but about designing interactive music *systems*, ones that are aware of player types and ones that attempt to resolve the conflicts inherent in musical interactivity in a more bespoke way. Being aware of how a player approaches a game could, and should, inform how the music works for that player.

6 | The Triple Lock of Synchronization

K. J. DONNELLY

Contemporary audiovisual objects unify sound and moving image in our heads via the screen and speakers/headphones. The synchronization of these two channels remains one of the defining aspects of contemporary culture. Video games follow their own particular form of synchronization, where not only sound and image, but also player input form a close unity.[1] This synchronization unifies the illusion of movement in time and space, and cements it to the crucial interactive dimension of gaming. In most cases, the game software's 'music engine' assembles the whole, fastening sound to the rest of the game, allowing skilled players to synchronize themselves and become 'in tune' with the game's merged audio and video. This constitutes the critical 'triple lock' of player input with audio and video that defines much gameplay in digital games.

This chapter will discuss the way that video games are premised upon a crucial link-up between image, sound and player, engaging with a succession of different games as examples to illustrate differences in relations of sound, image and player psychology. There has been surprisingly little interest in synchronization, not only in video games but also in other audiovisual culture.[2] In many video games, it is imperative that precise synchronization is achieved or else the unity of the gameworld and the player's interaction with it will be degraded and the illusion of immersion and the effectiveness of the game dissipated. Synchronization can be precise and momentary, geared around a so-called 'synch point'; or it might be less precise and more continuous but evincing matched

---

[1] With some games, a slight lack of synchrony between sound and image, between a player's input and the illusion of the event on screen, can be tolerable. For instance, with point-and-click narratives or detection games the player can mentally compensate for the discrepancy. However, the overwhelming majority of video games require rapid response to player input. What is sometimes called 'input lag' or 'latency', when a button is pressed and the in-game response to that activity is not immediate, can utterly ruin the gaming experience.

[2] I have discussed this in detail in relation to film and television in my book *Occult Aesthetics: Synchronization in Sound Film* (New York: Oxford University Press, 2014). Other relevant writing includes Jeff Rona, *Synchronization: From Reel to Reel: A Complete Guide for the Synchronization of Audio, Film and Video* (Milwaukee, WI: Hal Leonard Corporation, 1990) and Michael Sweet, *Writing Interactive Music for Video Games: A Composer's Guide* (London: Addison Wesley, 2014), 28–9.

dynamics between music and image actions; or the connections can be altogether less clear. Four types of synchronization in video games exist. The first division, precise synchronization, appears most evidently in interactive sounds where the game player delivers some sort of input that immediately has an effect on audiovisual output in the game. Clearest where diegetic sounds emanate directly from player activity, it also occurs in musical accompaniment that develops constantly in parallel to the image activity and mood. The second division, plesiochrony, involves the use of ambient sound or music which fits vaguely with the action, making a 'whole' of sound and image, and thus a unified and immersive environment as an important part of gameplay. The third strain would be music-led asynchrony, where the music dominates and sets time for the player. Finally, in parallel-path asynchrony, music accompanies action but evinces no direct weaving of its material with the on-screen activity or other sounds.

Synching It All Up

It is important to note that synchronization is both the technological fact of the gaming hardware pulling together sound, image and gamer, and simultaneously a critically important psychological process for the gamer. This is central to immersion, merging sensory stimuli and completing a sense of surrounding ambience that takes in coherently matched sound and image. Now, this may clearly be evident in the synchronization of sound effects with action, matching the world depicted on screen as well as the game player's activities. For instance, if we see a soldier fire a gun on screen we expect to hear the crack of the gunshot, and if the player (or the player's avatar) fires a gun in the game, we expect to hear a gunshot at the precise moment the action takes place. Sound effects may appear more directly synched than music in the majority of cases, yet accompanying music can also be an integrated part of such events, also matching and directing action, both emotionally and aesthetically. Synchronization holds together a unity of audio and visual, and their combination is added to player input. This is absolutely crucial to the process of immersion through holding together the illusion of sound and vision unity, as well as the player's connection with that amalgamation.

Sound provides a more concrete dimension of space for video games than image, serving a crucial function in expanding the surface of its flat images. The keystones of this illusion are synch points, which provide a structural relationship between sound, image and player input. Synch points unify the game experience as a perceptual unity and aesthetic encounter. Writing primarily about film but with relevance to all audiovisual culture, Michel Chion coined the term 'synchresis' to describe the spontaneous appearance of synchronized connection between sound and image.[3] This is a perceptual lock that magnetically draws together sound and image, as we expect the two to be attached. The illusory and immersive effect in gameplay is particularly strong when sound and image are perceived as a unity. While we, the audience, assume a strong bond between sounds and images occupying the same or similar space, the keystones of this process are moments of precise synchronization between sound and image events.[4] This illusion of sonic and visual unity is the heart of audiovisual culture. Being perceived as an utter unity disavows the basis in artifice and cements a sense of audiovisual culture as on some level being a 'reality'.[5]

The Gestalt psychology principle of isomorphism suggests that we understand objects, including cultural objects, as having a particular character, as a consequence of their structural features.[6] Certain structural features elicit an experience of expressive qualities, and these features recur across objects in different combinations. This notion of 'shared essential structure' accounts for the common pairing of certain things: small, fast-moving objects with high-pitched sounds; slow-moving music with static or slow-moving camerawork with nothing moving quickly within the frame, and so on. Isomorphism within Gestalt psychology emphasizes a sense of cohesion and unity of elements into a distinct whole, which in video games is premised upon a sense of synchronization, or at least 'fitting' together unremarkably; matching, if not obviously, then perhaps on some deeper level of unity. According to Rudolf Arnheim, such a 'structural kinship' works essentially on a psychological level,[7] as an

---

[3] Michel Chion, *Audio-Vision: Sound on Screen*, ed. and trans. Claudia Gorbman (New York: Columbia University Press, 1994), 5.

[4] Chion's synchresis matches the ideas of Lipscomb and Kendall, both of which note perceptual 'marking' by synch points. S. D. Lipscomb and R. A. Kendall, 'Sources of Accent in Musical Sound and Visual Motion', in the *Proceedings of the 4th International Conference for Music Perception and Cognition* (Liege: ICMPC, 1994), 451–2.

[5] Frans Mäyrä notes the surface and coding reality beneath. He discusses the 'dual structure of video games', where 'players access both a "shell" (representational layers) and the "core" (the gameplay)'. Frans Mäyrä, 'Getting into the Game: Doing Multidisciplinary Game Studies', in *The Video Game Theory Reader 2*, ed. Bernard Perron and Mark J. P. Wolf (New York: Routledge, 2008), 313–30 at 317.

[6] Rudolf Arnheim, 'The Gestalt Theory of Expression', in *Documents of Gestalt Psychology*, ed. Mary Henle (Los Angeles: University of California Press, 1961), 301–23 at 308.

[7] Rudolf Arnheim, *Art and Visual Perception: A Psychology of the Creative Eye* (Los Angeles: University of California Press, 1974), 450.

indispensable part of perceiving expressive similarity across forms, as we encounter similar features in different contexts and formulations. While this is, of course, bolstered by convention, it appears to have a basis in primary human perception.[8]

One might make an argument that many video games are based on a form of spatial exploration, concatenating the illusory visual screen space with that of stereo sound, and engaging a constant dynamic of both audio and visual movement and stasis. This works through isomorphism and dynamic relationships between sound and image that can remain in a broad synchronization, although not matching each other pleonastically blow for blow.[9] A good example here would be the first-person shooter *Quake* (1996), where the player sees their avatar's gun in the centre of the screen and has to move and shoot grotesque cyborg and organic enemies. Trent Reznor and Nine Inch Nails' incidental soundtrack consists of austere electronic music, dominated by ambient drones and treated electronic sounds. It is remarkable in itself but is also matched well to the visual aspects of the gameworld. The player moves in 3-D through a dark and grim setting that mixes an antiquated castle with futuristic high-tech architecture, corridors and underwater shafts and channels. This sound and image environment is an amalgam, often of angular, dark-coloured surfaces and low-pitched notes that sustain and are filtered to add and subtract overtones. It is not simply that sound and image fit together well, but that the tone of both is in accord on a deep level. Broad synchronization consists not simply of a mimetic copy of the world outside the game (where we hear the gunshot when we fire our avatar's gun) but also of a general cohesion of sound and image worlds which is derived from perceptual and cognitive horizons as well as cultural traditions. In other words, the cohesion of the sound with the image in the vast majority of cases is due to structural and tonal similarities between what are perhaps too often approached as utterly separate channels. However, apart from these deep- (rather than surface-) level similarities, coherence of sound and image can also vary due to the degree and mode of synchronization between the two.

---

[8] For further reading about games and Gestalt theory consult K. J. Donnelly, 'Lawn of the Dead: The Indifference of Musical Destiny in Plants vs. Zombies', in *Music In Video Games: Studying Play*, ed. K. J. Donnelly, William Gibbons and Neil Lerner (New York: Routledge, 2014), 151–65 at 160; Ingolf Ståhl, *Operational Gaming: An International Approach* (Oxford: Pergamon, 2013), 245; and Mark J. P. Wolf, 'Design', in *The Video Game Theory Reader 2*, ed. Bernard Perron and Mark J. P. Wolf (London: Routledge, 2008), 343–4.

[9] In other words, rather than 'Mickey-Mousing' (the music redundantly repeating the dynamics of the image activity), there is only a general sense of the music 'fitting' the action.

Finger on the Trigger

While synchronization may be an aesthetic strategy or foundation, a principle that produces a particular psychological engagement, it is also essentially a technological process. Broadly speaking, a computer CPU (central processing unit) has its own internal clocks that synchronizes and controls all its operations. There is also a system clock which controls things for the whole system (outside of the CPU). These clocks also need to be in synchronization.[10] While matters initially rest on CPU and console/computer architecture – the hardware – they also depend crucially on software.[11]

The principle of the synch point where image events and player inputs trigger developments in the music is a characteristic of video game music. Jesper Kaae discusses video games as 'hypertext', consisting of nodes and links, which are traversed in a non-linear fashion.[12] 'Nodes' might be understood as the synch points that underpin the structure of interactive video games, and have particular relevance for the triple lock of sound and image to player input. Specific to video games is how the disparate musical elements are triggered by gameplay and combined into a continuum of coherent development for the player's experience over time. Indeed, triggering is the key for development in such a non-linear environment, set in motion by the coalescence of the player's input with sound and image elements. A player moving the avatar into a new room, for example, can trigger a new piece of music or the addition of some musical aspects to existing looped music.[13] Michael Sweet notes that triggered musical changes can alter emotional state or general atmosphere, change the intensity of a battle, indicate a fall in the player's health rating, indicate an enemy's proximity and indicate successful completion of a task or battle.[14]

Triggered audio can be a simple process, where some games simply activate a loop of repeated music that continues ad infinitum as accompaniment to the player's screen actions, as in *Tetris* (Nintendo, 1989). However,

---

[10] See Randall Hyde, *The Art of Assembly* (N.p.: Randall Hyde, 1996), 92–6.

[11] MMORPGs (Massively Multiplayer Online Role-Playing Games) and games for multiple players require effective synchronization to hold the shared gameworld together.

[12] Jesper Kaae, 'Theoretical Approaches to Composing Dynamic Music for Video Games', in *From Pac-Man to Pop Music: Interactive Audio in Games and New Media*, ed. Karen Collins (Aldershot: Ashgate, 2008), 75–92 at 77.

[13] Richard Stevens and Dave Raybould, *The Game Audio Tutorial: A Practical Guide to Sound and Music for Interactive Games* (London: Focal Press, 2011), 112.

[14] Sweet, *Writing Interactive Music*, 28.

triggered audio often sets in train more complex programs where music is varied.[15] Karen Collins effectively differentiates between types of triggered audio in video games. 'Interactive audio' consists of 'Sound events that react to the player's direct input' like footsteps and gunshots, whereas 'adaptive audio' is 'Sound that reacts to the game states' such as location, mood or health.[16] The former relates to precise gameplay, while the latter is not so directly affected by player activity. In terms of music in video games, while much works on a level of providing accompanying atmosphere in different locations, for example, and so is adaptive, some programming allows for developing music to be triggered by a succession of player inputs (such as proximity of enemies). Adaptive music is particularly effective in sophisticated action role-playing games with possible multiple paths. Good examples of this would include the later iterations of the Elder Scrolls series games, such as *Skyrim* (2011). A particularly complex form of synchronization comes from branching (horizontal resequencing) and layering (vertical remixing) music to fit momentary developments in the gameplay instigated by the player.[17] The process of pulling together disparate musical 'cues' involves direct joins, crossfades and masks, with a dedicated program controlling a database of music in the form of fragmentary loops, short transitions and longer musical pieces of varying lengths (see, for example, *Halo* (2001) and sequels). These sophisticated procedures yield constant variation, where music is integrated with the experience of the player. This means momentary change, synchronized precisely to events in the game, and this precise matching of musical development to action on screen owes something to the film tradition of 'Mickey-Mousing' but is far more sophisticated.[18] The relationship of image, player input and soundtrack is retained at a constantly close level, controlled by the programming and with momentary changes often not consciously perceived by the player.

Tradition has led to strong conventions in video game audio and in the relationship between sound and image. Some of these conventions are derived from other, earlier forms of audiovisual culture,[19] while some others are more specific to game design. Synchronization is fundamental for video

---

[15] Ibid., 36.

[16] Karen Collins, *Game Sound: An Introduction to the History, Theory and Practice of Video Game Music and Sound Design* (Cambridge, MA: The MIT Press, 2008), 126.

[17] Tim van Geelen, 'Realising Groundbreaking Adaptive Music', in *From Pac-Man to Pop Music: Interactive Audio in Games and New Media*, ed. Karen Collins (Aldershot: Ashgate, 2008), 93–102.

[18] Tim Summers, *Understanding Video Game Music* (Cambridge, UK: Cambridge University Press, 2016), 190.

[19] Ibid., 176.

games, but the relationship between sound and image can take appreciably different forms. It might be divided into four types: precise synchronization to gameplay, plesiochrony, forcing gameplay to fit music and asynchrony.

Player-Led Synchrony

Player-led synchronization has a succession of synch points where player input aligns precisely with sound and image. Player input can change screen activity, and this renders musical developments in line with the changes in game activity. This is what Collins calls 'interactive audio', and this principle is most evident in interactive sound effects where the game player provides some sort of input that immediately has an effect in the audiovisual output of the game. For instance, the pulling of a gun's trigger by the player requires a corresponding immediate gunshot sound, and requires a corresponding resultant action on screen where a target is hit (or not) by the bullet. This is a crucial process that provides an immersive effect, making the player believe on some level in the 'reality' of the gameplay and gameworld on screen. It correlates with our experience of the real world,[20] or at least provides a sense of a coherent world on screen even if it does not resemble our own. This triple lock holds together sound and image as an illusory unity but also holds the player in place as the most essential function. Indeed, the continued coherent immersive illusion of the game is held together by the intermittent appearance of such moments of direct, precise synchronization. The coherence of the experience is also aided by synchronized music, which forms a precise unity of visuals on screen, other sounds and gameplay activity. Music in such situations is dynamic, following player input to match location, mood and activity. This is *reactive* music that can change in a real-time mix in response to the action, depending directly on some degree of variable input from the player. It lacks the linear development of music as it is traditionally understood and indeed, each time a particular section of a game is played, the music might never be exactly the same.

An interesting case in point is *Dead Space* (2008), which has a particularly convoluted and intricate approach to its music. The game is set in the twenty-sixth century, when engineer Isaac has to fight his way through the mining space ship Ishimura that is filled with 'Necromorphs', who are the zombified remnants of its crew. To destroy them, Isaac has to dismember

---

[20] Alison McMahan, 'Immersion, Engagement and Presence: A Method for Analyzing 3-D Video Games', in *The Video Game Theory Reader*, ed. Bernard Perron and Mark J. P. Wolf (London: Routledge, 2003), 67–86, at 72.

them. Played in third person, *Dead Space* includes zero-gravity vacuum sections, and puzzle solving as well as combat. Jason Graves, the game's composer, approached the game events as a drama like a film. He stated: 'I always think of this the way I would have scored a film . . . but it's getting cut up into a giant puzzle and then reassembled in different ways depending on the game play.'[21] So, the aim is to follow the model of incidental music from film,[22] but in order to achieve this, the music needs to follow a complex procedure of real-time mixing. While some games only offer a repetitive music on/off experience, *Dead Space* offers a more sophisticated atmospheric and immersive musical soundtrack. Rather than simply branching, the game has four separate but related music streams playing all the time. These are 'creepy', 'tense', 'very tense' and 'chaotic'. The relationship between these parallel tracks is controlled by what the game designers in this case call 'fear emitters', which are potential dangers anchored in particular locations in the gameworld. The avatar's proximity to these beacons shapes and mixes those four streams, while dynamically altering relative volume and applying filters and other digital signal processing. This means that a constant variation of soundtrack is continually evident throughout *Dead Space*.[23] Rather than being organized like a traditional film score, primarily around musical themes, the music in *Dead Space* is built around the synchronization of musical development precisely to avatar activity, and thus player input in relation to game geography and gameplay.

Plesiochrony

Plesiochrony aims not to match all dynamic changes of gameplay, but instead to provide a general ambience, making a unity of sound and

---

[21] Ken McGorry, 'Scoring to Picture', in *Post Magazine*, November 2009, 39, accessed 15 October 2020, https://web.archive.org/web/20100126001756/http://www.jasongraves.com:80/press.

[22] Mark Sweeney notes that the game has two musical sound worlds: a neo-romantic one in cut scenes and a modernist one inspired by twentieth-century art music (of the sort used in horror films) which works for gameplay. The latter is reminiscent of Penderecki's music as used in *The Exorcist* (1973) and *The Shining* (1980). 'Isaac's Silence: Purposive Aesthetics in Dead Space', in *Ludomusicology: Approaches to Video Game Music*, ed. Michiel Kamp, Tim Summers and Mark Sweeney (Sheffield: Equinox, 2016), 172–97 at 190, 192.

[23] Don Veca, the game's audio director, created a scripting system he called 'Dead Script', which was on top of low-level audio drivers and middleware. An important aspect of this was what he called 'the creepy ambi patch', which was a grouping of sounds that constantly reappeared but in different forms, pitch-shifted, filtered and processed. These were also controlled by the 'fear emitters' but appeared more frequently when no action or notable events were happening. Paul Mac, 'Game Sound Special: Dead Space', in *Audio Media*, July 2009, 2–3.

image, and thus an immersive environment for gameplay. Player input is less important and might merely be at a level of triggering different music by moving to different locations. The term describes a general, imprecise synchronization.[24] Plesiochrony works in an isomorphic manner (as discussed earlier), matching together atmosphere, location and general mood. Music and image fuse together to make a 'whole', such as a unified environment, following the principles of being isomorphically related to atmosphere, location and mood. This might be characterized as a 'soft synchrony' and corresponds to Collins' notion of 'adaptive audio'. The music modifies with respect to gameplay in a broad sense, but does not change constantly in direct response to a succession of player inputs. The music in these cases becomes part of the environment, and becomes instituted in the player's mind as an emotionally charged and phenomenologically immersive experience. The music is often simply triggered, and plays on regardless of momentary gameplay. However, it nevertheless accomplishes an important role as a crucial part of the environment and atmosphere, indirectly guiding and affecting player activity. Indeed, perhaps its principal function is a general furnishing of 'environmental' aspects to the game, emphasizing mood, tone and atmosphere.[25] For instance, in *Quake*, the music at times quite crudely starts and stops, often with almost no interactive aspect. It is simply triggered by the player's avatar entering a new location. The score has something of the quality of diegetic ambience and at times could be taken to be the sound of the location. However, the sounds do not change when the avatar becomes immersed underwater, indicating that it is outside the game's diegesis.

While 3-D games like *Quake* followed a model evident in most first-person shooters, other 3-D games have adopted different approaches. Indie game *The Old City: Leviathan* (2015) is not based on skilful fighting action or thoughtful puzzling. It is a first-person 'walking game', where a detailed visual environment is open to the player's exploration. This game engages with a margin of video games history, games that are about phenomenological experience rather than progressive achievement and gameplay in the conventional sense. The music was a featured aspect of *The Old City: Leviathan*'s publicity, and the 'lack' of action-packed gameplay allows music to be foregrounded. As a counterpart to the visuals, the extensive and atmospheric music soundtrack is by Swedish dark ambient

---

[24] For more discussion of plesiochrony, see Donnelly, *Occult Aesthetics*, 181–3.

[25] Gernot Böhme points to atmosphere as a form of integrated, concrete relationship between human and environment. Gernot Böhme, *The Aesthetics of Atmospheres*, ed. Jean-Paul Thibaud (London: Routledge, 2017), 14.

industrial musician Atrium Carceri. The game's texture is emphasized by the player's slow movement around the city location in first person, which allows and encourages appreciation of the landscape. Indeed, the game developers were obsessed with images and sounds: on their promotional website, the discussion alights on the difficulty of visually rendering puddles. More generally, the Postmod website states: 'Players have the option to simply walk from start to finish, but the real meat of the game lies in the hidden nooks and crannies of the world; in secret areas, behind closed doors . . . '. The music is not only an integrated part of the experience, but also follows a similar process of being open to exploration and contemplation, as ambient music tends to be quite 'static' and lacks a sense of developmental movement. The fact that there is little real gameplay, apart from walking, gives music a remarkable position in the proceedings, what might be called 'front stage'. There is no need for dynamic music, and the music has the character of Atrium Carceri's other music, as atmospheric ambience.[26] The music is an equivalent to landscape in an isomorphic manner. It is like a continuum, develops slowly and has no startling changes. The aim is at enveloping ambience, with a vaguely solemn mood that matches the player's slow movement around the large, deserted cityscape. In a way, the game 'fulfils' the potential of the music, in that its character is 'programmatic' or ambient music. While the music appears somewhat indifferent to the player, an interactive relationship is less important here as the music is an integrated component of the game environment (where the world to a degree dominates the player), and music functions as triggered isomorphic atmosphere. Less concerned with gameplay and more directly concerned with embodying environment, it lacks notable dynamic shifts and development. This decentres the player and makes them a visitor in a large dominant and independent sound- and image-scape. However, there is a coherence to the game's world that synchronizes sound and image on a fundamental level.

Music-Led Asynchrony

In the first configuration of asynchrony, music *articulates* and sets controls for action and gameplay. Collins and others are less interested in this form of game audio, perhaps because initially it appears to be less defining and less specific to video games than 'dynamic audio'. However, I would

---

[26] Of course, this is importing wholesale music of a style that is not particular to video games, yet fits these particular games well.

suggest that asynchrony marks a significant tradition in game audio. With games that are timebound, music often can appear to set the time for gameplay. This is most clear, perhaps, with music-based games like *Guitar Hero* (2005) or *Dance Dance Revolution* (1998), where the fixed song length dictates the gameplay. A fine example are the games corralled as the *Wii Fit* (2007) programme, a massively popular series of exercises that mix the use of a dedicated balancing board with the console's movement sensor to appraise performance. The music for each task is functional, providing a basic atmosphere but also providing a sense of aesthetic structure to the often repetitive exercises.[27] Each piece is fairly banal and does not aim to detract from concentration, but provides some neutral but bright, positive-sounding wallpaper (all major keys, basic melodies, gentle rhythmic pulses and regular four-bar structures). In almost every case, the music articulates exercise activity. It is not 'interactive' as such, and the precise duration of each exercise is matched by the music. In other words, each piece of music was written to a precise timing, and then the game player has to work to that. They should not, or cannot, make any changes to the music, as might be the case in other video games. The *Wii Fit* has a number of exercise options available, each of which lasts a relatively small period of time. These are based on yoga, muscle exercises or synchronized movement. There are also some balancing activities, which are the closest challenges to those of traditional video games, and include ski-jumping and dance moves coordinated to precisely timed movements. The crucial point for the player is that they can tell when the music is coming to an end, and thus when the particular burst of exercise is about to finish. Repetition of the same exercises causes the player to know the music particularly well and to anticipate its conclusion. This is clearly a crucial psychological process, where the player is forced to synchronize themselves and their activities directly to the game, dictated by the music.

Similarly, in *Plants vs. Zombies* (2009), changes in the musical fabric are based on the musical structure and requirements, not the gameplay. It is a tower defence game in which the player defends a house using a lawn (in the initial version), where they plant anthropomorphic defensive vegetables to halt an onrush of cartoon zombies. Each level of the game has a different piece of accompanying music, which comprises electronic approximations of tuned percussion and other traditional instrument sounds. The relation of music to action is almost negligible, with the

---

[27] Composers include Toru Minegishi (who had worked on the *Legend of Zelda* games and *Super Mario 3D World*), Shiho Fujii and Manaka Tomigana.

regularity of the music furnishing a rigid and mechanical character to gameplay. The music simply progresses, almost in parallel to the unfolding of the game, as a homology to the relentless shambling movement of the zombies. The first levels take place during the day on the front lawn of the player's unseen house and are accompanied by a piece of music that simply loops. The recorded piece mechanically restarts at the point where it finishes, irrespective of the events in the game.[28] Because the music is not subject to interruptions from dynamic music systems, the music is free to feature a strong, regular rhythmic profile. The cue is based on a tango or habanera dance rhythm. The very regularity of dances means that, as an accompaniment to audiovisual culture, they tend to marshal the proceedings, to make the action feel like it is moving to the beat of the dance rather than following any external logic. In *Plants vs. Zombies*, this effect is compounded by the totally regular structure of the music (based on four-bar units, with successive melodies featuring particular instruments: oboe, strings and pizzicato strings respectively).[29] There is a clear sense of integrity from the music's regular rhythmic structure in the face of variable timings in the gameplay. The harmony never strays too far from the key of A minor (despite an F 7th chord), and the slow tango rhythm is held in the bass line, which plays chord tones with the occasional short chromatic run between pitches. However, the continuity of this music is halted by the player's successful negotiation of the level, which triggers a burst of jazz guitar to crudely blot out the existing music. *Plants vs. Zombies'* music conceivably could fit another game with a profoundly different character. Having noted this, the cue's aptness might be connected most directly with the game on a deeper level, where the music's regularity relates to the unceasing regularity of the gameplay. The cue is not synchronized to the action, apart from the concluding segment of the level. In this, a drum beat enters as an accompaniment to the existing music, appearing kinetically to choreograph movement through grabbing proceedings by the scruff of the neck, as what is billed on screen as a 'massive wave of zombies' approaches at the level's conclusion. The assumption is that the beat matches the excitement of the action (and chaotic simultaneity on screen). However,

---

[28] Although the player's actions trigger musically derived sounds, forming something of a random sound 'soloing' performed over the top of the musical bed, it is difficult to conceive this as a coherent piece of music.

[29] The opening tango section comprises sixteen bars, followed by eight bars of oboe melody (the same four repeated), then an orphan four-bar drop-out section leading to pizzicato strings for eight bars, followed by the same section repeated, with added sustained strings for eight bars, and finally, a section of piano arpeggios of sixteen bars (the same four repeated four times), after which the whole piece simply repeats.

again, if we turn the sound off, it does not have a significant impact on the experience of the game and arguably none at all on the gameplay. In summary, the time of the music matches the game section's pre-existing structure, and the player has to work to this temporal and dynamic agenda rather than control it.

Parallel-Path Asynchrony

Unsynchronized music can also have a relationship of indifference to the game, and carry on irrespective of its action. It might simply co-exist with it, as a presence of ambiguous substance, and might easily be removed without significantly impairing the experience of the game. This situation is relatively common for mobile and iOS games and other games where sound is unimportant. Here, the music is not integrated strongly into the player's experience. This relationship of asynchrony between the music and gameplay is embodied by this form of 'non-functional' music that adds little or nothing to the game and might easily be removed or replaced. Such music often has its own integrity as a recording and can finish abruptly, when the player concludes a game section (either successfully or unsuccessfully), sometimes interrupted by another musical passage. This owes something to the tradition of earlier arcade games, and although it may seem crude in comparison with the processes of dynamic music, it is nevertheless an effective phenomenon and thus persists. The way this non-interactive music carries on irrespective of gameplay makes it correspond to so-called 'anempathetic' music, where music seems indifferent to the on-screen action. Anempathetic music has been theorized in relation to film, but clearly has a relevance in all audiovisual culture. Michel Chion discusses such situations, which have the potential to 'short-circuit' simple emotional congruence to replace it with a heightened state of emotional confusion.[30]

Some games simply trigger and loop their music. Although 'interactive dynamic music' can be a remarkable component of video games and is evident in many so-called 'four-star' prestige video games, in its sophisticated form, it is hardly the dominant form of video game music. Disconnected 'non-dynamic' music exemplifies a strong tradition in game music, which runs back to the arcade.[31] While some might imagine this is a retrogressive format, and that arcade games were simplistic and aesthetically unsophisticated, this earliest form of video game sound and

---

[30] Chion, *Audio-Vision*, 8–9.
[31] Donnelly, 'Lawn of the Dead', 154.

music remains a highly functional option for many contemporary games. For instance, this is highly evident in iOS and other mobile games, and games which lack dynamics and/or utilize highly restricted spatial schemes, such as simple puzzle games or games with heavily constrained gameplay. A good example is action platformer *Crash Bandicoot* (1996), which has a sonic backdrop of kinetic music emphasizing synthesized tuned percussion, while earcons/auditory icons and sound effects for game events occupy the sonic foreground. The music changes with each level, but has no requirement to enter a sophisticated process of adaptation to screen activity. Yet in purely sonic terms, the game achieves a complex interactive musical melange of the game score in the background with the highly musical sounds triggered by the avatar's activities in the gameplay. Yet the game can happily be played without sound. The musical background can add to the excitement of playing, evident in arcade games such as jet-ski simulator *Aqua Jet* (1996), which required the player to 'qualify' through completing sections in an allotted time. The music merely formed an indistinct but energetic sonic wall behind the loud sound effects. Similarly, in driving game *Crazy Taxi* (1999), 'game time' ticks down and then is replenished if the player is successful. Here, songs (including punk rock by The Offspring) keep going, irrespective of action. The music can chop and change when a section is finished, and when one song finishes another starts. The situation bears resemblance to the Grand Theft Auto series (1997–2013) with its radio station of songs that are not synchronized with action.

Candy Crush Saga (2012) is an extremely successful mobile game of the 'match three' puzzle variety. Music is less than essential for successful gameplay, although the game's music is highly effective despite many people playing the game 'silent'. The merest repetition of the music can convince the player of its qualities.[32] It is simply a looped recording and in no way dynamic in relation to the game. The music has a fairly basic character, with a swinging 12/8 rhythm and clearly articulated chord changes (I-IV-IVm-I-V) at regular intervals. However, one notable aspect of the music is that at times it is extremely *rubato*, speeding up and slowing down, which helps give a sense that the music is not regimented, and the player indeed can take variable time with making a move. The player's successive moves can sometimes be very rapid and sometimes taken at their leisure. Whatever happens, the music carries on regardless. However,

---

[32] The 'repetition effect' tests music's durability, although the cumulative effect of repetition can persuade a listener. I hated the music at first, but after playing the game, ended up appreciating it.

it is intriguing that the music contains a moment of drama that pulls slightly outside of the banal and predictable framework. The shift from major to minor chord on the same root note is a surprising flourish in a continuum of highly predictable music. This exists perhaps to make the music more interesting in itself, yet this (slightly) dramatic change signalled in the music is *not* tied to gameplay at all. It is subject to the random relationship between music and gameplay: the music can suggest some drama where there is none in the game. It might be argued that this applies a moment of psychological pressure to the player, who might be taking time over their next move, or it may not. However, while the music is a repeated recording with no connection to the gameplay, oddly it has a less mechanical character than some game music. The *rubato* performance and jazzy swing of the music can appear less strictly regimented than some dynamic music, which needs to deal in precise beats and quantified rhythms to hold together its disparate stem elements.[33]

Conclusion

The process of 'triggering' is the key to the whole process of synchronization in video games and may be noticeable for the player or not. In some cases, the trigger may simply inaugurate more variations in the musical accompaniment, but in others it can cue the beginning of a whole new piece of music. A certain activity embarked upon by the player triggers a change in the game audio. This locks the synchronization of the player's activity with sound and image elements in the game. Indeed, this might be taken as one of the defining aspects of video games more generally. This interactive point functions as a switch where the player triggers sound activity, such as when moving an avatar to a new location triggers changes in the music and ambient sound.[34] This physical, technological fact manifests the heart of the sound-and-image synch that holds video games together. However, we should remember that rather than simply being a technical procedure, crucially it is also a psychological one. It initiates and signals a significant change in the gameplay (more tense gameplay, the start of a new section of play, etc.).

[33] 'Stems' are musical parts that work through fitting intimately together rather than on their own. Arguably, the process of using stems comes from digital musical culture, where it is easy to group together recorded music channels in so-called 'submixes'.

[34] Sweet notes that these points are called 'hooks', which describe the commands sent from player input, through the game engine to the audio, so named for the game 'hooking into' the music engine. Sweet, *Writing Interactive Music*, 28.

There has been much writing by scholars and theorists of video game music about interactive audio.[35] However, 'interactivity' presents severe limits as a theoretical tool and analytical concept. Similarly, an analytical concept imported from film analysis used for dealing with video game audio – the distinction between diegetic and non-diegetic – also proves limited in its relevance and ability as a means of analysis. Instead of these two concepts, a division of music through attending to synchronization might be more fruitful for video game analysis. This would register the essential similarities between, for example, non-diegetic incidental music and diegetic sound environment for a particular location. Similarly, the dynamic changes that might take place in an interactive musical score could also follow a similar procedure in diegetic sound effects, when a player moves an avatar around a particular on-screen location. Analytical distinctions of music in video games should not be determined purely by mode of production. This has led to a focus on interactive video game music, which may well not be phenomenologically perceived by the player. This risks a focus on the underlying production, the coding level, to the detriment of addressing the phenomenological experience of the surface of gameplay.[36] The electro-mechanical perfection of time at the centre of modern culture endures at the heart of video games, whose mechanistic structures work invisibly to instil a specific psychological state in the player.

---

[35] Not only has Karen Collins written about different forms of interactive audio, but also Michael Liebe, who notes that there might be three broad categories of music interaction: 'Linear' (which cannot be changed by the player), 'Reactive' (which is triggered by player actions) and 'Proactive' (where the player must follow the game). Michael Liebe, 'Interactivity and Music in Computer Games', in *Music and Game: Perspectives on a Popular Alliance*, ed. Peter Moormann (Wiesbaden: Springer, 2013), 41–62, at 47–8.

[36] Frans Mäyrä notes that players, ' . . . access both a "shell" (representational layers) as well as the "core" (the gameplay).' Mäyrä, 'Getting into the Game,' 317.

7 | 'Less Music, Now!' New Contextual Approaches to Video Game Scoring

ROB BRIDGETT

In video games, music (in particular that which is considered 'the score') is automatically thought of as a fundamental requirement of the identity of any production. However, in this chapter, I will discuss how musical scores are often over-relied upon, formulaic and also, conceivably in some game titles, not required at all.

From the earliest availability of sound technologies, music has been present and marketed as a crucial part of a game's 'identity'. Most admirably, composers themselves have garnered an elevated status as auteurs within the industry, in a way that very few designers, animators, visual artists or sound artists have done. While this marks an important achievement for music and its presence in games, we are arguably in a phase of video game aesthetics where the function and use of music, particularly orchestral music, is becoming increasingly jaded, formulaic and repetitive, and where more subtle and fresh approaches appear to be garnering much higher critical praise.

While this chapter carries a provocative title and opening statement, I should state up front that I am a very big fan of video game music, composers and game scores. The premise of this chapter is not to question or discourage the involvement of composers and music in game development, but instead to challenge and further understand some of the motivations *behind* music use in video games. It is also to provoke the reader to see a future in which music can be integrated and considered much more thoughtfully, effectively and positively in order to serve the game's soundtrack in both production and aesthetic terms.

The Practicalities of Game (Music) Development

As a practitioner and audio director for the last twenty years in the video games industry, at both the triple-A and indie studio level, I have gained a good insight into how music is both commissioned and discussed amongst game developers, game directors, producers, composers and marketing departments.

Firstly, we need to consider some of the wider overall contexts in which music in contemporary video games production sits. Generally speaking, the **soundtrack** of a video game can be defined by three main food groups of voice-over,[1] sound effects and music. I would also add an additional area of consideration to this, perhaps almost a *fourth* food group, of 'mix', which is the artistic, technical and collaborative balance of all three of those food groups in their final contexts, and in which the audio developers are able to make decisions about which of the three to prioritize at any given moment or any given state or transition in a game. The mix is something that should be (but is very rarely) considered with as much vigour as music, voice and SFX, as early and often as possible during the process of working across a game's soundtrack.

To borrow from the production world of cinema sound, Ben Burtt and Randy Thom, both widely known and respected cinema sound designers and rerecording mixers, have often talked about what they refer to as 'the 100% theory'.[2] This is an observation whereby every different department on a film's soundtrack will consider it 100 per cent of their job to tell the story. The sound FX and Foley department consider it 100 per cent of their job to hit all the story beats and moments with FX, the writers consider it their job to hit and tell all the story moments with dialogue lines, and the composer and music department consider it 100 per cent of their job to hit all the storytelling moments with music cues. The result, most often, is arriving at the final mix stage, with premixes full of choices to be made about what plays when, and what is the most important element, or balance of elements, in any particular moment. It is essentially a process of deferring decision making until the very last minute on the mix stage, and is usually the result of a director working separately with each department, rather than having those departments present and coordinated as part of the overall sound team in general. Certainly, a similar thing can be said to be true of video game sound development, whereby the final 'shape' of the game experience is often unknown by those working on the game until very close to the end of post-production. This is mainly because game development is an 'iterative' process, whereby the members of a game

---

[1] Increasingly, because of either budgetary, aesthetic or cultural specificity, many video games do not actually contain any voice-over dialogue. They either display spoken content via on-screen text, or they contain no spoken dialogue or text at all. This decision can also be motivated because of the large budgetary impact that localizing these voice-overs into many different languages can incur on a production.

[2] Randy Thom, 'Designing a Move for Sound', in *Soundscape: The School of Sound Lectures, 1998–2001*, ed. Larry Sider and Diane Freeman (London: Wallflower, 2003), 121–37.

development team work out and refine the elements of the game, the story, the characters (quite often even the game engine itself) and the gameplay as they build it.

Iteration basically requires that something is first tried out on screen (a rough first pass at a gameplay feature or story element), then subjected to multi-disciplinary feedback, then refined from a list of required changes; and then that process of execution and review is repeated and repeated until the feedback becomes increasingly fine, and the feature or story element feels more and more satisfactory whenever played or viewed.

If we consider the difference between film and game preproduction for a moment, the sound teams in cinema are able to identify and articulate that the 100 per cent rule is being applied in their productions. They typically have a director and a pre-approved shooting script already in the bag before production begins, so they already *know* what they are making, who the characters are and what the story is, and likely all the shots in the movie: yet they still have every department thinking it is their job to tell 100 per cent of the story. The situation is even more exaggerated in games, because of the iterative nature of production and (often) highly segmented workflow, both of which keep a great many more factors in flux right the way through the cycle of creation. Developers know very little upfront about the story and the gameplay mechanics, and perhaps only understand the genre or the overall feeling and high-level rules of the initial creative vision as they set off into production. Coupled with the vast amount of work and re-work that occurs in game production in that iterative process, the 100 per cent theory is in overdrive, as creators work to cover what *may* be ultimately required by the game once the whole vision of the game has been figured out, and what is actually important has become apparent.

Deferring decisions to the mix in cinema, though less than ideal, is still very much something that can be done. There is time allotted at the end of the post-production period for this to occur, and there are craftspeople in the role of rerecording mixer who are heavily specialized in mixing. So, to further develop this picture of the production of game sound content, we also need to understand that mixing technology, practices, expertise and planning in video games have only recently come into existence in the last fifteen years, and are nowhere near anything that could be described as beyond rudimentary when compared with cinema. In contrast with those of games, because *cinema* mixes can be conceived and executed against a linear image, they are able to make sense of the overabundance of content in the three main food groups to a greater degree of sophistication. An interactive game experience, however, is being mixed at run-time – a mix which needs to take into account almost all possible gameplay situations that the player could initiate, and not just a linear timeline that is the same every time it is viewed.

One of the advantages that video game developers *do* have over those working in cinema is that their audio teams are very often, at least at the triple-A studio level, already embedded in the project from the earliest concept phases. This is something cinema sound designers and composers have long yearned for, as it would enable them to influence the other crafts and disciplines of the film-making process, such as script writing, set design and cinematography, in order to create better storytelling opportunities for sound and allow it to play the role of principal collaborator in the movie. In video games, the planning of financial and memory budgets, conversations about technology and so on begin very early in the concept phase. At the time of writing, at the end of the second decade of the twenty-first century, more than in the last ten years, the creative direction of the audio in a new title is also discussed and experimented on very early in the concept phase.

This organization enables musical style and tone, sound design elements and approaches, both artistic and technical, to be considered early on in the development. It also facilitates early collaborations across departments and helps to establish how audio content is to be used in the game. However, very little time or consideration is paid to the 'mix' portion of the sound-track, or basically, the thinking about what will play when, and how the three food groups of voice, sound and music will interact with, and complement, one another.

Ideally, being on the project and being able to map out what will play when and in what situation, gives a distinct advantage to those present on a preproduction or concept-phase development team, in that this work will actually inform the team as to what food group needs to be aesthetically prioritized in each situation. This way, for example, music cues can be planned with more accuracy and less 'overall coverage' in mind. Rather than making the mix decisions all at the 'back end' of the project during a final mix period, some of these decisions can be made upfront, thus saving a lot of time and money, and also allowing the prioritization of a composer's, or sound designer's tasks, on the areas of most importance in their work.

This is admittedly a utopian vision of how projects could work and be executed, and I know as well as anyone that as one works on a project, one needs to be prepared to react and pivot very quickly to cover something that was not discussed or even thought about the week before. Requests can emerge suddenly and quickly on a game team: for example, a new design feature can be requested and is taken on board as something that would be fun for the game to include, which completely changes one's budgeted music requirements. Conversely, a feature could be cut completely because it is not fun for the player, which can impact huge amounts of music and scheduled work that is no longer required, and with the clock ticking, one has to either reappropriate those existing cues to fit new contexts for which they were not composed, or completely scrap them and have a composer write brand new cues to fit the new contexts.

This is one of the inherent risks and challenges of video game development, that the iterative process of developing the game is focused on throwing away and cutting work that has been done, as often and early and continuously as possible in order to find the core essence of what the game is about. This means that a lot of work on both the music and sound side is carried out in 'sketch' mode, whereby everything is produced quite quickly and loosely (ready to be thrown away at a moment's notice), in order to not solidify and polish the intentions too soon. This often means a lot of the recording and refinement of the SFX and musical score does not occur until very late in production phases. So you will rarely really hear the final mastered, texture and mix of the score working in context until the all-too-short post-production phases.

In addition to the challenges added to the creation of this musical content by these continually moving goalposts, we should consider the great technical challenges of *implementing* a video game score to play back seamlessly in the game engine. One of the additional challenges of writing and working in this medium is that delivery and implementation of the musical score occurs through run-time audio engine tools (perhaps through middleware such as FMOD or Wwise). These systems require very specific music stem/loop/cue preparation and delivery, and scripted triggering logic must be applied, so that each cue starts, evolves and ends in the desired ways so as to support the emotion and action of the game's intensity seamlessly.

Given, then, that this is often the production process of working on music and sound in video games, we can start to understand how much of video game music has come into existence and how composers can spend two, three or four years (sometimes longer) on a single project, continually feeding it with music cues, loops, stingers and themes throughout the various milestones of a project's lifespan.

Another challenge that may not be evident is that music is often used during this iterative production period as a quick fix to supply or imply emotion, or evoke a particular feeling of excitement within the game, as a shortcut, and more of a Band-Aid solution than a balanced approach to the project's soundtrack.

The mechanical influences of a game's design also have a significant impact upon music content. A rigid structure and cadence of playback for music cues in each map or level may have been created as a *recipe* or template into which music functionally needs to fit, meaning that strict patterns and formulae about some of the more mechanical 'in-game', non-story music content act, not as emotional signifiers, but as mechanical Pavlovian signifiers to the players.

Game Music 101: When Less Is *Much* More

When I am not working on games, and am instead playing, I often notice that music is almost continual (often described as 'wall-to-wall'), in many game experiences. In these games, where music is initially established to be always present, in any subsequent moment when music is *not* present, the game somehow feels like it is missing something, or feels flat. In production, this would get flagged as a 'bug' by the QA (quality assurance) department. So an aesthetic trap very often lies in establishing music as an ever-present continuum right at the beginning, as from then on the audio direction becomes a slave to that established recipe of internalized logic in the game. For me, the danger of having ever-present music is not simply that ubiquitous music incurs a greater monetary burden on the project, but that this approach dilutes the power, significance and emotional impact of music through its continual presence.

Overused and omnipresent scores are a huge missed opportunity for the creative and aesthetic advancement of video game sound, and risk diluting the emotional impact of a game experience on an audience. Video game sound has largely been defined and understood aesthetically in a wider cultural context, over the last four decades, through its unsubtle use of repetitive music, dialogue and SFX. Though I understand, more than most, the huge pressure on game audio developers to implement and pack in as much heightened emotion and exaggerated impact into games as possible (depending much, of course, on already-established niche conventions and expectations of genre), it gives me great optimism that a more tempered and considered approach to the emotional and evocative power of game music and its relation to the other food groups of sound is already starting to be taken.

Development studio Naughty Dog have a consistent, highly cinematic and narrative-driven approach to their games, and subsequently their soundtracks feel aesthetically, and refreshingly, more like very contemporary movie soundtracks than 'video game soundtracks'. *The Last of Us* (2013), and Uncharted (2007–2017) series all have what would generally be considered quite sparse musical treatments. Much of the soundtracks are focused on voice and character performances, and are also about dynamic sound moments. Only when you get to very emotional 'key' elements in the plot of a game do you hear music cues being used to drive home the emotional impact. This mature approach on the part of the game directors and the sound teams is certainly helped by the studio's laser focus on narrative and cinematic experiences, which enables them to plot out and know much of what the player will be doing, in what order and in what environment far ahead of time during development.

Another fine example of a more sparse approach to a score is the Battlefield franchise by the developer DICE in Sweden. The game, being a first-person competitive shooter, necessitates an approach to the soundtrack where the player needs to hear all the intel and positional information available to them at all times during the chaos of the combat, with the utmost clarity. In this sense, a musical score would clearly get in the way of those needs during gameplay. In *Battlefield 3* (2011), a non-diegetic musical score is used only to establish the emotional states of the pre- and post-battle phases, and of the campaign mission itself; otherwise, the musical score is absent, entirely by design, and beautifully fitting the needs of the players.

In many of my projects I have been asked by game directors to always support the mood and the storytelling with music, often on a moment-to-moment basis. This is a battle that I have often had to fight to be able to demonstrate that music, when overused like this, will have the opposite effect on the player, and rather than immersing them in the emotion of the game, will make them feel fatigued and irritated, as a result of continually being bombarded with the score and forced moods telling them how they should feel about what is on screen. It is the musical equivalent of closed captioning when you do not need closed captioning. Sometimes I have been successful and at other times unsuccessful in making these points, but this is a part of the everyday collaborative and political work that is necessary on a team. I strongly believe that new approaches to music, sound and voice will gradually propagate across the industry, the more we see, analyse and celebrate successful titles doing something different.

Certainly, after working under continual 'use music to tell 100 per cent of the story' pressure like this, I can safely say that in order to move forwards aesthetically and adopt an integrated approach to the soundtrack, in most cases, sound needs to carry more of the storytelling, voice needs to do less, and music most certainly needs to do *a lot* less.

As we build games, movies, experiences and emotions together in our teams, perhaps music should be the weapon we reach for last, instead of first. This way, as developers, we could at least have a more accurate picture of where music is really needed and understand more what the actual role of the musical score is in our work.

For me, there are two more pivotal examples of a more sparse and mature music aesthetic that need to be highlighted, and both of them also have approaches in which the music for the game could also easily be considered as ambiguous, and sound-effect-like. Those two games are *Limbo* (2010) and *Inside* (2016), both from the Danish studio Playdead, with sound and music by Martin Stig Andersen. The refreshing aesthetic in these games is evident from the opening moments, when the focus of the game is solely on a boy walking through the woods (in both games). Foley and footsteps are the only sounds that establish this soundtrack, and gradually as the gameplay experience unfolds, more environmental sound and storytelling through SFX and ambience begin to occur. It is only when we get fairly deep into the game that we hear our first music cue. In *Limbo*, the first 'cue' is particularly striking, as it is a deep, disturbing low note, or tone, which sounds when the player jumps their character onto a floating corpse in order to get to the other side of a river. This low tone has such a visceral impact when synchronized with this disturbing moment (in most games this would be a trivial mechanical moment of simple navigation), that it takes the game into a completely different direction. Rather than a 'score', the game's 'music' seems in fact to be sound emanating from inside the soul of the character, or the dark black-and-white visuals of the world. And because the use of music is so sparse and rare – or at least, it is rare that you can identify particular sounds as specifically 'musical' – the impact of those cues and sounds becomes extremely intense. At the same time, the line between conventional musical materials and sound effects becomes blurred, allowing the sounds to gain a 'musical' quality. Many moments also stand out like this in the spiritual sequel to *Limbo*, *Inside*, the most memorable of which, for me, was the moment when the rhythmic gameplay of avoiding a sonic shockwave, and hiding behind metal doors, transitioned from being a purely sound-based moment to a purely musical one, and then back again. The way the transition was carried out elevated the experience to an entirely spiritual level, outside of the reality of the physics of sound, and into the realm of the intangible and the sacred.

Conclusions: Enjoy the Silence

Recently, I was very fortunate to work on a fantastic indie game called *Loot Hound* (2015) with some friends, and the interesting thing about that game was that it had absolutely no musical score and no musical cues whatsoever in the game. Even the menu and loading screen were devoid of music cues. The strange thing is that this approach was never consciously discussed between those of us working on the game. I am pretty sure this was not the first game with no music of any kind, but it was a very positive and renewing experience for me as someone who had come from working on triple-A, music-heavy games to be able to take time and express the game-play and the aesthetics through just sound, mix and voice. In the end, I do not think any of us working on that title played it and felt that it was lacking anything, or even that music would have brought anything significant to the table in terms of the experience.

In the end, the encouraging thing was: I do not think anyone who played it even mentioned or noticed that there was no music in this game. The game was released through Steam, where one could easily keep a track on feedback and comments, and I do not recall seeing anything about the game's lack of music, but did see quite a bit of praise for the sound and for the overall game experience itself. The game and process of its creation was certainly different and refreshing, and maybe one of many potential futures for game sound aesthetics to be celebrated and explored further in larger-scale productions to come.

A more integrated approach for all elements of the soundtrack is necessary to push games, and game scores, into new artistic and technical territories. This requires a lot of political and collaborative work on the part of game developers together in their teams, and also a desire to make something that breaks the mould of generic wall-to-wall game music. A part of establishing this new direction requires identifying, celebrating and elevating titles in which the soundtrack is fully more integrated, and where sound, music and voice gracefully handover meaning to one another, in a well-executed mix. A more integrated approach for music is also probably only possible once the contexts into which the music will fit can be understood more fully during all phases of production. And in that sense, the challenges are quite considerable, though not insurmountable. I believe that once the production and planning of music is integrated into game development schedules and production phases more carefully, the more integrated and enjoyable the score will be on an emotional level as a part of the overall experience of playing video games.

8 | Composing for Independent Games: The Music of *Kentucky Route Zero*

BEN BABBITT

Composer Ben Babbitt is one third of the game development team Cardboard Computer, along with Jake Elliott and Tamas Kemenczy. Cardboard Computer is best known for the critically lauded adventure game Kentucky Route Zero, *which was released in five instalments between 2013 and 2020. Here, Babbitt describes his background, philosophy and experiences writing music as part of a small team of game creators.*

Background

I grew up around music – both of my parents are employed as musicians, playing in orchestras and teaching. My father plays violin and viola and my mother plays cello. I was surrounded by a lot of what was primarily classical music growing up and there was always somebody practising or teaching or listening to music. I know my mother was practising a lot of Bach cello music when she was pregnant with me, so I must've been right up against the body of the cello for part of my time in utero. I'm sure that had some kind of prenatal influence on my developing brain. As I understand it, I became fascinated with music and sound very early on and started playing violin and piano when I was four or five. That fascination really took hold, though, and manifested as a desire to write my own music when I was around twelve or thirteen.

When I was growing up, my parents didn't allow my brothers and I to play video games, so we didn't have any consoles. I played at friends' houses but that was the extent of my relationship to the history of games. I never had games in mind as a context for my composition work, and only got involved when I met Jake Elliott (co-creator of *Kentucky Route Zero*) when we were in university together at the School of the Art Institute of Chicago (SAIC). He and Tamas Kemenczy were just starting to work on *Kentucky Route Zero*, and Jake asked me to write some music for it. Seven years later, we managed to complete the project.

I'd been writing my own music and playing in bands actually since I was about eleven or twelve, but I didn't focus on composition or think of my music that way until I went to study music when I was nineteen. I focused on composition at a conservatory in Chicago before I left and finished my degree at SAIC where I met Jake and Tamas. I'd done a few collaborations with a choreographer I went to school with but *Kentucky Route Zero* was actually the first project I was hired to work on as a composer. It was very much a learning process for me as I got deeper into the work. Because I didn't have much context for music in games beyond the little I'd experienced as a kid, in retrospect I think I approached it kind of blindly and intuitively. Conversations with Jake and Tamas helped a lot with finding an aesthetic direction for the music, but I was not drawing from a deeper set of experiences with other game music.

Composing for Games

I'm still becoming familiar with the process of creating music for other media, as I've only scored a few film projects so far. One major difference that strikes me is that when I'm working on a film, I'm able to create musical/sonic moments that correlate directly and specifically with visual moments on screen down to the frame, and that relationship remains intact – assuming everybody involved approves. There's arguably a wider range of possibility in terms of how music can interact with the image in games. Of course it's still possible to create music that relates to specific moments in a game as well, but it's a different kind of material inherently because it's unfrozen – it's always moving even when the activity in a scene can be slowed or stopped. I don't yet feel like I've explored the more real-time fluid relationship between music and image that's possible in games, but it's interesting to me. In some ways, it relates to an earlier tradition in music history where composers like John Cage and Morton Feldman were really interrogating the notion of authorship and distancing themselves from it via modes of chance and aleatoric processes. Games make that very easy to explore in the work itself, not only in the process of creating the music. One of my favorite composers and thinkers and game makers, David Kanaga (composer for *Proteus*, 2013), has explored what he calls the 'affordances' of games in relation to music and sound much more than I have.[1]

---

[1] See, for example, David Kanaga, 'Ecooperatic Music Game Theory', in *The Oxford Handbook of Algorithmic Music*, ed. Roger T. Dean and Alex McLean (New York: Oxford University Press, 2018), 451–70.

Kanaga is one of the most interesting and inspiring composers and thinkers working primarily in games. Our work is very different aesthetically but I think we share a lot of musical and philosophical interests. Liz Ryerson (*dys4ia*) is another composer working both in and outside of games making great work.[2] I return time and again to the music of twentieth-century French composer Olivier Messiaen, and his work had a clear influence on my music in *Kentucky Route Zero*. My relationship with music by other composers and artists took on a kind of research-based orientation for each new musical modality incorporated into the game. In other words, my influences varied from one part of the project to another, especially over the course of so many years. I've always wanted to continue working on my own music projects and collaborate with people in a music context, but it's been challenging to balance those interests with the workload of such a sprawling game as *Kentucky Route Zero* and other commercial interests I have. That continues to be a challenge, and I think anybody who works in a creative field can relate to that tension between investing in their 'career' or paid work, and investing in their own creative pursuits.

Working on Games

I don't think it's necessary to study composition for games specifically in order to work in that context. That said, I'm sure there are many aspects of a curriculum focused on composition for games that are useful and could help to cut down on the time it can take to find one's footing in a field when taking the trial-by-fire approach in learning 'on the job'. I think loving music and having some sense of curiosity about it and hunger to continue exploring musical possibilities is more useful than any kind of specific technical knowledge or traditional skill or facility on an instrument. For me, any technical knowledge or instrumental facility I've developed over time has grown out of that initial impulse to explore musical possibilities coming initially from my love for music as a listener, I think.

I became involved with *Kentucky Route Zero* through knowing Jake Elliott a little bit from a class we were in together at school. So I'd say that's a great place to start, whether someone is in school or not, there might already be people in one's community interested in making games and working with a composer. It can be really generative to work with

[2] See Ryerson's website, http://ellaguro.blogspot.com/ (accessed 8 May 2020) for more on her work.

friends and grow together and flatten the hierarchy a bit between employer/employee. In terms of finding jobs beyond one's own community, I know there are some really great resources on the Gamasutra website that has a jobs section, and also Twitter and Discord seem to be really active spaces for making new connections. Having work examples, even if one has never been hired to score a project, is very helpful in the process, especially when looking to work with people or studios outside of one's community or social circle.

For me, the most important thing to think about before starting a new project is whether the work sparks any real creative direction for me and if that's something I'm drawn to and connect to; in other words, does it seem exciting or interesting to work on? Of course, we don't always have the luxury of working only on the projects that are exciting to us, but I try to at least think about that before signing on to do something. I think if any money will be exchanged, having even just a simple contract or agreement in place before starting to work with someone is important. Also communicating one's needs to collaborators from the outset can be very helpful in establishing a clearly defined relationship that helps minimize the back and forth that can become tiresome.

I would advise aspiring composers to make the best music that you can make and judge that by how much you enjoy it and love the result, and then find ways to get that music to potential collaborators by any means. Don't be too self-critical at first, it can be difficult work on all fronts.

Kentucky Route Zero

Kentucky Route Zero *is a point-and-click adventure, which follows world-weary antiques delivery-driver Conway on his mission to complete what is apparently his 'final delivery'. As Conway seeks to locate the destination, he finds himself entangled in a series of curious events and is variously caught up in the lives of other characters. Adding to the sense of mystery, this 'magical realist adventure' frequently adopts an experimental approach to chronology, cause-and-effect, perspective and space.* Kentucky Route Zero *comprises five parts, called 'acts', split into 'scenes', each announced with a title card. Besides the acts, there are additional interludes and other satellite texts which serve to enrich the story and world of the game. The game includes ambient electronic underscore and sequences when characters are seen performing – in particular, a country band (credited as the Bedquilt Ramblers) are shown in silhouette performing Appalachian music and in Act*

III, players are introduced to an electronic musical duo, Junebug and Johnny. When Junebug and Johnny later perform a song at a gig, the player is able to select the lyrics of the song as it is performed.

The Project and Development

Kentucky Route Zero was a project developed over quite a long period of time, about nine years. I wrote the first pieces of music for it in 2011 and we published the fifth and final episode in January of 2020. The process unfolded organically in the sense that we were not working under prescribed production or release schedules coming from an outside source, like a producer or publisher; for almost the entire duration of the development process, there were only three people involved in the project. We did partner with Annapurna Interactive in the last two years of development, but that was to port the game to consoles; they were not directly involved in the development process, although they were immensely helpful in many ways. They became invaluable cheerleaders and enablers in those final hours.

At the beginning of my time working on the game, Jake, Tamas and I had a few conversations about the direction of the music and at that time they had some fairly specific ideas of what they wanted to hear. They asked me to record a set of traditional folk songs that they had selected and planned to use in each episode or 'act' of the game to provide a kind of meta-commentary on the events of the story. Additionally, they wanted me to create instrumental electronic 'ambient' versions of each of those songs that could be blended seamlessly with the acoustic versions. They also gave me a collection of old recordings from the 1930s of the songs by the Kentucky musician Bill Monroe that I could use as the primary reference for my own versions for the game. So at that point, I was really following their prompts and in many ways executing their vision for the music. I think this is not uncommon as a process between a composer and a director or game developer.

So I did my best to complete their request and turned in that first batch of work. It was after that point that Jake and Tamas reconfigured the project and found its five-act structure, and so that first set of pieces I had composed were mostly used in the first act. Over time as I became more involved as a collaborator and co-creator in the project, that initial process changed quite a bit. Although we continued to have conversations about the direction of the music that still included feedback and creative prompts from Jake and Tamas, they graciously allowed me to develop my own voice as composer and to bring my own ideas to whatever we were working on at the time. Of course, a lot of the music in the game still came from narrative decisions already made that involved a character perform-ing in a particular scene, for example, which were moments that had already been envisioned by the time I started working on them. But there was a balance between predetermined musical needs for any given scene and space for me to suggest new musical possibilities, in addition to having the creative freedom to inflect those predetermined musical moments with my own sensibilities.

Often before beginning to compose for any given scene or new section of the game, I would be able to read through Jake's script or play through works in progress delivered by Tamas that would be very helpful in my process of making music, hopefully feeling right at home in those scenes and moments when finally implemented. Although there were phases of the project where my work would come later in the process compared to where Jake and Tamas were, which would allow me to react to what they'd done, there were other portions of the development when we would all be working in tandem on the same thing. Especially towards the end of the project, the process became less linear and more simultaneous. We each had our siloed roles but were very often in dialogue with each other about what still needed to be done and the progress of our individual processes.

Early on in the development process of *Kentucky Route Zero*, it was decided that we would stop announcing release dates ahead of time because I think we'd given a release date for the second act and missed that dead-line, to vocal dismay from some of the players. As a result, we would work on a new act or interlude for however long it took to complete it, and almost always publish it without fanfare or warning as soon as it was finished. This was possible because we were self-publishing the work and were fortunate not to have to rely on traditional means of presenting new work with PR announcements and necessary lead times to secure coverage. It was never a priority, I don't think, to maximize the attention we might be able to garner for the project. It was more interesting to us – if I may speak on the others' behalf – to focus on the work itself and making it everything it could be. This certainly ended up shaping the timeline of development greatly, and as such it was a learning process with regard to pacing and planning our work in order for the project to remain feasible to complete.

Some time between publishing the fourth act and working on the interlude *Un Puebla De Nada*, we started working with Annapurna Interactive on the process of porting the game to PS4, Xbox One and Nintendo Switch, as well as localizing or translating all of the text in the game. This proved to be quite an intensive and time-consuming process, and also had an effect on the development of the game itself, despite our relationship with Annapurna being focused on the console port. This all relates back to the question of the scope of a project, and how that can impact the time it takes to complete it. I think, from my experience working on *Kentucky Route Zero*, it can be quite difficult to understand the scope of a project before diving into the development process and spending some time with it. That may have been more true for all of us who worked on *KRZ* because it was our first major project like this, but I think games are just inherently difficult to plan out accurately with regard to something like duration, for example, as opposed to knowing one is aiming to make a 90–120 minute feature film. I'm sure more experienced developers have a better sense of that relationship between scope and the timeline, but it's something I'm still striving to get a better grasp of.

It's interesting to have had both the experience of self-publishing and working with an outside publisher like Annapurna Interactive during the development process of *Kentucky Route Zero*. I think there are many benefits to both approaches, and both certainly come with their challenges. It does seem that in the time since we began developing *Kentucky Route Zero* in 2011, a number of interesting self-publishing open platforms have cropped up, like itch.io and Twine, and I'm sure there are others I don't know about. It is absolutely a privilege to work with a publisher like Annapurna to bring a project to a wider audience and make it available on more platforms than would be possible alone, but I think Jake, Tamas and I will always feel a kinship with the self-directed autodidactic relationship with our work that we cultivated over the years when we were making and publishing our work independently. It was very interesting to see everything that goes into planning a wider release, and actually participating more directly in the 'marketplace' and making an effort to engage an audience during the phase of wrapping up content on *Kentucky Route Zero*, and preparing to release the project on consoles simultaneous with the publication of the final act on PC.

The Music of Kentucky Route Zero

The music in *Kentucky Route Zero* grew directly out of those early conversations I had with Jake and Tamas back in 2011. At that time, they came to me with very specific musical needs for what the project was then and

I did my best to fulfil them. As I mentioned earlier, the traditional folk songs in each act and the ambient electronic score as foundational elements of the music in the game had been conceptualized by the time I was brought on to the project. They did, however, give me a lot of creative freedom when it came to my interpretation and execution of their prompts. Initially, I was not involved in selecting and placing the compositions that I made into the game itself. By the time I was more involved in a collaborative sense, working more closely with Jake and Tamas beginning with Act II, the sound world and the musical palette and their function within the story had already been established. As the project continued to develop and we encountered further beats of the story, and new characters and locations, there were more opportunities to introduce new types of music to the game.

In some ways, music in *Kentucky Route Zero* is used quite narratively in the sense that it's directly tied to and part of the storytelling; characters are often playing the music heard in the game. The traditional regional folk music performed by the Bedquilt Ramblers helps to anchor the story in a real location and hopefully transmits some sense of its cultural history. *KRZ* is a story about America, and as such it seemed necessary to draw on regional American vernacular music in some form given that it's such a part of the fabric of that culture.

To that end, I think that the music in the game might help to create a sense of occupying a specific 'world' or place, something that the text and imagery very much do as well. The music also helps to inflect different characters with qualities that might not come through in the same way otherwise. Junebug and Johnny display something about themselves when they are performing their music that is arguably ineffable and too subjective to concretize in any other way.

Another aspect of the role I think music serves in *KRZ* is related to the pace of the game itself. *KRZ* takes place almost entirely at night, and almost all of the story is delivered through a text window that appears on screen without voice actors reciting the lines. This nocturnal quality, in combination with the fact that the game involves a lot of reading, sort of dictates a certain slowness; tight and fast-paced action would not be compatible with these formal aspects of the project. The use of minimalist ambient electronic music, for example, might also help the player to slow down in a meditative sense, and become immersed in the pace of the story and encourage a certain kind of engagement with the story, to kind of drift into it, as it were. I hope that my music in *KRZ* helps to create the emotional textures specific to this story and its characters.

The performances by the Bedquilt Ramblers were already built into the role music would play throughout the project by the time I became involved. However, those were not necessarily intended to be central or even overtly performative events in the story. The role of the folk band calls back to that of the chorus in a Greek tragedy, which provided commentary about the events of the story from the sidelines. More central musical performances started to creep up in Act II, with a somewhat hidden performance of a piece of organ music in the Bureau of Reclaimed Spaces, but didn't really coalesce into being the focus of a scene until Junebug's performance in Act III. I think that sequence in particular might've been compelling to people because it was the first time in the course of the game where all of the different storytelling modalities were employed simultaneously; the text and the imagery and the music all became fused together, with the lyrics becoming dialogue choices and the visual focus of the scene also being the performance of the music.

Junebug and Johnny's performance in the third act was something that had been decided, I think, a long time before we actually got to that scene in the development process. Jake and Tamas had a number of references in mind for that character and the kind of music they might perform, the starting touchstone being '60s and '70s country singers like Loretta Lynn and Dolly Parton, both in terms of their musical and lyrical tropes and of their performance styles and stage personas. After some initial conversations about the direction for the music that also touched on presenting the song as an 'interactive' moment with selectable verses presented as karaoke-like text, I started working on it. It took a number of iterations before I arrived at a musical result I was happy with. Jake had written the lyrics so it was very much a collaborative effort. Given the fact that Junebug and Johnny were androids and not humans, Junebug's singing voice was a less straightforward albeit important component of the performance that needed to be figured out. After ruling out the option of using a vocoder,[3] or another overtly synthetic process for this, I experimented with treating my own voice through pitch and formant shifting and discovered a sort of uncanny instrument that fell somewhere between something palpably

---

[3] A vocoder is an electronic device or effect which allows the 'timbre and articulation of one sound source (usually a voice) to control another', often resulting in a 'talking' or 'singing' instruments effects. Hugh Davies, 'Vocoder', *Grove Music Online* (2001), www.oxfordmusiconline.com /grovemusic/view/10.1093/gmo/9781561592630.001.0001/omo-9781561592630-e-0000047646. Accessed 8 May 2020.

organic and human and something more heavily manipulated and artificial.

Reflecting on the Project

I have been continually surprised by the longevity of interest in this project, and the fact that it's found such a supportive audience. I don't think any of us could have foreseen most of the things that have happened with this project, least of all the kind of reception it's received. When Jake first asked me if I was interested in writing some music for it, I was very young and had never worked on anything like it. I had no context for what went into developing a game and how much time that could take. I'm not sure that Jake and Tamas did either. The risks in accepting the invitation did not occur to me at the time. I think if any of us had known that it would take so many years to complete, and come with some very challenging periods of work, we might've felt differently about taking something so ambitious in scope in the first place. I think the extent of its risks became more evident as we all got deeper into the process. That's certainly true for me. It proved at times to be very difficult to sustain the development and keep it viable for all of us to continue devoting the bulk of our time to it over the course of the project because of the unpredictable nature of its income. Because the development was funded through sales of the game, naturally that could be quite volatile and inconsistent and with it came stretches when very little money was coming in.

The process of making the work a viable means of earning a living continues to be a challenge, even if it is temporarily deferred from time to time. And aside from the practical challenges, working with and communicating with my collaborators will probably always come with its challenges as well as its evident benefits. Also, as I mentioned earlier, balancing my own creative interests with my obligations in the projects I take on is something that seems to only become more challenging, despite that tension existing to some degree the entire time I've been working as a composer.

The Broader Contexts and Meanings of Game Music

I think it's very important to consider the politics and ethics of representation when conceptualizing and choosing the music in a video game. All art is political, right? And as such all video games are political in terms of relating to or even reflecting a set of cultural values and interests through choices of representation, depiction and engagement with the conventions of the medium and its history. Although the decision to use traditional folk music from the region where *KRZ* is set was not mine initially, I think Jake and Tamas were conscious of the importance of respectful representation when they envisioned its place in the game. I recorded most of those songs in 2011 so I was much younger then and I think, generally less aware of some of these issues than I could've been. I actually took their initial prompts to record that set of songs based on the Bill Monroe records at face value; I did my best to recreate those historical recordings accurately, even mimicking recording techniques used at the time. Over the course of the project, I was compelled to move away from a kind of historical re-enactment approach to representing that music, and so the songs mutated into less straightforwardly traditional versions. That said, there are likely examples to be found of earlier interpretations of these songs that were just as unusual or divergent from the Bill Monroe interpretations.

With regard to the ways in which the music in *KRZ* engages with identity, the most overt example of that is the Junebug performance in Act III. Junebug and Johnny transform in an instant from rugged itinerant musicians into glossed up otherworldly performers, and despite having expressed their views with a dry and sarcastic sense of humour with no trace of sentimentality prior to the performance, Junebug becomes the vehicle for a heartfelt and heartbroken transmission of feeling and sentiment presented in the form of pop and country lyrical and musical tropes. The tension between the persona of the artist and the content of their work is made manifest. Junebug and Johnny relay parts of their origin story as involving having to remake themselves as they see fit, showing that their identities are an ever-shifting and alterable material. Their relationship with music is very much centred in their conscious embrace of the notion that identity itself is mutable, fluid and dynamic. Although I didn't make the conscious connection at the time, that ethos described by those characters informed my process in making that music, most specifically in the choice to use my own voice and transform it into something unrecognizable for Junebug's vocal performance.

PART III

Analytical Approaches to Video Game Music

Introduction

MELANIE FRITSCH AND TIM SUMMERS

One aspect of video game music that is both compelling and challenging is the question of *how* video game music should be studied. Game music is often sonically similar to classical music, popular musical styles and music in other media like film. Techniques from these other established fields of study can be applied to game music. Yet at the same time, game music exists as part of a medium with its own particular qualities. Indeed, many such aspects of games, including their interactivity, complicate assumptions that are normally made about how we study and analyse music.

Relationship with Film Music

Some scholars have examined game music by making fruitful comparisons with film music, noting the similarities and differences.[1] Neil Lerner has shown the similarities between musical techniques and materials of early cinema and those of early video game music like *Donkey Kong* (1981) and

---

[1] K. J. Donnelly, 'Emotional Sound Effects and Metal Machine Music: Soundworlds in Silent Hill Games and Films', in *The Palgrave Handbook of Sound Design and Music in Screen Media*, ed. Liz Greene and Danijela Kulezic-Wilson (London: Palgrave, 2016), 73–88; Miguel Mera, 'Invention/Re-invention', *Music, Sound and the Moving Image* 3, no. 1 (2009): 1–20; Florian Mundhenke, 'Resourceful Frames and Sensory Functions – Musical Transformations from Game to Film in *Silent Hill*', in *Music and Game: Perspectives on a Popular Alliance*, ed. Peter Moormann (Wiesbaden: Springer, 2013), 107–24; Zach Whalen, 'Case Study: Film Music vs. Video-Game Music: The Case of *Silent Hill*', in *Music, Sound and Multimedia: From the Live to the Virtual*, ed. Jamie Sexton (Edinburgh: Edinburgh University Press, 2007), 68–81.

Super Mario Bros. (1985).[2] William Gibbons has further suggested that the transition of silent film to 'talkies' provides a useful lens for understanding how some video games like *Grandia II* (2000) and the *Lunar* (1992, 1996) games dealt with integrating voice into their soundtracks.[3] Such parallels recognized, we must be wary of suggesting that films and games can be treated identically, even when they seem most similar: Giles Hooper has considered the varieties of different kinds of cutscenes in games, and the complex role(s) that music plays in such sequences.[4]

Film music scholars routinely differentiate between music that is part of the world of the characters (diegetic) and music that the characters cannot hear, like typically Hollywood orchestral underscore (non-diegetic). While discussing *Resident Evil 4* (2005) and *Guitar Hero* (2005), Isabella van Elferen has described how games complicate film models of music and diegesis. Van Elferen notes that, even if we assume an avatar-character cannot hear non-diegetic music, the player can hear that music, which influences how their avatar-character acts.[5] These kinds of observations reveal how powerful and influential music is in the video game medium, perhaps even more so than in film. Further, the distinct genre of music games poses a particular challenge to approaches from other fields, and reveals the necessity of a more tailored approach.

Borrowing Art Music Techniques

Just as thematic/motivic analysis has been useful in art music and film music studies, so it can reveal important insights in game music. Jason Brame analysed the recurrence of themes across *Legend of Zelda* games to show how the series creates connections and sense of familiarity in the various instalments,[6] while Guillaume Laroche and Andrew Schartmann have conducted extensive

---

[2] Neil Lerner, 'Mario's Dynamic Leaps: Musical Innovations (and the Specter of Early Cinema) in Donkey Kong and *Super Mario Bros.*', in *Music in Video Games: Studying Play*, ed. K. J. Donnelly, William Gibbons and Neil Lerner (New York: Routledge, 2014), 1–29.

[3] William Gibbons, 'Song and the Transition to "Part-Talkie" Japanese Role-Playing Games', in *Music in the Role-Playing Game: Heroes and Harmonies*, ed. William Gibbons and Steven Reale (New York: Routledge, 2019), 9–20.

[4] Giles Hooper, 'Sounding the Story: Videogame Cutscenes', in *Emotion in Video Game Soundtracking*, ed. Duncan Williams and Newton Lee (Cham: Springer, 2018), 115–42.

[5] Isabella van Elferen, 'Un Forastero! Issues of Virtuality and Diegesis in Videogame Music', *Music and the Moving Image* 4, no. 2 (2011): 30–9.

[6] Jason Brame, 'Thematic Unity Across a Video Game Series', *ACT. Zeitschrift für Musik & Performance*. 2 (2011), accessed 29 October 2020, www.act.uni-bayreuth.de/de/archiv/2011-02/ 03_Brame_Thematic_Unity/index.html.

motivic and melodic analyses of the music of the *Super Mario* games.[7] Frank Lehman has applied Neo-Riemannian theory, a method of analysing harmonic movement, to the example of *Portal 2* (2011).[8] Recently, topic theory – a way of considering the role of styles and types of musical materials – has been applied to games. Thomas Yee has used topic theory to investigate how games like *Xenoblade Chronicles* (2010) (amongst others) use religious and rock music for certain types of boss themes,[9] while Sean Atkinson has used a similar approach to reveal the musical approaches to flying sequences in *Final Fantasy IV* (1991) and *The Legend of Zelda: Skyward Sword* (2011).[10]

Peter Shultz has inverted such studies, and instead suggests that some video games themselves are a form of musical analysis.[11] He illustrates how *Guitar Hero* represents songs in gameplay, with varying degrees of simplification as the difficulty changes.

The Experience of Interactivity

Musical analysis has traditionally been able to rely on the assumption that each time a particular piece of music is played, the musical events will occur in the same order and last for approximately the same duration. Though analysts have always been aware of issues such as optional repeats, different editions, substituted parts and varying performance practices, art music analysis has often tended to treat a piece of music as highly consistent between performances. The interactive nature of games, however, means that the music accompanying a particular section of a game can sound radically different from one play session to the next. The degree of variation depends on the music programming of the game, but the way that game music is prompted by, and responds to, player action asks us to reconsider how we understand our relationships with the music in an interactive setting.

---

[7] Guillaume Laroche, 'Analyzing Musical Mario-Media: Variations in the Music of Super Mario Video Games' (MA thesis, McGill University 2012); Andrew Schartmann, *Koji Kondo's Super Mario Bros. Soundtrack* (New York: Bloomsbury, 2015).

[8] Frank Lehman, 'Methods and Challenges of Analyzing Screen Media', in *The Routledge Companion to Screen Music and Sound*, ed. Miguel Mera, Ronald Sadoff and Ben Winters (New York: Routledge, 2017), 497–516.

[9] Thomas B. Yee, 'Battle Hymn of the God-Slayers: Troping Rock and Sacred Music Topics in Xenoblade Chronicles', *Journal of Sound and Music in Games* 1, no. 1 (2020): 2–19.

[10] Sean E. Atkinson, 'Soaring Through the Sky: Topics and Tropes in Video Game Music', *Music Theory Online* 25, no. 2 (2019), accessed 29 October 2020, https://mtosmt.org/issues/mto.19.25.2/mto.19.25.2.atkinson.html.

[11] Peter Shultz, 'Music Theory in Video Games', in *From Pac-Man to Pop Music: Interactive Audio in Games and New Media*, ed. Karen Collins (Aldershot: Ashgate, 2008), 177–88.

Elizabeth Medina-Gray has advocated for a modular understanding of video game music. She writes,

modularity provides a fundamental basis for the dynamic music in video games. Real-time soundtracks usually arise from a collection of distinct musical modules stored in a game's code – each module being anywhere from a fraction of a second to several minutes in length – that become triggered and modified during gameplay. . . . [M]usical modularity requires, first of all, a collection of modules and a set of rules that dictate how the modules may combine.[12]

Medina-Gray's approach allows us to examine how these musical modules interact with each other. This includes how simultaneously sounding materials fit together, like the background cues and performed music in *The Legend of Zelda* games.[13] Medina-Gray analyses the musical 'seams' between one module of music and another. By comparing the metre, timbre, pitch and volume of one cue and another, as well as the abruptness of the transition between the two, we can assess the 'smoothness' of the seams.[14] Games deploy smooth and disjunct musical seams to achieve a variety of different effects, just like musical presence and musical silence are meaningful to players (see, for example, William Gibbons' exploration of the careful use of silence in *Shadow of the Colossus* (2005)).[15]

Another approach to dealing with the indeterminacy of games has come from scholars who adapt techniques originally used to discuss real-world sonic environments. Just like we might analyse the sound world of a village, countryside or city, we can discuss the virtual sonic worlds of games.[16]

---

[12] Elizabeth Medina-Gray, 'Modularity in Video Game Music', in *Ludomusicology: Approaches to Video Game Music*, ed. Michiel Kamp, Tim Summers and Mark Sweeney (Sheffield: Equinox, 2016), 53–72 at 53, 55.

[13] Elizabeth Medina-Gray, 'Meaningful Modular Combinations: Simultaneous Harp and Environmental Music in Two *Legend of Zelda* Games', in *Music in Video Games*, ed. K. J. Donnelly, William Gibbons and Neil Lerner (New York: Routledge, 2014), 104–21 and Elizabeth Medina-Gray, 'Musical Dreams and Nightmares: An Analysis of *Flower*', in *The Routledge Companion to Screen Music and Sounded*, ed. Miguel Mera, Ronald Sadoff and Ben Winters. (New York: Routledge, 2017), 562–76.

[14] Elizabeth Medina-Gray, 'Analyzing Modular Smoothness in Video Game Music', *Music Theory Online* 25, no. 3 (2019).

[15] William Gibbons, 'Wandering Tonalities: Silence, Sound, and Morality in *Shadow of the Colossus*', in *Music in Video Games*, ed. K. J. Donnelly, William Gibbons and Neil Lerner (New York: Routledge, 2014), 122–37.

[16] Kate Galloway, 'Soundwalking and the Aurality of Stardew Valley: An Ethnography of Listening to and Interacting with Environmental Game Audio', in *Music in the Role-Playing Game*, ed. William Gibbons and Steven Reale (New York: Routledge, 2019), 159–78; Elizabeth Hambleton, 'Gray Areas: Analyzing Navigable Narratives in the Not-So-Uncanny Valley Between Soundwalks, Video Games, and Literary Computer Games', *Journal of Sound and Music in Games* 1, no. 1 (2020): 20–43.

These approaches have two distinct advantages: they account for player agency to move around the world, and they contextualize music within the other non-musical elements of the soundtrack.

The interactive nature of games has made scholars fascinated by the experiences of engaging with music in the context of the video game. William Cheng's influential volume *Sound Play* draws on detailed inter-rogation of the author's personal experience to illuminate modes of inter-acting with music in games.[17] The book deals with player agency and ethical and aesthetic engagement with music in games. His case studies include morality and music in *Fallout 3* (2008), as well as how players exert a huge amount of interpretive effort when they engage with game music, such as in the case of the opera scene in *Final Fantasy VI* (1994). Small wonder that gamers should so frequently feel passionate about the music of games.

Michiel Kamp has described the experience of listening to video game music in a different way, by outlining what he calls 'four ways of hearing video game music'. They are:

1. Semiotic, when music is heard as providing the player 'with information about gameplay states or events';
2. Ludic, when we pay attention to the music and play '*to* the music or *along with* the music, such as running to the beat, or following a crescendo up a mountain';
3. Aesthetic, when 'we stop whatever we are doing to attend to and reflect on the music, or on a situation accompanied by music';
4. Background, which refers to when music 'does not attract our attention, but still affects us somehow'.[18]

Kamp emphasizes the multidimensional qualities of listening to music in games, and, by implication, the variety of ways of analysing it.

'Music Games'

In games, we become listeners, creators and performers all at once, so we might ask, what kind of musical experiences do games afford? One of the most useful

---

[17] William Cheng, *Sound Play: Video Games and the Musical Imagination* (New York: Oxford University Press, 2014).

[18] Michiel Kamp, 'Four Ways of Hearing Video Game Music' (PhD thesis, Cambridge University, 2014), 15, 89, 131.

places to start answering this question is in the context of so-called 'music games' that foreground players' interaction with music in one way or another.

Unsurprisingly, *Guitar Hero* and other music games have attracted much attention from musicians. It is obvious that playing instrument-performance games like *Guitar Hero* is not the same as playing the instrument in the traditional way, yet these games still represent important musical experiences. Kiri Miller has conducted extensive ethnographic research into *Guitar Hero* and *Rock Band* (2007). As well as revealing that these games appealed to gamers who also played a musical instrument, she reported that players 'emphasized that their musical experiences with Guitar Hero and Rock Band feel as "real" as the other musical experiences in their lives'.[19] With work by Henry Svec, Dominic Arsenault and David Roesner,[20] the scholarly consensus is that, within the musical constraints and possibilities represented by the games, *Guitar Hero* and *Rock Band* emphasize the performative aspects of playing music, especially in rock culture, and opening up questions of music making as well as of the liveness of music.[21] As Miller puts it, the games 'let players put the performance back into recorded music, reanimating it with their physical engagement and adrenaline'.[22] Most importantly, then, the games provide a new way to listen to, perform and engage with the music through the architecture of the games (not to mention the fan communities that surround them).

Beyond instrument-based games, a number of scholars have devised different methods of categorizing the kinds of musical interactivity afforded players. Martin Pichlmair and Fares Kayali outline common qualities of music games, including the simulation of synaesthesia and interaction with other elements in the game which affect the musical output.[23] Anahid

[19] Kiri Miller, 'Schizophonic Performance: Guitar Hero, Rock Band, and Virtual Virtuosity', *Journal of the Society for American Music* 3, no. 4 (2009): 395–429 at 408.

[20] Henry Adam Svec, 'Becoming Machinic Virtuosos: Guitar Hero, Rez, and Multitudinous Aesthetics', *Loading . . .* 2, no. 2 (2008), accessed 29 October 2020, https://journals.sfu.ca /loading/index.php/loading/article/view/30/28; Dominic Arsenault, 'Guitar Hero: 'Not Like Playing Guitar at All'?', *Loading . . .* 2, no. 2 (2008), accessed 29 October 2020, https://journals .sfu.ca/loading/index.php/loading/article/view/32/29; and David Roesner, 'The Guitar Hero's Performance', *Contemporary Theatre Review* 21, no. 3 (2011): 276–85.

[21] Melanie Fritsch and Stefan Strötgen, 'Relatively Live: How to Identify Live Music Performances', *Music and the Moving Image* 5, no. 1 (2012): 47–66.

[22] Kiri Miller, *Playing Along: Digital Games, YouTube, and Virtual Performance* (New York: Oxford University Press, 2011), 15.

[23] Martin Pichlmair and Fares Kayali, 'Levels of Sound: On the Principles of Interactivity in Music Video Games', *DiGRA '07 – Proceedings of the 2007 DiGRA International Conference: Situated Play*, University of Tokyo, September 2007, 424–30.

Kassabian and Freya Jarman emphasize musical choices and the different kinds of play in music games (from goal-based structures to creative free play).[24] Melanie Fritsch has discussed different approaches to world-building through the active engagement of players with music in several ways,[25] as well as the adoption of a musician's 'musical persona'[26] for game design by analysing games, turning on Michael Jackson as a case study.[27]

Opportunities to perform music in games are not limited to those specifically dedicated to music; see, for example, Stephanie Lind's discussion of *The Legend of Zelda: Ocarina of Time* (1998).[28] William Cheng and Mark Sweeney have described how musical communities have formed in multiplayer online games like *Lord of the Rings Online* (2007) and *Star Wars: Galaxies* (2003).[29] In the case of *Lord of the Rings Online*, players have the opportunity to perform on a musical instrument, which has given rise to bands and even in-game virtual musical festivals like Weatherstock, where players from across the world gather together to perform and listen to each other. These festivals are social and aesthetic experiences. These communities also exist in tandem with online fan culture beyond the boundary of the game (of which more elsewhere in the book; see Chapter 23 by Ryan Thompson).

Play Beyond Music Games

Music is important to many games that are not explicitly 'music games'. It is indicative of the significance of music in the medium of the video game that the boundaries of the 'music game' genre are ambiguous. For instance, Steven Reale provocatively asks whether the crime thriller game *L.A. Noire* (2011) is a music game. He writes,

---

[24] Anahid Kassabian and Freya Jarman, 'Game and Play in Music Video Games', in *Ludomusicology: Approaches to Video Game Music*, ed. Michiel Kamp, Tim Summers and Mark Sweeney (Sheffield: Equinox, 2016), 116–32.

[25] Melanie Fritsch, 'Worlds of Music: Strategies for Creating Music-Based Experiences in Video Games', in *The Oxford Handbook of Interactive Audio*, ed. Karen Collins, Holly Tessler and Bill Kapralos (New York: Oxford University Press, 2014), 167–177.

[26] Philip Auslander, 'Musical Personae', *TDR: The Drama Review* 50, no. 1 (2006): 100–19.

[27] Melanie Fritsch, 'Beat It! Playing the "King of Pop" in Video Games', in *Music Video Games: Performance, Politics, and Play*, ed. Michael Austin (New York: Bloomsbury, 2016), 153–76.

[28] Stephanie Lind, 'Active Interfaces and Thematic Events in *The Legend of Zelda: Ocarina of Time*', *Music Video Games: Performance, Politics, and Play*, ed. Michael Austin (New York: Bloomsbury, 2016), 83–106.

[29] Cheng, *Sound Play*; and Mark Sweeney, 'Aesthetics and Social Interactions in MMOs: The Gamification of Music in Lord of the Rings Online and Star Wars: Galaxies', *The Soundtrack* 8, no. 1–2 (2015): 25–40.

Guitar-shaped peripherals are not required for a game's music to be intractable from its gameplay ... the interaction of the game world with its audio invites the possibility that playing the game is playing its music.[30]

If games respond to action with musical material, the levels of games can become like musical scores which are performed by the gamer when they play. We may even begin to hear the game in terms of its music.

Reale's comments echo a broader theme in game music studies: the role of play and playfulness as an important connection between playing games and playing music. Perhaps the most famous advocate for this perspective is Roger Moseley, who writes that

Like a Mario game, the playing of a Mozart concerto primarily involves interactive digital input: in prompting both linear and looping motions through time and space, it responds to imaginative engagement ... [It makes] stringent yet negotiable demands of performers while affording them ample opportunity to display their virtuosity and ingenuity.[31]

Moseley argues that 'Music and the techniques that shape it simultaneously trace and are traced by the materials, technologies and metaphors of play.'[32] In games, musical play and game play are fused, through the player's interaction with both. In doing so, game music emphasizes the fun, playful aspects of music in human activity more generally. That, then, is part of the significance of video game music – not only is it important for gaming and its associated contexts, but video games reveal the all-too-often-ignored playful qualities of music.

Of course, there is no single way that video game music should be analysed. Rather, a huge variety of approaches are open to anyone seeking to investigate game music in depth. This section of the Companion presents several different methods and perspectives on understanding game music.

Further Reading

Cheng, William. *Sound Play: Video Games and the Musical Imagination.* New York: Oxford University Press, 2014.

Kamp, Michiel. 'Four Ways of Hearing Video Game Music.' PhD thesis, Cambridge University, 2014.

---

[30] Steven B. Reale, 'Transcribing Musical Worlds; or, Is *L.A. Noire* a Music Game?', in *Music in Video Games*, ed. K. J. Donnelly, William Gibbons and Neil Lerner (New York: Routledge, 2014), 77–103 at 100.

[31] Roger Moseley, *Keys to Play: Music as a Ludic Medium from Apollo to Nintendo* (Berkeley: University of California Press, 2016), 216–17.

[32] Moseley, *Keys to Play*, 22.

Kassabian, Anahid and Jarman, Freya. 'Game and Play in Music Video Games', in *Ludomusicology: Approaches to Video Game Music*, ed. Michiel Kamp, Tim Summers and Mark Sweeney. Sheffield: Equinox, 2016, 116–32.

Medina-Gray, Elizabeth. 'Analyzing Modular Smoothness in Video Game Music.' *Music Theory Online* 25, no. 3 (2019).

Miller, Kiri. *Playing Along: Digital Games, YouTube, and Virtual Performance.* New York: Oxford University Press, 2012.

Moseley, Roger. *Keys to Play: Music as a Ludic Medium from Apollo to Nintendo.* Berkeley: University of California Press, 2016.

9 | Music Games

MICHAEL L. AUSTIN

Within the field of game studies, much ink has been spilt in the quest to define and classify games based on their genre, that is, to determine in which category they belong based on the type of interaction each game affords. Some games lie clearly within an established genre; for example, it is rather difficult to mistake a racing game for a first-person shooter. Other games, however, can fall outside the boundaries of any particular genre, or lie within the perimeters of several genres at once. Such is the case with music games. While some may argue that a game can be considered to be a music game only if its formal elements, such as theme, mechanics or objectives, *centre* on music, musicians, music making or another music-related activity, in practice the defining characteristics of a music game are much less clear – or rather, are much broader – than with other genres. Many game publishers, players, scholars and critics classify a game as musical simply because it features a particular genre of music in its soundtrack or musicians make appearances as playable characters, despite the fact that little-to-no musical activity is taking place within the game.

In this chapter, I outline a number of types of music games. I also discuss the various physical interfaces and controllers that facilitate musical interaction within games, and briefly highlight a number of cultural issues related to music video games. As a conclusion, I will suggest a model for categorizing music games based on the kind of musical engagement they provide.

Music Game (Sub)Genres

Rhythm Games

Rhythm games, or rhythm action games, are titles in which the core game mechanics require players to match their actions to a given rhythm or musical beat. The ways in which players interact with the game can vary widely, ranging from manually 'playing' the rhythm with an instrument-shaped controller, to dancing, to moving an in-game character to the beat of a game's overworld music. Although proto-rhythm games have existed in some form since the 1970s, such as the handheld game *Simon* (1978), the genre became very successful in Japan during the late 1990s and early 2000s with titles such as *Beatmania* (1997), *Dance Dance Revolution* (1998) and *Taiko no Tatsujin* (2001). With *Guitar Hero* (2005), the genre came to the West and had its first worldwide smash hit. *Guitar Hero* achieved enormous commercial success in the mid-2000s before waning in popularity in the 2010s.[1]

Peripheral-based Rhythm Games

Perhaps the most well-known of all types of rhythm games, peripheral-based rhythm games, are those in which the primary interactive mechanics rely on a physical controller (called peripheral because it is usually an extra, external component used to control the game console). While peripheral controllers can take any number of shapes, those that control rhythm games are often shaped like guitars, drums, microphones, turntables or other musical instruments or equipment.

Quest for Fame (1995) was one of the first music games to utilize a strum-able peripheral controller – a plastic wedge called a 'VPick'. After connecting its cord into the second PlayStation controller port, players held the VPick like a guitar pick, strumming anything they had available – a tennis racket, their own thigh, and so on – like they would a guitar. The actions would be registered as electrical impulses that registered as soundwaves within the game. Players would progress through the game's various levels depending on their success in matching their soundwaves with the soundwaves of the in-game band.

Games in the Guitar Hero and Rock Band series are almost certainly the most well-known peripheral-based rhythm games (and arguably the most well-known music video games). *Guitar Hero* features a guitar-shaped peripheral controller with coloured buttons along its fretboard. As coloured gems that correspond to the buttons on the controller (and ostensibly to notes in the song being performed) scroll down the screen, players must press the matching coloured buttons in time to the music. The original *Rock Band* (2007) combined a number of various plastic instrument controllers, such as a guitar, drum kit and microphone, to form a complete virtual band. Titles in the Guitar Hero and Rock Band series

---

[1] Mario Dozal, 'Consumerism Hero: The "Selling Out" of Guitar Hero and Rock Band', in *Music Video Games: Performance, Politics and Play*, ed. Michael Austin (New York: Bloomsbury, 2016), 127–52.

also allow players to play a wide variety of songs and genres of music through a large number of available expansion packs.

Non-Peripheral Rhythm Games

PaRappa the Rapper (1996), considered by many to be one of the first popular music games, was a rhythm game that used the PlayStation controller to accomplish the rhythm-matching tasks set forth in the game, rather than a specialized peripheral controller.[2] In-game characters would teach PaRappa, a rapping dog, how to rap, providing him with lyrics and corresponding PlayStation controller buttons. Players were judged on their ability to press the correct controller button in rhythm to the rap. Similar non-peripheral rhythm games include *Vib-Ribbon* (1999).

Other rhythm games aim for a middle ground between peripheral and non-peripheral rhythm games. These rely on players using physical gestures to respond to the musical rhythm. Games in this category include *Wii Music* (2008), which uses the Wii's motion controls so that players' movements are synchronized with the musical materials. *Rhythm Heaven/ Rhythm Paradise* (2008) was released for the Nintendo DS, and to play the game's fifty rhythm mini-games, players held the DS like a book, tapping the touch screen with their thumbs or using the stylus to tap, flick or drag objects on the screen to the game's music.

Dance-based Rhythm Games

Dance-based rhythm games can also be subdivided into two categories. Corporeal dance-based rhythm games require players to use their bodies to dance, either by using dance pads on the floor, or dancing in the presence of sensors. Manual dance games achieve the required beat-matching through button-mashing that is synchronized with the dance moves of on-screen avatars using a traditional controller in the player's hands. These manual dance games include titles such as *Spice World* (1998) and *Space Channel 5* (1999).

Corporeal dance games were amongst the first rhythm games. *Dance Aerobics* (1987), called *Aerobics Studio* in Japan, utilized the Nintendo Entertainment System's Power Pad controller, a plastic floor-mat

---

[2] Andrew Webster, 'Roots of Rhythm: A Brief History of the Music Game Genre', *Ars Technica*, 3 March 2009, accessed 8 April 2020, http://arstechnica.com/gaming/2009/03/ne-music-game-feature.

controller activated when players stepped on red and blue circles, triggering the sensors imbedded inside. Players matched the motion of the 8-bit instructor, losing points for every misstep or rhythmic mistake. As players advanced through each class, the difficulty of matching the rhythmic movements of the instructor also increased. The 'Pad Antics Mode' of *Dance Aerobics* included a free-form musical mode called 'Tune Up' in which players could use the NES Power Pad to compose a melody, with each of the ten spots on the periphery of the Power Pad assigned a diatonic pitch; in 'Mat Melodies', players used these same spots to play tunes such as 'Twinkle, Twinkle Little Star' with their feet while following notes that appeared on a musical staff at the top of the screen. 'Ditto' mode featured a musical memory game similar to *Simon*.

Games in Konami's Bemani series include many of the best known in the rhythm games genre. The term 'Bemani' originated as a portmanteau in broken English of Konami's first rhythm game, *Beatmania*, and it stuck as a nickname for all music games produced by the publisher; the company even adopted the nickname as a brand name, replacing what was previously known as the Games & Music Division (GMD). *Dance Dance Revolution,* or *DDR* quickly became one of the most well-known games in this dance-based rhythm game genre. Usually located in public arcades, these games became spectacles as crowds would gather to watch players dance to match the speed and accuracy required to succeed within the game. *DDR* players stand on a special 3 x 3 square platform controller which features four buttons, each with arrows pointing forward, back, left or right. As arrows scroll upward from the bottom of the screen and pass over a stationary set of 'guide arrows', players must step on the corresponding arrow on the platform in rhythm with the game, and in doing so, they essentially dance to the music of the game.[3]

Although the first dance-based games required players to match dance steps alone, without regard to what they did with the rest of their body, motion-based games required players to involve their entire body. For instance, *Just Dance* (2009) is a dance-based rhythm game for the motion-controlled Wii console that requires players to match the full-body choreography that accompanies each song on the game's track list. As of the writing of this chapter in 2020, games were still being published in this incredibly popular series. When *Dance Central* (2010) was released for

---

[3] Joanna Demers, 'Dancing Machines: "Dance Dance Revolution", Cybernetic Dance, and Musical Taste', *Popular Music* 25, no. 3 (2006): 401–14; Jacob Smith, 'I Can See Tomorrow in Your Dance: A Study of Dance Dance Revolution and Music Video Games', *Journal of Popular Music Studies* 16, no. 1 (2004): 58–84.

Microsoft Kinect, players of dance games were finally rid of the need to hold any controllers or to dance on a mat or pad controller; rather than simply stepping in a certain place at a certain time, or waving a controller in the air to the music, players were actually asked to dance, as the console's motion-tracking sensors were able to detect the players' motion and choreography, assessing their ability to match the positions of on-screen dancing avatars.[4]

Musical Rail-Shooter Games

Rail-shooter games are those in which a player moves on a fixed path (which could literally be the rail of a train or rollercoaster) and cannot control the path of the in-game character/avatar or vehicle throughout the course of the level. From this path, the player is required to perform specific tasks, usually to shoot enemies while speeding towards the finish line. In musical rail-shooters, a player scores points or proves to be more successful in completing the level if they shoot enemies or execute other tasks in rhythm with music. Amongst the first of this type of game was *Frequency* (2001), which asked players to slide along an octagonal track, hitting controller buttons in rhythm in order to activate gems that represented small chunks of music. Other musical rail-shooters include *Rez* (2001), *Amplitude* (2003) and *Audiosurf* (2008).

Sampling/Sequencing and Sandbox Games

Some music games provide players with the ability to create music of their own. These games often began as music notation software or sequencing software programmes that were first marketed as toys, rather than serious music-creation software, such as *Will Harvey's Music Construction Set* (1984), *C.P.U. Bach* (1994) and *Music* (1998). *Otocky* (1987) was designed as a music-themed side-scrolling shoot-'em-up in which players were able to fire their weapon in eight directions. Shots fired in each direction produced a different note, allowing players a small bit of freedom to compose music depending upon in which direction they shot. *Mario Paint* (1992) included an in-game tool that allowed players to compose music to accompany the artistic works they created within the game; this

---

[4] Kiri Miller, 'Gaming the System: Gender Performance in Dance Central', *New Media and Society* 17, no. 5 (2015): 939–57 and Miller, *Playable Bodies: Dance Games and Intimate Media* (New York: Oxford University Press, 2017).

tool became so popular, it spurred on an online culture and spin-off software called *Mario Paint Composer* (Unfungames.com, 1992).[5]

Electroplankton (2005) was released for the Nintendo DS console and designed as a sequencing tool/game in which players interacted with ten species of plankton (represented as various shapes) through the use of the DS's microphone, stylus and touchscreen in the game's 'Performance Mode'. The species of a plankton indicated the action it performed in the game and the sound it produced. In 'Audience Mode', players could simply listen to music from the game. Despite its popularity, *Electroplankton* was not a successful music-creating platform due to its lack of a 'save' feature, which would have allowed players to keep a record of the music they created and share it.

KORG DS-10 (2008) was a fully fledged KORG synthesizer emulator designed to function like a physical synth in KORG's MS range, and was created for use on the Nintendo DS platform. Other iterations, such as *KORG DS-10 Plus* (2009) and *KORG iDS-10* (2015) were released for the Nintendo DSi and the iPhone, respectively. While it was released as synth emulator, *KORG DS-10* received positive reviews by game critics because it inspired playful exploration and music creation.[6]

Karaoke Music Games

Music games can also test a player's ability to perform using musical parameters beyond rhythm alone. Games such as *Karaoke Revolution* (2003) and others in the series, as well as those in the SingStar series (2004–2017) have similar game mechanics to rhythm games, but rather than requiring players to match a steady beat, these games require players to match pitch with their voices.

·*Def Jam Rapstar* (2010), perhaps the most critically acclaimed hip-hop-themed karaoke game, included a microphone controller in which players would rap along to a popular track's music video (or a graphic visualization when no video was available), matching the words and rhythms of the original song's lyrics; in instances where singing was required, a player's ability to match pitch was also graded.

---

[5]   Dana Plank, 'Mario Paint Composer and Musical (Re)Play on YouTube', in *Music Video Games: Performance, Politics, and Play*, ed. Michael Austin (New York: Bloomsbury, 2016), 43–82.

[6]   James Mielke, 'Korg DS-10 Review', *1up.com*, 2008, accessed 8 April 2020, https://web.archive.org/web/20160617012539/http://www.1up.com/reviews/korg-ds-10; Christopher Ewen, 'KORG DS-10 Review', *GameZone*, 2009, accessed 8 April 2020, https://web.archive.org/web/20100225131407/http://nds.gamezone.com/gzreviews/r35919.htm.

Mnemonic Music Games and Musical Puzzle Games

Many video games in this subgenre of music games have their roots in pre-digital games, and they rely on a player's ability to memorize a sequence of pitches or to recall information from their personal experience with music. *Simon*, considered by many to be the first electronic music game, tested a player's ability to recall a progressively complex sequence of tones and blinking lights by recreating the pattern using coloured buttons. Later games, such as *Loom* (1990) and *The Legend of Zelda: Ocarina of Time* (1998) relied, at least in part, on a similar game mechanic in which players needed to recall musical patterns in gameplay.

A variation on the 'name that tune' subgenre, *Musika* (2007) tapped into the library of song files players had loaded onto their iPod Touch. As they listen, players must quickly decide whether or not the letter slowly being uncovered on their screen appears in the title of that particular song. The faster they decide, the higher a player's potential score. *SongPop* (2012) affords players the chance to challenge one another to a race in naming the title or performer of popular tunes, albeit asynchronously, from a multiple-choice list.

Musician Video Games

The subgenre of what we might term 'musician video games' are those in which musicians (usually well-known musicians that perform in popular genres) or music industry insiders become heavily involved in the creation of a video game as a vehicle to promote themselves and their work beyond the video game itself. Games might even serve as the means of distribution for their music. Musicians or bands featured in a game may go on music-themed quests, perform at in-game concerts or do a myriad number of other things that have nothing at all to do with music. A wide variety of musicians are featured in this type of game, which include *Journey* (1983), *Frankie Goes to Hollywood* (1985), *Michael Jackson's Moonwalker* (1990), *Peter Gabriel: EVE* (1996) and *Devo Presents Adventures of the Smart Patrol* (1996).

Music Industry Games

In much the same way many musician video games allowed players to live the life of a rock star through an avatar, music industry-themed games put players in charge of musical empires, gamifying real-world, industry-related issues and tasks, such as budgets, publicity and promotion, and music video production. Games in this genre include *Rock Star Ate My Hamster* (1988), *Make My Video* (1992), *Power Factory Featuring C+C Music Factory* (1992), *Virtual VCR: The Colors of Modern Rock* (1992), *Rock Manager* (2001), *Recordshop Tycoon* (2010) and *TastemakerX* (2011).

Edutainment Music Games and Musical Gamification

Educators and video game publishers have long been keen on using video games as both a source of entertainment and as a potential tool for teaching various subjects, including music. Early edutainment games, such as *Miracle Piano Teaching System* (1990), sought to make learning music fun by incorporating video-game-style gameplay on a video game console or personal computer. Such endeavours must deal with the issue of how to incorporate instruments into the learning process. Some opt for MIDI interfaces (like *Miracle Piano*), while others use replica instruments. *Power Gig: Rise of the SixString* (2010) included an instrument very similar to an authentic guitar. This peripheral controller was designed to help teach players how to play an actual guitar, although it was 2/3 the size of a standard guitar and of poor quality, and besides teaching players various simplified power chords, the game really did not teach players how to play the guitar, instead simply mimicking the mechanics of *Guitar Hero* and other similar games. *Power Gig* also included a set of sensors that monitored the action of players who were air-drumming along with songs in the game. The game that has arguably come the closest to teaching game players to become actual instrument players is Ubisoft's *Rocksmith* (2011) and its sequels, which allowed players to plug in an actual electric guitar of their own (or acoustic guitar with a pickup), via a USB-to-1/4 inch TRS cable, into their Xbox 360 console to be used as a game controller. The game's mechanics are similar to those of other guitar-themed rhythm games: players place their fingers in particular locations on a fretboard to match pitch and strum in rhythm when notes are supposed to occur, rather than mashing one of four coloured buttons as in *Guitar Hero*-style rhythm games. Similarly, and taking the concept a step further, *BandFuse: Rock Legends* (2013) allows up to four players to plug in real electric guitars, bass guitars and microphones as a means of interacting with the video game by playing real music. In fact, the 'legends' referenced in the game's title are rock legends who, with the aid of other virtual instructors, teach players how to play their hit songs through interactive video lessons in the game's 'Practice' and 'Shred-U' modes.

Music Game Technology

Peripheral Controllers

Music games can frequently rely on specialized controllers or other accessories to give players the sense that they are actually making music. As previously discussed, these controllers are called 'peripheral' because they are often additional controllers used to provide input for a particular music game, not the standard controllers with which most other games are played. While some peripheral controllers look and react much like real, functioning instruments and give players the haptic sensation of playing an actual instrument, others rely on standard console controllers or other forms of player input.

Guitars

Games such as those in the Guitar Hero and Rock Band series rely on now-iconic guitar-shaped controllers to help players simulate the strumming and fretwork of a real guitar during gameplay. While pressing coloured buttons on the fretboard that correspond to notes appearing on the screen, players must flick a strum bar (button) as the notes pass through the cursor or target area. Some guitar controllers also feature whammy bars for pitch bends, additional effect switches and buttons and additional fret buttons or pads. These controllers can often resemble popular models of electric guitars, as with the standard guitar controller for *Guitar Hero*, which resembles a Gibson SG.

Drums and Other Percussion

Taiko: Drum Master (2004), known as *Taiko no Tatsujin* in Japan, is an arcade game that features two Japanese Taiko drums mounted to the console, allowing for a two-player mode; the home version employs the Taiko Tapping Controller, or 'TaTaCon', which is a small mounted drum with two *bachi* (i.e., the sticks used to play a taiko drum). Games in the Donkey Konga series (2003–2005) and *Donkey Kong Jungle Beat* (2004) require a peripheral set of bongo drums, called DK Bongos, to play on the GameCube console for which the games were created. *Samba de Amigo* (1999) is an arcade game, later developed for the Dreamcast console, played with a pair of peripheral controllers fashioned after maracas. Players shake the maracas at various heights to the beat of the music, positioning their maracas as indicated by coloured dots on the screen.

Turntables

Some hip-hop-themed music games based on turntablism, such as *DJ Hero* (2009), use turntable peripheral controllers to simulate the actions of a disc jockey. These controllers usually include moveable turntables, crossfaders and additional buttons that control various parameters within the game.

Microphones

Karaoke music games usually require a microphone peripheral in order to play them, and these controllers are notorious for their incompatibility with other games or consoles. Games such as *Karaoke Revolution* initially included headset microphones, but later editions featured handheld models. *LIPS* (2008) featured a glowing microphone with light that pulsed to the music.

Mats, Pads and Platforms

These controllers are flat mats or pads, usually placed on the ground, and in most cases, players use their feet to activate various buttons embedded in the mat. Now somewhat standardized, these mats are customarily found as 3 x 3 square grids with directional arrows printed on each square. As was previously mentioned, players use the NES Power Pad to play *Dance Aerobics*; this controller is a soft pad made of vinyl or plastic that can easily be rolled up and stored. Arcade music games like *Dance Dance Revolution* use hard pads, often accompanied by a rail behind the player to give them something to grab for stability during especially difficult dance moves and to prevent them from falling over. Some of these games now use solid-state pads that utilize a proximity sensor to detect a player's movement, rather than relying on the pressure of the player's step to activate the controller. *DropMix* (2017) is a music-mixing game which combines the use of a tabletop game plastic platform, cards with embedded microchips and a companion smartphone application to allow players to create mashups of popular songs. Using near-field communication and a smartphone's Bluetooth capabilities, players lay the cards on particular spots on the game's platform. Each card is colour-coded to represent a particular musical element, such as a vocal or drum track, and depending upon its power level, it will mix in or overtake the current mix playing from the smartphone. Players can also share their mixes on social media through the app.

Motion Controls

Taiko Drum Master: Drum 'n' Fun (2018) was released for Nintendo Switch and relies on the player using the console's motion controls. Taking a controller in each hand, the player swings the handheld controllers downwards for red notes and diagonally for the blue notes that scroll across the screen. In *Fantasia: Music Evolved* (2014), based on the 'Sorcerer's Apprentice' section of the film *Fantasia* (1940), players act as virtual conductors, moving their arms to trace arrows in time with music to accomplish goals within the game. These motions are registered by the Xbox Kinect's motion sensors, allowing players to move freely without needing to touch a physical controller.

Wii Nunchuks

Using the Wii's nunchuk controllers, players of *Wii Music* (2008) could cordlessly conduct an orchestra or play a number of musical instruments. Likewise, players of *Ultimate Band* (2008) played notes on a virtual guitar by pressing various combinations of buttons on the Wii nunchuk while strumming up and down with the Wii remote.

Smartphone or Portable Listening Device Touchscreens

Some games mimic the mechanics of a peripheral-based rhythm game, but without the need for the instrument controller. *Phase: Your Music Is the Game* (2007) is a touchscreen-based rhythm game for the Apple iPod Touch; using the music found on the iPod in the player's song library as the playable soundtrack, players tap the iPod's touchscreen, rather than colour-coded buttons on a plastic guitar. Likewise, *Tap Tap Revenge* (2008) also utilized the iPhone's touchscreen to simulate controller-based rhythm games such as *Guitar Hero*.

Wider Culture and Music Games

When popular music is included within a music game, copyright and licensing can often be the source of controversy and fodder for lawsuits. In its early days, players of *Def Jam Rapstar* were able to record videos of themselves performing the hip-hop songs featured in the game using their consoles or computers, and could upload these videos to an online community for recognition. In 2012, EMI and other rights holders brought up charges of copyright infringement, suing the game's makers for sampling large portions of hip-hop songs for which they owned the rights.[7] Because the game was a karaoke-style music game and players could further distribute the copyrighted songs in question through the online community, EMI sought even more damages, and the online community was subsequently shut down.

At the height of their popularity, rhythm games such as *Rock Band* and *Guitar Hero* featured frequently in popular culture; for example, on Season 2, Episode 15 (2009) of the popular television show *The Big Bang Theory*, characters are shown playing the Red Hot Chili Peppers' song 'Under the Bridge' on *Rock Band*. As these games gained popularity in their heyday, naysayers and musical purists insisted that these games had no inherent musical value since they did not seem to encourage anyone to actually play an instrument. As such, the games were often parodied in popular culture: the premise of the *South Park* episode 'Guitar Queer-O' (Season 11, Episode 3, 2007) revolves around the supposition that games such as *Guitar Hero* require no real musical skills. But these kinds of music games have also enjoyed a surge in popularity in educational arenas, and have been successfully put to instructive uses in classrooms, albeit not as a replacement for instrumental tuition.[8] There is some evidence to suggest that music games have actually inspired players to learn to play musical instruments outside of video games. In fact, seeing game characters play instruments in music games, such as the male protagonist Link who plays the ocarina in games in the Legend of Zelda series (Nintendo), has inspired male students to study the flute.[9] Also related to music, gender and performance, Kiri Miller writes in *Playable Bodies* that music games such as *Dance Central* also provide opportunities for players who chose to play as avatars that do not correspond with their own gender expression to engage in 'generic, stylized gender performances that may pose little risk or challenge to their own identities',[10] and in doing so, may denaturalize gender binaries.

---

[7] Eriq Gardner, 'EMI Sues Over Def Jam Rapstar Video Game', *The Hollywood Reporter*, 2012, accessed 8 April 2020, www.hollywoodreporter.com/thr-esq/emi-def-jam-rapstar-video-game-lawsuit-305434.

[8] See David Roesner, Anna Paisley and Gianna Cassidy, 'Guitar Heroes in the Classroom: The Creative Potential of Music Games', in *Music Video Games: Performance, Politics, and Play*, ed. Michael Austin (New York: Bloomsbury, 2016), 197–228.

[9] Donald M. Taylor, 'Support Structures Contributing to Instrument Choice and Achievement Among Texas All-State Male Flutists', *Bulletin of the Council for Research in Music Education* 179 (2009): 45–60.

[10] Miller, *Playable Bodies*, 84.

Types of Music Games

As we have seen, the term 'music games' covers a wide spectrum of games and subgenres. To conclude this chapter, I wish to introduce a model for categorization. While this type of analysis will never provide a definitive classification of music games, it does present a framework within which analysts can discuss what types of musical activities or opportunities a game affords its players and what types of musical play might be occurring within the course of a player's interaction with a game.

One useful way to describe music games is by asking whether, and to what extent, the player's musical engagement through the game is procedural (interacting with musical materials and procedures) and/or conceptual (explicitly themed around music-making contexts). These two aspects form a pair of axes which allow us to describe the musical experiences of games. It also allows us to recognize musical-interactive qualities of games that do not announce themselves as explicitly 'music games'.

Procedural and Conceptual Musical Aspects of Games

The procedural rhetoric of a music game denotes the rules, mechanics and objectives within a game – or beyond it – that encourage, facilitate or require musical activity or interaction. For example, in the rhythm game *Guitar Hero*, players must perform a musical activity in order to succeed in the game; in this case, a player must press coloured buttons on the game's peripheral guitar-shaped controller in time with the music, and with the notes that are scrolling by on the screen. Other games, such as *SongPop* require players to select a themed playlist, listen to music and race an opponent to select the name of the song or the artist performing the song they are hearing. It should be noted that the term *procedural* is used here to describe the elements of a game that facilitate a particular means or process of interaction, which is different from *procedural generation*, or a method of game design in which algorithms are used to automatically create visual and sonic elements of a video game based on player action and interaction within a game.

Amongst procedural games, some are strictly procedural, in that they rely on clear objectives, fixed rules and/or right or wrong answers. One such category of strictly procedural music games is that of rhythm- or pitch-matching games. Players of strictly procedural music games score points based on the accuracy with which they can match pitch or rhythm, synchronize their actions to music within the game, or otherwise comply with the explicit or implicit musical rules of the game. Loosely procedural music games rely less on rigorous adherence to rules or correct answers but rather facilitate improvisation and free-form exploration of music, or bring to bear a player's personal experience with the game's featured music. Games such as *Mario Paint Composer* or *My Singing Monsters* (2012) function as sandbox-type music-making or music-mixing games that allow players more freedom to create music by combining pre-recorded sonic elements in inventive ways. Other loosely procedural games take the form of quiz, puzzle or memory games that rely on a player's individual ability to recall musical material or match lyrics or recorded clips of songs to their titles (as is the case with the previously mentioned *SongPop*); even though the procedural rhetoric of these games requires players to accurately match music with information about it (that is to say, there is a right and a wrong answer), players bring their own memories and affective experiences to the game, and players without these experiences are likely much less successful when playing them.

Highly conceptual music games are those in which theme, genre, narrative, setting and other conceptual elements of the game are related to music or music making. Here, content and the context provide the musical materials for a music game. This contrasts with the 'procedural' axis which is concerned with the way the game is controlled. Conceptually musical aspects of games recognize how extra-ludic, real-world music experiences and affective memories create or influence the musical nature of the game. This is often accomplished by featuring a particular genre of music in the soundtrack or including famous musicians as playable characters within the game. We can think of procedural and conceptual musical qualities as the differences between 'inside-out' (procedural) or 'outside-in' (conceptual) relationships with music.

Games may be predominantly procedurally musical, predominantly conceptually musical or some combination of the two. Many music games employ both logics – they are not only procedurally musical, as they facilitate musical activity, but the games' music-related themes or narratives render them conceptually musical as well. We can also observe examples of games that are highly conceptually musical, but not procedural (like the artist games named above), and games that are procedural, but not conceptual (like games where players can attend to musical materials to help them win the game, but which are not explicitly themed around music, such as *L.A. Noire* (2011)).[11]

---

[11] See Steven B. Reale, 'Transcribing Musical Worlds; or, Is *L.A. Noire* a Music Game?', in *Music in Video Games: Studying Play*, ed. K. J. Donnelly, William Gibbons and Neil Lerner (New York: Routledge, 2014), 77–103.

Types of Conceptual Musical Content

Conceptual music games rely on rhetorical devices similar to those employed in rhetorical language, such as metonyms/synecdoches, which are used to describe strong, closely related conceptual ties, and epithets, for those with looser conceptual connections. A metonym is a figure of speech in which a thing or concept is used to represent another closely related thing or concept. For example, 'the White House' and 'Downing Street' are often used to represent the entire Executive Branches of the United States and British governments respectively. Similarly, the 'Ivy League' is literally a sports conference comprising eight universities in the Northeastern United States, but the term is more often used when discussing the academic endeavours or elite reputations of these universities. There are also musical metonyms, such as noting that someone has 'an ear for music' to mean not only that they hear or listen to music well, but that they are also able to understand and/or perform it well. Further, we often use the names of composers or performers to represent a particular style or genre of music as a synecdoche (a type of metonym in which a part represents the whole). For instance, Beethoven's name is often invoked to represent all Classical and Romantic music, both or either of these style periods, all symphonic music, or all 'art music' in general. Similarly, Britney Spears or Madonna can stand in for the genre of post-1970s pop music or sometimes even all popular music.

Metonymic music games are often considered musical because a prominent element of the game represents music writ large to the player or the general public, even if the procedural logic or mechanics of the game are not necessarily musical, or only include a small bit of musical interactivity. For example, *The Legend of Zelda: Ocarina of Time* is, by almost all accounts, an action-adventure game. Link, the game's main character, traverses the enormous gameworld of Hyrule to prevent Ganondorf from capturing the Triforce, battling various enemies along the way. Link plays an ocarina in the game, and, as one might be able to conclude based on the game's title, the ocarina plays a central role in the game's plot; therefore, the game could be considered a music game. Amongst the many other varied tasks Link completes, lands he explores, items he collects, and so on, he also learns twelve melodies (and writes one melody) to solve a few music-based puzzles, allowing him to teleport to other locations. For many, the amount of musical material in the game sufficiently substantiates an argument for labelling the game as a music game. Most of the game does not involve direct interaction with music. It is limited to isolated (albeit narratively important) moments. We can therefore describe *Ocarina of Time* as conceptually musical in a metonymic way, but with limited procedural musical content.

Music games that are even further removed from music and music-making than metonymic music games are epithetic music games. An epithet is a rhetorical device in which an adjective or adjectival phrase is used as a byname or nickname of sorts to characterize the person, place or thing being described. This descriptive nickname can be based on real or perceived characteristics, and may disparage or abuse the person being described. In the case of Richard the Lionheart, the epithet 'the Lionheart' is used both to distinguish Richard I from Richards II and III, and to serve as an honorific title based on the perceived personality trait of bravery. In *The Odyssey*, Homer writes about sailing across the 'wine-dark sea', whereas James Joyce describes the sea in *Ulysses* using epithetical descriptions such as 'the snot-green sea' and 'the scrotum-tightening sea'; in these instances, the authors chose to name the sea by focusing closely on only one of its many characteristics (in these cases, colour or temperature), and one could argue that colour or temperature are not even the most prominent or important characteristic of the sea being described.

Epithetic music games are video games classified by scholars, players and fans as music games, despite their obvious lack of musical elements or music making, due to a loose or tangential association with music through its characters, setting, visual elements, or other non-aural game assets, and so on. These games differ from metonymic games in that music is even further from the centre of thematic focus and gameplay, despite the musical nickname or label associated with them; in other words, the interaction with music within these games is only passive, with no direct musical action from the player required to play the game or interact with the game's plot.

These epithetic connections are often made with hip-hop games. Hip-hop games are sometimes classified as music games because, aside from the obvious utilization of hip-hop music in the game's score, many of the non-musical elements of hip-hop culture can be seen, controlled, or acted out within the game, even if music is not performed by the player, per se, through rapping/MC-ing or turntablism. Making music is not the primary (or secondary, or usually even tertiary) object of gameplay. For example, breakdancing is a para-musical activity central to hip-hop culture that can be found in many hip-hop games, but in non-rhythm hip-hop games, a player almost never directs the movements of the dancer. Boom boxes, or 'ghetto blasters', are also a marker of hip-hop culture and can be seen carried in a video game scene by non-player characters, or resting on urban apartment building stoops or basketball court sidelines in the backgrounds of many hip-hop-themed video games, but rarely are they controlled by the player. Games such as *Def Jam Vendetta* (2003), *50 Cent: Bulletproof* (2005) and *Wu-Tang: Shaolin Style* (1999) are sometimes classified as music games due to the overt and substantial depictions of famous hip-hop artists, despite the lack of musical objectives or themes within these fighting and adventure games. Here, particular rappers are used as icons for hip-hop music and musical culture. For example, *Def Jam Vendetta* is a fighting game wherein hip-hop artists such as DMX, Ghostface Killah and Ludacris face off in professional wrestling matches. Similarly, the NBA Street series features hip-hop artists such as Nelly, the St. Lunatics, the Beastie Boys and others as playable characters, but since the artists are seen playing basketball, rather than engaging in musical activities, they are epithetic and loosely conceptual music games.

While it might be tempting to classify games as either procedurally or conceptually musical (and often games do tend to emphasize one or the other), this does not allow for the complexity of the situation. Some games are especially musical both procedurally and conceptually, as is the case with games such as those in the Rock Band and Guitar Hero series which require players to perform musical activities (rhythm matching/performing) in a conceptually musical gameworld (as in a rock concert setting, playing with rock star avatars, etc.). It is perhaps more helpful to consider the two elements as different aspects, rather than mutually exclusive. The procedural–conceptual axes (Figure 9.1) can be used to analyse and compare various music games, plotting titles depending upon which traits were more prominent in each game. We can also note that the more a game includes one or both of these features, the more likely it is to be considered a 'music game' in popular discourse.

Using this model, *Rocksmith* would be plotted in the upper right-hand corner of the graph since the game is both especially procedurally musical (rhythm-matching game that uses a real electric guitar as a controller) and conceptually musical (the plot of the game revolves around the player's in-game career as a musician). *Rayman Origins* (2011) would be plotted closer to the middle of the graph since it is somewhat, but not especially, procedurally or conceptually musical; on the one hand, players that synch their movements to the overworld music tend to do better, and the game's plot does have some musical elements (such as a magical microphone and dancing non-playable characters); on the other hand, this game is

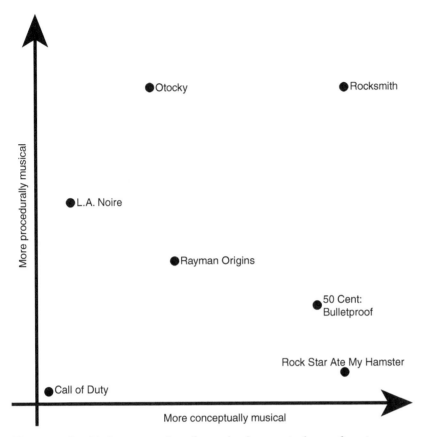

Figure 9.1 Graphical representation of procedural–conceptual axes of music games

a platform action game in which the object is to reach the end of each level, avoid enemies and pick up helpful items along the way, not necessarily to make music per se. Games in the Call of Duty or Mortal Kombat franchises, for example, would be plotted in the bottom-left corner of the graph because neither the games' mechanics nor the plot, setting, themes and so on, are musical in nature; thus, it is much less likely that these games would be considered by anyone to be a 'music game' compared to those plotted nearer the opposite corner of the graph.

Conclusions

Even if music video games never regain the blockbusting status they enjoyed in the mid-to-late 2000s, it is hard to imagine that game creators and publishers will ever discontinue production of games with musical mechanics or themes. While the categorical classification of the music game and its myriad forms and (sub)genres remains a perennial issue in the study of music video games, there exists great potential for research to emerge in the field of ludomusicology that dives deeper into the various types of play afforded by music games and the impact such play can have on the music industry, the academy and both Eastern and Western cultures more broadly.

10 | Autoethnography, Phenomenology and Hermeneutics

MICHIEL KAMP

When studying a video game's musical soundtrack, how do we account for the experience of hearing the music while playing the game? Let us pretend for a moment that a recording of *Bastion* (2011) is not from a game at all, but a clip from perhaps a cartoon series or an animated film.[1] We would immediately be struck by the peculiar camera angle. At first, when 'The Kid' is lying in bed, what we see could be an establishing shot of some sort (see Figure 10.1). The high-angle long shot captures the isolated mote of land that The Kid finds himself on through a contrast in focus between the bright and colourful ruins and the blurry ground far beneath him. As soon as he gets up and starts running, however, the camera starts tracking him, maintaining the isometric angle (from 0'02" in the clip). While tracking shots of characters are not uncommon in cinema, this particular angle is unusual, as is the rigidity with which the camera follows The Kid. Whereas the rigidity is reminiscent of the iconic tricycle shots from *The Shining* (1980), the angle is more similar to crane shots in Westerns like *High Noon* (1952). It would seem easy to argue that the high angle and the camera distance render The Kid diminutive and vulnerable, but David Bordwell and Kristin Thompson warn against interpreting such aspects of cinematography in absolute terms.[2] The major difference between traditional action sequences in film and the clip from *Bastion* is that the latter is essentially one long take, whereas typical (Hollywood) action sequences are composed of fast cuts between shots of varying camera distances and angles. The camerawork of this short sequence, then, creates a certain tension that remains unresolved, because there is no 'cut' to a next shot.

From this film-analysis standpoint, the music in the clip is less problematic. The drone with which the scene opens creates the same air of expectancy as the camera angle, but it almost immediately fulfils that expectation, as The Kid rises from his bed, a moment accentuated by the narrator's comment, 'He gets up'. The Kid's frantic pace through the assembling landscape is echoed in the

---

[1] Author's video, Hearing VGM, 'Bastion Clip 1', 19 September 2014, www.youtube.com/watch?v=pnqRWbJQIy8.

[2] David Bordwell and Kristin Thompson, *Film Art: An Introduction*, 8th ed. (New York: McGraw-Hill, 2008), 192.

Figure 10.1 *Bastion*'s 'opening shot'

snare drum and bass that form a shaky, staccato ground under the masculine reassurance of the narrator's gravelly voice (whose southern drawl sounds like a seasoned cowboy, perhaps a Sam Elliott character). As The Kid picks up his weapon, a giant hammer (which the narrator calls 'his lifelong friend'), a woodwind melody starts playing (0'19" in the clip). This common progression in the musical structure – a single drone leading into rhythmic accompaniment, in turn leading into melody – follows the progression in the narrative: The Kid gets his belongings and his journey is underway. But why does the camera not follow suit by cutting to the next 'shot'?

Consider now a clip I made when playing the same sequence in *Bastion* on another occasion.[3] We see The Kid lying in bed, a single drone accompanying his resting state. The drone creates an air of tension, in which we discern the distant sounds of gushing wind. These sounds draw our attention to the rising embers around The Kid's island high in the sky. Before we can start asking questions about the tension the drone creates – does it signify the emptiness of the sky, or the aftermath of the destruction that is implied in the ruined bedroom in the centre of the shot? – The Kid gets up, and a fast rhythm starts playing. As The Kid cautiously, haltingly, makes his way down a strip of land that starts forming around him in the sky (0'04" in the clip) – the camera following him step by step from afar – the frantic music suggests the confusion of the situation. The music heard in the first

---

[3] Author's video, Hearing VGM, 19 September 2014, 'Bastion Clip 2', www.youtube.com/watch?v=7bkIExk4PGI.

clip as underscoring the thrill and excitement of adventure now seems full of the anxiety and halting uncertainty of the protagonist. Yet the narrator suggests that 'he don't stop [*sic*] to wonder why'. So why does The Kid keep stopping?

Hearing Video Game Music

The questions that my analyses of *Bastion* prompted come from a misunderstanding of the medium of video games. The Kid stopped in the second clip because as my avatar, he was responding to my hesitant movements, probing the game for the source and logic of the appearing ground. I was trying to figure out if the ground would disappear if 'I' went back, and if it would stop appearing if 'I' stopped moving ('I' referring here to my avatar, an extension of myself in the gameworld, but when discussing the experience of playing a game, the two often become blurred). The camera does not cut to close-ups or other angles in the first clip because of the logic of the genre: this is an action-based role-playing game (RPG) that provides the player with an isometric, top-down view of the action, so that they have the best overview in combat situations, when enemies are appearing from all sides. So in order to accurately interpret the meaning of the camera angle, or of the actions of the characters, we need to have an understanding of what it is like to play a video game, rather than analyse it in terms of its audiovisual presentation. But what does this mean for our interpretation of the music?

In my example, I gave two slightly different accounts of the music in *Bastion*. In both accounts, it was subservient to the narrative and to the images, 'underscoring' the narrative arc of the first clip, and the confused movements of The Kid in the second. But do I actually hear these relationships when I am playing the game? What is it like to hear music when I am performing actions in a goal-oriented, rule-bound medium? Do I hear the musical 'underscoring' in *Bastion* as a suggestion of what actions to perform? I could, for instance, take the continuous drone at the beginning of the clip – a piece of dynamic music that triggers a musical transition when the player moves their avatar – as a sign to get up and do something. Or do I reflect on the music's relationship to my actions and to the game's visuals and narrative? While running along the pathway that the appearing ground makes, I could ask myself what the woodwind melody means in relation to the narrator's voice. Or, again, do I decide to play along to the music? As soon as I get up, I can hear the music as an invitation to run along with the frantic pace of the cue, taking me wherever I need to be to progress in the game. Or, finally, do I pay attention to the music at all? It could, after all, be no more than 'elevator music', the woodwinds having nothing particularly worthwhile to add to the narrator's words and the path leading me to where I need to be.

The questions I asked in the previous paragraph are all related to the broader question of 'what is it like to hear video game music while playing a game?' The three approaches that make up the title of this chapter – autoethnography, phenomenology and hermeneutics – revolve around this question. Each of the approaches can facilitate an account based in first-hand experience, of 'what it is like' to hear music while playing a video game, but each has its own methods and aims. With each also comes a different kind of knowledge, following Wilhelm Windelband's classic distinction between the nomothetic and idiographic.[4] Whereas the nomothetic aims to generalize from individual cases – or experiences in this case – to say something about *any* kind of experience, the idiographic is interested in the particularities of a case, what makes it unique. As we shall see, whereas hermeneutics tends towards the idiographic and phenomenology towards the nomothetic, autoethnography sits somewhere in-between the two. The three approaches can be categorized in another manner as well. To loosely paraphrase a central tenet of phenomenology, every experience consists of an experiencer, an experiential act and an experienced object.[5] Autoethnography focuses on the unique view of the experiencer, phenomenology on the essence of the act and hermeneutics on the idiosyncrasies of the object. These are very broad distinctions that come with a lot of caveats, but the chapter's aim is to show what each of these approaches can tell us about video game music. Since this chapter is about methodology, I will also compare a number of instances of existing scholarship on video game music in addition to returning to the example of *Bastion*. As it is currently the most common of the three approaches in the field, I will start with a discussion of hermeneutics. Autoethnography has not, until now, been employed as explicitly in video game music studies as in other disciplines, but there are clear examples of authors employing autoethnographic methods. Finally, phenomenology has been explored the least in the field, which is why I will end this chapter with a discussion of the potential of this approach as a complement to the other two.

---

[4] Wilhelm Windelband and Guy Oakes, 'History and Natural Science', *History and Theory* 19, no. 2 (1980): 165–8 at 167.

[5] 'The noetic-noematic structure of consciousness', in Husserl's terms. See, for example, Dermot Moran, *Introduction to Phenomenology* (London; New York: Routledge, 2000), 16.

Hermeneutics

Of the three approaches, hermeneutics is the one with the longest history within the humanities and the most applications in the fields of music, video games and video game music. As an approach, it is virtually synonymous with the idiographic, with its interest in the singular, idiosyncratic and unique. Hermeneutics is, simply put, both the practice and the study of interpretation. Interpretation is different from explanation, or even analysis, in that it aims to change or enhance the subject's understanding of the object. We can describe three forms of interpretation: functional, textual and artistic. First, interpretation, in the broadest sense of the word, is functional and ubiquitous. Drivers interpret traffic signs on a busy junction, orchestra musicians interpret the gestures of a conductor and video game players interpret gameplay mechanics to determine the best course of action. Second, in the more specialist, academic sense of the word, interpretation is first and foremost the interpretation of texts, and it derives from a long history going back to biblical exegesis.[6] This practice of textual interpretation involves a certain submission to the authority of a text or its author, and we can include the historian's interpretation of primary sources and the lawyer's interpretation of legal texts in this form as well. In contrast, there is a third mode of interpretation, a more creative, artistic form of interpreting artworks. The New Criticism in literary studies is an important part of this tradition in the twentieth century,[7] but the practice of ekphrasis – interpreting visual artworks through poetry or literary texts – is often seen to go much further back, to classical antiquity.[8] A hermeneutics of video game music involves navigating the differences between these three forms of interpretation.

Of particular importance in the case of video games is the difference between functional and artistic interpretation. Players interpret video game music for a number of practical or functional purposes.[9] The most often

---

[6] See, for example, Rudolf A. Makkreel, 'Wilhelm Dilthey', in *The Blackwell Companion to Hermeneutics*, ed. Niall Keane and Chris Lawn (Chichester: Wiley, 2016), 378–82 at 378; Paul H. Fry, *Theory of Literature* (New Haven; London: Yale University Press, 2012), 27.

[7] In this tradition, 'The Intentional Fallacy' by Wimsatt and Beardsley is usually seen as an important manifesto for a kind of interpretation that denies the authority of an author. See W. K. Wimsatt and M. C. Beardsley, 'The Intentional Fallacy', *The Sewanee Review* 54, no. 3 (1946): 468–88.

[8] James A. W. Heffernan, 'Ekphrasis and Representation', *New Literary History* 22, no. 2 (Spring 1991): 297–316 at 297.

[9] See also Tim Summers, *Understanding Video Game Music* (Cambridge, UK: Cambridge University Press, 2016), 41.

discussed example is Zach Whalen's idea of 'danger state music', or what Isabella van Elferen more broadly calls 'ludic music': music acts like a signpost, warning the player of the presence of enemies or other important events.[10] But the drone in *Bastion* warrants functional interpretation as well: as a player, I can understand its looping and uneventful qualities as signifying a temporary, waiting state, for me to break out of by pressing buttons. Artistic interpretation can certainly begin from such functional interpretation (I will return to this later), but it moves beyond that. It is not content with actions – pressing buttons – as a resolution of a hermeneutic issue but wants to understand the meaning of such musical material, in such a situation, in such a video game, in such a historical context and so on. This process of alternating focus on the musically specific and the contexts in which it sits is what is usually referred to as the hermeneutic circle, which is alternatively described as a going back and forth between parts and whole, between text and context, or between textual authority and the interpreter's prejudices.[11]

One of the most explicit proponents of artistic interpretation in musicology is Lawrence Kramer. First of all, what I referred to as a 'hermeneutic issue' is what Kramer calls a 'hermeneutic window': the notion that something in a piece stands out to the listener, that something is 'off' that requires shifting one's existential position or perspective in regard to it. In other words, something deviates from generic conventions.[12] Through this window, we step into a hermeneutic circle of interpretation, which navigates between two poles: 'ekphrastic fear' and 'ekphrastic hope'.[13] In every artistic interpretation, there is the fear that one's verbal paraphrase of a piece overtakes or supplants it. The interpretation then becomes more of a translation, missing out on the idiosyncrasies of the original and driving the interpreter and their readers further away from the piece, rather than towards an understanding of it. Ekphrastic fear means that one's prejudices fully overtake the authority of the work: it no longer speaks to us, but we

[10] Zach Whalen, 'Play Along – An Approach to Videogame Music', *Game Studies* 4, no. 1 (2004), www.gamestudies.org/0401/whalen/; Isabella van Elferen, 'Un Forastero! Issues of Virtuality and Diegesis in Videogame Music', *Music and the Moving Image* 4, no. 2 (2011): 30–9.

[11] The idea of interpretation as a circular process between parts and whole is usually associated with Friedrich Schleiermacher; the idea that interpretation involves working through one's preconceptions or prejudices of a text or object comes from Hans-Georg Gadamer, see Hans-Georg Gadamer, *Truth and Method*, trans. Joel Weinsheimer and Donald G. Marshall, 2nd ed. (London; New York: Continuum, 2004).

[12] Lawrence Kramer, *Interpreting Music* (Berkeley: University of California Press, 2011), 25.

[13] Lawrence Kramer, *Musical Meaning: Toward a Critical History* (Berkeley: University of California Press, 2002), 17–18.

speak for it. Ekphrastic hope, on the other hand, is the hope that a paraphrase triggers a spark of understanding, of seeing something new in the artwork, of letting it speak to us.

Game music hermeneutics involve another kind of fear that is often held by researchers and that is at the heart of this chapter: are we still interpreting from the perspective of a player of the game, or are we viewing the soundtrack as an outsider? This fear is best articulated by Whalen when he suggests that

[o]ne could imagine a player 'performing' by playing the game while an 'audience' listens in on headphones. By considering the musical content of a game as a kind of output, the critic has pre-empted analysis of the game itself. In other words, taking literally the implications of applying narrative structure to video-game music, one closes off the gameness of the game by making an arbitrary determination of its expressive content.[14]

In a sense, Whalen's 'audience' perspective is exactly what I took on in my introduction of *Bastion*. This kind of 'phenomenological fear' can be better understood and related to ekphrastic fear through an interesting commonality in the histories of video game and music hermeneutics. Both disciplines feature an infamous interpretation of a canonical work that is often used as an example of the dangers of hermeneutics by detractors. In the case of video games, it is Janet Murray describing *Tetris* as 'a perfect enactment of the overtasked lives of Americans in the 1990s – of the constant bombardment of tasks that demand our attention and that we must somehow fit into our overcrowded schedules and clear off our desks in order to make room for the next onslaught'.[15] In the case of music, this is Susan McClary's conception of a particular moment in Beethoven's Ninth Symphony as the 'unparalleled fusion of murderous rage and yet a kind of pleasure in its fulfilment of formal demands'.[16] These interpretations were made an example of by those unsympathetic to hermeneutic interpretation.[17] Murray's work was used

---

[14] Zach Whalen, 'Case Study: Film Music vs. Video-Game Music: The Case of Silent Hill', in *Music, Sound and Multimedia: From the Live to the Virtual*, ed. Jamie Sexton (Edinburgh: Edinburgh University Press, 2007), 68–81 at 74.

[15] Janet Murray, *Hamlet on the Holodeck: The Future of Narrative in Cyberspace*, Updated edition (Cambridge, MA: The MIT Press, 2017), 178.

[16] Susan McClary, *Feminine Endings: Music, Gender, and Sexuality* (Minneapolis: University of Minnesota Press, 1991), 128.

[17] It is telling that one of McClary's critics, Pieter van den Toorn, referred to an earlier version of McClary's text which contains the even more controversial characterization 'throttling, murderous rage of a rapist incapable of attaining release', instead of the more nuanced, edited phrasing from *Feminine Endings*. See Pieter C. van den Toorn, 'Politics, Feminism, and Contemporary Music Theory', *The Journal of Musicology* 9, no. 3 (1991): 275–99.

by ludologists to defend the player experience of video games from narrato-logical encroachment.[18] McClary's work was used by formalist musicologists (amongst others) to defend the listener's experience from the interpretations of New Musicology – a movement also influenced by literary studies. We might say that there is a certain formalism at play, then, in both the idea of phenomenological fear and ekphrastic fear: are we not going too far in our interpretations; and do both the experiencing of gameplay 'itself' and music 'itself' really involve much imaginative ekphrasis or critical analogizing at all?[19]

There are two remedies to hermeneutics' fears of overinterpretation and misrepresentation. First, there are questions surrounding what exactly the player's perspective pertains to. Is this just the experience of gameplay, or of a broader field of experiences pertaining to gaming? That might involve examining a game's paratexts (associated materials), the player and critical discourse surrounding a game and ultimately understanding the place of a game in culture. For instance, it is difficult to interpret a game like *Fortnite Battle Royale* (2017) or *Minecraft* (2011) without taking into account its huge cultural footprint and historical context. A music-related example would be K. J. Donnelly's case study of the soundtrack to *Plants vs. Zombies* (2009).[20] Like Kramer, Donnelly opens with a question that the game raises, a hermeneutic window. In this case, *Plants vs. Zombies* is a game with a 'simpler' non-dynamic soundtrack in an era in which game soundtracks are usually praised for and judged by their dynamicity, yet the soundtrack has received positive critical and popular reception. The question of why is not *solely* born out of the player's experience of music in relation to gameplay. Rather, it contraposes a deviation from compositional norms of the period. Donnelly then proceeds to interpret the soundtrack's non-dynamicity, not as lacking, but as an integral part to the game's meaning: a kind of indifference that 'seems particularly fitting to the relentless forward movement of zombies in *Plants vs. Zombies*'.[21] In other words, the soundtrack's indifference to the gameplay becomes an

---

[18] Markku Eskelinen, 'The Gaming Situation', *Game Studies* 1, no. 1 (2001), accessed 20 October 2020, http://gamestudies.org/0101/eskelinen/.

[19] Here, I am referring to another critique of hermeneutics in musicology by Carolyn Abbate, who gives the phrase 'doing this really fast is fun' as an example of what is in our minds when 'dealing with real music in real time'. See Carolyn Abbate, 'Music – Drastic or Gnostic?,' *Critical Inquiry* 30, no. 3 (2004): 505–36 at 511.

[20] K. J. Donnelly, 'Lawn of the Dead: The Indifference of Musical Destiny in Plants vs. Zombies', in *Music in Video Games: Studying Play*, ed. K. J. Donnelly, William Gibbons, and Neil Lerner (New York: Routledge, 2014), 151–65.

[21] Donnelly, 'Lawn of the Dead', 163.

important part of the game's meaning, which Donnelly then places in the context of a long history of arcade game soundtracks. By framing the interpretation through historical contextualization, Donnelly lends an authority to his account that a mere analogical insight ('musical difference matches the indifference of the zombies in the game') might not have had: experiencing *Plants vs. Zombies* in this manner sheds new light on a tradition of arcade game playing.

The second remedy involves keeping the player's experience in mind in one's interpretations. Context is essential to the understanding of every phenomenon, and it is difficult to ascertain where gameplay ends and context begins.[22] Even something as phenomenally simple as hearing the opening drone in *Bastion* as 'expectant' is based on a long tradition of musical conventions in other media, from *Also Sprach Zarathustra* in the opening scene of *2001: A Space Odyssey* (1968) to the beginning of Wagner's opera *Das Rheingold*. However, it is important to note that an explicit awareness of this tradition is not at all necessary for a player's understanding of the drone in that manner, for their functional interpretation of it. In fact, the player's functional interpretation relies on the conventionality of the expectant opening drone: without it, it would have formed a hermeneutic window that drove the player away from playing, and towards more artistic or textual forms of interpretation. These examples suggest that while the kind of functional interpreting that the experience of playing a game involves and artistic interpretation are to some extent complementary – the hermeneutic windows of artistic interpretation can certainly be rooted in musical experiences during gameplay – they can be antithetical as well. If the player's experience is often based in their understanding of game-musical conventions, it is only when a score breaks significantly with these conventions that a hermeneutics of the object comes into play. In other situations, the idiosyncrasies of the player or their experience of playing a game might be more interesting to the researcher, and it is this kind of interpretation that autoethnography and phenomenology allow for. Playing a game and paying special attention to the ways in which one is invited to interpret the game as a player might reveal opportunities for interpretation that steers clear of generalization or mischaracterization.

---

[22] This is essentially the same argument that Jacques Derrida makes in the case of text and context in his infamous aphorism 'Il n'y a pas de hors-texte' – 'there is no outside-text'; see Jacques Derrida, *Of Grammatology*, trans. Gayatri Chakravorty Spivak (Baltimore, MD; London: Johns Hopkins University Press, 1976), 158.

Autoethnography

If the three approaches discussed in this chapter are about verbalizing musical experience in games, the most obvious but perhaps also the most controversial of the three is autoethnography. It contends that the scholarly explication of experiences can be similar to the way in which we relate many of our daily experiences: by recounting them. This renders the method vulnerable to criticisms of introspection: what value can a personal account have in scholarly discourse? Questions dealing with experience take the form of 'what is it like to ... ?' When considering a question like this, it is always useful to ask 'why?' and 'who wants to know?' When I ask you what something is like, I usually do so because I have no (easy) way of finding out for myself. It could be that you have different physiological features ('what is it like to be 7-foot tall?'; 'what is it like to have synaesthesia?'), or have a different life history ('what is it like to have grown up in Japan?'; 'what is it like to be a veteran from the Iraq war?'). But why would I want to hear your description of what it is like to play a video game and hear the music, when I can find out for myself? What kind of privileged knowledge does video game music autoethnography give access to? This is one of the problems of autoethnography, with which I will deal first.

Carolyn Ellis, one of the pioneers of the method, describes autoethnography as involving 'systematic sociological introspection' and 'emotional recall', communicated through storytelling.[23] The kinds of stories told, then, are as much about the storyteller as they are about the stories' subjects. Indeed, Deborah Reed-Danahay suggests that the interest in autoethnography in the late 1990s came from a combination of anthropologists being 'increasingly explicit in their exploration of links between their own autobiographies and their ethnographic practices', and of '"natives" telling their own stories and [having] become ethnographers of their own cultures'.[24] She characterizes the autoethnographer as a 'boundary crosser', and this double role can be found in the case of the game music researcher as well: they are both player and scholar. As Tim Summers argues, '[i]n a situation where the analyst is intrinsically linked to

---

[23] Carolyn Ellis and Art Bochner, 'Autoethnography, Personal Narrative, Reflexivity: Researcher as Subject', in *Handbook of Qualitative Research*, ed. Norman K. Denzin and Yvonna S. Lincoln (Thousand Oaks, CA: Sage, 2000), 733–68 at 737.

[24] Deborah E. Reed-Danahay, 'Introduction', in *Auto/Ethnography: Rewriting the Self and the Social*, ed. Deborah E. Reed-Danahay (Oxford; New York: Berg, 1997), 1–17 at 2.

the sounded incarnation of the text, it is impossible to differentiate the listener, analyst, and gamer'.[25]

If the video game music analyser is already inextricably connected to their object, what does autoethnography add to analysis? Autoethnography makes explicit this connectedness by focusing the argument on the analyst. My opening description of *Bastion* was not explicitly autoethnographic, but it could be written as a more personal, autobiographic narrative. Writing as a researcher who is familiar with neoformalist approaches to film analysis, with the discourse on interactivity in video game music and with the game *Bastion*, I was able to 'feign' a perspective in which *Bastion* is not an interactive game but an animated film. If I were to have written about a less experimental approach to the game, one that was closer to my 'normal' mode of engagement with it, I could have remarked on how the transition between cues registers for me, as an experienced gamer who is familiar with the genre conventions of dynamic music systems. In other words, autoethnography would have revealed as much about me as a player as it would have about the soundtrack of the game.

This brings us to the second problem with autoethnography, namely the question of representation. Of course, my position as a gamer-cum-researcher is relatively idiosyncratic, but to what extent are *all* positions of gamers idiosyncratic? And to what extent is my position relevant at all to those interested in video game music? In other words: who cares what the musical experience of a game music researcher is like? Autoethnography occupies a somewhat ambiguous place in Windelband's distinction between nomothetic and idiographic knowledge. Most methodologies of autoethnography to a degree argue that the method is not merely idio-graphic: my account does not just represent my own experience, but to some extent that of a larger group, and from there it can derive some of its value. This is where the autoethnographic method, that of systematic introspection, plays an important role. Consider William Cheng's account of researching *Fallout 3* (2008).[26] While recording his playthrough, he finds himself pausing his progress through the game in order to sit back and enjoy a virtual sunrise, underscored by a Bach partita playing on the game's diegetic radio. This prompts him to wonder not just the extent to which the music influenced his actions, but the extent to which the fact that he was being recorded did as well. This reveals both his insider/outsider

---

[25] Summers, *Understanding Video Game Music*, 30–1.

[26] William Cheng, *Sound Play: Video Games and the Musical Imagination* (New York: Oxford University Press, 2014), 52–3.

perspective as a gamer/researcher and the idea that playing along to music is a form of role-playing. While the former revelation is perhaps idiosyncratic, the latter is something relatable to other, or perhaps all, forms of player engagement with musical soundtracks.

One argument why autoethnography lends itself well to the study of video game music is the length and scope of some video games. In particular, classic RPGs like the Final Fantasy series take many dozens of hours to complete. Although a busy researcher might opt for less 'costly' approaches, such as analysing a cue, looking at textual, audiovisual or ethnographic sources of the games' reception or focusing on aspects of production, they would be missing out on the experiential aspects of devoting a not insubstantial part of one's life to these games. The biographical connotations of RPG soundtracks – when and where players were in their lives when they played through an RPG – are the lifeblood of their reception. Relatively small soundtracks for games of sprawling lengths ensure that melodic and repetitive cues lodge themselves in the brains and memories of players and inspire all manners of reminiscing, from YouTube comments to concert performances. An autoethnographic account based on the researcher's own reminiscing would then straddle the nomothetic/idiographic and insider/outsider divides that are central to the perspective. Not only does an approach like this recognize both the player's and researcher's role in the construction of the musical experience, but it provides access to the essential role that lived experience plays in the historical, musical significance of these games.

Phenomenology

Both hermeneutic and autoethnographic approaches can benefit from a more detailed and systematic account of not just the experiencer or the experienced music, but of the experience itself. Phenomenology has not been employed extensively in the field, so this final section should then be seen as an exploration of what this approach might offer the study of video game music, rather than a survey of existing studies. Whereas autoethnography takes the charge of introspection and wears it proudly, the origins of phenomenology lie in a scholarly context in which it was considered a dirty word. Edmund Husserl, generally considered the father of phenomenology, strenuously distinguished his approach from introspection.[27] Rather

---

[27] Edmund Husserl, *Phenomenology and the Crisis of Philosophy*, trans. Quentin Lauer (New York: Harper & Row, 1965), 115. See also David R. Cerbone, 'Phenomenological Method: Reflection,

than an attempt at finding empirical aspects of experience by investigating one's own consciousness, phenomenology involves a reflection on conscious experience in order to find logical preconditions for those experiences. In other words, phenomenology deals not in empirical facts, but theoretical essences. It therefore aims to be closer in nature to logic and mathematics than to psychology and anthropology. It is unabashedly nomothetic, even if the experiential 'data' from which it starts are idiosyncratic to the experiencer. Husserl's intent was to follow through the line of philosophical thought that started with Descartes and continued through Kant, of finding absolute truths in non-empirical knowledge: if the existence of the world beyond its appearance to me is in doubt, then all I can do is study appearances or phenomena. This project neatly lines up with the problem of interpretation: if the meaning of a video game (score) as intended by its creators to me is in doubt, then I have to focus on my experience thereof. Where a phenomenological approach differs from hermeneutics is that it is ultimately not interested in the object of experience, but in the (player) experience itself – that is, what one might call 'hearing' or 'listening' to game music.

In order to study phenomena, one needs to suspend one's 'natural attitude', in which one assumes the existence of the world beyond our experiences of it. This is what is called the phenomenological *epoché*, transcendental reduction or simply 'bracketing'.[28] Our commonsensical, 'natural' ways of being in the world are so taken for granted that they 'pass by unnoticed', and so 'we must abstain from them for a moment in order to awaken them and make them appear' in a way as to understand them better.[29] In this mode, this *epoché*, we can begin to distinguish certain phenomena. For instance, in Husserlian terminology, all phenomena that we experience as existing outside our immediate consciousness (e.g., things that we perceive with our senses) are 'transcendent' phenomena; those phenomena that only exist in experience, such as imagined or remembered things, are 'immanent' phenomena. This leads to the insight that hearing a melody – a case of temporal perception – involves both transcendent objects, like a note C that I hear right now, and immanent objects, like a note D I remember hearing just a moment ago, and which informs my understanding of note C as being part of a descending motif.

Introspection, and Skepticism', in *The Oxford Handbook of Contemporary Phenomenology*, ed. Dan Zahavi (Oxford; New York: Oxford University Press, 2013), 7–24.

[28] Moran, *Introduction to Phenomenology*, 11–12.

[29] Maurice Merleau-Ponty, *Phenomenology of Perception*, trans. Donald A. Landes (London: Routledge, 2012), lxxvii.

After adopting the attitude of the *epoché*, the phenomenological method involves intuiting essences through imaginative variation, also known as the 'eidetic reduction'.[30] By imagining variations on a phenomenon, and considering at what point those variations would cease to be instances of that phenomenon, we can identify its essential characteristics. Consider, for instance, the opening drone in the *Bastion* sequence, which I suggested carried with it an air of expectancy in my experience as a player. As long, held notes, drones in general might be seen to have a static quality about them; after all, they are melodically directionless, and often harmonically as well. The attribute of expectancy in this particular experience of a drone is constantly at odds with this static quality: it seems to make the music want to go somewhere else. By imagining the *Bastion* opening drone as sounding or appearing different, it is possible to work out the way in which this 'expectantness' is an essential quality of this particular experienced drone. For instance, I can imagine the drone being higher or lower in volume or pitch, but it would still carry with it this same attribute in the context of my experience in *Bastion*. Only when I imagine hearing certain very specific other musical events with very specific musical and cultural contexts against the drone – for example, the Celtic folk melodies that are often accompanied throughout by bagpipe drones, or the drone-like early polyphony of Pérotin – is this attribute lost. This suggests that in this experience, qualities like 'static' and 'expectant' have more to do with context than with musical parameters of the *Bastion* drone itself. Taken as an essential quality of my experience of the drone, 'expectancy' reveals this context, and further imaginative variation might reveal more about its nature: the way in which audiovisual impressions or game-generic expectations are involved as preconditions for the experience, for instance.

Based on subjective experience, the phenomenological approach is ultimately theoretical rather than empirical. I can never say anything in general about *actual* experiences of the opening drone in *Bastion* – those had by other players – based on an examination of my own experiences, but I can say something about *possible* experiences of the opening drone. This means that as an approach, phenomenology lends itself best to experiences widely shared, but not thoroughly understood. This is why it has mostly been employed in investigations into some of the most basic and universal concepts: perception, art, technology and even existence and being itself.[31]

---

[30] Moran, *Introduction to Phenomenology*, 11–12.

[31] See Merleau-Ponty, *Phenomenology of Perception*. See also Martin Heidegger, 'The Origin of the Work of Art', in *Off the Beaten Track*, trans. Julian Young and Kenneth Haynes (Cambridge: Cambridge University Press, 2002), 1–56; Martin Heidegger, 'The Question Concerning

Husserl did discuss music, but only as a means of elucidating our conscious-ness of time.[32] Throughout the twentieth century, there have been more applied, sporadic attempts at investigating music in a phenomenological manner.[33] Scholars such as Alfred Schutz and Thomas Clifton have offered insights on music's relationship to time, from the experience of a musical work as an ideal, Platonic object, to the way a musical performance allows us to enter a 'flux' of inner time instead of outer 'clock' time.[34] All of these studies, however, are concerned with music as the exclusive object of atten-tion, whether it be in the concert hall or at home on the listener's couch as they listen to a recording.[35] Video games offer varied modes of engagement with music, whether they be more attentive (such as in *Guitar Hero*, 2005) or inattentive (such as in *Bastion*).[36] While earlier phenomenologies of music therefore are not necessarily directly applicable to video games, they do offer useful starting points for interrogating and refining existing theories of game music.

For example, Elizabeth Medina-Gray, in her analysis of modularity in game composition, makes a distinction between musical and non-musical choices.[37] For instance, pressing a button in *Guitar Hero* to play a note or phrase is a musical choice, based on rhythmic timing; pressing a button in *Bastion* to 'get up' is a non-musical choice, based on our desire to get our avatar moving. In both instances, the music responds to our actions, but the qualitative difference between the ways in which we hear that musical response can be described phenomenologically. A cursory glance would suggest that in the case of *Guitar Hero*, we are firmly in the 'inner time' of a song, whereas in the case of *Bastion*, this temporal experience is at the

---

Technology', in *The Question Concerning Technology and Other Essays*, trans. William Lovitt (New York; London: Garland, 1977), 3–35; Martin Heidegger, *Being and Time*, trans. John Macquarrie and Edward Robinson (Oxford: Blackwell, 1962).

[32] Edmund Husserl, *On the Phenomenology of the Consciousness of Internal Time (1893–1917)*, trans. John Barnett Brough (Dordrecht; Boston; London: Kluwer, 1991).

[33] See Thomas Clifton, *Music as Heard: A Study in Applied Phenomenology* (New Haven; London: Yale University Press, 1983); Alfred Schutz, 'Fragments on the Phenomenology of Music', trans. Fred Kersten, *Music and Man* 2, no. 1–2 (January 1, 1976): 5–71; David Lewin, 'Music Theory, Phenomenology, and Modes of Perception', *Music Perception: An Interdisciplinary Journal* 3, no. 4 (1986): 327–92.

[34] Schutz, 'Fragments on the Phenomenology of Music', 43. See also Jerrold Levinson, *Music in the Moment* (Ithaca, NY: Cornell University Press, 1997).

[35] See, for example, Schutz, 'Fragments on the Phenomenology of Music', 43. Schutz refers to this as 'pure' listening.

[36] Anahid Kassabian, *Ubiquitous Listening: Affect, Attention, and Distributed Subjectivity* (Berkeley: University of California Press, 2013).

[37] Elizabeth Medina-Gray, 'Modular Structure and Function in Early 21st-Century Video Game Music' (PhD dissertation, Yale University, 2014), 31–2.

very least a function of musical and non-musical expectations. However, looking closer at the music in *Bastion*, what exactly is the inner time of the musical drone with which the soundtrack opens? Jonathan Kramer might suggest that this is a form of 'vertical music' that has no clear directionality to it,[38] but then a drone can be expectant as well, depending on its context (cf. the opening to *Also Sprach Zarathustra*). While it is undoubtedly the case that the expectancy created by the drone is a soundtrack convention – in part a non-musical expectation – it is also a musical convention going back before Strauss' symphonic poem to, for instance, bagpipe playing. Moreover, to suggest that expectancy is an inessential attribute of *Bastion*'s opening drone is a misconstrual of my experience, of the phenomenon in question. Is 'getting up' in *Bastion* then a completely non-musical choice, if soundtrack conventions are so closely intertwined with video game and audiovisual narrative conventions?

To some extent, this kind of applied phenomenology resembles music theory in nature. It too attempts to abstract from empirical data – experiences as opposed to pieces of music – to find theoretical rules and patterns.[39] But as in music theory, these rules and patterns are historically and culturally contingent. And here lies the main challenge with phenomenologies of cultural phenomena such as video game music: it is hard to deduce when they stray from the universal and become 'too applied', because they are ultimately and inescapably rooted in subjective experience. As a critical complement to approaches such as hermeneutics and autoethnography, however, they can be an invaluable resource that helps us to unpack the specifics of what it is like to play a game and experience its music.

* * *

The three methods outlined in this chapter can be related to each other in a circular manner. Although an autoethnographic account of a game soundtrack can open up phenomenological questions, and these can be interpreted in a cultural-historical context, it is often a hermeneutic question or window that functions as the starting point of autoethnography: what is idiosyncratic about *this* particular experience, by this player, of this game? Although the player experience has been the central point of

---

[38] Jonathan D. Kramer, *The Time of Music: New Meanings, New Temporalities, New Listening Strategies* (New York; London: Schirmer Books, 1988), 375.

[39] Jonathan de Souza, for instance, also links phenomenology to music theory through the work of David Lewin. See Jonathan de Souza, *Music at Hand: Instruments, Bodies, and Cognition* (Oxford: Oxford University Press, 2017), 4.

concern for this chapter, it is by no means the exclusive object of investigation for these methods. David Bessell, for instance, autoethnographically approaches the creative process involved in designing the soundtrack to the unreleased horror game *Deal With the Devil*.[40] Moreover, in recent years, the lines between creation and consumption, between artists and audiences, have been blurred. Video game music is very much a part of participatory culture, as evidenced in the thousands of arrangements, covers and appropriations of popular soundtracks like that of *Super Mario Bros.* on platforms such as YouTube.[41] Not only should an account of the player experience involve this complicated web of material beyond the game, but this material itself could be construed as a modern form of ekphrasis. Academic approaches to the understanding of player experience might then be considered as just another strand of this wider web of interpretative practices.

---

[40] David Bessell, 'An Auto-Ethnographic Approach to Creating the Emotional Content of Horror Game Soundtracking', in *Emotion in Video Game Soundtracking*, ed. Duncan Williams and Newton Lee (Cham: Springer International Publishing, 2018), 39–50.

[41] See, for example, Melanie Fritsch, '"It's a-Me, Mario!" Playing with Video Game Music', in *Ludomusicology: Approaches to Video Game Music*, eds. Michiel Kamp, Tim Summers and Mark Sweeney (Sheffield: Equinox, 2016), 92–115.

11 | Interacting with Soundscapes: Music, Sound Effects and Dialogue in Video Games

ELIZABETH MEDINA-GRAY

Video games often incorporate a wide variety of sounds while presenting interactive virtual environments to players. Music is one critical element of video game audio – to which the bulk of the current volume attests – but it is not alone: sound effects (e.g., ambient sounds, interface sounds and sounds tied to gameworld actions) and dialogue (speaking voices) are also common and important elements of interactive video game soundscapes. Often, music, sound effects and dialogue together accompany and impact a player's experience playing a video game, and as Karen Collins points out, 'theorizing about a single auditory aspect without including the others would be to miss out on an important element of this experience, particularly since there is often considerable overlap between them'.[1] A broad approach that considers all components of video game soundscapes – and that acknowledges relationships and potentially blurred boundaries between these components – opens the way for a greater understanding not only of video game music but also of game audio more broadly and its effects for players.

This chapter focuses on music, sound effects and dialogue as three main categories of video game audio. In some ways, and in certain contexts, these three categories can be considered as clearly distinct and discrete. Indeed this chapter begins from the general premise – inherited from film audio – that enough of video game audio can be readily described as either 'music', 'sound effects' or 'dialogue' to warrant the existence of these separate categories. Such distinctions are reflected in various practical aspects of video game design: some games – many first-person shooter games, for instance – provide separate volume controls for music and sound effects,[2] and the Game Audio Network Guild's annual awards for video game audio achievement include categories for 'Music of the Year' and 'Best Dialogue'

---

[1] Karen Collins, *Playing with Sound: A Theory of Interacting with Sound and Music in Video Games* (Cambridge, MA: The MIT Press, 2013), 3.

[2] Mark Grimshaw, 'Sound and Player Immersion in Digital Games', in *The Oxford Handbook of Sound Studies*, ed. Trevor Pinch and Karin Bijsterveld (Oxford: Oxford University Press, 2011), 347–66 at 350.

(amongst others).[3] While music, sound effects and dialogue are generally recognizable categories of video game audio, the interactive, innovative and technologically grounded aspects of video games often lead to situations – throughout the history of video game audio – where the distinctions between these categories are not actually very clear: a particular sound may seem to fit into multiple categories, or sounds seemingly from different categories may interact in surprising ways. Such blurred boundaries between sonic elements raise intriguing questions about the nature of game audio, and they afford interpretive and affective layers beyond those available for more readily definable audio elements. These issues are not wholly unique to video games – John Richardson and Claudia Gorbman point to increasingly blurred boundaries and interrelationships across soundtrack elements in cinema, for example[4] – although the interactive aspect of games allows for certain effects and sonic situations that do not necessarily have parallels in other types of multimedia. In using the term 'soundscape' here, moreover, I acknowledge a tradition of soundscape studies, or acoustic ecology, built on the work of R. Murray Schafer and others, which encourages consideration of all perceptible sounds in an environment, including but by no means limited to music. Some authors have found it useful to apply a concept of soundscapes (or acoustic ecologies) specifically to those sounds that video games present as being within a virtual world (i.e., diegetic sounds).[5] I use the term more broadly here – in this chapter, 'soundscape' refers to any and all sounds produced by a game; these sounds comprise the audible component of a gameplay environment for a player. (An even broader consideration of gameplay soundscapes would also include sounds produced within a player's physical environment, but such sounds are outside the scope of the current chapter.)

This chapter first considers music, sound effects and dialogue in turn, and highlights the particular effects and benefits that each of these three audio categories may contribute to players' experiences with games. During the discussion of sound effects, this chapter further distinguishes between earcons and auditory icons (following definitions from the field of human–computer interaction, which this chapter will reference in some

---

[3] Game Audio Network Guild, '2018 Awards', www.audiogang.org/2018-awards/ (accessed 14 October 2018).

[4] John Richardson and Claudia Gorbman, 'Introduction', in *The Oxford Handbook of New Audiovisual Aesthetics*, ed. John Richardson, Claudia Gorbman and Carol Vernallis (New York: Oxford University Press, 2013), 3–35 at 29–30.

[5] Grimshaw, 'Sound and Player Immersion', 349–50.

detail) in order to help nuance the qualities and utilities of sounds in this larger audio category. The remaining portion of this chapter examines ways in which music, sound effects and dialogue sometimes interact or blur together, first in games that appeared relatively early in the history of video game technology (when game audio primarily relied on waveforms generated in real time via sound chips, rather than sampled or prerecorded audio), and then in some more recent games. This chapter especially considers the frequently blurred boundaries between music and sound effects, and suggests a framework through which to consider the musicality of non-score sounds in the larger context of the soundscape. Overall, this chapter encourages consideration across and beyond the apparent divides between music, sound effects and dialogue in games.

Individual Contributions of Music, Sound Effects and Dialogue in Video Games

Amongst the wide variety of audio elements in video game soundscapes, I find it useful to define the category of *music* in terms of content: I here consider music to be a category of sound that features some ongoing organization across time in terms of rhythm and/or pitch. In video games, music typically includes score that accompanies cutscenes (cinematics) or gameplay in particular environments, as well as, occasionally, music produced by characters within a game's virtual world. A sound might be considered at least *semi-musical* if it contains isolated components like pitch, or timbre from a musical instrument, but for the purposes of this chapter, I will reserve the term 'music' for elements of a soundscape that are organized in rhythm and/or pitch over time. (The time span for such organization can be brief: a two-second-long victory fanfare would be considered music, for example, as long as it contains enough onsets to convey some organization across its two seconds. By contrast, a sound consisting of only two pitched onsets is – at least by itself – semi-musical rather than music.) Music receives thorough treatment throughout this volume, so only a brief summary of its effects is necessary here. Amongst its many and multifaceted functions in video games, music can suggest emotional content, and provide information to players about environments and characters; moreover, if the extensive amount of fan activity (YouTube covers, etc.) and public concerts centred around game music are any indication, music inspires close and imaginative engagement with video games, even beyond the time of immediate gameplay.

While I define music here in terms of content, I define *sound effects* in terms of their gameplay context: Sound effects are the (usually brief) sounds that are tied to the actions of players and in-game characters and objects; these are the sounds of footsteps, sounds of obtaining items, sounds of selecting elements in a menu screen and so on, as well as ambient sounds (which are apparently produced within the virtual world of the game, but which may not have specific, visible sources in the environment). As functional elements of video game soundscapes, sound effects have significant capability to enrich virtual environments and impact players' experiences with games. As in film, sound effects in games can perceptually adhere to their apparent visual sources on the screen – an effect which Michel Chion terms *synchresis* – despite the fact that the visual source is not actually producing the sound (i.e., the visuals and sounds have different technical origins).[6] Beyond a visual connection, sound effects frequently take part in a process that Karen Collins calls *kinesonic synchresis*, where sounds fuse with corresponding actions or events.[7] For example, if a game produces a sound when a player obtains a particular in-game item, the sound becomes connected to that action, at least as much as (if not more so than) the same sound adheres to corresponding visual data (e.g., a visible object disappearing). Sound effects can adhere to actions initiated by a computer as well, as for example, in the case of a sound that plays when an in-game object appears or disappears without a player's input. Through repetition of sound together with action, kinesonically synchretic sounds can become familiar and predictable, and can reinforce the fact that a particular action has taken place (or, if a sound is absent when it is anticipated, that an expected action hasn't occurred). In this way, sound effects often serve as critical components of interactive gameplay: they provide an immediate channel of communication between computer and player, and players can use the feedback from such sounds to more easily and efficiently play a game.[8] Even when sound effects are neither connected to an apparent visible source nor obviously tied to a corresponding action (e.g., the first time a player hears a particular sound), they may serve important roles in gameplay: acousmatic sounds (sounds without visible sources), for instance, might help players to visualize the gameworld outside of what is immediately visible on the screen, by drawing from earlier experiences both playing the game and interacting with the real world.[9]

---

[6] Grimshaw, 'Sound and Player Immersion', 351–2; Michel Chion, *Audio-Vision: Sound on Screen*, ed. and trans. Claudia Gorbman (New York: Columbia University Press, 1994), 63.
[7] Collins, *Playing with Sound*, 32.
[8] Collins, *Playing with Sound*, 33.
[9] Grimshaw, 'Sound and Player Immersion', 360.

Within the context-defined category of sound effects, the *contents* of these sounds vary widely, from synthesized to prerecorded (similar to Foley in film sound), for example, and from realistic to abstract. To further consider the contributions of sound effects in video games, it can be helpful to delineate this larger category with respect to content. For this purpose, I here borrow concepts of *auditory icons* and *earcons* – types of non-speech audio feedback – from the field of Human–Computer Interaction (HCI, a field concerned with studying and designing interfaces between computers and their human users). In the HCI literature, *auditory icons* are 'natural, everyday sounds that can be used to represent actions and objects within an interface', while *earcons* 'use abstract, synthetic tones in structured combinations to create auditory messages'.[10] (The word 'earcon' is a play on the idea of an icon perceived via the ear rather than the eye.) Auditory icons capitalize on a relatively intuitive connection between a naturalistic sound and the action or object it represents in order to convey feedback or meaning to a user; for example, the sound of clinking glass when I empty my computer's trash folder is similar to the sounds one might hear when emptying an actual trash can, and this auditory icon tells me that the files in that folder have been successfully deleted. In video games, auditory icons might include footstep-like sounds when characters move, sword-like clanging when characters attack, material clicks or taps when selecting options in a menu, and so on; and all of these naturalistic sounds can suggest meanings or connections with gameplay even upon first listening. Earcons, by contrast, are constructed of pitches and/or rhythms, making these informative sounds abstract rather than naturalistic; the connection between an earcon and action, therefore, is not intuitive, and it may take more repetitions for a player to learn an earcon's meaning than it might to learn the meaning of an auditory icon. Earcons can bring additional functional capabilities, however. For instance, earcons may group into families through similarities in particular sonic aspects (e.g., timbre), so that similar sounds might correspond to logically similar actions or objects. (The HCI literature suggests various methods for constructing 'compound earcons' and 'hierarchical earcons', methods which

---

[10] Eve Hoggan and Stephen Brewster, 'Nonspeech Auditory and Crossmodal Output', in *The Human-Computer Interaction Handbook: Fundamentals, Evolving Technologies, and Emerging Applications*, ed. Julie A. Jacko, 3rd ed. (Boca Raton: CRC Press, 2012), 211–35 at 220, 222. See also William W. Gaver, 'Auditory Icons: Using Sound in Computer Interfaces', *Human-Computer Interaction* 2, no. 2 (1986): 167–77; Meera M. Blattner, Denise A. Sumikawa and Robert M. Greenberg, 'Earcons and Icons: Their Structure and Common Design Principles', *Human-Computer Interaction* 4, no. 1 (1989): 11–44.

capitalize on earcons' capacity to form relational structures,[11] but these more complex concepts are not strictly necessary for this chapter's purposes.) Moreover, the abstract qualities of earcons – and their pitched and/ or rhythmic content – may open up these sound effects to further interpretation and potentially musical treatment, as later portions of this chapter explore. In video games, earcons might appear as brief tones or motives when players obtain particular items, navigate through text boxes and so on. The jumping and coin-collecting sounds in *Super Mario Bros.* (1985) are earcons, as are many of the sound effects in early video games (since early games often lacked the capacity to produce more realistic sounds).

Note that other authors also use the terms 'auditory icons' and 'earcons' with respect to video game audio, with similar but not necessarily identical applications to how I use the terms here. For example, earcons in Kristine Jørgensen's treatment include any abstract and informative sound in video games, including score (when this music conveys information to players).[12] Here, I restrict my treatment of earcons to brief fragments, as these sounds typically appear in the HCI literature, and I do not extend the concept to include continuous music. In other words, for the purposes of this article, earcons and auditory icons are most useful as more specific descriptors for those sounds that I have already defined as sound effects.

In video game soundscapes, *dialogue* yields a further array of effects particular to this type of sound. Dialogue here refers to the sounds of characters speaking, including the voices of in-game characters as well as narration or voice-over. Typically, such dialogue equates to recordings of human speech (i.e., voice acting), although the technological limitations and affordances of video games can raise other possibilities for sounds that might also fit into this category. In video games, the semantic content of dialogue can provide direct information about character states, gameplay goals and narrative/story, while the sounds of human voices can carry additional affective and emotional content. In particular, a link between a sounding voice and the material body that produced it (e.g., the voice's 'grain', after Roland Barthes) might allow voices in games to reference physical bodies, potentially enhancing players' senses of identification with avatars.[13]

---

[11] Hoggan and Brewster, 'Nonspeech Auditory and Crossmodal Output', 222–3.

[12] Kristine Jørgensen, *A Comprehensive Study of Sound in Computer Games: How Audio Affects Player Action* (Lewiston, NY: Edwin Mellen Press, 2009), 84–90.

[13] Axel Stockburger, 'The Play of the Voice: The Role of the Voice in Contemporary Video and Computer Games', in *Voice: Vocal Aesthetics in Digital Arts and Media*, ed. Norie Neumark, Ross Gibson and Theo van Leeuwen (Cambridge, MA: The MIT Press, 2010), 281–99 at 285–7; Roland Barthes, 'The Grain of the Voice', in *Image-Music-Text*, trans. Stephen Heath (New York: Hill and Wang, 1977), 179–89.

A voice's affect might even augment a game's visuals by suggesting facial expressions.[14] When players add their own dialogue to game soundscapes, moreover – as in voice chat during online multiplayer games, for instance – these voices bring additional complex issues relating to players' bodies, identities and engagement with the game.[15]

Blurring Audio Categories in Early Video Game Soundscapes

As a result of extreme technological limitations, synthesized tones served as a main sonic resource in early video games, a feature which often led to a blurring of audio categories. The soundscape in *Pong* (1972), for example, consists entirely of pitched square-wave tones that play when a ball collides with a paddle or wall, and when a point is scored; Tim Summers notes that *Pong*'s sound 'sits at the boundary between sound effect and music – undeniably pitched, but synchronized to the on-screen action in a way more similar to a sound effect'.[16] In terms of the current chapter's definitions, the sounds in *Pong* indeed belong in the category of sound effects – more specifically, these abstract sounds are earcons – here made semi-musical because of their pitched content. But with continuous gameplay, multiple pitched earcons can string together across time to form their own gameplay-derived rhythms that are predictable in their timing (because of the associated visual cues), are at times repeated and regular, and can potentially result in a sounding phenomenon that can be defined as music. In the absence of any more obviously musical element in the soundscape – like, for example, a continuous score – these recurring sound effects may reasonably step in to fill that role.

Technological advances in the decades after *Pong* allowed 8-bit games of the mid-to-late 1980s, for example, to readily incorporate both a continuous score and sound effects, as well as a somewhat wider variety of possible timbres. Even so, distinctions between audio types in 8-bit games are frequently fuzzy, since this audio still relies mainly on synthesized sound

---

[14] Mark Ward, 'Voice, Videogames, and the Technologies of Immersion', in *Voice: Vocal Aesthetics in Digital Arts and Media*, ed. Norie Neumark, Ross Gibson and Theo van Leeuwen (Cambridge, MA: The MIT Press, 2010), 267–79 at 272.

[15] For more on players' voices in games, see Collins, *Playing with Sound*, 79–82; William Cheng, *Sound Play: Video Games and the Musical Imagination* (New York: Oxford University Press, 2014), 139–66; Stockburger, 'The Play of the Voice.'

[16] Tim Summers, 'Dimensions of Game Music History', in *The Routledge Companion to Screen Music and Sound*, ed. Miguel Mera, Ronald Sadoff and Ben Winters (New York: Routledge, 2017), 139–52 at 140.

(either regular/pitched waveforms or white noise), and since a single sound chip with limited capabilities typically produces all the sounds in a given game. The Nintendo Entertainment System (NES, known as the Family Computer or Famicom in Japan), for example, features a sound chip with five channels: two pulse-wave channels (each with four duty cycles allowing for some timbral variation), one triangle-wave channel, one noise channel and one channel that can play samples (which only some games use). In many NES/Famicom games, music and sound effects are designated to some of the same channels, so that gameplay yields a soundscape in which certain channels switch immediately, back and forth, between producing music and producing sound effects. This is the case in the opening level of *Super Mario Bros.*, for example, where various sound effects are produced by either of the two pulse-wave channels and/or the noise channel, and all of these channels (when they are not playing a sound effect) are otherwise engaged in playing a part in the score; certain sound effects (e.g., coin sounds) even use the pulse-wave channel designated for the melodic part in the score, which means that the melody drops out of the soundscape whenever those sound effects occur.[17] When a single channel's resources become divided between music (score) and sound effects in this way, I can hear two possible ramifications for these sounds: On the one hand, the score may invite the sound effects into a more musical space, highlighting the already semi-musical quality of many of these effects; on the other hand, the interjections of sound effects may help to reveal the music itself as a collection of discrete sounds, downplaying the musicality of the score. Either way, such a direct juxtaposition of music and sound effects reasonably destabilizes and blurs these sonic categories.

With only limited sampling capabilities (and only on some systems), early video games generally were not able to include recordings of voices with a high degree of regularity or fidelity, so the audio category of dialogue is often absent in early games. Even without directly recognizable reproductions of human voices, however, certain sounds in early games can sometimes be seen as evoking voices in surprising ways; Tom Langhorst, for example, has suggested that the pitch glides and decreasing volume in the failure sound in *Pac-Man* (1980) make this brief sound perhaps especially like speech, or even laughter.[18] Moreover, dialogue as an audio category *can* sometimes exist in early games, even without the use of

---

[17] See James Newman's chapter (Chapter 1) in this volume for further discussion of this game.

[18] Tom Langhorst, 'The Unanswered Question of Musical Meaning: A Cross-Domain Approach', in *The Oxford Handbook of Interactive Audio*, ed. Karen Collins, Bill Kapralos and Holly Tessler (Oxford: Oxford University Press, 2014), 95–116 at 109–13.

recorded voices. *Dragon Quest* (1986) provides an intriguing case study in which a particular sound bears productive examination in terms of all three audio categories: sound effect, music and dialogue. This case study closes the current examination of early game soundscapes, and introduces an approach to the boundaries between music and other sounds that remains useful beyond treatments of early games.

Dragon Quest (with music composed by Koichi Sugiyama) was originally published in 1986 in Japan on the Nintendo Famicom; in 1989, the game was published in North America on the NES with the title *Dragon Warrior*. An early and influential entry in the genre of Japanese Role-Playing Games (JRPGs), *Dragon Quest* casts the player in the role of a hero who must explore a fantastical world, battle monsters and interact with computer-controlled characters in order to progress through the game's quest. The game's sound is designed such that – unlike in *Super Mario Bros.* – simultaneous music and sound effects generally utilize different channels on the sound chip. For example, the music that accompanies exploration in castle, town, overworld and underworld areas and in battles, always uses only the first pulse-wave channel and the triangle-wave channel, while the various sound effects that can occur in these areas (including the sounds of menu selections, battle actions and so on) use only the second pulse-wave channel and/or the noise channel. This sound design separates music and sound effects by giving these elements distinct spaces in the sound chip, but many of the sound effects are still at least semi-musical in that they consist of pitched tones produced by a pulse-wave channel. When a player talks with other inhabitants of the game's virtual world, the resulting dialogue appears – gradually, symbol by symbol – as text within single quotation marks in a box on the screen. As long as the visual components of this speech are appearing, a very brief but repeated tone (on the pitch A5) plays on the second pulse-wave channel. Primarily, this repeated sound is a sound effect (an earcon): it is the sound of dialogue text appearing, and so can be reasonably described as adhering to this visual, textual source. Functionally, the sound confirms and reinforces for players the fact that dialogue text is appearing on screen. The sound's consistent tone, repeated at irregular time intervals, moreover, may evoke a larger category of sounds that accompany transmission of text through technological means, for example, the sounds of activated typewriter or computer keys, or Morse code.

At the same time, the dialogue-text sound can be understood in terms of music, first and most basically because of its semi-musical content (the pitch A5), but also especially because this sound frequently agrees (or fits

Example 11.1 Castle throne room (excerpt), *Dragon Quest*

together well) with simultaneous music in at least one critical aspect: pitch. Elsewhere, I have argued that sonic agreement – a quality that I call 'smoothness' – between simultaneous elements of video game audio arises through various aspects, in particular, through consonance between pitches, alignment between metres or onsets, shared timbres and similarities between volume levels.[19] Now, I suggest that any straightforward music component like a score – that is, any sonic material that clearly falls into the category of music – can absorb other simultaneous sounds into that same music classification as long as those simultaneous sonic elements agree with the score, especially in terms of both pitch and metre. (Timbre and volume seem less critical for these specifically musical situations; consider that it is fairly common for two instruments in an ensemble to contribute to the same piece of music while disagreeing in timbre or volume.) When a sound agrees with simultaneous score in only one aspect out of pitch or metre, and disagrees in the other aspect, the score can still emphasize at least a semi-musical quality in the sound. For instance, Example 11.1 provides an excerpt from the looping score that accompanies gameplay in the first area of *Dragon Quest*, the castle's throne room, where it is possible to speak at some length with several characters. While in the throne room, the dialogue-text sound (with the pitch A) can happen over any point in the sixteen-bar looping score for this area; in 27 per cent of those possible points of simultaneous combination, the score also contains a pitch A and so the two audio elements are related by octave or unison, making the combination especially smooth in terms of pitch; in 41 per cent of all possible combinations, the pitch A is not present in the score, but the combination of the dialogue-text sound with the score produces only consonant intervals (perfect fourths or fifths, or major or minor thirds or sixths, including octave equivalents). In short, 68 per cent of the time, while

[19] Elizabeth Medina-Gray, 'Analyzing Modular Smoothness in Video Game Music', *Music Theory Online* 25, no. 3 (2019), accessed 20 October 2020, www.mtosmt.org/issues/mto.19.25.3/mto.19.25.3.medina.gray.html.

a player reads dialogue text in the throne room, the accompanying sound agrees with the simultaneous score in terms of pitch. More broadly, almost all of the dialogue in this game happens in the castle and town locations, and around two-thirds of the time, the addition of an A on top of the music in any of these locations produces a smooth combination in terms of pitch. The dialogue-text sounds' onsets sometimes briefly align with the score's meter, but irregular pauses between the sound's repetitions keep the sound from fully or obviously becoming music, and keep it mainly distinct from the score. Even so, agreement in pitch frequently emphasizes this sound's semi-musical quality.

Further musical connections also exist between the dialogue-text sound and score. The throne room's score (see Example 11.1) establishes an A-minor tonality, as does the similar score for the castle's neighbouring courtyard area; in this tonal context, the pitch A gains special status as musically central and stable, and the repeated sounds of lengthy dialogue text can form a tonic drone (an upper-register pedal tone) against which the score's shifting harmonies push and pull, depart and return. The towns in *Dragon Quest* feature an accompanying score in F major, which casts the dialogue-text sound in a different – but still tonal – role, as the third scale degree (the mediant).

Finally, although the sound that accompanies dialogue text in *Dragon Quest* bears little resemblance to a human voice on its own, the game consistently attaches this sound to characters' speech, and so encourages an understanding of this sound as dialogue. Indeed, other boxes with textual messages for players (describing an item found in a chest, giving battle information, and so on), although visually very similar to boxes with dialogue text, do not trigger the repeated A5 tone with the appearing text, leading this dialogue-text sound to associate specifically with speech rather than the appearance of just any text. With such a context, this sound may reasonably be construed as adhering to the visible people as well as to their text – in other words, the sound can be understood as produced by the gameworld's inhabitants as much as it is produced by the appearance of dialogue text (and players' triggering of this text). In a game in which the bodies of human characters are visually represented by blocky pixels, only a few colours and limited motions, it does not seem much of a stretch to imagine that a single tone could represent the sounds produced by human characters' vocal chords. As William Cheng points out, in the context of early (technologically limited) games, acculturated listeners 'grew ears to extract maximum significance from minimal sounds'.[20] And if we consider

---

[20] Cheng, *Sound Play*, 58.

the Famicom/NES sound chip to be similar to a musical instrument, then *Dragon Quest* continues a long tradition in which musical instruments attempt to represent human voices; Theo van Leeuwen suggests that such instrumental representations 'have always been relatively abstract, perhaps in the first place seeking to provide a kind of discourse about the human voice, rather than seeking to be heard as realistic representations of human voices'.[21] Although the dialogue-text sound in *Dragon Quest* does not directly tap into the effects that recorded human voices can bring to games (see the discussion of the benefits of dialogue earlier in this chapter), *Dragon Quest*'s representational dialogue sound may at least reference such effects and open space for players to make imaginative connections between sound and body. Finally, in the moments when this sound's pitch (A5) fits well with the simultaneous score (and perhaps especially when it coincides with a tonic A-minor harmony in the castle's music), the score highlights the semi-musical qualities in this dialogue sound, so that characters may seem to be intoning or chanting, rather than merely speaking. In this game's fantastical world of magic and high adventure, I have little trouble imagining a populace that speaks in an affected tone that occasionally approaches song.

Blurring Sound Effects and Music in More Recent Games

As video game technology has advanced in recent decades, a much greater range and fidelity of sounds have become possible. Yet many video games continue to challenge the distinctions between music, sound effects and dialogue in a variety of ways. Even the practice of using abstract pitched sounds to accompany dialogue text – expanded beyond the single pulse-wave pitch of *Dragon Quest* – has continued in some recent games, despite the increased capability of games to include recorded voices; examples include *Undertale* (2015) and games in the Ace Attorney series (2001–2017).

The remainder of this chapter focuses primarily on ways in which the categories of sound effects and music sometimes blur in more recent games. Certain developers and certain genres of games blur these two elements of soundscapes with some frequency. Nintendo, for instance, has a tendency to musicalize sound effects, for example, in the company's

---

[21] Theo van Leeuwen, 'Vox Humana: The Instrumental Representation of the Human Voice', in *Voice: Vocal Aesthetics in Digital Arts and Media*, ed. Norie Neumark, Ross Gibson and Theo van Leeuwen (Cambridge, MA: The MIT Press, 2010), 5–15 at 5.

flagship Mario series, tying in with aesthetics of playfulness and joyful fun that are central to these games.[22] Horror games, for example, *Silent Hill* (1999), sometimes incorporate into their scores sounds that were apparently produced by non-musical objects (e.g., sounds of squealing metal, etc.) and so suggest themselves initially as sound effects (in the manner of auditory icons); William Cheng points out that such sounds in *Silent Hill* frequently blur the boundaries between diegetic and non-diegetic sounds, and can even confuse the issue of whether particular sounds are coming from within the game or from within players' real-world spaces, potentially leading to especially unsettling/horrifying experiences for players.[23] Overall, beyond any particular genre or company, an optional design aesthetic seems to exist in which sound effects can be considered at least potentially musical, and are worth considering together with the score; for instance, in a 2015 book about composing music for video games, Michael Sweet suggests that sound designers and composers should work together to 'make sure that the SFX don't clash with the music by, for example, being in the wrong key'.[24]

The distinction between auditory icons and earcons provides a further lens through which to help illuminate the capabilities of sound effects to act as music. The naturalistic sounds of auditory icons do not typically suggest themselves as musical, while the pitched and/or rhythmic content of earcons cast these sounds as at least semi-musical from the start; unlike auditory icons, earcons are poised to extend across the boundary into music, if a game's context allows them to do so.

Following the framework introduced during this chapter's analysis of sounds in *Dragon Quest*, a score provides an important context that can critically influence the musicality of simultaneous sound effects. Some games use repeated metric agreement with a simultaneous score to pull even auditory icons into the realm of music; these naturalistic sounds typically lack pitch with which to agree or disagree with a score, so metric agreement is enough to cast these sounds as musical. For example, in the Shy Guy Falls racing course in *Mario Kart 8* (2014), a regular pulse of mining sounds (hammers hitting rock, etc.), enters the soundscape as

---

[22] Tim Summers, *Understanding Video Game Music* (Cambridge, UK: Cambridge University Press, 2016), 193–7; Roger Moseley, *Keys to Play: Music as Ludic Medium from Apollo to Nintendo* (Berkeley: University of California Press, 2016), 236–74.

[23] Cheng, *Sound Play*, 99. For more on unsettling experiences arising from the use of sound-effect-like sounds in the music of *Silent Hill*, see Summers, *Understanding Video Game Music*, 127–30.

[24] Michael Sweet, *Writing Interactive Music for Video Games: A Composer's Guide* (Upper Saddle River, NJ: Addison-Wesley, 2015), 188.

a player drives past certain areas and this pulse aligns with the metre of the score, imbuing the game's music with an element of both action and location.

Frequently, though, when games of recent decades bring sound effects especially closely into the realm of music, those sound effects are earcons, and they contain pitch as well as rhythmic content (i.e., at least one onset). This is the case, for example, in *Bit.Trip Runner* (2010), a side-scrolling rhythm game in which the main character runs at a constant speed from left to right, and a player must perform various manoeuvres (jump, duck, etc.) to avoid obstacles, collect items and so on. Earcons accompany most of these actions, and these sound effects readily integrate into the ongoing simultaneous score through likely consonance between pitches as well as careful level design so that the various actions (when successful) and their corresponding earcons align with pulses in the score's metre (this is possible because the main character always runs at a set speed).[25] In this game, a player's actions – at least the successful ones – create earcons that are also music, and these physical motions and the gameworld actions they produce may become organized and dance-like.

In games without such strong ludic restrictions on the rhythms of players' actions and their resulting sounds, a musical treatment of earcons can allow for – or even encourage – a special kind of experimentation in gameplay. Elsewhere, I have examined this type of situation in the game *Flower* (2009), where the act of causing flowers to bloom produces pitched earcons that weave in and out of the score (to different degrees in different levels/environments of the game, and for various effects).[26] Many of Nintendo's recent games also include earcons as part of a flexible – yet distinctly musical – sound design; a detailed example from *Super Mario Galaxy* (2007) provides a final case study on the capability of sound effects to become music when their context allows it.

Much of *Super Mario Galaxy* involves gameplay in various galaxies, and players reach these galaxies by selecting them from maps within domes in the central Comet Observatory area. When a player points at

---

[25] For more details, see Steven Reale's transcription of portions of *Bit.Trip Runner*'s score and earcons: Steven B. Reale, 'Transcribing Musical Worlds; or, Is *L.A. Noire* a Music Game?', in *Music in Video Games: Studying Play*, ed. K. J. Donnelly, William Gibbons and Neil Lerner (New York: Routledge, 2014), 77–103 at 82–9.

[26] Elizabeth Medina-Gray, 'Musical Dreams and Nightmares: An Analysis of *Flower*', in *The Routledge Companion to Screen Music and Sound*, ed. Miguel Mera, Ronald Sadoff and Ben Winters (New York: Routledge, 2017), 562–76.

Example 11.2 The galaxy maps (excerpt), *Super Mario Galaxy*

a galaxy on one of these maps (with the Wii remote), the galaxy's name and additional information about the galaxy appear on the screen, the galaxy enlarges slightly, the controller vibrates briefly and an earcon consisting of a single high-register tone with a glockenspiel-like timbre plays; although this earcon always has the same timbre, high register and only one tone, the pitch of this tone is able to vary widely, depending on the current context of the simultaneous score that plays during gameplay in this environment. For every harmony in the looping score (i.e., every bar, with this music's harmonic rhythm), four or five pitches are available for the galaxy-pointing earcon; whenever a player points at a galaxy, the computer refers to the current position of the score and plays one tone (apparently at random) from the associated set. Example 11.2 shows an excerpt from the beginning of the score that accompanies the galaxy maps; the pitches available for the galaxy-pointing earcon appear above the notated score, aligned with the sections of the score over which they can occur. (The system in Example 11.2 applies to the typical dome map environments; in some special cases during gameplay, the domes use different scores and correspondingly different systems of earcon pitches.) All of these possible sounds can be considered instances of a single earcon with flexible pitch, or else several different earcons that all belong to a single close-knit family. Either way, the consistent components of these sounds (timbre, register and rhythm) allow them to adhere to the single action and provide consistent feedback (i.e., that a player has successfully highlighted a galaxy with the cursor), while distinguishing these sounds from other elements of the game's soundscape.

All of the available pitches for the galaxy-pointing earcons are members of the underlying harmony for the corresponding measure – this harmony appears in the most rhythmically consistent part of the score, the bottom two staves in Example 11.2. With this design, whenever a player points at a galaxy, it is extremely likely that the pitch of the resulting earcon will agree with the score, either because this pitch is already sounding at a lower register in the score (77 per cent of the time), or because the pitch is not already present but forms only consonant intervals with the score's pitches at that moment (11 per cent of the time). Since the pitches of the score's underlying harmony do not themselves sound throughout each full measure in the score, there is no guarantee that earcons that use pitches from this harmony will be consonant with the score; for example, if a player points at a galaxy during the first beat of the first bar of the score and the A♭ (or C) earcon sounds, this pitch will form a mild dissonance (a minor seventh) with the B♭ in the score at that moment. Such moments of dissonance are relatively rare (12 per cent of the time), however; and in any case, the decaying tail of such an earcon may still then become consonant once the rest of the pitches in the bar's harmony enter on the second beat.

The score's context (and careful programming) is thus very likely to reaffirm the semi-musical quality of each individual galaxy-pointing earcon through agreement in pitch. When a player points at additional galaxies after the first (or when the cursor slips off one galaxy and back on again – Wii sensors can be finicky), the variety of pitches in this flexible earcon system can start to come into play. Such a variety of musical sounds can open up a new way of interacting with what is functionally a level-selection menu; instead of a bare-bones and entirely functional static sound, the variety of musical pitches elicited by this single and otherwise mundane action might elevate the action to a more playful or joyful mode of engagement, and encourage a player to further experiment with the system (both the actions and the sounds).[27] A player could even decide to 'play' these sound effects by timing their pointing-at-galaxy actions in such a way that the earcons' onsets agree with the score's metre, thus bringing the sound effects fully into the realm of music. Flexible earcon systems

---

[27] For more on the sound design of *Super Mario Galaxy* and the developers' intentions, and an account of one author's experience of delight when encountering musical interactivity in this game, see Summers, *Understanding Video Game Music*, 193–7.

similar to the one examined here occur in several other places in *Super Mario Galaxy* (for example, the sound when a player selects a galaxy in the map after pointing at it, and when a second player interacts with an enemy). In short, the sound design in *Super Mario Galaxy* allows for – but does not insist on – a particular type of musical play that compliments and deepens this game's playful aesthetic.

Music, sound effects and dialogue each bring a wide variety of effects to video games, and the potential for innovative and engaging experiences with players only expands when the boundaries between these three sonic categories blur. This chapter provides an entry point into the complex issues of interactive soundscapes, and suggests some frameworks through which to examine the musicality of various non-score sounds, but the treatment of video game soundscapes here is by no means exhaustive. In the end, whether the aim is to analyse game audio or produce it, considering the multiple – and sometimes ambiguous – components of soundscapes leads to the discovery of new ways of understanding game music and sound.

12 | Analytical Traditions and Game Music: *Super Mario Galaxy* as a Case Study

STEVEN REALE[*]

Ludomusicologists generally agree that cinema and television represent the nearest siblings to video games, and so therefore adopt many methodologies familiar to film music scholarship in their work. For example, the influential concepts of *diegetic* and *non-diegetic*, which respectively describe sounds that exist either within or outside a narrative frame,[1] feature prominently in many accounts of game audio, and represent one axis of Karen Collins's model for the uses of game audio, the other being *dynamic* and *non-dynamic*, where dynamic audio can be further subcategorized as *adaptive* or *interactive*.[2] Ludomusicologists generally also agree that the interactive nature of video games marks its primary distinction from other forms of multimedia, and so a fundamental point of entry into studying game audio is to examine how composers and sound designers create scores and soundtracks that can adapt to indeterminate player actions.

Indeterminacy, though, creates a challenge for modern music theory, which is founded on the close study of musical scores, subjecting to detailed analysis the dots, curves and lines inscribed on their pages to reveal the musical structures and organizational patterns that drive their composition. For music theorists, who may be most comfortable examining music that has been fixed into notation in the form of a musical score, indeterminacy raises additional questions and problems: how does one analyse music for which there is no single agreed-upon structure, and which may be realized in a fundamentally different way every time it is heard? Because of this problem, music theory, alongside historical musicology, has been vulnerable to criticism for its tendency to privilege the notated score above other forms and artefacts of musical creativity.

---

[*] The author wishes to thank the editors of this volume, as well as Scott Murphy, for their considerable feedback and suggestions during the process of preparing this chapter.

[1] Claudia Gorbman, *Unheard Melodies: Narrative Film Music* (Indiana University Press, 1987), 22.

[2] Collins also notes that the interactive nature of video games creates further complications of the diegetic/non-diegetic divide. Karen Collins, *Game Sound: An Introduction to the History, Theory and Practice of Video Game Music and Sound Design* (Cambridge, MA: The MIT Press, 2008), 125–7.

Don Michael Randel has observed, for example, that in popular music, '"the work itself" is not so easily defined and certainly not in terms of musical notation'.[3] In that vein, Lydia Goehr's study, *The Imaginary Museum of Musical Works*, has become a gold-standard critical handbook of philosophical approaches to the concept of 'the musical work', and one of her first tasks is to dispense with the notion that the work (if such a thing exists at all) can be fully encapsulated by the musical score – even in the case of a common-practice composition for which an authoritative score exists.[4] Other scholarship, such as Jean-Jacques Nattiez's *Music and Discourse*,[5] has criticized the manner by which privileging the musical score presumes a direct communicative act between composer and listener that treats the role of the performer as ancillary. At worst, score-centric analysis may even suggest – or explicitly claim – that the need for musical performance reflects an unfortunate real-world compromise to an ideal situation in which musical ideas could be communicated from composer to listener without mediation. Heinrich Schenker's opening line of *The Art of Performance* makes this argument in a particularly bold and provocative way: 'Basically, a composition does not require a performance to exist.'[6] And what is more, some mid-twentieth-century composers embraced electronic music specifically for its potential to eliminate the need for human performance.[7]

At best, music theorists might isolate single improvised performances as case studies, freezing them into musical notation to subject them to conventional analytical methodologies. But such strategies fail when applied to the analysis of ever-changing video game music. While a single performance of Charlie Parker and Dizzy Gillespie performing Tadd Dameron's *Hot House* might achieve canonical heights worthy of

[3] Don Michael Randel, 'The Canons in the Musicological Toolbox', in *Disciplining Music: Musicology and Its Canons*, ed. Katherine Bergeron and Philip V. Bohlman (Chicago: The University of Chicago Press, 1992), 10–22 at 15.

[4] Lydia Goehr, *The Imaginary Museum of Musical Works* (Oxford: Clarendon, 1992).

[5] Jean-Jacques Nattiez's *Music and Discourse: Toward a Semiology of Music*, trans. Carolyn Abbate (Princeton: Princeton University Press, 1990).

[6] Heinrich Schenker, *The Art of Performance*, ed. Heribert Esser, trans. Irene Schreier Scott (New York: Oxford University Press, 2000), 3. Nicholas Cook, *Beyond the Score* (New York: Oxford University Press, 2013) provides a detailed account of the discursive problems attending music theory's emphasis of the score and relegation of performance.

[7] See Milton Babbitt, 'The Revolution in Sound: Electronic Music (1960)', in *The Collected Essays of Milton Babbitt*, ed. Stephen Peles with Stephen Dembski, Andrew Mead and Joseph N. Straus (Princeton University Press, 2003), 70–7; also Frank Zappa with Peter Occhiogrosso, *The Real Frank Zappa Book* (New York: Touchstone, 1989), 172–4.

transcription and close study, no single playthrough of a video game could ever be understood as definitive, and it is typically very difficult, if not impossible, to play a video game exactly the same way twice. A compelling analysis of a video game score, then, requires methodologies that are a bit alien to some assumptions that currently govern music-theoretical practice. We must heed David Lewin, who once described his analytic method 'as a space of theoretical potentialities, rather than a compendium of musical practicalities',[8] and yet go further, developing as we do approaches that can analyse music as both a set of theoretical potentialities and an adjoining set of *practical musical potentialities*, introduced whenever a video game score implements algorithmic solutions that provide satisfactory continuations to moments of musical indeterminacy. In short, many theoretical methodologies are not readily equipped to analyse game audio; existing toolsets must be reworked and new ones devised to grapple with this protean music.[9] This is a good thing: analytic methodologies are not destroyed but tempered and strengthened when reforged for use with new materials. This essay examines excerpts from *Super Mario Galaxy* (2007) through the lens of three music-theoretical methodologies in current practice – formal, reductive and transformational – demonstrating how the idiomatic nature of video game storytelling has a substantial impact on the utility of the analytical tools used to study its music.

The central conceit of *Super Mario Galaxy* is that the perennial villain Bowser has once again kidnapped Mario's beloved Princess Peach and is travelling through the universe with her as his prisoner. After some introductory levels, Mario finds himself on a space observatory, which, due to its low power levels, is only able to observe a small set of galaxies, the game's basic platforming stages. Each galaxy is associated with one or more missions; through completing them, Mario accumulates 'power stars', which re-energize the Observatory so that it is able to reach further out

---

[8] David Lewin, *Generalized Musical Intervals and Transformations* (New Haven: Yale University Press, 1987), 27.

[9] For some existing approaches, see Elizabeth Medina-Gray, 'Modular Structure and Function in Early 21st-Century Video Game Music' (PhD dissertation, Yale University, 2014); Tim Summers, 'Analysing Video Game Music: Sources, Methods and a Case Study', in *Ludomusicology: Approaches to Video Game Music*, ed. Michiel Kamp, Tim Summers and Mark Sweeney (Sheffield: Equinox Publishing, 2016), 8–31; and Steven Reale, 'Transcribing Musical Worlds; or, is *L.A. Noire* a Music Game?' in *Music in Video Games: Studying Play*, ed. K. J. Donnelly, William Gibbons and Neil Lerner (New York: Routledge, 2014), 77–103.

into space, allowing Mario access to more galaxies with more power stars, and ultimately Bowser's hideout.

Methodology 1: Formal Analysis – Theme and Variation

Elaine Sisman, in her article on variation in *The New Grove Dictionary of Music and Musicians*, defines it as 'A form founded on repetition, and as such an outgrowth of a fundamental musical and rhetorical principle, in which a discrete theme is repeated several or many times with various modifications', and she shows that one purpose of the form is *epideixis*, a rhetoric of ceremony and demonstration, where the purpose of the repetitions is to amplify, 'revealing in ever stronger terms the importance of the subject'.[10] In a classical set, the listener is often presented with variations of greater and greater complexity with the final variation serving as a climactic whirlwind of virtuosity that Roger Moseley has described as a musical *ilinx*, a 'dizzying, unruly play of motion'.[11] Musical variations appear in the score to *Super Mario Galaxy*, which features compositions that are readily understood as variations of others. I will consider two examples here: the developing orchestration to the Observatory Waltz, and the fragmenting of the Battlerock music in subsequent galaxies.

The waltz accompanies Mario's exploration of the Observatory, during which it becomes evident that because the Observatory is not fully powered, there are many dark, inaccessible sections in it (see Figure 12.1). The waltz is sparsely orchestrated: after an introductory standing-on-the-dominant, a vibraphone carries the melody with a simple bass accompaniment played by a cello; the harmonic progression of the passage is thus implied by a two-voice contrapuntal framework (see Example 12.1). As Mario explores the galaxy and accumulates power stars, the Observatory is re-energized, and more areas become illuminated and accessible (see Figure 12.2). As this happens, the waltz becomes more lushly orchestrated and new counter-melodies are added. Example 12.2 presents an excerpt from the final stage of musical development: the bassline, still articulated by the cello, is joined by horns that fill out the chords in an oom-pah-pah rhythm. Violins now carry the basic melody, adding an expressivity not present in the vibraphone, and the flute, which in the earlier iteration simply doubled the vibraphone upon

[10] Elaine Sisman, 'Variation', in *Grove Music Online*, http://oxfordmusiconline.com (accessed 26 November 2020).
[11] Roger Moseley, *Keys to Play: Music as a Ludic Medium from Apollo to Nintendo* (Oakland, CA: University of California Press, 2016), 27.

Figure 12.1 Comet Observatory, early; note darkened, inaccessible area in background*

* The author thanks Ryan Thompson and Dana and Joseph Plank for their assistance creating the gameplay stills in this chapter.

Example 12.1 Comet Observatory waltz, early (excerpt). All transcriptions by the author

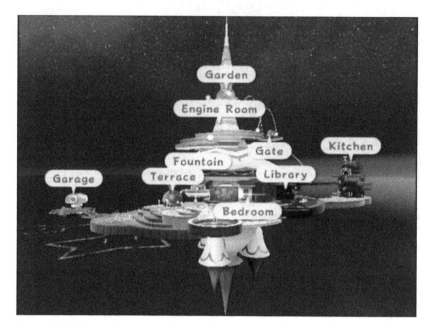

Figure 12.2 Comet Observatory, late; background now illuminated and accessible

Example 12.2 Comet Observatory waltz, late (excerpt)

Example 12.3 Reduction of Battlerock Galaxy music, first theme (excerpt)

repetition, now sounds a new melody in counterpoint with the violins. The rich variations of the basic waltz theme thus become an aural metaphor for the enlivened Observatory and the wide array of areas that are now open for play and exploration. Moreover, the variations do not appear simply as an exercise in progressive musical elaborations that we, the players, passively hear. Rather, the player, through Mario, is afforded a degree of agency in causing the variations' development: it is through our actions that the Observatory is re-energized, and so, within the fiction of the gameworld, it is we who bring about the subsequent variations.

In a case opposite to the first example, a theme is varied by stripping its elements down – reduction, rather than elaboration: in an early stage, the Battlerock Galaxy, Mario leaps between platforms and dodges bullets and force fields beside and through an enormous battle station built into an asteroid. The level's music, a brief reduction of which is excerpted in Example 12.3, features a martial and memorably tuneful scoring that alternates between two primary melodies with a march-like accompaniment, resembling countless science-fiction space epics, like *Star Wars* (1977), or the original *Battlestar Galactica* television series (1978–1979).

The music appears in an unaltered form in the later 'Dreadnought Galaxy', and the repetition of the theme connects the military qualities of the battleship with the earlier battle station. However, the initial introduction to this galaxy takes place in a sequence entitled 'Infiltrating the Dreadnought', in which Mario sneaks onto the ship by way of a pipe hidden on its side. During this portion of the level, the music that plays is a nearly unrecogniz-able, minimalistic version of the Battlerock tune: entitled 'Space Fantasy' on

Example 12.4 Reduction of 'Space Fantasy' (excerpt), same passage as that associated with Example 12.3. Although the surface chords change in the sixth bar of Example 12.3, the arpeggios that play beneath them at that point are the same as they appear here

the official soundtrack release,[12] the string melody has disappeared, and the basic chord progression is implied only by the frantic, unpredictably leaping arpeggios that appear deep in the mix of the Battlerock music (see Example 12.4). If we imagine the process of variation to be one of further elaboration of a basic structure, then the 'Space Fantasy' music serves as a kind of *anti-variation*, having stripped the Battlerock music of its elaborations to provide only its basic structure. There is a clever thematic parallel to the story taking place on screen: Mario's 'infiltration' of the Dreadnought implies that he stealthily evades detection during his entry – how fitting, then, that the musical accompaniment is a furtive echo of the bombastic battle tune, whose presence is so subtle that it may even elude detection by the player.

'Space Fantasy' underscores several other galaxies as well, including the 'Matter Splatter Galaxy'. Though this level mostly consists of a nebulous void, surfaces appear when droplets of matter fall in the manner of raindrops splattering on pavement, and as these 'dry up', the platforms that they comprise vanish until new ones fall in their place (see Figure 12.3). Once again, the appearance of the Battlerock tune invites the observant listener to conceptually connect these ostensibly disparate levels and to imagine a narrative thread that connects them. Perhaps the matter-splatter phenomenon is the result of a devastating battle that once took place, and just as the

---

[12] Mario Galaxy Orchestra, *Super Mario Galaxy: Official Soundtrack Platinum Edition* (Nintendo, 2007).

Figure 12.3 Matter Splatter Galaxy

'Space Fantasy' presents a disjointed, nearly unrecognizable anti-variation of the Battlerock theme, so too has all of the matter of the galaxy been fragmented, with only the sparsest bits being recognizable as traversable ground.

Elsewhere, I have examined the interaction of theme and variations with gameplay in *Portal 2* (Valve Corporation, 2011).[13] There, I showed that there was a distinct correlation of the game's procedures for training the player in its mechanics with a development in the musical accompaniments: that the gameplay itself is organized according to the musical principle of theme and variations. *Portal 2* is not unique in this regard; video games are often designed around iterative storytelling and gameplay mechanics: video game stories are often told and retold.[14] In the world of *Super Mario Bros.* this could mean an iterative story in which Mario explores three stages plus a fortress, only to find that 'OUR PRINCESS IS IN ANOTHER CASTLE', meaning that he must repeat the exercise seven more times in increasingly difficult challenges. It could also mean the iterative process by which almost all entries in the franchise involve Bowser kidnapping Peach and Mario exploring grander and grander spaces (Land ... World ... Galaxy) to rescue her, with each title introducing and requiring of the player more and more complex

13 Steven Reale, 'Variations on a Theme by a Rogue AI: Music, Gameplay, and Storytelling in *Portal 2*', *SMT-V: The Videocast Journal of the Society for Music Theory* 2, no. 2 and 2, no. 3 (August and December 2016), www.smt-v.org/archives/volume2.html#variations-on-a-theme-by-a-rogue-ai-music-gameplay-and-storytelling-in-portal-2-part-1-of-2 (accessed 26 November 2020).

14 On 'iterative narration', see Gérard Genette, *Narrative Discourse: An Essay in Method*, trans. Jane Levin (Ithaca, NY: Cornell University Press, 1980), 113–60.

gameplay techniques to do so.[15] Given this narratological structure, which is fundamental to the series, the similarly iterative musical principle of theme and variations offers a particularly well suited means of accompanying Mario's adventures.

Methodology 2: Reductive Analysis

Twentieth-century tonal music theory in North America was dominated by Schenkerian analysis, a methodology developed in the first half of the twentieth century by pianist, composer and editor Heinrich Schenker (1868–1935). Schenkerian analysis is a form of reductive analysis with two essential features: first, it examines a piece with the goal of determining which of its pitches are structural and which are ornamental. A structural pitch is emblematic of a governing harmony at a particular moment, and may be decorated, or *prolonged*, by ornamental ones. The process occurs on several levels of resolution, referred to as the foreground, middleground and background. A foreground analysis accounts for nearly every note of a work's outer voices (bass and soprano). Notes determined to be structural at the foreground level are then reproduced at a middleground level, and are once again examined to determine their relative structural or ornamental significance in that higher-order context. The process can continue through several layers of middleground, but eventually the analysis will identify a specific set of tones that cannot be reduced further: these pitches constitute the background. One of the greatest insights of Schenker's theory is the idea that tonal processes are *self-similar* – that is, those that govern the musical surface *also* govern the deepest structure of a work, up to and including the background.

The background level also highlights the second essential feature of the methodology: for Schenker, tonal music is organized around a teleological

---

[15] Video game reviewer Ben ('Yahtzee') Croshaw humorously observes that the world design of most games in the Super Mario franchise have an iterative structure as well; from his review of *Super Mario Odyssey* (2017): 'You guessed it: it's the classic ditty: "Grasslands, Desert, Ocean, Jungle, Ice World, Fire World, Boss"'. Ben Croshaw, 'Zero Punctuation: Super Mario Odyssey', *Escapistmagazine.com* (8 November 2017; accessed 26 November 2020) https://v1.escapistmagazine.com/videos/view/zero-punctuation/117154-Yahtzee-Reviews-Super-Mario-Odyssey. In his own meta-iterative way, Croshaw self-referentially echoes the same joke he has made in other reviews of franchise entries, such as 'Zero Punctuation: Mario & Luigi Paper Jam', *Escapistmagazine.com* (20 January 2016; accessed 26 November 2020) http://v1.escapistmagazine.com/videos/view/zero-punctuation/116678-Mario-Luigi-Paper-Jam-Review.

Figure 12.4 The two archetypal Schenkerian backgrounds (*Ursätze*). Schenker also allows for the theoretical possibility of a background that descends by octave, but these are rare in practice

principle whereby the pitch representing either scale degree 3 or scale degree 5 undertakes a descent to arrive at scale degree 1, accompanied by a bass arpeggiation outlining a I–V–I progression – the combination of the melodic descent and the bass arpeggiation is called the work's *Ursatz*, or fundamental structure (see Figure 12.4).[16] Tonal processes being self-similar, as noted above, a Schenkerian analysis is likely to identify many analogous teleological descents taking place in short form over the course of an entire work.

To some degree, Schenkerian methodologies have fallen out of favour, in part due to criticism from musicology for their ideological privileging of the Austro-Germanic musical tradition and assumptions about the relationship between organicism and genius, amongst others.[17] Indeed, a principal criticism of the theory is its circularity, in that it prioritizes a certain kind of musical organization, and then deems as 'good' works that conform to its desired criteria, such works having been carefully selected from the common-practice canon.[18] But perhaps even more importantly, the late twentieth century saw a general disciplinary widening of American music theory, from the purviews of both methodology and repertoire. On the one hand, this meant that music theorists began analysing works from outside the canon of Western art music, the tonal compositions in which Schenkerian elucidation finds its richest rewards. On the other hand, new analytical methodologies arose that, if not entirely supplanted, then at least displaced Schenkerian analysis from

---

[16] For detailed overviews of Schenkerian techniques, see Allen Cadwallader, David Gagné and Frank Samarotto, *Analysis of Tonal Music: A Schenkerian Approach*, 4th ed. (New York: Oxford University Press, 2019); and Allen Forte and Steven E. Gilbert, *Introduction to Schenkerian Analysis* (New York: Norton, 1982).

[17] Joseph Kerman, 'How We Got into Analysis, and How to Get Out', *Critical Inquiry* 7, no. 2 (1990): 311–31.

[18] Eugene Narmour, *Beyond Schenkerism: The Need for Alternatives in Music Analysis* (Chicago: University of Chicago Press, 1977), 28–30.

its position as the dominant toolset for studying triadic music – one of these, neo-Riemannian analysis, we will consider below.[19]

But while many criticisms of the theory as a whole are legitimate, that does not mean that it needs to be rejected wholesale: the techniques of reductive analysis that Schenker pioneered are powerful and can be employed without being oriented towards its problematic ends.[20] It is, for example, perfectly reasonable to assign structural significance to certain musical tones without needing to implicate them as part of a controversial *Ursatz*, and when I teach Schenkerian analysis to my own students, I emphasize how identifying the relative structural weight of specific notes in a melody can contribute to their vision for an artful performance regardless of how well those tones group on the background level in the abstract. Certainly, other productive ends are possible, too, and this section will focus on one sequence in *Super Mario Galaxy* – the battle with the boss character King Kaliente – to show how the musical logic of the encounter proposes a hearing that is captured particularly well through a reductive reading that departs from many of the central tenets of conventional Schenkerian theory.[21]

---

[19] Patrick McCreless offers a detailed and compelling account of the history of music theory as a twentieth-century North American academic discipline, including the rise and subsequent criticism of Schenkerian analysis. See his 'Rethinking Contemporary Music Theory', in *Keeping Score: Music Disciplinarity, Culture*, ed. David Schwarz, Anahid Kassabian and Lawrence Seigel (Charlottesville: University Press of Virginia, 1997), 13–53.

[20] As this book went to press, a new controversy arose that, as a consequence, severely undermines this position. During the plenary session of the 2019 meeting of the Society for Music Theory, Philip Ewell offered a presentation showing that a 'white racial frame' continues to permeate the discipline of music theory ('Music Theory's White Racial Frame', Society for Music Theory, Columbus, OH, 9 November 2019). As part of the presentation, Ewell included excerpts of Heinrich Schenker's writing in which he celebrates whiteness and castigates 'inferior races', and argued that Schenker's racist views not only cannot be isolated from his theory of music, but that they are in fact fundamental to it. In response, the *Journal of Schenkerian Studies* published a special issue responding to Ewell's paper (Volume 12, 2019). The issue drew considerable criticism, as the journal included an essay by an anonymous author, published ad hominem attacks against Ewell while failing to invite him to submit a response or any other kind of contribution and appeared to sidestep the peer-review process. On 7 July 2020, the Executive Board of the Society for Music Theory released a statement condemning the issue: 'The conception of this symposium failed to meet the ethical, professional, and scholarly standards of our discipline.' As Schenkerian analysis is a methodology at the core of American music theory (see McCreless, 'Rethinking Contemporary Music Theory'), the discipline can no longer wait to reckon with the ugly nature of its past, and Schenkerian practitioners can no longer bulwark by claiming as their purview the purely musical, believing it to be a realm cloistered from the messy humanity of music making. Ewell published an expanded version of his keynote talk in Philip Ewell, 'Music Theory and the White Racial Frame', *Music Theory Online* 26, no. 2 (September 2020).

[21] Two other modified Schenkerian applications to video music include Jason Brame, 'Thematic Unity in a Video Game Series', *Act: Zeitschrift für Musik und Performance 2* (2011), accessed 26 November 2020, www.act.uni-bayreuth.de/de/archiv/2011-02/03_Brame_Thematic_Unity/;

Figure 12.5 Mario volleys a coconut at King Kaliente

King Kaliente is encountered as part of a mission in the early Good Egg Galaxy. After navigating through the level, the player arrives on a planetoid on which is a pool of lava surrounded by a small ring of land. King Kaliente spits out two kinds of projectiles at Mario: fireballs, which must be dodged, and coconuts, which Mario must volley back at him (see Figure 12.5). The pattern of the battle is typical for Mario games: the first volley strikes the boss; on the second volley, the boss returns the coconut, which Mario must strike a second time before it connects; and on the third volley, the boss returns the coconut a second time, so Mario must strike it three consecutive times before it hits. Once it does, the encounter ends. In sum, on the first volley there are two hits – the first when Mario returns the coconut, and the second when it strikes King Kaliente; on the second volley there are four hits, and on the third volley six. Each hit is accompanied by a different tone, so on each successive volley two new tones are heard. The music that accompanies the battle alternates between two principal themes, and the pitches that sound with each hit change depending on which theme is playing. Table 12.1 presents the pitches that sound during the first theme only, but it is worth noting that both versions end on the same B♭.

and Peter Shultz, 'Music Theory in Music Games', in *From Pac-Man to Pop Music: Interactive Audio in Games and New Media*, ed. Karen Collins (Brookfield, VT: Ashgate Publishing Company, 2008), 177–88.

Table 12.1 Number of hits and pitches sounded
during each volley of the King Kaliente battle

Volley #	Number of hits	Pitches sounded
1	2	C, G
2	4	C, E♭, F, G
3	6	C, E♭, F, F♯, G, B♭

Figure 12.6 Reductive analysis of the King Kaliente hits

Figure 12.6 presents each of the three volleys in a rudimentary
Schenkerian notation. In so doing, it suggests a reading wherein each of
the successive volleys 'composes out' the preceding. Hence, the E♭ in
the second volley is seen as a consonant skip from the opening C, and the
F as an incomplete lower neighbour to the closing G: these additional tones
thus ornament the structural perfect fifth. In the third volley, the notes from
the second are given stems to indicate their relative structural weight as
compared to the newly added tones: the F♯, a chromatic passing tone
between the incomplete neighbour F and the structural G, and the B♭,
a consonant skip from the structural G.

Although the techniques used to create Figure 12.6 are heavily drawn
from Schenkerian practices, its interpretive implications are quite different. First, a conventional Schenkerian reading presupposes that the various levels examine the same passage of music at different degrees of
resolution: the background level presents only its most structurally significant tones, the middleground level presents all tones above a certain
threshold of structural significance and the foreground level replicates
most tones, if not every tone of the outer voices. In typical practice,
Schenkerian backgrounds and middlegrounds are not intended to reflect
passages that are literally heard in performance, let alone in serial

presentation,[22] yet here, the three successive volleys present, in order, background, middleground and foreground readings of a singular musical idea.

Figure 12.6 thus suggests that each successive volley is a *more musically detailed* version of the preceding one – that the tones accompanying the initial volley present only the background structure of the attack's musical logic, and that the successive attacks come closer and closer to its musical surface. That musical observation may cause us to recast our experience of the gameplay challenge presented to us. In principle, the structure of the encounter will be familiar to most gamers: once players master a simple gameplay mechanic, they are then asked to contend with more difficult and complicated variations of it. In this view, the first volley may be understood as a prototype that is developed and varied in the successive volleys. Instead, rather than seeing later iterations of the attack as complications of a basic process, the Schenkerian reading allows us to read the final volley as the fundamental process. Rather than the encounter representing the growth and development of a simple technique, it can be understood as an enacted actualization of a complex task through an iterative presentation of versions that begin simply and become progressively more complex. This way of thinking is not only native to gameplay design;[23] Jeffrey Swinkin has also shown that such a 'thematic actualization' is a productive lens for understanding Romantic variation sets, where 'variations retroactively define what the theme is' and 'themes often do not reside at a determinate point in musical space [i.e., at the beginning] but rather come into being gradually as the piece unfolds'.[24]

Second, Schenkerian logic takes the position that the move from foreground to background reveals the basic tonal structure of a composition through the revelation that each tone of the foreground in some way participates in the prolongation of the tones of the *Ursatz*, which features a descending scale in either the major or minor mode – a suitable enough distinction for the common-practice tonal works for which Schenkerian analysis is most effectively deployed.[25] Notably, the background presented

---

[22] A conventional scenario in which this might occur would be in a set of variations on a theme, but even there it would be unusual for successive variations to do nothing more than add additional ornamental tones to the version that came immediately before it.

[23] Frank L. Greitzer, Olga Anna Kuchar and Kristy Huston, 'Cognitive Science Implications for Enhancing Training Effectiveness in a Serious Gaming Context', *Journal on Educational Resources in Computing* 7, no. 3 (November, 2007), Article 2, accessed 26 November 2020, https://doi.org/10.1145/1281320.1281322.

[24] Jeffrey Swinkin, 'Variation as Thematic Actualisation: The Case of Brahms's Op. 9', *Music Analysis* 31, no. 1 (2012): 38–9.

[25] Although later theorists proposed other kinds of background structures besides those presented in Figure 12.4. See Walter Everett, 'Deep-Level Portrayals of Directed and Misdirected Motions in Nineteenth-Century Lyric Song', *Journal of Music Theory* 48, no. 1 (2004): 25–68.

Figure 12.7 Reductive analysis of first half of synth melody

Example 12.5 King Kaliente battle music (A theme only) (excerpt)

in Figure 12.6 does not resemble the conventional backgrounds of Figure 12.4. Furthermore, the King Kaliente battle music is composed in a modal idiom that is not well captured by a major/minor binary: specifically, the C-minor blues scale, the complete collection of which not only appears in the third volley, but also constitutes the basic piano vamp accompanying the encounter (see Example 12.5). Thus, it is the foreground, rather than the background level, that clarifies the tune's basic tonal language.

Crucially, notwithstanding the ways in which the present reductive reading diverges from conventional Schenkerian practice, it is still able to engage with the first of the central Schenkerian insights: that being the relationship between background structures and foreground gestures. Specifically, as already noted, the foreground version of the hits exactly replicate the piano vamp; moreover, as shown in Figure 12.7, the background of Figure 12.6 is identical to the background of the synth melody, which also features structural motion from C up to G – also note the resemblance of the foreground of Figure 12.6 to that of Figure 12.7: each features an initial consonant skip from C to E♭, an F# approach to G and registral and melodic prominence of a high B♭.

The nuances elucidated by a reductive analysis of the King Kaliente theme further provide an explanation for something that long ago caught my attention, and this relates to the second feature of Schenkerian methodology. Video games and Schenkerian analysis are similarly goal-oriented: in this example, the player's goal is to defeat the enemy, while in the *Ursätze* of Figure 12.4, the music's goal is to descend to C. When first encountering this boss fight and experiencing the musical coordination of pitch hits with Mario's attacks, I had expected that the final note would be the high C, thereby allowing the six-note figure of the third volley to cadence, thus co-ordinating musical closure with the end of the battle. Such a resolution would align well with other teleological theories, like Eugene Narmour's implication-realization model,[26] but a high C here would *not* serve a reductive reading well. First, as a cadential pitch, it would be tempting to grant it structural significance, but since it would only appear in the fore-ground version of the motive, there would be no compelling way to add it to the background version. Second, the presence of the B♭ is not only necessary to flesh out the complete blues scale, but it also ensures complete pitch variety for the third volley attack: a high C would replicate the pitch class of the first note. Finally, a high C does not participate at all in the musical surface of Example 12.5, except for a brief appearance as an incomplete upper neighbour to the B♭ in the second half of the melody – and so again, it would be a mistake to afford the high C the structural significance it would need to be a goal tone for the passage.

All told, then, the reductive reading presents a more compelling expla-nation for the pitch selection of the third volley than might a competing theory based on realized implications. In my modified Schenkerian view, the structural pitches of the encounter are C and G – a motive established in the first volley and confirmed in the second. But, and I thank Scott Murphy for phrasing it thusly, 'permanently vanquishing is categorically different than temporarily stunning',[27] and the third volley makes the distinction audibly clear. While the hits for each volley feature the same musical structure, it is only the final, successful volley that transcends the structural G to land on the vanquishing upper B♭.

---

[26] Eugene Narmour, *The Analysis and Cognition of Melodic Complexity: The Implication-Realization Model* (Chicago: University of Chicago Press, 1992).

[27] Personal email to the author, 27 January 2019.

The criticisms of the late twentieth century certainly impacted Schenkerian analysis's dominance within the field of North American music theory, but a thoughtful analysis can still carefully tailor the undeniably powerful and unique insights that the methodology is capable of elucidating while avoiding the larger ideological and contextual problems that hazard its practice. In my view, this is to be embraced: on the one hand, the jazzy King Kaliente music, like much music of the post-common-practice era, is not composed according to the assumptions that Schenkerian practice is designed to accommodate, and any attempt to 'Schenkerize' it according to them would be doomed to fail. On the other hand, the Observatory waltz of Examples 12.1 and 12.2 could, with relative ease, submit to a conventional Schenkerian reading with a normative *Ursatz*, but it is hard to imagine what the purpose of such an exercise would be, beyond making a claim that the Observatory waltz fulfils the tonal expectations of the common-practice idiom after which it is modelled, a fact that should already be obvious to anyone with enough background in music theory to 'Schenkerize' it. By contrast, reading the King Kaliente hits through a more flexible reductive instrument can certainly amplify and enhance our understanding of their specific idiomatic construction.

Methodology 3: Transformational Analysis

Current trends in transformational music theories began with the publication of David Lewin's *Generalized Musical Intervals and Transformations* (*GMIT*), and although Lewin's adaptation of mathematical group theory is designed to be applicable to any kind of musical structure, its most common current application is known as neo-Riemannian theory, which explores relationships between major and minor triads not from the standpoint of function (as did Hugo Riemann, the *fin-de-siècle* music theorist for whom it is named), but rather from the standpoint of voice-leading. As a theory that does not require that the tonal organizations it analyses orient chords with respect to a central tonic, neo-Riemannian theory is well equipped to handle triadic music of the late Romantic period and neo-Romantic music, where the latter enjoys a particular prominence in film scores.[28]

---

[28]   See, for example, Frank Lehman, 'Transformational Analysis and the Representation of Genius in Film Music', *Music Theory Spectrum* 35, no. 1 (Spring 2013): 1–22; Frank Lehman, *Hollywood Harmony: Musical Wonder and the Sound of Cinema* (New York: Oxford University Press, 2018); Scott Murphy, 'Transformational Theory and the Analysis of Film Music', in *The Oxford Handbook of Film Music Studies*, ed. David Neumeyer (New York: Oxford University

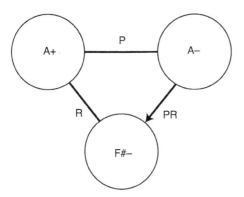

Figure 12.8 A neo-Riemannian network

A central technique of neo-Riemannian analysis – as early as its inception in *GMIT* – is the creation of visual networks that describe transformational relationships amongst chords. Figure 12.8 provides a sample neo-Riemannian network for a hypothetical musical passage with the chords A major, A minor and F♯ minor.

The diagram indicates that the closest relationship between A major and A minor is a **P** (Parallel) transformation, which holds the perfect fifth of a triad fixed and moves the remaining note by a half step. It also indicates that the closest relationship between A major and F♯ minor is an **R** (Relative) transformation, which holds the major third of a triad fixed and moves the remaining note by whole step. Finally, it indicates that the closest relationship between A minor and F♯ minor is a composite move where **P** is followed by **R**. The arrow between these latter two nodes indicates that the composite transformation **PR** will only transform A minor to F♯ minor; reversing the move requires reversing the transformations, so getting from F♯ minor to A minor requires the composite transformation **RP**.

There are three atomic transformations in neo-Riemannian theory: in addition to **P** and **R**, there is an **L** (Leading-tone exchange) transformation, which holds the minor third of a triad fixed and moves the remaining note by a half step. Any triad may be transformed into any other triad using some combination of these three basic moves. These basic transformations can be combined to form compound transformations, where, for example, **S** (Slide) = **LPR** or **RPL**, **H** (Hexatonic pole) = **PLP** or **LPL**, and **N** (Neighbour) = **PLR** or **RLP**. Some accounts of neo-Riemannian theory

Press, 2013), 471–99; and Guy Capuzzo, 'Neo-Riemannian Theory and the Analysis of Pop-Rock Music', *Music Theory Spectrum* 26, no. 2 (2004): 196–7.

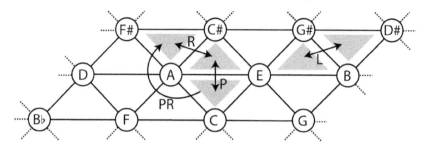

Figure 12.9 *Tonnetz* representation of the network in Figure 12.8 (left), and of the third atomic transformation, **L** (right)

treat these compound transformations as unary in their own right.[29] For the purposes of this chapter, I will be counting individual **P**, **L** and **R** moves when considering tonal distance, so that the compound transformations will be treated as three individual moves.

By itself, Figure 12.8 is of limited usefulness: ideally, networks will be deployed in the interest of a larger analytical point; say, drawing a hermeneutic meaning from its arrangement, like Frank Lehman's discussion of the Argonath sequence in *The Fellowship of the Ring* (Peter Jackson, 2001),[30] or showing that two disparate passages operate under the same transformational logic, such as David Lewin's comparison of the Tarnhelm and Valhalla motives in *Das Rheingold*.[31] Often such networks are treated according to the presumptions of mathematical graph theory – in such cases, all that matters is the specific relationship amongst the network's nodes and edges (here, chords and transformations) and its actual geometrical arrangement on the page is ancillary. Other times, theorists use a graph's visual appearance to suggest a specific analytical interpretation – for example, as is often the case in Lewin's diagrams, there could be a presumed temporal dimension that reads from left to right;[32] in Figure 12.8, perhaps the triads are heard in the order A major, F♯ minor, A minor.

In addition to analytic networks, another common way of visualizing harmonic motion is through a *Tonnetz* (see Figure 12.9). In such diagrams, pitch-classes are arranged along three axes – the horizontals represent

[29]   See, for example, Richard Cohn, *Audacious Euphony* (New York: Oxford University Press, 2012), 30.

[30]   Lehman, *Hollywood Harmony*, 192–7.

[31]   David Lewin, 'Some Notes on Analyzing Wagner: "The Ring" and "Parsifal"', *19th Century Music* 16, no. 1 (Summer 1992): 49–58.

[32]   Julian Hook, 'David Lewin and the Complexity of the Beautiful', *Intégral* 21 (2007): 155–90.

perfect fifths; the ascending diagonals major thirds; and the descending diagonals minor thirds. Triads are then represented by the triangles established by the axes: upward-pointing triangles represent major triads while downward-pointing triangles represent minor triads. Neo-Riemannian thinking presumes enharmonic equivalence; so, resembling the logic of *Pac-Man* (Namco, 1980), the diagram wraps around itself, establishing the doughnut-shaped geometric figure called a *torus*. To clarify: continuing along the lower horizontal past G leads to the D on the middle left; continuing down along the descending diagonal past the G leads to the B♭ on the lower left; and continuing down along the ascending diagonal from the G leads to the D♯ in the upper right, which is enharmonically equivalent to E♭. The *Tonnetz* makes visually clear how combinations of the atomic transformations create greater tonal distances – how, for example, the PR transformation is more tonally remote than any of the atomic transformations alone.[33]

A potentially puzzling aspect of neo-Riemannian networks is that we often understand music to be a *linear* art form, by which I mean that its events are usually performed and experienced through time in one specific order, and yet its diagrams present music on a plane, suggesting that its nodes can be explored in any number of ways. According to this logic, the chords in Figures 12.8 and 12.9 could appear in any order, with any number of internal repetitions. How can we reconcile the *planar, non-linear* aspect of neo-Riemannian theory's geometric representations with the conventionally *temporal, linear* manner in which music is experienced?

The problem is compounded when we consider that Lewin would prefer not to understand analytical networks from a bird's-eye perspective (what he calls the 'Cartesian view'), but rather wants to imagine a listener inhabiting the networks, experiencing them from a first-person perspective, which he calls the 'transformational attitude': "'If I am *at* [a point] s and wish to get to [a point] t'", Lewin asks, "'what characteristic gesture ...

---

[33] Amongst music theorists of a neo-Riemannian bent, it is not universally agreed that measuring tonal distance on the basis of counting individual neo-Riemannian transformations provides an unproblematic account of the voice-leading procedures it is intended to model. Tymoczko, for example, has shown that transforming F minor to C major (**PLR** or **RLP**) requires one more transformation than does transforming F major to C major (**LR**), whereas comparing the half-step between A♭ and G on the one hand and the whole-step between A and G on the other implies that the F minor is tonally closer to C major than is F major. Dmitri Tymoczko, 'Three Conceptions of Musical Distance', in *Mathematics and Computation and Music*, ed. Elaine Chew, Adrian Childs and Ching-Hua Chuan (Heidelberg: Springer, 2009), 258–72 at 264–7. For a detailed discussion of ways that the discrepancy may be reconciled, see Scott Murphy, 'Review of Richard Cohn, *Audacious Harmony: Chromaticism and the Triad's Second Nature*', *Journal of Music Theory* 58, no. 1 (2014): 79–101.

should I perform in order to arrive there?" . . . This attitude', he continues, 'is by and large the attitude of someone *inside* the music, as idealized dancer and/or singer. No external observer (analyst, listener) is needed'.[34] Considering again Figure 12.8, if we imagine ourselves *inside* the network, hearing these three chords from a first-person perspective, then what exactly would it mean for our musical experience to move 'clockwise' or 'counterclockwise'? And is there a conceptual difference between these two experiences that should dictate the placement of the network's nodes?

In contrast to instrumental music, and even music that accompanies opera, film, musical theatre or television – perhaps game music's closest relatives – video games are inherently spatial: when we play, we are very frequently tasked with directing a character – our in-game avatar – through a digital world.[35] Given that distinction, it is comparatively quite easy to imagine moving through a musical space, if that musical space is somehow co-ordinated with the virtual space the player moves through.

In *Super Mario Galaxy*, the principle way that the game space is organized is that the Comet Observatory serves as a central hub for a handful of domes; in each dome is a portal to a galaxy cluster, allowing Mario to select a specific galaxy to travel to. Some of these galaxies feature boss battles or other one-off tasks, and in such cases, the musical material is usually borrowed from similar levels elsewhere in the game. Table 12.2, then, lists each primary galaxy for each dome and the key centre for its principle musical accompaniment; I here define 'primary' galaxy to be one for which the game offers more than one mission. Observing that the Engine Room and Garden employ a lot of reused music (and one atonal tune without a clear key centre), the following discussion restricts its purview to the first four domes, which also happen to be the four domes that are accessible from the first floor of the Observatory.

Figure 12.10 reimagines the first four domes, along with the Comet Observatory as a central hub, as part of a transformational network. In so doing, it extends the logic of the neo-Riemannian transformations beyond labelling voice-leadings between adjacent chords in a local progression to encompass modulations between key areas, and describes them by the

---

[34] David Lewin, *Generalized Musical Intervals and Transformations*, 159. Emphasis original.

[35] Although theorizing a distinction between concepts like 'digital world', 'virtual space' and 'game space' is outside the scope of the present work, it is worth noting Melanie Fritsch's careful distinction between the concepts of 'gameworld' and 'diegetic environment'. See Melanie Fritsch, 'Worlds of Music: Strategies for Creating Music-based Experiences in Videogames', in *The Oxford Handbook of Interactive Audio*, ed. Karen Collins, Bill Kapralos and Holly Tessler (New York: Oxford University Press, 2014), 167–78 at 170.

Table 12.2 Primary galaxies with their key centres in *Super Mario Galaxy*

Dome	Galaxy	Key Centre	Notes
Terrace	Good Egg	C major	
	Honeyhive	C major	
Fountain	Space Junk	A♭ major	
	Battlerock	E major	
Kitchen	Beach Bowl	A major	
	Ghostly	D minor	
Bedroom	Gusty Garden	D♭ major	
	Freezeflame	D minor	
	Dusty Dune	E major	
Engine Room	Gold Leaf	C major	Reuses 'Honeyhive' music
	Sea Slide	A major	Reuses 'Beach Bowl' music
	Toy Time	C major	Uses theme from very first *Super Mario Bros.* game (Nintendo, 1985)
Garden	Deep Dark	N/A	Atonal – no clear key centre
	Dreadnought	E major	Reuses 'Battlerock' music
	Melty Molten	D minor	

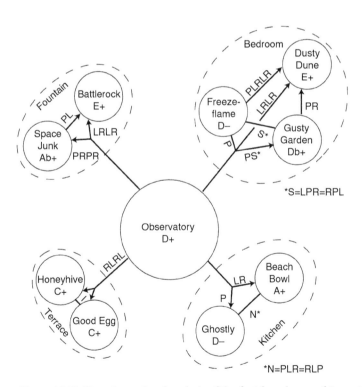

Figure 12.10 Transformational analysis of the first four domes of *Super Mario Galaxy*

transformations that would be required to move from one tonic triad to the next.[36] The diagram analyses the transformations needed to get from the key centre of the Observatory to any of the included galaxies, and also analyses transformations amongst galaxies that appear in a single dome. The length of each segment in the diagram is relative to the number of transformational moves it takes to get from key to key. Consider first the transformational connections within each dome: for domes 1, 2 and 3, there are only two primary galaxies, and therefore there is only one transformation: in the first dome, the Identity transformation maps C major onto C major; in the second dome, a composite **PL** transforms A♭ major into E major, for a total of two moves; and in the third dome, a composite transformation **N**, which requires three moves as shown in the figure, turns A major to D minor. The growth in transformational complexity is indicated by the relative lengths of the edges between the nodes, and as a result, the space of the tonal galaxy clusters gets progressively larger. The largest tonal galaxy cluster of the four, of course, is the Bedroom, owing to the multiplicity of transformational edges required to connect all of the nodes. Significantly, the player's access to each dome is unlocked in precisely the order from smallest to largest: Terrace, Fountain, Kitchen and Bedroom. Thus, progress through the available galaxy clusters is correlated with their internal tonal complexity.

Note too, that in almost every case, the tonal distance between galaxies within a dome is smaller than the tonal distance between the Observatory and the galaxy cluster, where this distance is measured as the combined number of transformational moves to get from the Observatory to the galaxies in one cluster. Thus, it takes a total of four transformations to get from the Observatory to the galaxies in the Terrace, eight to get to the Fountain, three to the Kitchen and nine to the Bedroom. These distances nicely capture the implied vast astronomical space between the Observatory and each cluster, relative to the smaller astronomical distance

---

[36] Dmitri Tymoczko has argued that voice-leading operations apply just as well to scales and modulations as they do to chords and progressions. See *A Geometry of Music: Harmony and Counterpoint in the Extended Common Practice* (New York: Oxford University Press, 2011), 17–19. Similarly, Steven Rings introduces the concept of 'pivot intervals' in his system of transformational analysis to describe modulations between keys. See *Tonality and Transformation* (New York: Oxford University Press, 2011), 58–66. It should be noted that both authors consider voice-leading operations as they operate on *scales* rather than tonic triads. By contrast, René Rusch proposes a 'Toveyian' blending of Schenkerian and neo-Riemannian procedures that examines modulations through Tovey's conception of key relations, which relates triads through modal mixture in a diatonic universe, and suggests the plausibility of the present approach. See René Rusch, 'Schenkerian Theory, Neo-Riemannian Theory and Late Schubert: A Lesson from Tovey', *Journal of the Society for Musicology in Ireland* 8 (2012–2013): 3–20.

between galaxies in any one cluster. Moreover, ordering the domes about the hub from shortest distance to longest replicates the order of the physical locations of each dome around the central hub of the Observatory. This implies a ready metaphor between the locations of each dome on the tonal map and their physical locations in the gameworld.

Whereas the planar logic of transformational networks often chafes against a typically linear listening experience, in the case of Figure 12.10, the spatial, exploratory nature of *Super Mario Galaxy*'s design readily lends itself to thinking about its musical score in a similarly spatial way. It is not difficult to imagine ourselves as listeners moving through Figure 12.10 in a first-person perspective, going from key area to key area in a manner isomorphic to the way that Mario travels between the Observatory and the various galaxies, because there is a ready metaphor that connects tonal distances with segment length and another that correlates size with tonal complexity; these metaphors are at the heart of a powerful interpretative resonance between the geography of the game and the geometry of the diagram. The composite tonal distances between the Observatory waltz and the galaxies of each cluster are correlated with the physical layout of the Comet Observatory. Tonal complexity within a cluster is correlated with the order in which Mario gains access to these four domes, which further suggests a reading that tonal complexity is also correlated with the game's power stars. This means that greater power to the Comet Observatory implies a capacity for listener-Mario to negotiate greater tonal complexity, just as character-Mario is being asked to negotiate more and more difficult platforming tasks. When transformational moves are correlated with astronomical distance, the organization of Figure 12.10 can imply how remote each cluster is from the Comet Observatory relative to how close they are to each other. And finally, there is a happy coincidence that Figure 12.10 itself resembles the star maps in the various domes that Mario uses to travel to the game's galaxies (see Figure 12.11). In these ways, Figure 12.10 presents a particularly apt representation of the musical – but also physical – adventures of Mario.

Conclusions

I began my research for this chapter by taking seriously two existential problems with modern music theory: first, the notion that a musical work can exist as a singular entity frozen in time through musical notation treats the act of musical performance as a supplement to the 'real' musical work

Figure 12.11 Travelling to the Good Egg Galaxy from the Terrace Dome

that takes place between composer and listener. The second is that the techniques and methodologies that underpin modern music theory are well suited to music frozen in time, but strain when asked to account for music that cannot be fixed in such a way. As a result, modern music theory is incentivized to privilege notated music and to downplay non-notated and improvised musics, even if these are vastly more characteristic of the grand scope of human music-making than the former.

As a practising music theorist, though, my experience has been that most analysts are sensitive musicians in their own right, who use theoretical tools to advance deeply musical insights that can inform performance. At the same time, it is certainly true that most analytical methodologies rely on treating some kind of fixed musical notation as an input and begin to break down when such notation can be neither acquired nor self-produced through transcription. But since there continues to exist vast amounts of music that can be fixed into notation, there has not generally been felt a widespread, urgent need to rework or revise existing methodologies to accommodate those that cannot. This has been true despite the experiments in the 1960s with chance-based, or *aleatoric*, music; or the rise of the cultural importance of jazz, rock, jam-band or dee-jayed electronic music, genres that may all rely on moment-by-moment indeterminacy. Furthermore, this is true despite the historical reality that the vast majority of human music-making has been improvised and non-notated: as Philip V. Bohlman has observed, 'The fundamentally oral nature of music notwithstanding, musicology's canons arise from the field's penchant for working with texts.'[37] In the end, the problem is a specific case of a general one, identified by literary theorists, that overlooks the reality that a present-day conception of artworks as unified, static entities is both recent and anomalous, stemming from a nineteenth-century European shift in patterns of cultural consumption.[38]

Each of the three methodologies in this chapter was intentionally selected to apply an analytical technique in current practice in the field – and, equivalently, a technique designed with fixed, notated music in mind – to a genre of music that is often dynamic and indeterminate. What excites me as a music theorist is that the theories did not break, but were instead refracted by the logic of the game's design. To adopt a video-gaming metaphor, the theories 'levelled-up': more than just proven in battle, they are enhanced and ready to take on new, challenging analytical encounters.

But of even greater significance than our ability to apply music-theoretical approaches to a new, underrepresented musical medium, is the realization that the indeterminate nature of video game play perhaps aligns the medium more closely with other improvised artistic practices than do its more static relatives in film, television or opera. Video game musical analysis requires that music theories grapple with uncertainty, and the toolsets used to analyse video game music can be adapted to shed light on other kinds of improvised musics. We can and should invert the obvious question – 'what can music theory tell us about game audio?' – and instead ask how video game music can transform music theory, and in so doing, create for it opportunities to study musics that at first glance seem wholly unrelated to those that accompany Mario's journeys through the universe.

---

[37] Philip V. Bohlman, 'Epilogue: Musics and Canons', in *Disciplining Music: Musicology and Its Canons*, ed. Katherine Bergeron and Philip V. Bohlman (Chicago: The University of Chicago Press, 1992), 197–210 at 202.

[38] See Terry Eagleton, *Literary Theory: An Introduction* (Minneapolis: University of Minnesota Press, 1983) and Walter J. Ong, *Orality and Literacy: 30th Anniversary Edition*, 3rd ed. (New York: Routledge, 2013).

13 | Semiotics in Game Music

IAIN HART

Introduction: Semiotics Is Not Hard

Playing a video game is a very communicative activity. Set aside the ideas that communication only happens between humans and that communication only happens with words. We communicate with animals, machines and the built environment all the time, conveying our needs, aspirations, designs and emotions as we live in and shape our world. We do the same when we play video games, inhabiting a virtual space and forging our path through it. Understanding how we communicate with a video game, and how a video game communicates with us, helps us understand the fundamental elements of the video game text (like graphics, sound, narrative and music) and how they fit together. It also helps us to be able to shape and direct those communications, if we are in the business of constructing or composing for video games.

One of the best ways to understand communication is to analyse the signs that are shared back and forth in communication and what they mean. This is known as 'semiotics'. There is an enduring and erroneous belief amongst the general population that semiotics is difficult and perhaps a little dry. The purpose of this chapter is to demonstrate firstly that semiotics is not all that complicated, and secondly, that semiotics can make sense of a lot of how video game music works. In fact, a lot of the core functions of game music are semiotic processes so simple we barely notice them, but so effective that they utterly transform gameplay.

Semiotics

What Are Signs?

Semiotics is the study of signs. Charles Sanders Peirce, who was the founder of one of the two main branches of semiotics (the more universal of the branches; the founder of the other, more linguistic branch was Ferdinand de Saussure), described a sign as 'anything, of whatsoever mode of being, which mediates between an object and an interpretant'.[1] The 'object' in Peirce's definition is relatively straightforward; it is a thing that exists, whether as a tangible lump of matter or as an abstract concept. The 'interpretant', meanwhile, is the effect of the object on one's mind – the idea that would typically pop into your mind in relation to that object. The 'sign', then, is the intermediary between a thing and an idea, or between the external world and the thought world. In fact, Peirce wrote that 'every concept and every thought beyond immediate perception is a sign'.[2] Furthermore, signs can be the likeness of the object, like a photograph; they can be an indication towards the object, like an emergency exit sign; or they can be a symbol that only represents the object by convention or by abstract relationship, like a word or the concept of tonality.[3]

Adopting such a broad definition of the term and concept of the 'sign' presents us with a massive scope of investigation from the very outset, which the astute semiotician will find profoundly liberating. If anything that represents something to us is a sign, then we are not bound by analogies to language systems or by prescriptive semantics. We can address meanings on the terms in which they are transmitted – describing them with words as humans are wont to do, but not assuming they will map neatly or even consistently to a set of words or concepts. This is quite handy when we look at music, which is a largely non-verbal and abstract medium (even singers can convey abstract and non-verbal meanings, like emotions, alongside the words being sung).[4] It becomes especially useful when we look at music in video games, where music can be directly associated with events, characters and areas, even while maintaining some level of abstraction from these things.

How Signs Are Used to Communicate

However, semiotics is *not necessarily* the study of communication. Jean-Jacques Nattiez, who developed a Peircean semiotics for music, observed that while communication through music is possible, it cannot be

---

[1] Charles Sanders Peirce, *The Essential Peirce: Selected Philosophical Writings*, ed. Peirce Edition Project, vol. 2 (Bloomington, IN: Indiana University Press, 1998), 410.

[2] Peirce, *The Essential Peirce*, 402.

[3] Peirce, *The Essential Peirce*, 5.

[4] Jean-Jacques Nattiez, *Music and Discourse: Toward a Semiology of Music*, trans. Carolyn Abbate (Princeton, NJ: Princeton University Press, 1990), 37; Philip Tagg, *Music's Meanings: A Modern Musicology for Non-Musos* (New York: The Mass Media Music Scholars' Press, 2013), 171.

guaranteed.[5] Communication depends on a meaning being inscribed by one person, then a corresponding meaning being interpreted by another person. It is possible for the other person to interpret a meaning that is completely different to the meaning inscribed by the first person – we might call this a *mis*-communication.[6] And music is generally very open to interpretation.

Music cannot prescribe its own meanings, except within cultural and textual conventions and relationships. It can 'connote' meanings by implying relationships outside of itself – evoking emotions like the sadness we feel in Beethoven's 'Moonlight Sonata',[7] or suggesting scenes like the flowing waters of Smetana's *Vltava*[8] – but it does not typically have a mechanism to 'denote' or exactly specify meanings. Any denotations we hear in music (and even many of its connotations) are contingent on external relationships. For example, Smetana's *Vltava* may suggest to us the movement of a grand river, but to do so it relies on our familiarity with Western musical tropes (such as the relationship between conjunct motion and the concept of 'flow'); to link the music to the eponymous Czech river itself requires the composer's direct explication in the title of the work.

Like all human creative output, music exists within contexts that provide such conventions, and it moves between contexts as it is encountered by people, in the process forming relationships between contexts. Even musical analysis (sometimes described as an investigation of 'the music itself') is what Theo van Leeuwen calls a 'recontextualization'; meanings tend to attach themselves to works as they are experienced and distributed, even (or especially?) when this is done with an analytical purpose.[9] The ever-present existence and never-ending negotiation of context allows music to be denotative, within specific bounds. For van Leeuwen, 'musical systems (systems of melody, harmony, rhythm, timbre, etc.) do have "independent" meaning, in the sense that they constitute meaning potentials which specify what kinds of things can be "said". . . . Meaning potentials delimit what *can* be said, the social context what *will* be said'.[10] So when we start playing a video game and hear its music, we are not accidentally listening to some tunes with no meaningful relationship to the images we see or the interactions we perform. Each element of a video game has an influence over the

---

[5] Nattiez, *Music and Discourse*, 17.

[6] Tagg, *Music's Meanings*, 177–8.

[7] Ludwig van Beethoven, Piano Sonata No. 14, Opus 27, No. 2, 1802.

[8] Bedřich Smetana, *Vltava* (or *The Moldau*), JB 1:112/2, 1874.

[9] Theo van Leeuwen, 'Music and Ideology: Notes Toward a Sociosemiotics of Mass Media Music', *Popular Music and Society* 22, no. 4 (1998): 25–6.

[10] Van Leeuwen, 'Music and Ideology', 26.

meanings we interpret in the other elements, resulting in a cohesive and semiotically rich experience filled with the *potential*, at least, for communication.

For a 'meaning potential' to turn into a 'meaning', the potential just needs to be fulfilled through experience, much like how specific decisions can affect the final stages of some games, giving you one ending from a set of possible endings. For a 'potential communication' to turn into a 'communication', however, there needs to be a correlation between the composer's intended meanings and the meaning suggested by the interpretants in the player's mind. This is a minefield. Game composers and developers can try to influence the interpretants that music will form in the player's mind by creating specific contexts for the music, such as by co-ordinating or juxtaposing music with other game elements. However, there are other factors that affect how the player's mind works (everything from their past gaming experience, to their personality, to what they had for dinner). Every experience the player has during gameplay has a meaning, but these meanings form part of a negotiation of communication between the player and the game – a negotiation that involves sounds, images, movements and inputs. Musical signs form part of this negotiation, and their meanings can depend as much on the player themselves as on the music's initial composition. Tracking down the source of musical meanings, and tracing how these meanings move through and influence gameplay, are key to understanding game music's signs and communications.

Semiotics in Game Music

Two Semiotic Domains

Next time you play a game, take notice of the things you are observing. Take notice of the characters: how they are dressed, how they move, how they interact with you. Take notice of the scenery: its colours, shapes and textures; its architecture, time period, planet of origin or state of repair. Take notice of the sounds of the concrete jungle, or the living forest, or the competitors' race cars or the zombie horde. Take notice of the music: the shape of its tune, the texture of its harmonies and rhythms, how it alerts you to characters or objects, how its ebbs and flows guide your emotional responses. The video game is providing you with a constant stream of signs that signify many different things in many different ways; your entire perception of the gameworld is constructed by communications through visual, aural and/or textural signs.

While you are at it, take notice of the things that you are communicating to the game. You are making inputs through a keyboard, mouse, controller, joystick or motion detector. Your inputs may be directional ('move my character to the left'), functional ('change up a gear') or metafunctional ('open the inventory menu'). Many of your inputs are reactions, prompted by conscious needs ('I need to see what is in my inventory') or by semi-conscious or unconscious needs (flinching when you hear a monster right behind your character). Many are the result of your choices, whether to move towards a strange sound, to cast a particular spell or to turn up the music volume. Your actions are providing the game program with a stream of input signs that come from you and that represent how you want to interact with the gameworld; your interactions are constructed of signs that could take the form of keystrokes, button presses, movements, keywords, voice commands, configuration file changes and so on.

The game music's communications to you, and your communications with the game and its music, come from two separate semiotic domains that have distinct (though related) sets of semiotic activity. The first semiotic domain is centred around the creation of the video game and the composition of the music: this is when musical (and other) elements of the game are put into the video game program based on creative and developmental choices. The second semiotic domain is centred on your actions in gameplay: this is when the musical (and other) elements of the game program are actualized into your experience of the game through your interactions. When you are playing a game, you are hearing musical signs from both semiotic domains – in the most basic sense, you hear the composer's original musical signs (initial composition) in the way they are being configured by your interactions (gameplay). And while it often makes sense to look at these together (since games are made to be played), there is some valuable information about both the game and how you play it, and the music and how you hear it, that can be obtained from looking at them separately.

Initial Composition and Initial Meanings

There are two kinds of signs that are put into video game music when it is composed and put into the game program: musical signs and configurative signs. Musical signs are the things that we typically think of as music, like notes, melody, harmony, instrumentation, dynamics and so on. These typically function the same way in video games as they could be expected to in any other context. For example, if you remove a music file from a video game's program folder and play it in an audio player, it will often sound like regular non-interactive music.[11] You can also analyse these signs much as you would any other piece of music. Accordingly, these are often the first signs to be analysed when we look at video game music. These are the signs that bear most resemblance to film music, that are transposed into orchestral settings, that are played on the radio, and that you buy as part of an *Official Soundtrack* album. And, if adequately accounting for the cultural contexts of both composition and analysis, investigating the musical signs as at initial composition can reveal a lot about the music and its role within the game.

Configurative signs, meanwhile, are the signs that turn music into video game music. These are things that come into the music through the functions and designs of the video game program, and can include timing, repetition, layering and responses to interactivity. They take musical signs and configure them to work as part of the game. For example, the video game *Halo 3* (2007) plays music as the player enters certain spaces filled with enemies. The timing of the start of the music, and the consequent correspondence between the music and the newly entered space, are configurative signs. Like earlier games in the *Halo* series, *Halo 3* also turns off the music after the player has spent too long in the one space to encourage them along and to minimize repetition, and this is also a configurative sign.[12] Configurative signs contextualize musical signs within the game program by determining how the music will fit in with the other game elements. They are, therefore, very important in determining how (and how effectively) music can denote meanings within the game. The musical signs in *Halo 3*'s soundtrack may independently connote a sense of action, but the configurative signs that line up the start of the music with entering a theatre of action are what allow the music to denote the experience of battle.

Unlike musical signs, configurative signs are hard to remove from the video game and analyse separately. The functions built into the game program can be difficult to observe independently without access to the video game source code and the requisite knowledge to interpret it. Likewise, the precise mechanisms used by audio subsystems or middleware

---

[11] Tim Summers, *Understanding Video Game Music* (Cambridge, UK: Cambridge University Press, 2016), 38–9.

[12] Karen Collins, *Game Sound: An Introduction to the History, Theory, and Practice of Video Game Music and Sound Design* (Cambridge, MA: The MIT Press, 2008), 141.

require a certain amount of technical expertise to both implement and interpret. However, we can make educated deductions about these functions based on gameplay experience. Battles in *Halo 3* tend to take place in open spaces that are joined by corridors, roads or canyons. After entering several of the open spaces and hearing the music start, we can infer that the game contains a function to start music when entering open spaces. Further gameplay can confirm or qualify the hypothesis, and then analysis can focus on when and why these configurative signs are implemented in the game and what effect they have on the music. This must be done with a little care, however, as there are additional semiotic processes taking place during gameplay.

Gameplay and the Player's Influence

Gameplay simultaneously changes nothing and everything about video game music. Just as in the semiotic domain of initial composition, music within gameplay consists of musical signs and configurative signs. These are, for the most part, the same sets of signs that were present at initial composition. However, during gameplay, the player's interactivity actuates the configurative signs, which then act on the musical signs to determine what music the player hears and how the player hears it. So, while the *Halo 3* game program contains both the music cues to play in certain areas and the program functions to make the music stop playing after a specific amount of time to hurry the player along, it is only the player's choice to linger that cements the cessation of music in that area as a fact of the musical experience. If the player chose to clear the area and move on quickly, they would hear a transition to another music cue, but the cessation of music in that area would not be part of their gameplay experience. The player's choices add and exclude musical potentials in the played experience (an important thing to remember when analysing music from within gameplay); they can activate a different set of configurative signs than another player and end up with a subtly but observably different experience.

However, the player brings more to the game experience than just the power to activate configurative signs. They bring a set of signs that correspond to them personally. These can include the choices they make and the reasons they make them, their musical, gameplay or stylistic preferences, their mood, their cognitive associations or even artefacts of the world around them. These personal signs strongly influence which of the configurative signs built into the game the player will activate during gameplay. The activated configurative signs subsequently act on the musical signs of

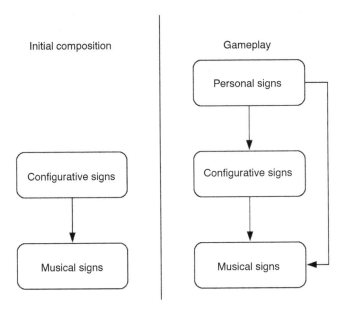

Initial composition

Gameplay

Configurative signs

Musical signs

Personal signs

Configurative signs

Musical signs

Figure 13.1 Actions of signs in the semiotic domains of interactive configuration and gameplay

the game, crystallizing a musical experience from the potentials that were built into the game mixed with the effects of the player's personal experiences. One of the simplest examples of the influence of personal signs is the way your mood affects how you drive in a racing game. If you are having a bad day, you are more likely to drive rashly, make errors, spin out and lose the race. In this circumstance, not hearing the victory music at the end of the race is a result of the negative signs floating around in your mind being expressed in your interactions.

Figure 13.1 demonstrates how each set of signs relates to other sets of signs within the semiotic domains of initial composition and gameplay; an arrow from X to Y in this diagram indicates an 'X acts on Y' relationship. The arrow from personal signs to musical signs may be unexpected; it indicates that there are circumstances in which the player can add musical signs directly to the game (such as by playing their own music instead of the soundtrack, or by providing a music file to be played within and as part of the game like in *Audiosurf*, 2008) or in which the player's perception of certain musical signs is strongly influenced by their personal experience (such as dancing to 'I Don't Want to Set the World on Fire' by the Ink Spots at their wedding, then hearing the song played in association with a post-apocalyptic wasteland in *Fallout 3*, 2008).

Because the musical experience of gameplay is constructed from a combination of signs from the music's initial composition and signs from the player themselves, every player's experience of a game's music is unique. Of course, all experiences of a game are similar, since they are built from the same musical and configurative potentials that were originally put into the game. However, it is important to be mindful that approaching video game music through gameplay changes the semiotic domain in which listening and analysis occur, and that there are more sources of signs in the semiotic domain of gameplay than just 'the text itself'. This is one of the great differences between video games and other texts, such as films; while any viewer of a film brings a lot of their own thoughts, opinions and signs to the task of interpreting a film, they (usually) do not change the film itself in the process of viewing it. Espen Aarseth describes texts like video games as 'ergodic', meaning that work has to be done to them in order to interpret them.[13] Video games and their music are not the only kinds of ergodic texts, but they are arguably the most widespread (or, at least, commercially successful) examples in today's world. Furthermore, an interesting corollary of doing work to a text is that, as Hanna Wirman points out, the player can be considered as an author of the text (especially when considering the 'text' to be the played experience of the game).[14] So video game music is simultaneously just 'regular old music', and a relatively 'new' kind of text with potentials for expression and creativity that we have barely started to explore. The following case studies of musical examples from the Elder Scrolls games demonstrate both aspects of this duality.

Case Studies: Music of the Elder Scrolls Series

The Elder Scrolls video games are a popular series of high fantasy role-playing games published by Bethesda Softworks. The series was cemented as a fixture of video game culture with the third instalment, *The Elder Scrolls III: Morrowind* (2002, hereafter *Morrowind*), a position reinforced by the subsequent two instalments, *The Elder Scrolls IV: Oblivion* (2006, hereafter *Oblivion*) and *The Elder Scrolls V: Skyrim* (2011, hereafter *Skyrim*). In each of these three games, the player character starts the story as a prisoner of unknown heritage and ends it as the hero of the world,

---

[13] Espen Aarseth, *Cybertext: Perspectives on Ergodic Literature* (Baltimore, MD: Johns Hopkins University Press, 1997), 1.

[14] Hanna Wirman, 'On Productivity and Game Fandom', *Transformative Works and Cultures* 3 (2009), ¶ 2.4, http://journal.transformativeworks.org/index.php/twc/article/view/145/115.

having risen to glory through battle, magic, theft, assassination, vampirism, lycanthropy, alchemy, commerce and/or homemaking. The unrivalled stars of the games, however, are their expansive, explorable and exquisite open worlds. Each game is set in a different province on a continent called Tamriel, and each provides a vast landscape filled with forests and grasslands, lakes and rivers, settlements and towns, mountains and ruins, along with caves and underground structures that serve as the loci of many missions. Finding the location of some missions requires a good deal of exploration, and free exploration can allow the player to stumble upon side quests, so the player can spend a lot of time in the great digital outdoors of Tamriel.

Accompanying Tamriel in games from *Morrowind* onwards are scores by composer Jeremy Soule. The scores are orchestral, keeping quite close to a Western cinematic aesthetic, but with occasional influences from northern European folk music. They infuse gameplay within their gameworlds and they link the gameworlds to each other, assisting the tapestry of the games' stories, sights and sounds to envelop the player's senses. The first case study below examines themes that run through the title music of each game, demonstrating the signifying power of novelty and nostalgia in musical introductions. The second case study shows how game music often acts as a sign for the player to take notice, and how the player's learned lessons translate into personal signs that affect further gameplay.

Linking Games Through Musical Composition: Elder Scrolls Title Music

The scores for the Elder Scrolls games maintain an aesthetic congruence with the story world of each game. For example, *Skyrim*'s score frequently makes use of a male choir to invoke an aesthetic aligned with modern imaginations of Vikings, an overt expression of Scandinavian inspirations that are also built into the game's musical foundations in references to Scandinavian nationalist symphonic music.[15] However, the scores of each game also maintain congruence with the scores of the other games using variations on several shared melodic and rhythmic themes, creating the potential for familiarity. This is a powerful mechanism for drawing the player into a video game series, and the Elder Scrolls games begin this work

---

[15] Sun-ha Hong, 'When Life Mattered: The Politics of the Real in Video Games' Reappropriation of History, Myth, and Ritual', *Games and Culture* 10, no. 1 (2015): 42–3; Mark Sweeney, 'The Aesthetics of Video Game Music' (PhD thesis, University of Oxford, 2014), 219.

Example 13.1 Excerpt of title music melody from *Morrowind*

even before gameplay proper, as the title themes of each game exhibit some of the clearest thematic parallels. When a player plays *Oblivion* for several hundred hours, for instance, and then begins to play *Morrowind* because they want to experience the earlier game's story as well, there are musical signs in *Morrowind* that suggest they are in the same gameworld that they enjoyed in *Oblivion*.

The title music from *Morrowind* uses a melodic theme that can be separated into three melody fragments, marked A, B and C in Example 13.1. Fragment A initiates a sense of action by moving quickly from the tonic to an emphasized minor third (a note which, as tonic of the relative major, suggests optimism in this context), and then repeating the action with further upward progress. The roundabout return to the tonic is like heading home after a mission with a momentary detour to pick a flower that you need to make a potion. Each 'action' in Fragment A is made up of a rhythmic figure of a minim on the first beat of the bar preceded by two quavers (which may be counted out as 'three-and-one') – a figure that occurs frequently in this theme and features prominently in the themes of subsequent games. Fragment B repeats the first 'actions' of Fragment A but then achieves and affirms the higher tonic. Fragment C triumphantly pushes on upwards to the relative major's higher tonic – the fulfilment of the optimism of Fragment A – and then descends progressively to where this journey all began. *Morrowind*'s title music repeats this sequence three times, each with increasing volume and orchestral richness, each time attempting to draw the player deeper into a sense of adventure with which to better enjoy the imminent gameplay.

The primary melodic theme from *Oblivion* is a variation on the first two parts of *Morrowind*'s theme (each variation marked in Example 13.2 as A2 and B2). There is a marked increase in the pace of *Oblivion*'s version of the theme, which is somewhat disguised in this transcription by the shift to 6/8 time, a shift which results in an aesthetic more akin to that of a mainstream

Example 13.2 Excerpt of title music melody from *Oblivion*

Example 13.3 Later excerpt of title music melody from *Oblivion*

pirate film than of a high fantasy epic. The 'three-and-one' rhythmic figure is carried over, though here as 'three-and-four/six-and-one' figures. The additional pace of this theme gives the figures a somewhat more adventurous feel, bringing to mind swordplay or the sound of a horse's galloping hooves. Notably, the primary melodic theme of *Oblivion* does not use *Morrowind*'s Fragment C at all – following Fragment B2, the title music instead enters a series of dramatic variations on Fragments A2 and B2. However, Fragment C does make a (somewhat veiled) appearance later in *Oblivion*'s title theme. Though Fragment C3 in Example 13.3 is a very simplified version of Fragment C, its rhythm and downward shape are both suggestive of the *Morrowind* fragment and fulfil a similar homeward purpose. The return to the tonic is, however, attained with much less certainty. With the benefit of hindsight, this could be seen as an allegory for the uneasy peace achieved at the resolution of *Oblivion*'s main quest line, which is revealed in *Skyrim* to have been very much temporary.

Skyrim's primary melodic theme is varied even more substantially from the original *Morrowind* material than was *Oblivion*'s primary theme, to the point that it may be more accurate to describe *Skyrim*'s primary melodic theme as a variation on *Oblivion*'s theme rather than that of *Morrowind*. It continues and expounds upon some of the ideas behind *Oblivion*'s variations, such as pacing, a 6/8 time signature and an air of adventurousness. Like that of *Oblivion*, the *Skyrim* title music initially uses only variations of Fragments A and B (marked as A4 and B4 respectively in Example 13.4), which it then repeats with slight variations (Fragments A4* and B4* in Example 13.4). The theme as a whole

Example 13.4 Excerpt of title music melody from *Skyrim*

Example 13.5 Later excerpt of title music melody from *Skyrim* (with trumpet accompaniment)

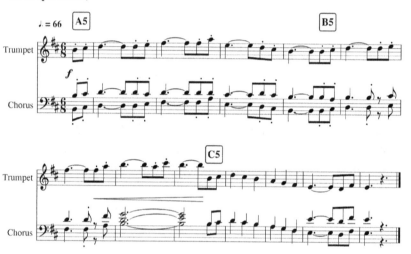

also has a much smaller pitch range than earlier themes, though it makes up for this in loudness. The main element that links *Skyrim*'s primary melodic theme back to *Morrowind* is the rhythmic figures or 'actions', as these are again featured prominently. It may even be argued that, at this stage, the rhythmic figures are the most significant shared elements tying the title music of *Morrowind*, *Oblivion* and *Skyrim* together, and the main musical sign to the player of commonality between the games (prior to the start of gameplay, at least).

However, later in *Skyrim*'s theme the original *Morrowind* theme returns in an almost pure state. Example 13.5 shows an excerpt from *Skyrim*'s title music including the two most prominent vocal parts and a trumpet accompaniment. The three original Fragments from *Morrowind* are reproduced very closely in Fragments A5, B5 and C5, most prominently in the lower vocal part and the trumpet line. This is arguably more of a choral and orchestral arrangement of the *Morrowind* theme than a variation upon it.

From a semiotic point of view, the melody that I have called the *Morrowind* theme above is a sign, as are the Fragments A, B and C that constitute the theme, and even the rhythmic figures or 'actions' that recur throughout the theme and its variations. All of these fragments are capable of bearing meaning, both as small elements (sometimes called 'musemes')[16] and combined into larger structures. At the time of *Morrowind*'s release, these were symbols of the game *Morrowind* and, after gameplay, of the experience of playing *Morrowind*. Through the variations on the theme presented in the scores of the subsequent games, they have been extended into symbols of the experience of playing an Elder Scrolls game. The particular instances of the theme still refer to the game in which that instance is found (that is, *Skyrim*'s versions of the theme as sung by a 'Nordic' choir are still very much symbols of *Skyrim*), but they also refer laterally to the sequels and/or prequels of that game and to the series as a whole.

The latter example is a good illustration of this twofold signification, as it is functionally a part of the *Skyrim* theme but is also clearly derived from *Morrowind*. Its inclusion is, in fact, rather fascinating. The excerpt in Example 13.5 begins at 2 minutes 8 seconds into *Skyrim*'s title music, but *Skyrim*'s title menu is remarkably simple, presenting new players with only three options (start a new game, view the credits or quit). It is entirely possible that a first-time player could spend less than 20 seconds in the menu before starting a game and so could miss the close reproduction of the *Morrowind* theme entirely. Its inclusion allows *Skyrim*'s title music to powerfully signify both nostalgia for past games and the novelty of a fresh variation to long-term fans of the series,[17] while its delayed start prevents it from interfering with the title music's essential function of priming seasoned Elder Scrolls players and neophytes alike for the imminent quest through established musical tropes of adventure and place.[18] Different groups of people may experience a different balance of nostalgia, novelty and expectation, which is both testament to the richness of the score's

---

[16] Tagg, *Music's Meanings*, 232–8.

[17] On nostalgia in video game music, see Sarah Pozderac-Chenevey, 'A Direct Link to the Past: Nostalgia and Semiotics in Video Game Music', *Divergence Press*, no. 2 (2014), http://divergencepress.net/2014/06/02/2016-11-3-a-direct-link-to-the-past-nostalgia-and-semiotics-in-video-game-music/

[18] See Isabella van Elferen, 'Analysing Game Musical Immersion: The ALI Model', in *Ludomusicology: Approaches to Video Game Music*, ed. Michiel Kamp, Tim Summers and Mark Sweeney (Sheffield: Equinox, 2016), 34–7.

weave of musical and configurative signs, and an example of how the semiotic content of music can be altered by the semiotic processes of gameplay.

Linking Experiences Through Musical Gameplay: Skyrim's Action Music

Playing *Skyrim* takes you on many journeys. Some of these journeys give you a chance to discover new parts of the gameworld, new sights and sounds and characters and challenges. Other journeys are strangely similar to journeys past (all dungeons start to look the same after a while). The journeys are all somewhat alike, of course, on account of being made of the same basic elements: the parts that make up the game *Skyrim*. Building familiarity with gameplay mechanisms and signifiers early in gameplay can help the player engage with the game's world and story. As long as familiarity avoids crossing the line into boredom, it can be a useful tool in the player's arsenal for success. In a game like *Skyrim*, success can be achieved in large and small ways: finishing quests (both major and minor) and winning battles.

The data files of *Skyrim* contain eight full-length (between one- and two-minute) cues of combat music that are played during battles (there are also some derivative and/or smaller versions that are not considered here). These cues share several commonalities, including fast tempi, minor keys, high-pitch repeated staccato or accented notes and dramatic percussion that emphasizes the first beat of each bar – traits that align with the typical role of combat music, which is to increase the sense of action and tension in the sonic environment during combat scenarios.[19] *Skyrim* and its prequels are open-world games and the player can enter combat scenarios inadvertently; the pleasant music that accompanies exploration of the countryside can be suddenly interrupted by combat music, and this is sometimes (if the enemy has not yet been seen or heard) the first thing that alerts the player to danger. Helpfully, *Skyrim*'s combat music has a sign at the start of each combat music cue to point out what is happening. Figure 13.2 shows waveforms of the first five seconds of each of the main combat music cues. Each cue has an abrupt start that is, in most cases, louder than the ensuing music. Loud strikes on deep drums emphasize the shift from bucolic exploration to dangerous combat and prompt the player to respond accordingly.

---

[19] Winifred Phillips, *A Composer's Guide to Game Music* (Cambridge, MA: The MIT Press, 2014), 151–2.

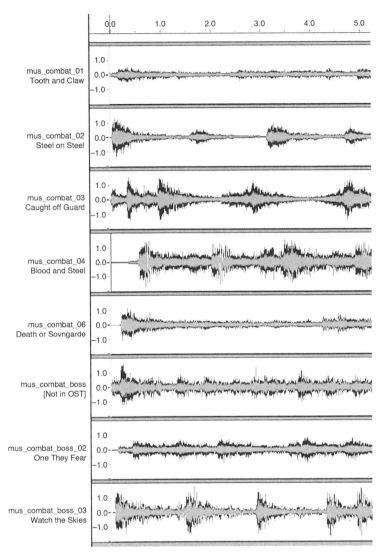

Figure 13.2 Graphical representation in Audacity of waveforms of combat music from *Skyrim* (mixed down to mono for simplicity; cues listed by filename with *Original Game Soundtrack* titles indicated) [author's screenshot]

The first time a player encounters combat music in *Skyrim* is during the introductory scenes of the game, when the player's newly minted character has their head on the executioner's block in the town of Helgen. Proceedings are interrupted by the appearance of the dragon Alduin, the prophesied consumer of the world, who flies in and attacks the town. The musical

Figure 13.3 Alduin's appearance at Helgen (silhouette between tower and mountain), and moment of first combat music in *Skyrim* [author's screenshot]

accompaniment to this world-changing event is the cue 'mus_combat_04' (named 'Blood and Steel' on the *Original Game Soundtrack*).[20] Immediately preceding the initial crash of percussion in the music is Alduin's ominous roar and visual appearance (see Figure 13.3). The sign linking combat music and danger could scarcely be more obvious.

Having been introduced to combat music in this way, the player can more easily recognize combat scenarios later in *Skyrim*. Down the road from Helgen, the player may come across a wild wolf and once again hear combat music. A wolf is a smaller threat than a dragon, though likely still a test of the new character's mettle. On hearing the initial blast of drums, the player can whip out their war axe or sword and take care of the situation. Yet, as previously mentioned, *Skyrim* is an open-world game and threats may come from any direction. The next wolf to attack may come from behind a tree (the music begins when an enemy becomes aware of the character's presence, not the other way around), so the music may be the first sign of danger. It can operate in this way because it was initialized as denoting threats from the very start.

As the player learns more about how gameplay in *Skyrim* works, they may choose a play style that emphasizes strategic combat over brawn. The skill of 'sneaking' involves both moving quietly and staying out of sight in

---

[20] Jeremy Soule, *The Elder Scrolls V: Skyrim (Original Game Soundtrack)* (DirectSong, 2011), digital audio.

order to move close enough to an enemy to strike a critical blow, ideally without the enemy becoming aware of the character's presence until it is too late. The player has learned that combat music starts when an enemy becomes aware of the character's presence and starts to attack, so the absence of combat music becomes the sign of successful sneaking. Combat music during an attempt to sneak up on an enemy indicates to the player that the game is up – they have to run or fight, and quickly. Sneaking is a semiotic negotiation, wherein the player is trying to convey the right combination of signs to the game to get the desired combination of signs in return. It depends both on the game initializing combat music as a sign of danger, and on the player learning and subsequently manipulating the game's signs for their own ends.

Conclusion

Semiotics is rather like mathematics: it describes the world rather well, and while you can live most of your life without it, it can give you a different, different, clearer, more precise, and rather exciting perspective on the things that you see every day. The semiotics of video game music shows how communication between the player and the game involves everything from physical movements, to the mental effects of emotions, to the nostalgic pull of past experiences. There are meanings placed into game music at its creation, and there are meanings you hear in video game music that come not from the composer, but from yourself. We communicate with the games we play as they communicate with us, weaving meanings into musical experiences and throughout gameworlds, and we do it almost without thinking. Semiotics is not hard – it is just an extension of that meaning-making process into conscious and deliberate thought, a description of video game music that helps make sense of the communication that is already happening.

14 | Game – Music – Performance: Introducing a Ludomusicological Theory and Framework

MELANIE FRITSCH

Introduction

Since the late 2000s, the distinct field of ludomusicology has gained momentum. Reportedly, the neologism ludomusicology was coined by Guillaume Laroche and his fellow student Nicholas Tam, with the prefix 'ludo' referring to ludology, the study of games.[1] In early 2008, Roger Moseley also used this term and introduced an additional dimension to the meaning:

> Whereas Laroche's deployment of the term has reflected a primary interest in music *within* games, I am more concerned with the extent to which music might be understood as a mode of gameplay. . . . Bringing music and play into contact in this way offers access to the undocumented means by which composers, designers, programmers, performers, players, and audiences interact with music, games, and one another.[2]

In this chapter, I will outline my approach I have developed at full length in my 2018 book towards a distinct ludomusicological theory that studies both games and music as playful performative practices and is based on that broader understanding. This approach is explicitly rooted both in performance theory and in the musicological discourse of music as

---

[1] On Guillaume Laroche and Nicholas Tam's use of the term see Tasneem Karbani, 'Music to a Gamer's Ears', *University of Alberta Faculty of Arts News* (22 August 2007), accessed 10 April 2020, https://web.archive.org/web/20070915071528/http://www.uofaweb.ualberta.ca /arts/news.cfm?story=63769 and Nicholas Tam, 'Ludomorphballogy', *Ntuple Indemnity* (7 September 2007), accessed 10 April 2020, www.nicholastam.ca/2007/09/07/ludomorphballogy. Unlike narratologists, who proposed to study games as a form of text or narrative using established methods from other fields, ludologists favoured the idea of finding subject-specific approaches. On this debate in game studies and more information on the field in general see Frans Mäyrä, *An Introduction to Game Studies: Games in Culture* (London: Sage, 2008).

[2] Roger Moseley, 'Playing Games with Music (and Vice Versa): Ludomusicological Perspectives on *Guitar Hero* and *Rock Band*', in *Taking It to the Bridge: Music as Performance*, ed. Nicholas Cook and Richard Pettengill (Ann Arbor: University of Michigan Press, 2013), 279–318 at 283.

performance.[3] The basic idea is that with the help of a subject-specific performance concept, a framework can be developed which provides a concrete method of analysis. Applying this framework further allows us to study music games as well as music as a design element in games, and performances of game music beyond the games themselves. It is therefore possible to address all three ludomusicological subject areas within the frame of an overarching theory.

Performance – *Performanz* – Performativity

Performance theory is a complicated matter, due to firstly, the manifold uses of the term 'performance' and secondly, the multiple intersections with two other concepts, namely performativity and *Performanz* (usually translated to 'performance' in English, which makes it even more confusing). Due to these issues and a ramified terminological history, the three concepts as used today cannot be unambiguously traced back to one basic definition, but to three basic models as identified by Klaus Hempfer: the theatrical model (performance), the speech act model of linguistic philosophy (performativity) and the model of generative grammatics (*Performanz*).[4] Despite offering new and productive views, the evolution of the three concepts and their intersections has led to misreadings and misinterpretations that I have untangled elsewhere.[5] For the purpose of this chapter, it is sufficient to be only generally aware of this conceptual history, therefore I will confine the discussion to some aspects that are needed for our understanding.

The concept of performativity was originally introduced by linguistic philosopher John L. Austin during a lecture series entitled *How to Do Things with Words* in 1955.[6] He suggested a basic differentiation between a constative and a performative utterance: While a constative utterance can only be true or false and is used to state something, performatives are neither true nor false, but can perform an action when being used (for example, 'I hereby declare you husband and wife'). This idea was taken up, further

---

[3] The full development of the approach summarized here can be found in Melanie Fritsch, *Performing Bytes: Musikperformances der Computerspielkultur* (Würzburg: Königshausen & Neumann, 2018), chs. 2, 3 and 4.

[4] Klaus W. Hempfer, '*Performance*, Performanz, Performativität. Einige Unterscheidungen zur Ausdifferenzierung eines Theoriefeldes', in *Theorien des Performativen: Sprache – Wissen – Praxis. Eine kritische Bestandsaufnahme*, ed. Klaus W. Hempfer and Jörg Volbers (Bielefeld: transcript, 2011), 13–41, here 13.

[5] Fritsch, *Performing Bytes*, 18–35.

[6] John L. Austin, *How to Do Things with Words: The William James Lectures Delivered at Harvard University in 1955*, 2nd ed. (Oxford: Clarendon, 1975).

discussed and reshaped within philosophy of language and linguistics.[7] Additionally, it was adopted in the cultural and social sciences, where it sparked the 'performative turn', and the power of performatives to create social realities was particularly discussed (for example, the couple actually being wedded after an authorized person has uttered the respective phrase in the correct context such as in a church or registry office). On its way through the disciplines, it was mixed or used interchangeably with the other two widely debated concepts of performance (as derived, for example, from cultural anthropology including game and ritual studies as e.g. conducted by Victor Turner) and *Performanz* (as discussed in generative grammatics e.g. by Noam Chomsky). In performance research as conducted by gender studies, performance studies or theatre studies scholars, the term performativity was not only referred to, but further politicized. A major question was (and still is) the relation between the (non-)autonomous individual and society, between free individual behaviour and the acting out of patterns according to (social) rules. Another major issue is the relationship between live and mediatized performances, as scholars such as Peggy Phelan,[8] Erika Fischer-Lichte[9] or Phillip Auslander have emphasized.[10] The evanescence and ephemerality of live performances and the creation of an artistic space that was seen to be potentially free from underlying schemata of behaviour and their related politics (e.g. in art forms such as Happenings as opposed to art forms such as the bourgeois theatre of representation), were set in harsh opposition to recorded performances that were returned into an 'economy of reproduction'.[11]

When trying to understand games and music as performances, it is therefore necessary to state clearly which concept one is referring to. There are two options: Either one uses an existent concept as introduced by a specific scholar, or one needs to develop a subject-specific approach that is informed by the respective terminological history, and takes the entanglements with the other two concepts into account.

The goal of this chapter is to approach the three subject areas of ludomusicology from the perspective of performance studies using performance theory.[12]

---

[7] See also James Loxley, *Performativity* (London: Routledge, 2007).

[8] Peggy Phelan, *Unmarked: The Politics of Performance* (New York: Routledge, 1993).

[9] Erike Fischer-Lichte, *Ästhetik des Performativen* (Frankfurt am Main: Suhrkamp, 2004).

[10] Phillip Auslander, *Liveness. Performance in a Mediatized Culture* (New York: Routledge, 2008); see also Melanie Fritsch and Stefan Strötgen, 'Relatively Live: How to Identify Live Music Performances?', *Music and the Moving Image* 5, no. 1 (2012): 47–66.

[11] Phelan, *Unmarked*, 146.

[12] For an approach informed by performativity, see Iain Hart's chapter, Chapter 13 in this volume.

Analysing Games as Performances

The concept of 'performance' that we chose as our starting point has two basic dimensions of meaning. To illustrate these, a classic example from the field of music games is helpful: *Guitar Hero*. In this so-called rhythm-action game, that is played using a guitar-shaped peripheral,[13] the player is challenged to push coloured buttons and strum a plastic bar in time with the respectively coloured 'notes' represented on screen to score points and make the corresponding sound event audible. As Kiri Miller has observed, two basic playing styles have been adopted by regular players: 'The score-oriented [players] treat these games as well-defined rule-bound systems, in which the main challenge and satisfaction lies in determining how to exploit the scoring mechanism to best advantage'.[14] On the other hand, she describes

Rock-oriented players [who] recognize that rock authenticity is performative. They generally do value their videogame high scores, but they also believe creative performance is its own reward. As they play these games, they explore the implications of their role as live performers of prerecorded songs.[15]

This second playing style has particularly been highlighted in advertisements, in which we see 'typical' rock star behaviours such as making the 'guitar face',[16] or even smashing the guitar, thereby inviting potential players to 'unleash your inner rock star'. Beyond hitting buttons to score points, these rock-oriented players are demonstrating further competencies: the knowledge of the cultural frame of rock music, and their ability to mimic rock-star-ish behaviours. As Miller highlights, 'Members of both groups are generally performance-oriented, but they employ different performance-evaluation criteria'.[17]

With the performance concept formulated by theorist Marvin Carlson we can specify what these different evaluation criteria are: 'If we … ask what makes performing arts performative, I imagine the answer would somehow suggest that these arts require the physical presence of trained or skilled human beings whose demonstration of their skills is the performance.'[18] Carlson concludes that '[w]e have two rather different

---

[13] For more information on this genre see Michael Austin's chapter, Chapter 9, in this volume.

[14] Kiri Miller, 'Schizophonic Performance: Guitar Hero, Rock Band, and Virtual Virtuosity', *Journal of the Society for American Music* 3, no. 4 (2009): 395–429 at 418.

[15] Ibid.

[16] David Roesner, 'The Guitar Hero's Performance', *Contemporary Theatre Review* 21, no. 3 (2012): 276–85 at 278.

[17] Miller, 'Schizophonic Performance', 418.

[18] Marvin Carlson, *Performance: A Critical Introduction* (New York: Routledge, 1996), 3.

concepts of performance, one involving the display of skills, the other also involving display, but less of particular skills than of a recognized and culturally coded pattern of behavior'.[19] This can be applied to the two playing styles Miller has identified, with the former relating to Miller's score-oriented players, and the latter to the rock-oriented players. Carlson further argues that performance can also be understood as a form of efficiency or competence (*Leistung*) that is evaluated 'in light of some standard of achievement that may not itself be precisely articulated'.[20] It is not important whether there is an external audience present, because 'all performance involves a consciousness of doubleness, through which the actual execution of an action is placed in mental comparison with a potential, an ideal, or a remembered original model of that action'.[21] In other words: someone has to make meaning of the performance, but it does not matter whether this someone is another person, or the performer themselves.

In summary, this dimension of performance in the sense of *Leistung* consists of three elements: firstly, a display of (playing) skills, that secondly happens within the frame and according to the behavioural rule sets of a referent (in our case musical) culture, and that, thirdly, someone has to make meaning out of, be it the performer themselves or an external audience.

Additionally, the term performance addresses the *Aufführung*, the aesthetic event. This understanding of performance as an evanescent, unique occurrence is a key concept in German *Theaterwissenschaft*.[22] At this point it is worthwhile noting that the debate on games and/as performances reveals linguistic tripwires: The English term 'performance' can be translated to both *Leistung* and *Aufführung* in German, which allows us to clearly separate these two dimensions. But due to the outlined focus of German *Theaterwissenschaft*, when used in the respective scholarly German-language discourse, the English word 'performance' usually refers to this understanding of *Aufführung*. As Erika Fischer-Lichte has described it:

The performance [in the sense of *Aufführung*, M. F.] obtains its artistic character – its *aesthetics* – not because of a work that it would create, but because of the event

---

[19] Carlson, *Performance*, 4–5.

[20] Carlson, *Performance*, 5.

[21] Ibid.

[22] Regarding the differences between German *Theaterwissenschaft* and the Anglo-American disciplines of theatre studies and performance studies see Marvin Carlson, 'Introduction. Perspectives on Performance: Germany and America', in Erika Fischer-Lichte, *The Transformative Power of Performance: A New Aesthetics*, ed. Erika Fischer-Lichte, trans. Saskya Iris Jain (New York: Routledge 2008), 1–11.

that takes place. Because in the performance, ... there is a unique, unrepeatable, usually only partially influenceable and controllable constellation, during which something happens that can only occur once[.][23]

While offering a clear-cut definition, the focus on this dimension of performance in the German-language discourse has at the same time led to a tendency to neglect or even antagonize the dimension of *Leistung* (also because of the aforementioned politicization of the term). This concept of performance that was also championed by Phelan leads to a problem that has been hotly debated: If the *Aufführung* aspect of performance (as an aesthetic event) is potentially freed from the societal context, external structures and frames of interpretation – how can we make meaning out of it?

Therefore, 'performance' in our framework not only describes the moment of the unique event, but argues for a broader understanding that purposely includes both dimensions. The term connects the *Aufführung* with the dimension of *Leistung* by including the work and training (competence acquisition) of the individual that is necessary to, firstly, enable a repeatable mastery of one's own body and all other involved material during the moment of a performance (*Aufführung*) and, secondly, make the performance meaningful, either in the role of an actor/performer or as a recipient/audience, or as both in one person. The same applies to the recipient, who has to become competent in perceiving, decoding and understanding the perceived performance in terms of the respective cultural contexts. Furthermore, a performance can leave traces by being described or recorded in the form of artefacts or documents, which again can be perceived and interpreted.[24]

But how can we describe these two dimensions of performance (the aesthetic *Aufführung* and the systematic *Leistung*), when talking about digital games?

Dimensions of Game Performance: *Leistung*

In a comprehensive study of games from the perspective of competencies and media education, Christa Gebel, Michael Gurt and Ulrike Wagner distinguish between five competence and skill areas needed to successfully play a game:

1. cognitive competence,
2. social competence,

---

[23] Fischer-Lichte, *Ästhetik des Performativen*, 53–4. Translation by the author.
[24] See Fritsch 2018, *Performing Bytes*, 34–35.

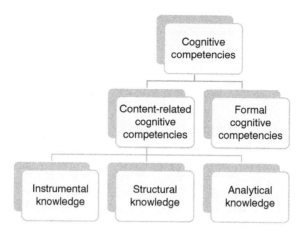

Figure 14.1 The area of cognitive competency following Gebel (2010)

3. personality-related competence,
4. sensorimotor skills,
5. media competence.[25]

In this system, the area of cognitive competence comprises skills such as abstraction, drawing conclusions, understanding of structure, understanding of meaning, action planning and solving new tasks and problems, all of which can easily be identified in the process of playing *Guitar Hero*. In an article from 2010, Gebel further divides cognitive competence into formal cognitive and content-related cognitive competencies (Figure 14.1).[26]

Formal cognitive competencies include skills such as attention, concentration or the competence of framing (which in the case of *Guitar Hero*, for example, means understanding the difference between playing a real guitar and the game).

Content-related cognitive competencies concern using and expanding one's existing game- and gaming-specific knowledge, and are further subdivided into areas of instrumental, analytical and structural knowledge. Instrumental knowledge includes skills such as learning, recognizing and applying control principles. In short, instrumental knowledge concerns the

---

[25] Christa Gebel, Michael Gurt and Ulrike Wagner, *Kompetenzförderliche Potenziale populärer Computerspiele: Kurzfassung der Ergebnisse des Projekts 'Kompetenzförderliche und kompetenzhemmende Faktoren in Computerspielen'* (Berlin: JFF – Institut für Medienpädagogik in Forschung und Praxis, 2004), www.jff.de/fileadmin/user_upload/jff/veroeffentlichungen/vor_2015/2004_kompetenzfoerderliche_potenziale_von_computerspielen/2004_Kurzfassung_computerspiele_jff_website.pdf (accessed 11 April 2020).

[26] Christa Gebel, 'Kompetenz Erspielen – Kompetent Spielen?', *merz. medien + erziehung* 54, no. 4 (2010): 45–50.

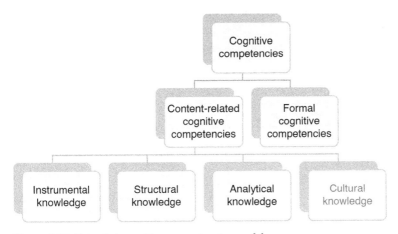

Figure 14.2 Extended cognitive competencies model

use of the technical apparatus. For example, that might involve dealing with complex menu structures.

Analytical and structural knowledge means, firstly, that players quickly recognize the specific features and requirements of a game genre and are able to adjust their actions to succeed in the game. For example, experienced music game players will immediately understand what they need to do in a game of this genre for successful play, and how UI (User Interface) and controls will most likely be organized.

However, as we have seen in the *Guitar Hero* example, content-related cognitive competency does not only include game- and gaming-specific knowledge, but also knowledge from a wider cultural context (in our case rock music culture). This area of competence, the knowledge of the cultural contexts and practices to which a game refers or uses in any form, is not explicitly addressed in Gebel's model, but can be vital for understanding a game. Therefore, we need to add such general cultural knowledge to the category of content-related cognitive skills (Figure 14.2).

The area of social competency includes social skills such as empathy, ambiguity tolerance or co-operation skills as well as moral judgement. This area is closely linked to personality-related competence, which includes self-observation, self-criticism/reflection, identity preservation and emotional self-control. Sensorimotor competence contains skills such as reaction speed and hand–eye co-ordination. The fifth area of competence relates to media literacy and explicitly addresses digital games as a digital medium. This comprises the components of media-specific knowledge, autonomous action, active communication and media design.

Regarding this last aspect, considerations from the discourse on game literacy particularly help to understand the different roles players adopt during gameplay.[27] In this context, we have already stated that players can adopt either the role of an actor/performer or that of a recipient/audience of a game, or even both at the same time (Carlson's double consciousness). In the case of *Guitar Hero*, players can watch each other play or do without any external audience at all. When playing alone at home, they can make meaning out of their performances themselves by placing the actual performance in mental comparison with their idea of the 'guitar hero' as a model.

But players do not always play given games as intended by the designers.[28] In fact, oftentimes they either try to find out what is possible in the game, or even look for ways in which to break the rules and do something completely different than the intended manner of playing. In *Ultima IX*, for example, players found out that the game allowed for building bridges using material such as bread, corpses or brooms. Subsequently, some of them started bridge-building competitions, thereby playfully (mis)using the technology and the given game as the material basis for staging their own gameplay performances by following their own rule set.[29] Eric Zimmerman addresses such practices when he includes 'the ability to understand and create specific kinds of meaning' in his concept of gaming literacy.[30] From his point of view, players must be literate on three levels: systems, play and design, because 'play is far more than just play *within* a structure. Play can *play with* structures. . . . [B]eing literate in play means *being playful* – having a *ludic attitude* that sees the world's structures as opportunities for playful engagement'.[31] He emphasizes that he explicitly names his concept gaming literacy

because of the mischievous double-meaning of "gaming", which can signify exploiting or taking clever advantage of something. Gaming a system means finding hidden shortcuts and cheats, and bending and modifying rules in order

---

[27] See José Zagal, *Ludoliteracy: Defining, Understanding, and Supporting Games Education* (Pittsburgh: Figshare, 2010) and Eric Zimmerman, 'Gaming Literacy: Game Design as a Model for Literacy in the Twenty-First Century', in *The Video Game Theory Reader 2*, ed. Bernard Perron and Mark J. P. Wolf (New York: Routledge, 2009), 23–31.

[28] See James Newman, *Playing with Videogames* (New York: Routledge, 2008); Karen Collins, *Playing with Sound: A Theory of Interacting with Music and Sound in Video Games* (Cambridge, MA: The MIT Press, 2013) and Fritsch, *Performing Bytes*, chapter 3.

[29] Danny Kringiel, 'Spielen gegen jede Regel: Wahnsinn mit Methode', *Spiegel Online*, 30 September 2005, www.spiegel.de/netzwelt/web/spielen-gegen-jede-regel-wahnsinn-mit-methode-a-377417.html (last accessed 15 September 2016).

[30] Zimmerman, 'Gaming Literacy', 25.

[31] Zimmerman, 'Gaming Literacy', 27.

to move through the system more efficiently – perhaps to misbehave, but perhaps to change that system for the better.[32]

Hence, gaming literacy includes the competencies and knowledge to playfully explore and squeeze everything out of a given structure, be it successfully finishing a game by playing it as intended, or by exploiting emergent behaviour such as the creative use of bugs or other types of uncommon play to create one's own game. It further entails breaking the system, and making creative use of singular components, for example by hacking. That way, players can become designers themselves. But in order to do so, it is necessary to be competent regarding design. In his reasoning, Zimmerman relies on his and Katie Salen's definition of design as 'the process by which a *designer* creates a *context* to be encountered by a *participant*, from which *meaning* emerges'.[33] A designer might be one single person or a group, such as a professional design team, or in the case of folk or fan cultural gaming practices, 'culture at large'.[34] That way, players do not just inhabit the traditional roles of performer and/or audience, but can even themselves become designers of new contexts, 'from which meaning emerges' by playing *with* the given material. But this play does not occur randomly. Instead, the emerging participatory practices happen within the frames of players' own cultural contexts according to the specific rule systems that are negotiated by the practitioners themselves. Breaking the rules of such a practice could, at worst, lead to dismissal by this expert audience, as I have outlined elsewhere.[35] For example, when writing a fan song about a game, it is important to have reasonably good musical skills (regarding composing, writing lyrics and performing the song), and technological skills (knowing how to create a decent recording and posting it online), but also to be literate both in the game's lore and its respective fan culture as well as in gaming culture in general, which can for example be demonstrated by including witty references or puns in the music or the lyrics.[36] A similarly competent audience on video platforms such as YouTube will most certainly give feedback and evaluate the performance regarding all these skills.

With this framework, the dimension of *Leistung* can be helpfully broken down into different areas of competence. In particular, the complex area of

---

[32] Zimmerman, 'Gaming Literacy', 25.

[33] Katie Salen and Eric Zimmerman, *Rules of Play: Game Design Fundamentals* Cambridge, MA: The MIT Press, 2004), 41.

[34] Ibid.

[35] See Melanie Fritsch, "It's a-me, Mario!' – Playing with Video Game Music', in *Ludomusicology: Approaches to Video Game Music*, ed. Michiel Kamp, Tim Summers and Mark Sweeney (Sheffield: Equinox, 2016), 92–115.

[36] See Fritsch, *Performing Bytes*, 268–90.

cognitive competencies and knowledge can be structured for analysis by helping to identify and address specific skill sets.

Dimensions of Game Performance: *Aufführung*

As game designer Jesse Schell has stated, '[t]he game is not the experience. The game enables the experience, but it *is not the experience*'.[37] On a phenomenological level, a game (be it digital or otherwise) only manifests itself during the current act of play, the unique event, as a unique ephemeral structure (the *Aufführung*) that can be perceived and interpreted by a competent recipient. Considering games in play as a gestalt phenomenon against the backdrop of gestalt theory may be helpful.[38] A useful concept that applies gestalt theory for a subject-specific description of this structure can be found in Craig Lindley's concept of a gameplay gestalt: '[I]t is a particular way of thinking about the game state, together with a pattern of perceptual, cognitive, and motor operations. . . . [T]he gestalt is more of an interaction pattern involving both the in-game and out-of-game being of the player'.[39] So, a gameplay gestalt is one founded on a process, centred on

the act of playing a game as performative activity based on the game as an object. On the part of the players, any information given by the game that is relevant for playing on the level of rules as well as on the level of narrative, need interpretation, before carrying out the appropriate bodily (re)action,[40]

thereby bringing the gestalt into existence and enabling the experience. But how can we describe experiences beyond personal impressions?

Regarding the aesthetic dimension of *Aufführung*, a slightly adjusted version of Steve Swink's concept of game feel can be made fruitful. He

---

[37] Jesse Schell, *The Art of Game Design: A Book of Lenses* (San Francisco: Taylor & Francis, 2008), 10.

[38] Gestalt theory originally derives from an area of psychological theory introduced in the early twentieth century, which underwent changes in the different research areas by which it was adopted, such as musicology. See, for example, Mark Reybrouk, 'Gestalt Concepts and Music: Limitations and Possibilities', in *Music, Gestalt, and Computing: Studies in Cognitive and Systematic Musicology*, ed. Marc Leman (Berlin: Springer, 1997), 57–69.

[39] Craig A. Lindley, 'The Gameplay Gestalt, Narrative, and Interactive Storytelling', in *Computer Games and Digital Cultures Conference Proceedings*, Tampere 2002, 203–15 at 207, www.digra.org/wp-content/uploads/digital-library/05164.54179.pdf (last accessed 5 March 2020).

[40] Melanie Fritsch, 'Worlds of Music: Strategies for Creating Music-based Experiences in Videogames', in *The Oxford Handbook of Interactive Audio*, ed. by Karen Collins, Bill Kapralos and Holly Tessler (New York: Oxford University Press, 2014), 167–78 at 170.

defines game feel as '**Real-time control of virtual objects in a simulated space, with interactions emphasized by polish**'.[41] He emphasizes that playing a game allows for five different experiences:

- The aesthetic sensation of control,
- The pleasure of learning, practising and mastering a skill,
- Extension of the senses,
- Extension of identity,
- Interaction with a unique physical reality within the game.[42]

In other words, game feel highlights aspects of embodiment and describes the current bodily and sensual experience of the player as a co-creator of the *Aufführung* (in the sense of Fischer-Lichte). Therefore, the concept can be used to describe the aesthetic experience of performing (*aufführen*) during the actual execution (*ausführen*) offered by the game as a concept of possibilities. Taking up the example of *Guitar Hero*: Players learn to handle the plastic guitar to expertly score points (the pleasure of learning, practising and mastering a skill), thereby controlling the musical output (the aesthetic sensation of control) and incorporating the guitar-shaped controller into their body scheme (extension of the senses). When playing the game, they do not just press buttons to score points, but also perform the 'rock star fantasy', embodying the guitar hero (extension of identity). This works in any case: No matter which playing style players choose regarding the dimension of *Leistung*, during the performance in the sense of *Aufführung* both can be matched with the 'guitar hero' as a cultural pattern of behaviour – the button-mashing virtuoso or the rocking-out show person. Even the practising mode is tied to the rock star fantasy, when players struggle through the journey from garage band to stadium-filling act by acquiring necessary playing skills (the pleasure of learning, practising and mastering a skill). In other words, during every possible performance of the game (including practising) the emergent music-based gameplay gestalt[43] is in all cases tied to the promised subjective experience project of 'unleash[ing] your inner rock star', and is in this way charged with meaning. Even an ironic, exaggerated approach can work in this case, as this is also an accepted pattern in rock and heavy metal culture as comedy bands such as JBO or Tenacious D demonstrate.

---

[41] Steve Swink, *Game Feel: A Game Designer's Guide to Virtual Sensation* (Burlington: Morgan Kaufmann Publishing, 2009), 6.

[42] Swink, *Game Feel*, 10.

[43] See Fritsch, 'Worlds of Music.'

In summary: Regarding digital game playing as performance, the dimension of *Aufführung* can helpfully be addressed with Swink's concept of game feel, and broken down for description into his five experiential categories. It further becomes clear that the dimensions of *Leistung* and *Aufführung* are interlocked. The respective competencies and skill sets need to be acquired for the competent creation and understanding of an aesthetically pleasing gameplay gestalt.

As it is the goal of this chapter to introduce my basic ludomusicological framework that studies both games and music as playful performative practices, we need to address the two dimensions of performance regarding music in the next step.

Music as Performance: *Leistung*

As we have seen, for the analysis of a game such as *Guitar Hero*, a broader understanding of music beyond that of a written textual work is vital. In this context, the theorization about music as performance as conducted by researchers such as Nicholas Cook,[44] Christopher Small,[45] Carolyn Abbate[46] and others comes to mind. In this discourse the idea of music being a performative art form and a social practice is emphasized. But how should this be described in analysis?

In his book *Markenmusik*, Stefan Strötgen proposes a terminological framework that approaches music as a sounding but also as a socio-cultural phenomenon.[47] The basis for his argument is a five-tier model by music-semiotician Gino Stefani responding to the question 'in what ways does our culture produce sense with music?'[48] Stefani differentiates between the general codes (the psychoacoustic principles of auditory perception), and in a second step, the social practices on which basis 'musical techniques' are developed as organizational principles for sounds. Strötgen summarizes that with 'social practices' Stefani describes a 'network of sense' on which 'the relationships between music and society or, rather, between the various social practices of a culture' are built.[49] He further concretizes Stefani's

---

[44] See for example Nicholas Cook, *Beyond the Score: Music as Performance* (New York: Oxford University Press, 2013).

[45] Christopher Small, *Musicking: The Meanings of Performing and Listening* (Hanover, NH: Wesleyan University Press, 1998).

[46] Carolyn Abbate, 'Music – Drastic or Gnostic?', *Critical Inquiry* 30, no. 3 (2004): 505–36.

[47] Stefan Strötgen, *Markenmusik* (Würzburg: Königshausen & Neumann, 2014).

[48] Gino Stefani, 'A Theory of Musical Competence', *Semiotica* 66, no. 1–3 (1987): 7.

[49] Strötgen, *Markenmusik*, 119–50. Here Stefani as quoted and summarized by Strötgen on 129.

model: Different musical styles do not just sound different. Music also becomes meaningful through its use in society by linking it with other content such as pictorial worlds, shared ideas about the philosophy behind it, performer and fan behaviours, body images, or social rule sets regarding who is 'allowed' to perform which music in what context and so on, thus becoming part of a social network of meaning. These meanings have to be learned and are not inherent in the music itself as text or aural event. These three factors (general codes, social practices, musical techniques) then provide the basis for the emergence of 'styles', and in the end of a concrete-sounding 'opus' performed by competent performers and understood by competent recipients.[50]

At this point, one aspect needs to be highlighted that we have addressed regarding performance theory in general and that is also vital for the debate on music as performance: the politics of (musical) play and reception. This aspect is a core facet of Small's concept of musicking:

A theory of musicking, like the act itself, is not just an affair for intellectuals and 'cultured' people but an important component of our understanding of ourselves and of our relationships with other people and the other creatures with which we share our planet. It is a political matter in the widest sense. If everyone is born musical, then everyone's musical experience is valid.[51]

Musicking, defined as taking part 'in any capacity, in a musical performance, whether by performing, by listening, by rehearsing or practising, by providing material for performance (what is called composing), or by dancing'[52] demands a radical de-hierarchization of musical participation not only in terms of performers, but also in terms of recipients and designers. As Abbate and Strötgen also stress, audiences contribute their own meanings and interpretive paths when attending a musical performance. Subsequently, not only is everyone allowed to musick, but everyone is also allowed to talk about it and step into the role of designer by contributing in whatever capacity to the social discourse, for example, around a certain piece and how it has to be performed. Musicking means moving away from the idea of the one correct meaning that a composer has laid down in the musical text, which a passive recipient understands either correctly or not at all. This aspect of musical participation and music as a (recorded) commodity is also discussed by Cook and Abbate. According to Cook, a constant social (and therefore political) renegotiation of what, for example, a string quartet is supposed to be, which instruments are

---

[50] For the full discussion see Strötgen, *Markenmusik*, 119–137.
[51] Small, *Musicking*, 13.
[52] Small, *Musicking*, 9.

allowed in it, how to talk about it, how a specific one is to be performed and so on is the very core of how music-related social practices are established.[53] But similar to social practices, when and where we have the right to musick and play games is constantly being renegotiated against the backdrop of the respective cultural discourses.[54] Regarding music and the right to play it and play with it, we have seen this prominently in the sometimes harsh debates around *Guitar Hero*, when musicians such as Jack White or Jimmy Page strongly opposed such games and advocated 'kids' learning to play a real guitar instead of playing the game. Looking at the social practices of rock and its discourses of authenticity and liveness, it is quite obvious why they rejected the game: They accused game players of finagling an experience ('Unleash your inner rock star') they have no right to experience, since they have avoided the years of blood, sweat and tears of learning to play a real guitar.[55]

Music as Performance: *Aufführung*

Regarding the dimension of *Aufführung*, the aesthetic dimension, again the game feel concept as explained above comes in handy. In her seminal text Carolyn Abbate makes the case for a 'drastic musicology' that also includes personal experiences, as well as bodily and sensual experiences that occur during performances.[56] In our context, Abbate's example, in which she describes her experience of playing 'Non temer, amato bene' from Mozart's *Idomeneo* at the very moment of performance is quite interesting: '*doing this really fast is fun*' is not just a description of her momentarily playing experience, but also refers to the fact that she has acquired the necessary skills firstly, to play this piece of music at all and

---

[53] Nicholas Cook, 'Between Process and Product: Music and/as Performance', *Music Theory Online* 7, no. 2 (2001), accessed 16 October 2020, https://mtosmt.org/issues/mto.01.7.2/mto.01.7.2.cook.html

[54] This can either happen in a constructive or destructive way. A common phenomenon is gatekeeping; for example when game music started to enter the concert halls, not every classical music fan or critic was in favour of this development. Game culture itself has cut a bad figure in terms of inclusivity, with certain mostly straight-white-male-dominated groups not accepting non-white, non-male-identifying people as gamers. As the Gamergate debate has proven, this is not only fan culture being discussed, but a complex and highly political controversy, which cannot be laid out here in detail.

[55] See also Fritsch and Strötgen, 'Relatively Live'; and Moseley, 'Playing Games with Music.'

[56] Abbate, 'Music – Drastic or Gnostic?', 505–36. For a ludomusicological reading of Abbate's approach see Isabella van Elferen, 'Ludomusicology and the New Drastic', *Journal of Sound and Music in Games* 1, no. 1 (2020): 103–12.

secondly, to play it fast.[57] This points to the fact that both dimensions of performance are not only linked in terms of knowledge but also in terms of embodiment. In other words: In order to play a piece of music or, more generally speaking, create a musical performance, not only the acquisition of the respective knowledge is required, but equally the above-mentioned sensorimotoric and other playing competencies in order to create a satisfying *Aufführung* in the form of a coherent gestalt, the sounding 'opus'. Her description of musical movement with '*here comes a big jump*'[58] also follows this logic: on the one hand, she hereby refers to an option in the written work understood as a concept of possibilities that allows for this moment, which she can anticipate and master (the aesthetic sensation of control) thanks to her already acquired skills and knowledge (the pleasure of learning, practising and mastering a skill). On the other hand, she also describes her playing experience regarding the dimension of aesthetics using a metaphor of embodiment (extension of identity).

Table 14.1 summarizes the terminological framework we have developed so far, both for games and music understood as playful performative practices.

With the *Guitar Hero* example, we have already seen how this model can be usefully applied when studying music games. But what about the other two areas of ludomusicology, namely music as a design element in games, and game music beyond games?

Music as a Design Element in Games: *Super Mario Bros.*

Super Mario Bros. (1985) is one of the best-selling games of all time and started a long-running franchise that have been sold and played worldwide. Further, the title has been extensively studied in ludomusicological writing.[59] The game was designed under the lead of Shigeru Miyamoto and was distributed in a bundle with the Nintendo Entertainment System in North America and Europe, making it one of the first game experiences many players had on this console.

The staging of *Super Mario Bros.* is not intended to be realistic, neither in terms of its visual design, presenting a colourful comic-styled 8-bit diegetic environment, nor in terms of what the player can do. As I have stated before,

---

[57] Abbate, 'Music – Drastic or Gnostic?', 511.

[58] Ibid.

[59] A full version of this case study can be found in Fritsch, *Performing Bytes*, 130–44. See also Zach Whalen, 'Play Along – An Approach to Videogame Music', *Game Studies* 4, no. 1 (2004); Andrew Schartmann, *Koji Kondo's Super Mario Bros. Soundtrack* (New York: Bloomsbury, 2015).

Table 14.1 Overview of the ludomusicological framework

Competence (*Leistung*)	Presentation (*Aufführung*)

1. Concepts of media education
Five areas of competence and skills[a]
 	
• Social skills
• Personal competence
• Sensomotoric skills
• Media competence
• Cognitive competence
• following Gebel, subdivided into:[c]
1. Formal cognitive skills
2. Content-related cognitive competencies
   a. Instrumental knowledge
   b. Analytical knowledge
   c. Structural knowledge
   d. + Cultural knowledge
	Slightly modified game-feel-model, after Steve Swink[b]
	
	= the aesthetic experience of performing (*aufführen*) during the execution (*ausführen*) Offered by the game as concept of possibilities; it highlights the aspect of embodiment and describes the current bodily and sensual experience of the player as a co-creator of the performance (in the sense of *Aufführung*, after Fischer-Lichte)[d]

2. Game Literacy/Gaming Literacy Literacy model, after Zagal and Zimmerman.[e] Areas of competence enable the player to perform in several roles 1. As actor 2. As recipient 3. As designer	Five experiential dimensions 1. The aesthetic sensation of control 2. The pleasure of learning, practising and mastering a skill 3. Extension of the sense 4. Extension of identity 5. Interaction with a unique physical reality within the game

a   Gebel, Gurt and Wagner, *Kompetenzförderliche Potenziale populärer Computerspiele.*
b   Swink, *Game Feel.*
c   Gebel 'Kompetenz Erspielen – Kompetent Spielen?'
d   Fischer-Lichte, *Ästhetik des Performativen.*
e   Zagal, *Ludoliteracy* and Zimmerman, 'Gaming Literacy.'

I describe the *performative space* in which all actions induced by the game take place, including those in front of the screen, as the gameworld. In this gameworld, the game's narrative, the specific and unique sequence of fictional and non-fictional events happening while playing the game, unfolds. In order to address the *world*, which can be seen on screen, and set this apart from the gameworld, I will henceforth refer to this as the diegetic environment. I use the term diegesis here in the sense of Genette: 'diegesis is not the story, but the universe in which it takes place'[.][60]

Super Mario Bros.' diegetic environment presents the player with manifold challenges such as abysses, multifarious enemies, moving platforms and other traps and obstacles. In the words of Swink,

---

[60] Fritsch, 'Worlds of Music', 170.

In general, the creatures and objects represented have very little grounding in meaning or reality. Their meaning is conveyed by their functionality in the game, which is to present danger and to dominate areas of space. ... [W]e're not grounded in expectations about how these things should behave.[61]

The game does not offer an introduction or a tutorial, but gameplay starts immediately. That way, players have to understand the specific rules of the abstract diegetic environment, and either already possess or acquire all the necessary cognitive competencies and instrumental knowledge required to master all challenges. The avatar Mario also possesses specific features, such as his three states (Mario, Super Mario, Fire Mario) or the ability to execute high and wide jumps, which never change through the entire game. Regarding the dimension of *Leistung*, in addition to developing sensorimotor skills such as reaction speed and hand–eye co-ordination, learning and applying a whole range of cognitive skills and game-related knowledge is therefore necessary to successfully master the game. Formal cognitive (for example, attention, concentration, memory) and personality-related skills (coping with frustration and emotional self-control) are vital. The experience offered during the *Aufführung* while manoeuvring Mario through the diegetic environment featuring its own rules (interacting with a unique physical reality within the game) can be understood as the player discovering and mastering challenges by increasing not the avatar's skill set, but their own playing skills (the pleasure of learning, practising and mastering a skill). This is done through embodiment by getting a feel for Mario (extending the player's own identity) and the surrounding world (extending their senses). For example, as Steve Swink notes, 'Super Mario Brothers has something resembling a simulation of physical forces ... there are in fact stored values for acceleration, velocity and position. ... If Mario's running forward and suddenly I stop touching the controller, Mario will slide gently to a halt'.[62] A skilled player who has mastered the controls (experiencing the aesthetic sensation of control) and developed a feel for Mario's movements (extending the player's identity), can make use of this, for example by running towards a low-hanging block, ducking and gently sliding under it, thereby getting to places that are normally only accessible with a small Mario.

But how do music and gameplay come together? Composer Koji Kondo created six basic pieces for the game, namely the Overworld, Underworld, Starman and Castle themes, the Underwater Waltz and the ending theme. As detailed musicological analyses and explanations of the technological

---

[61] Swink, *Game Feel*, 225.
[62] Swink, *Game Feel*, 206–9.

preconditions and subsequent choices can be found elsewhere, as noted above, I will confine myself here to highlighting how the music and sound effects are perfectly designed to create a coherent gameplay gestalt.

In an interview Kondo explains that, based on the specifications initially communicated to him, the Underwater Waltz was the first melody he wrote for the game, since it was easy for him to imagine how underwater music must sound.[63] This indicates that for certain representations on the visual level such as water, swimming and weightlessness, cultural ideas exist on how these should be underscored, namely in the form of a waltz. Kondo further states that a first version of the Overworld theme that he had also written on the basis of the specifications did not work (which were for-mulated: 'Above ground, Western-sounding, percussion and a sound like a whip'). He describes that he had tried to underscore the visual appearance of the game, namely the light blue skies and the green bushes. But when Kondo played the prototype, the melody did not fit Mario's jumping and running movements, therefore it felt wrong. As players have only a specific amount of time to succeed in a level, the music as well as the level design encourage them to not play carefully, but rather to adopt a 'Fortune Favours the Bold'[64] playing style. Kondo's second approach, now based on the actual embodied experience of gameplay, reflected this very game feel. As Schartmann puts it:

Instead of using music to incite a particular emotional response (e. g., using faster notes to increase tension), he tried to anticipate the physical experience of the gamer based on the rhythm and movement of gameplay. . . . In essence, if music does not reflect the rhythm of the game, and, by extension, that of the gamer, it becomes background music.[65]

That way, the distinct laws and rhythms of the diegetic world, and the way in which the player should move Mario through them using their own learned skills and the subsequent 'extension of the senses' are both acous-tically transported by the music and by the sound effects, also by using techniques such as movement analogy, better known as Mickey-Mousing (the 'ka-ching' of the coins, the uprising jumping sound, the booming sound of Bullet Bills etc.). In addition to game-specific competencies, general cultural knowledge from other media types, namely cartoons and movies regarding the logic of how these are underscored, help to develop

[63] Satoru Iwata, 'Iwata Asks: Volume 5: Original Super Mario Developers', *Iwata Asks* (2010), accessed 11 April 2020, http://iwataasks.nintendo.com/interviews/#/wii/mario25th/4/4.

[64] Swink, *Game Feel*, 221.

[65] Schartmann, *Super Mario Bros.*, 32–3.

a quick understanding of the inner workings of the abstract world presented on screen.

Kondo conceptualized the soundtrack in close connection with the game feel evoked by the game performance, understood as the player's sensual and physical experience as they follow the intended scheme of play that is encouraged by the level design. The game's music sounds for as long as the player performs the game, which is determined by their skill level (unskilled players may have to restart many times over) and by their actions. The sounding musical performance is therefore directed by their gameplay and their (game-) playing skills. Playing *Super Mario Bros.* can be understood as a musical performance; firstly, when understood in terms of *Leistung,* the generation of this performance requires not only knowledge but also the physical skills needed to play the game at all; and secondly, it requires the ability to adopt the intended speed and playing style encouraged by the level design, play time limit and music.[66] All elements of the staging (gameplay, diegetic world, level design, music, etc.) are from a functionalist point of view designed to support game feel in the sense of an interlocking of both dimensions of performance, so that a coherent gameplay gestalt can be created during the current act of play, which involves the player in the gameworld as defined above. The player constantly shifts between the role of performer and that of recipient and continuously develops their respective skills in the course of the game's performance.

Music Beyond Games: Chip Music as a 'Gaming-a-System' Practice

Since the late 1970s, game sounds and music have found an audience outside the games themselves. They can be heard in TV shows, commercials, films and other musical genres. In Japan the first original soundtrack album of Namco titles was released in 1984, and the first dedicated label for chip music – G.M.O. Records, as an imprint of Alfa Records – was founded in 1986.[67]

---

[66] The creators of another game in the franchise, namely *Super Mario Galaxy*, mentioned this very philosophy as the basic idea behind their game's soundtrack. See Satoru Iwata, 'Mario Is Like a Musical Instrument', *Iwata Asks* (2010), accessed 11 April 2020, http://iwataasks.nintendo.com/interviews/#/wii/supermariogalaxy2/1/4.

[67] See, for example, Melanie Fritsch, 'Heroines Unsung: The (Mostly) Untold History of Female Japanese Composers', in *Women's Music for the Screen: Diverse Narratives in Sound*, ed. Felicity Wilcox (New York: Routledge, in press). A full version of this case study can be found in Fritsch, *Performing Bytes*, 252–67.

As explained in the introduction to Part I of this book, thanks to the coming of affordable home computers and video game systems, a participatory music culture emerged at the same time. Instead of simply playing computer games, groups banded together to remove the copy protection of commercial titles. Successfully 'cracked' games were put into circulation within the scene and marked by the respective cracker group with an intro so that everyone knew who had cracked the title first. Due to the playful competition behind this, the intros became more and more complex and the groups invented programming tricks to push the existing hardware beyond its boundaries. As Anders Carlsson describes:

> Just as a theatre director can play with the rules of what theatre is supposed to be, the demosceners and chip music composers found ways to work beyond techno-logical boundaries thought to be unbreakable. . . . These tricks were not rational mathematical programming, but rather trial and error based on in-depth knowl-edge of the computer used. Demosceners managed to accomplish things not intended by the designers of the computers.[68]

In addition to the idea of competition, an additional goal can be described as an independent accumulation of knowledge and competencies through playful exploration and 'gaming a system' in the sense of Zimmerman, but according to a specific rule set as negotiated in the community. The goal of this self-invented meta-game with the personal goal of 'technology mas-tery' (the pleasure of learning and mastering a skill, seamlessly merging in an aesthetic sensation of control) is an optimization of the staging – in the sense of an exhibition – of skills during the actual performance of the songs. These skills include knowing the specific sound characteristics and technological features of the respective sound chip, as well as optimizing and generating sounds that had been thought to be impossible. The finished composition and concrete opus sounds as a musical performance when the practitioner plays their work themselves or when someone else performs their composition based on the staging of the technical appara-tus (that is the computer technology). Such a media-mediated music performance can in turn be evaluated accordingly by a competent recipi-ent, savvy in the evaluation rules negotiated in the chip music scene. Aesthetic notions relate not only to the composition and the sounding opus, but also to the elegance or extravagance of the staging, that is, the use of hardware and software. Further, practitioners constantly renegotiate

---

[68] Anders Carlsson, 'Chip Music: Low-Tech Data Music Sharing', in *From Pac-Man to Pop Music: Interactive Audio in Games and New Media*, ed. Karen Collins (Aldershot: Ashgate, 2008), 153–62 at 155.

how a well-made artefact is to be created, which affordances it must fulfil, how it should be judged and so on.

Additionally, demosceners and chip musicians do not keep the knowledge they have gained through 'gaming a system' to themselves, but share their insights with the community, for example by publishing their programming routines, or self-created accessible software such as Hülsbeck's Soundmonitor or the Soundtracker 2, a hacked, improved and freely distributed version of Karsten Obarski's Soundtracker, created by the Dutch hacker Exterminator.[69] As the songs produced with these trackers were saved in the MOD format, they are effectively open books for competent users, as Anders Carlsson describes:

[I]t was possible to look into the memory to see how the songs worked in terms of the routine that defines how to access the sound chip, and the key was to tweak the chip to its fullest. . . . [I]t was possible for users to access the player routines, along with instruments, note data, effects and samples. Even though these elements could be hidden with various techniques, there would usually be a way to hack into the code[.] As long as a user has the tracker that was used for making the song, it is possible to load the song into an editor and gain total control of the song.[70]

By creating and openly sharing their tools and knowledge, chip musicians actively practised the democratization of musical participation advocated by Small. The resulting music performances were also shared within the community, were increasingly made available free of charge via the Internet and were made available to others for use or further processing, thereby undermining the idea of music as a commodity to be paid for. 'Gaming a system' therefore does not only take place in relation to the hard- and software, but also avoids the usual distribution and performance rules of Western music, thereby creating new genres and giving musicians access to musical production that they would otherwise have been denied, and allowing everyone to musick. As for example Bizzy B., 'godfather of breakbeat hardcore and drum 'n' bass, responsible for overseeing hardcore's transition into jungle' (as he is described by the interviewer Mat Ombler) explains in an interview about the role of the Amiga and the tracker OctaMED, written by Teijo Kinnunen:

It allowed me to have a doorway into the music business. . . . I wouldn't have been able to afford the money for a recording studio; I wouldn't have been able to

---

[69] Regarding hacker ethics and ideas, see Kenneth B. McAlpine's chapter (Chapter 2) in this volume.

[70] Carlsson, 'Chip Music', 158.

practice music production and take my music to the next level if it wasn't for the Commodore Amiga.[71]

Since the early days, the community has diversified into what Leonard J. Paul calls the 'old school' and the 'new school'.[72] Whereas the old school practitioners focus on using the original systems or instruments to create their performances, the new school evolved with the new technological possibilities of 1990s personal computers, as well as the trackers and other tools developed by the scene itself, and is interested in on-stage performances which include the performers themselves being on the stage. They further explore new hybrid forms by combining the chip sound – which does not have to be created with the original systems; instead new synthesizers are used – with other instruments,[73] thereby gaming a third system by freely combining the systems of different musical genres.

Chip musicians invented their own meta-game with the goal of creating music performances with the given materials. Participation is only restricted in that they must have access to the respective technology and must be literate, firstly in using the technology and secondly in the socially negotiated rules of the meta-game; this demands all five above-mentioned areas of competence outlined by Gebel, Gurt and Wagner,[74] and the acquisition of these respective skills to create chip music performances. Over time, these rules have changed, and the new school have developed their own social practices and rules for 'gaming a system'.

Conclusions

Using this terminological framework, we can respectively describe and analyse the design-based use of music as an element of staging, and the resulting

---

[71] Mat Ombler, 'Megadrive to Mega Hit: Why Video Games Are So Tied to Club Music', *Vice* (2018), accessed 11 April 2020, https://www.vice.com/en_uk/article/a3pb45/video-games-90s-club-music-commodore-amiga.

[72] Leonard J. Paul, 'For the Love of Chiptune', in *The Oxford Handbook of Interactive Audio*, ed. Karen Collins, Bill Kapralos and Holly Tessler (New York: Oxford University Press, 2014), 507–30 at 510.

[73] See also Matthias Pasdzierny, 'Geeks on Stage? Investigations in the World of (Live) Chipmusic', in *Music and Game Perspectives on a Popular Alliance*, ed. Peter Moormann (Wiesbaden: Springer, 2013), 171–90 and Chris Tonelli, 'The Chiptuning of the World: Game Boys, Imagined Travel, and Musical Meaning', in *The Oxford Handbook of Mobile Music Studies Volume. 2*, ed. Sumanth Gopinath and Jason Stanyek (New York: Oxford University Press, 2014), 402–26.

[74] Gebel, Gurt and Wagner, *Kompetenzförderliche Potenziale populärer Computerspiele*.

relationship between players, music and game, in the context of play on the two dimensions of performance. It further enables a differentiated distinction between the performance dimensions of *Leistung* and *Aufführung*, as well as a differentiation between music- and game-specific competencies regarding the *Leistung* dimension. Understood as forms of performance, both music and games can also be addressed as social acts, and aspects of embodiment can be taken into account thanks to the adapted game feel concept. Used in addition to other approaches introduced in this book, this framework can help to describe specific relationships and highlight aspects of these in order to further our understanding of games and music.

PART IV

Realities, Perception and Psychology

Introduction

MELANIE FRITSCH AND TIM SUMMERS

Games present us with virtual spaces and universes, and ask us to interact with them. These worlds are virtual, because they cannot be sensed directly like our everyday reality, but instead, we perceive them through the channels of audio, video and, sometimes, touch, that the game apparatus provides. Audio and music are part of how we come to understand the game environments that are shown to us – sound helps to construct the worlds and shapes how we engage with them.

It has been well documented that audio contributes to a sense of orientation, awareness and engagement with virtual realities. Kristine Jørgensen studied the experience of players when sound was removed during playing games. From the players' reports, she concluded that 'the absence of sound decreases the sense of control' and 'the sense of a presence and lifelike universe is affected'.[1] Audio in games deals both with functional and aesthetic aspects of the game. Sound can at once provide gameplay-relevant information (like indicating that an event has occurred, proximity of enemies, etc.), and it serves part of the artistic experience of the game (creating a mood, manipulating emotions, etc.). Music may similarly easily do both. As Axel Stockburger notes, 'Score sound objects can also be connected to locations in the game, which makes them significant for the spatial practice of a game',[2] but these musical functions are also part of the characterization of these locations, creating a vivid and engaging world, not just serving as signposts.

---

[1] Kristine Jørgensen, 'Left in the Dark: Playing Computer Games with the Sound Turned Off', in *From Pac-Man to Pop Music: Interactive Audio in Games and New Media*, ed. Karen Collins (Aldershot: Ashgate, 2008), 163–76 at 167.

[2] Axel Stockburger, 'The Game Environment from an Auditive Perspective', in *Proceedings: Level Up: Digital Games Research Conference* (DiGRA), ed. Marinka Copier and Joost Raessens (Utrecht, 4–6 November), 2003 at 5.

Though game music may have functional qualities, it is not as straight-forward as music simply making a game 'easier' or improving player achievement. Music may distract the player's attention away from impor-tant in-game information, add to the cognitive load of the player or create a mood that is not optimum for high-scoring performance. Empirical research on this topic has been conducted in the domain of racing games. Some projects found that car speed and lap times increased with music, but produced the most errors,[3] while others found that participants' fastest times were attained without music.[4] As a further contrast beyond racing games, a study using *The Legend of Zelda: Twilight Princess* (2006) reported the best player performance with background music unrelated to the game.[5] Yet analysis of the discourse in player forums of *Left 4 Dead* (2008) clearly indicates that a well-crafted implementation that conveys clear and accurate information can help players to increase their gameplay performance, or at least give them the *impression* that they are performing better.[6]

Unsurprisingly, empirical studies have also supported our assumptions that music alters the enjoyment of games,[7] and affects the way players approach playing through games, for example by impacting behaviours such as risk-taking.[8] Beyond performance, there is evidence of the physio-logical effect of listening to music in games. Heart rate, blood pressure and

[3] Gianna Cassidy and Raymond MacDonald, 'The Effects of Music Choice on Task Performance: A Study of the Impact of Self-Selected and Experimenter-Selected Music on Driving Game Performance and Experience', *Musicae Scientiae* 13, no. 2 (2009): 357–86; and Gianna Cassidy and Raymond MacDonald, 'The Effects of Music on Time Perception and Performance of a Driving Game', *Scandinavian Journal of Psychology* 51 (2010): 455–64.

[4] Masashi Yamada, Nozomu Fujisawa and Shigenobu Komori, 'The Effect of Music on the Performance and Impression in a Racing Video Game', *Journal of Music Perception & Cognition*, 7 (2001): 65–76 and Masashi Yamada, 'The Effect of Music on the Performance and Impression in a Racing Video Game', in *Proceedings of the 7th International Conference on Music Perception and Cognition*, ed. Catherine J. Stevens, Denis K. Burnham, Gary McPherson et al. (Casual Productions: Adelaide, 2002), 340–3, reported in Scott Lipscomb and Sean Zehnder, 'Immersion in the Virtual Environment: The Effect of a Musical Score on the Video Gaming Experience', *Journal of Physiological Anthropology and Applied Human Sciences* 23, no. 6 (2004): 337–43.

[5] Siu-Lan Tan, John Baxa and Matthew P. Spackman, 'Effects of Built-In Audio Versus Unrelated Background Music on Performance in an Adventure Roleplaying Game', *International Journal of Gaming and Computer-Mediated Simulations*, 2, no. 3 (2010): 1–23.

[6] Melanie Fritsch, 'Musik', in *Game Studies*, ed. Benjamin Beil, Thomas Hensel and Andreas Rauscher (Wiesbaden: Springer, 2018), 87–107 at 101–3.

[7] Christoph Klimmt, Daniel Possler, Nicolas May, Hendrik Auge, Louisa Wanjek and Anna-Lena Wolf, 'Effects of Soundtrack Music on the Video Game Experience', *Media Psychology* 22, no. 5 (2019): 689–713.

[8] Katja Rogers, Matthias Jörg and Michael Weber, 'Effects of Background Music on Risk-Taking and General Player Experience', in *CHI PLAY '19: Proceedings of the Annual Symposium on Computer-Human Interaction in Play* (Association for Computing Machinery, 2019), 213–24.

cortisol levels (all indicators of stress) have all been recorded as increased in participants playing first-person shooters with music compared to those playing without.[9] As can be gleaned from the above discussion, empirical psychological research into game music is still an underexplored area, with many apparent contradictions yet to be fully explored or explained. Rather more extensive is research into the conceptual basis of the experience of music while gaming.

The word 'immersion' is used extensively in both casual and academic writing about games and their music. Unfortunately, the term is unstable and can refer to very different meanings depending on the context. As Gordon Calleja summarizes, 'There is a lack of consensus on the use of *immersion* to refer to either general involvement in a medium . . . or to the sense of being transported to another reality'.[10] These definitions are sometimes compatible, but at other times lead to opposing views – Katie Salen and Eric Zimmerman criticize what they call the 'immersive fallacy', 'the idea that the pleasure of the media experience lies in its ability to sensually transport the participant into an illusory, simulated reality'.[11] Instead, they believe that immersion lies in engaging gameplay, as does Elena Gorfinkel, who notes that 'one can get immersed in *Tetris*. Therefore, immersion into gameplay seems at least as important as immersion in a game's representational space.'[12]

Scholars have approached sound and immersion in games in a variety of ways, usually avoiding defining immersion, but instead focusing on factors that encourage the multifaceted experience(s) of immersion. Most concentrate on the ways in which games use sound and music to engage players. Mark Grimshaw and Karen Collins specifically emphasize the interactive connection between player agency and sound. Grimshaw describes how players and the game systems work together to form a sonic environment. Grimshaw analyses

the sound of first-person shooters, particularly where the ability of the player to contribute sound to the acoustic ecology of the game (the triggering of audio

---

[9] Sylvie Hébert, Renée Béland, Odrée Dionne-Fournelle, Martine Crête and Sonia J. Lupien, 'Physiological Stress Response to Video-Game Playing: The Contribution of Built-In Music', *Life Sciences* 76, no. 20 (2005): 2371–80; Richard Tafalla, 'Gender Differences in Cardiovascular Reactivity and Game Performance Related to Sensory Modality in Violent Video Game Play', *Journal of Applied Social Psychology* 37, no. 9 (2007): 2008–23.

[10] Gordon Calleja, *In-Game: From Immersion to Incorporation* (Cambridge, MA: MIT Press, 2011), 32.

[11] Katie Salen and Eric Zimmerman, *Rules of Play: Game Design Fundamentals* (Cambridge, MIT Press, 2004), 450.

[12] Quoted in Salen and Zimmerman, *Rules of Play,* 452.

samples through player action and presence in the game world) is a key factor in player immersion in that ecology and, thus, the game world.[13]

Karen Collins uses a similar idea of 'kinesonic synchresis'.

Interactive sound in games is kinesonically synchretic: sounds are fused not to image but to action. In other words, interactive sound is event-driven, and the sound is controlled by an action or occurrence that is initiated by the game or by the player.[14]

This embodied interaction, Collins suggests, is part of the process of creating an immersive experience.

Other scholars have attended to the musical materials involved in immersion. Rod Munday, for instance, treats immersion as 'deep involvement' and proposes that music encourages 'mythic immersion'. This occurs where players become involved with the game, leave behind elements of their own sense of self and engage with the avatar to act as the hero of a game.[15]

Isabella van Elferen proposes a model for musical immersion that outlines the varied roles of music in player engagement. Her framework is called the 'ALI model', an acronym that reflects the three dimensions of musical affect, literacy and interaction.

Affect: 'personal investment in a given situation through memory, emotion and identification',
Literacy: 'gamers recognize certain composing styles [and] are able to interpret gaming events and feel involved in gameplay, game worlds and game plots',
Interaction: 'Musical interaction in video games establishes a direct connection between player actions and the game soundtrack'.[16]

This approach recognizes the multidimensionality of music and immersion in games, and allows the different aspects to be considered not only separately, but also with an awareness of how they interact. Perhaps player involvement is likely to be most intense where the three areas of the framework overlap.

---

[13] Mark Grimshaw, 'Sound', in *The Routledge Companion to Video Game Studies*, ed. Mark J. P. Wolf and Bernard Perron (New York: Routledge, 2014), 117–24 at 121.

[14] Karen Collins, *Playing With Sound: A Theory of Interacting with Sound and Music in Video Games* (Cambridge, MA: The MIT Press, 2013), 32.

[15] Rod Munday, 'Music in Video Games', in *Music, Sound and Multimedia: From the Live to the Virtual*, ed. Jamie Sexton (Edinburgh: Edinburgh University Press, 2007), 51–67 at 56.

[16] Isabella van Elferen, 'Analysing Game Musical Immersion: The ALI Model', in *Ludomusicology: Approaches to Video Game Music*, ed. Michiel Kamp, Tim Summers and Mark Sweeney (Sheffield: Equinox, 2016), 32–52 at 34–7.

Beyond focus on the issue of 'immersion' specifically, sound can be instrumental in forging our relationship with the worlds and realities of games. Games may use so-called 'informative sound' for notifications and interactions with game interfaces. 'Auditory icons' are based on references to our everyday reality, while 'earcons' are more abstracted and use musical features like pitch and timbre to communicate information. Sometimes sounds are used to draw the player's attention to gameplay features or events. Kristine Jørgensen would call these 'emphatic' sounds, given that they communicate information about aspects of the gameworld, emphasizing or augmenting the event.[17] These can be entirely compatible with a 'realistic style'.

Even though a game may strive to be realistic in terms of its aesthetic style, that is not necessarily achieved through fidelity to reality. Even 'realistic' games use music in unrealistic ways. Richard Stevens and Dave Raybould have outlined how sounds that are less close to reality can sometimes give the impression of being more 'realistic'.[18] Signs of realism can be more effective than fidelity to reality. Similar approaches are found with musical strategies in games. Andra Ivănescu shows how *L.A. Noire* (2011) uses music to create a compelling, realistic historical world of 1940s Los Angeles, but the representation has more in common with Hollywood imagery than the historical reality of the time period and setting.[19] Ivănescu has explored extensively how popular music is used anachronistically, and how radically chronologically juxtaposed situations leverage nostalgia to create aesthetically compelling realities.[20] For example, she explores how the *BioShock* (2007–2016) and *Fallout* (1997–2018) games place American popular music from the earlier and mid-twentieth century alongside their futuristic settings to immerse the player in their distinctive worlds.[21] Games often use music as a way to give their virtual worlds a sense of history and cultural identity – games like *Dishonored 2* (2016) and *Wolfenstein: The New Order* (2014) use newly-written music in the fictional reality to 'texture' and provide character to the world.

---

[17] Kristine Jørgensen, 'Emphatic and Ecological Sounds in Gameworld Interfaces', in *The Routledge Companion to Screen Music and Sound*, ed. Miguel Mera, Ronald Sadoff and Ben Winters (New York: Routledge, 2017), 72–84 at 79.

[18] Richard Stevens and Dave Raybould, 'The Reality Paradox: Authenticity, Fidelity and the Real in Battlefield 4', *The Soundtrack* 8, no. 1–2 (2015): 57–75.

[19] Andra Ivănescu, 'Torched Song: The Hyperreal and the Music of *L.A. Noire*', *The Soundtrack* 8, no. 1–2 (2015): 41–56.

[20] Andra Ivănescu, *Popular Music in the Nostalgia Video Game: The Way it Never Sounded* (Cham: Palgrave, 2019).

[21] On these games see also William Cheng, *Sound Play: Video Games and the Musical Imagination* (New York: Oxford University Press, 2014) and William Gibbons, 'Wrap Your Troubles in Dreams: Popular Music, Narrative and Dystopia in BioShock', *Game Studies* 11 (2011).

Discussions of music and virtual environments have also sought to understand how exploring virtual environments can relate to the music we so often hear while roaming game spaces. Mark Sweeney and Michiel Kamp have connected discussions of music and landscape with the virtual gameworlds.[22] They outline how musical features connote landscapes: examples include music that has a sense of internal surface-level motion, but overall musical stasis (which is apt for the looped and repeated music so often found in games). They describe how 'cues can support experiences akin to those of natural landscapes', and thus how music becomes part of how we engage with the virtual geography.[23]

Music and sound are extraordinarily important elements of how we engage with the worlds of games. In this Part, Mark Grimshaw-Aagaard provides a broad conceptual background on the importance of sound for presence and the nature of reality we experience in games. Dana Plank outlines how aspects of music and cognition are evident in game music, and finally Duncan Williams describes some of the present and future possibilities presented by the intersection of music and physiological responses in the context of games.

Further Reading

Collins, Karen. *Playing With Sound: A Theory of Interacting with Sound and Music in Video Games*. Cambridge, MA: The MIT Press, 2013.

Grimshaw, Mark, Tan, Siu-Lan and Lipscomb, Scott D. 'Playing With Sound: The Role of Music and Sound Effects in Gaming', in *The Psychology of Music in Multimedia*, ed. Siu-Lan Tan, Annabel J. Cohen, Scott D. Lipscomb and Roger A. Kendall. Oxford: Oxford University Press, 2013, 289–314.

Ivănescu, Andra. *Popular Music in the Nostalgia Video Game: The Way It Never Sounded*. Cham: Palgrave, 2019.

Jørgensen, Kristine. 'Left in the Dark: Playing Computer Games with the Sound Turned Off', in *From Pac-Man to Pop Music: Interactive Audio in Games and New Media*, ed. Karen Collins. Aldershot: Ashgate, 2008, 163–76.

van Elferen, Isabella. 'Analysing Game Musical Immersion: The ALI Model', in *Ludomusicology: Approaches to Video Game Music*, ed. Michiel Kamp, Tim Summers and Mark Sweeney. Sheffield: Equinox, 2016, 32–52.

---

[22] Michiel Kamp and Mark Sweeney, 'Musical Landscapes in Skyrim', in *Music in the Role-Playing Game*, ed. William Gibbons and Steven Reale (New York: Routledge, 2020), 179–96.

[23] Kamp and Sweeney, 'Musical Landscapes', 186.

15 | A Step Back from Reality: Sound and Presence in Computer Games and Other Worlds

MARK GRIMSHAW-AAGAARD

Introduction

If, as suggested by Donald T. Campbell,[1] the result of our particular abilities to sense and perceive is that we are distanced from a fundamental reality,[2] then what precisely is the nature and role of presence with respect to that reality? Furthermore, given the theme of this companion, what is the role of sound in relation to presence in virtual gameworlds? These are the two questions that underpin this chapter and to which I provide some answers. One question that might be asked, but which I do not attempt to answer, is: what is the role, if any, of *music* in presence in virtual gameworlds? The answer to this particular question I leave to the reader to attempt once the companion has been read. Other chapters in this companion deal more directly with music and its relationship to narrative and ludic processes or its abilities to provoke emotion in the game player and to establish meaning. These are areas, I suggest, that might be helpfully informed by answering questions about music and presence. Here, I content myself merely with providing some of the groundwork that will help the reader attempt the question. Before moving on to deal with *my* two questions, I must first clarify some terminology in order to furnish a framework from within which I can then debate them. I begin with a definition of sound.

---

[1] Donald T. Campbell, 'Evolutionary Epistemology', in *The Philosophy of Karl Popper*, Vol. XIV Book 1, ed. Paul Arthur Schilpp (La Salle, IL: Open Court, 1974), 413–63.

[2] This is explained further in the chapter subsection 'Stepping Back from Reality', but, briefly, our sensory system provides a very filtered window on reality – aurally, we sense and perceive only between approximately 20 Hz and 20 kHz, and so miss out on aural aspects of that reality that, for example, dogs and cats are aware of.

The Framework

What Is Sound?

In agreement with Pasnau,[3] I would describe the standard definition of sound, various forms of which are to be found in dictionaries and acoustics textbooks – namely that sound is an audible pressure wave propagating in a medium – as incoherent. Incoherent in that the definition and its use to explain our relationship to sound holds up neither to scrutiny nor to experience. Furthermore, I would describe the definition's use within physics and acoustics as inconsistent and imprecise. Such instances abound and are, perhaps, manifestations of the incoherency of the standard definition. Elsewhere,[4] I have given a more detailed exegesis of the problems with the definition and its use, so here, a few examples of inconsistency and imprecision will suffice to support my contention; the matter of incoherency I also deal with in the following discussion.

Consider the following quotations from John Tyndall: 'It is the motion imparted to this, the auditory nerve, which, in the brain, is translated into sound' (so sound arises in the brain), but 'thus is sound conveyed from particle to particle through the air' (so sound is a physical phenomenon in the air), and yet it is in the brain that 'the vibrations are translated into sound'.[5] Here, sound seems to be at once a physical acoustic phenomenon and a neurological phenomenon. Admittedly, these are from a book published in 1867 when the new scientific discipline of acoustics was beginning to find its feet, so perhaps I should not be so harsh. Yet, such muddled thinking persists, as demonstrated by the following description from the 2010s: 'The [hearing] implant is placed . . . in the area [in the brain] where the axons (nerve fibres) and cochlear nucleus (synapses) – which transport sounds picked up by the ear to the cerebral cortex – are found'.[6] What is wrong with the statements is that the brain comprises electrical energy, while sound (i.e., a sound wave) comprises acoustic energy – sound waves cannot be phenomena both in the air and in the brain, or indeed, as suggested by Tyndall's last statement, something only to be found in the

---

[3] Robert Pasnau, 'What Is Sound?', *The Philosophical Quarterly* 49, no. 196 (1999): 309–24.
[4] Mark Grimshaw, 'A Brief Argument For, and Summary of, the Concept of Sonic Virtuality', *Danish Musicology Online – Special Issue on Sound and Music Production* (2015), 81–98.
[5] John Tyndall, *Sound* (London: Longmans, Green, and Co., 1867), 2–4.
[6] Denis Pouliot, 'Hearing Without Ears (Auditory Brainstem Implant)', *Lobe*, c.2014, https://web.archive.org/web/20140513004625/https://www.lobe.ca/en/non-classee/hearing-without-ears-auditory-brainstem-implant/.

brain. The American National Standards Institute (ANSI) documentation provides, in fact, two definitions of sound:

a. Oscillation in pressure, stress, particle displacement, particle velocity etc., propagated in a medium with internal forces (e.g. elastic or viscous) or the superposition of such propagated oscillation ...

b. Auditory sensation evoked by the oscillation described in (a).[7]

The second of these could, with great latitude in the definition of the word 'sensation', be taken to be sound in the brain, but they should not be used interchangeably in the same sentence (otherwise one can easily end up with the amusing but absurd statement that *sound is evoked by sound*).[8]

The standard definition of sound is more precisely and usefully a definition of sound waves, and, in this, it is a perfectly adequate definition, if used a little inconsistently in the literature. It is not, though, a sufficient or coherent definition of sound, and for this reason, in the book *Sonic Virtuality*, Tom Garner and I devised a new definition to account for various sonic anomalies and inconsistencies that are found when regarding sound solely as the physical phenomenon that is a sound wave: 'Sound is an emergent perception arising primarily in the auditory cortex and that is formed through spatio-temporal processes in an embodied system'.[9]

One advantage of this new definition is that it accounts for the multimodality[10] of our hearing in a way that the standard definition does not. This multimodality is clearly evidenced by the McGurk effect. In this demonstration, two films are shot of someone repeatedly enunciating 'baa' and 'faa' respectively. The audio from the 'baa' video is then superimposed and synchronized to the 'faa' video. One hears 'baa' on the 'baa' video (as would be expected), but one hears 'faa' on the 'faa' video: in the latter case, the sight of a mouth articulating 'faa' overrides the sound wave that is 'baa'. How can it be that one perceives different sounds even though the sound waves are identical?

In psychoacoustics, the McGurk effect is described as an illusion, a perceptual error if you like, because it does not square with the standard definition of sound. However, since every one of the hundreds of people to whom I have now demonstrated the effect experiences that 'error', I prefer

---

[7] American National Standard, *Acoustical Terminology*. ANSI/ASA S1.1–2013.

[8] Grimshaw, 'A Brief Argument For, and Summary of, the Concept of Sonic Virtuality.'

[9] Mark Grimshaw and Tom A. Garner, *Sonic Virtuality: Sound as Emergent Perception* (New York: Oxford University Press, 2015), 1.

[10] Multimodality refers to the formation of percepts (perceptual artefacts) from two or more sensory channels.

instead to question the coherency of the definition: how can sound be just a sound wave if everyone perceives two different sounds while sensing the same sound wave?[11]

Before moving onto an exposition of presence, I will present one more aspect of the sonic virtuality definition of sound that will prove particularly useful when it comes to discussing presence in the context of reality. This aspect is best illustrated by asking the question *where is sound?* In acoustics and psychoacoustics, explanations for this come under the banner of 'sound localization'. In this regard, we can understand sound as a sound wave as being at a point distant from us, hence distal: sound is thus where the object or objects that produce the sound wave are, and our stereophonic hearing (i.e., the use of two physically separated ears) is the means to such localization. Sound seems to be happening 'over there'. Yet sound, in the standard conception of it, is travelling through the medium (typically air for humans) to us, and so the location of sound is a moving, medial location somewhere between the sound wave source and our ears. So, sound seems to be 'coming towards us'. A third theory is that the location of sound is proximal, at our ears. Here, sound is 'what we are hearing' at our particular point of audition. As noted above, the ANSI acoustics documentation provides a second definition of sound that, while contradicting the first ANSI definition of sound, supports the proximal notion. This proximal-based definition of sound as sensation contrasts with the medial-based definition of sound as a sound wave, and both contrast with the distal-based concept of the localization of sound as a sound wave. In summary, sound is variously described as being located a) at a particular point (distal), b) somewhere between the source and us (medial), or c) at our ears (proximal). Inconsistency, indeed.[12]

In *Sonic Virtuality*, Garner and I proposed a different theory of the localization of sound. In this case, sound as a perception is actively localized by us through superimposing it mentally on various artefacts from the world. The sonic virtuality definition of sound defines aural imaging, the imagining of sound, as sound no less than sound perceived in the presence of a sound wave. Should the sound be perceived in the presence of sound waves, very

---

[11] I recently discovered that this worked even when just visualizing the two videos while sensing the sound waves. Playing the McGurk effect for the umpteenth time (to my wife this time instead of students or conference delegates), I found that, while watching for her reaction as I faced her from behind the screen, I clearly heard 'faa' when I knew – and imagined – the 'faa' video was playing on the screen. This discovery simply provides further credence to the sonic virtuality definition of sound.

[12] For a useful exposition of theories concerning the location of sound, see Roberto Casati and Jerome Dokic, 'Sounds', *Stanford Encyclopedia of Philosophy*, ed. Edward N. Zalta (Stanford: Stanford University, 2005), accessed 9 April 2020, http://plato.stanford.edu/entries/sounds/.

often the location of the sound is quite distinct to the location of the sound wave source. Imagine yourself in a cinema, watching a dialogue scene. Where do you perceive the sound to be: at one of the loudspeakers ranged along the side or back walls, or somewhere between those loudspeakers and your ears, or even at your ears, or is it located on the mouth of the screen character now talking? Most cinemagoers would suggest the last option: the sound has been superimposed on the artefact in question (here, the character). This is an example of what Chion calls 'synchresis'.[13] This common perceptual phenomenon demonstrates the problems with the acoustics and psychoacoustics conceptualization of sound localization. While the sonic virtuality concept of sound localization suffices to explain synchresis, also known as the ventriloquism effect and related to the binding problem, it can also be used to explain how we fashion a perceptual model of reality.

In recent work,[14] I have explored the idea of the environment as being a perception rather than something physical, and have shown how the sonic virtuality notion of sound localization aids in explaining the process of constructing this model of the physical world. Briefly, Walther-Hansen and I reduced reality (the world of sensory things) to a salient world (the set of sensory things of which we are aware at any one time), then to the environment that, in our conceptualization, is a perceptual model of the salient world. The environment is that model of the salient world chosen from a number of alternate models that are tested and refined as we are subjected to sensory stimuli, and this process continues unabated as the salient world changes. In this, I base my conception on work by Clark, who developed further the notion of perceptual models of the world in order to account for knowledge of that world.[15] The theory behind such hypothetical modelling of the world has been used by others in connection with presence, such as Slater and Brenton et al.[16] Clark explains it as a rolling

---

[13] Michel Chion, *Audio-Vision: Sound on Screen*, Claudia Gorbman, ed. and trans. (New York: Columbia University Press, 1994), 5.

[14] Mads Walther-Hansen and Mark Grimshaw, 'Being in a Virtual World: Presence, Environment, Salience, Sound' (Paper presented at Audio Mostly 2016, 2–4 October, Norrköping), see *AM '16: Proceedings of Audio Mostly 2016* (New York: ACM, 2016), 77–84; Mark Grimshaw-Aagaard, 'Presence, Environment, and Sound and the Role of Imagination', in *The Oxford Handbook of Sound and Imagination Volume 1*, ed. Mark Grimshaw-Aagaard, Mads Walther-Hansen and Martin Knakkergaard (New York: Oxford University Press, 2019b), 669–82.

[15] Andy Clark, 'Expecting the World: Perception, Prediction, and the Origins of Human Knowledge', *Journal of Philosophy*, CX, no. 9 (2013): 469–96.

[16] Mel Slater, 'Presence and the Sixth Sense', *Presence: Teleoperators and Virtual Environments* 11, no. 4 (2002): 435–9; Harry Brenton, Marco Gillies, Daniel Ballin and David Chatting, 'The Uncanny Valley: Does it Exist and Is it Related to Presence?' (paper presented at Conference of

generation and testing (according to experience) of hypotheses that proceed under time pressure until a best-fit model is arrived at. In my conception, this hypothetical model of the salient world is the environment. That is, our perceptual 'environment' is a particular constructed version of reality, based on our sensory experiences.

I come back to this environment in relation to presence and sound, and so, for now, I content myself with suggesting that we construct, test and refine our model environment in large part through the localization of sound. I now turn my attention to presence, for it is in the environment, at a remove from reality, that we are present.

A Brief Exposition of Presence

It is not my intention here to enumerate all the extant definitions of and explanations for the hotly debated topic of presence. I and others, to various extents, have already undertaken this task.[17] Rather, I prefer to draw attention to the main threads common to many discussions on presence, the main bones of contention in the debates and the relationship of presence to immersion (the term that is more widely used in computer games literature but which is not necessarily synonymous with presence).

The concept of presence is typically used in the field of Virtual Reality (VR), a field and an industry that is now (once again) converging with that of computer games. Here, presence is usually defined as the sense or feeling of being there, where 'there' is a place in which one might be able to act (and which one might typically have an effect on). The definition arises from the concept of telepresence and betrays the origin of presence research, which was originally concerned with remote control of robots (moon rovers and so on). Slater provides a succinct definition of presence that, in its broad sweep, encapsulates many others: '[presence] is the extent to which the unification of *simulated* sensory data and perceptual processing produces a coherent "place" that you are "in" and in which there may be the potential for you to act'.[18] Leaving aside the question of what

Human Computer Interaction, Workshop on Human Animated Character Interaction, Edinburgh, Napier University, 6 September 2005).

[17] Matthew Lombard and Theresa Ditton, 'At the Heart of it All: The Concept of Presence', *Journal of Computer-Mediated Communication* 3, no. 2 (1997); Mark Grimshaw-Aagaard, 'Presence and Biofeedback in First-Person Perspective Computer Games: The Potential of Sound', in *Foundations in Sound Design for Interactive Media*, ed. Michael Filimowicz (New York: Routledge, 2019), 78–94.

[18] Mel Slater, 'A Note on Presence Terminology', *Presence Connect* 3, no. 3 (2003): 1–5 at 2, my italics.

'simulated data' are,[19] the definition is notable for its limiting of presence only to virtual worlds (hence the simulation). Presence, in this definition, only occurs through the mediating effects of the type of technology to be found in VR systems: it is thus not possible to be present outside such systems, such as when one is in the real world. This is problematic to say the least, for how precisely does presence in virtual worlds (being there, potential to act and so forth) differ from the same sense or feeling when we experience it (as we do) in the real world? Although Slater goes on to suggest that there *is* such a thing as presence in the real world (in which case his definition is imprecise), much of the presence literature deals with presence in virtual worlds with little effort to explain what presence is in the real world (if indeed there is such a thing).

There is a debate in presence theory as to the relationship between attaining presence and the level of fidelity of the virtual world's sensory simulation to sensations in the real world. Similarly, there is a debate as to whether presence arises solely from the fidelity of the sensations or whether other factors need to be taken into account. Slater's definition implies a directly proportional relationship between fidelity and reality in the production of sensory data and level of presence. IJsselsteijn, Freeman and de Ridder are more explicit in stating that 'more accurate reproductions of and/or simulations of reality' are the means to enhance presence.[20] Slater further states that '[p]resence is about form',[21] where that form is dictated by the level of fidelity of the VR system to *sensory* reality – the *content* of the virtual world can be engaging or not, but this has nothing to do with presence. Yet, as I and others have noted,[22] it is possible to be absent even in the real world, and presence requires attention (is one present when one sleeps or is presence only possible when one is awake and alert?)[23]

---

[19] Sensory data cannot be simulated – they just 'are' – though their effects might be simulated via technologies such as transcranial magnetic stimulation. Sensory data can indeed be simulations *of* something.

[20] Wijnand A. IJsselsteijn, Jonathan Freeman, and Huib De Ridder, 'Presence: Where Are We?', *Cyberpsychology & Behavior* 4, no. 2 (2001): 179–82, at 180.

[21] Slater, 'Presence Terminology', 2.

[22] For example, Grimshaw-Aagaard, 'Presence and Biofeedback in First-Person Perspective Computer Games', and John A. Waterworth and Eva L. Waterworth, 'Distributed Embodiment: Real Presence in Virtual Bodies', in *The Oxford Handbook of Virtuality*, ed. Mark Grimshaw (New York: Oxford University Press, 2014), 589–601 at 589.

[23] One is always bathed, immersed sensorially, by the 'technology' of reality, but one is not necessarily aware of this. Thus, when sleeping, there is a limited salient world from which to construct perceptual models of reality. Perhaps this is an explanation of the mechanism of dreams that must, out of necessity, draw upon a greater share of memory and latent desire, in

Immersion is a term that is widely synonymous to presence when used in computer game research and industry marketing, but in presence research it means something else. Here, most follow Slater's view that immersion is 'what the technology delivers from an objective point of view [while presence] is a human reaction to immersion'.[24] Immersion can thus be objectively measured as a property of the technology – such-and-such a piece of equipment provides 91.5 per cent immersion in terms of its fidelity to reality – while presence is a subjective experience that lends itself less readily to precise measurement. This seems a reasonable distinction to me, but, as noted above, one should not make the mistake of assuming (a) that there is a direct proportionality between immersion and presence or (b) that immersive technology, and its level of simulative fidelity, is all that is required for presence.

There is surprisingly little empirical research on the role of sound in presence in virtual worlds. Much of it is to do with testing the fidelity-to-the-real-world (i.e., immersiveness) of the audio technology – particularly in regard to the production and function of 'realistic' sounds[25] – and spatiality and/or localization of sound wave sources.[26] A large part of this research implicitly assumes that an increase in fidelity of real-world simulation equals an increase in presence: this might well be true for spatial positioning of audio in the virtual world, but is doubtful when it comes to the use of 'realistic' sounds. Most of this research neglects to discuss what 'realistic' means but, assuming 'authentic' is meant, then one might well wonder at the authenticity of a computer game's inherently unrealistic, but carefully crafted dinosaur roar or the explosion of a plasma rifle, even if we do not doubt their power to contribute to presence.[27] Verisimilitude would

---

order to devise their wondrous models of a reality. One is no longer present, and is thus absent, in a model environment drawn from the salient world of reality.

[24] Slater, 'Presence Terminology', 1–2.

[25] For example, Kees van den Doel and Dinesh K. Pai, 'The Sounds of Physical Shapes', *Presence: Teleoperators and Virtual Environments* 7, no. 4 (1998): 382–95; Roberta L. Klatzky, Dinesh K. Pai and Eric P. Krotkov, 'Perception of Material from Contact Sounds', *Presence: Teleoperators and Virtual Environments* 9, no. 4 (2000): 399–410.

[26] For example, Elizabeth M. Wenzel, 'Localization in Virtual Acoustic Displays', *Presence: Teleoperators and Virtual Environments* 1, no. 1 (1992): 80–107; Claudia Hendrix and Woodrow Barfield, 'The Sense of Presence Within Auditory Virtual Environments', *Presence: Teleoperators and Virtual Environments* 5, no. 3 (1996): 290–301; Karsten Bormann, 'Presence and the Utility of Audio Spatialization', *Presence: Teleoperators and Virtual Environments* 14, no. 3 (2005): 278–97; Maori Kobayashi, Kanako Ueno and Shiro Ise, 'The Effects of Spatialized Sounds on the Sense of Presence in Auditory Virtual Environments: A Psychological and Physiological Study', *Presence: Teleoperators and Virtual Environments* 24, no. 2 (2015): 163–74.

[27] See, for example, Richard Stevens and Dave Raybould, 'The Reality Paradox: Authenticity, Fidelity and the Real in Battlefield 4', *The Soundtrack* 8, no. 1–2 (2015): 57–75.

be the better word for such a quality, but this often has little to do with reality or authenticity, so is of little concern to those designing VR audio technology, for whom the mantra tends to be one of realism and objectivity over experience and subjectivity.

Some empirical research on sound and presence has taken place in the field of computer games under the banner of immersion,[28] and there has been a fair bit of philosophical or otherwise theoretical research on the role of sound in the formation of presence/immersion.[29] Of particular interest are those few works championing the necessity of sound to presence that base their ideas on studies of hearing loss. An especially notable example is a study of World War II veterans in which it is argued that hearing is the primary means of 'coupling' people to the world.[30] Such 'coupling' has been suggested to be a synonym for presence by researchers who argue that the use of background or ambient sounds is crucial to presence.[31]

---

[28] For example, Mark Grimshaw, Craig A. Lindley and Lennart E. Nacke, 'Sound and Immersion in the First-Person Shooter: Mixed Measurement of the Player's Sonic Experience', paper presented at Audio Mostly 2008, 22–23 October 2008, Piteå, Sweden; Lennart E. Nacke, Mark N. Grimshaw and Craig A. Lindley, 'More Than a Feeling: Measurement of Sonic User Experience and Psychophysiology in a First-Person Shooter Game', *Interacting with Computers* 22, no. 5 (2010): 336–43.

[29] For example, much of my recent work cited elsewhere in this chapter but also, amongst others, Sander Huiberts, 'Captivating Sound: The Role of Audio for Immersion in Games' (PhD thesis, University of Portsmouth and Utrecht School of the Arts, 2010).

[30] D. A. Ramsdell, 'The Psychology of the Hard-Of-Hearing and the Deafened Adult', *Hearing and Deafness*, 4th ed., ed. Hallowell Davis and S. Richard Silverman (New York: Holt, Rinehart and Winston, 1978), 499–510.

[31] Robert H. Gilkey and Janet M. Weisenberger, 'The Sense of Presence for the Suddenly Deafened Adult: Implications for Virtual Environments', *Presence: Teleoperators and Virtual Environments* 4, no.4 (1995): 357–63; Craig D. Murray, Paul Arnold and Ben Thornton , 'Presence Accompanying Induced Hearing Loss: Implications for Immersive Virtual Environments', *Presence: Teleoperators and Virtual Environments* 9, no. 2 (2000): 137–48. One might reasonably ask, then, if a deaf person ever experiences presence as it is currently conceived, given the emphasis there is on the visual in presence research, or if any presence they attain is different to that attained by those who hear (my opinion is that there are different sensory means to attaining presence, and, with respect to environmental modelling, those lacking a sense more than make up for it with increased acuity of other senses). Deafness increases the risk of social isolation in the literature cited and so perhaps sociality is a far greater factor in inducing presence than is usually considered – this risk is greater in those who become deaf as adults, as for the subjects in the Ramsdell study, and who might lose copresence or social presence (see Lee) while still having a form of physical presence. And, for that matter, what is the role in presence formation of the other classical senses, taste, smell, touch not to mention the sensing of temperature and gravity (most, if not all, of which are conspicuous by their absence in the immersive technology of VR)? Kwan Min Lee, 'Why Presence Occurs: Evolutionary Psychology, Media Equation, and Presence', *Presence: Teleoperators and Virtual Environments* 13, no.4 (2004): 494–505.

Stepping Back from Reality

I am now in a position to return to the suggestion with which I began this chapter – that the end result of sensation and perception is to distance us from reality – and I separate the discussion first into a section dealing with presence and reality in the context of virtual worlds and then, second, a section embedding sound into that thinking.

Presence and Reality

As Lee notes, while there has been much research on the mechanism of presence and factors contributing to it, there is little research on *why* humans are capable of feeling presence.[32] Lee was writing in 2004, and the situation he describes is much the same today: most research conducted on presence is of the empirical type, experimentally attempting to find the factors causing presence, the belief being that results will lead to improvements in the efficacy of VR technology in inducing presence (namely, the immersiveness of the technology). Lee, using research from the field of evolutionary psychology, suggests that humans cannot help but be present in virtual worlds because humans have a natural tendency to accept sensory stimuli first as being sourced from reality, and then to reject this instinctive assumption, if necessary, following longer assessment (and, I might add, should such time for reflection be available): 'Humans are psychologically compelled to believe in relatively stable cause-effect structures in the world, even though they are not a perfect reflection of reality'.[33] Put another way, humans naturally tend to the logical post hoc fallacy (*after this, therefore because of this*), where we tend to assume causality between events, one occurring after the other. Additionally, despite knowing that virtual objects and effects are not real, 'people keep using their old brains',[34] and so their first reaction is to treat virtuality as real, and this is why we feel presence in virtual worlds.[35] Lee's suggestion is a worthy one (and one that allows for the feeling of presence outside virtual worlds) but he implies that we already know what reality definitively *is*, which conflicts with the ideas of Campbell with which I began this chapter.

---

[32] Lee, 'Why Presence Occurs.'

[33] Lee, 'Why Presence Occurs', 498.

[34] Lee, 'Why Presence Occurs', 499.

[35] *Post hoc ergo propter hoc* is also fundamental to a proposed basis for the temporal binding of sensations (see the binding problem noted below) – how do we know that a sequence of sensations (e.g., watching a bird in flight) is part of the same perceptual event?

Like Lee, Campbell is inspired by theories of evolution for his ideas concerning the development of knowledge. Both authors deal with the purpose or effect of sensation and perception, and converge on what it is to know reality when virtuality (Lee) or illusion (Campbell) come into play. Campbell's view, where it differs to Lee's, is best expressed by an example he provides: 'Perceived solidity is not illusory for its ordinary uses: what it diagnoses is one of the "surfaces" modern physics also describes. But when reified as exclusive, when creating expectations of opaqueness and impermeability to all types of probes, it becomes illusory'.[36] In other words, the sensations we receive from our eyes and our fingertips might persuade us that the table top in front of us is solid and smooth, and, on a day-to-day level, this works perfectly well, but, when the table top is subjected to closer inspection (either through technological means or through the sensory apparatus of smaller organisms), its impermeability and opaqueness are shown to be illusions. This neatly encapsulates a broad philosophical framework extending back through Kant (the impossibility of knowing the true nature of an object, the thing-in-itself[37]) to the hoary Platonic Allegory of the Cave. Campbell extends this further through the framework of evolution: 'Biological theories of evolution . . . are profoundly committed to an organism-environment dualism, which when extended into the evolution of sense organ, perceptual and learning functions, becomes a dualism of an organism's knowledge of the environment versus the environment itself'.[38] Thus, the evolution of sensation and perception as the basis for cognition (learning and knowing) goes hand in hand with a distancing from the reality of the world. We have to summarize, simplify and filter reality to function and survive. In the case of humans, I would be more explicit in stating that conceptual and abstract thinking have as their *purpose* a distancing from reality, the better (a) to safeguard us from the all-too-real dangers of that reality and (b) to enable us to rearrange reality's building blocks by constructing a more commodious reality to suit our species' trajectory.[39]

---

[36] Campbell, 'Evolutionary Epistemology', 448.

[37] The *Ding an sich*. (An introduction to this concept can be found at the *Stanford Encyclopedia of Philosophy*: Nicholas F. Stang, 'Kant's Transcendental Idealism', *Stanford Encyclopedia of Philosophy*, ed. Edward N. Zalta (Stanford: Stanford University, 2005), accessed 9 April 2020, https://plato.stanford.edu/entries/kant-transcendental-idealism/.)

[38] Campbell, 'Evolutionary Epistemology', 449.

[39] An analogy for this second suggestion might be one drawn from the philosophy of creativity: imagine a board covered with Post-it notes, each succinctly expressing a concept abstracted from some fundamental motivation. These can be rearranged and recombined in any manner and sense can still be made if it must be. Other analogies are the Word for Word game of the BBC Radio show *I'm Sorry I Haven't a Clue* and, as some might assert, the axiomatic basis of much of (natural/Western) scientific thought.

Sound and the Feeling of Presence

From the above, if the purpose of sensation (and all that follows) is indeed to distance us from a, by now, unknowable reality, then the sensory data of virtual worlds, being at best somewhat poor simulations of what we experience outside such worlds, merely ease this task and this is why we can experience presence in such worlds. Having used the preceding section to lead up to this suggestion, I now turn my attention to the role of sound in the attainment of presence.

In order to do this, I concentrate on the function of sound in constructing an environment. As I have previously noted, where we are present is in the environment,[40] and the environment is a perception that is the result of the evolutionary imperative to distinguish self from everything that is not the self (the non-self). In other words, sensation, as the experience of the boundary between self and non-self, is the initial means to impose a distance between ourselves and reality.

The environment, as a perception, is a metonym of (stands for) the non-self that is the salient world, and, like all metonyms, it encapsulates a conceptualization that is lacking in its details (thus distancing from what it represents) but that is perfectly functional for what we require (presence, a place in which to act). There are many sensations that contribute to the construction of the environment, but, in terms of sound, I will concentrate on the role of sound localization. The localization of sound, as stated above, is the mental projection of sound onto perceptions of artefacts from the world. What we perceive forms part of the environment as a model of the world, and thus the localization of sound onto other perceptions (e.g., visual percepts) constructs in large part the spatio-temporality of that model.

Although there are sounds that I can locate as being of me – breathing, my pen scratching the surface of the paper as I write – most sounds of which I am aware, that are within my saliency horizon, are not of me. I make this distinction from experience and thus this basic distinction becomes part of the process of distinguishing self from non-self, the perceptual carving out of a space in which I can be present. By saliency, I mean not only conscious attending to sound waves but also subconscious awareness. There are many sound waves in the world that can be sensed, and, though I do not necessarily attend to and focus on them, my perceptual apparatus is aware of them and is processing them. Such sound waves

---

[40] Grimshaw-Aagaard, 'Presence, Environment, and Sound and the Role of Imagination.'

become conspicuous by their absence. For example, in an anechoic chamber (a room without reverberation),[41] bar the auditory modality, there is as much richness of sensory stimuli as in any other room. Here though, there are no background or ambient sound waves due to the soundproofing, and the absorption and lack of reflection of sound waves in the room further contribute to the lack of ambience – these are sound waves one is not typically consciously aware of. Ramsdell defines three levels of hearing of which the 'primitive level' comprises ambient sounds that

maintain our feeling of being part of a living world and contribute to our own sense of being alive. We are not conscious of the important role that these background sounds play in our comfortable merging of ourselves with the life around us because we are not aware that we hear them. Nor is the deaf person [i.e. the adult who has become deaf] aware that he has lost these sounds; he only knows that he feels as if the world were dead … By far the most efficient and indispensable mechanism for 'coupling' the constant activity of the human organism to nature's activity is the primitive function of hearing.[42]

Thus it is with the anechoic chamber; lacking the ambient sound waves, one loses one's coupling to the world. One is unable to fully distinguish self from non-self because we are accustomed to making use of a full complement of our familiar sensory stimuli in order to do so. At the very least, presence begins to slip away and the world closes in on the self.

Ambient sound thus has a role in presence in establishing a basic environmental spatiality – other selves and events, and distances from self to nearby surfaces – in which the self can be present. But those sound waves of which we are consciously aware also contribute to distinguishing between self and non-self by means of sound (as an emergent perception) that is then localized on other perceptions drawn from the world (mainly through vision) to be combined into percepts (objects that are perceived). Additionally, the spatiality of the environment is further developed by this sound localization as a topography of the salient world. Unlike vision, auditory sensation takes place omnidirectionally, and so the topography and artefactuality of the unseen world can be modelled through hearing – my feet under the table shifting position on the floor, birds singing in the garden behind me, dogs barking in the distance. The temporality of the

---

[41] I have been in several anechoic chambers and the experience is always thoroughly disorientating and, after a while, uncomfortable. To speculate, this discomfort might be because the lack of acoustic ambience means we are unable to reliably model the spatial aspects of the environment we must be present in and so are left uncomfortably closer to reality than we normally are in our everyday existence.

[42] Ramsdell, 'Psychology of the Hard-Of-Hearing and the Deafened Adult', 501–2.

environment is again in large part contributed to by the localization of sound. In this case, percepts provide a form of interface to the reality that cannot be fully apprehended by our senses, and interfaces have potential to initiate actions and events, an unfolding future, hence the basic temporality of the environment. But temporality also derives from the knowledge of the relationship between moving object (vision) and hearing of the event (audition) – we know that, compared to light, sound waves take a perceptible amount of time to travel between their source and our ears. The localization of sound (in the active, sonic virtuality sense) makes use of the benefit of experience in its probing of the salient world, in its binding[43] of different modalities (e.g., vision and audition) together into multimodal percepts (objects and events – the substrate of the spatio-temporality of the environment).

Although the above description is of the role of sound in establishing presence in an environment modelled on the real world, it can equally be applied to presence in virtual worlds, particularly if the assumption is that the mechanisms of achieving presence are the same in both realities. One significant difference should be briefly noted, though, especially where it brings me back to my contention that conceptual and abstract thinking, being founded on sensation and perception, have as their purpose a distancing from reality. This is that the sensations provided by a virtual world represent a particular model of reality (in the form of the sensations if not always the content); the environment we then make from this virtual world is, then, perceptually poorer than those made of the real world (not only because the number of sensations available is fewer and their dispositions more primitive but also because the number of modalities used is fewer) – the abstraction that is the environment is itself based on an abstraction. The ease with which we appear to be present in certain forms of computer games might then be not because of the virtual world's attempted 'realism' but, perversely, because of the virtual world's imposition of an even greater distance from reality than that we normally experience.

---

[43] This is a deliberate reference to the binding problem, specifically BP2. One of the major problems of neuroscience is how the brain binds different perceptions into a unified percept of an object or event (for an exposition of this issue with regard to presence see Michael A. Harvey and Maria V. Sanchez-Vives, 'The Binding Problem in Presence Research', *Presence: Teleoperators and Virtual Environments* 14, no. 5 (2005): 616–21). Not being a neuroscientist, I merely offer a humble philosophical explanation within a limited and particular set of sensations.

In Summary

I have argued for the role of sound in constructing the fundamental spatio-temporality of the perceptual model of the salient world that is the environment. I have further argued that it is in the environment that we feel present, and that the environment arises under time constraints and the evolutionary requirement to distinguish self from non-self that aids in the need to survive. Thus, the modelling of the environment, as triggered by sensation (and refined by cognition), is a means to distance one from a reality that by now is not, if indeed it ever was, knowable. As a model, the environment is an abstraction (with all the loss of detail that implies); it is a topographically arranged container of interfaces to an inscrutable reality. The interfaces contained within are the percepts of which sounds are one form. Sound, in its active localization, provides spatiality to the environment, and the experience of the relative speeds of light and sound waves creates temporality, while the potential for action inherent in the interfaces provides a futurity and therefore further temporality to the environment. Thus, one is present in the environment, and, though one is buffered from reality by it, one is able to act within and upon reality through the interfaces of that environment.

16 | Audio and the Experience of Gaming: A Cognitive-Emotional Approach to Video Game Sound

DANA PLANK

It was June of 1990; I was four years old, waiting with my mom in our car, which was parked on the searing hot asphalt of a mall parking lot. My brother, who was nine, was inside with my father picking out his birthday present. When they finally returned, my brother was carrying a huge grey, black and red box with the words 'Nintendo Entertainment System' printed on the side. Without this day, impatient and blazing hot in my memory, I might never have known Mario and Link and Kid Icarus and Mega Man, and my life would have been much poorer for it. We brought home two games that day: the promotional 3-in-1 game that came with the system (*Super Mario Bros./Duck Hunt/Track Meet*; 1985), and *The Legend of Zelda* (1986). It is almost impossible to imagine the rich, diverse game world of *Zelda*'s Hyrule without its characteristic sounds. How would the player experience the same level of satisfaction in restoring their health by picking up a heart container or lining their coffers with currency without that full, round plucking sound as they apprehend the heart, or the tinny cha-ching of picking up a gemlike rupee (see Example 16.1)?

Without a variety of sounds, video games would lose a great deal of their vitality and power. Without the occasional punctuation of ostensibly diegetic sound effects, the player would not feel as deeply engrossed in a game and could grow irritated with its musical tracks, which are looped throughout the duration of a particular zone. Without sound effects to flesh out the world of a game, the aural dimension could fall flat, lacking novel stimuli to keep the player motivated and invested in the outcome of play. Aural stimuli elicit emotional, psychological and physiological responses from players, whether that response is ultimately meant to support narrative, influence gameplay decisions, foster player agency or facilitate incorporation into the game body. This discussion draws on empirical literature from music cognition and psychology, indicating the potent effects of sound. Video games add one more dimension to this conversation that will be discussed later in the chapter: interactivity. The soundscape is a site of incorporation, a dynamic

Example 16.1 *The Legend of Zelda*, small treasure sound effect

and vital bridge between the bodies of player and avatar. In this chapter, I argue that sound is one of the most important modalities through which the game incorporates its players into a complexly embodied hybrid of the material and virtual; sound largely determines the experience of play.

Game Sound, Arousal and Communication

Music and game sound serve as a source of intense and immediate communication with the player by engaging our physiological and psychological systems of arousal and attention. Our bodies do not remain fully alert at all times; a state of perpetual readiness to respond to the environment would be particularly taxing on physical resources, a costly expenditure of energy.[1] Therefore, the body undergoes many changes in arousal levels throughout the day, both on the order of minutes or hours (called tonic arousal, as in the diurnal cycle of sleep and wakefulness) and on the order of seconds or minutes (called phasic arousal, as triggered by various stimuli in the environment). Phasic arousal relates to the appearance of salient stimuli in the auditory environment. For example, the sound of a slamming door will drastically raise phasic arousal for a brief moment, until the cortex assesses the sound and determines that it is not an impending threat. There are many studies that explore the connection of music and sound to phasic arousal, focusing on elements such as dynamics and tempo.[2]

---

[1] David Huron, 'Arousal', *An Ear for Music* (n.d.), https://web.archive.org/web/20100620200546/http://csml.som.ohio-state.edu/Music838/course.notes/ear04.html. Huron states that music engages four of our 'readiness' mechanisms: arousal, attention, habituation and expectation. He also demonstrates how costly constant arousal would be: 'if a person were in a constant state of high arousal, they would need to consume 6 to 10 times their normal caloric intake.'

[2] Francesca R. Dillman Carpentier and Robert F. Potter, 'Effects of Music on Physiological Arousal: Explorations into Tempo and Genre', *Media Psychology* 10, no. 3 (2007): 339–63; Gabriela Husain, William Forde Thompson and E. Glenn Schellenberg, 'Effects of Musical Tempo and Mode on Arousal, Mood, and Spatial Abilities', *Music Perception* 20, no. 2 (2002): 151–71; Alf Gabrielsson, 'Emotions in Strong Experiences with Music', in *Music and Emotion: Theory and Research*, ed. Patrik N. Juslin and John A. Sloboda (New York: Oxford University Press; 2001), 431–49; Carol L. Krumhansl, 'An Exploratory Study of Musical Emotions and Psychophysiology', *Canadian Journal of Experimental Psychology* 51 (1997): 336–52; Isabelle Peretz, 'Listen to the Brain: A Biological Perspective on Musical Emotions', in *Music and*

A new sound in a game soundscape is a stimulus that increases phasic arousal, causing the temporary activation of the sympathetic nervous system (SNS). SNS activation leads to a number of physiological changes that prime the body for a fight-or-flight response until the sense of danger is assessed by the cortex as being either hazardous or innocuous. The physiological responses to SNS activation include: (a) the release of epinephrine (also known as adrenaline) from the adrenal gland, acting in the body to raise heart rate and increase muscle tension to prepare for potential flight; (b) the release of norepinephrine (or noradrenaline) in an area of the brain called the *locus coeruleus*, leading to raised sensitivity of the sensory systems, making the player more alert and mentally focused; (c) the release of acetylcholine in the nervous system, a neurotransmitter that increases muscle response; (d) increased blood pressure; (e) increased perspiration; and (f) increased oxygen consumption.[3] The stimulus startling the player will be relayed to the thalamus and then move into the amygdala, causing an automatic, quick fear response.[4] From there, the signal will travel to the sensory cortex in the brain, which evaluates the signal and then sends either an inhibitory or reinforcing signal back to the amygdala. In the video game, the 'danger' is virtual instead of proximate, and so these startle responses are most likely to evoke an eventual inhibitory signal from the sensory cortex. However, activation of the SNS by sound in the video game will lead to short bursts of energy – physiological changes that lead to a spike in the player's overall alertness, priming them for action.

There are several acoustical features that affect this kind of sympathetic arousal, such as: an increase in the loudness and speed of the stimulus; physically proximal sounds (aka, close sounds); approaching sounds, unexpected or surprising sounds; highly emotional sounds, and sounds that

---

Emotion: Theory and Research, ed. Patrik N. Juslin and John A. Sloboda (New York: Oxford University Press, 2001), 105–134; Louis A. Schmidt and Laurel J. Trainor, 'Frontal Brain Electrical Activity (EEG) Distinguishes Valence and Intensity of Musical Emotions', *Cognition and Emotion 15* (2001): 487–500; John A. Sloboda and Patrik N. Juslin, 'Psychological Perspectives on Music and Emotion', in *Music and Emotion: Theory and Research*, ed. Patrik N. Juslin and John A. Sloboda (New York: Oxford University Press, 2001), 71–104.

[3] Epinephrine/adrenaline, norepinephrine/noradrenaline and acetylcholine are all neurotransmitters – organic chemical substances in the body that transfer impulses between nerves, muscle fibres and other structures. In other words, neurotransmitters are compounds that foster communication between the brain and various parts of the body.

[4] The thalamus relays sensory and motor signals to other parts of the brain and has the vital function of regulating consciousness, sleep and alertness. The amygdala is composed of two almond-shaped structures deep in the middle of the brain; the amygdala handles memory processing, decision-making and emotional responses (such as fear, anxiety and aggression), and is therefore vital in recognizing and responding to a startling signal.

Example 16.2 *The Legend of Zelda*, secret

have a learned association with danger or opportunity or that are personally addressed to the player (e.g., using the player's name in a line of dialogue). Video game sound effects often serve many of these functions at once: they tend to be louder than, or otherwise distinguished from, the background musical texture in order to stick out; they are often surprising; they tend to invoke the player's learned association with the meaning of the effect (danger, reward, opportunity, discovery of a secret, etc.; see Example 16.2); and all are directly addressed to the player as a communicative device conveying information about the gameplay state.[5]

A sound effect is meant to evoke an orienting response – in other words, it commands attention from the player.[6] If an orienting response is triggered, the player will experience additional physiological changes: pupil dilation, a bradycardic heart response (where the heart rate goes down, then up and then back to the base line), cephalic vasodilation (the blood vessels

---

[5] Sound effects are usually short clips lasting a couple of seconds or less that serve a signalling function to the player and are typically triggered by direct operator (player) actions on the console controller. Sound effects – whether they are samples or recordings of real-world sounds, short musical cues, or abstract inventions for fantasy or science-fiction sounds – can be utilized for several purposes in the game context: confirming the spatiality of the playing field (making the space sound realistic or conveying its size through reverberation), aiding in identification with the game character and serving as multimodal sensory feedback (by connecting button presses and other player actions to the game character's responses) and modifying player behaviour. Definitions of sound effects can also include Foley, the reproduction of human-generated sounds such as footsteps (or atmospheric sounds such as wind and rain). Foley sounds provide subtlety and depth to the gameworld, and are typically mixed behind the musical cues as a backdrop to the more salient aural elements. Most early games use Foley rather sparingly, due to the lack of channel space to accommodate fully independent Foley, sound effects and musical tracks. For example, on the Nintendo Entertainment System, sound effects often impede on one of the five audio channels, briefly interrupting the melody or harmony in order to signal the player. Sound effects based on player actions are privileged in these early soundscapes for their communicative function – conveying critical information and serving as multimodal feedback to the player. For more on these distinctions, see Axel Stockburger, 'The Game Environment from an Auditive Perspective', in *Level Up: Proceedings from DiGRA* (2003), 1–5 at 5, accessed 9 April 2020, www.audiogames.net/pics/upload/gameenvironment.htm; Kristine Jørgensen, 'Audio and Gameplay: An Analysis of PvP Battlegrounds in World of Warcraft', *Game Studies: The International Journal of Computer Game Research* 8, no. 2 (2008), accessed 29 October 2020, http://gamestudies.org/0802/articles/jorgensen.

[6] Alvin Bernstein, 'The Orienting Response and Direction of Stimulus Change', *Psychonomic Science* 12, no. 4 (1968): 127–8.

in the head become dilated), peripheral vasoconstriction (blood vessels in the extremities constrict) and increased skin conductance.[7] All of these physiological changes due to SNS activation or orienting response prime the player for action by temporarily raising their phasic arousal via short, deliberate signals. However, it is not ideal to remain at a high level of phasic arousal; not only is this a costly energy expenditure, it can cause fatigue and stress. In the context of a game, a player will be less likely to continue play if they experience an incessant barrage of stimuli activating the SNS.

Just as sound can increase phasic arousal, it can also reduce it, especially when it is low-energy; for example, slow, predictable or soft. Effective game sound design will seek a balance; maintaining or lowering phasic arousal (e.g., with background music and silence) to maintain player concentration while raising it to draw attention to particular elements and prime the player to respond (e.g., with sound effects). Repetitive background sounds may serve an additional function, beyond merely preventing player stress from overstimulation of the SNS. According to the Yerkes–Dodson law, for simple tasks, higher phasic arousal leads to better performance. For complex tasks, lower phasic arousal leads to better performance.[8] Therefore, the more complicated the video game task (in terms of motor skills and/or critical thinking), the less active, arousing and attention-getting the soundscape should be – if the goal of the game developers is to enhance player performance. Effective sounds work alongside other elements of the soundscape (such as background music for a particular area) to pique the player's phasic arousal to a level optimal for game performance at any given moment.

Game composers may opt to intentionally manipulate the player, however, and use short musical cues as sound effects that will lead to a higher arousal level in a simpler area, in order to increase the difficulty of the level (and increase player satisfaction upon successful completion of the level). Koji Kondo famously used music this way in *Super Mario Bros.* (1985), doubling the tempo of the background-level track as a signal that the player was running out of time; at the 100-second mark a short ascending chromatic signal would play, startling the player and potentially raising their heart rate and stress levels (see Example 16.3). The question remains

[7] John W. Rohrbaugh, 'The Orienting Reflex: Performance and Central Nervous System Manifestations', in *Varieties of Attention*, ed. Raja Parasuraman and D. R. Davies (Orlando, FL: Academic Press, 1984), 325–48; Evgeny N. Sokolov, 'The Neural Model of the Stimulus and the Orienting Reflex', *Problems in Psychology* 4 (1960): 61–72; Evgeny N. Sokolov, *Perception and the Conditioned Reflex* (New York: Macmillan, 1963).

[8] Robert M. Yerkes and John Dillingham Dodson, 'The Relation of Strength of Stimulus to Rapidity of Habit-Formation', *Journal of Comparative Neurology and Psychology* 18 (1908): 459–82.

Example 16.3 *Super Mario Bros.*, 'Hurry!'

whether this sound signal inherently spikes a player's arousal through its acoustic features, or the physiological response arises from familiarity with the sound's meaning from previous play attempts or from similarly structured musical cues in other games.

Game Sound and Attention

Attention relates directly to arousal; an orienting response occurs when a sound commands a player's attention. Sounds that lower phasic arousal can help a player to concentrate or remain invested in a task. However, attention is not synonymous with arousal. In the real world, we learn how to filter sounds in a noisy environment to determine which ones are the most important. This process of focusing on certain sounds is known as the cocktail party effect (or selective attention), first described by E. C. Cherry in 1953.[9] In games, however, the sound design must perform some of this work for us, bringing elements to the forefront to highlight their importance and convey information to the player.[10] If we remove the need for the player to selectively attend to game sound, there are greater opportunities to manipulate the two other forms of attention: exogenous (also known as passive attention; when an event in the environment commands awareness, as in a sudden sound effect that startles the player), and endogenous (when the player wilfully focuses on a stimulus or thought, as when the player is concentrating intently on their task in the game).

---

[9] E. C. Cherry, 'Some Experiments on the Recognition of Speech, with One and Two Ears', *Journal of the Acoustical Society of America* 25 (1953): 975–9.

[10] There are often options in the main menu screen to control for the volume of the dialogue, sound effects and music separately. An experienced player can thus customize the soundscape to avoid audio fatigue or to become more sensitive and responsive to auditory cues, but a novice might want to rely on the default mix for optimal performance.

Music, in addition to potentially lowering phasic arousal, can shift players into a mode of endogenous attention, which could be one reason for the pervasive use of wall-to-wall background music in early video games.[11] The musical loops facilitate endogenous attention, so that the introduction of communicative sound effects could act as exogenous attentional cues and raise phasic arousal as needed. A study by MacLean et al. from 2009 investigated whether a sudden-onset stimulus could improve sensitivity during a task that required participants to sustain attention; they found that exogenous attention can enhance perceptual sensitivity, so it would appear that the combination of music (facilitating endogenous attention) with effects (facilitating exogenous attention) can help players to focus and stay involved in their task.[12] This manipulation of attention has a powerful effect on neural patterns during play.[13] After game sounds engage attentional processes, they can then do other work, such as communicating information about the game state or eliciting emotion.

The most important function of sound effects is to provide information to the player; therefore, game sounds have several of the same features as signals in the animal kingdom. They are obvious (standing out from the background track in terms of tempo, register, timbre or harmonic implication); frequently multi-modal (e.g., the sound is often joined to a visual component; and, in later games, haptic feedback through 'rumble packs' on controllers); employ specific sounds for a singular purpose (sound effects rarely represent multiple meanings); and are meant to influence the behaviour of the player (informing a player of impending danger will make them more cautious, whereas a sound indicating a secret in the room helps the player to recognize an opportunity). Signals are meant to influence or change the behaviour of the observer, just as game sounds may serve to alter a player's strategic choices during play.

Background musical loops typically play over and over again while the player navigates a specific area. Depending on the number of times the

---

[11] Thomas Schäfer and Jörg Fachner, 'Listening to Music Reduces Eye Movements', *Attention, Perception & Psychophysics* 77, no. 2 (2015): 551–9.

[12] Katherina A. MacLean, Stephen R. Aichele, David A. Bridwell, George R. Mangun, Ewa Wojciulik and Clifford D. Saron, 'Interactions between Endogenous and Exogenous Attention During Vigilance', *Attention, Perception, & Psychophysics* 71, no. 5 (2009): 1042–58; when the stimulus was unpredictable, sensitivity went up, but performance did not. When the sudden-onset stimulus was more predictable (as in a video game, when a certain action prompts a sound and the player knows to expect this response), the participant did not suffer the decrement in performance.

[13] Annabel J. Cohen, 'Music as a Source of Emotion in Film', in *Handbook of Music and Emotion: Theory, Research, Applications*, ed. Patrik N. Juslin and John A. Sloboda (New York: Oxford University Press, 2010), 879–908 at 894.

track repeats, this incessant looping will likely lead to habituation, a decreased sensitivity to a musical stimulus due to its repeated presentation.[14] A level loop that repeats over and over will eventually be less salient in the soundscape; the player will eventually forget the music is even present. However, the music will continue to exert influence on the player, maintaining arousal levels even if the music falls away from conscious awareness. One can regain responsiveness to the initial stimulus if a novel, dishabituating stimulus is presented (engaging exogenous attentional mechanisms and raising phasic arousal); in the case of the video game, this is usually in the form of a sound effect. Thus, depending on the specific conditions of gameplay, game sound can serve two main functions with regards to attention and arousal. First, sound can create a muzak-like maintenance of optimal player arousal without attracting attention.[15] The second function is to directly manipulate the player's attention and arousal levels through dishabituating, obvious musical changes in dynamics, tempo or texture. Combining music's regulatory capabilities with the signalling mechanisms of sound effects, the game composer can have a tremendous amount of control over the player's affective experience of the video game.

Emotion and Measurement

Affect is a broad, general term involving cognitive evaluation of objects, and comprising preference (liking or disliking), mood (a general state), aesthetic evaluation and emotion.[16] Emotion is thus a specific type of affective phenomenon. Many definitions emphasize that emotions require an eliciting object or stimulus, differentiating them from moods.[17] Music often serves as the eliciting object, a potentially important event that engenders a response.[18] Changes in emotion can be captured in terms of

[14] David Huron, 'A Psychological Approach to Musical Form: The Habituation-Fluency Theory of Repetition', *Current Musicology* 96 (2013): 7–35 at 9.

[15] David Huron, 'The Ramp Archetype and the Maintenance of Passive Auditory Attention', *Music Perception* 10, no. 1 (1992): 83–92.

[16] Patrik N. Juslin, 'Emotional Reactions to Music', in *The Oxford Handbook of Music Psychology*, 2nd ed., ed. Susan Hallam, Ian Cross and Michael Thaut (Oxford: Oxford University Press, 2009), 197–214 at 198.

[17] Nicholas Cook, *Analysing Musical Multimedia* (Oxford: Clarendon, 1997), 23; Cohen, 'Music as a Source of Emotion in Film', 880.

[18] Ian Cross and Caroline Tolbert, 'Music and Meaning', in *The Oxford Handbook of Music Psychology*, 2nd ed., ed. Susan Hallam, Ian Cross and Michael Thaut (Oxford: Oxford University Press, 2009), 33–46.

shifts in arousal levels (as described in the preceding section) or valence (positive or negative attributions).[19]

Empirical studies have shown consistently that music has a measurable effect on the bodies of listeners.[20] Researchers can monitor psychophysiological changes induced by musical stimuli in order to access internal, invisible or pre-conscious responses to music that may belie self-reported arousal levels or perceived emotional changes; these measures can include heart rate, systolic and diastolic blood pressure, blood volume, respiration rates, skin conductance, muscular tension, temperature, gastric motility, pupillary action or startle reflexes.[21] Additionally, researchers have used mismatch negativity (MMN) from electroencephalogram (EEG) data to understand neuronal responses to the event-related potentials (ERP) of particular sounds; these neural processes result in increased oxygenation of the blood that changes the local magnetic properties of certain tissues, allowing researchers to capture these changes through the use of functional magnetic resonance imaging (fMRI).[22] In other words, a person's body can register responses to the eliciting stimulus at a pre-conscious level, even if they report that they are not experiencing an emotion. However, some bodily responses might be idiosyncratic and influenced by the subjective experiences of the player.[23] Though emotions have a biological basis, there are also a range of socio-cultural influences on the expression of particular emotions, and psychological mechanisms that serve as mediators between external events and the emotional response they elicit.[24]

---

[19] James A. Russell, 'A Circumplex Model of Affect', *Journal of Personality and Social Psychology* 39 (1980): 1161–78.

[20] Ivan Nyklíček, Julian F. Thayer and Lorenz J. P. Van Doornen, 'Cardiorespiratory Differentiation of Musically-Induced Emotions', *Journal of Psychophysiology* 11, no. 4 (1997): 304–21; this study investigated autonomic differentiation of emotions – whether cardiorespiratory measures could differentiate between discrete emotions. They found successful differentiation based on two components: respiratory (relating to arousal levels) and chronotropic effects (changes in heart rate).

[21] David A. Hodges, 'Bodily Responses to Music', in *The Oxford Handbook of Music Psychology*, 2nd ed., ed. Susan Hallam, Ian Cross and Michael Thaut (Oxford: Oxford University Press, 2009), 183–96.

[22] Laurel J. Trainor and Robert J. Zatorre, 'The Neurobiology of Musical Expectations from Perception to Emotion', in *The Oxford Handbook of Music Psychology*, 2nd ed., ed. Susan Hallam, Ian Cross and Michael Thaut (Oxford: Oxford University Press, 2009), 285–306.

[23] Hodges, 'Bodily Responses to Music.'

[24] It is worth noting that there is a small but developing literature specifically on the psychology of game music; see for example Mark Grimshaw, Siu-Lan Tan and Scott D. Lipscomb, 'Playing with Sound: The Role of Music and Sound Effects in Gaming', in *The Psychology of Music in Multimedia*, ed. Siu-Lan Tan, Annabel J. Cohen, Scott D. Lipscomb and Roger A. Kendall (Oxford: Oxford University Press, 2013), 289–314; Inger Ekman, 'A Cognitive Approach to the Emotional Function of Game Sound', in *The Oxford Handbook of Interactive Audio*, ed.

The BRECVEMA Framework

One thing is clear from the existing bodies of research: sound induces emotional responses with direct physiological implications that are objectively measurable. However, researchers are still exploring exactly *what* emotions music can evoke, and the mechanisms behind *how* sound or music influences listeners. One influential model for understanding this process is the 'BRECVEMA framework', developed by Juslin and Västfjäll.[25] The BRECVEMA framework comprises eight mechanisms by which music can evoke an emotion:

- *Brain Stem Reflex:* an automatic, unlearned response to a musical stimulus that increases arousal (e.g., when a player is startled).
- *Rhythmic Entrainment:* a process where a listener's internal rhythms (such as breathing or heart rate) synchronize with that of the musical rhythm.
- *Evaluative Conditioning:* when a musical structure (such as a melody) has become linked to a particular emotional experience through repeated exposure to the two together.
- *Contagion:* a process where the brain responds to features of the musical stimulus as if 'to mimic the moving expression internally'.[26]
- *Visual Imagery:* wherein the listener creates internal imagery to fit the features of the musical stimulus.
- *Episodic Memory:* the induction of emotion due to the association of the music with a particular personal experience.
- *Musical Expectancy:* emotion induced due to the music either failing to conform to the listener's expectations about its progression, delaying an anticipated resolution or confirming an internal musical prediction.
- *Aesthetic Judgement:* arising from a listener's appraisal of the aesthetic value of the musical stimulus.

Video game sounds can involve several domains from this framework. For example, a tense sound might cause an anxious response in the player, demonstrating contagion; a sound of injury to the avatar might cause a player to recoil as if they have been hit (which could draw on entrainment, evaluative conditioning and visual imagery). Players might activate

---

Karen Collins, Bill Kapralos and Holly Tessler (New York: Oxford University Press, 2009), 196–214.

[25] Juslin, 'Emotional Reactions to Music', 206–7; Patrik N. Juslin and Daniel Västfjäll, 'Emotional Responses to Music: The Need to Consider Underlying Mechanisms', *Behavioral and Brain Sciences* 3, no. 5 (2008): 555–75.

[26] Juslin, 'Emotional Reactions to Music', 204.

one or more of these mechanisms when listening; this may account for
individual differences in emotional responses to particular sound stimuli.
While studies of game sound in isolation can demonstrate clear effects on
the bodies of players, sound in context is appraised continuously and
combined with other stimuli.[27] Mark Grimshaw suggests a connection
between aural and visual modalities while highlighting the primacy of
sound for evaluating situations in games.[28] Inger Ekman suggests that
although the visual mode is privileged in games, this is precisely what
grants sound its power.[29]

Emotion and Game Sound

Although I have been reviewing some of the literature from *music* psychology and cognition, we have seen that many of the same processes apply to
communicative *sounds* in the game. The functional boundaries between
categories of sounds are largely perceptual, based on the clarity of the
auditory image evoked by each stimulus. And yet, there is slippage, and
the boundaries are not finite or absolute: Walter Murch has written that
even in film, most sound effects are like 'sound-centaurs'; simultaneously
communicative and musical.[30] As William Gibbons asked of the iconic
descending tetrachord figure in *Space Invaders* (Taito, 1978), 'Is this tetrachord the sound of the aliens' inexorable march, is it a musical underscore,
or is it both?'[31] As a result of this inherent ambiguity, the BRECVEMA
framework serves as a useful starting point for understanding some of the
potential sources of emotion in game sound. Emotion is a clear site of
bodily investment, implicating a player's physiological responses to stimuli,
phenomenological experiences and subjective processes of making and
articulating meaning. As we have also seen, emotion relates to perception,
attention and memory – other emphases in the broader field of cognitive
psychology.

---

[27] Ekman, 'Cognitive Approach', 197.

[28] Mark Grimshaw, 'Sound and Player Immersion in Digital Games', in *The Oxford Handbook of
Sound Studies*, ed. Trevor Pinch and Karin Bijsterveld (New York: Oxford University Press,
2009), 347–66 at 347–8; Cook, *Analysing Musical Multimedia*, 22.

[29] Ekman, 'Cognitive Approach', 200; Karen Collins, *Playing With Sound: A Theory of Interacting
with Sound and Music in Games* (Cambridge, MA: The MIT Press, 2013), 27.

[30] Walter Murch, 'Dense Clarity – Clear Density', *Transom Review* 5, no. 1 (2005): 7–23 at 9.

[31] William Gibbons, 'The Sounds in the Machine: Hirokazu Tanaka's Cybernetic Soundscape for
Metroid', in *The Palgrave Handbook of Sound Design and Music in Screen Media*, ed. Liz Greene
and Danijela Kulezic-Wilson (London: Palgrave, 2016), 347–59 at 348.

If emotion comprises responses to potentially important events in the environment, then sound effects in a video game serve as potent stimuli. These sounds represent salient events that are cognitively appraised by the player using any number of mechanisms from the BRECVEMA framework, leading to changes in their emotional and physiological state and behaviour during gameplay. The sounds also serve as important sites of incorporation, linking the game body of the avatar to that of the player.

Aki Järvinen describes five different categories of emotional response in video games: prospect-based, fortunes-of-others, attribution, attraction and well-being.[32] Prospect-based emotions are associated with events and causal sequence and involve expectations (eliciting emotions such as hope, fear, satisfaction, relief, shock, surprise and suspense). Fortunes-of-others emotions are displays of player goodwill and are most often triggered in response to events in massively multiplayer online role-playing games (MMORPGS), where the player feels happy or sorry for another player. Attribution emotions are reactions geared towards agents (other human players, a figure in the game or the game itself): Järvinen states that the intensity of these emotions 'is related to how the behavior deviates from expected behavior'; thus, a player may experience resentment of an enemy, or frustration at the game for its perceived difficulty.[33] Attraction emotions are object-based, including liking or disliking elements of the game settings, graphics, soundtrack or level design. These emotions can change based on familiarity and are invoked musically by the player's aesthetic appraisal of the music and sound effects. Finally, well-being emotions relate to desirable or undesirable events in gameplay, including delight, pleasant surprise at winning or achieving a goal, distress or dissatisfaction at game loss. Well-being emotions are often triggered (or at least bolstered) musically, through short fanfares representing minor victories like obtaining items (see Example 16.4), or music representing death (Example 16.5). The intensity of the elicited emotion is proportional to the extent that the event is desirable or undesirable, expected or unexpected in the game context. Well-being emotions frequently relate to gameplay as a whole (victory or failure), as opposed to the more proximal goal-oriented category of prospect emotions. Sound is an important elicitor of ludic emotion (if not *the* elicitor) in four out of Järvinen's five categories.

---

[32] Aki Järvinen, 'Understanding Video Games as Emotional Experiences', in *The Video Game Theory Reader*, ed. Bernard Perron and Mark J. P. Wolf (New York: Routledge, 2008), 85–108.

[33] Järvinen, 'Emotional Experiences', 91.

Example 16.4 *Metroid*, 'Item Found'

Example 16.5 *The Legend of Zelda*, 'Death'

Interactivity, Immersion, Identification, Incorporation and Embodiment

In discussing the invented space between the real world and the bare code, game scholars speak of interactivity, immersion, transportation, presence, involvement, engagement, incorporation and embodiment, often conflating the terms or using them as approximate synonyms. What these terms have in common is that they evoke a sense of motion towards or into the game. Interactivity is sometimes broken down into two related domains depending on which end of the process the researcher wants to explore: the experience of the user (sometimes described as spatial presence) and the affordances of the system that allow for this experience (immersion).[34] The player does not enter the console, but instead a world between; represented and actively, imaginatively constructed. Discussions of terms such as interactivity have tended to privilege either the player or the system, rather than the *process* of incorporation through play.[35] Sound helps to create both a site of interactive potential and the process, incorporating the body of the player into the avatar. It is to these modes of traversing and inhabiting the game that I now turn, in order to bring my arguments about sound and gamer experience to a close.

[34] Werner Wirth, Tilo Hartmann, Saskia Böcking, et al., 'A Process Model of the Formation of Spatial Presence Experiences', *Media Psychology* 9 (2007): 493–525.

[35] Lev Manovich, *The Language of New Media* (Cambridge, MA: The MIT Press, 2001), 56.

Example 16.6 *Super Mario Bros.*, jump and stomp enemy sound effects

Definitions of immersion use a somewhat literal metaphor – a feeling of being surrounded by the game or submerged as if into a liquid.[36] However, Gordon Calleja's definition of incorporation involves a process of obtaining fluency through the avatar, 'the subjective experience of inhabiting a virtual environment facilitated by the potential to act meaningfully within it while being present to others'.[37] Conscious attention becomes internalized knowledge after a certain amount of play.[38] Calleja's work emphasizes process; a player becomes more fluid in each domain over time.[39] Incorporation is a more cybernetic connection between player and game; instead of merely surrounding the player, the feedback mechanisms of the game code 'make the game world present to the player while simultaneously placing a representation of the player within it through the avatar'.[40] Incorporation invokes both presence and the process; it suggests both a *site* in which the bodies of the player and avatar intertwine, and the *stages of becoming*, involving simultaneous disembodiment and embodiment.

As Mark Grimshaw suggests, immersion resulting from game sound is 'based primarily on contextual realism rather than object realism, verisimilitude of action rather than authenticity of sample'.[41] Sounds related to jumping and landing in platformer games help the player to feel the weight and presence of their actions and give them information about when to move next. The speed of play in *Mega Man* (1987) is faster than in *Super Mario Bros.*; the sound effect is tied to landing rather than springing off the momentum of stomping an enemy (see Example 16.6), but it still has an upward contour. Rather than suggesting the downward motion of landing,

---

[36] Winifred Phillips, *A Composer's Guide to Game Music* (Cambridge: The MIT Press, 2014), 38; she describes immersion as 'sinking completely within' a game.

[37] Gordon Calleja, 'Digital Games Involvement: A Conceptual Model', *Games and Culture* 2, no. 3 (2007): 236–60 at 254.

[38] Gordon Calleja, 'Digital Games and Escapism', *Games and Culture* 5, no. 4 (2010): 254–7.

[39] Calleja, 'Digital Game Involvement', 254.

[40] Ibid.

[41] Grimshaw, 'Sound and Player Immersion', 362; see also Mark Grimshaw, 'Sound', in *The Routledge Companion to Video Game Studies*, ed. Mark J. P. Wolf and Bernard Perron (New York: Routledge, 2014), 117–24 at 119: 'What typically characterizes these sound effects is that they conform to a realism of action; *do a sound, hear a sound* (a play on the film sound design mantra of *see a sound, hear a sound*) . . . Through synchronization and realism of action, the sound *becomes* the sound of the depicted event.'

Example 16.7 *Mega Man*, Mega Man landing

this effect gives the player a precise indication of the instant when they can jump again (see Example 16.7).[42] Jump sounds are immersive because of their unrealism (rather than in spite of it), because of how they engage with the player's cognitive processes and embodied image schema.

James Paul Gee theorizes video games according to studies of situated cognition, arguing that embodied thinking is characteristic of most video games.[43] Gee describes the avatar as a 'surrogate', and describes the process of play in this way: 'we players are both imposed on by the character we play (i.e., we must take on the character's goals) and impose ourselves on that character (i.e., we make the character take on our goals)'.[44] Waggoner takes up the notion of a projective identity as a liminal space where games do their most interesting and important work by influencing and inflecting the bodies of players and game characters.[45] In his ethnographic work on MMORPG players and their avatars, Waggoner found that players tended to distance themselves from their avatars when speaking about them, claiming that the avatar was a distinct entity or a tool with which to explore the game. Yet, those same players tended to unconsciously shift between first- and third-person language when talking about the avatar, slippage between the real and the virtual that suggests a lack of clear boundaries – in other words, experienced players tended to speak from this space of projected identity.

The avatar's body is unusual in that it becomes something both inhabited and invisible; a site of both ergodic effort and erasure.[46] This has led

---

[42] The speed of this effect evokes a sensation of one foot landing just slightly before the other.

[43] James Paul Gee, 'Video Games and Embodiment', *Games and Culture* 3, nos. 3–4 (2008): 253–63 at 258; I was similarly inspired to explore this topic after a realization that not only are most games embodied, but they use health and ability as a core game mechanic.

[44] Gee, 'Video Games and Embodiment', 260; see also James Paul Gee, *Why Video Games are Good for Your Soul* (Altona, Victoria: Common Ground, 2005), 56; James Paul Gee, *What Video Games Have to Teach Us About Learning and Literacy* (New York: Palgrave Macmillan, 2007).

[45] Zach Waggoner, *My Avatar, My Self: Identity in Video Role-Playing Games* (Jefferson: McFarland, 2009), 15.

[46] Espen Aarseth, *Cybertext: Perspectives on Ergodic Literature* (Baltimore, MD: The Johns Hopkins University Press, 1997), 1; Aarseth gives several examples of ergodic (or non-trivial) effort in traversing a text, such as eye movement and the turning of pages. But, on page 94 he gives a very different (and less-cited) definition of particular use to game studies: 'a situation in which a chain of events (a path, a sequence of actions, etc.) has been produced by the nontrivial efforts of one or more individuals or mechanisms'. Both imply qualities of the text itself that are

some theorists to treat games as a 'simultaneous experience of disembodied perception and yet an embodied relation to technology', a notion I find compelling in its complexity.[47] Despite the myriad contested models, what is clear is that gameplay creates a unique relationship to embodied experience, collapsing boundaries between the real and virtual and suggesting that a person can exist in multiple modes simultaneously through identifying *with* and *as* a digital avatar. The player body remains intact, allowing the sensation and perception of the gameworld that is vital to begin the process of incorporation.[48] The controller serves as a mediator and even as a kind of musical instrument or conductor's baton through which the player summons sound, improvises and co-constitutes the soundscape with the game. Through the elicitation of sound and movement in the game, the controller allows for the player's body to become technologically mediated and more powerfully incorporated. But the controller does not extend the body into the screen – our embodied sensations and perceptions of the gameworld do that. Sound is the modality through which the gameworld begins to extend out from the screen and immerse us; sound powerfully engages our cognitive and physiological mechanisms to incorporate us into our avatars. The controller summons sound so that we may absorb it and, in turn, become absorbed.

Despite the numerous technological shifts in game audio in the past thirty years, my response to the sounds and musical signals is just as powerful as it was at the age of four. It is *still* impossible to imagine Hyrule without its characteristic sounds, though the shape and timbre of these cues in 2017's *The Legend of Zelda: Breath of the Wild* have a slightly different flavour from those of the original games in the franchise, with sparse, pianistic motives cleverly playing against the expansiveness of the open world map. I still experience a sense of achievement and fulfilment finding one of the hundreds of Korok seeds hidden throughout the land (Example 16.8), the

---

activated by the audience or player. The word (particularly its association with non-trivial effort) appears often in work on cybertexts, electronic literature, interactive fiction and game studies, as in the work of Noah Wardrip-Fruin.

47 Martti Lahti, 'As We Become Machines: Corporealized Pleasures in Video Games', in *The Video Game Theory Reader*, ed. Mark J. P. Wolf and Bernard Perron (London: Routledge, 2003), 157–70 at 168.

48 Timothy Crick, 'The Game Body: Toward a Phenomenology of Contemporary Video Gaming', *Games and Culture* 6, no. 3 (2011): 259–69 at 266: 'If there were no reasons to assume that the virtual body in a game world is the same as our body in the actual world, then the US Marines' licensing of the classic FPC video game Doom (Id Software, 1993) in the mid-1990s may suggest otherwise. Licensed and rebuilt as 'Marine Doom', the use of video games as military training tools is particularly instructive in establishing a phenomenological link between embodied perception in the virtual and real world.'

Example 16.8 *The Legend of Zelda: Breath of the Wild*, Korok seed/small collectible item sound effect

Example 16.9 *The Legend of Zelda: Breath of the Wild*, heart container/stamina vessel sound effect

Example 16.10 *The Legend of Zelda: Breath of the Wild*, spotted by a Guardian cue, bars 1–2

flush of pride and triumph from exchanging spirit orbs for heart containers or stamina vessels (Example 16.9) and a rush of panic from the erratic tingling figure that indicates that I have been spotted by a Guardian and have mere seconds to avoid its searing laser attack (Example 16.10).

Game sound is one of the most important elicitors of ludic emotion. Sound is uniquely invasive among the senses used to consume most media; while the player can close their eyes or turn away from the screen, sound will continue to play, emitting acoustical vibrations, frequencies that travel deep inside the ear and are transmitted as electrical signals to the auditory processing centres of the brain. Simply muting the sound would be detrimental to game performance, as most important information about the game state is communicated, or at least reinforced, through the audio track in the form of sound effects.[49]

---

[49] Kristine Jørgensen, 'Left in the Dark: Playing Computer Games with the Sound Turned Off', in *From Pac-Man to Pop Music: Interactive Audio in Games and New Media.*, ed. Karen Collins (Aldershot: Ashgate, 2008), 163–76 at 167; Jørgensen's work suggests that turning off the sound results in decreased performance in the game and increased anxiety for players.

Thus, the game composers and sound designers hold the player enthralled, immersing them in affect, manipulating their emotions, their physiological arousal levels, their exogenous and endogenous attention and their orienting responses. The player cannot escape the immense affective power of the soundscape of the game. Empirical work in game studies and the psychology of music has a lot of work to do in order to fully understand the mechanics behind these processes, but an appreciation for the intensity of the auditory domain in determining the player's affective experience will help direct future investigation. Through all of these mechanisms and processes, game sound critically involves the body of the player into the game by way of the soundscape; I argue that the soundscape is vital to the process of incorporation, joining the material body of the player to those in the game.

17 | Psychophysiological Approaches to Sound and Music in Games

DUNCAN WILLIAMS

Psychological research investigating sound and music has increasingly been adapted to the evaluation of soundtracking for games, and is now being considered in the development and design stages of some titles. This chapter summarizes the main findings of this body of knowledge. It also describes the application of emotional measurement techniques and player responses using biophysiological metering and analysis. The distinction between different types of psychophysiological responses to sound and music are explored, with the advantages and limitations of such techniques considered. The distinction between musically induced and perceived emotional response is of particular relevance to future game design, and the use of biophysiological metering presents a unique opportunity to create fast, continuous control signals for gaming and game sound to maximize player experiences. The world of game soundtracking also presents a unique opportunity to explore sound and music evaluation in ways which traditional musicology might not offer (for example, deliberately antagonistic music, non-linear sound design and so on). The chapter concludes with directions for future research based on the paradigm of biofeedback and bio-controlled game audio.

Introduction

As readers of this book will doubtlessly be very much aware, creating effective soundtracking for games (which readers should take to include music, dialogue and/or sound effects), presents particular challenges that are distinct from creating music for its own sake, or music for static sound-to-picture formats (films, TV). This is because gameplay typically affords players agency over the timing of events in the game. One of the great benefits of effective soundtracking is the ability to enhance emotional engagement and immersion with the gameplay narrative for the player – accentuating danger, success, challenges and so on. Different types of game can employ established musical grammars which are often borrowed from linear musical domains.

Emotional Engagement through Avatar and Control

There is a distinction to be made between active and passive physiological control over the audio (or indeed, more generally over the game environment). Active control means that the user must be able to exert clear agency over the resulting actions, for example, by imagining an action and seeing an avatar follow this input with a direct correlation in the resulting sound world. Passive control would include detection of control signals which are not directly controllable by the end user (for example, heart rate, or galvanic skin response for emotional state estimation). This has been proposed as a control signal in horror games such as 2011's *Nevermind*,[1] in which the gameplay is responsive to electro-dermal activity – world designs which elicit higher sweat responses from the player are chosen over worlds with less player response[2] – and becomes particularly interesting in game contexts when the possibility of adapting the music to biofeedback is introduced.[3] Here, the potential to harness unconscious processes (passive control) for music and sound generation may be realized, for example, through individually adaptive, responsive or context-dependent remixing. Such technology could be married together with the recent significant advances in music information retrieval (MIR), non-linear music creation[4] and context-adaptive music selection. For example, it could be used to create systems for unsupervised music selection based on individual player preference, performance, narrative or directly from biophysiological activity. As with any such system, there are ethical concerns, not just in the storage of individual data, but also in the potential to cause harm to the player, for example by creating an experience that is too intense or scary in this context.

---

[1] Barbara Giżycka and Grzegorz J. Nalepa, 'Emotion in Models Meets Emotion in Design: Building True Affective Games', in *2018 IEEE Games, Entertainment, Media Conference (GEM)*, Galway (2018), 1–5.

[2] Eduardo Velloso, Thomas Löhnert, and Hans Gellersen, 'The Body Language of Fear: Fearful Nonverbal Signals in Survival-Horror Games', Proceedings of DiGRA 2015 Conference, 14–17 May 2015, Lüneburg, Germany.

[3] Richard Teitelbaum, 'In Tune: Some Early Experiments in Biofeedback Music (1966–1974)', in *Biofeedback and the Arts, Results of Early Experiments*, ed. David Rosenbloom (Vancouver: Aesthetic Research Center of Canada Publications, 1976), 35–56; Boris Blumenstein, Michael Bar-Eli and Gershon Tenenbaum, 'The Augmenting Role of Biofeedback: Effects of Autogenic, Imagery and Music Training on Physiological Indices and Athletic Performance', *Journal of Sports Sciences* 13 (1995): 343–54; Elise Labbé, Nicholas Schmidt, Jonathan Babin and Martha Pharr, 'Coping with Stress: The Effectiveness of Different Types of Music', *Applied Psychophysiology and Biofeedback* 32 (2007): 163–8.

[4] Axel Berndt, 'Musical Nonlinearity in Interactive Narrative Environments', Proceedings of the International Computer Music Conference (ICMC), Montreal, Canada, 16–21 August 2009, 355–8.

*Psychophysiological Assessment as a Useful Tool for Both Analysing
Player Response to Music in Games, and Creating New Interactive
Musical Experiences*

Psychophysiological assessment can provide clues as to player states and
how previous experience with sound and music in linear domains
(traditional non-interactive music and media) might influence a player
in a game context (learned associations with major or minor keys, for
example). Moreover, it suggests that these states are not necessarily
distinct (for example, a player might be both afraid and excited – consider, for example, riding a rollercoaster, which can be both scary and
invigorating, with the balance depending on the individual). In other
words, there is not necessarily an emotional state which is universally
'unwanted' in gameplay, but there may be states which are 'inappropriate' or emotionally incongruous. These are difficult phenomena to evaluate through traditional measurement techniques, especially in the
midst of gameplay, yet they remain of vital importance for the game
sound designer or composer. Biophysiological measurement, which
includes central and peripheral nervous system measurement (i.e.,
heart and brain activity, as well as sweat and muscle myography) can
be used both to detect emotional states, and to use physical responses to
control functional music, for example, in the design of new procedural
audio techniques for gaming.[5] Music can have a huge impact on our day-
to-day lives, and is increasingly being correlated with mental health and
well-being.[6] In such contexts, music has been shown to reduce stress,
improve athletic performance, aid mindfulness and increase concentration. With such functional qualities in mind, there is significant potential
for music in game soundtracking, which might benefit from biophysio-
logically informed computer-aided music or sound design. This chapter
gives an overview of this type of technology and considers how biosensors might be married with traditional game audio strategies (e.g.,
procedural audio, or algorithmically generated music), but the general
methodology for design and application might be equally suited to
a wide variety of artistic applications. Biophysiological measurement
hardware is becoming increasingly affordable and accessible, giving

---

[5] Omar AlZoubi, Irena Koprinska and Rafael A. Calvo, 'Classification of Brain-Computer
Interface Data', in *Proceedings of the 7th Australasian Data Mining Conference-Volume 87*
(Sydney: Australian Computer Society, 2008), 123–31.
[6] Raymond MacDonald, Gunter Kreutz and Laura Mitchell 'What Is Music, Health, and
Wellbeing and Why Is it Important?', in *Music, Health and Wellbeing*, ed. Raymond MacDonald,
Gunter Kreutz and Laura Mitchell (New York: Oxford University Press, 2012), 3–11.

rise to music-specific applications in the emerging field of brain–computer music interfacing (BCMI).[7]

For these types of system to be truly successful, the mapping between neurophysiological cues and audio parameters must be intuitive for the audience (players) and for the composer/sound designers involved. Several such systems have been presented in research,[8] but commercial take-up is limited. To understand why this might be, we must first consider how biosensors might be used in a game music context, and how emotions are generally measured in psychological practice, as well as how game music might otherwise adapt to game contexts which require non-linear, emotionally congruous soundtracking in order to maximize immersion. Therefore, this chapter will provide an overview of emotion and measurement strategies, including duration, scale and dimensionality, before considering experimental techniques using biosensors, including a discussion of the use of biosensors in overcoming the difficulty between differentiation of perceived and induced emotional states. This section will include a brief overview of potential biosensors for use in game audio contexts. We will then review examples of non-linearity and adaptive audio in game soundtracking, before considering some possible examples of potential future applications.

Theoretical Overview of Emotion

There are generally three categories of emotional response to music:

[7] Yee Chieh (Denise) Chew and Eric Caspary, 'MusEEGk: A Brain Computer Musical Interface', in *Proceedings of the 2011 Annual Conference Extended Abstracts on Human factors in Computing Systems*, CHI '11: CHI Conference on Human Factors in Computing Systems, Vancouver BC, Canada, May 2011 (New York: ACM Press), 1417–22; Ian Daly, Duncan Williams, Alexis Kirke, James Weaver, Asad Malik, Faustina Hwang, Eduardo Miranda and Slawomir J. Nasuto, 'Affective Brain–Computer Music Interfacing', *Journal of Neural Engineering* 13 (2016): 46022–35.

[8] Mirjam Palosaari Eladhari, Rik Nieuwdorp and Mikael Fridenfalk, 'The Soundtrack of Your Mind: Mind Music – Adaptive Audio For Game Characters', *ACE '06: Proceedings of the 2006 ACM SIGCHI International Conference On Advances In Computer Entertainment Technology*, Hollywood, California, 14–16 June 2006 (New York: ACM Press), 54–61; Axel Berndt, 'Diegetic Music: New Interactive Experiences', in *Game Sound Technology and Player Interaction: Concepts and Developments*, ed. Mark Grimshaw (Hershey, PA: IGI-Global, 2011), 60–76; Duncan Williams, Alexis Kirke, Eduardo R. Miranda, Ian Daly, James Hallowell, Faustina Hwang, Asad Malik, James Weaver, Slawomir J. Nasuto and Joel Eaton, 'Dynamic Game Soundtrack Generation in Response to a Continuously Varying Emotional Trajectory', in *Proceedings of the 56th Audio Engineering Society Conference 2015* (Queen Mary, University of London: Audio Engineering Society, 2015).

- *Emotion*: A shorter response; usually to an identifiable stimulus, giving rise to a direct perception and possibly an action (e.g., fight/flight).
- *Affect/Subjective feeling*: A longer evoked experiential episode.
- *Mood*: The most diverse and diffuse category. Perhaps indiscriminate to particular eliciting events, and as such less pertinent to gameplay, though it may influence cognitive state and ability (e.g., negative or depressed moods).

Emotion (in response to action) is the most relevant to gameplay scenarios, where player state might be influenced by soundtracking, and as such this chapter will henceforth refer to emotion unilaterally.

Emotional Descriptions and Terms

Psychological evaluations of music as a holistic activity (composition, performance and listening) exist, as do evaluations of the specific contributions of individual musical features to overall perception. These generally use self-report mechanisms (asking the composer, performer or listener what they think or feel in response to stimulus sets which often feature multiple varying factors). The domain of psychoacoustics tends to consider the contribution of individual, quantifiable acoustic features to perception (for example, correlation between amplitude and perceived loudness, spectro-temporal properties and timbral quality, or acoustic frequency and pitch perception). More recently this work has begun to consider how such factors contribute to emotional communication in a performance and an emotional state in a listener (for research which considers such acoustic cues as emotional correlates in the context of speech and dialogue).[9]

At this stage it is useful to define common terminology and the concepts that shape psychophysiological assessments of perceptual responses to sound and music. Immersion is a popular criterion in the design and evaluation of gaming.

The term 'immersion' is often used interchangeably in this context with 'flow',[10] yet empirical research on the impact of music on immersion in the context of video games is still in its infancy. A player-focused definition (as

---

[9] See, for example, Patrik N. Juslin and Petri Laukka, 'Expression, Perception, and Induction of Musical Emotions: A Review and a Questionnaire Study of Everyday Listening', *Journal of New Music Research* 33 (2004): 217–38.

[10] David Weibel and Bartholomäus Wissmath, 'Immersion in Computer Games: The Role of Spatial Presence and Flow', *International Journal of Computer Games Technology* (2011): 14 pp. at 6, accessed 29 October 2020, https://dl.acm.org/doi/pdf/10.1155/2011/282345.

opposed to the perceptual definition of Slater,[11] wherein simulated environments combine with perception to create coherence) has been suggested
as a sense of the loss of time perception,[12] but this was contested in later
work as anecdotal.[13] Some studies have considered players' perceived, self-
reported state in an ecological context,[14] that is, while actually playing –
suggesting that players underestimate how long they actually play for if
asked retrospectively. Later research has suggested that attention might be
better correlated to immersion.[15]

Whichever definition the reader prefers, the cognitive processes involved
are likely to be contextually dependent; in other words the music needs to be
emotionally congruent with gameplay events.[16] This has implications for
soundtrack timing, and for emotional matching of soundtrack elements with
gameplay narrative.[17]

Despite the increasing acknowledgement of the effect of sound or music
on immersion in multimodal scenarios (which would include video game
soundtracking, sound in film, interactive media, virtual reality (VR) and so
on), there is a problem in the traditional psychophysical evaluation of such
a process: simply put, the experimenter will break immersion if they ask
players to actively react to a change in the stimulus (e.g., stop playing when
music changes), and clearly this makes self-report mechanisms problematic
when evaluating game music in an authentic manner.

Distinguishing Felt Emotion

We must consider the distinction between perceived and induced emotions, which is typically individual depending on the listeners' preferences and current emotional state. The player might ask themselves:
'*I understand this section of play is supposed to make me feel sad*' as
opposed to '*I feel sad right now at this point in the game*'. We might

[11] Mel Slater, 'A Note on Presence Terminology', *Presence Connect* 3, no. 3 (2003): 1–5.
[12] Timothy Sanders and Paul Cairns, 'Time Perception, Immersion and Music in Videogames', in
      Proceedings of the 24th BCS interaction specialist group conference 2010 (Swindon: BCS Learning
      & Development Ltd., 2010), 160–7.
[13] A. Imran Nordin, Jaron Ali, Aishat Animashaun, Josh Asch, Josh Adams and Paul Cairns,
      'Attention, Time Perception and Immersion in Games', in *CHI'13 Extended Abstracts on
      Human Factors in Computing Systems* (New York: ACM, 2013), 1089–94.
[14] Simon Tobin, Nicolas Bisson and Simon Grondin, 'An Ecological Approach to Prospective and
      Retrospective Timing of Long Durations: A Study Involving Gamers', *PloS one* 5 (2010): e9271.
[15] Nordin et al., 'Attention, Time Perception and Immersion in Games.'
[16] Kristine Jørgensen, 'Left in the Dark: Playing Computer Games with the Sound Turned Off', in
      From Pac-Man to Pop Music: Interactive Audio in Games and New Media, ed. Karen Collins
      (Aldershot: Ashgate, 2008), 163–76.
[17] D. Williams et al., 'Dynamic Game Soundtrack Generation.'

look for increased heart rate variability, skin conductance (in other words, more sweat), particular patterns of brain activity (particularly frontal asymmetry or beta frequencies)[18] and so on, as evidence of induced, as opposed to perceived emotions. Methods for measuring listeners' emotional responses to musical stimuli have included self-reporting and biophysiological measurement, and in many cases combinations thereof.

The distinction between perceived and induced or experienced emotions in response to musical stimuli is very important. For example, induced emotions might be described as '*I felt this*', or '*I experienced this*', while perceived emotions could be reported as '*this was intended to communicate*', or '*I observed*', and so on. The difference has been well documented,[19] though the precise terminology used can vary widely.

Perceived emotions are more commonly noted than induced emotions: 'Generally speaking, emotions were less frequently felt in response to music than they were perceived as expressive properties of the music.'[20] This represents a challenge, which becomes more important when considering game soundtracking that aims to induce emotionally congruent states in the player, rather than to simply communicate them. In other words, rather than communicating an explicit goal, for example '*play sad music = sad player*', the goal is rather to measure the player's own bioresponse and adapt the music to their actual arousal as an emotional indicator as interpreted by the system: biophysiological responses help us to investigate *induced* rather than *perceived* emotions. Does the music communicate an intended emotion, or does the player really feel this emotion?

---

[18] John Allen and John Kline, 'Frontal EEG Asymmetry, Emotion, and Psychopathology: The First, and the Next 25 Years', *Biological Psychology* 67 (2004): 1–5.

[19] Daniel Västfjäll, 'Emotion Induction through Music: A Review of the Musical Mood Induction Procedure', *Musicae Scientiae* 5, supplement 1 (2001–2002): 173–211; Jonna K. Vuoskoski and Tuomas Eerola, 'Measuring Music-Induced Emotion: A Comparison of Emotion Models, Personality Biases, and Intensity of Experiences', *Musicae Scientiae* 15, no. 2 (2011): 159–73.

[20] Marcel Zentner, Didier Grandjean and Klaus R. Scherer, 'Emotions Evoked by the Sound of Music: Characterization, Classification, and Measurement', *Emotion* 8 (2008): 494–521 at 502. For more information on method and epistemology in regards to perceived and induced emotional responses to music, the interested reader may wish to refer to Marcel Zentner, S. Meylan and Klaus R. Scherer, 'Exploring Musical Emotions Across Five Genres of Music', *Sixth International Conference of the Society for Music Perception and Cognition (ICMPC)* Keele, UK, 5 August 2000, 5–10; Alf Gabrielsson, 'Emotion Perceived and Emotion Felt: Same or Different?', *Musicae Scientiae* 5, supplement 1 (2001–2002): 123–47; and Klaus R. Scherer, Marcel Zentner and Annekathrin Schacht, 'Emotional States Generated by Music: An Exploratory Study of Music Experts', *Musicae Scientiae*, supplement 1 (2001–2002): 149–71.

Models of Mapping Emotion

A very common model for emotions is the two-dimensional or circumplex model of affect,[21] wherein positivity of emotion (valence) is placed on the horizontal axis, and intensity of emotion (arousal) on the vertical axis of the Cartesian space. This space has been proposed to represent the blend of interacting neurophysiological systems dedicated to the processing of hedonicity (pleasure–displeasure) and arousal (quiet–activated).[22] In similar ways, the Geneva Emotion Music Scale (GEMS) describes nine dimensions that represent the semantic space of musically evoked emotions,[23] but unlike the circumplex model, no assumption is made as to the neural circuitry underlying these semantic dimensions.[24] Other common approaches include single bipolar dimensions (such as *happy/sad*), or multiple bipolar dimensions (*happy/sad, boredom/surprise, pleasant/frightening* etc.). Finally, some models utilize free-choice responses to musical stimuli to determine emotional correlations. Perhaps unsurprisingly, many of these approaches share commonality in the specific emotional descriptors used. Game music systems that are meant to produce emotionally loaded music could potentially be mapped to these dimensional theories of emotion drawn from psychology. Finally, much of the literature on emotion and music uses descriptive qualifiers for the emotion expressed by the composer or experienced by the listener in terms of basic emotions, like 'sad', 'happy'.[25] We feel it is important to note here that, even though listeners may experience these emotions in isolation, the affective response to music in a gameplay context is more likely to reflect collections and blends of emotions, including, of course, those coloured by gameplay narrative.

Interested readers can find more exhaustive reviews on the link between music and emotion in writing by Klaus R. Scherer,[26] and a special issue of

---

[21] James A. Russell, 'A Circumplex Model of Affect', *Journal of Personality and Social Psychology* 39, no. 6 (1980), 1161–78.

[22] James Russell and Lisa Feldman Barrett, 'Core Affect, Prototypical Emotional Episodes, and Other Things Called Emotion: Dissecting the Elephant', *Journal of Personality and Social Psychology* 76, no. 5 (1999), 805–19; James Russell, 'Core Affect and the Psychological Construction of Emotion', *Psychological Review* 110, no. 1 (2003): 145–72.

[23] Zentner at al., 'Emotions Evoked by the Sound of Music.'

[24] Klaus R. Scherer, 'Which Emotions Can Be Induced by Music? What Are the Underlying Mechanisms? And How Can We Measure Them?', *Journal of New Music Research* 33, no. 3 (2004): 239–51.

[25] Paul Ekman, *Emotions Revealed: Recognizing Faces and Feelings to Improve Communication and Emotional Life* (London: Phoenix, 2004); Carroll E. Izard, 'Basic Emotions, Natural Kinds, Emotion Schemas, and a New Paradigm', *Perspectives on Psychological Science* 2 (2007): 260–80.

[26] Scherer, 'Which Emotions Can Be Induced by Music?'

Musicae Scientiae.[27] Much of this literature describes models of affect, including definitions of emotions, emotional components and emotional correlates that may be modulated by musical features.

Introduction to Techniques of Psychophysiological Measurement

While biosensors are now becoming more established, with major brands like Fitbit and Apple Watch giving consumers access to bio-physiological data, harnessing this technology for game music, or even more general interaction with music (for example, using sensors to select music playlists autonomously) is less common and something of an emerging field. The challenges can be broadly surmised as (1) extracting meaningful control information from the raw data with a high degree of accuracy and signal clarity (*utility*), and (2) designing game audio soundtracks which respond in a way that is congruent with both the game progress and the player state as measured in the extracted control signal (*congruence*).

Types of Sensor and Their Uses

Often research has a tendency to focus on issues of technical implementation, beyond the selection and definition of signal collection metrics outlined above. For example, it can be challenging to remove misleading data artefacts caused by blinking, eye movement, head movement and other muscle movement.[28] Related research challenges include increased speed of classification of player emotional state (as measured by biofeedback), for example, by means of machine-learning techniques,[29] or

[27] Alexandra Lamont and Tuomas Eerola, 'Music and Emotion: Themes and Development', *Musicae Scientiae* 15, no. 2 (2011): 139–45.

[28] P. N. Jadhav, D. Shanmughan, A. Chourasia, A. R. Ghole, A. Acharyya and G. Naik, 'Automated Detection and Correction of Eye Blink and Muscular Artefacts in EEG Signal for Analysis of Autism Spectrum Disorder', *Engineering in Medicine and Biology Society (EMBC), 2014 36th Annual International Conference of the IEEE*, 26–30 August 2014, Chicago (Piscataway, NJ: IEEE, 2014), 1881–4; Swati Bhardwaj, Pranit Jadhav, Bhagyaraja Adapa, Amit Acharyya, and Ganesh R. Naik, 'Online and Automated Reliable System Design to Remove Blink and Muscle Artefact in EEG', *Engineering in Medicine and Biology Society (EMBC), 2015 37th Annual International Conference of the IEEE* 25–29 August 2015, Milan (Piscataway, New Jersey: IEEE, 2015), 6784–7.

[29] Arthur K. Liu, Anders M Dale and John W Belliveau, 'Monte Carlo Simulation Studies of EEG and MEG Localization Accuracy', *Human Brain Mapping* 16 (2002): 47–62.

accuracy of the interface.[30] Generally these are challenges related to the type of data processing employed, and can be addressed either by statistical data reduction or noise reduction and artefact removal techniques, which can be borrowed from other measurement paradigms, such as functional magnetic resonance imaging (fMRI).[31] Hybrid systems, utilizing more than one method of measurement, include joint sensor studies correlating affective induction by means of music with neurophysiological cues;[32] measurement of subconscious emotional state as adapted to musical control;[33] and systems combining galvanic skin responses (GSR) for the emotional assessment of audio and music.[34] One such sensor which has yet to find mainstream use in game soundtracking but is making steady advances in the research community is the electroencephalogram (EEG), a device for measuring electrical activity across the brain via electrodes placed across the scalp.[35] Electrode placement varies in practice, although there is a standard 10/20 arrangement [36] – however, the number of electrodes, and potential difficulties with successful placement and quality of signal are all barriers to mainstream use in gaming at the time of writing, and are potentially insurmountable in VR contexts due to the need to place equipment around the scalp (which might interfere with VR headsets, and be adversely affected by the magnetic field induced by headphones or speakers).

---

[30] Aimé Lay-Ekuakille, Patrizia Vergallo, Diego Caratelli, Francesco Conversano, Sergio Casciaro and Antonio Trabacca, 'Multispectrum Approach in Quantitative EEG: Accuracy and Physical Effort', *IEEE Sensors Journal* 13 (2013): 3331–40.

[31] Rogier Feis, Stephen M. Smith, Nicola Filippini, Gwenaëlle Douaud, Elise G. P. Dopper, Verena Heise, Aaron J. Trachtenberg et al. 'ICA-Based Artifact Removal Diminishes Scan Site Differences in Multi-Center Resting-State fMRI', *Frontiers in Neuroscience* 9 (2015): 395.

[32] Nicoletta Nicolaou, Asad Malik, Ian Daly, James Weaver, Faustina Hwang, Alexis Kirke, Etienne B. Roesch, Duncan Williams, Eduardo Reck Miranda and Slawomir Nasuto, 'Directed Motor-Auditory EEG Connectivity Is Modulated by Music Tempo', *Frontiers in Human Neuroscience* 11 (2017): 1–16.

[33] Rafael Ramirez and Zacharias Vamvakousis, 'Detecting Emotion from EEG Signals Using the Emotive Epoc Device', in *Brain Informatics*, ed. Fabio Massimo Zanzotto, Shusaku Tsumoto, Niels Taatgen and Yiyu Yao (Berlin: Springer, 2012), 175–84.

[34] Ian Daly, Asad Malik, James Weaver, Faustina Hwang, Slawomir J. Nasuto, Duncan Williams, Alexis Kirke and Eduardo Miranda, 'Towards Human-Computer Music Interaction: Evaluation of an Affectively-Driven Music Generator via Galvanic Skin Response Measures', *2015 7th Computer Science and Electronic Engineering Conference (CEEC)*, 24–25 September 2015 (Piscataway, NJ: IEEE, 2015), 87–92.

[35] Ernst Niedermeyer and Fernando Henrique Lopes da Silva, *Electroencephalography: Basic Principles, Clinical Applications, and Related Fields* (Philadelphia, PA: Lippincott Williams and Wilkins, 2005).

[36] Allen and Kline, 'Frontal EEG Asymmetry, Emotion, and Psychopathology.'

Mapping Sensory Data

There is a marked difference between systems for controlling music in a game directly by means of these biosensors, and systems that translate the biophysiological data itself into audio (*sonification* or *musification*).[37] In turn, the distinction between *sonification* and *musification* is the complexity and intent of the mapping, and I have discussed this further elsewhere.[38] Several metrics for extracting control data from EEG for music are becoming common. The P300 ERP (Event Related Potential, or 'oddball' paradigm) has been used to allow active control over note selection for real-time sound synthesis.[39] In this type of research, the goal is that the user might consciously control music selection using thought alone. Such methods are not dissimilar to systems that use biophysiological data for spelling words, which are now increasingly common in the BCI (brain–computer interface) world,[40] though the system is adapted to musical notes rather than text input. Stimulus-responsive input measures, for example, SSVEP responses (a measurable response to visual stimulation at a given frequency)[41] have been adapted

---

[37] Thilo Hinterberger and Gerold Baier, 'Poser: Parametric Orchestral Sonification of EEG in Real-Time for the Self-Regulation of Brain States', *IEEE Trans. Multimedia* 12 (2005): 70–9; Gerold Baier, Thomas Hermann, and Ulrich Stephani, 'Multi-Channel Sonification of Human EEG', in *Proceedings of the 13th International Conference on Auditory Display*, ed. W. L. Martens (Montreal, Canada: Schulich School of Music, McGill University, 2007): 491–6.

[38] Duncan Williams, 'Utility Versus Creativity in Biomedical Musification', *Journal of Creative Music Systems* 1, no. 1 (2016).

[39] Mick Grierson, 'Composing With Brainwaves: Minimal Trial P300b Recognition as an Indication of Subjective Preference for the Control of a Musical Instrument', in *Proceedings of International Cryogenic Materials Conference (ICMC'08)* (Belfast, 2008); Mick Grierson and Chris Kiefer, 'Better Brain Interfacing for the Masses: Progress in Event-Related Potential Detection Using Commercial Brain Computer Interfaces', in *CHI EA '11: CHI '11 Extended Abstracts on Human Factors in Computing Systems* (New York ACM, 2011), 1681–6.

[40] See, for example, Dean J. Krusienski, Eric W. Sellers, François Cabestaing, Sabri Bayoudh, Dennis J. McFarland, Theresa M. Vaughan and Jonathan R Wolpaw, 'A Comparison of Classification Techniques for the P300 Speller', *Journal of Neural Engineering* 3 (2006): 299–305; Christa Neuper, Gernot R. Müller-Putz, Reinhold Scherer and Gert Pfurtscheller, 'Motor Imagery and EEG-based Control of Spelling Devices and Neuroprostheses', *Progress in Brain Research* 159 (2006): 393–409.

[41] Matthew Middendorf, Grant McMillan, Gloria Calhoun, Keith S. Jones et al., 'Brain-Computer Interfaces Based on the Steady-State Visual-Evoked Response', *IEEE Transactions on Rehabilitation Engineering* 8 (2000): 211–14. SSVEP is a measurable response to visual stimulation at a given frequency seen in the visual cortex. For a detailed explanation the reader is referred to Middendorf, 'Brain-Computer Interfaces', and Gernot R. Müller-Putz, Reinhold Scherer, Christian Brauneis and Gert Pfurtscheller , 'Steady-State Visual Evoked Potential (SSVEP)-based Communication: Impact of Harmonic Frequency Components', *Journal of Neural Engineering* 2 (2005): 123. For a review of use in various music-related cases, see Duncan Williams and Eduardo Miranda, 'BCI for Music Making: Then, Now, and Next', in

to real-time score selection.[42] SSVEP allows users to focus their gaze on a visual stimulus oscillating at a given rate. As well as active selection in a manner which is analogous to the ERP, described above, SSVEP also allows for a second level of control by mapping the duration of the gaze with non-linear features. This has clear possibilities in game soundtracking, wherein non-linearity is crucial, as it might allow for a degree of continuous control: for example, after selecting a specific musical motif or instrument set, the duration of a user's gaze can be used to adjust the ratio for the selected passages accordingly. A similar effect could be achieved using eye-tracking in a hybrid system, utilizing duration of gaze as a secondary non-linear control. Active control by means of brain patterns (Mu frequency rhythm) and the player's imagination of motor movement are also becoming popular as control signals for various applications, including avatar movement in virtual reality, operation of spelling devices, and neuroprostheses.[43] The challenge, then, is in devising and evaluating the kinds of mappings which are most suited to game-specific control (non-linear and narratively congruent mappings).

Non-Linearity

Non-linearity is a relatively straightforward concept for game soundtracking – music with a static duration may not fit synchronously with player actions. Emotional congruence can also be quickly explained: Let us imagine a MMORPG such as *World of Warcraft*. The player might be in a part of a sequence, which requires generically happy-sounding music – no immediate threat, for example. The tune which is selected by the audio engine might be stylistically related to ambient, relaxing music, but in this particular case, wind chimes and drone notes have negative connotations for the player. This soundscape might then create the opposite of the intended emotional state in the player. In related work, there is a growing body of evidence which suggests that when sad music is played to listeners who are in a similar emotional state, the net effect can actually be that the listeners' emotional response is positive, due to an emotional mirroring

Brain-Computer Interfaces Handbook, ed. Chang S. Nam, Anton Nijholt and Fabien Lotte (Boca Raton, FL: CRC Press, 2018), 191–205.

[42] Eduardo Miranda and Julien Castet (eds), *Guide to Brain-Computer Music Interfacing* (London: Springer, 2014).

[43] Dennis McFarland, Laurie Miner, Theresa Vaughan and Jonathan Wolpaw, 'Mu and Beta Rhythm Topographies During Motor Imagery and Actual Movements', *Brain Topography* 12 (2000): 177–186 and Neuper et al., 'Motor Imagery and EEG-based Control of Spelling Devices and Neuroprostheses.'

effect which releases some neurosympathetic responses.[44] There is some suggestion that music has the power to make the hearer feel as though it is a sympathetic listener, and to make people in negative emotional states feel listened to – essentially, by mirroring. So, simply giving generically sad music to the player at a challenging point in the narrative (e.g., low player health, death of an NPC or similar point in the narrative) might not achieve the originally intended effect.

One solution might be to apply procedural audio techniques to an individual player's own selection of music (a little like the way in which *Grand Theft Auto* games allow players to switch between radio stations), or in an ideal world, to use biophysiological measures of emotion to manipulate a soundtrack according to biofeedback response in order to best maximize the intended, induced emotional response in an individual player on a case-by-case basis.

Figure 17.1 shows a suggested signal flow illustrating how existing biosensor research might be implemented in this fashion, in for example a non-linear, biofeedback-informed game audio system, based on metrics including heart rate, electro-dermal activity, and so on, as previously mentioned.

In Figure 17.1, real-time input is analysed and filtered, including artefact removal to produce simple control signals. Control signals are then mapped to mixer parameters, for example, combining different instrumentation or musical motifs. In the case of a horror game, is the user 'scared' enough? If not, adjust the music. Is the user 'bored'? If so, adjust the music, and so on. Any number of statistical data reduction techniques might be used in the signal analysis block. For details of previous studies using principal component analysis for music measurement when analysing EEG, the interested reader is referred to previous work.[45]

If we consider one of the best-known examples of interactive, narrative congruous music, the iMUSE system by LucasArts (popularized in *Monkey*

---

[44] Joanna K. Vuoskoski and Tuomas Eerola, 'Can Sad Music Really Make You Sad? Indirect Measures of Affective States Induced by Music and Autobiographical Memories', *Psychology of Aesthetics, Creativity, and the Arts* 6 (2012): 204–13; Joanna K. Vuoskoski, William F. Thompson, Doris McIlwain and Tuomas Eerola, 'Who Enjoys Listening to Sad Music and Why?', *Music Perception* 29 (2012): 311–17.

[45] Ian Daly, Duncan Williams, James Hallowell, Faustina Hwang, Alexis Kirke, Asad Malik, James Weaver, Eduardo Miranda and Slawomir J. Nasuto, 'Music-Induced Emotions Can Be Predicted from a Combination of Brain Activity and Acoustic Features', *Brain and Cognition* 101 (2016): 1–11; Ian Daly, Asad Malik, Faustina Hwang, Etienne Roesch, James Weaver, Alexis Kirke, Duncan Williams, Eduardo Miranda and Slawomir J. Nasuto, 'Neural Correlates of Emotional Responses to Music: An EEG Study', *Neuroscience Letters* 573 (2014): 52–7; Daly et al., 'Affective Brain–Computer Music Interfacing'; Nicolaou et al., 'Directed Motor-Auditory EEG Connectivity.'

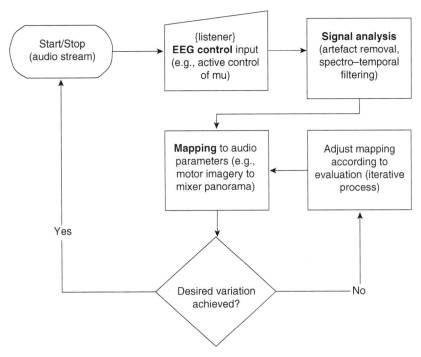

Figure 17.1 Overview of signal flow and iterative evaluation process

Island 2, amongst other games), musical material adapts to the player character's location and the game action.[46] For example, musical transformations include vertical sequencing (adding or removing instrumentation), and horizontal (time-based) resequencing (such as looping sections, or jumping to different sections of a theme). Adding biosensor feedback would allow such changes to respond to a further control signal: that of the player's emotional state.

There are ethical concerns when collecting a player's biophysiological responses, beyond the immediate data protection requirements. Should the game report when it notes unusual biophysiological responses? The hardware is likely to be well below medical grade, and false reporting could create psychological trauma. What if in the case of a game like *Nevermind*, the adaptations using biofeedback are too effective? Again, this could result in psychological trauma. Perhaps we should borrow the principle of the Hippocratic oath – firstly do no harm – when considering these scenarios,

---

[46] Willem Strank, 'The Legacy of iMuse: Interactive Video Game Music in the 1990s', *Music and Game: Perspectives on a Popular Alliance*, ed. Peter Moormann (Wiesbaden: Springer, 2013), 81–91.

and moreover it could be argued that playing a game gives some degree of informed consent in the case of extremely immersive experiences. Within the context of gameplay, the idea of 'harm' becomes somewhat nebulous, but there is certainly room to consider levels of consent for the player in particularly intense games.

Adaptive Game Soundtracking: Biofeedback-Driven Soundtracks?

For video game soundtracking to move towards enhancing player immersion, we might suggest that simple modulation and procedural audio techniques need to be made more sophisticated to be able to adapt musical features to players' emotional responses to music in full synchronization. A fully realized system might also need to incorporate elements of surprise, for example. Biomarkers indicating lack of attention or focus could be used as control signals for such audio cues, depending on the gameplay – ERP in brain activity would be one readily available biophysiological cue. As such, there is a serious argument to be made for the use of active biophysiological sensor mapping to assist access in terms of inclusion for gaming: players who might otherwise be unable to enjoy gaming could potentially take part using this technology, for example in the field of EEG games.[47] EEG games remain primarily the domain of research activity rather than commercial practice at the time of writing, though Facebook have very recently announced the acquisition of the MYO brand of 'mind-reading wrist wearables'. Significant advances have already been made in the field of brain–computer music interfacing. Might bio-responsive control signals be able to take these advances to the next level by providing inclusive soundtrack design for players with a wide range of access issues, as in the case of the EEG games above? The use of musical stimuli to mediate or entrain a player's emotional state (i.e., through biofeedback) also remains a fertile area for research activity.[48] Neurofeedback is becoming increasingly

---

[47] Damien Coyle, Jhonatan Garcia, Abdul R. Satti and T. Martin McGinnit, 'EEG-Based Continuous Control of a Game Using a 3 Channel Motor Imagery BCI: BCI Game', in *2011 IEEE Symposium on Computational Intelligence, Cognitive Algorithms, Mind, and Brain (CCMB)* 11–15 April, Paris (Piscataway, NJ: IEEE, 2011), 1–7; Kavitha Thomas, A. Prasad Vinod and Cuntai Guan, 'Design of an Online EEG Based Neurofeedback Game for Enhancing Attention and Memory', in *2013 35th Annual International Conference of the IEEE Engineering in Medicine and Biology Society (EMBC)* 3–7 July 2013, Osaka (Piscataway, NJ: IEEE, 2013), 433–6.

[48] Hinterberger and Baier, 'Poser: Parametric Orchestral Sonification of EEG'; Daly et al., 'Towards Human-Computer Music Interaction.'

common in the design of brain–computer music interfacing for specific purposes such as therapeutic applications, and this emerging field might be readily adaptable to gaming scenarios. This would potentially offer game soundtrack augmentation to listeners who would benefit from context-specific or adaptive audio, including non-linear immersive audio in gaming or virtual reality, by harnessing the power of music to facilitate emotional contagion, communication and perhaps most importantly, *interaction* with other players in the context of multiplayer games (e.g., MMORPG games).

Conclusions

Music has been shown to induce physical responses on conscious and unconscious levels.[49] Such measurements can be used as indicators of affective states. There are established methods for evaluating emotional responses in traditional psychology and cognitive sciences. These can be, and have been, adapted to the evaluation of emotional responses to music. One such popular model is the two-dimensional (or circumplex) model of affect. However, this type of model is not without its problems. For example, let us consider a state, which is very negative and also very active (low valence and high arousal). How would you describe the player in this condition, afraid? Or angry? Both are very active, negative states, but both are quite different types of emotional response. Hence many other dimensional or descriptive approaches to emotion measurement have been proposed by music psychologists. This is a difficult question to answer based on the current state of research – we might at this stage simply have to say that existing models do not yet currently give us the full range we need when thinking about emotional response in active gameplay. Again, biosensors potentially offer a solution to overcoming these challenges in evaluating player emotional states.[50] However, player immersion remains well understood by the gaming community and as such is a desirable,

[49] Oliver Grewe, Frederik Nagel, Reinhard Kopiez and Eckart Altenmüller, 'How Does Music Arouse "Chills"?', *Annals of the New York Academy of Sciences* 1060 (2005): 446–9; Oliver Grewe, Frederik Nagel, Reinhard Kopiez and Eckart Altenmüller, 'Emotions Over Time: Synchronicity and Development of Subjective, Physiological, and Facial Affective Reactions to Music', *Emotion* 7 (2007): 774–88.

[50] Boris Reuderink, Christian Mühl and Mannes Poel, 'Valence, Arousal and Dominance in the EEG During Game Play', *International Journal of Autonomous and Adaptive Communications Systems* 6 (2013): 45–62.

measurable attribute.[51] Emotional congruence between soundtracking and gameplay is also a measurable attribute, providing the players evaluating this attribute have a shared understanding of exactly what it is they are being asked to evaluate. Considering the affective potential of music in video games is a useful way of understanding a player's experience of emotion in the gameplay.

These solutions sound somewhat far-fetched, but we have already seen a vast increase in consumer-level wearable biosensor technology, and decreasing computational cost associated with technology like facial recognition of emotional state – so these science-fiction ideas may well become commercially viable in the world of game audio soon. Scholarship in musicology has shown an increasing interest in the psychology of music, and the impact of music on emotions – but the impact of music, emotion and play more generally remains a fertile area for further work, which this type of research may help to facilitate.

---

[51] Scott D. Lipscomb and Sean M. Zehnder, 'Immersion in the Virtual Environment: The Effect of a Musical Score on the Video Gaming Experience', *Journal of Physiological Anthropology and Applied Human Science* 23 (2004): 337–43.

PART V

────

Game Music, Contexts and Identities

Introduction

MELANIE FRITSCH AND TIM SUMMERS

Though video game music is a distinct type of music for the moving image, game music does not exist in isolation. It engages with a huge range of contextual issues. That includes other musical traditions and styles, especially when it borrows, or draws inspiration from, pre-existing music. Beyond (or sometimes through) musical citation and allusion, video game music is also inevitably connected to social and cultural concerns.

Perhaps the most straightforward way that game music refers to wider contexts is through musical borrowing. Since the 1970s, video games have quoted classical music and opera. When the player loses in *Circus* (1977), for example, the game plays a snippet of Chopin's Second Piano Sonata – the familiar 'funeral march'.[1] Though many quotations of classical music in games draw on long-standing film music conventions, the use of classical music in games is far broader than just second-hand borrowing from cinema.

Much attention has been given to the widespread quotation of classical music in games of the 1980s and 1990s. For example, at least fourteen games made between 1982 and 1993 use significant quotations from just the Toccata and Fugue in D Minor attributed to Bach.[2] William Gibbons suggests several reasons for the use of classical music in early games:

---

[1] Neil Lerner, 'The Origins of Musical Style in Video Games, 1977–1983', in *The Oxford Handbook of Film Music Studies*, ed. David Neumeyer (New York: Oxford University Press, 2013), 319–49 at 321.

[2] Dana Plank, 'From the Concert Hall to the Console: Three 8-Bit Translations of the Toccata and Fugue in D Minor', *Bach* 50, no. 1 (2019), 32–62 at 33.

- Pre-existing, copyright-free music saved the time and expense associated with the composition of original music
- Classical music was an alternative when programmers lacked the confidence to act as composers themselves
- Classical, particularly contrapuntal baroque music, was well suited to the limited polyphony and voices of sound chip technology
- Repetitious classical music could be easily looped
- Classical music could draw on cultural connotations of prestige and 'high art', along with other associations of the music in wider culture (for example, for indicating a chronological/geographic setting, or drawing on film references).[3]

The influence of classical music on games extends well beyond specific quotations, and can also be found in stylistic pastiche, which serves many of the same functions as the direct quotations, particularly by drawing on pre-existing cultural associations of particular musical styles.[4]

Quotations of, and allusions to older musical styles are by no means exclusive features of older games. Karen Cook has written extensively on aspects of music and history in games, particularly how games use and reconfigure musical meanings. For instance, Cook traces the use of sacred chant, such as the Dies Irae, in game music from the 1980s to the 2010s.[5] In using older musical styles in the context of games, video games present particular visions of (music) history. Cook notes how games like *Civilization IV* (2005), which use large amount of pre-existing Western 'classical' music, enact an ideologically loaded version of history, defining universal progress and cultural improvement in terms of a linear development of Western art music.[6] Both Karen Cook and James Cook have explored how games use particular musical materials to conjure a vision

---

[3] William Gibbons, '"Blip, Bloop, Bach"? Some Uses of Classical Music on the Nintendo Entertainment System', *Music and the Moving Image* 2, no. 1 (2009): 40–52; and William Gibbons, *Unlimited Replays: Video Games and Classical Music* (New York: Oxford University Press, 2018).

[4] William Gibbons, 'Little Harmonic Labyrinths: Baroque Musical Style on the Nintendo Entertainment System', in *Recomposing the Past: Representations of Early Music on Stage and Screen*, ed. James Cook, Alexander Kolassa and Adam Whittaker (New York: Routledge, 2018), 139–152.

[5] Karen M. Cook, 'Beyond the Grave: The "Dies irae" in Video Games', *Sounding Out!* (2017), accessed 9 April 2020, https://soundstudiesblog.com/2017/12/18/beyond-the-grave-the-dies-irae-in-video-game-music/; and Karen M. Cook, 'Beyond (the) Halo: Plainchant in Video Games,' in *Studies in Medievalism XXVII: Authenticity, Medievalism, Music*, ed. Karl Fugelso (Woodbridge, UK: Boydell & Brewer, 2018), 183–200.

[6] Karen M. Cook, 'Music, History, and Progress in Sid Meier's Civilization IV', in *Music in Video Games: Studying Play*, ed. K. J. Donnelly, William Gibbons and Neil Lerner (New York: Routledge, 2014), 166–82.

of the Middle Ages,[7] as part of 'medievalism' in games (of which more in Cook's chapter in this volume, Chapter 19), while Jessica Kizzire has noted how baroque and Renaissance musical styles are used in *Final Fantasy IX* (2000) to create a nostalgic musical mood.[8]

Gibbons suggests that 'combining classical music with video games involves a kind of transgression, a crossing of boundaries that begs for explanation and interpretation',[9] because of the tension from the highbrow cultural associations of classical music and supposedly lowbrow video games. Perhaps, however, these combinations might accentuate and argue for the similarities, rather than differences, between games and classical music experiences. In any case, they remain moments in which musical and cultural concerns are deployed and played out in the realm of video games.

In games, we are often asked to engage with an avatar with a different identity to our own, and visit worlds beyond our personal experience. It is unsurprising, then, that music in games should engage (deliberately or otherwise) with a wide variety of social and cultural issues.

Race

Kiri Miller argues that in *Grand Theft Auto: San Andreas* (2004), the music on the car radios (as well as the presentation of the songs) emphasizes urban black culture and encourages players to identify with the African-American protagonist, CJ, and hear with his ears, irrespective of the gamer's own background.[10] Black men are underrepresented in games, though DJ games like *Beatmania* (1997) and *DJ Hero* (2009) tend to present DJs as male and black, either visually or sonically through the involvement of particular celebrities. Michael Austin has investigated a similar situation for other games themed around hip-hop, which can also involve complex

---

[7] Karen M. Cook, 'Medievalism and Emotions in Video Game Music', *Postmedieval: A Journal of Medieval Cultural Studies* 10 (2019): 482–97 and James Cook, 'Sonic Medievalism, World Building, and Cultural Identity in Fantasy Video Games', in *Studies in Medievalism XXIX*, ed. Karl Fugelso (Cambridge, UK: D. S. Brewer, 2020), 217–238.

[8] Jessica Kizzire, '"The Place I'll Return to Someday": Musical Nostalgia in Final Fantasy IX', in *Music in Video Games: Studying Play*, ed. K. J. Donnelly, William Gibbons, Neil Lerner (New York: Routledge, 2014), 183–98.

[9] Gibbons, *Unlimited Replays*, 4.

[10] Kiri Miller, 'Jacking the Dial: Radio, Race, and Place in "Grand Theft Auto"', *Ethnomusicology* 51, no. 3 (2007): 402–38.

racial identity politics.[11] Even games set in fantastical worlds can use music as part of racial discussions.[12] More problematically, games have often used national and racial musical stereotypes as shorthand for representing the heritage of characters (as in, for example, the cartoony and comedic Punch Out!! (1983–2009)).

Class

Game music can be used to depict class, as shown by Andra Ivănescu, who uses *Beneath a Steel Sky* (1994) as a case study to illustrate this aspect of game music.[13] This game presents an image of a highly stratified society. Music here is used to implicitly represent the class structure and the dynamics of social mobility as the player's character journeys through the world. Music and class also intersects with other kinds of musical representation in games, including how particular socio-economic groups are portrayed. Aspects of musical depiction of class can be part of, for example, the representation of economically underprivileged rural communities (*Far Cry 5*, 2018). Additionally, classical or classical-styled music and its institutions such as an opera house can be used as a stand-in for a 'world in order' that is still structured and cultured (such as in the opera house scene in *Final Fantasy VI*, 1994, or the Fort Frolic scene in *BioShock*, 2007) as opposed to a dystopian or otherwise 'uncivilized' world that has turned towards chaos.[14]

Gender

Given that games and film often share similar musical aesthetics, it is unsur-prising that many of the same issues of music and gender representation occur

[11] Michael L. Austin, '"Playas" and Players: Racial and Spatial Trespassing in Hip Hop Culture Through Video Games', in *Oxford Handbook of Hip Hop Music Studies*, ed. Justin D. Burton and Jason Lee Oakes (New York: Oxford University Press, 2018), n.p.

[12] See, for example, John Maenhout's work on *Fire Emblem* games. John Joseph Maenhout, 'Sonic Representations of Categorical Difference in Diegetic Video Game Music' (MA thesis, University of North Carolina at Chapel Hill, 2018).

[13] Andra Ivănescu, 'Beneath a Steel Sky: A Musical Characterisation of Class Structure', *The Computer Games Journal* 7 (2018): 231–42.

[14] See, on these examples, William Cheng, *Sound Play: Video Games and the Musical Imagination* (New York: Oxford University Press, 2014), 57–92 and Melanie Fritsch, *Performing Bytes: Musikperformances der Computerspielkultur* (Würzburg: Königshausen and Neumann, 2018), 152–63.

in both.[15] For games that involve physical performance, like dance games, aspects of gender performance become embodied.[16] Sometimes, games may end up reproducing and reinforcing gendered messages and representations from existing music cultures. For instance, Elisa Meléndez has outlined how *Rock Band* and *Guitar Hero* replicate some problematic aspects of music and gender from rock music cultures.[17] Yet, as Meléndez describes, in the context of video games, the interactivity provides opportunities for players to challenge gendered assumptions and images through their performances. Games also allow players access to subjectivities they would not otherwise inhabit – music can be part and parcel of that process. For instance, Rowan Tulloch, Catherine Hoad and Helen Young consider how *Gone Home* (2013) presents players with a 'riot grrrl' feminist punk perspective.[18] Players adopt that subject position, irrespective of their own gender.

Disability

Dana Plank has outlined many aspects of how games use sound and music to represent impairment (physical and/or mental).[19] She notes that the ludic context of games means that such disability is often treated as some kind of threat or gameplay obstacle. For instance, Plank describes how the music for *Final Fantasy VI*'s antagonist, Kefka, serves his characterization as mentally unbalanced. We might also recognize the increasing willingness of games to engage with representation of impairment in a more thoughtful manner, such as games which use music to ask us to empathize with, rather than 'other', disabled characters.[20]

---

[15] Michael Austin, 'Orchestrating Difference: Representing Gender in Video Game Music', in *Masculinity at Play*, ed. Nicholas Taylor and Gerald Voorhees (London: Palgrave Macmillan, 2018), 165–83.

[16] Kiri Miller, 'Gaming the System: Gender Performance in Dance Central', *New Media and Society* 17, no. 5 (2015): 939–57; *Playable Bodies: Dance Games and Intimate Media* (New York: Oxford University Press, 2017).

[17] Elisa Meléndez, 'For Those About to Rock: Gender Codes in the Rock Music Video Games Rock Band and Rocksmith' (PhD thesis, Miami: Florida International University, 2018).

[18] Rowan Tulloch, Catherine Hoad and Helen Young, 'Riot Grrrl Gaming: Gender, Sexuality, Race, and the Politics of Choice in Gone Home', *Continuum* 3 (2019), 337–50.

[19] Dana Plank, 'Bodies in Play: Representations of Disability in 8- and 16-bit Video Game Soundscapes' (PhD dissertation, Ohio State University, 2018).

[20] See, for example, Hyeonjin Park, '"I Got Nightmare Eyes!": Understanding Madness from Players' Interpretation of Diegetic and Nondiegetic Music in Night in the Woods', paper presented at Ludo 2019, Leeds, UK, 26–28 April 2019.

Geography and Politics

Games have long made use of music beyond Western classical and pop traditions. In the Nintendo Game Boy version of *Tetris* (1989), a Russian folk song, 'Korobeiniki', is heard as the main default theme. This was part of the marketing of *Tetris* as an attractively exotic product from Russia. In the context of thawing Cold War politics, such an approach represented a more positive image of Russia, rather than the portrayal as a threatening adversary that had been typical of Russian characterizations in games.[21] More direct depictions of traditional musical cultures are also made in games – for instance, in *Kentucky Route Zero* (2020), Appalachian folk is performed to depict the game's setting. Other games create new music in traditional styles: *Assassin's Creed Syndicate* (2015), set in Victorian London, uses newly composed street ballads typical of the period and location.

Given the fictional worlds of games, it is not uncommon for game music to draw inspiration from non-Western musics, and to adapt musical elements to the game's own ends. These adaptations can be more or less problematic. Music in the medieval fantasy RPG *The Witcher 3: Wild Hunt* (2015) alludes to medieval and folk traditions, and includes materials created in collaboration with Polish folk musicians, even though it does not recreate a specific musical culture.[22] Similarly, composers for *Assassin's Creed Odyssey* (2018), set in Ancient Greece, devised a musical language inspired by traditional music and records from antiquity, but clearly refracted through a modern lens. Of course, it is not difficult to find less thoughtful adaptations of traditional music in games, and games have not avoided the exoticist and orientalist appropriations of music found across screen media. Vice versa, Japanese composers such as Nobuo Uematsu and many others have drawn on Western musical styles, mixed them and given them their own flavour by ignoring traditional compositional rule sets and conventions.[23]

With respect to geographic difference, it is worth noting that the musical content of individual games can vary depending on region-

---

[21] Dana Plank, '"From Russia with Fun": Tetris, Korobeiniki and the Ludic Soviet', *The Soundtrack* 8, no. 1–2 (2015): 7–24.

[22] Barnabas Smith and Brendan Lamb, 'From Skyrim to Skellige: Fantasy Video Game Music Within a Neo-Mediaevalist Paradigm', *Musicology Australia* 40, no. 2 (2018): 79–100.

[23] Matthew Belinkie, 'Video Game Music: Not Just Kid Stuff', *VGMusic.com* (1999), accessed 9 April 2020, www.vgmusic.com/information/vgpaper.html, and Nicholas Gervais, 'Harmonic Language in The Legend of Zelda: Ocarina of Time', *Nota Bene: Canadian Undergraduate Journal of Musicology* 8 (2015): 26–42.

specific releases, and that geographical traditions of games often have different musical conventions compared to those from elsewhere. For instance, we can clearly recognize the different musical approaches of Western and Japanese role-playing games.[24]

A further issue is the dominance of European and North American voices in a subject area that focuses on a significant amount of music from East Asia. Little scholarship from Asian perspectives has been integrated into discussions of game music in the Western academy. Doubtless, language barriers have had a part to play in this situation. Discussions of game music are certainly widespread in Japan (not least through the prolific historian and chiptune musician Haruhisa Tanaka),[25] and some research on the topic occurs in academic environments.[26]

That recognized, more research has begun to take into account the implications of the Japanese context for interpretation and meanings of game music.[27] Ultimately, video games, their music and even video game music studies are all beginning to engage with wider contexts.

Sometimes, discussing game music with an awareness of these kinds of contextual issues and power dynamics can be rather uncomfortable, particularly when we recognize problematic aspects of video games and music that we love. However, we can still appreciate and enjoy games (and game music) that we are keenly aware have less laudable aspects. Such contextual awareness also illustrates the importance of game music: it shows how game music is not an isolated musical practice, but intersects with broader questions and discourse about music in culture and society.

---

[24] William Gibbons, 'Music, Genre, and Nationality in the Postmillennial Fantasy Role-Playing Game', in *The Routledge Companion to Screen Music and Sound*, ed. Miguel Mera, Ronald Sadoff and Ben Winters (New York: Routledge, 2017), 412–427.

[25] Haruhisa 'hally' Tanaka, *History of Computer Game Music* (Tokyo: Rittor Music, 2014).

[26] See, for example, Yôhei Yamakami and Mathieu Barbosa, 'Formation et Développement des Cultures Autour de la 'Geemu ongaku' (1980–1990)', *Kinephanos. Revue d'Etudes des Médias et de Culture Populaire* 5, no. 1 (2015): 142–60; Masashi Yamada, 'Continuous Features of Emotion in Classical, Popular and Game Music', *Proceedings of Meetings on Acoustics* 19 (2013), 6 pp; Hiroshi Yoshida, 'Epistemic Sounds in Video Games', paper presented at Ludo 2018, University of Leipzig, Leipzig, Germany, 14 April 2018.

[27] See, for example, Andrew Schartmann, 'Music of the Nintendo Entertainment System: Technique, Form, and Style' (PhD thesis, Yale University, 2018) and Thomas B. Yee, 'Battle Hymn of the God-Slayers: Troping Rock and Sacred Music Topics in Xenoblade Chronicles', *Journal of Sound and Music in Games* 1, no. 1 (2020): 2–19.

Further Reading

Cook, Karen M. 'Beyond (the) Halo: Plainchant in Video Games', in *Studies in Medievalism XXVII: Authenticity, Medievalism, Music*, ed. Karl Fugelso. Woodbridge, UK: Boydell & Brewer, 2018, 183–200.

Gibbons, William. *Unlimited Replays: Video Games and Classical Music*. New York: Oxford University Press, 2018.

Ivănescu, Andra. 'Beneath a Steel Sky: A Musical Characterisation of Class Structure.' *The Computer Games Journal* 7 (2018): 231–42.

Miller, Kiri. 'Jacking the Dial: Radio, Race, and Place in "Grand Theft Auto."' *Ethnomusicology* 51, no. 3 (2007): 402–38.

Plank, Dana. 'Bodies in Play: Representations of Disability in 8- and 16-bit Video Game Soundscapes'. PhD dissertation, Ohio State University, 2018.

18 | Game Music and Identity

CHRIS TONELLI

Terry Eagleton perfectly stated the most fundamental lesson about identity when he penned the line: 'Nothing ever happens twice, precisely because it has happened once already.'[1] In other words, a second iteration of an event is always different to a first occurrence, and changes in context, temporal or spatial, reconfigure the meanings of objects and events. When we posit sameness, even sameness to self, there's always something we're missing, some difference we're failing to account for. Our failure to realize that the secondness of the later happening in Eagleton's sequence makes it different from the first stands in nicely for all the differences we fail to consider when we experience people or things as possessing identities.

Jean-Luc Nancy puts it a different way. He points to how we are prone to look at the formula A=A and see both As as identical, ignoring that they are in different positions on the page and in distinct relations to one another.[2] The perception of identity requires reductiveness, because it identifies sameness in different contexts and ignores the ways relations between those contexts exist as a part of what an object or event means. But this 'failure' is inevitable, despite the advantages we gain when we remind ourselves of the many differences that perceptions of identity obscure. The fact is that we are users of language, and language forces us to experience the world in terms of identity. No matter how deeply we consider the truth of Eagleton's statement or Nancy's intervention, we are bound to forget it at times; we are bound, all of us, to reduce our perception of eternal difference to reductive (but sometimes empowering) cognitive constructions of categorical sameness.

We are all also bound, it seems, to crave identification for ourselves. As much as we might try, we do not seem capable of consistently viewing ourselves as constantly renewing entities, distinct in substantial ways from what we were moments ago and possessing meaningful differences from any reified identity category others might want to slot us into. We crave two

[1] Terry Eagleton, *After Theory* (New York, Basic Books, 2003), 66.
[2] Jean-Luc Nancy, 'Identity and Trembling', in *The Birth to Presence*, trans. Brian Holmes (Stanford, CA: Stanford University Press, 1993), 9–35 at 11.

distinct types of identity: *qualitative group identity*, which indicates identities that are perceived or felt as existing and shared amongst groups of
individuals, and *personal identity*, our feelings of our, or others', or things'
sameness to our/themselves across time. Personal identity encompasses
our sense of what matters most about who we are, or who others are as
individuals, beyond our belongingness to shared reified qualitative group
identities like African, Texan, Deaf, male, white, Black, and so on.

In this chapter, we will reflect on the ways game music contributes to the
processes that generate and constantly renegotiate personal identity and
qualitative group identity. We will consider both self-identity and our
perception of the identities of others in the world around us.

But before we start to talk about game music, I'll acknowledge one more
awful truth: identification is often fuelled by a process cultural theorists call
Othering, with a capital 'O'. Othering means coming to understand one's
own identity by positioning another perceived identity group as an inferior
opposite. This deleterious process is signified by the capital 'O'. Othering is
an element in the process through which slavery has been justified –
enslaved groups have been constructed in a multitude of ways as less
human than their captors – and Othering is part of the process through
which governments and individuals in recent years have justified not acting
to eliminate and prevent widespread forms of suffering and death in the
contexts of recent national policies towards refugees. All forms of media
hold the potential to contribute to processes of identification and Othering.
The musical choices made by game designers and players are part of
a broader constantly shifting mediascape in which every musical choice
plays some small role in the unfolding of these processes. The stakes are
high in the micropolitics of everyday aesthetics. Or, in other words: game
music matters.

Some Key Terms Before We Click Start

The word 'affordance' is important throughout this chapter, as is its
counterpart 'articulation'. To speak about musical meaning we need to
understand that the sounds of music only give rise to meanings when
listeners *articulate* meanings with those sounds. To *articulate* is to attach.
Think of an image of an articulated vehicle: the attachment of two or more
parts together by a pivot joint articulates the parts of the vehicle together.
As the sounds of music manifest in different contexts, the meanings
listeners articulate with those sounds will not necessarily be the same.

For certain meanings to arise, listeners need to have been exposed to the idea that meaning x is connected to sound y and they need to recall that connection in the act of listening; they need to *re-articulate* that sound and that idea. Affordance refers to the opposite side of this process; it refers to the agency of sounds in determining what meanings might be articulated with them. While I could potentially associate any sound with any meaning, the sounds themselves always play a role in the process of determining which meanings come to mind, which meanings remain articulated, which dearticulate and disappear quickly. Concerning articulation, it is important to note that the attachments are *always* temporary; even very well-established and broadly shared associations will not be present when certain listeners encounter the sounds in question. The material properties of the sound play a role in shaping the articulation process. This does not mean they determine the meaning or that every time a particular quality of sound manifests for a listener, no matter who the listener is, they will experience the same meanings or feelings. This simply means the material qualities of the sound are present and their presence contributes to, or frustrates, the articulation process. The material presence of certain kinds of game music trigger certain players to make certain associations – *they afford a process of articulation*. Other players will experience the same music without being affected in the same way by this affordance, but that property remains an affordance of that particular music; it remains part of what that music might give rise to in a distinct encounter or context.

Just like we are not good at recognizing the irreducible singularity of everything around us, we are also not good at being aware that musical meaning (and the meanings we associate with all the materiality we encounter) is always contingent and temporary. We often speak as if types of music *have* meaning rather than *afford* meaning in a new way in every instance of their appearance. This is a shortcut that sometimes saves us time but often leads us into false assumptions and problematic claims. In fact, it often leads us into the kinds of problematic claims that serve the process of Othering. It leads us to claim that the music our identity group has created or is associated with *means*, for example, the nobility of the human spirit while the music of our Others is primitive or less valuable or sophisticated.

To begin to understand what the many kinds of video game music in existence 'are', or what they 'do' – what processes of identification and Othering they serve – we need to look at particular examples without falling into the trap of reducing music's ability to *afford* meaning to a notion that musical sounds or structures *have* meaning. Because of the nature of the processes of articulation and affordance, music that sounds in distinct temporal and spatial contexts will have distinct effects. The full extent of these effects are unknowable, but as game music researchers we can begin to understand what certain kinds of game and game music design afford in certain environments and encounters. We can begin to hear some of the ways game music fuels identificatory processes.

Civilization IV: Articulating European Art Music with 'Civilizedness'

One of the most widely analysed examples of game music fuelling identity categories via articulation of meanings to the sounds of game music is *Civilization IV* (2005). Game music scholars Tim Summers and Karen M. Cook have both written on the ways music operates in this game, and their work can be consulted for greater detail than I will include here. What is important at this point is that in this turn-based strategy game the player is responsible for shaping the development of their 'civilization' over 6000 years, from 'ancient' to 'modern' times. Cook points out that 'the overwhelming majority of *Civ IV*'s terrain soundtrack consists of compositions from the Western art music tradition' and that 'the commencement of the terrain soundtrack ... aurally represents the first successful milestone in [the] cultural progress [the game stages]'.[3] As the gameplay of *Civ IV* progresses, the game reinforces pre-existing articulations between European culture, art music, notions of progress and notions of civilizedness. Some might argue that by articulating European art music with notions of progress, the game is not necessarily articulating the non-European with the binary opposites of 'civilized' and 'progressive'. However, by rearticulating these concepts the game contributes to a broader process of *naturalization* of these associations, a process through which these associations come to seem unquestionable in certain contexts. This naturalization can then play a role in contexts in which Othering occurs, bolstering various European or European-associated identities; because of this process the associations often come to feel less like cultural constructions and more like unchanging universal truths because the articulations have been reasserted in so many media texts – video games being one of many – that they make up the fabric of what many people feel to be real

[3] Karen M. Cook, 'Music, History, and Progress in Sid Meier's Civilization IV', in *Music in Video Games: Studying Play*, ed. K. J. Donnelly, William Gibbons and Neil Lerner (New York: Routledge, 2014), 166–82 at 170.

and true. Games, of course, function as part of a broader mediascape and symbolic mythscape.

However, *Civ IV* also directly contributes to the articulation of certain identities with negative associations. The music that was chosen for the earliest stages of civilization in the game 'draw on stereotypical sound-images of pan-African, Native American, or Aboriginal music'.[4] The alignment in the earliest stages of the game of these three identity categories with the idea of 'less civilized' or 'less developed' via the appearance of musical features associated with these groups operates alongside articulation of Europeanness with the opposite sides of these binaries, contributing to a long destructive history of aligning various non-European people with primitiveness.

Cook is careful to point out that players engage with *Civ IV* in different ways. Players may play while remaining aware of and critical of the associations the game design is encouraging. Other players might read the articulations as ironic and find humour in the notion that the European elite, a group historically responsible for so much of the history of slavery and the economic and institutional results of that slavery that still linger in the present, is being musically associated with 'civilizedness' and 'progress'. And the game itself complicates the civilized/primitive binary by acknowledging the ways in which 'highly developed' societies have caused environmental crises that threaten the existence of those societies. Complicating these issues further, we need to recognize that some players may be playing with the soundtrack muted or replaced by different music of their choosing. Our study of the ways game music comes into play in processes of identification needs to remain open to the ability of the player to engage in oppositional readings and/or modifications of the gaming experience. Yet, at the same time, we cannot let our awareness of the presence of actual or potential oppositional readings lead us to dismiss the potential effects that standard encounters with existing game and game music design seem to give rise to. Most encounters with the music of *Civ IV* likely reinforce a damaging but widespread association of Europeanness with civilizedness and non-Europeanness with primitiveness.

The Last of Us: Affording Masculinities

One of the medium-specific dimensions of video gaming lies in the ways it is distinctly interactive in comparison with media like film, television, radio

---

[4] Ibid., 173.

and literature. All media forms afford interaction, as their effects emerge from the ways individuals interpret and attend to texts. Media users add imagined elements as they engage with media, they ignore and misunderstand elements, they make unique associations based on their personal histories: they each play a foundational role in reconstituting media texts. Gaming is not *more* interactive than other media forms – as interaction cannot be holistically quantified – but it is *differently* interactive. Nearly all video games involve control of some form of avatar and some understanding that you as the player both are and are not that avatar, both are and are not the protagonist at the centre of the game. The relationship between player and avatar is *intersubjective* provided we create the sense that our avatar is a kind of subject, has some qualities that make it a unique (imaginary) entity, as we control that avatar and imagine their perspective. We should also acknowledge here that the player is not the only individual on whom the game music is acting in regards to identity-related processes; streaming audiences or other non-players in audible range of music from games can also be affected by the sounds of gaming as they develop relationships to other avatar and non-avatar bodies/identities.

Intersubjectivity is a term for the illusory sensation that we are sensing, feeling and thinking from the subject position of another subject. It is a sensation of a kind of blurring between self and Other. Disidentification is the theorist Jose Esteban Muñoz's term for a kind of intersubjective experience with an identity we have Othered and/or that has Othered an identity we claim. While most media and media texts offer opportunities for intersubjective experience across reified categories of identity distinction, games often place players into long durations of interactivity with particular avatars that may or may not be identified in ways that align with or coherently extend the players' own identity (or identities). The way game players dwell for long periods of time in an intersubjective middle space between their RL (real-life) selves and the avatars they control has a range of implications for the dynamics of identity. Studying these dynamics and these implications can help us understand the extent to which game music functions to make identities manifest that players 'try on' during gameplay. The intersubjective encounter, when it occurs across lines of (dis)identification, might give us temporary imaginary access to identities we do not feel entitled to occupy at any other time. This might have the effect of reinforcing senses of Otherness or disidentification, or, conversely, it might chip away at them.

I will now discuss in detail an example that displays identificatory, counter-identificatory (Othering) and disidentificatory (complex or oscillating blending of Othering plus identification) dynamics involving encounters with both game avatars and game music through a close reading of the game *The Last of Us: Remastered* (hereafter *TLOU*) (2014). Though this example is just one amongst a vast range of distinct types of games and approaches to game music, this close reading can model some of the medium-specific considerations we encounter when we study the intersections of game music and identification.

Like countless action-adventure films, *TLOU* centres on framing working-class white masculinity as heroic. The main character is Joel. In the game's first sequence, a cinematic cutscene, Joel is marked with working-class precariousness, depicted on his mobile phone discussing how he can't afford to lose his job. As the avatar we control through most of the game, Joel is the game's narrative focal point. *TLOU* offers a third-person perspective, and so we see the body of this avatar, our working-class hero, throughout nearly every moment of the game.

The term 'leitmotif' is used to describe musical elements associated with particular characters or specific referents/concepts in a narrative context. Though 'motif' most often refers to a melodic device, it is not unconventional to refer to 'timbral' or 'instrumental leitmotifs', which are uses of particular musical instruments or instrument timbres in association with particular characters. The melodic, timbral and instrumental leitmotifs used in the *TLOU* game soundtrack help to construct Joel as a hero. The dominant soundtrack feature is the foregrounding of guitars. This choice of guitar as instrumental leitmotif is not surprising. The guitar as instrumental leitmotif for a male hero is a well-established film music convention, especially in the Western film genre (in films like *For a Few Dollars More*, for example). This convention has bled out of Westerns into countless other filmic, televisual, radio and digital media works, such that many media users who have never seen a Western still know that particular guitar timbres have been strongly articulated with masculine heroes (such as in films like the genre-blending film *Bubba Ho-Tep*, which draws heavily on Western conventions in the context of a comedy horror film about Elvis Presley saving his nursing home from a murderous mummy). *TLOU* makes extensive use of three distinct guitar timbres, all of which have been repeatedly articulated with male media heroes. Each of these three timbral leitmotifs function as markers of different dimensions of Joel's character. These include a tremolo-drenched electric guitar sound associated with Joel's heroism, a nylon-stringed guitar that comes to be associated with Joel's feelings towards his daughter and a steel-string acoustic guitar sound that comes to be associated with his feelings about Ellie, a substitute daughter figure that appears later in the game. Since all three guitar timbres are associated with Joel, the leitmotifs are unified on the instrumental level, but differentiated on the timbral level, as the distinct guitar timbres represent different aspects of the same character.

The game establishes Joel's working-classness and masculinity in ways that make it difficult (not impossible, however) for players to ignore. The game also works to mark Joel as Texan. However, this articulation operates in a weak way and players are capable of missing or resisting this construction. Music plays a role in affording and encouraging these associations. Like the more general articulation of Texan or Southern as part of Joel's character through non-musical means, the success of music in affording these articulations is achieved to varying degrees that range from total to strong to weak to non-existent. Westerns, of course, also often invoke the American South, and all three of the guitar timbres in question here have been employed widely in this genre (the examples above all employ electric guitars most prominently, but we hear and often see nylon- and steel-string acoustic guitars in countless Western films like *Rio Bravo*, *Along the Navajo Trail* or the comedy Western *Three Amigos*). Beyond film, the tremolo soaked heavy-stringed electric guitar is strongly associated with 'Texas blues' and Texan 'guitar heroes' like Stevie Ray Vaughan. The nylon-string guitar is associated with Spanish music, Mexican music and, subsequently, the border cultures of the Southern states. The steel-string acoustic guitar has a wide variety of associations, yet, when it appears in the game it often employs scalar qualities that underscore its association with the blues genre, which, of course, developed in the American South.

The opening sequence of *TLOU*, where we first meet Joel, is set in Austin, Texas, but references to the setting are not so apparent that they will be acknowledged by every player. Troy Baker's voice acting of Joel in English-language versions of the game avoids a strong Southern accent, and many of the elements that reveal the setting would be recognizable only to those familiar with the Austin area.[5] Game dialogue referring to Joel as 'Texas' has the potential to establish him as Texan, but judging from streamed gameplay, players can often miss or resist this implication. One such instance can be witnessed in a gameplay livestream by a streamer who identifies as Gibi. After twenty-five minutes of gameplay, non-player

---

[5] During Gibi's liveplay stream that I discuss below (see www.twitch.tv/videos/279324500) one viewer revealed via a chat post that for her/hir/him the setting is unambiguous. S/z/he recognizes the freeways referenced in the game's second cutscene are roads s/z/he drives in Austin. The game design does include road signs that reference Texan cities Austin, Deerwood, Pleasant Valley, San Marcos and San Antonio, but they flash by fairly quickly and might not be attended to by the player.

character Tess refers to Joel as 'Texas', saying: 'Alright Texas, boost me up'.[6] In her playthrough, Gibi repeats Tess's line in a flat tone, seemingly contemplating the sudden interpellation of her avatar into the identity of 'Texan'. She seems unexcited by this interpellation, perhaps slightly unsettled by a line that altered the non-Southern identity she may have been ascribing to Joel.[7] After about three hours of gameplay, prompted by her navigation of Joel though an 'old museum' with display cases full of maps and uniforms, Gibi asks: 'What city are we in? Texas? I know Texas isn't a city but what city of Texas are we in? Or, no, he's not in Texas anymore. He's from Texas?'[8] This questioning of an identity that has been so frequently underscored musically, as well as in the game dialogue, seems to indicate a resistance to the articulation of Joel in terms of Southernness or a Texan identity.

On the other hand, it is also worth considering the media users for whom this articulation is strongly present. On a stream of the game by streamer NairoMK, after a portion of the opening cutscene that features a minor-key highly ornamented solo nylon-string guitar passage, one stream viewer posted the comment: '20 minute banjo solo?'[9] The association of this style of guitar playing with a distinct instrument, the banjo, that itself possesses associations with the American South, reveals that the game's music is affording the idea of Southernness to some players. Despite its African origins and histories of African-American use, the banjo has come to be strongly articulated with white American Southernness.[10] The fact that the nylon-string guitar playing is, when paired with the visual and narrative elements of this opening cutscene, invoking an absent banjo for this viewer, might suggest that the

---

[6] At the time of writing, the gameplay stream I refer to was available here: ggGibi, 'Gibi Plays Last of Us – Part 2', Twitch Stream www.twitch.tv/videos/279332170, accessed 10 April 2020.

[7] Throughout her stream Gibi repeatedly comments on the resemblance between Joel and the character Dylan McDermott plays in the first season of the television series *American Horror Story*. The game's construction of Joel is decidedly not the only force constructing Joel's character; Gibi's transmedial and intertextual conflation of the two characters is informing how she is co-constructing Joel. McDermott's character, Ben, is American, but neither Texan nor Southern.

[8] At the time Gibi posed this question, she was playing a sequence set in Boston.

[9] Previously available in the chat bar of www.twitch.tv/videos/287187464 at 10:06.

[10] The association of the banjo with the bluegrass genre and the association of the bluegrass genre with the south-eastern state of Kentucky and with 'white' rather than African-American musicians is one strong chain of association that often codes the banjo as white and Southern. Despite the dominance of associations of bluegrass with white musicians, scholars are working to make African-American histories in and around bluegrass more audible. For more on this, see Robert Winans's book *Banjo Roots and Branches* (Urbana, IL: University of Illinois Press, 2018), or the website African Bluegrass, www.africanbluegrass.com, accessed 10 April 2020.

Southernness and whiteness of the characters is strongly, perhaps disidentificatorily, felt by this particular viewer. The reference to this guitar as a banjo may have been a means of counter-identifying or disidentifying with these instruments and/or certain genres with which these instruments are associated, and, by extension, the social groups and identities most strongly associated with those genres.[11] Regardless of whether this reading was, in fact, the identificatory assertion the commenter intended to perform, the fact that she/ze/he invoked the banjo in their comment seems to suggest the guitar was strongly invoking associations with the American South at moments when Joel is the game's focal point. It seems clear from these instances of gameplay that certain players will, and others will not, experience Joel's working-class masculinity as Southern or Texan. The music carries associations with Texas, but these associations themselves do not ensure that Joel's working-class masculinity will be experienced as Southern or Texan.

This distinction between players who attend to Joel's Southernness and those who do not points us to the diversity of ways gamers read game texts and paratexts. The functions of music always depend, in part, on what the listener brings to the experience. One of the medium-specific aspects of game music is that when and how music manifests in the gaming experience will often depend, to greater or lesser extents, on the choices the player makes in the game. This is important to keep in mind as I move on to explain how the musical devices in *TLOU* shape the identificatory aspects of the gaming experience. For example, the electric guitar timbre is present in the very first musical moment of *TLOU*, the song that sounds on the start screen. Players who have never played the game or encountered others playing it cannot associate that timbre with the character of Joel, since they have not yet been introduced to the character (the visual on the start screen is an open window with curtains swaying; it does not contain an image of game characters). The timbre and the harmonic minor modality it sounds in this sequence may suggest various meanings, but it will not yet suggest the interiority of a particular character. Players encountering the start screen after witnessing or participating in gameplay, however, may feel

---

[11] The reference to excessive duration (solos do not usually last 20 minutes) suggests counter- or disidentification with the way the nylon-string guitar manifests in this sequence. Also, the frequency with which the banjo is singled out for mockery compels me to read this comment's reference to excessive duration along with a reference to the non-present banjo to be an invocation of the banjo as a means of rejecting the nylon-string guitar playing as too 'country'. For more on the politics of anti-banjo bias see Jeannie B. Thomas and Doug Enders, 'Bluegrass and "White Trash": A Case Study Concerning the Name "Folklore" and Class Bias', *Journal of Folklore Research* 37, no. 1, (2000): 23–52.

intersubjectively connected to the subject position and/or identities of Joel, and may associate Joel with the minor modality of this opening. The same is true for the loading music that follows the start screen.

As mentioned above, *TLOU*'s opening cutscene deals with Joel's working-class uncertainty. The first image we see, however, is of Joel's tween daughter, Sarah. The loading music ends before this image and the cutscene unfolds and articulates the father–daughter relationship. Music re-enters after this sequence. The nylon-string guitar accompanies Joel carrying a sleeping Sarah to her bed and, in so doing, gains the potential to be heard as a timbral leitmotif signifying the father–daughter relationship or the side of Joel concerning his parental feelings. We may at this point also associate the timbre with Sarah. However, as the game progresses and the notion that the guitar symbolizes Joel's interiority becomes better established, a connection with Sarah alone, rather than with father–daughter feelings specific to Joel, is less likely to be maintained.

The electric guitar from the start screen re-enters after two gameplay sequences separated by a cutscene. In the second of these, the player navigates Joel carrying Sarah through a chaotic urban environment, where humans infected by a fungus are attacking the not-yet-infected. When this play sequence ends, a cutscene occurs in which Sarah is shot by a soldier. The melodic motif from the start screen recurs and then our reverberant guitar re-emerges with a VI-i chord succession at the moment it appears Sarah dies.[12] The movement to the minor root chord is likely to afford a sense of simultaneous closure and despair, and though we are actually the ones affected by these feelings, the visual components prompt us to associate these feelings with Joel, a father whose daughter appears to have just died in his arms. With Sarah's apparent death, the electric guitar takes over as the foreground of the music. Joel is all that is left and this guitar sound becomes strongly associated with him and his solitude in this moment.

A title sequence and theme song appear at this point, closing the game's introductory section. This is followed by another cutscene that establishes the setting for the post-introduction section and begins to unfold the game's plot. The electric guitar sounds again as the cutscene transitions into the next sequence of gameplay, where the player begins what, for most players, will be a substantial period of intersubjective relation with Joel as

---

[12] The melody here begins in a bowed string voice that is associated with Sarah and later Ellie, blurring the identity of the two characters. See the following note for further comment on the fact there are some minor attempts in the game to develop the female characters musically.

they navigate him through the game. In this appearance of the timbral/ instrumental leitmotif, the guitar sounds alone. The solitary musical voice sounding an improvisatory, free-rhythmic melodic sequence is linked with the image of a solitary male hero remaining in control in the face of adversity. As the player becomes Joel, the music positions Joel, and the player-as-Joel, as a new hero in a lineage of male heroes who have faced adversity boldly, on their own.

While Gibi, who is female, gives no indication she identifies in terms of qualitative group identity with Joel's maleness or Southernness or his working-classness, she seems to perform an easy attachment to Joel that is distinct in kind from her attachment to other characters in the game. One of the unique qualities of *TLOU* is that Joel is not the only avatar the player must control. No matter what your gender identity, you navigate three avatars if you play through the entirety of *TLOU*: one male avatar, Joel, and two female avatars, Sarah and Ellie. The amount of time you spend in distinct sequences of the game depends on how you play. However, if you play through *TLOU* in a relatively conventional manner, you spend about nine times as much time in control of Joel than in control of the two female characters. And while you play, the timbral, instrumental and melodic leitmotifs of the game are positioned in a manner that affords a sense of access to Joel's interiority and a sense of his heroic presence. The relatively short durations of gameplay as the female characters leaves far less opportunity for development of their interiority via musical devices, and relatively little is done during these sequences to develop the female characters musically.[13] Throughout her gameplay, attachment to Joel seemed to have been performed by Gibi far more frequently and strongly than attachment to Ellie, Sarah or any of the non-player characters. Attachment to Joel seems to have been felt by Gibi as an element of her personal identity, and the holistic depiction of Joel's internality via, in part, the game's music – the way it constructs a personal identity for Joel in a way it does not for any other character in *TLOU* – makes Joel the most nuanced subject for identification that *TLOU* offers. Since Joel is by far the most fully developed, emotionally textured character in the game – thanks in no small measure to the game music – there are many aspects about Joel's character that Gibi may have felt as points of connection that affirm both her own personal identity and the sense that Joel has qualities she identifies with.

---

[13] Relatively little, but not nothing. Following dominant norms related to the gendering of Western musical instruments, upper-range bowed string playing (violin) serves as an instrumental leitmotif shared by both of the female characters.

Though Gibi does not align with Joel in terms of certain of Joel's qualitative group identities (male, Texan, Southern), forms of identification with Joel nevertheless unfolded during, and were afforded by, her gameplay and its musical aspects.

Game Music Styles, Affect and Intersections of Personal and Qualitative Group Identity

Considerations of personal identity in relation to game music is a complex topic that is distinct from, but cannot ever be fully isolated from, qualitative group identity. As Adrienne Shaw points out in her study *Gaming at the Edge: Sexuality and Gender at the Margins of Gamer Culture*: 'There is empirical evidence that identities are experienced at the nexus of the individual and the social.'[14] Our tastes and attachments are almost always informed to some degree by the ways we feel belongingness to or exclusion from certain shared group identities, but these group identities are never fully deterministic of the ways we negotiate our personal identity or perceive the identities of other people or things. It is clear that game music is a vehicle for formation and maintenance of aspects of personal identity for many gamers (and some non-gamers!). Their celebrations of these aspects of their identities have led elements of game music to shape musical activities that occur outside of the experience of gameplay.

In the opening chapter of his book *Understanding Video Game Music*, Tim Summers discusses the system start cues of various gaming consoles. These are short musical gestures that sound when gaming consoles are turned on. They serve the functions of letting users know the console is working and that it is properly connected to working speakers, and, at the same time, these musical cues act as a sonic marker of the brand of the console. For some gamers, these might remain mere markers of brand identity. But for others they become entangled with both personal and qualitative group identities. Summers points to the fact that because 'these cues are so frequently heard by players they gain significant nostalgic capital'.[15] The secondness that Eagleton points us to in the quote that opened this chapter manifests in the repetition that Summers points to. When we re-hear these start-up cues we are often cognizant on some level

---

[14] Adrienne Shaw, *Gaming at the Edge* (Minneapolis, MN: University of Minnesota Press, 2015), 43.
[15] Tim Summers, *Understanding Video Game Music* (Cambridge, UK: Cambridge University Press, 2016), 16.

of both the previous times we have heard the cues, and aspects of the gaming experiences that followed. We articulate these memories with the sounds, and these memories then become part of the meaning afforded by those sounds. These affordances and articulations of memory and sound may, as Summers argues, lead to nostalgic feelings, but they may alternately lead to feelings better described not as the kind of longing for a return to the past that is central to nostalgia, but as a broader variety of feelings of connectedness to past experiences we have had. If we strongly value those experiences, these system start cues, and other sonic components unique to gaming or to specific games, may afford a feeling of connectedness to experiences we feel have played a role in defining us; they may trigger feelings that inform our sense of personal identity.

We may come to understand that we are not the only ones subjectivated by rehearings of these sounds. When we hear these cues, or witness others being subjectivated by these cues, we may experience feelings of interpersonal connectedness to others. These feelings of co-subjectivation may or may not afford, or be articulated with, the concept of a shared belongingness to a qualitative group identity. They may remain senses of parallel personal-identity construction, rather than characteristics and/or results of a shared group identity. Summers discusses the fact that hip-hop artist Frank Ocean began his 2012 album *Channel Orange* with a sample of the system start-up cue of the first PlayStation gaming console. A listener who feels subjectivated by hearing this cue might listen to Ocean's sample and feel that she/ze/he shares a belongingness to the practice-based qualitative group identity category of 'gamer' with Ocean, but this is not the inevitable or only possible affordance.

Regardless of what Ocean's inclusion of the start-up cue might afford, the presence of the sample on *Channel Orange* is one in a wide variety of examples of game music flowing beyond the spaces of gaming. However, the fact that the game is not present does not mean that the games are not brought to mind. The sounds will likely afford memories of gaming's other affordances for listeners who possess those memories. The music is primed to consciously or unconsciously re-articulate those memories with the sounds affording the memories. For individuals whose personal identities are afforded in part by their experiences as game players, game music (or music that sounds like game music) provides a tool they can use to structure non-game spaces. It allows them to perform their personal or qualitative group identities, prolong or reshape feelings of identificatory attachment or create an environment conducive to their preferred modes of sociability. Elements of the chiptune scene (described in detail in Chapter 2), the now common practice of orchestral performances of versions of works composed for games, game music cover bands, personal practices of marketing and listening to game soundtrack recordings apart from the experience of gaming, and many other practices, are widespread and relevant to study of game music's intersections with identity.

Credit Music

Game music's (re-)articulation of meanings with group identity categories is an important process with real-world consequences. Some gamers do, and others do not, identify intersubjectively with their avatars. Yet Adrienne Shaw's work convincingly argues that media users are often not terribly concerned about whether the media they are consuming represents the qualitative group identities they align with in RL (despite the important sociopolitical benefits media representation of visible minorities can often lead to). The game players she interviewed for her study, she argues, 'connected more with texts that were affectively familiar, even if the identities of the characters were radically different from theirs'.[16] These kinds of affective identifications operate on the level of personal identity, or what Shaw refers to as *identification with* rather than *identification as*. Though her study is not primarily about music, she discusses how for several of her consultants 'music engendered a great deal more identification than did other media'.[17] This too, like her discussion of identification with media characters, operates largely on the level of affect and, as in the case of the music, with or without the mediation of the avatar-as-imagined-subject. Her respondents describe their connection with the emotions they feel certain music conveys and/or the emotional and imaginative affordances of that music. One of her respondents, Evan, discussed how listening to music while running allowed him to imagine 'he was a heroic figure'.[18] This emotional configuration points to the ways in which personal identity is a process, not an object we possess, and music is a tool that commonly helps us negotiate feelings that we register and then expand into a sense of self-understanding, a sense that feeling this way matters, it is part of who we are. Conversely, music can emotionally configure us in ways we know we prefer not to be configured; it can put us in touch with feelings we counter-identify with, feelings we know we prefer not to feel, and we can perform and affirm our identity by marking our distaste for these varieties of emotion.

---

[16] Shaw, *Gaming at the Edge*, 78.
[17] Ibid., 71.
[18] Ibid.

Certain game music can configure us emotionally in ways where we become the versions of ourselves we most identify with, while other game music fails to affect us in that way. While these processes can unfold entirely in ways that remain in the domain of personal identity, they can also spill over into and inform processes related to qualitative group identity. Game music makes listeners like Evan feel heroic when he's running and this may feed associations he has with qualitative group identities he holds or doesn't hold (like males as heroic, Americans as heroic, working-class individuals as heroic, etc.).

One final angle from which we can approach the study of game music's intersection with identity is related to the fact that, contrary to games like *TLOU* that predetermine (most) aspects of the identities the game avatars represent, many recent games include the option for users to shape aspects of their avatar like race, gender, sexuality and other dimensions. Shaw's work argues that we need to recognize the problematic aspects of this practice alongside its positive affordances. She discusses how this shifts the burden of representation onto the player and, as such, is part of the broader contemporary neoliberal mindset that erodes social narratives advocating societies that are based on shared responsibility for the well-being of each member.[19] In a neoliberal society, we are all on our own, competing in the free market for survival with no social contract guaranteeing our well-being or obliging us to one another. If we want to navigate an avatar that aligns with our RL identity, says a neoliberal attitude, we need to labour to make our own. Another related result of these adjustable avatars is, of course, that they can sometimes diminish the potential good that might come out of games forcing us to control an avatar whose identities might be distinct from our own and might foster identification across reified identity categories and/or challenge our impulses to Other.

The vast world of video gaming is getting more diverse. Pre-programmed avatars that represent RL identity categories that are not dominant in our mediascapes are slowly but surely coming to be encountered by both individuals who identify with those categories and players who do not. And as we get the chance to control a hero that mirrors our qualitative group identities, or one that allows us to intersubjectively imagine identities whose social locations we can never occupy in RL, music will be sounding, affording meanings that shape that experience, whether or not, at the same time, we are embracing the reductive and strategic comforts of identification.

[19] Ibid., 35.

JAMES COOK

Introduction

Video games have frequently been associated with newness, the present or even the future. Despite this, they have long had a close and creative relationship with history. While many early games dealt with ahistorical topics such as digital versions of already-extant analogue games (billiards, chess, tennis or ping-pong) or futuristic ideas such as *Spacewar!* (1962), it was not long before games began to deal with history. *Hamurabi* (1968), for example, was one of the earliest strategy games, in which, through a text-based interface, the player acted as the ancient Babylonian king Hammurabi (*c*.1810–*c*.1750 BC) in the management of their kingdom.

Whether set in 'real' historical situations or imagined worlds motivated and animated by a shared understanding of history, games have long drawn on the past as a source of inspiration and continue to do so today. This essay is concerned not just with history but with music *and* history. I therefore mean to touch briefly on various ways in which music history and games interact. Though far from an exhaustive treatment of the topic, these case studies may stand as staging points for further investigations. In the main, they demonstrate the mutual interactions between representations of history in games and other media, showing both intermedial shared aspects, and those seemingly unique to, or at least originating in games.

Intermedial Trends and Game Technology

The use of historical music to underscore historical topics is not a phenomenon particular to games. Long before the advent of video games, it had already found full vent in the world of film from at least as early as Miklós Rósza's score for *Ivanhoe* (1952), for which he professed to have 'gone back to mediaeval music sources' and his earlier score for *Quo Vadis* (1951) which drew on the Ancient Greek *Epitaph of Seiklos*.[1]

The relationship, in historically situated film, of 'historical music' to 'real' or 'authentic' music history (to risk wading into a debate best left to a different essay) is complex.[2] History is not something discovered, but something made. It is a 'site from which new narratives spring, conditioned and coloured by the perspectives and technologies of the age'.[3] What is considered an 'authentic' musical expression of a time period changes through time and cultural context, and is impacted upon by technological constraints and opportunities. We must be mindful too of the popular conception of history, which is often coloured by trends in and across genres, rather than necessarily springing from the minds of our best historians and musicologists.

Though this relationship is complex in film it is perhaps further problematized in video games. The capabilities of the technology involved in the latter act as both constraining and motivating forces for the composition of music in a manner which is often considered unique to the medium. This uniqueness is, I would argue, largely illusory however: the very fact of non-diegetic music's ubiquitous deployment in film is, of course, predicated on an analogous artistic response to the technological constraints of silent-era films.[4] In both media, we grapple with the aesthetic legacies of earlier technological constraints, even though the constraints themselves no longer apply.

Though the very presence of a film score is clearly predicated on technological development, it is still arguable that changes in technology have had a more obvious impact on video games than film in recent years, through the number and kinds of sounds that have become available to composers. We will return to this point later in the essay. While some compositional trends may have evolved from technological concerns inherent to games, many historical tropes in games come from those

---

[1] Miklós Rózsa, *Double Life: The Autobiography of Miklós Rózsa* (Tunbridge Wells: Midas, 1982), 155; Stephen C. Meyer 'The Politics of Authenticity in Miklós Rózsa's Score to El Cid', in *Music in Epic Film: Listening to Spectacle*, ed. Stephen C. Meyer (New York: Routledge, 2016), 86–101 at 90.

[2] For a discussion see James Cook, Alexander Kolassa and Adam Whittaker 'Introduction: Understanding the Present through the Past and the Past through the Present', in *Recomposing the Past: Representations of Early Music on Stage and Screen*, ed. James Cook, Alexander Kolassa and Adam Whittaker (Abingdon: Routledge, 2018), 1–15.

[3] Ibid., 1.

[4] For more on this concept, see Claudia Gorbman, *Unheard Melodies: Narrative Film Music* (Bloomington, IN and London: Indiana University Press and BFI Publishing, 1987), 4.

already prevalent in film music. Something that is less frequently discussed is the degree to which this influence seems to have been mutual.

Video game music has a complex and multifaceted relationship with the sounds of history, borrowing from and lending to our shared, intermedial popular conceptions of the past built through decades of common gestures, drawing upon historical and musicological research, and filtering all of this through the limitations and opportunities offered by the technology of the time.

Tropes from Film into Game

Perhaps the most obvious broad trope to move from film and other media into game is medievalism. Medievalism is essentially the creative afterlife of the middle ages. It does not therefore mean 'real' medieval music, but musics from other historical periods that are understood 'as medieval' in popular culture (from baroque, to folk, to heavy metal), and newly composed works that draw on readily understood symbols of the medieval. It is one of the primary animating forces behind fantasy, and has a rich history in its own right.[5]

In film, medievalism plays out as a variety of tropes, both visual and sonic. I wish to focus here particularly on 'Celtic' medievalism. In essence, it draws on aspects of Celtic and Northern (i.e. Northern European and especially Scandinavian) culture, which are held as a shorthand for a particular representation of the middle ages. Examples include *Robin Hood* (2010), which makes use of the Irish song 'Mná na hÉireann' (composed by the twentieth-century composer Seán Ó Riada to an eighteenth-century text) to underscore a scene set in medieval Nottingham; or the *How to Train Your Dragon* series (2010–2019), which displays a mixture of Celtic and Viking imagery, alongside Celtic-style music to represent an imaginary, yet clearly Northern setting.[6]

On screen, a clear Celtic/Northern medievalist aesthetic is often vital to narrative and scene-setting. It often signals a kind of rough-hewn but honest, democratic, community-based society, with elements of nostalgia, as well as a closeness to nature. Writers such as Gael Baudino and Patricia Kennealy-Morrison often draw on pagan Celtic sources as an alternative to

---

[5] Stephen C. Meyer and Kirsten Yri (eds), *The Oxford Handbook of Music and Medievalism* (New York: Oxford University Press, in press).

[6] Simon Nugent, 'Celtic Music and Hollywood Cinema: Representation, Stereotype, and Affect', in *Recomposing the Past* ed. James Cook, Alex Kolassa and Adam Whittaker (Abingdon: Routledge, 2018), 107–23.

what they perceive as the medieval Christian degradation of women,[7] and this association with relative freedom for women is often borne out in other Celtic medievalist representations.

An example of medievalism in games is *The Witcher 3: Wild Hunt* (2015), which combines several distinct medievalisms to characterize each of the areas of the gameworld, as I have noted elsewhere.[8] I will focus on two contrasting examples here. One of the clearest is in the region called Skellige, a Hebridean-type archipelago, which oozes Celtic/Northern medievalism. This is manifest in the presence of Viking longboats, longship burials and widow sacrifice,[9] as well as of tartans, clans and Irish accents.

Celtic/Northern medievalism is utterly vital to the narrative in Skellige; it helps us immediately to situate ourselves within a believable world, in which we expect and can understand the social interactions we observe. The associations with Celtic medievalism, paganism and freedom for women strongly apply to Skellige too. Unlike the rest of the game world, the dominant religion in the region is headed by the female priestesses of Freya; there are several female warriors in evidence and a woman may become the leader of the region, depending on player choices.

Sound and music are integral to the medievalism. The score borrows heavily from Celtic folk, using bagpipes and flutes and, in a nod to the association of Celtic medivalism with freedom for women, female voice. The cue 'The Fields of Ard Skellig', which acts as non-diegetic backing throughout open-world exploration of Skellige, can stand as exemplary. We have a Hardanger fiddle, a Norwegian folk instrument that is a clear sign of Northern medievalism in popular culture.[10] The Hardanger fiddle is used predominantly to support the vocals, which borrow the text from a Scots-Gaelic poem called 'Fear a' Bhàta'. Despite its eighteenth-century origins, it has clear Northern medievalist narrative potential here. Unintelligible or obscure text, be that Latin, faux-Latin, open vowel sounds, minority languages or even invented languages, has a long history in

---

[7] Jane Tolmie, 'Medievalism and the Fantasy Heroine', *Journal of Gender Studies* 15, no. 2 (2006): 145–58 at 152.

[8] James Cook, 'Sonic Medievalism, World Building, and Cultural Identity in Fantasy Video Games', *Studies in Medievalism XXIX*, ed. Karl Fugelso (Cambridge, UK: D. S. Brewer, 2020), 217–238.

[9] As noted in Cook, 'Sonic Medievalism', Celtic medievalism is a subset of Northern medievalism and it therefore often borrows from Viking imagery as much as it does from Celtic.

[10] This instrument is perhaps best recognized as the instrument that often plays the 'Rohirrim' leitmotif in *The Lord of the Rings* as well as other games, such as the similarly Northern medievalist *Age of Conan: Hyborian Adventures* (2008).

medievalist representation,[11] and the use of Gaelic in this song exploits this adroitly, while adding to the generally Celtic aesthetic. The vocal delivery is free, expressive and heavily ornamented, and supported by a harmonically static and modal arrangement.

These Celtic/Northern medievalist aspects contrast with the urban areas of the game, Oxenfurt and Novigrad. This contrast is redolent of an animating tension at the heart of many fantasy narratives: modernity vs premodernity, rationalism vs irrationality, pre-industrial vs industrial. Here, it helps differentiate the areas of the game. The cities of Oxenfurt and Novigrad are architecturally Early Modern. The famous university of Oxenfurt, with a coat of arms drawing on that of the University of Cambridge, and a name redolent of Oxford, adds an association with rationality that is often evoked in the dialogue of the non-player characters, or NPCs (who ask 'what will you do when all the monsters are dead', for instance). The sound world too plays on this contrast. The music is more frequently diegetic, the result of live performances by in-game Renaissance dance bands, rather than the non-diegetic sound of the environment as heard in Skellige. It is also more metrical, and focuses on hammered and plucked strings, as well as percussion.

Sonic representations of religion in the cities and Skellige are markedly different too. Unlike Skellige, Oxenfurt and Novigrad follow the Church of the Eternal Fire, which has clear parallels with aspects of medieval Christian history (with witch burnings etc.). Musically, its representation follows one of the clearest markers of sacred medievalism in introducing chanting male voices (which are unique at this point of the game) as the player approaches the Great Temple of the Eternal Fire.

In all, while the urban areas of the game still draw on popular medievalism, it is clearly one of a contrasting narrative power, enabling the game regions to feel linked but still distinct. There are a variety of medieval modes in play here, which provide shifting, varied images and all of which draw on associations built up in film and other media.

Technology and Tropes

One of the best examples of technology impacting on historical game music is manifest in the use of baroque counterpoint. As has been discussed

---

[11] Adam Whittaker, 'Musical Divisions of the Sacred and Secular in "The Hunchback of Notre Dame"', in *Recomposing the Past: Representations of Early Music on Stage and Screen*, ed. James Cook, Alex Kolassa and Adam Whittaker (Abingdon: Routledge, 2018), 89–106.

elsewhere in this volume, the capabilities of games within the chiptune era created some interesting compositional challenges. Due to limitations in memory and available hardware,[12] composers devised novel approaches to composing both for a limited number of voices, and for non-equal temperament. As Kenneth B. McAlpine has noted, one approach was to borrow the baroque technique of implied pedal, rapidly alternating semiquavers between a moving note and repeated note. Some games, such as *Fahrenheit 3000* (1984), would borrow pre-existent examples of this wholesale – in this case the opening to Bach's famous Toccata and Fugue in D minor – while others, such as Ben Daglish's *Krakout* (1987) composed new works making use of the same techniques to allow implied polyphony on a one-voice beeper.[13]

There are obvious practical and aesthetic advantages to baroque allusion in slightly later games too. As William Gibbons has noted,[14] a console such as the NES was essentially capable of three voices, two upper parts (the square-wave channel) and one lower part (the triangle-wave channel).[15] This complicates attempts at explicitly Romantic or jazz harmony, which must be implied contrapuntally, rather than stated in explicit polyphony. It does lend itself to contrapuntal styles such as the baroque trio sonata or simple keyboard works, however. The 'closed-off harmonic and melodic patterns' and the 'repeats inherent in [the] binary structures' of these works are also very well suited to the demands of loop-based game scores which need to repeat relatively short sections of music several times.[16] Nonetheless, as Gibbons has shown, what may have once been simple technological expedience instead developed into a trend of dramatic and narrative power.

As Gibbons has noted, medieval castles and labyrinths were common in game design during the 1980s and 1990s, offering both a recognizable location and aesthetic common to many role-playing games of the time, and a logical game mechanic allowing for dungeons and towers to be conquered one at a time. Frequently, the musical backing for castles and

---

[12] Kenneth B. McAlpine, *Bits and Pieces: A History of Chiptunes* (New York: Oxford University Press, 2019), 1–102.

[13] Ibid., 45–8.

[14] William Gibbons, 'Little Harmonic Labyrinths: Baroque Musical Style on the Nintendo Entertainment System', in *Recomposing the Past: Representations of Early Music on Stage and Screen*, ed. James Cook, Alex Kolassa and Adam Whittaker (Abingdon: Routledge, 2018), 139–51.

[15] The noise channel and DCPM are also important for compositional effects, though they cannot contribute to the harmony.

[16] Ibid., 141.

labyrinths either exploited pre-existent baroque music or period pastiche. The associations between baroque music and grandeur may have been partly responsible for this choice of music; baroque architecture and baroque music are often linked in scholarship and in the popular imagination. Magnificent castles, such as Tantagel in *Dragon Warrior/Dragon Quest* (1986) for instance, often struggle to convey a sense of opulence within the limitations of their graphics. This is particularly the case for top-down views, which tend to elide tapestries, paintings, rugs, or furniture. The baroque aesthetic of the music here seeks to fill in the visual lacunae.

The links go deeper, however, drawing on popular medievalism. Gibbons has situated this use of baroque to underscore fantasy as part of a 'complex intertextual – indeed intermedial – web of associations that connects video games with progressive rock and heavy metal, fantasy literature and films, and table-top role-playing games';[17] all of these draw on medievalism. Many early fantasy games began as an attempt to translate the gameplay and aesthetics of *Dungeons and Dragons* (*D&D*) into video game form. They also frequently drew on the imagery of 1980s 'sword-and-sorcery' fantasy, such as the *Conan* series – often going so far as to model box art on analogous film imagery – and wove a healthy dose of Tolkien throughout all of this. These disparate strands are tied together through music. A number of progressive rock and heavy metal bands from the 1960s to the 1980s had very similar influences, drawing on Tolkien, *D&D* and the fantasy imagery of sword-and-sorcery films. They also drew heavily on baroque music alongside these influences, from allusions to Bach's Air on a G String in Procol Harum's 'A Whiter Shade of Pale' (1967), to following baroque-style ornamentation and harmonic patterns, as Robert Walser has argued.[18] That all these elements therefore combine in the fantasy medievalism of the NES-era console is unsurprising.

Tropes from Game Back into Film

So far, I have treated video games as a medium which translates influences from other media and filters them through certain technological constraints. But this does disservice to the important influences that the sound of video games seems to have had on other media, and particularly their representations or creative uses of the past. I wish to point to two

---

17 Ibid., 146–50.
18 Robert Walser, *Running with the Devil: Power, Gender, and Madness in Heavy Metal* (Middletown, CT: Wesleyan University Press, 1993), 57–107.

specific examples. The first of these is an indirect product of the baroque contrapuntal nature of many early fantasy game soundtracks, as discussed above, which I hold at least partly responsible for the tendency, in recent years, to conflate all pre-classical music in popular historical film and television. In effect, baroque music comes to stand for the medieval and Renaissance. Though baroque may have mingled with medievalist fantasy in prog rock and metal, it was generally not something usually seen in filmic depictions of the medieval. More recent examples abound, however: the diegetic use of *Zadok the Priest* on the march to Rodrigo Borgia's coronation as Pope Alexander Sextus in 1492 in *The Borgias* (2011), some 193 years before the birth of its composer,[19] or the non-diegetic use of Bach's St Matthew Passion (1727) heard as the ceiling of a twelfth-century cathedral collapses in *The Pillars of the Earth* (2010), for instance. The advantages of using pre-existent baroque music over pre-existent medieval or Renaissance music is obvious. This music has a greater currency in popular culture; people are more likely to recognize it. This has obvious advantages for the idea of building 'affiliating' identifications,[20] which relies on the listener making intertextual connections. For the example of *The Borgias*, hearing *Zadok the Priest* has obvious connotations of a coronation – more chronologically appropriate music almost certainly would not have this same symbolic meaning to the vast majority of listeners. Baroque music is often more familiar than medieval and Renaissance music, which is not tonal, and is played on a variety of unusual instruments. Much very early music is so far outside of most listeners' experience as to sound simply 'other', rather than necessarily early. Baroque music, however, is familiar to many – but still recognizably 'early'. Nonetheless, despite the clear advantages for directors/producers/designers in using baroque music as part of a medieval or Renaissance sound world, it nonetheless does depend on a popular conception of history that collapses these time periods together, and this seems to be a direct consequence of the tendency for baroque music to be used in medievalist-themed games over the last thirty to forty years.[21]

---

[19] James Cook, 'Representing Renaissance Rome: Beyond Anachronism in Showtime's *The Borgias* (2011)', in *Recomposing the Past: Representations of Early Music on Stage and Screen*, ed. James Cook, Alex Kolassa and Adam Whittaker (Abingdon: Routledge, 2018), 17–31.

[20] Anahid Kassabian, *Hearing Film: Tracking Identifications in Contemporary Hollywood Film Music* (London: Routledge, 2001), 3.

[21] It must be noted that such a use is not unique to film music post-video-game: see for instance Walton's score for the 1944 film version of *Henry V* which, alongside a recomposition of the famous *Agincourt Carol*, certainly did make use of harpsichord throughout – a baroque instrument and one not in existence during the time of Henry V. Nonetheless, I would argue

The second example is seemingly even more unique to a post-video-game world and, while not relating strictly to music, is still very much a part of the overall phenomenon of sonic medievalism. This particular trope is one that has remarkable currency across all visual fantasy media, namely the portrayal of dwarfs as Scottish. I have previously argued that the dialect and accent of voice actors is an extremely important aspect of sonic medievalism,[22] and that the tendency to represent the medieval period in particular with characteristically 'Northern' accents (Scotland, the North of England, Scandinavia) is related to the common trope of Northern medievalism. A great many films, televisions, books and video games draw on associated characteristics of this. Within this complex and shifting semantic area, the Scottishness of dwarfs seems remarkably fixed. Many will point to *The Lord of the Rings* (2001–2003) film franchise as the moment that the national identity of dwarfs was set in stone, but there is a far earlier game example: *Warcraft II: Tides of Darkness* (1995). Predating *LOTR* by six years, *Warcraft II* is clear that dwarfs are Scottish, and they remain so for subsequent iterations in the same game world. The game series Baldur's Gate (1998–2016) continues this very same trend and it seems clear that video game dwarfs were recognizably Scottish long before the same trend was concretized in film. Some may argue that the subsequent choice of accent for *LOTR* is incidental and related to the natural accent of the character Gimli, who most prominently displays the accent at the start of the series. However, John Rhys-Davies, who plays Gimli, is Welsh, and the accent is therefore clearly a choice, supressing both the actor's natural accent and the Received Pronunciation English accent that he often adopts for his acting work. While it is true that the same aspects of sonic medievalism may have independently influenced both the ludic and filmic approaches to voice acting, it seems more plausible that some influence was taken from game into film.

In all, while we can point to trends moving from historical TV and film into games, filtered through different technological concerns, it seems clear that some aspects have moved the other way too. The association of fantasy dwarfs and the Scottish accent seems good evidence of this, as does the currency of the baroque as a marker of the medieval which seems, in part, to have come about specifically through the technical limitations of certain games.

that the extreme currency of baroque-as-medieval/Renaissance music in video games has dramatically increased the prominence of this historical trope in television and film representations of pre-baroque music.

[22] Cook, 'Sonic Medievalism.'

Representations of 'Real' History in Games

So far, I have discussed the creative use of history in fantasy games, but what of the representation of 'real' history in video games? To an extent, the distinction is arbitrary. At the start of this chapter, I argued that history is something that is creative, not reproductive, that there is an element of at least fiction, if not fantasy, in every historical work. Nonetheless, for all the somewhat porous boundaries, some games are, to greater or lesser extents, rooted in real history. An excellent example is the Civilization series (1991–present). Rather than presenting an historical story, this series instead allows the player to take control of a nation and to guide its historical development. History is an important part of the game nonetheless, with real historical figures, technological developments and buildings. Real historical music also plays an important role.

Karen Cook has focused attention on the *Civilization IV* soundtrack.[23] She notes that music here acts 'to signify chronological motion and technological progress' and that, while supporting an underlying American hegemonic ideology, it nonetheless allows the player to interact with this within a postmodern framework. Music forms only part of the soundtrack, and is always non-diegetic, cycling through a number of pre-composed pieces from the Western art music tradition, with the choice of piece depending on the level of advancement that the player has achieved. Before advancement to the Classical era (i.e. the era of Classical civilization, rather than 'classical music'), there is no music in the soundtrack (though other sound effects are present), seemingly identifying the Classical period as being the first that is 'technologically capable of, and culturally interested in, music making itself'.[24] Once the Classical era is entered, the score begins to contain music but, unlike all other eras of the game, it includes no pre-existent music, presumably due to the scarcity of surviving music from the Classical world, and its unfamiliarity to the majority of listeners. Instead, new music is composed which draws from 'stereotypical sound-images of pan-African, Native America, or Aboriginal music'.[25] This is a far cry from descriptions of music from antiquity, and from the few surviving notated examples of it, but it draws on a pervasive sense of exoticism whereby music of the distant past is seen to be discernible in music of cultures

---

[23] Karen M. Cook, 'Music, History, and Progress in Sid Meier's Civilization IV', in *Music in Video Games: Studying Play*, ed. K. J. Donnelly, William Gibbons and Neil Lerner (New York: Routledge, 2014), 166–82.

[24] Ibid., 170.

[25] Ibid., 173.

geographically distant from Western civilization. This reinforces a major criticism of the game series, that Western civilization is seen as the natural culmination of progress.

The next game period – the Middle Ages – is the first to use pre-existent music, though almost none is medieval. The only medieval music is monophonic chant, which remains a part of the modern liturgy in many parts of the world, while the polyphonic music is entirely Renaissance, including works by Ockeghem and Sheppard. None of these Renaissance choices are included in the Renaissance era of the game, which instead uses music by Bach, Beethoven and Mozart. Again, we seem to have a sense of musical chronology collapsing in upon itself. The pre-medieval world is represented purely by newly composed music indebted to an exoticist colonialist historiography, the medieval by the sounds of Renaissance polyphony (presumably since medieval polyphony would have sounded too foreign and exotic) and music from later than this period is represented by a collection of predominantly Classical and Romantic composers, with a bit of baroque in the Renaissance. In all, this game showcases the fascinating degree to which music can historicize in the popular imagination in a manner not always indebted to temporal reality.

'Real' History and 'Real' Music History

For the remainder of this essay I wish to focus on an extraordinary musical moment that occurs in the *Gods and Kings* expansion of *Civilization V* (2012). As the player transitions from the set-up screen to the voice-over and loading screen at the start of the 'Into the Renaissance' scenario, the player is treated to a recomposition, by Geoff Knorr, of Guillaume de Machaut's Messe de Nostre Dame, here titled 'The medieval world'.

Machaut, a fourteenth-century French composer, is particularly revered for his polyphonic works. These pieces from the late Middle Ages represent important landmarks in European music history. His Messe de Nostre Dame is perhaps his most famous work, written in the early 1360s.[26]

To the best of my knowledge, this is a unique instance of a piece of pre-existent medieval polyphony in a video game. The manner of its presentation is remarkably subtle and effective, altering the original medieval musical text to make it sound *more medieval* (to a popular audience). Situating this track at the opening of the 'Into the Renaissance' scenario

---

[26] Daniel Leech-Wilkinson, 'Le Voir Dit and La Messe de Nostre Dame: Aspects of Genre and Style in Late Works of Machaut', *Plainsong and Medieval Music* 2, no. 1 (1993): 43–73 at 44.

is a remarkable nod to certain historiographical narratives: the Mass cycle was seen by Bukofzer as paradigmatic of the Renaissance, the perfect musical expression of its time.[27] Many see Machaut's Mass, the very earliest surviving attempt by a composer to organize a full cycle of each movement of the Mass Ordinary, as the first steps on the path to the Renaissance Mass cycle. Situating Machaut's Mass at the opening of this scenario, as representative of 'the medieval world' and its transition 'into the Renaissance' is therefore a deeply symbolic gesture.

The recomposition opens not with the start of Machaut's Mass, but with a new choral opening (see Example 19.1, bb. 1–15). It deploys a male choir, singing Latin text – an important signal of sacred space in medievalist renderings.[28] This choir begins with an opening rising minor third gesture, but with the countertenor and tenor, and baritone and bass parts respectively paired at the fifth (bb. 1–2). This, combined with the triple metre, the clear Dorian modality and the supporting open-fifth drones, immediately situates us within a medievalist sound world. The paired open-fifth movement continues for much of the opening phrase, mirroring the early descriptions of improvised polyphonic decoration of chant from the *Musica enchiriadis,* in which parallel doubling of the melody forms the basis of the polyphony. To this is added a sprinkling of 4–3 suspensions (for example in b. 3) which add some harmonic colour, without dispelling the sense of medievalism. Bar 8 reaches a particularly striking moment in which accidentals are introduced for the first time and an extraordinary unprepared fourth leaps out of the texture. As with the opening, the voices are paired, but this time at a perfect fourth. This rejection of common-practice harmony is striking and gives an antiquated feeling to the harmony, even if it is also rather unlike Machaut's own harmonic practice. The introduction of additional chromaticism is clearly a nod to the *musica ficta* of the medieval period too.[29]

Despite the many changes, this opening is based on that of Machaut's Mass (Example 19.2), which also opens with paired open-fifth Ds and As (bb. 1–2), though quickly departs from this parallelism. The striking moment at bar 8 of 'The medieval world' may be seen as an adaptation of bar 5 of Machaut's Mass, where the first accidental is used – here too giving

---

[27] Manfred Bukofzer, *Studies in Medieval and Renaissance Music* (London: J. M. Dent & Sons Ltd., 1951), 217–19.

[28] Whittaker, 'Musical Divisions of the Sacred and Secular.'

[29] The application of *musica ficta* relates to the addition of sharps and flats outside of the usual range of notes available to the composer in order to avoid tritones and false relations, and to ensure that cadences were correctly prepared through semitone movement.

Example 19.1 'Into the Renaissance' (excerpt), *Civilization V: Gods and Kings*, showing the adaptation of Machaut's Messe de Nostre Dame

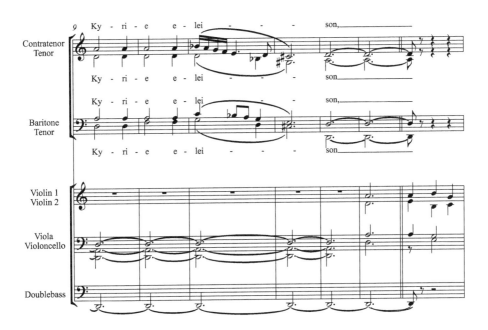

an F♯ against a B. In Machaut's Mass, the contrapuntal context is clear – the B and F♯ are inverted, giving a perfect fifth, and the descending D to C figure in the bass (not found in the recomposition) clearly gives the

Example 19.1 (cont.)

Example 19.2 Machaut, Messe de Nostre Dame

context of a traditional cadence of this period. Knorr seemingly found this moment of Machaut's Mass striking and wished to give it even greater prominence in his recomposition. In doing so, he has created something which sounds to most ears more authentically medieval than the medieval original. The final cadence of this section, with its strident G♯ and C♯ (Example 19.1, b. 12), is taken directly from the cadence at the end of the first Kyrie of Machaut's Mass. It requires no adaptation here, as perhaps the most recognizable moment of the entire piece, which is again an aural marker of absolute alterity from the common-practice period – parallel octaves, fifths and chromaticism, which were all theoretically justifiable in Machaut's day but sound alien to many modern ears. The opening of this movement therefore is an interesting moment of recomposition. It takes the most medieval-sounding aspects of the piece whole, but reinforces them with many tropes of popular medievalism missing from its original.

After this opening (from b. 15), the orchestration catapults us into the world of the post-Romantic film score, to match the rest of the soundtrack. The strings play an exact transcription of the opening of Machaut's Mass (compare Example 19.1, bb. 15–27 and Example 19.2), and this is gradually augmented by brass and wind. This moment is, to my mind, unique in game music, in that real medieval polyphony is used – presented as an exact transcription that has merely been re-orchestrated. Ironically, it is perhaps the least medieval-sounding moment in the entire piece. The transcription of the Mass dissolves shortly before the obviously medieval cadence, allowing a contrasting entry to take over which builds in even more contrasting medievalist approaches, derived from quintessential folk-style dance-type pieces. We have percussion added for the first time, most notably including the tambourine, which draws specific connotations with on-screen representations of medieval peasant dancing. Again, for the popular imagination, this rendition is arguably more medieval sounding than the direct transcription of the real medieval music.

Conclusions

Attitudes to music history found in games are part of a mutually supportive nexus of ideas regarding the popular understanding of the sounds of the past shared between a number of different media, and indeed outside of these too. As we have seen, games like *The Witcher 3* borrow their medievalism directly from film and television, allowing enormous amounts of complicated exposition to be afforded simply through audiovisual associations to intermedial shorthands. Other forms of musical expression, though connected to associations from outside of the genre, were filtered through the technological constraints of certain game systems leading, for instance, to the ubiquity of real and pastiche baroque music within fantasy games of the 1980s and 1990s. That some of these trends from games, some initially purely practical and some seemingly creative licence, later returned to influence film and television also seems clear. One thing that differentiates historical games from other audiovisual media seems to be the extent to which 'real' pre-baroque music is avoided. Knorr's recomposition of the Messe de Nostre Dame is seemingly an isolated example of pre-baroque polyphony, and even this is recomposed to make it more medievalist.

20 | Open Worlds: Globalization, Localization and Video Game Music

WILLIAM GIBBONS[*]

Video games are an international phenomenon. That statement is true both in the colloquial sense – games are a tremendously popular media form enjoyed by more than a billion players around the globe – but also in the sense that they are profoundly *international*. Games on my phone, computer or shelf right now were created in countries including: Canada (*Assassin's Creed*), Germany (*Risen*), Japan (*Final Fantasy XV*), Poland (*The Witcher 3*), South Africa (*Desktop Dungeons*), South Korea (*Magna Carta*), the United Kingdom (*The Room*), the United States (*Fallout*) and Uruguay (*Kingdom Rush*) – amongst others. Despite this diversity, however, relatively few video games are overtly identified as products of any particular geographic region. Instead, developers often deliberately eliminate or minimize region-specific identifiers through a process called localization, in which aspects of a game are adapted to fit the perceived cultural norms and preferences of a target market.[1] This process most obviously includes translation of all game text into different languages, which can be in itself a fraught process. Yet localization also involves a wide range of minor, or possibly major, alterations to game content.[2] The

---

[*] I am very grateful to Dana Plank as well as to this volume's editors, Tim Summers and Melanie Fritsch, for their helpful comments and suggestions in preparing this chapter.

[1] Localization is a multifaceted process, but following Keiran J. Dunne, I adopt a general definition as: 'The process by which digital content and products developed in one locale (defined in terms of geographical area, language and culture) are adapted for sale and use in another locale. Localization involves: (a) translation of textual content into the language and textual conventions of the target locale; and (b) adaptation of non-textual content (from colors, icons and bitmaps, to packaging, form factors, etc.) as well as input, output and delivery mechanisms to take into account the cultural, technical and regulatory requirements of that locale.' Keiran J. Dunne, 'A Copernican Revolution: Focusing on the Big Picture of Localization', in *Perspectives on Localization*, ed. Kieran J. Dunne (Philadelphia: John Benjamins, 2006), 1–11 at 4. For in-depth perspectives on the history and general principles of localization, see Minako O'Hagan and Carmen Mangiron, *Game Localization: Translation for the Global Digital Entertainment Industry* (Philadelphia: John Benjamins, 2013); and Miguel Ángel Bernal-Merino, 'The Localisation of Video Games' (PhD Dissertation, Imperial College London, 2013).

[2] The processes of translation and localization are creative and complicated enough that some scholars and practitioners prefer the term 'transcreation' rather than 'translation', and use 'culturization' to refer to the adaptation of games to suit local cultural practices and beliefs. For an overview of 'culturization', see for example O'Hagan and Mangiron, *Game Localization*, ch. 5, 201–41.

economic allure of localization is immense, and well documented. As Rebecca Carlson and Jonathan Corliss have noted, the fundamental concept is that 'products must appear as if they were manufactured domestically, suggesting that consumers only want goods that feel familiar and "local"'.[3] Moreover, in some cases developers must localize games to accommodate legal restrictions, as in the case of Germany, where certain types of imagery and violence are restricted in games.

The localization process can also have a profound effect on video game music and how players perceive it.[4] At its best, localizing music can help a diverse range of players connect with games in a personally meaningful way; at its worst, it obscures the artistic achievements of composers and sound designers across the globe, and homogenizes musical culture in a potentially detrimental way. Localization is, at its core, an erasure of cultural difference – an erasure that can change gameplay, as well as audiovisual components.[5] Whether actively or passively, music always factors into that process of erasure. A given musical cue may be altered or swapped out entirely for each target market, composers might opt to write in a less regionally identifiable style, or players may simply understand the music in a different way because the context has changed.

My goals in this chapter are to begin building a framework for understanding how musical localization creates unique challenges and opportunities for the study of game music—and more generally to consider how and why scholars might approach game music as a product of place. To that end, I suggest ways in which we can adapt three broad categories of localization to the study of video game music:[6]

---

[3] Rebecca Carlson and Jonathan Corliss, 'Imagined Commodities: Video Game Localization and Mythologies of Cultural Difference', *Games and Culture* 6 (2011): 61–82 at 67.

[4] Previous studies of game music have not investigated the impact of localization in detail, although some have acknowledged its existence. Karen Collins's assessment is fairly typical: 'Localization is necessary to create a realistic game environment . . . and the audio must be as realistic and engaging as the original. . . . Different music may need to be selected for different target markets'. Karen Collins, *Game Sound: An Introduction to the History, Theory and Practice of Video Game Music and Sound Design* (Cambridge, MA: MIT Press, 2008), 99.

[5] Carlson and Corliss, for example, note that 'Images, animations, and overall design aesthetics, game mechanics and interface, narrative, and even button mapping might be modified to accommodate the perceived differences between regional markets.' Carlson and Corliss, 'Imagined Commodities', 64. It is also worth noting that, while I focus on music here, localization often results in other significant audio changes, such as the necessity to record large amounts of voiced dialogue in a wide range of languages.

[6] Although the terminology related to game localization is highly fluid, my three categories here are based on those briefly outlined in Alexander Thayer and Beth E. Kolko, 'Localization of Digital Games: The Process of Blending for the Global Games Market', *Technical Communication* 51 (2004): 477–88.

1. **Basic localization**. Only essential information is localized for target markets (e.g., subtitles), with few or no musical changes. This choice can result from budget constraints, but can also occur when developers intend for particular products to *emphasize* (rather than downplay) cultural origins. As a result, music may play into specific cultural tropes or regional styles.

2. **Complex localization**. Culture-specific musical markers are removed or altered, typically with the goal of making a game seem internationalized, or perhaps universal. Musically, this could involve minor changes to music to suit target demographics, or composers adopting 'stateless' compositional styles.

3. **Blending**. The music is significantly or completely altered for international release, typically to strip the game of markers of cultural identification and replace those markers with those of the target demographic's culture. This can include composing, rewriting, removing and/or replacing a significant amount of in-game audio.[7]

In the sections that follow, I offer a brief case study of each type, using long-running games series to illustrate sustained models for musical localization. Although I intend for this framework to be widely applicable, for the sake of continuity, I will focus on one very common localization path: the adaptation of Japanese games for the North American market.[8]

Japanese games make an ideal case study for this kind of cultural transfer, as they have long occupied a central position in the North American market both economically and aesthetically. Yet as Mia Consalvo notes in her thoughtful book, *Atari to Zelda: Japan's Videogames in Global Contexts*: 'in the early days of arcades and Nintendo, many Western players did not recognize that Japanese games were coming from Japan. They were simply new and interesting games to

---

[7] For a brief overview of blending and the impact of localization on game audio in general, see Karen Collins, *Game Sound*, 97–9. O'Hagan and Mangiron note that whether voice-over acting is rerecorded is the major distinction between whether an international release is considered a 'full localization' or 'partial localization'. O'Hagan and Mangiron, *Game Localization*, 17.

[8] O'Hagan and Mangiron, for example, note the 'well-recognized trade imbalance' that results in a tremendous number of Japanese games being successfully exported to the rest of the world, with a relatively small number of games making the opposite journey. O'Hagan and Mangiron, *Game Localization*, 18. For clarity, I should also note that in this chapter I am concerned with 'official' processes of game localization – those undertaken by the developers and publishers themselves – as opposed to 'unofficial' fan localizations.

play.'[9] As Consalvo demonstrates, Japanese developers have for decades vacillated on the extent to which the 'Japaneseness' of their products should be erased or emphasized, and the musical efforts in both directions make for intriguing case studies. Finally, it is worth noting that localization is an economic imperative for most Japanese developers, as their share of the global market declined markedly after 2000, such that 'Japanese companies have become more aggressive and experimental in their [localization] strategies.'[10] I argue that music plays a significant role in those strategies, variously obscuring and reinforcing games' cultural context.

Basic Localization: The Katamari Series

Localization is usually about maximizing accessibility (and thus sales) by making games feel 'local' to each target region. On occasion, however, developers (often their marketing teams) may choose instead to actively reinforce a game's origins – emphasizing, rather than minimizing, its 'Otherness'. As Carlson and Corliss point out, building on the work of Koichi Iwabuchi:

> some products develop 'cultural odor' – the association of (stereotypical) images or ideas of a culture with a product when it is consumed. . . . When the international appeal of a video game, a video game franchise, or even the success of a particular developer, is linked with perceptions of the product's foreignness, as is increasingly often the case, localization can no longer be oversimplified as a purely domesticating endeavor.[11]

One relatively straightforward example might be the Yakuza series of action-adventure games (2005–2018), which emphasize their Japanese settings and plots through a relative lack of localization (including, with one exception, a lack of English voice acting). In the case of Yakuza, limiting localization to the bare necessities reinforces the game's setting, helping players immerse themselves in the contemporary Japanese criminal underworld – a setting that can, as in my case, feel extremely foreign to

---

[9] Mia Consalvo, *Atari to Zelda: Japan's Videogames in Global Contexts* (Cambridge, MA: MIT Press, 2016), 4.

[10] Consalvo, *Atari to Zelda*, 122.

[11] Carlson and Corliss, 'Imagined Commodities', 73. See also the work of Koichi Iwabuchi, in particular *Recentering Globalization: Popular Culture and Japanese Transnationalism* (Durham, NC: Duke University Press, 2002).

the player. The music – often diegetic – likewise reinforces the geographical and chronological setting.

Music has, of course, long been a part of establishing setting in video games in precisely this way, just as it has in film and other multimedia forms.[12] In some cases, however, the music becomes less about identifying the diegetic setting and more about identifying the game itself as being an exotic product. Consider, for example, Nintendo's marketing of *Tetris* as an explicitly 'Russian' product in the 1980s – an effort that involved visual elements, marketing ('From Russia With Fun!'), and the inclusion of Russian music on the soundtracks of the Nintendo Entertainment System and Game Boy versions.[13] There is nothing fundamentally Russian about *Tetris*, aside from its creator, Alexey Pajitnov – yet the game was specifically designed and marketed that way.

The same trend is evident on a larger scale in the developer Namco's Katamari series, which began with the PlayStation 2 title *Katamari Damacy* (2004). The game's simplicity of play, unique aesthetics and broad appeal across demographic lines garnered a significant fan base and widespread critical approval, and the eight years after *Katamari Damacy* saw the near-annual release of a new Katamari game (see Table 20.1).[14] The series has recently come full circle: after a lull in the mid-2010s, Namco released *Katamari Damacy Reroll*, a remake of the original 2004 *Katamari Damacy* for PC and the Nintendo Switch console.

The details of the Katamari games vary somewhat, but in nearly all cases the player takes on the role of the Prince of All Cosmos, who must create a series of ever-larger clumps (*katamaris*) by rolling up whatever happens to be around, starting with tiny objects and ending with entire countries, or even planets. Although there is nothing specifically Japanese about this narrative,

---

[12] Kiri Miller, for example, has pointed to the use of popular music in the Grand Theft Auto series as a key part of establishing the setting of each game, and Dana Plank has identified the exoticized musical representation of ancient Egypt in an NES game. Kiri Miller, *Playing Along: Digital Games, YouTube, and Virtual Performance* (New York: Oxford University Press, 2012); Dana Plank, 'The Penultimate Fantasy: Nobuo Uematsu's score for *Cleopatra no Ma Takara*', in *Music in the Role-Playing Game: Heroes & Harmonies*, ed. William Gibbons and Steven Reale (New York: Routledge, 2019), 76–96.

[13] On the branding of *Tetris* as a Russian product, see Dana Plank-Blasko, '"From Russia with Fun!" *Tetris*, Korobeiniki and the Ludic Soviet', *The Soundtrack* 8 (2015): 7–24; and William Gibbons, *Unlimited Replays: Video Games and Classical Music* (New York: Oxford University Press, 2018), 23–6.

[14] In a testament to the game's beloved status, in 2012, *Katamari Damacy* was part of a group of games added to the permanent collection of the New York Museum of Modern Art. See the item description at Museum of Modern Art, www.moma.org/collection/works/164919, accessed 15 October 2020.

Table 20.1 Main Katamari series releases, 2004–2018

Title (North American)	Release Date (Japan/North America)
Katamari Damacy	2004
We Love Katamari	2005
Me & My Katamari	2005/2006
Beautiful Katamari	2007
I Love Katamari	2008
Katamari Forever	2009
Katamari Amore	2011
Touch My Katamari	2011/2012
Katamari Damacy Reroll (remake of *Katamari Damacy*)	2018

Steven Jones and Mia Consalvo have both suggested that 'the central activity of the game – collecting things – is a commentary on the somewhat obsessive collecting activities of *otaku*[15] in Japan (and likely elsewhere), thus drawing from Japanese culture again for a central gameplay mechanic'.[16] Indeed, the first level of *Katamari Damacy* begins in a small Japanese home before progressing to a larger neighbourhood. Everything else about the game, from its aesthetic to its marketing to its music, likewise exudes Japaneseness. Even the title resists translation. A transliteration of *katamari* ('clump') *tamashii* ('soul'), the two *kanji* characters of the title are displayed prominently even on the North American box art, which also depicts a rainbow above a giant *katamari*, a large city (presumably Tokyo), and Mount Fuji. And although the game's text-only dialogue is translated into English, the unusual speech patterns of the King character seem reminiscent of the quirky Japanese-to-English translations of 1980s titles. In short, the game was presented to North American audiences as a product intentionally redolent with the 'fragrance' of Japaneseness, to use the sociologist Koichi Iwabuchi's preferred term.

The soundtracks of the Katamari games are equally indicative of their Japanese origins. As Steven Reale has argued persuasively in a study of

---

[15] An otaku is a person who is obsessed with a specific aspect of popular culture (such as manga, anime, computer games). The term can be used as an equivalent to geek or nerd, but over its history it has also caught a negative connotation due to the case of the 'Otaku Murderer' Tsutomu Miyazaki, who murdered young girls in 1988 and 1989 and was obsessed with anime and horror videos.

[16] Consalvo, *From Atari to Zelda*, 29. See also Steven E. Jones, *The Meaning of Video Games: Gaming and Textual Strategies* (New York: Routledge, 2008), ch. 2, 47–68.

Katamari Damacy's music, the Japanese culture of naïve cuteness, or *kawaii*, is the game's prevailing visual and sonic aesthetic.[17] In a trend continued by the later Katamari games, *Katamari Damacy*'s soundtrack – identical, to the best of my knowledge, in the Japanese and North American releases – is an eclectic compilation of popular songs contributed by various Japanese artists, loosely united by the frequent incorporation of the series' main theme.[18] The musical style varies wildly from stage to stage, touching on everything from big band jazz to J-pop to electronica. Uncommonly, even in the North American releases the (surreal) lyrics to these levels remain in Japanese – or in a combination of Japanese and English that could feel equally foreign to speakers of both languages.

The choice to export the Katamari games with only basic localization – and with no musical alterations to fit the target demographic – has a few possible interpretations. On one level, it might reflect budgetary concerns, or, after *Katamari Damacy*'s unexpected North American success, a desire for later games to adhere as closely as possible to its aggressively quirky aesthetic. Alternatively, we can understand the games as part of the 'Cool Japan' soft-power strategy of the 2000s.[19] As Christine Yano notes, since the early 2000s, Japanese government and industry have chosen 'to capitalize on cuteness as a new, youth-oriented way to brand Japan – relinquishing images of samurai warriors and dark-suited bureaucrats for a newer, frankly commercial, overtly playful aesthetic'.[20] The Katamari games, and their music, certainly fit that

---

[17] Steven Reale, 'Chaos in the Cosmos: The Play of Contradictions in the Music of *Katamari Damacy*', *ACT: Zeitschrift für Musik & Performance* 2 (2011): 2.

[18] The Katamari series' lead sound designer, Yuu Miyake, has indicated that although the music went in some unexpected directions in later games, they originally intended for an increasing globalization of the music: in his words, 'I originally had plans for up to two *Katamari* sequels. The first game would feature all Japanese artists, the second game would feature artists from around the world (unfortunately we didn't have enough experience in English negotiations for this to happen), and the third game's soundtrack would feature remixes from producers around the world.' Jayson Napolitano, 'Katamari Music Maestro: Yu Miyake Interview', *Original Sound Version* (December 15, 2009), accessed 10 April 2020, www.originalsoundversion.com/katamari-music-maestro-yu-miyake-interview/.

[19] On the complexities and contractions of 'Cool Japan', see for example Koichi Iwabuchi, 'Pop-Culture Diplomacy in Japan: Soft Power, Nation Branding and the Question of "International Cultural Exchange"', *International Journal of Cultural Policy* 21 (2015): 419–32; and Christine R. Yano, 'Wink on Pink: Interpreting Japanese Cute as It Grabs the Global Headlines', *The Journal of Asian Studies* 68 (2009): 681–8.

[20] Yano, 'Wink on Pink', 684. Yano points to this *kawaii* movement as a demasculinisation of Japanese culture, and a playful embrace of 'femininity' – an element also visible in the vibrant rainbow visuals and dominant female vocals of the Katamari games.

description. In either case, the music is a central part of situating the series as an explicitly Japanese cultural product. The next case study is more complex, in that this Japaneseness is simultaneously emphasized and minimized, as the games are presented as both regional and universal products.

Complex Localization: The Tales Series

Video game genres are typically identified by narrative content and gameplay style, not by geographic origin. In one case, however, these concepts overlap: the Japanese role-playing game (or JRPG). JRPGs trace their origins back to the 1980s, with early examples such as *Dragon Quest* (1986), *Phantasy Star* (1987) and *Final Fantasy* (1987). The genre has since diversified in a number of directions, but calling a title a JRPG nonetheless generates several expectations.[21] The player will likely control a party of adventurers who set off to prevent some kind of global disaster, for example, and the gameplay will likely reward exploration, levelling up characters and strategy versus the player's technical skill. Despite their original indebtedness to Western computer RPG series like *Wizardry* (1980) and *Ultima* (1981), JRPGs quickly developed into a distinct genre. Indeed, as Douglas Schules points out, 'for fans, the genre is typically framed as a foil to Western role-playing games (WRPGs), locating the differences between the two in some alchemical arrangement of narrative (story engagement), aesthetic (visuals), and ludic (sandbox vs. confinement) properties'.[22] Similarly, there are likewise a range of musical expectations for JRPGs, typically in terms of the function and placement of music; following in the steps of early genre games like *Dragon Quest*, JRPGs very often feature non-dynamic, looped musical cues designated for specific locations (towns, dungeons, etc.).

There also remains a core expectation of Japaneseness in JRPGs – a sense that some part of the games' authenticity rests in their country of origin.[23] Yet as narrative- and text-heavy JRPGs have become increasingly popular

---

[21] For an overview of the JRPG and its generic expectations, see William Gibbons, 'Music, Genre, and Nationality in the Postmillennial Fantasy Role-Playing Game', in *The Routledge Companion to Screen Music and Sound*, ed. Miguel Mera, Ronald Sadoff and Ben Winters (New York: Routledge, 2017), 412–27.

[22] Douglas Schules, '*Kawaii* Japan: Defining JRPGs through the Cultural Media Mix', *Kinephanos* 5 (2015): 53–76 at 54.

[23] As with the Katamari games, Schules locates part of the cultural authenticity of JRPGs in their incorporation of *kawaii* aesthetics. Schules, '*Kawaii* Japan.'

outside Japan, localization has become a crucial part of their worldwide distribution. Schules has pointed out, for example, how bad or insufficient localization of JRPGs can adversely affect player experience, and consequently sales.[24] This localization is more than just translation (although that is also important); it involves making the aspects of Japanese culture that are embedded in JRPGs accessible to the widest possible audience by rendering them innocuous. Iwabuchi identifies Japan by its 'peculiar position in the global audiovisual market as an exporter of what may be called "culturally odourless" products, that is, products which … do not immediately conjure images of the country of origin in the minds of consumers'.[25] In other words, JRPGs must be somehow both Japanese and not-Japanese, regional and universal.

As a result, JRPGs can get entangled in a liminal space during the localization process – or even before, if developers take a game's eventual worldwide distribution into account from the beginning of its creation. As O'Hagan and Mangiron put it, 'When games become objects of translation, they come under a complex array of forces: on the one hand pressure for international uniformity for ease of localization, on the other, the obligation to retain the distinctive flavor of the original.'[26] The end result is often a 'complex localization', where some aspects of games *beyond* those essential to playability may be altered for international audiences. Again, music reflects this position. Seldom is anything in the musical language coded as 'Japanese' or even 'non-Western'. In fact, quite the opposite – the music often seems to intentionally eschew Japaneseness, and is in some cases altered for international distribution.

Consider, for example, the Tales series of JRPGs. This perennial franchise may fall short of the massive international success of *Final Fantasy* or *Dragon Quest*, but it has a number of localized games with a dedicated fan base in North American markets (see Table 20.2). When a Tales game is released in North America (and, to be clear, not all have been), the localization process typically takes at least six to eight months, and sometimes significantly longer; several games have left Japan only after two or more years. These are lengthy, narrative-heavy games, often requiring

[24] Douglas Schules, 'When Language Goes Bad: Localization's Effect on the Gameplay of Japanese RPGs', in *Dungeons, Dragons, and Digital Denizens: The Digital Role-Playing Game*, ed. Gerald Voorhees, Josh Call and Katie Whitlock (New York: Continuum, 2012), 88–112.

[25] Koichi Iwabuchi, 'From Western Gaze to Global Gaze: Japanese Cultural Presence in Asia', in *Global Culture: Media, Arts, Policy, and Globalization*, ed. Diana Crane, Nobuko Kawashima and Kenichi Kawasaki (New York: Routledge, 2002), 256–74 at 232.

[26] O'Hagan and Mangiron, *Game Localization*, 91.

Table 20.2 Tales games released in North America (NA)

Title (NA)	Release Date (JP/NA)
Tales of Phantasia	1995/2006
Tales of Destiny	1997/1998
Tales of Eternia	2000/2001
Tales of Symphonia	2003/2004
Tales of Legendia	2005/2006
Tales of the Abyss	2005/2006
Tales of Vesperia	2008/2014
Tales of Hearts	2008
Tales of Graces	2009/2012
Tales of Xillia	2011/2013
Tales of Xillia 2	2012/2014
Tales of Zestiria	2015
Tales of Berseria	2016/2017

80–100 hours to complete. Consequently, they require a great deal of translation work, followed by rerecording of voice-over tracks for international release.[27] With regard to music, I argue that there are, broadly speaking, two forms of localization at work: one obvious, and one much subtler.

The composer Motoi Sakuraba (joined by various collaborators) has contributed the score for each game except *Tales of Legendia*, marking the series with an idiosyncratic style that, like its visual aesthetic, is highly influenced by anime. One of the most prominent and consistent features of Tales games is a lengthy title cutscene in the manner of an anime television programme. In Japanese Tales games, the music for this sequence has typically been a pre-existing song by a popular J-pop musician or group. *Tales of Graces*, for example, made use of the song 'Mamoritai (White Wishes)' from the South Korean singer BoA, whose music is also popular in Japan. For the first several games in the series, however, in the North American versions these songs were replaced by new music from Sakuraba, composed in a style more in keeping with the in-game music. Although this change does not affect gameplay (or the visuals), it is nonetheless

---

[27] *Tales of Symphonia*, for example – far from the largest title in the series, although the first to gain a large North American audience – required the translation of over 500,000 words and rerecording of 7 hours of voice-over work, according to a 2004 interview. 'Pre-E3 2004: *Tales of Symphonia* Interview', *IGN* (30 April 2004), accessed 10 April 2020, www.ign.com/articles/2004/04/30/pre-e3-2004-tales-of-symphonia-interview?page=3.

a significant alternation; these sequences introduce the game's characters, and more generally provide a framing device that establishes players' expectations and immerses them in the experience.

The reasoning behind the differences in the Japanese and North American versions boiled down to demographic targeting. *Tales of Symphonia* was amongst the first Tales games marketed to North American audience in particular, and its musical strategies are revealing. In an interview with the online game magazine *IGN*, *Symphonia*'s Localization Producer, Nao Higo, noted that: 'one of the things I changed for the US was the opening theme song. The Japanese version had a song done by a pop group, but for the US we changed it so that we have the in-game music composer do the opening theme and I think he did a fantastic job. I think the US market will like it a lot.'[28] An FAQ article on *IGN* a few months later made the point even more explicit:

Q: What's changed for the US build?

A: In an effort to make *Tales of Symphonia* appeal to a US audience, [game developer] Namco has taken several steps to 'make' it a US product. The J-Pop opening theme song has been replaced by an orchestral anthem. . . .

Q: Why did they change the opening theme?

A: Namco felt that the *Tales of Symphonia's* presentation was 'too Japanese'. During the localization process, it made several changes to help make *TOS* appeal to a US audience. The first thing changed was the opening theme, which featured 'Starry Heavens' by Day After Tomorrow. The new anthem was created by Motoi Sakuraba, who composed *TOS*'s score.[29]

Assuming this FAQ article gets its facts correct, swapping out the theme song was more than a musical afterthought – it was the first thing the localization team changed to make the game more appealing to a North American audience. Intriguingly, *Tales of Symphonia* was released in the same year – and even by the same developer (Namco) – as *Katamari Damacy*. Yet the approaches to localization could not be more different. *Katamari*'s basic localization emphasized the Japanese 'Otherness' of the soundtrack, while *Symphonia*'s complex localization minimized the same elements.

More recent games in the Tales series, such as *Tales of Zestiria* and its prequel *Tales of Berseria*, have kept the music the same between the

---

[28] 'Pre-E3 2004: *Tales of Symphonia* Interview.'

[29] Staff, '*Tales of Symphonia* FAQ', *IGN* (18 June 2004), accessed 10 April 2020, www.ign.com/articles/2004/06/18/tales-of-symphonia-faq?page=4.

Japanese and North American versions of the intro video, but made changes to the lyrics. The former game removes the Japanese lyrics entirely for the North American release, resulting in an instrumental-only track, in keeping with previous North American Tales games. *Zestiria*, however, features a separate English-language version of the song. In both cases, however, it is a shift in musical style for the series – hard rock instead of J-pop – that makes it possible for the two versions to musically co-exist. This stylistic change reflects the second large-scale musical strategy in complex localization: the avoidance of geographically specific musical styles in the first place, which developers sometimes call 'internationalization'. In the words of O'Hagan and Mangiron, 'developers strive through the internationalization process to design games with an international appeal that do not require much modification for different territories' – and the way developers often limit the amount of *ex post facto* localization is by 'keeping cultural references to a minimum and developing games in as culturally neutral a way as possible'.[30]

As regards character design, for example, Japanese game developers (and, relatedly, animators) often adhere to a principle of *mukokuseki*, or 'statelessness,' meaning that characters' ethnic identities are obscured. Many JRPG characters, including in the Tales series, fall into this category, sporting bright blue hair or ambiguous facial features that avoid lending the characters any specific ethnic or cultural markers. This ideology of cultural erasure has a broader impact on the reception and understanding of Japanese products and their localization. As Iwabuchi observes, 'the international spread of mukokuseki popular culture from Japan simultaneously articulates the universal appeal of Japanese cultural products and the disappearance of any perceptible "Japaneseness", which ... is subtly incorporated into the "localization" strategies of the media industries'.[31]

Applying *mukokuseki* to the music of the Tales series suggests some significant parallels. The title music is a clear example – the culturally fragrant J-pop of earlier games has been jettisoned for a comparatively odourless rock style. Or, one could alternatively make a persuasive argument that the music has become increasingly Westernized, which North American audiences might simply perceive as universal. Sakuraba's scores present a somewhat more complex case. As I noted above, in the case of many of the earlier Tales games, he composed new title music to replace the title

---

[30] O'Hagan and Mangiron, *Game Localization*, 208. Localization of a game after it has been officially released is also called 'post-gold' localization.
[31] Iwabuchi, *Recentering Globalization*, 33.

sequence. We might, then, wonder why his music was not 'too Japanese', as Namco evidently considered the J-pop song to be. Were Sakuraba – and, by extension, other JRPG composers with similar musical styles – composing in a form of musical *mukokuseki*, designed to avoid markers of its own Japaneseness? Given the interconnectedness of Japanese media (film, anime, games) and Western cinematic traditions, that question is difficult to answer with any certainty. Yet Sakuraba's musical style and orchestration (predominantly piano and Western orchestra) seems for the most part calculated to avoid overt Japanese musical markers, and JRPGs as a genre have long borrowed from Western classical and cinematic music history.[32]

Viewed from this angle, in some cases complex musical localization of this kind takes on a more troubling dimension. Players may associate JRPG music with being 'Japanese' – indeed, for many North American players it may be their only exposure to Japanese music. Yet we can also understand that music as intentionally 'stateless', or even as a rejection of Japanese musical identity. The situation is again analogous to *mukokuseki* character design; as Iwabuchi astutely notes, 'If it is indeed the case that the Japaneseness of Japanese animation derives . . . from its erasure of physical signs of Japaneseness, is not the Japan that Western audiences are at long last coming to appreciate . . . an animated, race-less and culture-less, virtual version of "Japan"?'[33] That is to say, the kinds of approaches composers like Sakuraba employ in anticipating the preferences of North American audiences are part of a larger pattern of cultural erasure. In my final example, that erasure becomes almost complete, as the Japanese score is either entirely or in large part replaced by different music for North American audiences.

Blending: The Gran Turismo series

Blending is the most complex and sweeping type of localization game developers employ. While complex localization may entail a series of

---

[32] Significantly, while composers like Sakuraba and Nobuo Uematsu had more significant backgrounds in Japanese prog rock, the classical training of Koichi Sugiyama (composer of the Dragon Quest games) likely influenced the tone of subsequent JRPGs. Moreover, I have argued elsewhere that a number of games for the Nintendo Entertainment System (including early JRPGs such as the Dragon Quest series) employed musical styles derived from eighteenth-century Western counterpoint. See William Gibbons, 'Little Harmonic Labyrinths: Baroque Musical Style on the Nintendo Entertainment System', in *Recomposing the Past: Representations of Early Music on Stage and Screen*, ed. James Cook, Alexander Kolassa and Adam Whittaker (New York: Routledge, 2018): 139–52.

[33] Iwabuchi, *Recentering Globalization*, 33.

relatively minor adjustments to audio, visual and narrative elements to 'internationalize' a title, blending requires major alterations. Entire narrative arcs may be scrapped, added or rewritten; a character's design may be completely transformed; or, most interestingly for this chapter, an entirely new soundtrack may be provided.[34] Blending for narrative and visual reasons often results from adapting games to divergent cultural expectations, or to accommodate various international rating systems. For example, in the 1990s, animations featuring blood or references to alcoholic beverages were routinely excised from Japanese exports to North America. This type of reasoning is less likely to result in changes to game music – although there have indeed been instances in which games were negatively affected by their inclusion of music that could be perceived as culturally offensive.[35]

Although never common, musical blending most often occurs when there is a need to replace an entire soundtrack to appeal to a target demographic. That need may result from practical or aesthetic concerns – or possibly both. For example, Sony Computer Entertainment's SingStar series of karaoke-based games often featured radically different track lists depending on the country of release, for obvious reasons. Audiences had to be familiar enough with the pop songs on the soundtracks to sing along with them, or the game would be both much less appealing and much more difficult. On the other hand, Sega's *Sonic CD* (1993) received a new soundtrack for its North American release, apparently because developers were concerned about the Japanese soundtrack's ability to appeal to North American audiences. To the chagrin of a number of fans, Sega removed the majority of the techno-influenced original music by Naofumi Hataya and Masafumi Ogata, and replaced it with an eclectic, predominantly prog rock score from Spencer Nilsen and David Young.

The purpose of musical blending is not always entirely clear, beyond a vague attempt to anticipate (correctly or incorrectly) the preferences of a given regional audience. The most obvious example of such a practice is the Gran Turismo series of racing simulators (see Table 20.3), all of which have been released on Sony PlayStation consoles. As Tim Summers explains regarding the first game in the series:

---

[34] For a brief overview of blending, see Thayer and Kolko, 'Localization of Digital Games', 481.

[35] In perhaps the best-known example, though not directly related to localization, the Fire Temple music of *The Legend of Zelda: Ocarina of Time* (1998) originally contained an Islamic prayer chant, which Nintendo quietly removed from subsequent versions of the game. Likewise, the Microsoft-developed fighting game *Kakuto Chojin* (2002) was removed from shelves in both the United States and Japan for including Islamic prayer chant in its soundtrack.

Table 20.3 Gran Turismo primary titles

Title	Year of Release (JP/NA)
Gran Turismo	1997/1998
Gran Turismo 2	1999
Gran Turismo 3: A-Spec	2001
Gran Turismo 4	2004
Gran Turismo 5	2010
Gran Turismo 6	2013
Gran Turismo Sport	2017

In Japan, the game features a newly commissioned score in a generic rock style, while the game heard in North American, Australasia and Europe includes pre-existing rock, electronica and pop songs from well-known artists. A definitive reason for this difference is elusive, but plausible factors include the commercial potential for Western pop music in those regions and that the original Japanese soundtrack, in a 1980s rock style, sounded unfashionably dated for a Western audience.[36]

In contrast to the SingStar example, the rejection of the original Japanese soundtrack (by composers Masahiro Andoh and Isamu Ohira) was not a practical concern; there is no gameplay-related requirement for familiar music. Yet clearly the developers believed an entirely new soundtrack geared to Western tastes was important enough to license an expensive track list featuring artists including David Bowie, Blur and The Dandy Warhols. *Gran Turismo 2* followed a similar pattern to the first game, with a separate soundtrack for the Japanese and North American releases of the game.

Beginning with *Gran Turismo 3: A-Spec*, however, the series adopted a more ecumenical approach to music, including both licensed popular music and an original score by a range of Japanese composers. There are a few practical reasons for a shared, rather than blended, soundtrack. For one thing, the enhanced storage of the PlayStation 2 and later consoles allowed for more music; perhaps this change prompted the developers to allow players to choose. For another, using the same soundtrack allowed for a near-simultaneous release of the game in all geographic regions, with very little necessity for localization. On the other hand, there remain some significant musical differences. Most notably, the Japanese and North

---

[36] Tim Summers, *Understanding Video Game Music* (Cambridge, UK: Cambridge University Press, 2016), 26.

American (and European) versions feature different music for the opening video. In the case of *Gran Turismo 3*, the Japanese version features, as usual, a new version of 'Moon Over the Castle' (the Gran Turismo theme song); the North American release, by contrast, features a remix of Lenny Kravitz's 'Are You Gonna Go My Way' (1993). Later Gran Turismo games follow this trend – a 'universal' soundtrack mixing original Japanese game music with Western (predominantly North American) popular music, and demographically targeted intro videos.

Gran Turismo's shift away from fully blended soundtracks – while still remaining a globally popular franchise – reveals a change in perception about the necessity of musical blending in order to appeal to global audiences. As Carlson and Corliss point out regarding gameplay alterations, often the assumptions underlying localization choices rely on cultural stereotypes, and 'misleading generalizations often reveal more about distributors' motives or preconceptions than the tastes of international game audiences'.[37] Perhaps owing to concerns over these cultural stereotypes – and of course avoiding the expense of creating two or more soundtracks – blended musical scores seem to be giving way to complex localization and composers aiming for musical 'statelessness' (although those techniques are not free from their own cultural challenges, as we have already seen). Yet whenever present, blended scores present particular challenges to the study of game music. When multiple soundtracks exist for a game, which is the 'real' one? Is it fair for scholars to give primacy to 'their' versions of games, or does that choice itself reinforce cultural hegemony? And, as a practical consideration, how can researchers even ascertain what differences exist between games in the first place, when it is often difficult or impossible to obtain and play all regional versions?

***

As these final questions make clear, the localization of video game music is a multifaceted topic, and this essay only begins to scratch its surface. On a basic level, the very existence of multiple, equally 'official' versions of a game eradicates the notion of any stable text for analysis.[38] Indeed, the state of localization can be far more complex and multidirectional than

---

[37] Carlson and Corliss, 'Imagined Commodities', 69.

[38] Tim Summers identifies localization as one of a set of ontological challenges posed by studying games in *Understanding Video Game Music*, 25–6. For more on music's role in the destabilization of the video game text, see Steven Reale, 'Barriers to Listening in *World of Warcraft*', in *Music in the Role-Playing Game: Heroes & Harmonies*, ed. William Gibbons and Steven Reale (New York: Routledge, 2019): 197–215; see also Reale's contribution to this volume (Chapter 12).

these case studies have indicated. In some cases, for example, Japanese games even receive a 'recursive import' – a reverse localization of the North American version of an originally Japanese title, as in the Japan-only 'International' versions of several *Final Fantasy* games in the 2000s.[39] In those cases, a Japanese audience might consume – or indeed prefer – music that was specifically altered from a Japanese soundtrack in order to appeal to an entirely *different* regional demographic. Despite its challenging and occasionally frustrating nature, however, engaging meaningfully with musical localization is crucial, and my intention here has been to begin moving in that direction rather than to provide concrete answers. All musical works are products of place, and considering video game music as a cultural rather than 'universal' product provides significant new insights into how game music affects audiences (and vice versa). Localization inevitably shapes how players (including scholars) understand and interpret games and their music, and recognizing its impact helps situate game music, its creators and its audiences as part of an expansive open world.

---

[39] On recursive imports, see for example Minako O'Hagan, 'Putting Pleasure First: Localizing Japanese Video Games', *TTR: Traduction, Terminologie, Rédaction* 22 (2009): 147–65.

21 | Female Credit: Excavating Recognition for the Capcom Sound Team

ANDREW LEMON AND HILLEGONDA C. RIETVELD

This chapter focuses on the Japanese game development company Capcom (CAPsule COMputers), arguably 'a well-established developer and publisher',[1] known for some of the most popular action arcade games of the 1980s and early 1990s, including *Ghosts 'n Goblins* (1985), *Commando* (1985), *Bionic Commando* (1987), *Final Fight* (1989), *Ghouls 'n Ghosts* (1988) and *Street Fighter II* (1991), developed with male players in mind. The music for these action games was provided by the mostly female Capcom Sound Team. Ayako Mori and Tamayo Kawamoto joined Capcom in 1984, and other core members of the team included Junko Tamiya, Manami Matsumae, Harumi Fujita, Yoko Shimomura and Tamayo Kawamoto, most of whom left the company in 1990 shortly after their seminal soundtrack work as a team on the arcade game *Final Fight* had been completed. Yoko Shimomura, who composed the memorable themes for *Street Fighter II*, left Capcom for the game developer Square in 1993 to pursue her dream of scoring orchestral music for role-playing game (RPG) titles, bringing to an end the domination of Capcom's female Sound Team. This collective of female composers went on to influence a host of game composers through their pioneering work on early arcade hardware. Yet in versions of games ported from the arcade to home consoles and computers, their work was left uncredited. Popular recognition for their work has been relatively slow, due to a number of factors that include the use of pseudonyms and the company's crediting policy, as well as the routine exscription[2] of women in a male-dominated game industry.

Versions of the original compositions were created for various game publishers when these arcade games were ported for home play. In such cases, the versioning work carried out by composers, such as the UK-based Rob Hubbard and Tim Follin, was usually credited, sometimes for the music, other times for the sound of the game, while the composers of the original music stems were not named. Even retrospective developer-interview material on Capcom's own website makes no mention of the composition and music

---

[1] Mia Consalvo, *Atari to Zelda: Japan's Videogames in Global Contexts* (Cambridge, MA: MIT Press, 2016), 170.

[2] Robert Walser, *Running with the Devil: Power, Gender, and Madness in Heavy Metal Music* (Middletown CT: Wesleyan University Press, 1993), 114–115.

work for its popular games.[3] Capcom had a policy in place from the early 1980s of only identifying creators via non-gender-specific pseudonyms in its titles; these pseudonyms were sometimes rotated amongst members of staff, who may have had up to eight different handles under which they produced content for the company.[4] In this context, it was near impossible to identify the composers and, due to the way in which surnames are presented,[5] neither could their gender be inferred. This may be partly because 'the commercial, functional nature of this work sets it free from the stranglehold of auteurism'.[6] Game composers work to briefs, in a similar manner to visual designers, rather than create work in order to stand out as individual artists. For example, when discussing her move to game publisher Square, after her time at Capcom, Yoko Shimomura comments that, '(g)etting my name out there had never been a major goal of mine, but now here I was in a situation where I found I had to attach my name to my music where if I didn't, I didn't belong there'.[7] Crediting practices are a perennial issue in the industry, and one which, as far back as 2003, had already eventually led the International Game Designer Association (IGDA) to develop its Credit Standards Committee: it stated in 2014 that

Employees are often mislabeled, unlabeled, or left off the credits. In fact, a 2006 IGDA Game Writers Special Interest Group survey revealed that 35% of respondents (48 out of 134) either 'don't ever' or 'only sometimes' receive official credit for their efforts ... we believe that employers effectively and accurately assigning credits are crucial.[8]

---

[3] Anonymous, 'Final Fight Developer Interview', *Capcom.com* (8 February 2019), https://game.capcom.com/cfn/sfv/column/list/cat4768. Accessed 28 April 2020.

[4] Alexander Brandon and Chris Greening, 'Junko Tamiya Interview: Creating Capcom's Incredible NES Scores', *VGMOnline,* trans. Mohammed Taher (19 May 2014), www.vgmonline.net/junkotamiyainterview/; Chris Greening, 'Harumi Fujita Interview: Ghosts, Goblins, and Gargoyles', *VGMOnline,* trans. Alex Aniel (5 December 2015), www.vgmonline.net/harumifujitainterview/. Both accessed 28 April 2020.

[5] Richard Moss, 'How Bad Crediting Hurts the Game Industry and Muddles History', *Gamasutra* (6 November 2018), https://www.gamasutra.com/view/news/329003/ How_bad_crediting_hurts_the_game_industry_and_muddles_history.php. Accessed 28 April 2020.

[6] Daniel Martin-McCormick, 'Various Artists. Diggin' in the Carts: A Collection of Pioneering Japanese Video Game Music', *Pitchfork* (16 December 2017), https://pitchfork.com/reviews/ albums/various-artists-diggin-in-the-carts-a-collection-of-pioneering-japanese-video-game-music/. Accessed 28 April 2020.

[7] Nick Dwyer, *Digging in the Carts [Radio].* Series 2/Episode 6. Red Bull Radio (6 December 2017), accessed 29 October 2020, www.mixcloud.com/VGmix/2017-12-07-nick-dwyer-diggin-in-the-carts-season-2-episode-6-rbma-radio/ at 39:00.

[8] IGDA, *Game Crediting Guide 9.2* (NP: International Game Developers' Association, 2014), accessed 29 October 2020, https://igda.org/resources-archive/crediting-standards-guide-ver -9-2-en-jp-2014/.

Nevertheless, the Crediting Standards Guide is a guide, and is therefore not necessarily enforceable,[9] as game cultures and concomitant legal frameworks differ across the world.

During the late 1980s and early 1990s, when Capcom's Sound Team laid the musical ground rules for subsequent action games, Capcom's policy on crediting also seemed to differ from non-Japanese crediting practices. In particular, in the United States and United Kingdom, composers who provide music and sound effects for video games tended to work as individuals,[10] whether as freelancers joining single projects or as solo artists working in-house at game-developing companies.[11] By contrast, Japanese video game companies took a team-based approach to audio for arcade games, and their musicians also performed on music albums and during live concerts of the video game soundtracks. For example, between 1988 and 1997, Capcom had an in-house band, Alfh Lyra wa Lyra, which included some members of the Capcom Sound Team.[12] Capcom's band was resurrected for the 2002's rerelease of the *Capcom Game Music Series* (SCITRON DISCS).[13] The credits on recent album releases of video game material provide more detail than the games, acknowledging the original composers, as well as the arrangers who follow up by porting and/or remixing the original source material. Examples of such soundtrack albums include *Bionic Commando* in 2008,[14] and the 2014 reboot.[15] The availability of online databases cataloguing both game credits (MobyGames) and soundtrack album releases (VGMDb) also aids the project of identifying and crediting these musicians.[16] Further recognition for the team of

[9] Anonymous [Editorial], 'Giving Credit Where Credit Is Due', *Gamasutra* (3 October 2008), www.gamasutra.com/view/feature/132202/giving_credit_where_credit_is_due.php. Accessed 28 April 2020.

[10] Andreas Wallström, 'Rob Hubbard Interview', *C64.com* (n.d.). www.c64.com/interviews/hubbard.html. Accessed 28 April 2020.

[11] Frank Cifaldi, 'Catching up with Tim Follin', *Gamasutra* (26 December 2009), https://www.gamasutra.com/view/news/97596/Playing_CatchUp_Tim_Follin.php. Accessed 28 April 2020.

[12] Alfh Lyra wa Lyra aka Alph Lyra was comprised of the following members of Capcom's Sound Team at the time: Isao Abe, Yasuaki Fujita, Tamayo Kawamoto, Manami Matsumae, Shun Nishigaki and Yoko Shimomura.

[13] Alfh Lyra wa Lyra, *Capcom Game Music VOL 2* [CD] (Tokyo, Japan: SCITRON DISCS, 2002); Alfh Lyra wa Lyra, *Capcom Game Music VOL 3* [CD] (Tokyo, Japan: SCITRON DISCS, 2002).

[14] Simon Viklund, *Bionic Commando Rearmed (The Soundtrack)* [CD] (New York: Sumthing Else Music Works, 2009).

[15] Simon Viklund, *Bionic Commando Rearmed 2 Original Soundtrack* [CD] (New York: Sumthing Else Music Works, 2014).

[16] 'Bionic Commando: Rearmed (The Soundtrack)', VGMdb [Video Game Music Database] (28 May 2008), https://vgmdb.net/album/8726. Accessed 28 April 2020.

composers is therefore improving, as illustrated by two documentaries, *Diggin'*
in the Carts on Japanese video game composers,[17] and *Beep: A Documentary*
History of Game Sound,[18] which includes an extensive set of interviews with
video game composers and sound designers. Interviews with individual game
composers have also been valuable sources of information, such as those
published by VideoGameMusic Online (VGMO) between 2015 and 2017.

Despite a changing game industry, improvements in acknowledgement,
a widening demographic of players and developers (including initiatives
such as Women in Games) and even a well-received guide to video game
composition by the successful game composer Winifred Phillips,[19] female
game composers have more often than not been *exscripted* from game
histories. For the discussion here, the question remains why this female
team of Capcom's composers were not given due credit at the height of
their works' popularity in the arcades, as well as when their work was ported
for gameplay at home. Although the video game industry may be thought of
as a monument valley of men, where bygone assumptions of male dominance and power are 'being built again into new structures',[20] the perception
persists of a male-dominated industry where, as Carly A. Kocurek puts it,
young competitive 'technomasculinity' is foregrounded:

The common assumption that gaming is and rightly should be for boys and men
even in the empirical evidence that women make up a large percentage of gamers is
neither natural nor logical. It is the product of a long-standing historical and
cultural construction of video gaming among video gamers begun during the
golden era of the video game arcade.[21]

Such masculinist narrative is partly sustained through the manner in which
(in Laine Nooney's words) 'our sense that videogame history is "all about
the boys" is the consequence of a certain mode of historical writing,
preservation, memory and temporally specific affective attachments, all of
which produce the way we tell the history of videogames'.[22] Also, in the
currently developing field of study of game music, a focused discussion of

---

[17] Nick Dwyer and Tu Neill (dir.), *Diggin' in the Carts* (Red Bull Academy, 2014),
https://daily.redbullmusicacademy.com/2014/10/diggin-in-the-carts-series. Accessed
28 April 2020.

[18] Karen Collins (dir.), *Beep: A Documentary History of Game Sound* (Canada: Ehtonal, 2016).

[19] Winifred Phillips, *A Composer's Guide to Game Music* (Cambridge, MA: The MIT Press, 2014).

[20] Shira Chess, *Ready Player Two: Women Gamers and Designed Identity* (Minneapolis: University
of Minnesota Press, 2017), 173, 177.

[21] Carly A. Kocurek, *Coin-Operated Americans: Rebooting Boyhood at the Video Game Arcade*
(Minneapolis: University of Minnesota Press, 2015), 191.

[22] Laine Nooney, 'A Pedestal, a Table, a Love Letter: Archaeologies of Gender in Videogame
History', *Game Studies* 13, no. 2 (2013). http://gamestudies.org/1302/articles/nooney

issues in sexuality and gender has only relatively recently commenced, for example in terms of gameplay,[23] game music culture[24] and composition.[25] In this chapter, we wish to contribute to this area of knowledge. Resonating with Nooney's archaeological approach to gender politics in video game history, the discussion that follows here is based on an excavation of game archives and game versions in order to evidence how the composers of Capcom's successful arcade game titles found themselves in a position of invisibility, a state of affairs which is quite persistent and has only sporadically been corrected and updated. In the context of her archaeological approach to game sound, Collins explains that this 'allows us to not only revisit current media objects and texts within a new framework, but also allow us [sic] to revisit the histories and chronicles of our media'[26] in order to achieve an understanding that circumvents, and can be critical of, dominant historical discourse.

To understand how the original composers for Capcom's arcade games were credited in comparison to the producers responsible for porting their musical compositions for home play, we focus first on three examples: *Commando* (1985), *Bionic Commando* (1987) and *Ghouls 'n Ghosts* (1988). These were all first created for Capcom's 1980s arcade game library and then ported for home computers, the Commodore 64, Nintendo Entertainment System (NES) and ZX Spectrum. Taking an archival approach, the capture of data for this chapter was performed by carefully checking for the credit information, which was retrieved through hands-on gameplay of the three selected titles on their various platforms, where possible via hardware, including the Commodore 64 and the NES/Nintendo Famicom.[27] Where the hardware was unavailable, the crediting information was checked through emulation, in addition to an investigation into the ROM programme data for each of the arcade games in

---

[23] Melanie Fritsch, 'Beat It! – Playing the "King of Pop" in Video Games', in *Music Video Games: Performance, Politics and Play*, ed. Michael Austin (New York: Bloomsbury, 2016), 153–76.

[24] Rob Gallagher, '"All the Other Players Want to Look at My Pad": Grime, Gaming, and Digital Identity', *GAME: Italian Journal of Game Studies*, 6, no.1 (2017).

[25] David Machin and Theo van Leeuwen 'Sound, Music and Gender in Mobile Games', *Gender and Language* 10, no. 3 (2016): 412–32; Michael Austin, 'Orchestrating Difference: Representing Gender in Video Game Music', in *Masculinity at Play*, ed. Nicholas Taylor and Gerald Voorhees (London: Palgrave Macmillan, 2018), 165–83; Hillegonda C. Rietveld and Andrew Lemon, 'The Street Fighter Lady: Invisibility and Gender in Game Composition', *ToDiGRA: Transactions of the Digital Games Research Association* 5, no. 1 (2019), 107–33.

[26] Karen Collins, 'Game Sound in the Mechanical Arcades: An Audio Archaeology', *Game Studies* 16, no. 1 (2016), accessed 29 October 2020, http://gamestudies.org/1601/articles/collins.

[27] The Nintendo Famicom is the original Japanese version of the Nintendo Entertainment System (NES).

question. Additional archival research was conducted in the historical digital databases of *Digital Magazine* and *Digital Fanzine* via emulated Commodore 64 disc images; these were retrieved and checked using the VICE Commodore 64 emulator (Version 3.4; Viceteam, 2019). Additionally, *Game Magazine* articles were accessed via archives of print media preserved digitally at the Internet Archive (Archive.org). In order to review and check the data obtained, extensive use was also made of long-play video content (full gameplay videos) present on both archive.org and YouTube, as well as more traditional sources of information. These include online game-credit databases such as the VGMDb.net, which provides an archive of game soundtrack album credits; MobyGames.com, a site dedicated to video game credits; and The Cutting Room Floor, a site dedicated to preserving information on material that is present inside the game data, but not normally accessible or used in gameplay.

According to game historian John Szczepaniak, '[y]ou cannot even begin to imagine the Herculean task of disentangling Japanese credit listings … And once you find a thread and follow it down the rabbit hole, you just bring up more questions than answers'.[28] Here, we did exactly that, and jumped into the proverbial rabbit hole. As Capcom was not always transparent in providing credits for the individual contributions by its team members, assessing credit for the work performed by members of the Capcom Sound Team in the 1980s and early 1990s is, indeed, challenging. For example, *Video Game Music Online*'s interviews with composers Junko Tamiya[29] and Harumi Fujita[30] show that it was Capcom's policy at the time to only credit via pseudonyms, which were often rotated, with a number of different names in use for each person. For example, Junko Tamiya had several pseudonyms, including Gon, Gonzou and Gondamin. In addition to this layer of obfuscation, memory storage limitations in early arcade games often resulted in an absence of a staff roll or a post-game credit sequence. In this context, it is a challenge for researchers (particularly video game music database administrators) to seek out proper credit information for titles, with many relying on decoding high-score tables' default values,[31] and hidden data inside game code,[32]

---

[28] Moss, 'Bad Crediting.'
[29] Brandon and Greening, 'Junko Tamiya Interview.'
[30] Greening, 'Harumi Fujita Interview.'
[31] Adding credit information (in heavily abbreviated form) was a common practice at the time, as the high-score table was a possible place to insert default values which would display at boot-up of the arcade machine – these would be written over by players during gameplay until the machine was switched off, and then would revert to the default values.
[32] Adding abbreviated credit information into padded areas of ROM storage was also common at the time; this would only be accessible by reading the chips out as this data was superfluous to

as well as interview sources, in order to establish who contributed music to a game. This policy of anonymity was also motivated by an attempt to prevent the poaching of staff by competitor companies, especially during the fledgling years of arcade development in Japan.[33] In seeking out the actual credits for composition work, our research identified regular staff changes at Capcom during its early years, with staff who began their game music careers at Capcom moving on to perform work for other titans of the arcade industry including Namco, Taito, SNK and even home consoles. Notably, Yoko Shimomura went on to work at Square after her time at Capcom. Ultimately, this tactic did not really help with retaining staff in the long term.

In home-computer ports of arcade game software, there is also a lack of credit or attribution for composition work due to size optimization requirements that often lead to the truncating or omission of full ending credits and attributions of the original work when these are converted by the porting team. In addition, the composition credits for many of the home console and micro-computer versions of original game music have routinely been attributed wrongly to the (albeit impressive) reversioning porting team. Coupled with the very different attitude of solo practitioners in the West, which contrasts with the more team-based approach of Japanese developers to crediting, all of the aforementioned factors have led to many of the original works by these female composers being inextricably linked to the covers and arrangements produced by those responsible for home conversions of these classic arcade games. As a result, the credit for the music composition for those titles has effectively been misattributed, if not in the raw data, then certainly in the public consciousness. This is further complicated by the porting arranger at times gaining inspiration from Capcom's own console conversion process. Observing this is certainly not a slight on the game musicians who arranged these conversions and whose work is highly regarded, especially within the technical limitations of the hardware they were working with; and we also recognize that the original game composers were influenced by other popular music sources in their work. Here, though, we wish to note the game composers who produced the original compositions and, in particular, the melodies that many of the home ports are based on.

the game. John Aycock and Patrick Finn, 'Uncivil Engineering: A Textual Divide in Game Studies', *Game Studies* 19, no. 3 (2019).

[33] Moss, 'Bad Crediting.'

Within the context of archival opaqueness, we first discuss three examples of crediting practices during home-computer conversions of Capcom original arcade game material, *Commando, Bionic Commando* and *Ghouls 'n Ghosts*. In the process, we review how crediting was handled in-game, starting with the home conversions of these arcade titles, in chronological order. *Commando* is a top-down arcade shooter game title produced by Capcom, and features a non-stop barrage of war-game thrills, where the protagonist pursues and rescues prisoners of war while defeating enemy combatants, in a one-man army setting. The game's music score was written by Capcom Sound Team member Tamayo Kawamoto, drawing influences from war film soundtracks. For example, her percussive solo reminds the listener of the main theme of Frank de Vol's score for *The Dirty Dozen* (1967), referring to its 95-bpm (beats per minute) martial percussion solo in her own composition, albeit at a much faster tempo, around three times that of the original.[34] Another point of reference can be found in Jay Chattaway's Main Theme score for *Missing in Action* (1984);[35] a helicopter sound effect that is very similar to the film's opening sound design can be heard over Kawamoto's *Commando* theme music when starting the arcade game. The original arcade machine did not credit Kawamoto, lacking both a full credit roll and any hidden material in the high-score table, instead merely listing other Capcom arcade games from previous years.

The driving groove of Rob Hubbard, for the ported Commodore 64 home-play version, feels funkier than Tamayo Kawamoto's original soundtrack. Covering the original composition quite closely, it takes inspiration from the 'insert coin' sound effect that Kawamoto had initially created for the arcade game.[36] Hubbard claims he created the new version in one night:

I went down to their [Elite Systems] office and started working on it late at night, and worked on it through the night. I took one listen to the original arcade version and started working on the c64 version [*sic*]. I think they wanted some resemblance to the arcade version, but I just did what I wanted to do. By the time everyone arrived at 8.00 am in the morning, I had loaded the main tune on every C64 in the building! I got my cheque and was on a train home by 10.00 am.[37]

---

[34] See Frank De Vol, 'Main Title From "The Dirty Dozen"', on *The Dirty Dozen (Music From The Original Sound Track)* [Vinyl] (Hollywood, CA: MGM Records, 1967).

[35] See Jay Chattaway, 'Main Theme' for *Missing in Action* (dir. Joseph Zito, 1984).

[36] See Insert Coin SFX from Commando (1985, Capcom, Arcade), recorded here: '01 – Credit – Commando (Arcade) – Soundtrack – Arcade', video, 0:02, 10 May 2016, posted by VintaGamers Paradise, https://youtu.be/j4WT8jAVwgg.

[37] 'Waz' and 'Kenz', 'Interviews with Rob Hubbard', *The SID Homepage* (*c*.1997), www.sidmusic.org/sid/rhubbard.html. Accessed 28 April 2020.

On loading the ported Commodore 64 game, a simple text screen of credits appears. The screen makes no mention of the original producers of material for the arcade game and solely credits Rob Hubbard for 'Sound', the line denoting the copyright marking '©' to Japan Capsule Computers UK. It may well be that the lack of a reference to the original composer of material is chip-memory- and screen-space-related. According to Chris Butler, programmer of the Commodore 64 version of *Commando*, the porting company Elite Systems[38] required its team to store the entire game in memory to avoid loading extra material from tape for the title,[39] which led to the home conversion being cut back quite a bit from the arcade original. The lack of information about the developer and production team adds to the game's enigmatic mystery, yet it also opens a space for assumptions that a masculinist game industry has *exscripted* not only the original game music composer, but also her gender.

Bionic Commando was released by Capcom in 1987 for the arcade platform featuring a novel bionic-arm-swinging mechanic and an archetypal lone protagonist railing against a seemingly far stronger enemy, an army on the side of an authoritarian regime. The title features a distinctive, varied and, for its time, experimental soundtrack by Harumi Fujita. A mix of music genres ranges from the merengue and bossa nova, to a stereotypical military-style marching theme that adds a layer of humour. Fujita explains that she is particularly proud of her tone generation (instrument design) in this soundtrack; she makes very good use of the game's FM-based sound chip in creating a varied, rich set of instrument tones and percussion for the title's score.[40] Musician Tim Follin handled the conversion work for the software developer Software Creations and publisher US Gold (under their Go! label) in 1988, making the game playable on home computers such as the ZX Spectrum and Commodore 64 in European territories. The result is an original set of complex interpretations of Fujita's original themes, style and tonal structure. In the case of Fujita's Level 1 'Forest Theme' for the arcade release, Follin uses the original material as a starting point, but at around forty-five seconds into the music, the interpretation significantly veers away from this, building on the original music material to create something new through extensive use of arpeggiation and extreme ring modulation effects, to float back to the original composition in a looping manner. Elsewhere in the conversion, the

[38] Gary Penn, 'The Butler Did It!', *ZZap64* 17 (September 1986), 104–5.
[39] The music file was 6 kilobytes in size, which in the early days of game development was substantial, given the total memory size of 64 kilobytes available on the Commodore 64.
[40] Greening, 'Harumi Fujita Interview.'

composition is nevertheless built, with added flair, directly on Fujita's recognizable original compositions. In *Lethal News*, a Commodore 64 disc-based scene magazine, Tim Follin famously comments that, 'it started like an arcade conversion! ... I started converting the title tune, and it just developed, slipped out of my grip and became something, that was very different from what I had in mind, at the beginning. Quite messy!'[41] As for *Commando*, Harumi Fujita is not credited as the original composer. The in-game credits are sparse, offering a small opening screen on the version for the Commodore 64 that merely gives credit to the conversion team, partly in response to screen space and memory-size constraints on the home-computer versions of the game. The ending screen, in particular, is even more minimal, simply showing a congratulatory message to the victorious player.

Bionic Commando was remade in 2008 as *Bionic Commando: Rearmed*[42] by Capcom for home console and computer platforms for a modern audience. The composer of the music stems for this title, Simon Viklund, has made it clear that his work on the score is formulated from covers of Junko Tamiya's original work on the NES version of the game, stating that:

I just don't want to take too much credit for it, I mean, these songs are remakes. They have the same melodies and harmonies. I didn't write those, those are from back in the original game, and a lot of the reasons that people like them is the nostalgia factor. They recognize the melodies and appreciate how they've been treated.[43]

Earlier versions of *Bionic Commando* include a re-imagining of the arcade game on the NES/Nintendo Famicom, released in July in 1988, for which Junko Tamiya, a colleague of Harumi Fujita in the Capcom Sound Team, handled the conversion, adding new material. Only two of the tracks from the original arcade release appear in the converted version. In turn, the NES version became a source of inspiration to Follin's later conversion and composition work for home-computer releases in September 1988, in which he incorporated Tamiya's NES *Bionic Commando* composition. This in itself takes Fujita's original arcade 'Bionic Commando Theme' and 'Heat Wave', as the starting points for Follin's arrangement of the

---

[41] Kwon [Metin Aydin], 'Tim Follin Interview', *Lethal News* 6 (December 1990).

[42] Titled *Bionic Commando: Master D Fukkatsu Keikaku* in Japan.

[43] Jayson Napolitano, 'Comic Con 08: Interview With Bionic Commando Rearmed Composer/Director Simon Viklund', *Original Sound Version* (28 July 2008), www.originalsoundversion.com/comic-con-08-interview-with-bionic-commando-rearmed-composerdirector-simon-viklund/. Accessed 28 April 2020.

'Stage 2 Theme' in the Commodore 64 and ZX Spectrum home-computer ports. This demonstrates a dynamic process of influence and reinterpretation. Yet, again, the original composers do not appear on the credits roll of *Bionic Commando: Rearmed.*[44] A sequel to this version was released in 2011 on home console and computer platforms, again scored by Simon Viklund, utilizing original material alongside some covers of Tamiya's NES soundtrack. Again, Junko Tamiya does not appear in the end credit roll at all.[45] Both of these omissions have been fixed on the soundtrack albums of the two remakes, where Junko Tamiya has been credited as one of the source composers, alongside Harumi Fujita.[46]

The final game score conversion under discussion here is the game *Ghouls 'n Ghosts*, produced in 1988 by Capcom on their fledgling CPS (Capcom Play System) hardware platform for arcade. The game is a sequel to their successful 1985 arcade game *Ghosts 'n Goblins*. As is common in the arcade action genre, it features a male lone protagonist knight on a quest to save a kidnapped princess from the clutches of Lucifer. The game is notable for its extreme difficulty and the necessity of performing a 'double run' to complete it, requiring the game to be finished twice in order for the player to be successful. The music for the arcade title was composed by Tamayo Kawamoto, who built on the sound and composition work by her colleague Ayako Mori for the earlier *Ghosts 'n Goblins* arcade title. In the 'Ending Theme' to the arcade game, Tamayo Kawamoto pays tribute to *Bionic Commando*, taking cues from her fellow team member Harumi Fujita's 'Forest' theme. The game provides a rich audio experience. The music and sound design benefited from the expanded sound capabilities of Capcom's new CPS (Capcom Play System) arcade system platform, which featured both upgraded FM synthesis and 8-bit sound sample capabilities for both music and sound effects. This allowed for a wider range of possibilities for the composer, especially in terms of tone generation and percussion.

Credits in the home port are sparse once again; a single screen in the game's opening acknowledges the porting team, crediting Tim Follin as 'Musician'. Although Kawamoto's original baroque themes as well as the musician's tone, instrument design, and thematic, ornamentation and composition choices in the original works reside at the core of the

---

[44] MahaloVideoGames, 'Bionic Commando Walkthrough – Credits', video, 7:17, 28 May 2009, www.youtube.com/watch?v=Ak-wbtb62Xc.

[45] MahaloVideoGames, 'Bionic Commando Rearmed 2 End Credits', video, 4:06, 15 February 2011, www.youtube.com/watch?v=3JS3LCrfq5c.

[46] 'Bionic Commando: Master D Fukkatsu Keikaku (The Soundtrack)', VGMdb [Video Game Music Database] (8 August 2009), https://vgmdb.net/album/14901. Accessed 28 April 2020.

soundtrack, a portion of the material is new. Follin took inspiration from the original themes, such as 'Village of Decay' and 'Crystal Forest', to re-imagine the soundtrack for the ported version. Despite the 3-channel limitations of the hardware, in particular, Follin's score for the Commodore 64 platform is widely regarded as a classic of the genre,[47] creating a realistic and atmospheric set of music tracks that morph into an underscore soundscape.

In discussing the three examples of *Commando*, *Bionic Commando* and *Ghouls 'n Ghosts*, it is apparent that the Japanese style of crediting in-game and at the back end of the game is accessible or visible only by completing the game in one play, on a single credit, or by inputting a cheat through a combination of buttons.[48] The original arcade versions only present the logo or name of the production company, Capcom, at the start of the game loading process, with credits often being hidden in high-score tables or in hard-to-access ending screens. By contrast, the Western method employed in all the home-computer ports we have looked at credit the porting team at the start of the game. On loading the game (which can be a lengthy process) the credits are presented on the title screen, or rotated as part of the attract mode of the game in question, making a bold statement regarding their creators. This insight suggests that beyond constraints of data memory and screen space, there are also cultural differences that contribute to the invisibility of the Japanese Capcom Sound Team.

In summary, by applying a game archaeological methodology to the crediting practices of three of Capcom's titles, and in turn excavating their porting processes during the late 1980s and 1990s, we identified a diverse set of crediting practices that had obscured the female members of the Capcom Sound Team. As we have shown, a complex set of industry politics played a role in preventing the attribution of proper credit to the team for their iconic and memorable video game music compositions at the height of their popularity. For example, there is the challenging issue of the use of pseudonyms, and a company crediting policy that anonymizes and hides the identities of its creative staff members. Furthermore, when games are ported, the porting musicians are credited, but not the names of the original composers, partly due to their anonymity, and partly due to

---

[47] High Voltage SID Collection Team, 'HVSC's Top 100 SIDs, As Voted on by SID Fans', *High Voltage SID Collection* (5 July 2000), www.transbyte.org/SID/HVSC_Top100.html. Accessed 28 April 2020.

[48] 'Ghouls 'n Ghosts (Arcade)', *The Cutting Room Floor* (29 September 2019), https://tcrf.net/Ghouls%27n_Ghosts_(Arcade)#Hidden_Credits. Accessed 28 April 2020.

limited game screen and memory space. This is exacerbated by the routine exscription of women in popular video game histories. The idea that the ideal gamer is young and male stems from the action-game era in the arcades, and by extension, as no information is available about the creators, there also seems an unspoken assumption that these games were most likely created by young men.

However, during the last decade, there has been a marked change in the awareness and acknowledgement of the contributions of these Japanese female composers to historical classic game titles and global music culture, due to ongoing endeavours in documentaries, in-depth interviews and databases. Remakes and re-imaginings of video game titles, such as the Bionic Commando: Rearmed series and its remixed soundtrack, have helped to push awareness about the original composers into the public consciousness. However, more research is necessary, as demonstrated by our findings. Although credit is emerging where credit is due outside of the actual video games, this is some thirty years late for the creative and, at times, innovative contributions by the original composers. Our conclusion is therefore not only that game industry histories need revisions that take into account the hidden and marginalized identities of video game creators, but also that there is an urgent need to improve the protection of creators in the game industry, perhaps even a need for the standardization of crediting practices, comparable to that in the film industry. This is especially pertinent for remixed or arranged in-game music, which carries over into the game releases themselves.

PART VI

Beyond the Game

Introduction

MELANIE FRITSCH AND TIM SUMMERS

The significance of video game music does not end when we turn off the console, shut down the PC or leave the arcade. It has an extended life far beyond the boundaries of the game itself. Perhaps the most obvious way that video game music is encountered outside the game is through recordings and performances of game music.

Albums of video game music have been produced since the mid-1980s.[1] Once video games began to include substantial musical material, it was not long before albums started to capture that music. *Video Game Music* (Yen Records, 1984) featured music from Namco games, arranged by Haruomi Hosono, an influential musician and founder member of Yellow Magic Orchestra. Some of the tracks on the album were simply captures of the sonic output of a game round, while others were more elaborate reworkings with additional instruments. Similar records quickly followed. The same year, Hosono also produced a twelve-inch record in the same vein, with music from *Super Xevious, Gaplus* and *The Tower of Druaga*, written by Yuriko Keino and Junko Ozawa, while a full-length album, *The Return of Video Game Music*, arrived in 1985. It would not be long until albums for particular games companies and even specific games began to appear. G.M.O. records specialized in the former, rapidly producing numerous company-specific compilations from 1986 to 1988. A notable example of a game-specific album was the *Dragon Quest* LP (1986, Apollon), one of the

---

[1] Chris Kohler, *Power-Up: How Japanese Video Games Gave the World an Extra Life* (Indianapolis, IN: Bradygames, 2005), 131–64; Melanie Fritsch, *Performing Bytes: Musikperformances der Computerspielkultur* (Würzburg: Königshausen and Neumann, 2018), 236–45; Melanie Fritsch, 'Heroines Unsung: The (Mostly) Untold History of Female Japanese Composers', in *Women's Music for the Screen: Diverse Narratives in Sound*, ed. Felicity Wilcox (New York: Routledge, in press).

first game music albums recorded with orchestral musicians. The album featured three versions of the game's music: an orchestral recording, a version as it sounds in the NES game and a version performed on a higher-quality synthesizer. The tradition of arranging and rearranging video game music into multiple versions was thus embedded into game music recordings from the earliest days of the practice.

Now, soundtrack albums of video game music are commonplace. Furthermore, that tradition of arranging and adapting music into multiple formats has continued: the same game's music might be adapted into any number of different recorded and performed versions. Game music arrangements span orchestral music, jazz, electronic dance music, piano solos, folk traditions and so on. Almost any musical style imaginable has featured some kind of game music adaptation. More so than film music, game music is open to multiple radically different interpretations; rarely does one performed or recorded version of a piece stand as definitive. This is likely because the process of taking game music out of its interactive context necessitates at least some kind of adaptation, even if that is just deciding how many repetitions to include of a looped cue, or whether or not to replicate the timbres of the original game sounds.

Recordings of game music have facilitated radio programmes about game music (BBC Radio 3's *Sound of Gaming*, Classic FM's *High Score*, MPR's *Top Score*), not to mention circulation on YouTube and streaming services, where official releases sit alongside amateur and fan projects. Many of these recordings go hand in hand with live performances. Concerts of game music have been consistently produced since *Dragon Quest*'s music was performed at a special concert in Tokyo on 20 August 1987. Game music concert culture has a complex relationship with classical music culture,[2] and can often be a force for creating a particular problematic canon of 'great' game music. Of course, live performances of game music are by no means the preserve of the classical-style concert. There is a thriving culture of game music cover bands,[3] not to mention the innumerable ensembles and soloists who play game music as part of their repertoire. Often, these performances, whether as part of public concerts or just personal performances, are then documented and uploaded to YouTube where they become part of the broader online culture.

[2] William Gibbons, *Unlimited Replays: Video Games and Classical Music* (New York: Oxford University Press, 2018), 157–71.

[3] See Sebastian Diaz-Gasca, 'Super Smash Covers! Performance and Audience Engagement in Australian Videogame Music Cover Bands', *Perfect Beat* 19, no. 1 (2018): 51–67.

The vast online game music fandom motivates the continual production and reproduction of game music. Nostalgia is an important factor for engaging with game music; players are reminded of the past experiences of playing the games that they share with each other.[4] Yet, it would be erroneous to characterize game music fandom as exclusively an exercise in nostalgia. The participatory culture(s) of game music include remixes, adaptations, mashups and all kinds of musical creativity. These extend into hardware and software experimentations, or the reworking of the game's materials in any number of ways. As in the chiptune scene, discussed earlier in this book (see Chapter 2), players recontextualize and adapt the materials of games to create new meanings and cultural objects themselves.[5]

A neat example is *Mario Paint Composer*, discussed in detail by Dana Plank.[6] This adaptation of *Mario Paint* (1992) is a highly restrictive music sequencer. An online culture has developed in which innovative ways are found to circumvent the limitations of *Mario Paint Composer* to enable it to play pre-existing songs or new compositions. A lively community consists of gamer-musicians sharing techniques, organizing collaborations, critiquing each other's work and providing each other with support and mentorship. As Plank argues, this is not a culture based on nostalgia for the original *Mario Paint*; instead the appeal comes from the social practice and participatory culture founded on the game. While *Mario Paint Composer* is an extreme example, similar dynamics of participatory cultures built on game-musical materials can be seen across game modding and remix cultures.[7] As Karen Collins puts it, game sound is 'an interaction between player and game, between players, and between player and society'.[8]

Aside from fan activities, commercial music endeavours have borrowed audio from games. From 'Pac-Man Fever' (Buckner & Garcia, 1981) to 'Tetris' (Doctor Spin, aka Andrew Lloyd Webber and Nigel Wright, 1992)

---

4 Diaz-Gasca, 'Super Smash Covers.'

5 See Melanie Fritsch, '"It's-a-me, Mario!' Playing with Video Game Music', in *Ludomusicology: Approaches to Video Game Music*, ed. Michiel Kamp, Tim Summers and Mark Sweeney (Sheffield: Equinox, 2016), 92–115, and, more extensively, Fritsch, *Performing Bytes*, 222–93.

6 Dana Plank, 'Mario Paint Composer and Musical (Re)Play on YouTube', in *Music Video Games: Performance, Politics, and Play*, ed. Michael Austin (New York: Bloomsbury, 2016), 43–82.

7 Jared O'Leary and Evan Tobias, 'Sonic Participatory Cultures Within, Through, and Around Video Games', in *The Oxford Handbook of Music Making and Leisure*, ed. Roger Mantie and Gareth Dylan Smith (New York: Oxford University Press, 2017), 543–66; Kyle Stedman, 'Remix Literacy and Fan Compositions', *Computers and Composition* 29, no. 2 (2012): 107–23.

8 Karen Collins, *Playing With Sound: A Theory of Interacting with Sound and Music in Video Games* (Cambridge, MA: The MIT Press, 2013), 123.

and 'Super Mario Land' (Ambassadors of Funk, 1992), there is no shortage of novelty records based on games. More subtle integrations of game music into popular music include Charli XCX's adaptation of the *Super Mario Bros.* coin sound in 'Boys', Drake using music from *Sonic the Hedgehog* (2006) on 'KMT', Kanye West's sampling of *Street Fighter II* on 'Facts', Wiz Khalifa's *Chrono Trigger* samples on 'Never Been' and Burial's use of *Metal Gear Solid 2* on 'Archangel'. Some musicians do not sample game music directly, but their work is nonetheless influenced by game music, such as jazz pianist Dominic J. Marshall's 'Deku Tree' on his album *The Triolithic*. These examples indicate the extent to which game music has permeated modern musical consciousness. Games have also provided many opportunities for the presentation and promotion of pop music and artists. These include tie-in games like *Journey Escape* (1982) and *The Thompson Twins Adventure* (1984), app albums like Björk's *Biophilia* (2011),[9] or even the playlists for yearly editions of sports games.[10]

Classical music, too, has been integrated into games in a substantial way, both in the service of fun, and as part of an educational agenda. *Eternal Sonata* (2007) features Frédéric Chopin as the main playable character, and the plot of *Gabriel Knight 2: The Beast Within* (1995) focuses on the lives of Richard Wagner and his patron Ludwig II.[11] We have already mentioned the integration of classical music into games elsewhere in this volume, but it is worth reiterating that this is another way in which games and broader culture (musical and otherwise) intersect.

In more formal educational settings, games have been integrated into classroom teaching,[12] and video games have been used as a pedagogical

---

[9] See Samantha Blickhan, '"Listening" Through Digital interaction in Björk's Biophilia', in *Ludomusicology: Approaches to Video Game Music*, ed. Michiel Kamp, Tim Summers and Mark Sweneey (Sheffield: Equinox, 2016), 133–51.

[10] See Holly Tessler, 'The New MTV? Electronic Arts and "Playing" Music', in *From Pac-Man to Pop Music: Interactive Audio in Games and New Media*, ed. Karen Collins (Aldershot: Ashgate, 2008), 13–26 and Antti-Ville Kärja, 'Marketing Music Through Computer Games: The Case of Poets of the Fall and Max Payne 2', in *From Pac-Man to Pop Music*, ed. Karen Collins (Aldershot: Ashgate, 2008), 27–44.

[11] On Chopin and *Eternal Sonata*, see Gibbons, *Unlimited Replays*, 126–40.

[12] Gianna Cassidy and Anna Paisley, 'Music-Games: A Case Study of Their Impact', *Research Studies in Music Education* 35, no. 1 (2013): 119–38; Jen Jenson, Suzanne De Castell, Rachel Muehrer and Milena Droumeva, 'So You Think You Can Play: An Exploratory Study of Music Video Games', *Journal of Music, Technology and Education* 9, no. 3 (2016), 273–88; David Roesner, Anna Paisley and Gianna Cassidy, 'Guitar Heroes in the Classroom: The Creative Potential of Music Games', in *Music Video Games: Performance, Politics and Play*, ed. Michael Austin (New York: Bloomsbury, 2016), 197–228; Andrew Lesser, 'An Investigation of Digital Game-Based Learning Software in the Elementary General Music Classroom', *Journal of Sound and Music in Games* 1, no. 2 (2020), 1–24.

model for teaching music.[13] Video game music is now mentioned on syllabi for national music qualifications in the UK, and game music is included in some Japanese schoolbooks, which use them to teach musical skills through performance. Once again, these examples testify that game music is not a sealed subgenre of music, but bound up with other areas of musical activity.

This mobility of game music is also clearly evident when game music moves across media, being used in advertisements, TV shows or films. Films based on games may replicate and adapt music from games. For instance, the *Silent Hill* (2006) film soundtrack is closely modelled on the game's score.[14] Media that draws on geek culture more generally may also feature game music (as in the use of music from Zelda games in *Scott Pilgrim vs. the World* (2010) or the *Super Mario Bros.* theme in an episode of *The Big Bang Theory*).[15] Games are part of multimedia franchises, and draw on, and contribute to, these networks. In the case of the game *Star Trek: Klingon* (1996), not only did the game share a musical style (and composer) with the series, but a song introduced into the fictional world in the game was later reprised in the television series. These examples all emphasize that music is part of the fabric that binds together media networks.

Ultimately, to consider game music only within the bounds of the game text is to only see part of the story. Similarly, to limit our understanding of games and music to compositions written for games is to underestimate the ways in which games can shape our musical engagements and understandings more generally. Instead, by recognizing the ways that games draw on, contribute to, enable and reconfigure musical activities and meanings, we can better appreciate the significance of video games as a musical medium.

Further Reading

Collins, Karen. *Playing With Sound: A Theory of Interacting with Sound and Music in Games*. Cambridge, MA: The MIT Press, 2013.

---

[13] Meghan Naxer, 'A Hidden Harmony: Music Theory Pedagogy and Role-Playing Games', in *Music in the Role-Playing Game: Heroes and Harmonies*, ed. William Gibbons and Steven Reale (New York: Routledge, 2020), 146–58.

[14] On *Silent Hill* games and films, see K. J. Donnelly, 'Emotional Sound Effects and Metal Machine Music: Soundworlds in Silent Hill Games and Films', in *The Palgrave Handbook of Sound Design and Music in Screen Media*, ed. Liz Greene and Danijela Kulezic-Wilson (London: Palgrave, 2016), 73–88 and Florian Mundhenke, 'Resourceful Frames and Sensory Functions – Musical Transformations from Game to Film in *Silent Hill*', in *Music and Game: Perspectives on a Popular Alliance*, ed. Peter Moormann (Wiesbaden: Springer, 2013), 107–24.

[15] *The Big Bang Theory*, 'The Launch Acceleration', Series 5 Episode 23 (2012).

Diaz-Gasca, Sebastian. 'Super Smash Covers! Performance and Audience Engagement in Australian Videogame Music Cover Bands.' *Perfect Beat* 19, no. 1 (2018): 51–67.

Fritsch, Melanie. "It's a-me, Mario!' Playing with Video Game Music', in *Ludomusicology: Approaches to Video Game Music*, ed. Michiel Kamp, Tim Summers and Mark Sweeney. Sheffield: Equinox, 2016, 92–115.

O'Leary, Jared and Tobias, Evan. 'Sonic Participatory Cultures Within, Through, and Around Video Games', in *The Oxford Handbook of Music Making and Leisure*, ed. Roger Mantie and Gareth Dylan Smith. New York: Oxford University Press, 2016, 543–66.

Plank, Dana. 'Mario Paint Composer and Musical (Re)Play on YouTube', in *Music Video Games: Performance, Politics, and Play*, ed. Michael Austin. New York: Bloomsbury, 2016, 43–82.

Tessler, Holly. 'The New MTV? Electronic Arts and 'Playing Music', in *From Pac-Man to Pop Music: Interactive Audio in Games and New Media*, ed. Karen Collins. Aldershot: Ashgate, 2008, 13–26.

22 | Pop Music, Economics and Marketing

ANDRA IVĂNESCU

Introduction

Nearly two decades into the twenty-first century, it has become a cliché to emphasize the economic power of the video games industry. The phrase 'Video games are big business', or some variation thereof, has been a staple of writing on the topic for decades, with early iterations lauding the commercial successes of arcades,[1] later iterations citing it as motivation for the academic study of games[2] and more recent versions citing the staggering billions in income they have generated, which has formed the basis of several transnational empires.[3]

At the same time, over the past thirty years many have lamented the multiple shifts the music industry has undergone as a series of demises. The music industry has now 'died' many times over. Sinnreich metaphorically describes this as 'a kind of industrial murder', itself 'constructed and promoted aggressively by the music industry itself', which has fingered 'nearly everyone for the blame, from digital music startups to major companies like Google and Apple to the hundreds of millions of people who use their products. P2P file sharing even plays the role of the butler, as the inevitable primary suspect.'[4] Within this particular narrative, in which the games industry thrives while the music industry is being killed, a favourite exaggeration of the media, and to a certain degree of the games industry itself, the two industries are compared, on the basis of an argument that the games industry has surpassed the music industry and the film industry combined.[5] This narrative is not new, and

---

[1] Edward H. Ziegler, Jr., 'Regulating Videogames: Mixed Results in the Courts', *Land Use Law and Zoning Digest* 34, no. 4 (1982): 4–8.

[2] James Newman, *Videogames* (London: Routledge, 2004), 3.

[3] Holly Tessler, 'The New MTV? Electronic Arts and "Playing" Music', in *From Pac-Man to Pop Music: Interactive Audio in Games and New Media*, ed. Karen Collins (Aldershot: Ashgate, 2008), 13–26 at 14.

[4] Aram Sinnreich, *The Piracy Crusade* (Boston, MA: University of Massachusetts Press, 2013), 69

[5] For example, Jeff Parsons, 'Video Games Are Now Bigger than Music and Movies Combined', *Metro Online* (3 January 2019), accessed 10 April 2020, https://metro.co.uk/2019/01/03/video-games-now-popular-music-movies-combined-8304980/?ito=cbshare.

neither are the types of figures it quotes. As Kline, Dyer-Witheford and de Peuter note, the early 1980s already saw the arcade game industry 'grossing eight billion dollars', when 'pop music had international sales of four billion, and Hollywood brought in three billion' and 'revenue from the game Pac-Man alone probably exceeded the box-office success of Star Wars'.[6]

The comparison is problematic on a number of levels, not only since secondary and tertiary markets for film and music are usually not accounted for in this particular calculation, but also, more importantly, as the comparison does not take into account the affinities between cultural industries, and it becomes particularly ineffectual when trying to understand the commercial machinations of a neoliberal world in which the transmedia empire rules supreme. As Kärjä noted over a decade ago, 'there is no reason to forsake conglomeration, as the mutual cross-promotion of music and audio-visual media is a long-lived convention by now'.[7] Even when looking beyond the varieties of integration (vertical, horizontal, lateral) that are central to these empires, the connections between these industries are more important than ever before. In her seminal 2008 book *Game Sound*, Karen Collins argued that 'there is a growing symbiotic relationship between the music industry and the games industry', adding that 'commonly, games are being used to promote and sell music, and recording artists are being used to sell games'.[8] This symbiotic relationship has grown and evolved since 2008, but while there are potentially endless variations on this basic relationship, there are few instances in which pop music, video games and economics meet that do not fall within this basic description. What is important to note is that even when they exist as separate entities (which is itself increasingly rare), cultural industries do not *operate* separately, as this chapter will continue to demonstrate by looking at the complex relationships between popular music and video games.

Popular Music in Video Games

Popular music permeates the history of digital games in many forms, from the stylistic allusions and even covers of songs found in video game scores

---

[6] Stephen Kline, Nick Dyer-Witheford and Grieg de Peuter, *Digital Play: The Interaction of Technology, Culture, and Marketing* (Montreal: McGill-Queen's University Press, 2003), 104.

[7] Antti-Ville Kärja, 'Marketing Music Through Computer Games: The Case of Poets of the Fall and Max Payne 2', in *From Pac-Man to Pop Music*, ed. Karen Collins (Aldershot: Ashgate, 2008), 27–44 at 29.

[8] Karen Collins, *Game Sound: An Introduction to the History, Theory and Practice of Video Game Music and Sound Design* (Cambridge, MA: The MIT Press, 2008), 111.

from earlier days, to the direct use of popular music recordings made possible by the evolution of gaming technologies. As Collins notes, because of the nature of music in games at the time (it existed primarily as code rather than samples), there was 'little understanding of copyright law', resulting in 'significant borrowing of music without copyright clearance'.[9] This would soon change, and the use of recorded popular music in video games would intensify significantly in the twenty-first century. Although there are significant precursors here, and numerous other developers which are important in their own way, the three developers that have defined this relationship as we know it are EA Sports, Harmonix and Rockstar.

Sports games played an instrumental role in demonstrating the aesthetic and commercial role that popular music can play in digital games. One of the earliest sports games to which popular music was integral was Psygnosis's futuristic racing game *Wipeout* (1995), which featured both an original soundtrack by Tim Wright and a number of tracks from popular electronica artists of the time including Leftfield, The Chemical Brothers and Orbital. Music was a significant part of the marketing of the game, and a *Wipeout: The Music* LP was released on CD and vinyl. Cross-promotion also entailed distributing the soundtrack to *Wipeout XL* to dance clubs in London and New York.[10] It is also important to note that *Wipeout* was also a release title for the PlayStation in the UK, which emphasizes not only how pre-recorded music was part of the demonstrative aspect of the technology in play, but also the link between game music and UK club culture in the 1990s.[11]

EA Sports have taken this to a higher level in the twenty-first century, with now Worldwide Executive and President of EA Music Group Steve Schnur in the role of the evangelist. Tessler draws on a talk from Schnur when examining the now-almost-quaint premise that video games are 'the new MTV'; she argues that 'video games are new cultural and industrial intermediaries, forging new customer-motivated and consumer-driven business partnerships', and that, like the music video, video games have had a considerable impact on 'the vertical integration of the music

---

[9] Collins, *Game Sound*, 115.

[10] Ibid.

[11] This was not the first, nor would it be the last time that music games, or games in which music played a significant role, were launched and/or marketed in relation to club culture. The handheld game *Simon* was launched at Studio 54, while Rockstar sponsored nights at nightclubs at the beginning of the twenty-first century. See William Knoblauch, 'SIMON: The Prelude to Modern Music Video Games', in *Music Video Games*, ed. Michael Austin (New York: Bloomsbury, 2016), 25–42 at 5 and Kline, Dyer-Witheford and de Peuter, *Digital Play*, 235.

industry'.[12] As Summers contends, these games both take advantage of pre-existing musical associations and forge new ones, even to the point of influencing musical performances at real-life sports competitions.[13] While the MTV comparison may today seem somewhat outdated, and Schnur's claims are at times exaggerated, it remains clear that the impact of video games, and particularly EA Sports, on the music industry is not to be underestimated; it functions in particular as a gatekeeper and marketing machine, whereby players get exposed to new, carefully curated playlists every year, over and over throughout tens of hours of gameplay, which leads directly to purchases, and even to the launch of now-well-known indie artists.[14]

Music games – particularly rhythm-action games – were naturally also significant in terms of the development of commercial relationships between video game developers and the music industry. Harmonix are perhaps the most successful developer of pop-based rhythm-action games, most notably with franchises like Guitar Hero (2005–2015), Rock Band (2007–2017) and Dance Central (2010–2019). *Guitar Hero* was originally designed by Harmonix in partnership with RedOctane, who developed accessories such as dance pads and special joysticks for games, but when Harmonix was acquired by MTV Games and RedOctane by Activision (which would become Activision Blizzard following a significant merger in 2008), *Guitar Hero* became an Activision product and was developed by Neversoft. Meanwhile, Harmonix started developing a direct competitor, *Rock Band* (which would later be published by Microsoft Studios and then by Oculus, themselves owned by Facebook). Competing publishers also led to competition in terms of the acquisition of rights for the different music available in the subsequent games. Successful rights acquisitions were celebrated and special editions were released, while additional songs were purchased in droves, urging comparisons to the much older industry of mass-produced sheet music.[15] For the most part this was a mutually beneficial relationship, although it did, at times, create conflicts and dissatisfaction. An interesting moment was the *Death Magnetic* controversy, whereby the aforementioned Metallica

---

[12] Tessler, 'The New MTV?', 14.

[13] Tim Summers, *Understanding Video Game Music* (Cambridge, UK: Cambridge University Press, 2016), 112–13.

[14] Tessler, 'The New MTV?', 15.

[15] Kiri Miller, *Playing Along: Digital Games, YouTube, and Virtual Performance* (New York: Oxford University Press, 2012), 89. Interestingly, *Guitar Hero*-branded sheet music was also produced (Summers, *Understanding Video Game Music*, 183).

album was mastered differently (and in the view of many, significantly better) on the *Guitar Hero 3* version than the album version released on the same day. The album was considered to be a victim of the music industry 'loudness wars' and was affected by serious dynamic range compression, an issue which was simply avoided in the video game version, which did not suffer the same clipping issues.[16]

Beyond relatively small issues such as this, the success of these franchises created clear tensions between the games industry and the music industry. These were evident in the exchange between Edgar Bronfman, chief executive of Warner Music, and Robert Kotick, chief executive of Activision Blizzard, whereby the former was dissatisfied with the amount of royalties paid to record companies,[17] while the latter argued that the commercial advantages of having your music featured in such games far outweighed the disadvantages.[18] Statistics did support Kotick's assertion, particularly in terms of exposure to new music and short-term sales, with Universal Music Group COO Zach Horowitz claiming that sales for songs included in games had spiked by up to 1000 per cent.[19] Such convincing figures were quite commonly quoted at the time, with an Electric Artists white paper claiming that 40 per cent of hard-core gamers will buy music after hearing it in a game and that 73 per cent of gamers believe that game soundtracks help sell music.[20] This moment was telling, in terms of both the popularity of the genre and of the industrial tensions created by the rise of the video game industry more broadly. While the genre reached its peak around the mid- to late-2000s, some rhythm games continue to thrive, like the mobile hit *Beat Fever* (2017), *NEXT Music* (2018), which provides people with a link to Spotify to stream a song after it has been successfully played in the app, or the virtual reality (VR) game *Beat Saber* (2019), a launch title for the Oculus Quest system, available on multiple VR platforms, which was not

---

[16] Eric Smialek, 'The Unforgiven: A Reception Study of Metallica Fans and "Sell-Out" Accusations', in *Global Metal Music and Culture: Current Directions in Metal Studies*, ed. Andy Brown, Karl Spracklen, Keith Kahn-Harris and Niall Scott (New York: Routledge, 2016), 106–24.

[17] Eliot van Buskirk, 'Warner Threatens to Pull Music from Guitar Hero, Rock Band', *Wired* (8 August 2008), accessed 10 April 2020, www.wired.com/2008/08/warner-threaten/.

[18] Matthew Garrahan and Chrystia Freeland, 'Warner Chief Slammed in "Guitar Hero" Row', *Financial Times* (14 August 2008), accessed 10 April 2020, www.ft.com/content/cb6e2106-6a23-11dd-83e8-0000779fd18c.

[19] Marc Graser, 'Videogames Rock Song Sales', *Variety* (21 August 2009), accessed 10 April 2020, https://variety.com/2009/digital/news/videogames-rock-song-sales-1118007573/.

[20] Quoted after Collins, *Game Sound*, 116.

only perhaps the most familiar rhythm game of the 2010s, but also one of the few commercially successful VR titles.[21]

The third developer that has arguably defined the relationship between pop music and video games is British giant Rockstar. As Kline, Dyer-Witheford and de Peuter note, 'marketing synergies are at the centre of Rockstar's business strategy'.[22] While many of Rockstar's games include popular music, its flagship franchise Grand Theft Auto (or GTA: 1997–2013) is the most significant here. The first of the games to include a significant amount of popular music was the nostalgia-laden *Grand Theft Auto: Vice City* (2002), closely followed by *Grand Theft Auto: San Andreas* (2004). These followed up on the critical and commercial success of *Grand Theft Auto III* (2001) and built their innovative sandbox worlds on an arguably satirical vision of the United States, reaching record sales which would only increase with subsequent instalments; the latest game in the series, *Grand Theft Auto V* (2013) broke seven Guinness World Records, reflecting its popularity and commercial success.[23] Miller emphasizes that the figures associated with the sales of these games are significant as they are 'less casual purchases' as a result of their cost; their high price is justified by the 'buyer's expectation of spending something like a hundred hours in the gameworld'.[24] The music of *Vice City* and *San Andreas* was featured prominently on radio stations in the games and became an integral part of the *GTA* experience. As Miller argues in her seminal ethnographic and ethnomusicological study of *San Andreas*, 'the only direct product place-ment in the games is the music on the radio, a design choice that creates a powerful musical connection between the gameworlds and the real world'.[25] Importantly, some of these musical imports are advertised in the game's instruction booklet, including a two-page spread for Capitol Records.[26] The 'soundtracks' to these games have also been released sepa-rately, to further commercial success. Miller discusses the attention devoted to the radio station system by the developers and argues that 'their playlists have instructional force, teaching millions of players how to recognize and value certain artists, songs, and musical characteristics

---

[21] Lucas Matney, 'How Beat Saber Beat the Odds', *TechCrunch* (8 May 2019), accessed 10 April 2020, https://techcrunch.com/2019/05/08/how-beat-saber-beat-the-odds/.

[22] Kline, Dyer-Witheford and de Peuter, *Digital Play*, 234.

[23] Jenna Pitcher, 'Grand Theft Auto 5 Smashes 7 Guinness World Records', *Polygon* (9 October 2013) accessed 10 April 2020, www.polygon.com/2013/10/9/4819272/grand-theft-auto-5-smashes-7-guinness-world-records.

[24] Miller, *Playing Along*, 24.

[25] Miller, *Playing Along*, 55.

[26] Miller, *Playing Along*, 74.

within a given genre'.[27] While both *Grand Theft Auto IV* and *Grand Theft Auto V* built on these experiences and expanded their playlists significantly, it was *Vice City* and *San Andreas* that paved the way for nostalgic radio stations in numerous franchises to come, including BioShock (2007–2013) and Mafia, particularly *Mafia III* (2016).

Video Games and Popular Musicians

Collins describes musician-themed games as one of the three types of games in which music is 'the primary driving motive', alongside the already-discussed category of rhythm-action games and the more loosely defined category of 'creative games', which rarely involve popular music directly.[28] Here, Collins cites a number of arcade games which are musician-themed, including Journey's *Journey Escape* (1982), Aerosmith's *Revolution X* (1994), Wu-Tang Clan's *Wu-Tang: Shaolin Style* (1999), and perhaps the best known example, *Michael Jackson's Moonwalker* (1990). More recent iterations of the genre include *50 Cent: Bulletproof* (2005) and *50 Cent: Blood on the Sand* (2009), as well as the metal parody *Brütal Legend* (2009), which features Jack Black as the protagonist Eddie Riggs,[29] as well as including a number of guest appearances from rock stars such as Ozzy Osbourne. Collins argues that 'the music is a peripheral or secondary aspect of these types of games, with the attention instead on the marketing power of celebrities'.[30] While the musician-themed game was arguably never a popular genre (although individual games may have been), popular musicians have been involved in the creation of video games, their sound and their music in a number of ways.

On the one hand, popular musicians have been involved in the creation of video game music itself. According to Collins, this occurred more frequently 'after the development of Red Book (CD) audio games machines in the mid 1990s', but notes that Brian May's work for *Rise of the Robots* (1994) is a notable early example of this.[31] Trent Reznor's involvement in the sound of *Quake* (1996) and subsequent soundtracks for id Software games is also a significant example. Credited as Trent Reznor and Nine Inch Nails, the well-known rock star created the sound of *Quake*, including

---

[27] Miller, *Playing Along*, 55–9.

[28] Collins, *Game Sound*, 36.

[29] Although Jack Black does not play himself in this game, the musical theming of the game and Black's identifiable voice and performances allow this to sit comfortably within the subgenre.

[30] Collins, *Game Sound*, 112.

[31] Collins, *Game Sound*, 8.

the music and the sound effects, contributing to the unique atmosphere of the game, which built on its predecessors (most notably *Doom*, 1993) to kick-start the FPS (first-person-shooter) genre. Reznor was certainly neither the first nor the last popular musician to be involved in the production of video game sound, and was followed by many others, whose contributions ranged from full soundtrack development, to rere-cording existing tracks in Simlish (the fictional language of the EA sub-sidiary Maxis franchise The Sims), to the performance of a single track for the game. Notable artists here include Paul McCartney, Metallica, Skrillex, Amon Tobin and Leona Lewis. Some even lent their likenesses to char-acters in the games; for instance, Phil Collins appears as himself (complete with concert) in *Grand Theft Auto: Vice City Stories* (2006), while David Bowie's contribution to *Omikron: The Last Nomad* (1999) included both playing an important character and contributing significantly to the sound-track of this somewhat eccentric sci-fi production. Musicians lend their image to the outside promotion of these games as well; for instance Jay Kay, lead singer of Jamiroquai, linked his 2005 tour to the *Need for Speed: Most Wanted* (2005) launch and the *Need for Speed* franchise more broadly, including special EA-sponsored competitions.[32]

Video games have also provided numerous avenues for musicians to launch or further their careers. Kärjä examines the case of the band Poets of the Fall, and their 2005 rise to fame due to the game *Max Payne 2: The Fall of Max Payne* (2003). The Poets of the Fall track 'Late Goodbye' appears on the end credits of *Max Payne 2*, which led it to become a surprise hit; its success was all the more surprising considering the band did not have a record label behind them and had played very few gigs at the time. In other words, their success operated in parallel to traditional music industry systems and marketing strategies. Similarly, Jonathan Coulton, who wrote the famous 'Still Alive' song which appeared on the end credits of *Portal* (2007), releases his songs outside of traditional publishing contracts and under a creative commons licence, focusing on alternative revenue streams. Both Poets of the Fall and Jonathan Coulton are exceptions here, of course, and the majority of songs promoted through video games are part of larger industrial synergies. For instance, while EA Sports franchises are well known for 'breaking' new talent, only 25 per cent of the songs on the soundtrack of *FIFA 2005* (2004), for instance, were from independent record labels;[33] this was enough to maintain an edge without posing a financial risk.

---

[32] Kärja, 'Marketing Music Through Computer Games', 33.
[33] Tessler, '"The New MTV?"', 15.

Video games also provide varieties of cultural capital to musicians beyond the games themselves. Video games have been the subject of numerous pop songs and, at times, entire albums, with artists both inspired by the new art form and capitalizing on its popularity. The novelty niche has been a significant part of the genre, with early examples such as Buckner & Garcia's *Pac-Man Fever* album (1982) including songs dedicated to the eponymous game, as well as to games like *Frogger, Donkey Kong* and *Centipede*. At the same time, video games have provided inspiration for innovative artists, ranging from electronic music pioneers Yellow Magic Orchestra, to the entire genre of chiptune.

Synergy and Transmedia Storytelling

Beyond these evident cross-fertilizations, whereby the two industries act symbiotically (as do arguably all cultural industries), there are areas of consumption which both lie outside of what is traditionally thought of as the fields of games and music, and yet are inextricably linked to both. Synergy becomes essential here. As Kline, Dyer-Witheford and de Peuter note, synergy is 'about the intensification of growth and expansion through integration across the many spheres of production, technology, taste culture, and promotion'.[34] Trailers and other promotional materials for games fall into this loosely defined category and act as synergistic nodes, often connecting different media.

Modern video game trailers operate in ways that are both similar to and distinct from film trailers, lying, as Švelch argues, 'between the ludic and the cinematic'.[35] Kline, Dyer-Witheford and de Peuter argue that 'because the television screen displays both video game play and advertisements about such play, the game and the image of the game fuse'.[36] While a certain genre of video game trailer shares formal qualities with film trailers, specifically those which present fully CGI-animated or live-action content, as well as promotional intent, focusing on the promotion of a full game (either upcoming or newly released), many others diverge from this model. Švelch developed two typologies of video game trailers, which centre on either their formal qualities, or the relationship between the games themselves and these paratextual materials; both are helpful in terms of understanding what differentiates video game trailers from trailers for other media, particularly film, and the roles that popular music plays in these aspects of game

---

[34] Kline, Dyer-Witheford and de Peuter, *Digital Play*, 225.
[35] Jan Švelch, 'Towards a Typology of Video Game Trailers: Between the Ludic and the Cinematic', *GAME: Italian Journal of Game Studies* 4 (2015): 17–21 at 17.
[36] Kline, Dyer-Witheford and de Peuter, *Digital Play*, 225.

marketing. Specifically, as games tend to simply have more trailers than other media, because of their longer development cycles and the necessity to create and maintain interest, that game trailers can also differ from them in terms of content (focusing on gameplay footage, pre-rendered animation, or live-action footage); in the fact that they do not necessarily promote a full game (but may promote certain aspects of it); and in that the relationship of these paratexts to the games themselves may focus on either the performance of play, cross-promotion and/or transmedia storytelling,[37] or replicating the interactivity of the medium.[38] The role of popular music in video game trailers reflects these varying criteria.

Performance trailers will often use popular music that aims to promote a particular experience. In the case of games that use a significant amount of licensed music, their trailers will reflect this. For instance, trailers for sports video games will often feature popular music prominently, often cross-promoting relatively new or popular artists. Music games, specifically rhythm games, will often feature not only the popular music featured in the games, but often the popstars themselves, or even animated versions of them, as is the case of *The Beatles: Rock Band* (2009), which fully capitalizes on the rights obtained. Transmedia trailers, on the other hand, will use popular music, or often covers of popular music, to, as Švelch describes, expand 'the fictional world of a video game beyond the boundaries of a video game as a medium'.[39] Some trailers interestingly bridge the two categories, focusing on identification and presenting a 'projected identity'[40] whereby escapism is at the forefront and the player/character distinction is blurred. Thompson has noted this phenomenon in *League of Legends* promotional music videos,[41] but it is a widespread strategy prominent amongst a number of game genres. With sports games, for instance, it is common that a trailer will initially feature players in their homes enjoying a game, only for them to suddenly break the fourth wall and become the professional athletes portrayed.[42] Music is important throughout these

---

[37] Henry Jenkins, *Convergence Culture: Where Old and New Media Collide* (New York: New York University Press, 2006).

[38] Švelch, 'Towards a Typology of Video Game Trailers.'

[39] Švelch, 'Towards a Typology of Video Game Trailers', 20.

[40] James Paul Gee, *What Video Games Have to Teach Us About Learning and Literacy* (New York: Palgrave Macmillan, 2003).

[41] Ryan Thompson, 'Putting the "E" in ESports: Analyzing Music Videos from League of Legends', paper presented at NACVGM 2019, University of Hartford, Connecticut, 30–31 March 2019.

[42] The FIFA 19 *Champions Rise* launch trailer makes this explicit as we see game players helpfully espouse their feelings of identification through phrases like: 'They all wanna meet [Brazilian professional footballer] Neymar, but me, I *am* Neymar.'

types of trailers, as becomes particularly evident in a number of live-action trailers for the Call of Duty franchise, where a classic rock soundtrack is as integral to the power fantasy sold as celebrity cameos and slow-motion explosions.

The use of popular music in video game trailers becomes particularly synergetic not only when developers and music labels are part of a larger corporation (as is the case with many Sony franchises), and when third-party content creation focuses on both games and music (as is the case with MTV games), but also when music labels develop related games or, as happens more often, video game developers delve into music production. As Collins noted, 'some games companies are becoming full multi-media conglomerates, and are aligning themselves with particular social groups and taste cultures, which are themselves often developed around genres of music'.[43] There are earlier examples of this, like Sega's Twitch Records,[44] or Nintendo's live performances as part of their Fusion Tour,[45] but more contemporary instances takes this further, as is the case with *League of Legends* (2009).

On 3 November 2018, millions of viewers tuned in to watch the Opening Ceremony of the League of Legends 2018 World Championship, the largest e-sports event of the year, and, according to some sources, the e-sports event with the largest viewership of all time. Like many sporting events of this scale, the ceremony started with a musical performance, and the artists who walked on stage were both brand new and very familiar to fans of this successful MOBA (multiplayer online battle arena). The band were K/DA, a virtual band composed of Ahri, Akali, Evelynn and Kai'sa, four *League of Legends* (*LoL*) champions. These characters, created by Riot Games, were voiced by Miyeon and Soyeon (of K-pop group (G)I-dle), Madison Beer and Jaira Burns, respectively. The accompanying video was released on the same day, and garnered a large number of views – 104 million over its first 30 days,[46] and at the time of writing it stands at over 270 million. Furthermore, the song debuted at no. 1 in the digital pop charts, and also ranked #1 on Google Play Top Songs and #1 on the iTunes K-pop charts. Overall, the song, its accompanying AR (augmented reality) performance at the World Championships, and its accompanying animated music video, have been Riot Games's most successful foray into popular music, also earning the company a Shorty Award – 'Honoring the Best of Social Media'

---

[43] Collins, *Game Sound*, 117.
[44] Tessler, 'The New MTV?', 21.
[45] Tessler, 'The New MTV?', 18.
[46] Shorty Awards 2019, accessed 10 April 2020, https://shortyawards.com/11th/kda-popstars.

for 'Best in Games' in 2019, but music – and pop music in particular – plays a central role in the developer's business strategy.

As Consalvo and North note, *LoL*, Riot Games's only title for the first decade of its existence, is 'possibly one of the most influential titles in normalizing the free-to-play game model for core gamers and the games media'.[47] Essential to the game's commercial success is its permanent free status, and its monetization through micro-transactions, largely in the form of new champions (playable characters) and new skins for existing champions (aesthetic changes to champions). While Riot Games produce and release a significant amount of music, including music from the games themselves, and additional material by their bands, their music videos (or those videos explicitly marketed as music videos) fall into one of two categories: promotional videos for upcoming e-sports championships, or promotional videos for new champions and skins, both of which act as trailers for either events or new in-game content.

K/DA's big moment in November 2018 thus encapsulates a myriad of relationships between video games and popular music and acted as a complex promotional machine. As Kline, Dyer-Witheford and de Peuter argue: 'The synergistic marketing of interactive games involves the coordination of promotional messages to saturate diverse cultural niches, a heightened emphasis on the binding of game design and advertising, and the weaving of a branded network of cultural products, practices, and signs to create multiple entry points for consumer-players, hence multiple revenue streams for game corporations.'[48] Following K/DA's 'Pop/Stars' music video and performance release, the K/DA Official Skins Trailer was also released, illustrating the aesthetic qualities of the K/DA 'members' in-game, including how elements of the choreography are incorporated. In December 2018, VR developer Oculus released a video on YouTube featuring Madison Beer (one of the performers of the song) playing the *Beat Saber* version of 'Pop/Stars' on Oculus Rift. As one of the most popular rhythm games of the past decade, this introduced a new level of monetization to the song, and a new connection to traditional music video games.

Overall, the song, its videos and its uses both typify and complicate the traditional relationships between pop music and video games on a number of levels. Riot Games has released music which has been distributed through the largest channels for distributing music currently available – YouTube,

[47] Christopher A. Paul and Mia Consalvo, *Real Games: What's Legitimate and What's Not in Contemporary Videogames* (Cambridge, MA: MIT Press, 2019), 101.

[48] Kline, Dyer-Witheford and de Peuter, *Digital Play*, 225–6.

the biggest platform for streaming music in the world, but also Spotify, Apple Music and so on – as part of large marketing campaigns promoting new content for its free-to-play game, music also made available as part of new iterations of traditional rhythm games like *Beat Saber*, where it is also used to illustrate and promote new VR technologies. These commercial endeavours are only made more complex by their ephemerality, in that Riot Games rarely use one of their manufactured bands as part of long-term marketing,[49] but also by the fact that Riot themselves are owned by Chinese giant Tencent – the most profitable video game (and arguably media) conglomerate in the world. The commercial and political implications of this and other transnational conglomerates for the industries under question are yet to be fully explored.

Conclusions

The cultural field of video games extends far beyond games themselves, into a wider network of paratextual and intertextual machinations: some directly related to the marketing and sale of video games and acting as an integral part of the industry, some operating at the margins; both inextricably linked to the industry, depending on it and existing outside of it.

While this chapter has primarily focused on triple-A games (although some of the developers included can be considered independent, particularly in terms of their relationships with outside publishers), the relationship between popular music and video games changes somewhat beyond these limited borders. At the same time, alternative revenue streams, including video game music covers, remixes and mashups, make their way into the mainstream through popular platforms like YouTube, while samples and tracks of video game music, as well as video game hardware, are commonly used in music production. While not many of these avenues are commercially relevant, particularly when compared to the commercial impact of other video game YouTubers, Twitch streamers and e-sports stars, they demonstrate how these relationships pervade cultures. As Kline, Dyer-Witheford and de Peuter note, 'The basic logic in synergies is that, just like a high-quality interactive gaming experience, one path always spawns ten more.'[50] More research into the commercial and economic impact of these platforms in relation to music would benefit our understanding of these synergies or their potential subversion.

---

[49] Although K/DA themselves would be the focus of a significant comeback in 2020 in the form of new singles, an EP, and considerable additional marketing material.

[50] Kline, Dyer-Witheford and de Peuter, *Digital Play*, 226.

Dyer-Witheford and de Peuter argue that video games are 'a paradigmatic media of Empire – planetary, militarized hypercapitalism, and of some of the forces presently challenging it'.[51] The economics and marketing of popular music and video games operate as integral parts of transnational capitalist machines, hypercapitalism at its best and worst. At the same time, as Miller warns, 'while it would be a mistake to ignore the role of commercial forces in structuring the practices described ..., it would be equally myopic to dismiss ordinary players' practices as nothing but compliant consumption'.[52] Indeed, Svec focuses explicitly on how the musical properties of games – the 'grim realities of cultural production under capitalism' re-enacted in *Guitar Hero*, and the 'simulation of machinic virtuosity' in *Rez* – can offer '"lines of flight", however humble'.[53] In other words, the seeds of the disruption of hypercapitalist machines exist both within them and at their margins, but whether their impact on the culture industries will sufficiently challenge existing matrices remains to be seen.

---

[51] Nick Dyer-Witheford and Greig de Peuter, *Games of Empire* (Minneapolis: University of Minnesota Press, 2009), 15.

[52] Miller, *Playing Along*, 225.

[53] Henry Svec, 'Becoming Machinic Virtuosos: Guitar Hero, Rez, and Multitudinous Aesthetics', *Loading ...* 2, no. 2 (2008), 11 pp. at 1, date accessed 29 October 2020, https://journals.sfu.ca/loading/index.php/loading/article/view/30/28.

23

Game Music Beyond the Games

RYAN THOMPSON

The influence of games, and their music, extends well beyond the boundaries of the game texts. Outside of Jesper Juul's 'magic circle', the imagined space in which the rules of the game apply and play occurs, are worlds of meaning, consumption and community that reflect and serve to transmit our own lived experience with the medium.[1] This chapter investigates game music removed from the context of the video games that contain it, instead focusing on the role of game music in the context of wider culture. As part of that exploration, this chapter marks how the availability of communication and audio production tools from the year 2000 to the present affords fan communities surrounding game audio an ever-increasing potential for discussing, transmitting, remixing and otherwise exploring the music of the games we play. I say 'we' in the inclusive sense intentionally, as an insider of a number of fan groups engaging with game audio. Though this essay attempts to remain relatively detached throughout, I follow scholar Henry Jenkins in describing myself as a fan, and in pointing out that even when writing on subjects that 'are not explicitly personal, [I] deal with forms of culture that have captured my imagination and sparked my passion'.[2]

That disclaimer aside, this chapter is especially concerned with one game music fan group: OverClocked ReMix – and their primary output hosted at ocremix.org, which today is one of the largest centres of organized fan activity surrounding game audio. OC ReMix (to use the site's own preferred abbreviation) provides a window into how fan efforts have been facilitated over time as new technologies have become available. This is in large part due to the longevity of the website, but also the size of the community, and the scope and scale of the efforts that community has been able to produce. In the process, such labour demonstrates how technology is entwined with creative potential on the part of fans and amateurs. This essay serves as an introduction to OC ReMix, the twenty-year history of

---

[1] Jesper Juul, *Half-Real: Video Games Between Real Rules and Fictional Worlds* (Cambridge, MA: MIT Press, 2008), 164–5.

[2] Henry Jenkins, *Fans, Bloggers, and Gamers: Exploring Participatory Culture* (New York: New York University Press, 2006), 6.

which is briefly covered below. I then make specific claims about how the organization's long history provides an opportunity to study how fan activity and output has changed in the wake of more accessible production and publication technologies. Ultimately, fandom provides a lens through which we can observe part of a larger cultural conversation about game audio's significance to players long after they put down controllers and step away from the games.

History of OverClocked ReMix

OC ReMix was founded in 1999 by David Lloyd as a spin-off of Overclocked.org, a site hosting various resources including a webcomic about emulation (in this context, the process of running video game console code and materials on one's home computer). Lloyd had 'a real interest in just the art of arranging and composing music more than playing any given instrument', and a passion for video game music – as a result, the site was created as 'a way to get better at . . . and explore making music'.[3] While some other sites concerning fan-created video game music predate OC ReMix, they were constrained by the technological limitations of the pre-broadband mid-1990s.[4] One of the contributions OC ReMix makes to fan-driven game audio culture is that it was amongst the first sites in game audio fandom to host music using the MP3 file format (rather than low-quality, low-file-size MIDI files) tailored for wide distribution.[5]

OC ReMix began as a one-man operation, with Lloyd (using the moniker 'djpretzel') uploading musical arrangements (hereafter 'remixes', following the site's parlance) either composed by him or (after the first few dozen mixes were posted) sent his way by fellow game audio fans. By 2002 the volume of submissions had grown beyond the capacity of Lloyd's own spare time, and a panel of judges was established to help keep up with the ever-increasing volume of submissions. Today, the site receives multiple thousands of submissions per year.

---

[3] David Lloyd, interview with Emily Reese. Emily Reese, 'Video Game Music Fan Site OC ReMix on Top Score', *Classical MPR* (15 November 2012), accessed 10 April 2020, https://www.classicalmpr.org/story/2012/11/15/ocremix-top-score-larry-oji-david-lloyd.

[4] One example of this still exists in its original form today: the MIDI-only website vgmusic.com, which features over 31,000 fan transcriptions. See *VGMusic.com Video Game Music Archive*, accessed 10 April 2020, https://vgmusic.com/.

[5] Also in 1999, Napster was launched, bringing with it widespread public awareness of the MP3 file format.

The website's use of the term 'judges' panel' correctly suggests that the site's music constitutes a curated collection: only 10–15 per cent of music submissions are posted to the website. Via the judges' panel, site staff make evaluations of the quality of its submissions, maintaining a dual emphasis on both the originality of arrangement and the quality of sound production (enabled by the focus on MP3 submissions rather than MIDI files).[6] OC ReMix actively acknowledges that this is a subjective process, one in which remixers must situate their arrangement submissions between two seemingly opposing ideas: they 'must be different enough from the source material to clearly illustrate the contributions, modifications, and enhancements you have made' while simultaneously they 'must not modify the source material beyond recognition'.[7] William Cheng, addressing the topic of speedrunning, writes about navigating the boundaries between what is possible and what is expected:

To be sure, it is possible for an act to be so radical that it comes off as more alienating than impressive ... Distinguished players are not ordinarily those who zip completely ... out of bounds. Rather, they are the ones dancing precariously along the edges ... testing its boundaries while abiding as verifiable participants within.[8]

A subjective decision process might well involve opinions on the game in question being remixed. OC ReMix actively works against any notions of canon formation within the game audio community. Judge and long-time contributor Andrew 'zircon' Aversa notes that 'we DEFINITELY don't want to only promote the popular titles. That's why we've repeatedly rejected the idea of a rating system or anything involving mix popularity. The results would immediately skew towards those really popular games.'[9] It's likely that at least part of why the site staff feels so strongly about this can be attributed to Lloyd's nostalgia for older games (both in game audio

---

[6] This process is visible to the public, and judges are strongly encouraged to articulate why they voted a certain way to maintain transparency for future submitters. One such example is here: Gario, 'OCR03958 – *YES* Tangledeep & Dungeonmans "In the Heart of Home"', *OverClocked ReMix* (March 2019), accessed 10 April 2020, https://ocremix.org/community/topic/48099/.

[7] OverClocked ReMix, 'Wiki: Submission Standards and Instructions', *OverClocked ReMix*, accessed 10 April 2020, http://ocremix.org/info/Submission_Standards_and_Instructions.

[8] William Cheng, *Sound Play: Video Games and the Musical Imagination* (New York: Oxford University Press, 2014), 6.

[9] Andrew Aversa, 'r/IAmA – We Are OverClocked ReMix, Creating Free Game Remixes since 1999. We Just Released a 6 Hour Free Album of Final Fantasy VI Arrangements after a $150,000 Kickstarter Last Year. Nobuo Uematsu Loved Our Take on the Opera. Ask Us Anything!', *Reddit.com* (2013), accessed 4 March 2020, www.reddit.com/r/IAmA/comments/1hkxo1/ we_are_overclocked_remix_creating_free_game/cavo2wv.

and emulation), rooted in his love of the Sega Master System, rather than the much better known Nintendo Entertainment System.[10]

Lloyd also contributes a great deal of written material to the website – he creates a short write-up of each new posted ReMix (the capitalization here follows the website's own nomenclature) as a means of introduction to the new piece. Originally, these were one- or two-sentence constructions, but as the website has grown, so has the scope of these introductions, which today feature citations from the artist's submission, quotes from the vote of the judges' panel and intertextual references noted by Lloyd as he listens to every piece.[11] When read in full alongside the decisions of the judges' panel (also available on the website) for each mix, it's clear that these write-ups do more than provide an introduction for someone unfamiliar with the source material – they situate every arrangement in the history of OC ReMix itself and in the body of music created for video games writ large.

Starting with remix number 1000, Lloyd has turned every 500th site post (that is, remix number 1500, 2000, etc.) into a reflection on the state of the website and the trajectory of the fandom surrounding video game audio. For the thousandth posted remix, one of his own covering *Super Mario RPG: Legend of the Seven Stars*, Lloyd writes:

OC ReMix is not about numbers, in the end, nor should it be. However . . . taking a retrospective look back from OCR01000 to OCR00001 – however arbitrary those numbers are – reflects on what I think are amazing accomplishments on the parts of the site's many contributors. The listeners, reviewers, judges, forum members, #ocremix regulars, mirrorers and file sharers, and of course the ReMixers themselves, have all put together something that, even were it all to end abruptly tomorrow, is to me a singular and wonderful contribution to both music and games.[12]

---

[10] Nintendo's public data lists sales of the NES in 'the Americas' as 34 million consoles sold to date. Nintendo, 'Nintendo Co., Ltd.: Library-Historical Data', *Nintendo* (n.d.), accessed 4 March 2020, www.nintendo.co.jp/ir/finance/historical_data/xls/consolidated_sales_e1906.xlsx, accessed 10 April 2020. In 1988, the *New York Times* claimed that Nintendo held 83 per cent of the market share of video games sold in the country. Douglas McGill, 'Nintendo Scores Big', *New York Times* (4 December 1988), accessed 4 March 2020, retrieved from https://web.archive.org/web/20130524041326/http://www.nytimes.com/1988/12/04/business/nintendo-scores-big.html?sec=&spon=&pagewanted=2.

[11] Though, of course, Lloyd's writing is not the same as scholarly publications on the subject, it is very likely that Lloyd has written more about video game music than any single scholar has to date.

[12] A 'mirrorer' refers to someone who hosts backups of site content to alleviate server stress and cost. Write-up post by David Lloyd, 'Super Mario RPG: Legend of the Seven Stars "Booster Tarantino"', *OverClocked ReMix* (30 June 2003), accessed 10 April 2020, https://ocremix.org/remix/OCR01000.

The post for remix number 1500 is more forward-looking than a celebration of what came before, with announcements about Chipamp, a plugin installer for Winamp that automatically adds functionality for a variety of chiptune formats, keeping neatly in line with Lloyd's ongoing passion for emulation and history as core reasons why OC ReMix exists. Lloyd's write-up for the 2000th posted remix is a celebration of a 'celebrity' contribution – a collaboration between David Wise, Grant Kirkhope and Robin Beanland covering Wise's own score to *Donkey Kong Country 2* that foreshadows the *Donkey Kong Country*-inspired score of *Yooka-Laylee* (though, of course, nobody could have known that at the time).

Alongside the release of individual mixes, OC ReMix has also released 'albums': these are more focused collections of music with either a single game or concept in mind. Lloyd reflects about the history of album releases on the site:

Kong in Concert ... while it wasn't the very first OC ReMix album, it took the concept originally established by *Relics* [the first album, a solo project by user Protricity] one step further and made many intelligent decisions regarding the playlist, website, and overall package/presentation that I think have been fairly influential. *Relics* was the conceptual innovator and set the overall precedent, but *KiC* ran with that and has served as a blueprint and barometer for many albums since.[13]

The title above, *Kong in Concert*, positions the release both as aspiring towards and standing against more traditional concert releases.[14] The album is clearly not 'in concert', as many tracks contain no live instruments. Calling attention to this distinction serves to reinforce the difference in status between fan activity and official activity, such as official arranged editions of game soundtracks or concert events such as Video Games Live.[15]

Occasionally, albums mark significant events in the life of OC ReMix. The remix album of *Super Street Fighter II Turbo*, *Blood on the Asphalt*, released in 2006, caused Capcom (the creators of *Street Fighter*), then in the process of creating a remastered edition of the same game, to contact OC

---

[13] Write-up post by David Lloyd, 'Donkey Kong Country 2: Diddy's Kong Quest "Re-Skewed" OC ReMix', *OverClocked ReMix* (15 March 2010), accessed 10 April 2020, https://ocremix.org/remix/OCR02000.

[14] See, on this topic, William Gibbons, *Unlimited Replays: Video Games and Classical Music* (New York: Oxford University Press, 2018), 174.

[15] The use of the phrase 'in concert' mirrors a juxtaposition between common understandings of 'highbrow' classical music and 'lowbrow' video games discussed extensively in Gibbons, *Unlimited Replays*, to which I direct readers interested in pulling at this thread longer than the scope of this chapter allows.

ReMix (first the album's director Shael Riley, who pointed them to Lloyd). Lloyd had 'recently enacted an End User License Agreement at OverClocked ReMix that could ... grant Capcom license to use the arrangements from *Blood on the Asphalt*.'[16] The group of musicians on the album, coordinated by Lloyd, 'tried hard to ensure that working with a large fan community was as close as possible for Capcom to working with a single composer. We didn't want to squander the opportunity [to participate in an official release] by risking drama or miscommunication.'[17]

The partnership was a success, and *Super Street Fighter II Turbo HD Remix,* released in 2008, featured the first score of a commercially released game to be created entirely by fans. Lloyd remarks:

Capcom were cautious but ultimately pretty flexible with the contract we signed, which ... allows us to distribute the music from HD Remix ourselves, independent of Capcom, as long as we don't charge a profit ... Ultimately, everyone wins: we retain the ability to treat the music as fan works and make it freely available online, and Capcom gets what we think is a pretty badass soundtrack for free.[18]

The partnership between Capcom and OC ReMix continues to serve as a model for corporations engaging fan communities; in the years following the release of *HD Remix,* Capcom again reached out to the site for the twenty-fifth anniversary of *Mega Man*'s release, and commissioned a commercial album celebrating all of the different Mega Man franchises across two discs. OC ReMix has also collaborated with other fan groups; for APEX 2013, a premiere video game tournament, the organizers commissioned OC ReMix to produce an album that celebrated each of the games featured at the tournament. This was the first time an OC ReMix album had been created in association with a specific event, and a number of albums have been created for subsequent APEX years.

Another milestone release for OC ReMix was *Voices of the Lifestream,* which established a new scale for what the community could do with their album format. *Voices* features a complete re-envisioning of every cue from *Final Fantasy VII*; in total, the album contains forty-five tracks from more than forty artists across four discs.

Five years later, OC ReMix (in an effort led by Andrew Aversa) attempted to build on the success of *Voices*: 'Back in 2007, I directed an

---

[16] Shael Riley quoted in Ben Kuchera, 'Fans Go Pro: How OC ReMix Put Its Stamp on Street Fighter II HD Remix', *Ars Technica* (18 July 2008), accessed 10 April 2020, https://arstechnica.com/gaming/2008/07/ocremix/2/.

[17] David Lloyd, quoted in ibid.

[18] Ibid.

album project based on *Final Fantasy VII.* Now, I'm working together with McVaffe on an even grander tribute for *Final Fantasy VI,* in celebration of the series' 25th birthday.'[19] In order to make the release as good as possible – as *Final Fantasy VI (FFVI)* holds a special place in the game audio community for a number of reasons outside the present scope – the site attempted to raise funds on the crowdfunding site Kickstarter.[20] This original effort was met with a cease-and-desist notice from Square Enix, which caused the Kickstarter to be taken down before the original campaign ended.

Though the specifics remain unclear (the site staff involved, including both Lloyd and Aversa, are bound by a non-disclosure agreement), OC ReMix and Square Enix reached an agreement and a month later, the Kickstarter campaign was relaunched, with a pointed disclaimer added ensuring that backers knew the project was unofficial. The campaign ultimately raised over $150,000 from backers, though the website ended up losing some money on the release, due to the cost of royalties to Square Enix, the physical production of the albums themselves and other associated costs.[21] Despite these challenges, the album release marks the first time a video game fan organization has successfully negotiated with a company to allow for release of a fan work that had been taken down via a cease-and-desist order, speaking to the centrality of OC ReMix in the larger space of game audio fandom.

It bears mentioning that part of the reason the organization was able to succeed in negotiating with Square Enix is that no one – neither David Lloyd nor anyone else involved with staffing OC ReMix – has ever received monetary compensation for work related to the website. Any money that comes in (via YouTube ad revenue, donations and sales of the Mega Man album described above) is re-invested into the hosting costs associated with keeping the site up and running. However, being a central hub for game audio fandom over twenty years certainly lends a certain amount of corporate authority amongst the community outside of economic terms. An accumulation of prestige and 'the exchange of curatorial expertise' are

[19] Andrew Aversa, Kickstarter campaign, 'An EPIC 5-Disc FF6 Fan Album from OC ReMix ... Take Two!', *Kickstarter* (11 June 2014), accessed 10 April 2020, www.kickstarter.com/projects/ocremix/an-epic-5-disc-ff6-fan-album-from-oc-remix-take-tw

[20] Both William Cheng and Ryan Thompson have written book chapters focused around *Final Fantasy VI.* See Cheng, *Sound Play,* 57–92 and Ryan Thompson, 'Operatic Conventions and Expectations in *Final Fantasy VI*', in *Music in the Role-Playing Game: Heroes and Harmonies,* ed. William Gibbons and Steven Reale (New York: Routledge, 2020), 177–28.

[21] Again, the specifics of royalties and payments to Square Enix are not publicly available, even to people otherwise considered community insiders.

part of 'an informal economy, which coexists and complexly interacts with the commercial economy'.[22]

In its twenty-year history, OC ReMix has had a number of musicians start as fans and ReMixers (that is, those folks creating music published to the site) before going onwards to professional careers in music. Andrew Aversa (*SoulCalibur V*, *Tangledeep*), Wilbert Roget II (*Call of Duty: WWII*, *Mortal Kombat 11*), Jake Kaufman (*Shovel Knight*, *Shantae*), Danny Baranowsky (*Super Meat Boy*, *The Binding of Isaac*), Jimmy Hinson (*Mass Effect 2*, *Threes!*), Pete Lepley (*Wargroove*) and Nabeel Ansari (*Sole*) have all composed game soundtracks after posting music to OC ReMix. Many others, including Doug Perry, Jillian Aversa, John Stacy, Mattias Häggström Gerdt and Ben Briggs all have full-time careers in music as performers, software developers (of music-production software), audio engineers, or DJs and in related fields.[23] Similarly, a number of established industry composers have contributed remixes to the site in support of its mission: these include George Sanger (*The 7th Guest*), Joe McDermott (*Zombies Ate My Neighbors*), David Wise (*Donkey Kong Country*), Grant Kirkhope (*Banjo-Kazooie*), Norihiko Hibino (*Zone of the Enders*, *Metal Gear Solid*) and Rich Vreeland (*Fez*, *Hyper Light Drifter*).

Over the span of twenty years, the group has further spurred a number of other fan communities to take root, operating outside the parameters of the OC ReMix submission guidelines. One important such community is Dwelling of Duels, which places more of an emphasis on live performance – no such restriction exists in the OC ReMix submission guidelines. Another site, now defunct, was VGMix, created by composer and fan remixer Jake Kaufman (then using the moniker 'virt'), who was prompted to do so by two factors. First, that OC ReMix had too high a bar to clear regarding its submission standards, causing many good fan creations to fall outside the guidelines (medleys, mixes using material across multiple games and franchises, lo-fi chiptunes, etc.) without a prominent venue for publication. Second – and perhaps more importantly, to Kaufman – that a distrust had grown concerning the authority invested in OC ReMix and Lloyd specifically, which (at the time) Kaufman perceived not merely as a locus for participatory culture, but as a corporate entity seeking 'to court and capture

---

[22] Henry Jenkins, *Spreadable Media: Creating Value and Meaning in a Networked Culture* (New York: NYU Press, 2013), 61.

[23] This list of people engaged as music professionals outside composition specifically is likely incomplete; for instance, one might broadly include the author (a posted ReMixer) as having a career in music.

the participatory energies of desired markets and to harness them toward their own ends'.[24]

Specifically, the 'About' section of the VGMix.com website reads, in places, as a pointed rebuke of OC ReMix's practices:

No month-long waits to have your music approved . . . We're not about brand loyalty or buzzwords, we're about giving you a place to speak your mind . . . some of us prefer not to put our music at Overclocked because of the fundamental way it's run . . . [.][25]

This was not just a private debate between people in a back room; rather, throughout game audio fandom online, these two opinions caused division within the larger community. In OC ReMix's own posting history, there is a gap of almost ten years (between late 2001 and early 2010) during which Kaufman did not submit to the website, preferring other fan outlets (including VGMix). Upon the ReMix heralding Kaufman's return to the website (and as a result, the OC ReMix community), Lloyd notes (in an extra-long write-up):

In the many years since the infamous ocremix-vgmix split, a lot of things have happened that make this writeup possible, I think. We all got older, for one, and while age doesn't guarantee wisdom, it can certainly facilitate it . . . I debated even saying anything, and instead just posting this mix like it was any other album track, but even if the past didn't warrant some commentary, the truth is that Jake's reputation and growth as a game composer would have demanded some special words, regardless . . . Hopefully the few folks that are operating under the mis-impression that I feel otherwise . . . can finally come around, as I believe we have.[26]

That such a reconciliation warranted public comment on the OC ReMix website speaks to the centrality of the organization to the larger sphere of game audio fandom. Today, the group is rapidly approaching remix number 4,000, and is thinking about what might happen when the original founders retire. In 2016, the organization moved 'under the umbrella and sponsorship of *Game Music Initiative, Inc*, a 501c3 non-profit charitable organization' in order to ensure the preservation and continuation of the OC ReMix mission in the event something happens to one of the core staff members.[27]

---

[24] Jenkins, *Spreadable Media*, 297.

[25] Jake Kaufman, 'About', *VGmix.com* (c.2002), accessed 10 April 2020, https://web.archive.org/web/20020602143137/http://www.vgmix.com/faq.php.

[26] Write-up post by David Lloyd, 'Donkey Kong Country 2: Diddy's Kong Quest "Dance of the Zinger"', *OverClocked ReMix* (16 March 2010), accessed 10 April 2020, https://ocremix.org/remix/OCR02005

[27] OverClocked ReMix, 'Wiki: About Us' (n.d.), accessed 10 April 2020, http://ocremix.org/info/ ` About_Us.

Game Music (Remixes) as Art

The mission statement of OC ReMix reads as follows: 'Founded in 1999, OverClocked ReMix is a community dedicated to the appreciation and promotion of video game music as an art form.'[28] That the notion of game music as artistic endeavour needs to be promoted suggests that it, and by extension, video games themselves, might not be considered art. Similarly, Video Games Live, a touring concert series created and produced by composer Tommy Tallarico, defines itself as 'a concert event put on by the video game industry to help encourage and support the culture and art that video games have become', as if games of the past (which past? Is there an arbitrary line somewhere?) were somehow neither culture nor art.[29] Both groups – one amateur, one professional – are formed out of a belief that game audio deserves a place amongst the cultured; that is, it deserves to be recognized as 'art'.

In describing the relationship between video games and classical music (in the broad sense), William Gibbons notes:

the fundamental principle on which classical music as a concept is based: some music is art and some music isn't. Despite what their opponents might claim, it isn't that these fans want to eradicate musical hierarchies – it's that they want to ensure that their preferred music makes the cut. The barbarians at the gates aren't tearing down the walls; they just want to come in for tea.[30]

Given a world where an audience perceives the orchestra (classical music) as art, and chiptunes (video games) as entertainment, it makes sense that a number of people might want to recreate music written for the latter medium in styles that might mask its ludic origins. This sort of hierarchical thinking (with classical music at the top) is pervasive enough not only to warrant Gibbons dedicating an entire book to the subject, but also to shape the public reception of OC ReMix. The site staff has occasionally both recognized that this sort of argument about what is and is not art exists, and has challenged it, promoting diversity amongst musical genres. In particular, electronic dance music and techno are often derided as 'less than' in critiques of the site, as a note on the OC ReMix Facebook pages acknowledges even as it defends electronic music:

---

[28] Ibid.

[29] For more on Tallarico's framing, see William Gibbons, 'Rewritable Memory: Concerts, Canons, and Game Music History', *Journal of Sound and Music in Games* 1, no. 1 (2020), 75–81.

[30] Gibbons, *Unlimited Replays*, 165.

From YouTube today: 'I love OC ReMix, I really do, but I'm getting sick of hearing techno ALL THE TIME.' If YOU see someone say this, don't take that BS lying down. They don't listen to all of our music (or know what techno is). Most of our music is not techno. Even IF our music was all techno and electronica, we'd be PROUD of it.[31]

Similarly, another note from a few years later reads:

Recently on Tumblr: 'Has OC ReMix ever hosted a music file that wasn't just some sound mixing techno/trance rendition? There *are* multiple genres of music in life.' As always, if you ever see anyone say something like this about OC ReMix, they don't really know what music we post . . . In 2014 so far, we've posted 153 ReMixes. 127 aren't 'techno/trance', i.e. 83%. Skeptical? Here's the 127 [linked below the post individually] to check out! Enjoy, and don't be afraid to embrace electronica too. 'Teknoz' is also great, and we welcome whatever genres are sent to us![32]

Getting into the weeds of specific arguments about what is and isn't art is well outside the scope of the present chapter. I will note that this type of reception speaks to a point made by Melanie Fritsch: 'in order to under-stand fan-made creations . . . fans need to become literate in the respective fandom as well as in the practices, discourses and aesthetics of the sur-rounding fan culture.'[33] In other words, the priorities of OC ReMix as an organization might be in conflict with a broader fan base of remixed video game music. Music made for the site is, of course, made for the site, and therefore crafted with the site's mission in mind. Acknowledging that disagreement about mission across a broader audience of listeners (beyond OC ReMix) not only exists but that there are groups of people emotionally invested in it provides a lens through which we can understand why fans choose to remix video game music in the first place.

Jenkins and Fandom Through Time

Fandom scholar Henry Jenkins writes about a number of trends in fan-dom – one of the most repeated themes in his own work is that technology

---

[31] Facebook note by OverClocked ReMix, *Facebook* (2010), accessed 10 April 2020, www.facebook.com/notes/overclocked-remix/i-love-oc-remix-i-really-do-but-im-getting-sick-of-hearing-techno-all-the-time/10150248557170585.

[32] Facebook note by OverClocked ReMix, *Facebook* (2014), accessed 10 April 2020, www.facebook.com/notes/overclocked-remix/has-oc-remix-ever-hosted-a-music-file-that-wasnt-just-technotrance/10154483637755585.

[33] Melanie Fritsch, "It's a-me, Mario!' Playing with Video Game Music', in *Ludomusicology: Approaches to Video Game Music*, ed. Michiel Kamp, Tim Summers and Mark Sweeney (Sheffield: Equinox, 2016), 92–115 at 99.

continues to shift our understanding of what fandom means. Today, an engaged, active audience is simply 'taken for granted by everyone involved in and around the media industry'.[34] This is especially true in comparison to the state of affairs described by Jenkins in *Textual Poachers*, published in 1992, when 'fans were marginal to the operation of our culture, ridiculed in the media, shrouded with social stigma', a time when communication effectively worked in one direction only, from platform holders to end consumers.[35]

Jenkins, writing in 2006, articulates a number of points about a then-emerging participatory culture, noting that 'new tools and technologies enable consumers to archive, annotate, appropriate, and recirculate media content'.[36] Perhaps the biggest technological change was the general global shift from less stable, slower dial-up Internet to the modern always-connected broadband Internet over the years 2000–2010, with more people globally using a broadband connection from 2004 on.[37]

In the context of OC ReMix specifically, the affordability and availability of audio production software has grown drastically in the period from when the site was founded to the present day. In 1998 (a year before OC ReMix was founded), the core version of Pro Tools – a premiere, industry-standard audio production suite – carried a list price of $7,995, well beyond what even a committed hobbyist can afford to spend.[38] By 2003 the list price for Pro Tools LE (a somewhat pared-down version, targeted for individuals and beginners) was $495 (including the two-channel MBox interface), and today, Pro Tools is available at a subscription rate of $29.99 per month, or $299 per year. In addition, other digital audio work-stations (DAWs) entered the market, creating competition and accessibility for new users; many DAWs (including Pro Tools) now have free trials or extremely limited free editions. Other notable audio software releases in this timespan include Audacity (free, open source audio editor) in 2000, GarageBand by Apple in 2004 (free in the Mac OSX ecosystem) and Reaper (a $60, fully featured DAW) in 2006.

A difference in quality over time is especially noticeable when reading reviews of early remixes written by users years after their release. Andrew

---

[34] Jenkins, *Fans, Bloggers, and Gamers*, 1.

[35] Ibid.

[36] Ibid., 135.

[37] The Organisation for Economic Co-operation and Development (OECD), *The Future of the Internet Economy: A Statistical Profile*, 2011. www.oecd.org/internet/ieconomy/48255770.pdf.

[38] Pro Tools 24 MIX was priced at $7,995: www.pro-tools-expert.com/home-page/2018/2/22/the-history-of-pro-tools-1994-to-2000.

Luers, under the moniker 'OA', closes his (mostly negative) remarks on one early remix by writing 'Regardless, this mix is ancient, so I can understand the difference between then and now.'[39] Similar suggestions about production quality (quality of sample libraries, bitrate, mixing techniques employed, etc.) abound in reviews of early remixes. This is likely because both creativity and quality of musical arrangement (that is, orchestration, instrumentation, etc.) is both more difficult to subjectively evaluate and less constrained by the limitations of 1999 technology, compared to production quality.

OC ReMix specifically addresses this in its submission guidelines, which once stated that revisions were not permitted unless fixing an error with a recently posted mix, 'in keeping [with] the idea that OCR represents a history of video and computer game remixes, not just a collection of them, and that rewriting or replacing pieces of that history would have negative repercussions'.[40] It is clear that Lloyd and the judges' panel think of OC ReMix as a locus for a larger community, one with a history worthy of preservation.[41]

Without dwelling on a history of technology specifically, a few other developments not geared specifically towards audio that are nonetheless important to the present conversation are the launch of YouTube in 2005, Twitch.tv in 2011 and Discord in 2015. Each are part of 'an era of communication' demonstrating 'some decisive steps ... expanding access to the means of cultural production (through ease-of-access-and-use tools) and to cultural circulation within and across diverse communities'.[42] Today, OC ReMix now cross-publishes all of its musical output on YouTube, with a short reel explaining the website running over the top of the audio of each remix. Discord has served to replace IRC (Internet Relay Chat, an older chat system) chatrooms for many communities, including OC ReMix, which maintains an active Discord server – similarly, the 'bulletin board' style of forum, while still used, is seeing less and less traffic as site members gravitate towards Discord as a preferred platform for communication.

---

[39] Comment from user 'OA', reviewing mix #00021. http://ocremix.org/remix/OCR00021.

[40] From an older, archived version of the Submission Standards, dated May 7, 2006. https://ocremix.org/wiki/index.php?%20title=Submission_Standards_and_Instructions&direction=prev&oldid=1366

[41] The submission standards today have removed explanations for policies in an effort to make the document easier to process; that said, it still reads that 'Submissions that are revisions or new versions of existing, posted ReMixes will only be evaluated as additions, not as replacements, and must be substantially different. Revisions are not encouraged and may be held to higher standards.' http://ocremix.org/info/Submission_Standards_and_Instructions.

[42] Jenkins, *Spreadable Media*, 161.

Closing Remarks

The growth of OC ReMix and other fan groups was made possible via the continuing trend towards availability of both broadband Internet and music-production technologies. Without that infrastructure in place, fandom might still have organized around shared interests, but the centrality of 'digitally empowered consumers' in 'shaping the production, distribution, and reception of media content' – what Jenkins describes as grassroots convergence – would not have been achieved on the same scale.[43] OC ReMix, and the wider community of game audio fandom it helps foster, illustrates 'the many ways that expanding access to the tools of media production and circulation is transforming the media landscape, allowing . . . for greater support for independent media producers'.[44]

As newly disruptive technologies such as Twitch.tv enable amateur and fan activity in live broadcast spaces, we can look forward to observing how these relationships between fans and rights holders continue to develop. Despite continuously changing technologies, I suspect it will be some time before a new organization is formed that traces the effects of technological change as readily as OC ReMix has done during the transformations throughout all of our society in the wake of broadband Internet, web hosting, social media and participatory culture.

What started as a project by a single person is today a larger enterprise, with 4,000 posted ReMixers, thousands more forum members and millions of listeners. As listeners continue to respond emotionally to games and the music contained within them, OC ReMix serves as a locus for the larger community of players (and viewers, in the age of Twitch.tv etc.) who are moved by the musical material of video games. I believe that remixing these works is a means to inject them with our own personality, putting something of ourselves into a conversation about meaning. David Lloyd writes:

As much as it is a site dedicated to games, and to music, OCR is a site dedicated to the infinite possibilities of musical arrangement, *specifically,* and commercial markets *tend* to resist individual artists moving too far & too often along the spectrum of stylistic diversity & influence . . . To be clear, I'm not throwing shade on the emergent commercial mixing scene, which I view as both fantastic AND inevitable, but I do think meaningfully distinct & vital work remains possible outside of that space.[45]

---

[43] Jenkins, *Fans, Bloggers, and Gamers*, 155.
[44] Jenkins, *Spreadable Media*, 294–5.
[45] Write-up post by David Lloyd, 'OCR4000', *OverClocked ReMix* (18 November 2019), accessed 10 April 2020, https://ocremix.org/remix/OCR04000.

The 'work' he references is about this ongoing, continually unfolding conversation. What do games mean for us – as individuals, and as a larger audience? Fan-made responses to this music not only help elucidate meanings of the video games themselves, but also enrich an ever-growing community of players, composers, listeners and fans that have something to say about video game music.

24

Producing Game Music Concerts

THOMAS BÖCKER, WITH MELANIE FRITSCH AND
TIM SUMMERS

Thomas Böcker is a concert producer specializing in staging orchestral concerts of video game music. After initially working as a producer, music director and music consultant in the game industry (on titles such as Cold Zero – The Last Stand, Knights of the Temple *and* Stalker: Shadow of Chernobyl*), Böcker was responsible for the first commercial concerts of video game music outside Japan, encouraging some of the highest profile orchestras to embrace the genre alongside their more traditional repertoire. Here, he recounts the history of the concerts, explains his approach to designing the events, and reflects on their cultural context.*

Background

When the First Symphonic Game Music Concert was held on 20 August 2003 at Leipzig's Gewandhaus, it was both the realization of a long-held ambition and the start of a new tradition. It achieved the goal of staging a concert of video game music outside Japan and launched a series of orchestral concerts that continue to diversify and grow, now playing game music to audiences in concert halls across Europe, North America, Australia and East Asia.

Like any ambitious concert project, the origins and motivations lie in the appeal of the music. As a child, I was enraptured by the music of video games. I started recognizing the names of the composers, such as Chris Hülsbeck, Yuzo Koshiro and Nobuo Uematsu; I became a fan of their music, and video game music in general. As much as I loved being a listener, I was always driven by the idea of creating something by myself. The predecessor to the Symphonic Game Music Concerts were two album projects that I produced, *Merregnon* (2000) and *Merregnon 2: Video Game World Symphony* (2004). Initiated in 1999, *Merregnon* combined the work of video game composers from all over the world, who wrote exclusive music for a fantasy story I devised. Story, music and art were combined in CD albums, where one could listen and read along to the protagonist's adventures. The first album was made with samplers, but the success of the project meant that the sequel was able to use live performers. Strings and chorus were recorded in Prague, and additional instruments in New York. For the majority of the composers involved, this was their first time recording this kind of music with live musicians; certainly in Germany, no orchestral recording had yet been done for a video game production. The recording for *Merregnon 2* saw me working closely with conductor Andy Brick, and orchestra manager Petr Pycha. Having created orchestral recordings for the album, a concert seemed feasible. These records helped to create networks that would ultimately facilitate the production of the concerts.

Staging the concert was my first project as an entrepreneur, after I had made the decision to start my own business. The most logical approach to realizing the concert seemed to be to hold it alongside a well-established industry event, so I proposed a Symphonic Game Music Concert to the Games Convention trade fair in Leipzig. The concert was ultimately held as the opening ceremony of the 2003 convention. It was performed to a sold-out audience of 2,000 listeners, dismantling the common assumption that there was no market for such a concert.

The Initial Concerts

Of course, the inspiration for the Symphonic Game Music Concerts came partly from Japanese game concerts such as the Dragon Quest concerts helmed by composer Koichi Sugiyama (starting 1987) and the Orchestral Game Concert series (1991–1996). Indeed, the First Symphonic Game Music Concert was performed sixteen years to the day after Sugiyama had held his first Dragon Quest concert. However, these forerunner concerts had a focus on Japanese productions and especially games on the Nintendo consoles, whereas the Symphonic Game Music Concerts were to have a broader repertoire: the goal was to feature video game music from all platforms, from all over the world. The first concert mainly honoured the few publishers who had invested money into live orchestra recordings for their games. This focus provided the first theme for the concert. As the concert series became more well known, and with the growing willingness of publishers to get involved (such as by sponsoring arrangements), there were fewer limits to the choice of music for the concerts. The repertoire had few constraints: it extended from early 8-bit games to the latest PC titles, included games that were not given a European release (such as *Chrono Cross*), and even featured world premieres of music that was performed in the concert hall prior to the game being released, as was the case for *Stalker: Shadow of Chernobyl.*

The initial team consisted of Andy Brick, who reviewed and edited the scores; Petr Pycha, who booked the orchestra and managed the logistics; and myself as the creator and producer, who managed the whole process, came up with the programme, obtained all required permissions and liaised with various external partners. The production started four months before the concert and most of the early preparation involved protracted conversations to obtain the legal permission to perform the music. Some rights holders required persuasion, but many discussions simply involved trying to identify the person who had responsibility for granting such permission. Aside from the legal barriers, a more practical problem became finding the original sheet music to use as the basis for our orchestrations. Some cues had to be recreated, as the original production materials had not been preserved. We contacted original composers to keep them involved in the arrangement of their music for the concert. The orchestra, the Czech National Symphony Orchestra, had two days of rehearsal in Prague, and a dress rehearsal in the hours before the concert in Leipzig. Andy Brick conducted the performance, which received ten minutes of standing ovations, and was covered by several major media outlets, including German TV stations, the BBC and the *New York Times.* We were honoured that several composers attended the concert to hear their work being performed (including Nobuo Uematsu, Christopher Lennertz, Olof Gustafsson, Richard Jacques and Andrew Barnabas). The success of the concert prompted us to stage another concert the following year, and we continued to produce opening ceremony concerts every year up to 2007, each one a sell-out event.

Since the first concerts, we have been continually finding ways to reach new audiences, and not just through touring the world. Feeling that my concerts would benefit from a new approach, having reached the peak of what was possible in cooperation with the Games Convention, I invited the former manager of the WDR Radio Orchestra, Winfried Fechner, to attend what would be my last Symphonic Game Music Concert in Leipzig in 2007. He was amazed at both the music and by the young and attentive audience, and so we agreed to continue the series in Cologne the following year. Our concert Symphonic Shades (2008) at the Funkhaus Wallrafplatz was the first concert of game music to be given a live radio broadcast, and later, the Symphonic Fantasies (2009) concert at the Philharmonie Köln broke new ground as being the first audiovisual live-streamed concert of game music.

Through the internet, we reached a worldwide audience and engaged a huge online community.

Later, my company funded and produced live album recordings (such as *Symphonic Fantasies Tokyo* with the Tokyo Philharmonic Orchestra, recorded at Tokyo Bunka Kaikan) and studio recordings (such as *Final Symphony*, performed by the London Symphony Orchestra, recorded at Abbey Road Studios), which gave audiences the opportunity to re-experience the concerts at home, and in terms of promotional activities, these albums help us to show orchestra managers what video game music – or rather, our video game music arrangements – are all about.

Programming and Repertoire

Especially in the beginning, I was guided in my musical choices by what I liked myself and what I thought would be appreciated by others as well. Beyond following my own taste, it was important to learn what the audience would like to hear. Over the years, it became easier to glean this information from online discussions. Forums provided a great opportunity to find suggestions for cues that might be suitable for the concerts. Especially in the case of *Final Symphony*, the concert of music from *Final Fantasy*, I put a lot of time into researching fan favourites and analysing which titles from the soundtracks were played most often. I sent a list of these to the arrangers, who, of course, had done their own research already, and who had their own favourites.

Initially, the concerts took the form of 'best of' programmes, featuring many different styles. Individual shorter items were played alongside bigger medleys, all in a format quite close to that of the original music in the game. In this sense, they were similar to typical film music concerts. However, when the concerts moved to Cologne, where they were held from 2008 to 2012, arrangers were engaged to create more elaborate and integrated musical structures, specifically for concert performance, in the tradition of classical music. Now, the aim was to incorporate melodies in different contexts, to tell the story of the games musically.

The boldest step was certainly made with my production Final Symphony, an ongoing tour which was planned in 2012 and premiered in 2013. Conducted by former Chief Conductor of the Auckland Philharmonia Orchestra, Eckehard Stier, this concert featured music from *Final Fantasy VI, VII* and *X*, in arrangements by Masashi Hamauzu, Jonne Valtonen and Roger Wanamo. This video game music concert featured a symphonic poem, a piano concerto and a full symphony, something that had never been done before. The symphony lasts forty-five minutes, with structures and musical processes directly modelled on classical symphonies. We see audiences in the USA, Europe, Japan, China and Australasia sitting with rapt attention to every moment in the piece, because of the connection they have to the music. This closer emulation of traditional Western classical musical genres made it possible to convince orchestras like the London Symphony Orchestra, the San Francisco Symphony and the Melbourne Symphony Orchestra to perform game music. Funded by my company, the London Symphony Orchestra recorded *Final Symphony* at Abbey Road Studios in 2014 with composer Nobuo Uematsu in attendance. It topped the iTunes Classical Charts in more than ten countries and entered the Classical Album Top 5 of both the Billboard Charts and the Official UK Charts, further demonstrating the public appetite for game music in this form.

The arrangements are specifically tailored for orchestral performance, which requires transforming the originals to work naturally within the new environment. Granted, this causes divergence from the original scores, and perhaps not every fan likes it. But from an aesthetic point of view, it offers the best result, rather than forcing orchestras to perform unsuitable music that is a more direct translation of the soundtrack.

A common theme in all of the concerts has been the absence of video projection at the performances, which distinguishes them from many other concerts of game and film music. The reason is that right from the beginning, I wanted the focus to be on the music, on the musicians. The audience – often first-timers in the concert hall – were meant to actually see how the sound is produced, and not be distracted by videos. The thought was that people are there for the music only, and might come back for other concerts as well, establishing a connection between the orchestra and the audience. I would not want to characterize the project as a mission to convert people to orchestral music, but I thought it would be a wonderful way to awaken their interest in classical music.

My concerts are truly focused on the music part, while other major tours are probably about the games in general, as a whole, with the visuals being very important for the overall experience. Having said this, I am not against video projection in general. What I am not convinced about is the way it is typically implemented in video game music concerts. It is often similar to a simple clip show. There is no creative approach that would be comparable to what we do with the arrangements, and hence it takes away from the overall experience, at least for me. A concert with equally sophisticated audio and video parts complementing each other would, however, be definitely to my liking; though there would undoubtedly be practical challenges, including gaining the additional support of licensors and investment from promoters.

Working with Partners

The concerts require us to work with several partners, ranging from performers to composers and corporate entities. Our arrangements are usually not straightforward orchestrations of original music, and therefore always require the permission of the rights owners if we want to work with the material. Naturally, this involves discussions with composers and developers, and, fortunately, especially the Japanese composers have been very open to our own interpretations.

When it comes to orchestras, although we have definitely seen huge improvements in attitudes to game music over the years, there is still a certain scepticism from some more conservative ensembles – especially in Germany – when it comes to performing video game music. Often, those responsible for management did not grow up playing games themselves, so it makes it harder for them to see what we are trying to achieve right from the start. Also, my concerts are certainly different to other productions, which are more about pop orchestral arrangements. Sometimes it takes a little effort to make orchestras aware of the fact that, after all, what we are doing is very much in line with music from the traditional orchestral repertoire, such as the symphonic poems of Richard Strauss, and the orchestras do not have to feel underused at all. Perhaps, however, our audiences can relate more to Cloud, Sephiroth and Aerith than Till Eulenspiegel.

Project partners always need to be convinced of the value of the concerts, but I do not see this as a burden; I see it as part of my job. If I were an orchestra manager, I would be cautious; they have to protect their ensembles from bad programmes, and poor performances can damage the reputation of an orchestra. Today, with seventeen years of experience, and orchestras such as the London Symphony Orchestra, the San Francisco Symphony, the Royal Stockholm Philharmonic Orchestra, the Melbourne Symphony Orchestra and the Tokyo Philharmonic Orchestra on our list, it is certainly easier to reassure project partners; these endorsements indicate to managers that there must be some value to our productions.

The Changing Landscape

As the concert series continues, we are faced with the challenge of achieving a balance between innovation and retaining the qualities that appealed to audiences in the first place. One approach to this issue is encapsulated in the extended pieces of the Final Symphony concerts, which keep the main melodies from the Final Fantasy games intact and recognizable, while at the same time offering something new and fresh, to make the listener experience exciting even for people who have heard the music many times before. These pieces benefit from the storytelling principle, as it allows us to combine and layer melodies, so that they are appearing in a new context.

We continue to use public opinion to inform our programming and we keep an eye on modern games, so we can introduce new music into the repertoire. That process includes playing games, reading reviews and watching playthroughs. However, the new addition has to have musical appeal and integrate with the rest of the programme – we never force anything into our concerts just because of fan service.

While it was initially difficult to introduce the idea of a concert of video game music to a broader public, now such concerts are common. It is a huge achievement that the gaming industry should be proud of, although if a little criticism is allowed, it sometimes leads to carelessness; the excitement and passion of the beginning have faded into routine at times. We see increasing numbers of themed concerts, such as those dedicated to music from Final Fantasy, Legend of Zelda, Kingdom Hearts and so on. While this is a fantastic development and allows great musical coherence within one concert, it dramatically favours the biggest franchises which have the most marketing power. A side effect of these concerts is that many other gems are not getting performed; the producers of concerts dedicated to lesser-known franchises would struggle to break even. Overall, however, the quality of performance has increased and to see top class orchestras playing the music is deeply gratifying

I can imagine a concert with both classical repertoire and game music, but the programming would have to be done with skill and knowledge. An arbitrary selection of classical music performed alongside game cues might leave both audiences dissatisfied, or, at the other extreme, fail to gain any attention. However, a more careful approach, such as programming Uematsu alongside Prokofiev and Tchaikovsky, might be a way to introduce two different audiences to each other's music. It is challenging to find such programme combinations that are both artistically successful and appeal to orchestra managers, who are wary of attempts to mix (what they perceive as) incompatible audiences. I would love, however, to see audiences of both kinds of music enjoying the orchestra together.

I would like producers to take more liberties and try something new. At the moment, many of the performances are more about random clip shows and selling merchandise, not so much about the music and its interpretation. In order to be relevant as an art form, I believe the game music concert needs more than that. The music needs to be appropriately arranged and adapted, so that it has a distinct identity and independent form, so that it can stand on its own musical strength, rather than purely as a second-degree derivative product. This is why Masashi Hamauzu once told me he believes that the concert Final Symphony is here to stay, and while other productions might be forgotten in 10 or 20 years, Final Symphony will still be remembered, and most likely even still performed in concert halls around the world. In my opinion, one cannot think of a better compliment.

Culture and Aesthetics

Game music concerts can be situated in a broader context of the changing cultural attitudes to games and their music. Germany has always had quite a strong interest in video game music, with figures such as Chris Hülsbeck widely known in gaming circles. His importance became obvious to more people when in 2008, both performances of our Chris Hülsbeck concert – Symphonic Shades – sold out very quickly. In particular, Germany has seen a shift in a broad cultural attitude to video games, from games having something of a bad reputation to being officially recognized by the government as a cultural asset. Game music concerts can be understood as part of this cultural shift. Besides regular concertgoers, the five performances I produced in Leipzig always attracted a large number of special guests, such as those from the political arena, including former Minister Presidents Georg Milbradt, Head of the Government of Saxony, and his successor, Stanislaw Tillich. As they were held as official opening ceremonies of the Game Convention, we had an audience that probably would not have considered attending a game music concert, but that in the end was pleasantly surprised by the quality that was on offer. That was the report that I received from the management of the Leipzig Trade Fair. In addition, without this response within the circles of politics and industry, there certainly would not have been more than one concert in Leipzig. In 2015 I was presented with the national Cultural and Creative Pilots Award by the

German Federal Government for my work with game concerts, an award which recognizes outstanding entrepreneurs within Germany's cultural and creative industries. It gave me the opportunity to introduce the concept of game concerts to Germany's Minister of State for Culture and the Media, Prof. Monika Grütters, which I believe was a huge step forward for further awareness of the genre.

That said, it will be a few more years before game music concerts have significant power for cultural change; they are too young, too new to be taken entirely seriously by everyone. I think the best thing we can say about video game music today is that it is accepted as high-quality work; it is for others to decide whether it can be considered 'art' in the years to come.

Select Bibliography

Austin, Michael (ed.). *Music Video Games: Performance, Politics, and Play.* New York: Bloomsbury, 2016.

Braguinski, Nikita. *RANDOM: Die Archäologie der Elektronischen Spielzeugklänge.* Bochum: Projekt Verlag, 2018.

Cheng, William. *Sound Play: Video Games and the Musical Imagination.* New York: Oxford University Press, 2014.

Collins, Karen. 'Flat Twos and the Musical Aesthetic of the Atari VCS.' *Popular Musicology Online* 1 (2006).

'From Bits to Hits: Video Games Music Changes Its Tune.' *Film International* 12 (2005): 4–19.

Game Sound: An Introduction to the History, Theory and Practice of Video Game Music and Sound Design. Cambridge, MA: The MIT Press, 2008.

'An Introduction to Procedural Audio in Video Games.' *Contemporary Music Review* 28, no. 1 (2009): 5–15.

Playing With Sound: A Theory of Interacting with Sound and Music in Video Games. Cambridge, MA: The MIT Press, 2013.

Cook, Karen M. 'Beyond (the) Halo: Plainchant in Video Games', in *Studies in Medievalism XXVII: Authenticity, Medievalism, Music*, ed. Karl Fugelso. Woodbridge, UK: Boydell & Brewer, 2018, 183–200.

Diaz-Gasca, Sebastian. 'Super Smash Covers! Performance and Audience Engagement in Australian Videogame Music Cover Bands.' *Perfect Beat* 19, no. 1 (2018): 51–67.

Donnelly, K. J., Gibbons, William and Lerner, Neil (eds). *Music in Video Games: Studying Play.* New York: Routledge, 2014.

Fritsch, Melanie. 'History of Video Game Music', in Peter Moormann (ed.), *Music and Game: Perspectives on a Popular Alliance.* Wiesbaden: Springer, 2013, 11–40.

'"It's a-me, Mario!" Playing with Video Game Music', in *Ludomusicology: Approaches to Video Game Music*, ed. Michiel Kamp, Tim Summers and Mark Sweeney. Sheffield: Equinox, 2016, 92–115.

Performing Bytes: Musikperformances der Computerspielkultur. Würzburg: Königshausen & Neumann, 2018.

Gibbons, William. 'Music, Genre and Nationality in the Postmillennial Fantasy Role-Playing Game', in *The Routledge Companion to Screen Music and Sound*, ed. Miguel Mera, Ronald Sadoff and Ben Winters. New York: Routledge, 2017, 412–27.

Unlimited Replays: Video Games and Classical Music. New York: Oxford University Press, 2018.

Gibbons, William and Reale, Steven (eds). *Music in the Role-Playing Game: Heroes and Harmonies*. New York: Routledge, 2020.

Grimshaw, Mark. 'Sound', in *The Routledge Companion to Video Game Studies*, ed. Mark J. P. Wolf and Bernard Perron. London: Routledge, 2014, 117–24.

Grimshaw, Mark, Tan, Siu-Lan and Lipscomb, Scott D. 'Playing With Sound: The Role of Music and Sound Effects in Gaming', in *The Psychology of Music in Multimedia*, ed. Siu-Lan Tan, Annabel J. Cohen, Scott D. Lipscomb and Roger A. Kendall. Oxford: Oxford University Press, 2013, 289–314.

Ivănescu, Andra. 'Beneath a Steel Sky: A Musical Characterisation of Class Structure.' *The Computer Games Journal* 7 (2018): 231–42.

Popular Music in the Nostalgia Video Game: The Way It Never Sounded. Cham: Palgrave, 2019.

Jørgensen, Kristine. 'Left in the Dark: Playing Computer Games with the Sound Turned Off', in *From Pac-Man to Pop Music: Interactive Audio in Games and New Media*, ed. Karen Collins. Aldershot: Ashgate, 2008, 163–76.

Kamp, Michiel. 'Four Ways of Hearing Video Game Music.' PhD thesis, Cambridge University (2014).

Kamp, Michiel, Summers, Tim and Sweeney, Mark (eds). *Ludomusicology: Approaches to Video Game Music*. Sheffield: Equinox, 2016.

Kassabian, Anahid and Jarman, Freya. 'Game and Play in Music Video Games', in *Ludomusicology: Approaches to Video Game Music*, ed. Michiel Kamp, Tim Summers and Mark Sweeney. Sheffield: Equinox, 2016, 116–32.

McAlpine, Kenneth B. *Bits and Pieces: A History of Chiptunes*. New York: Oxford University Press, 2018.

Medina-Gray, Elizabeth. 'Analyzing Modular Smoothness in Video Game Music.' *Music Theory Online* 25, no. 3 (2019), accessed 29 October 2020, www.mtosmt.org/issues/mto.19.25.3/mto.19.25.3.medina.gray.html

Miller, Kiri. 'Jacking the Dial: Radio, Race, and Place in "Grand Theft Auto."' *Ethnomusicology* 51, no. 3 (2007): 402–38.

Playable Bodies: Dance Games and Intimate Media. New York: Oxford University Press, 2017.

Playing Along: Digital Games, YouTube, and Virtual Performance. New York: Oxford University Press, 2012.

Moormann, Peter (ed.). *Music and Game: Perspectives on a Popular Alliance*. Wiesbaden: Springer, 2013.

Moseley, Roger. *Keys to Play: Music as a Ludic Medium from Apollo to Nintendo*. Oakland, CA: University of California Press, 2016.

Newman, James. 'The Music of Microswitches: Preserving Videogame Sound – A Proposal.' *The Computer Games Journal* 7 (2018): 261–78.

O'Leary, Jared and Tobias, Evan. 'Sonic Participatory Cultures Within, Through, and Around Video Games', in *The Oxford Handbook of Music Making and*

Leisure, ed. Roger Mantie and Gareth Dylan Smith. New York: Oxford University Press, 2017, 541–564.

Paul, Leonard J. 'Droppin' Science: Video Game Audio Breakdown', in *Music and Game: Perspectives on a Popular Alliance*, ed. Peter Moormann. Wiesbaden: Springer, 2013, 63–80.

Phillips, Winifred. *A Composer's Guide to Game Music*. Cambridge, MA: The MIT Press, 2014.

Plank, Dana. 'Bodies in Play: Representations of Disability in 8- and 16-bit Video Game Soundscapes.' PhD dissertation, Ohio State University (2018).

'Mario Paint Composer and Musical (Re)Play on YouTube', in *Music Video Games: Performance, Politics, and Play*, ed. Michael Austin. New York: Bloomsbury, 2016, 43–82.

Summers, Tim. *Understanding Video Game Music*. Cambridge, UK: Cambridge University Press, 2016.

Tanaka, Haruhisa 'hally'. *All About Chiptune*. Tokyo: Seibundo-shinkosha, 2017.

Tessler, Holly. 'The New MTV? Electronic Arts and "Playing" Music', in *From Pac-Man to Pop Music: Interactive Audio in Games and New Media*, ed. Karen Collins. Aldershot: Ashgate, 2008, 13–26.

Troise, Blake. 'The 1-Bit Instrument: The Fundamentals of 1-Bit Synthesis, Their Implementational Implications, and Instrumental Possibilities.' *Journal of Sound and Music in Games* 1, no. 1 (2020): 44–74.

van Elferen, Isabella. 'Analysing Game Musical Immersion: The ALI Model', in *Ludomusicology: Approaches to Video Game Music*, ed. Michiel Kamp, Tim Summers and Mark Sweeney. Sheffield: Equinox, 2016, 32–52.

Whalen, Zach. 'Play Along – An Approach to Videogame Music.' *Game Studies* 4, no. 1 (2004). www.gamestudies.org/0401/whalen/

Zdanowicz, Gina and Bambrick, Spencer. *The Game Audio Strategy Guide: A Practical Course*. New York: Routledge, 2020.

Index

CPSIA information can be obtained
at www.ICGtesting.com
Printed in the USA
LVHW060852030821
694401LV00007B/452